CW01456524

The

Call na h-*Iolaire*

DARKEST DAWN

The Story of the Iolaire Tragedy

STORNOWAY

Goat Hill

Melbost

Carse of Melbost

Cnoc Dubhaig

Moss End

Hospital

Sandwickhill

Sandwick

Upper Holm

Luidhe na' Ron

Cnoc a Sgaite

Chubag

Gob Shilldinish

Gob nan Van

Holm Farm

Mol Shilldinish

Rudha Shilldinish

Eil.n nan Caorach

Eilean nan Van (Lamb I.)

Holm B.

Sgeir Liath

Stac a Chaise

Holm I.

Holm Pt.

Biastan Holm

Sandwick Loch

Stoney Field Loch

Cemetery

School

Stoney Field

Ruin

STORNOWAY HARBOUR
(See plate 1919)

Mol Sandwick

Mol Sandwick Beg

Sandwick Pt.

Eilean na Gobhail

Peninsular Pt.

Poll a'Choire

Craggan Feach

Glumag H.

Arnish Pt.

Arnish

Smearing B.

Cnoc Arnish

Loch Arnish

Mol Dhubicaill

Tob Leirabhaigh

Amhainn Leirabhaidh

Loch Bualabhig

Cnoc Bualabhig

Rugh'a Bhaigh Uaine

Bagh Uaine

Loch nan Stiar

ish Moor

Sgeir na Faodal

The Outer building on the
Western Pier just open West of
Eilean na Gobhail. (N.21°W.)

Tidal streams are weak

Var.n 20°20' W. (1915)
decreasing about 5' annually

MAGNETIC

EYE PENINSULA

Stac Mòr Gharrabost
Geodha nan Cliabh
Geann Dhibidill
Bayble School Ho.
Rudha na Shean Eich
Allt Tuath
Agaish
Cnocan Gorm
Langa Sgeir Mhòr
Langa Sgeir Bheag
Uidhe
Old Kirk of Eye (Part in ruins)
School Ho.
New Church
Agaish Hill
Clach Stein
Pabail Àrd
Cnoc
Pabail Iosal
HUIE BAY
(gh nah-Uidhe)
Cnoc Ramadail
Gob Ramadail (Cnoc Pt.)
Suordal
Loch Shuordail
Clatha Pabail (Bayble Quay)
Geodh'a Gharaidh
Bagh Shuordail
Allt Driseach
Bagh Pabail
Bible Ba
Ben Pabail (Ben Bibie)
Rudha na Geodha Bàine
Rudha nan Caorach
Steidshall
L. an Dùn
Budha na Sgriangaich
Geodha Fada
Geodha na h'Inghinn
Stac Shuordail
Cnoc na h'Iolair
Geodh'a Gharaidh
Rudha Dubh
Sgeir Phadric
Geodha na Gràine
Mol an Droighin
Rudha na Geodha Duibhe
Sgeir a Chabhrig
Geodha na Sithannan
Rudha nan Sgarbh
L. Cùite
Gob Grutha
Leabaidh a Mhinisteir
Eilean na Crotach (Crotha Rk.)
Chicken Head
(Ceann na Circ)
Gob Rk.
Geodha na Laradh
Rudha an Laraig
Rudha an Teampuill
Hen & Chickens
Red Beacon
(18 feet high)
Light house open

Part of the Iolaire 100 Years project.
Project partners: Acair, An Lanntair and Museum nan Eilean

The Publishers are grateful for all the assistance received from many organisations during the preparation of this book
We are particularly grateful to all the individuals who provided photographs, letters and other memorabilia.

The Publishers are grateful for financial assistance received from
Comhairle nan Eilean Siar
Museums Galleries Scotland
Point and Sandwick Trust

The publishers are grateful to BBC Radio nan Gàidheal for permission to quote from interviews.

First published in 2018 by Acair, An Tosgan, Seaforth Road, Stornoway, Isle of Lewis, Scotland HS1 2SD
www.acairbooks.com
info@acairbooks.com

© Text Malcolm Macdonald, and the estate of Donald John MacLeod
© National Portrait Gallery, London, Robert Francis Boyle by Walter Stoneman

Reproduced by permission of Duncan Macpherson Collection, Skye and Lochalsh Archive Centre
(High Life Highland). The Kyle photographs appear on pages 66 and 67
Reproduced by permission of the National Library of Scotland. The map appears on page 2-3, 222, 490-491.

All rights reserved.
The right of Malcolm Macdonald and the estate of Donald John MacLeod to be identified as the author
of the work has been asserted by them in accordance with the Copyright, Designs and Patent Act 1998.
No part of this publication may be reproduced, stored in a retrieval system nor reproduced or transmitted by
any means, electronic, mechanical, photocopying or otherwise, without the prior permission of the publisher.

The Cover and interior design by Margaret Ann MacLeod for Acair.

Chuidich Comhairle nan Leabhraichean am foillsichear le cosgaisean an leabhar seo.

Tha Acair a' faighean taic bho Bhòrd na Gàidhlig.

A CIP catalogue record for this title is available from the British Library

Printed by Hussar Books, Poland.

ISBN: 978-1-78907-024-8

Riaghladair Carthannas na h-Alba

Carthannas Clàraichte/
Registered Charity SC047866

The
DARKEST DAWN

Call na h-*Iolaire*

The *Story* of the *Iolaire Tragedy*

Malcolm Macdonald   Donald John MacLeod

edited by
Annie Delin

acair

This book owes much to Donald John MacLeod (1933–2018)
who was its co-author and contributed a wealth of material.
Sadly he did not live to see the final publication.

During research and writing I also lost my wife Isobel
(1951–2012) and only sister Kay (1941–2018), to both
of whom I pay loving tribute.

The book is dedicated to my grandfather,
Malcolm Macdonald (1873–1919), and the 279 other
men aboard His Majesty's Yacht *Iolaire* on the dark
morning of New Year's Day 1919.

Malcolm Macdonald

At the authors' request all royalties from the sale of this book
will be donated to Bethesda Hospice in Stornoway.

At 1.55am on 1st January 1919, a naval yacht carrying sailors home on leave ran aground on rocks near the village of Holm, a mere 20 yards from the shore of the Isle of Lewis and less than a mile from the safe harbour of Stornoway. HMY *Iolaire* was crowded with 280 men, mostly naval reservists returning to the safety and comfort of their homes after the horrors of the Great War. On this dark night of winter a force ten gale was blowing from the south, hard onto the shore, and there was a heavy sea running. Men drowned as they jumped or slid into the sea from the pitching decks, were flung back into the angry foam from lifeboats awash and overloaded, were dashed against jagged rocks, or managed to swim and crawl ashore, only to die before they could reach shelter or aid. By the time the first New Year's Day of peacetime dawned, 201 men had lost their lives, 181 of them on the very shores of the island they called home.

"No one now alive in Lewis can ever forget the 1st of January 1919, and future generations will speak of it as the blackest day in the history of the island, for on it 200 of our bravest and best perished on the very threshold of their home under the most tragic of circumstances. The terrible disaster at Holm on New Year's morning has plunged every home and every heart in Lewis into grief unutterable. Language cannot express the desolation, the despair which this awful catastrophe has inflicted.

"One thinks of the wide circle of blood relations affected by the loss of even one of these gallant lads, and imagination sees these circles multiplied by the number of the dead, overlapping and overlapping each other till the whole island - every hearth and home in it - is shrouded in deepest gloom.

"All the island's war losses in the past four cruel years - although these number fully four times the death roll of New Year's Day morning - are not comparable to this unspeakable calamity. The black tragedy has not a redeeming feature."

William Grant, founder of the Stornoway Gazette, January 1919.
(Reprinted in the *Loyal Lewis Roll of Honour*, 1920)

A note on pronunciation
The word '*iolaire*' means, in Scottish Gaelic, 'eagle', and is pronounced 'yuh-la-rah'. The ship named the *Iolaire*, which was so tragically wrecked on New Year's Day 1919, is always pronounced in the English way, as 'Eye-oh-lair'

Contents

I am most touched to have been asked to provide a foreword for this important publication. 'The Darkest Dawn' is a deeply poignant tribute to all those who so tragically lost their lives when H.M.Y. IOLAIRE sank a century ago, in the early hours of 1st January 1919.

This is a profoundly moving record of a disaster which has had a truly lasting effect on the communities of Lewis, Harris and Berneray. It must also not be forgotten that there were an additional twenty-six people on board from communities stretching from Aberdeen to Penzance. This book enables present and future generations to know something of the indescribable grief of those families, relatives, neighbours and friends who were so cruelly affected by the loss of their loved ones. After miraculously surviving their military service during the First World War, they perished only a few hundred yards from their final destination.

It is perhaps understandable that, until recently, the circumstances surrounding this most tragic of events in the history of the Islands have not been widely discussed. This book, therefore, provides us with a fitting legacy with which to mark the loss of 201 passengers and crew of H.M.Y. IOLAIRE.

Acair are to be congratulated for producing this most comprehensive publication; its detailed and personal narrative, coupled with rare photographs of those caught up in this tragedy, has created a fitting epitaph to those Servicemen whose loss had such a devastating effect on the island communities.

Author's Introduction

Anyone growing up in the Isle of Lewis after the war could not help but be aware of the catastrophe that struck the island on New Year's morning 1919, when HMY *Iolaire* foundered outside Stornoway harbour, drowning over two hundred seamen coming home on leave. The sinking was still an emotional issue long after the Second World War, as many people were still living who, along with their families, had suffered profound distress due to the tragedy.

During the First World War the Western Isles had already lost many sons at sea, but nobody expected islanders who had survived the war to perish within yards of their native shore while returning home. All the islanders drowned in the *Iolaire* disaster were naval ratings or mercantile marine seamen coming home on leave.

Rumours as to the cause of the disaster were for many years still widespread and the *Iolaire* Inquiry was considered by the islanders to be a whitewash – used to exonerate the Admiralty from any imputation or responsibility for the deaths of the island seamen, many of whom had survived over four years of bloody carnage during the war.

Even the number of those who died has remained uncertain for a century and we have made it a priority, in establishing the identities of all those lost and all those saved, to establish once and for all the figures connected with the disaster. In doing so, we have arrived at a figure of the men lost which totals 18 crew, two men returning to the naval base from leave, 174 Lewismen and seven men from Harris – a total of 201 men lost. For many years it has been taken as fact that the figure given at the Public Inquiry in February 1919 – of 205 men lost – was accurate, but our examination of the papers in the Admiralty file 116/1695, the whole record of the Public Inquiry, now held at the Public Records Office (National Archive) at Kew in London, turned up the information put before the court:

> "Of the crew of 24 there were 18 drowned and of these 14 bodies have been recovered. From the naval depot there were 2 men on board, both were drowned and 1 body has been recovered. From Lewis 174 men are missing, and of those 110 bodies were recovered, and from Harris 7 missing, 5 recovered. Six of the crewmen were survivors. All the officers were drowned."

These figures for casualties match exactly with those apportioned and contained in this book. This disproves the Admiralty's later claim, reported in the Inquiry findings, reproduced by the press and recorded on the *Iolaire* monument, stating that 205 men were lost. It has taken 100 years to establish that the Public Inquiry findings were factually inaccurate and contrary to the evidence presented – in this important matter as, perhaps, in others.

Hopefully, this book will provide a fresh perspective on other little-known aspects of the disaster, and remind people of the heartache, anguish, agony, despair, sorrow and want that the people of Lewis and Harris experienced due to the drowning of their kith and kin, virtually on their own doorstep, on New Year's morning, 1919.

Malcolm Macdonald, 2018

Editorial note on personal names

In the Western Isles of Scotland, personal names for both men and women have great variety, flexibility and depth of meaning. At the time when the First World War came to an end, most people were known to family and friends by their own Gaelic name (Iain, Dòmhnall, Aonghas) by a nickname (Am Patch, Teenie, Càdham) and by a name relating them to their father/mother and grandparents (Dhòmhnaill – of Donald, Mhagaidh – of Maggie). When it came to serving with the Royal Naval Reserve, or to speaking before a Public Inquiry, they would be named by their English equivalent name (John instead of Iain, Norman for Tarmod, Malcolm for Calum) and by their surname of Macleod, Macdonald, Campbell and so on. This effectively means that the reader could find the same man under up to five different names. Survivor Norman Mackenzie of Cross, Ness was also called Làrag (his nickname) and Tarmod Dhòmhnaill 'an Bhàin (Norman son of Donald son of Fair John) for example. We have tried, wherever possible, to clarify who each person is, although the formal English name under which each man registered to serve is most commonly used. Other names are included, where we know them, in the chapters listing survivors and those lost on the *Iolaire*.

Index of abbreviations

2nd Eng – Second Engineer

AB – Able Bodied Seaman

AMC – Armed Merchant Cruiser

Asst Stwd – Assistant Steward

Carp – Carpenter

Cdr – Commander

CPO – Chief Petty Officer

DAMS – Defensively Armed Merchant Ship

DH – Deckhand

ERA – Engine Room Artificer

Frmn – Fireman

HMD – His Majesty's Drifter

HMML – His Majesty's Motor Launch – carrying a three-pounder Hotchkiss gun, machine guns and depth charges, with a 10-man crew, for inshore minesweeping and anti-submarine work.

HMS – His Majesty's Ship (includes shore bases)

HMT – His Majesty's Trawler

HMY – His Majesty's Yacht

L/DH – Leading Deckhand

L/Sigmn – Leading Signalman

L/Smn – Leading Seaman

Lt – Lieutenant

LVA – Leading Victualling Assistant

MM – Mercantile Marine

MMR – Mercantile Marine Reserve

Ord Smn – Ordinary Seaman RN

PO – Petty Officer

Pte RMLI – Private, Royal Marine Light Infantry

Q-boat – decoy vessel

RN – Royal Navy

RNR – Royal Naval Reserve

RNVR – Royal Naval Volunteer Reserve

Sig Boy – Signal Boy

Sigmn – Signalman

Smn – Seaman

SS – Steamship

Stkr – Stoker

Sub Lt (E) – Sub Lieutenant (Engineer)

Stwd – Steward

T124X Rates – rates of pay made to Mercantile Marines

T-124Y – rate of pay received by Mercantile Marine men serving with the Royal Navy on a temporary basis under full naval discipline.

Teleg – Telegraphist

Trmr – Trimmer

U-boat – German submarine

Chapter 1

Lewis and Harris Before the War

"The rhythm of the crofting year was dictated by seasonal work which would fit around the rigours of the weather.... they knew who was related to who and had listened to the stories around the fire on winters' evenings."

The Outer Hebrides

The Isles of Lewis and Harris form a single island in the archipelago north-west of Scotland, known as the Outer Hebrides, the Western Isles and, in Scots Gaelic, Innse Gall or na h-Eileanan an Iar. Appearing as a fragment, a fringe of islands left behind to the west of Scotland, the backbone of Lewis and Harris is, in fact, Europe's first and oldest rock. Lewisian gneisses pre-date the volcanic eruptions of the Scottish Highlands and give the landscape its unique, unchanging aspect. In places ground smooth by glaciation, sometimes thinly covered with turf, and interspersed with countless lochans (small ponds), deep sea lochs and swathes of peat bog, fringed to the west by superb, sweeping sandy beaches and dunes, it is a landscape with its own distinct character.

It's customary to consider this chain of islands as remote, an outpost of the British Isles, but for centuries the isles were at the crossroads of busy sea-faring communities including the Norse lands of Scandinavia, Ireland and mainland Scotland. With a constant stream of incoming visitors – whether raiders, settlers or shipwrecked sailors – and an equal outflow of emigrants, seafarers and captured wives for Vikings, the world view of islanders through the centuries was anything but insular. New arrivals came from Norway, Spain and all of Scotland and it was not uncommon for an island man to have seen ports in Europe, Asia, Africa and the Americas before he was 30.

The island left behind by departing soldiers and sailors in 1914 was a complex, tightly bound and sometimes contrary community. Religion, morality and faith created a strict code, the crofting seasons were relentless in their physical demands and the weather set its own challenges for families struggling to survive. Yet the language, folklore and culture were rich and nuanced, written clearly on the landscape and alive in the vigorous speech, song and poetry of the people. Living conditions that appeared primitive and unhealthy to visitors bred close companionship and sheltered a robust population. This was the world that young men left to serve their country in August 1914.

Island life before 1914

For most islanders, the rhythm of the crofting year was dictated by seasonal work which would fit around the rigours of the weather. Many of the year's major tasks – the planting of crops, lambing, grazing cattle and lifting peats – were communal and young people were, from a very early age, familiar with the neighbours who came to help. Children of the same age-group played outside each other's homes and explored their home shores and moors. They worked together too – boys would fish from the rocks and scramble to help the men pull up the returning fishing boats, girls learnt how to bait fish hooks and to tend livestock. Planting and lifting crops, seeing lambs safely delivered and sheep shorn were tasks for everyone, while the annual cutting of peat and the later lifting and bringing it home was a great gathering of all age-groups, and children would be expected to do their part.

Young men already knew each other well by the time they were allowed to join fishing crews heading out to lay the long lines or to cast the nets for herring. They had played together and been to school together at the primary schools in their own villages. They knew who was related to who, and had listened to the stories around the fire on winter's evenings. There was very little they did not know about each other's lives and families.

Working together in this way from day to day bred a tough community spirit, reinforced by moments of rest – by song, by worship and by story-telling. The strength of the community lay in a spirit of mutual interdependence, the weak supported by the stronger and everyone with a part to play. There is no doubt that Hebridean communities suffered deprivations in many ways, but they always united to ensure that those less fortunate in their midst had peats, fish, potatoes and milk, the basic essentials for life, as well as companionship from neighbours and relatives of all generations. That community spirit bonded islanders into a doughty people who respected the sea and who worshiped God each day, not just on Sunday, for His provision to them.

Prayer was an absolute part of daily life. There would be prayers in homes each day and any stray child who found themselves in a friend or relative's home at the time would simply join the family worship and the reading of the Bible. Psalms would be led by the men both at home and before tasks such as fishing or harvesting, as a way of blessing the work in hand, the family drawn together. Going to church was, especially in the rural areas, the way of life for almost everyone. Services were held not just on Sundays but on midweek days, for funerals and on special dates such as New Year's Day. The churches would be full, and people walked miles together in all weathers to attend, catching up with news as they walked.

Beyond Stornoway, the conversation at these gatherings would be almost exclusively in Gaelic, the language of home and hearth, the language of memories, story-telling and of worship. Most church ministers were Gaelic-speaking and used it forcefully from the pulpit. Headmasters were often Gaelic-speakers too, but would speak English to reinforce power and social class. Most adults in the country villages spoke some English if they needed to for officialdom, but in the town of Stornoway English was more prevalent, partly as a practical response to the greater integration here of newcomers to the islands.

For children, the first brush with English came when they went to school. Since 1872 Scotland had a system of free schools run by local school boards, education being compulsory from five to thirteen. There were primary schools in every district and school rolls were high as the villages flourished before the war. New five-year-olds would be shocked to find that the language they had learnt at the hearth was not to be spoken in the classroom, but a new language begun from day one.

Royal Naval Reserve sailors who originally trained in Stornoway before state education was introduced had their first significant exposure to English when they joined the RNR:

"As some of them were not over-conversant with English, the drill orders had to be given to them in Gaelic. For instance the order to 'Slope Arms' was given literally as 'air do ghuailinn àrd' ('on your shoulders high'). 'Present Arms' was 'Ma choinneamh do mhionaich' ('In front of your stomach'). As time passed, however, these recruits became familiar with English and were able to execute orders given in that language."[1]

But this was all over by the turn of the century, when English was a language which could be used, when needed, by most. The men who joined the RNR before 1914 were comfortable following orders in English, even if conversation between themselves remained in their own language. In this and many other respects, the life that islanders left behind when they went to serve their country in 1914 differed from the lives known by men who answered the call from other parts of Britain.

How islanders lived

We are fortunate to have a detailed historic picture of the islands' physical living conditions in the early 20th century, thanks to a 19th century Government Inquiry. In 1884 the Napier Commission published its detailed and thorough examination of rural circumstances after an inquiry commissioned by William Gladstone's Liberal government, chaired by the 10th Lord Napier, who was appointed in 1883. He and his colleagues got quickly to work and were in Lewis in June 1883, gathering evidence at hearings including at Ness – after which they had their own alarming encounter with the perils of island life. They were proceeding by sea to Stornoway on 7th June when their vessel, the armed paddle steamer HMS *Lively,* was wrecked on the Chicken Rock near Swordale, Point, some five miles from her destination. Nobody was lost and the Commission carried on with their gathering of evidence. During the full course of their inquiry they held 71 evidence sessions in 61 locations, including church halls and bothies[2] all over the Highlands and Islands, so that the poorest and most frail could play a part on their home turf. In all 775 witnesses were examined.

The Napier Commission gave exact descriptions of the dwellings in the islands. Blackhouses predominated in the Western Isles and still formed 80% of the housing stock in 1912, when a new squad of government officials came to inspect for the Royal Commission on Housing in Scotland. Blackhouses were not uniform in character; in their lowest form they were:

> "Sordid hovels in which horses, cows, and pigs occupied one end of the undivided tenement, while the human inhabitants, accompanied by pigs and poultry, were immersed in obscurity and dirt at the other."[3]

The better sort were thatched with grass or heather, floored with clay and built with un-tempered stones, might possess a chimney and a window in the wall, a door unshared by cattle, a partition between the stall and the lodging and, when kept clean, did not offer an unpleasant aspect.

But in the Outer Hebrides the blackhouses were most insanitary. The typical Lewis crofter's house was built by the crofter himself:

> "It had double low thick walls of loose stone, united by a packing of earth or clay intended to stop the wind blowing through. The roof was composed of a framework of wooden rafters and couples (resting on the inner wall), covered over with turf divots and straw, bound with ropes of heather, straw, or coarse thatch-rope, and weighted down with stones. It was never airtight nor watertight, and what rain did not come through, ran down to the earth-packing forming the centre of the walls, which were thus kept perpetually damp. There was no chimney and

Blackhouse interior, Lionel, Ness, about 1899. Note the fire on the floor front right of the picture and the bed in the alcove on the left

Croft houses around the turn of the century, regarded by visiting inspectors as 'unfit for human habitation'.

The crofting township of Kneep in Uig, showing the low roofline of blackhouses.

19

often no window; if windows were fixed in the wall or roof, they were not made to open. Sometimes there was a round porthole made to open in the roof, but this was not favoured, because it reduced valuable manurial product. These houses had only one door, used by the cattle and family alike. Inside, the house usually contained three compartments. In the middle was the living room with a blazing peat-fire filling the house with smoke. Rough stones covered with clay made a cold and damp floor. On one side of this middle compartment was the sleeping room, on the other the byre. The byre had no paving, and the manure liquids percolated into the ground, and at times found their way into neighbouring dwelling-houses and even into drinking wells. The dung was allowed to accumulate in the byre till spring, when, having by this time increased the height of the floor by several feet, it was carted or carried in creels away to the fields. The roof with the adherent soot was stripped to the cabers and also used to manure the land. New divots for the roof were then obtained from the hill-side, and this process proved very detrimental to the pasturage. Many of these houses were built back to back, and sometimes in rows three deep."[4]

By contrast, there were also in Lewis white houses – they formed the majority of housing in the town of Stornoway and were scattered here and there elsewhere. The Napier Report describes them thus:

"The white house, in its usual form, consisted of two rooms, often with a bed closet between them, and sometimes with garrets in the roof. It had two chimneys in the gables and windows designed to open and shut; the walls were built of mortar; one end was floored with boards, the other with earth or flags; the partitions and ceilings were of wood and clay roughly put together; the roofing was of boards covered with thatch, or felt daubed with tar, or exceptionally with slates."[5]

The Napier Report led directly to the Crofters Holdings (Scotland) Act 1886, which established rights for crofters – the right to a reasonable rent, to pass their croft on to their families and, if the crofter decided to give up the tenancy of his croft, the Act also stated that they would have to be paid for any improvements made to it. But it left unsolved the problem of living conditions in the islands.

Just five years later more inspectors called, and wrote:

"The attention of the Board has been directed to the condition of the dwellings of the labouring classes in the Western Highlands and Islands. Many of these dwellings throughout extensive districts would, no doubt, be regarded by modern scientific sanitarians as utterly unfit for human habitation, and the Board fear that in not a few cases such an opinion might be entertained on good grounds. On the other hand, the Board feel that any attempt to secure the sanitary improvement of these dwellings is attended with quite exceptional difficulties. The people, as a rule, it is believed, are satisfied with, and even attached to, their miserable hovels, and it is impossible to change in a day the confirmed habits of a whole people. …. The Board are of opinion that in these circumstances any proposal involving sudden or sweeping change would almost certainly tend to excite popular resentment and defeat the objects which the Board have in view. Moreover, the local assessments are already so oppressive in many of these districts that the imposition of further burdens even for the most excellent object is to be deprecated."[6]

In 1893 the Lewis District Committee warned the people that they intended to insist on a complete separation of the byre – where the animals were kept – from the living-room. Four test cases were brought before Sheriff George Campbell in 1895, and structural alterations were ordered. The Harris Committee took a census of offenders and legal proceedings were instituted against 28 householders. This did effect change – in 1896 there were in Harris 167 houses containing 431 animals, but by 1898 only 13 houses contained 23 animals.[7]

In 1905 the attention of Parliament was once again called to the island's sanitary conditions and the Secretary for Scotland had to answer parliamentary questions. As a result, the Local Government Board for Scotland sent two officials to investigate and report. They visited seven townships, and their account was considered appalling. Precise figures were only given for four townships – Back, Arnol, Bragar and Leurbost. Here just 42 of the total number of 314 houses were found to be fit and the remainder grossly insanitary and unfit for habitation. The Report on the Sanitary Condition of the Lews gave distressing details:

"The house occupied by two paupers (brother and sister) may be singled out for a fuller description as it presented the worst features we have yet met among houses of this shockingly insanitary type…. Immediately on opening the swing door one was met by the ammoniacal odour from the byre and was conscious of walking on and sinking into manure…. Three cows occupied about two thirds of the available space, and the darkness was so profound that one rubbed against them before seeing them. In a space about half as large …. was the living and sleeping room…. In this awful den, not fit for a pig, there are housed two wretched old paupers, who are compelled to crouch over the peat fire all night as there is no bed to retire to. One of the cows had a most suspicious hacking cough."[8]

The Royal Commission on Housing in Scotland, appointed in 1912, reported in 1917. In Harris:

"Public Health officials agreed that it was hopeless to do anything with the greater part of the black houses in the parish, and these are apparently 60 or 70 per cent of the whole."[9]

In Lewis, probably 80 per cent of the houses were still blackhouse type and cattle-housing remained general. The medical officer for health testified that:

"The death-rate from phthisis (tuberculosis) is more than double what it was forty years ago, while in the county generally[10] it has gone down about 40 per cent. I am convinced that the housing conditions are the main factor in causing the annual toll of fifty deaths from consumption."[11]

The report stated:

"That such a condition of affairs as we found in Lewis should exist within twenty-four hours of Westminster is scarcely credible. Nor is it creditable from a national standpoint."[12]

There were other causes for health concern found by inspectors. The water supply in Lewis and Harris was generally obtained from wells, mountain streams or lochs. The wells were liable to surface pollution, prone to dry up in summer and, in some areas, the distance to a loch or stream was great. Considerable improvements to wells were made after they were described in 1891 as: *'little better than cesspools for surface soakings'.*[13] Wells were repositioned or cleaned out, protected with concrete walls, covered in and a pump installed.

Much of this damning information about the living conditions in the islands was collated into a single volume, published in 1918 by J. P. Day. Reviewing *Public Administration in the Highlands and Islands of Scotland*, the *Spectator* magazine wrote:

"In Lewis there is a larger population than the island can support in comfort, even if every acre of land capable of cultivation were given to the crofters…. Mr. Day would have us recognize frankly that the crofter districts are valuable to the State as a nursery of healthy men and women, and that they should be put under a special administration of their own with a generous subvention from the Exchequer."[14]

The beginning of the 20th century was a period of change and improvement in island health conditions. In Stornoway the Lewis Hospital opened in 1896 and by 1915 there were three medical staff, two trained nurses, two nurses in training and two domestics. The Mossend Fever Hospital, built in 1875-76, had one nurse and dealt specifically with cases of typhoid, typhus fevers and other forms of disease attributed to bad sanitary arrangements. The Lewis Combination Poorhouse in Stornoway served the whole island and could accommodate 66 persons. In 1911, the poorhouse was licensed to provide accommodation for patients suffering from mental illness, who otherwise were transferred to Inverness. The fact that, in 1918, electors in the Western Isles chose as their first ever Member of Parliament Dr Donald Murray MOH (Medical Officer of Health) is testimony to his trojan work in trying to improve health and conditions within the islands.

Work and economy

With most men away from home regularly at the fishing, the rest of the family were occupied with peats, crops, water, laundry, weaving, knitting, cooking, housekeeping and the care of young children, the old and frail in their villages and the all-important animals. The men when ashore maintained the boats, thatched and repaired the houses, ploughed and helped with harvesting. Summer was a busy time, with little daylight wasted.

Fishing provided the staple diet of islanders, and the waters around the islands and further afield were a rich larder. Scottish fishing boats of the 1700s and early 1800s were mainly small, open boats, wooden and clinker-built, with each plank overlapping the one below. They were powered by sails and could be used close to shore, launched off beaches or from small harbours. It was from vessels

Zulu fishing boat Muirneag leaving harbour

Launching of fishing boat from the beach - the baskets are full of baited long lines.

such as these that crofters could catch enough fish for their families, friends, neighbours and to generate a small income with a good catch.

After the 18th century, larger herring busses of up to 80 tons fished in deeper water and stayed at sea for several weeks. The herring were caught using drift nets and a Dutch method of preserving herring in salt, known as curing, was adopted. A government bounty was paid to Scottish fishermen, calculated on the amount of fish caught. More fishermen began to catch herring and they were able to buy new and bigger boats, some of which were built at Stornoway. With salt, brine, drying and other means of preserving the 'silver darlings', markets further afield were reachable.

Launching and beaching a fishing boat could not be done without a team of strong men.

From the mid-nineteenth century the island girls and women who gutted, graded and salted herring locally had a change in lifestyle. From as young as 15 years old they began to follow the shoals around the coast, from the East Coast and Shetland in the spring and summer down to East Anglia in the autumn. Ports like Lerwick, Peterhead and Yarmouth became familiar to them, and many would work this way for several seasons. They took their kists (chests) with them by boat and train to each location where they lived, often with other girls from the islands and elsewhere, in boarding houses or lofts. After months of hard work, the fishcurer finally paid them for the season and they returned home. Island boats also worked these ports and romances and marriages blossomed, thanks to the herring, between island girls and boys and even between island girls and mainland fishermen.

Catches in the 19th century boomed and so did Stornoway. As the eminent author and local historian Frank Thompson wrote:

"By the 1850s, Stornoway was fast becoming a town of some commercial importance, based on its reputation as the best harbour on Scotland's north-west coast. It had a major ship-building and repair facility and its harbour also catered for the lucrative shipping trade in Atlantic waters. But it was to be the humble herring that would establish Stornoway as a centre for the industry. By 1876, the demand for fishing stations in Stornoway harbour was so great that they were let out to the highest bidders. Before long, the town was recognised as the major herring port of Britain - if not of Europe."[15]

Thompson describes late 19th century Stornoway as a town thronged with people, where the summer population tripled to 9,000 souls and one reporter counted 930 fishing boats in the harbour at one time. Herring were exported from Stornoway to Germany, Russia and other Baltic countries, while Liverpool and London were among the markets for kippered herring, smoked in Stornoway.

Thompson adds:

"When the Stornoway Town Council decided to design a Burgh Coat of Arms, they made sure to include in the armorial bearing three small fish and the motto "God's Providence is our Inheritance" in recognition of the vital role played by the herring in the island's economic development."

Other areas of the islands also had their fishing centres. Castlebay in Barra and Carloway on the west coast of Lewis enjoyed notable herring exports, while areas like Ness pursued the home white fish markets.

Hard work around the croft was an ordinary part of daily life for women such as these two in Bernera in 1913.

And, of course, fish was a staple in the island diet, to be had freely or cheaply, and transformed into a number of island specialities from herring with potatoes (sgadan 's buntàta) to stuffed cod's head (ceann-cropaig).

The Lewis herring industry was beginning to decline by 1914 – soon to be dealt a body blow by war and the collapse of trade with the Baltic states – but another industry was just coming into bloom, from early origins as a home industry for crofters. Harris Tweed had been woven in island homes for many years, but in 1846 Lady Catherine Murray, Countess of Dunmore, saw its potential as a new cottage industry which could be developed to the benefit of the islands. Her husband was Alexander Murray, the Earl of Dunmore and owner of the Isle of Harris. Lady Dunmore oversaw the copying of the Murray family tartan into Harris Tweed and had it woven for the gamekeepers and gillies on her estate, starting a new fashion among the gentry which saw the reputation of the clò mòr grow. A cottage industry grew with it throughout Lewis and Harris.

The Congested Districts Board, established in 1897, had powers to aid and develop spinning, weaving and other home industries in the Highlands and Islands. They provided instruction under the guidance of local committees, supplied dye-pots free of charge and advanced interest-free loans for purchasing looms. The success of their work in Lewis was reflected in the figures – there were 53 looms in Lewis in 1899, 161 in 1906 and 300 looms in 1911. The Harris Tweed 'Orb' Certification Trade-Mark was registered in 1910 and the first cloth was stamped in 1911, protecting the cloth from both British and European copies. To be identified as Harris Tweed the tweed had to be hand-spun, hand-woven and finished by hand in the Outer Hebrides.

Travel and communication

Islanders have been setting out for new lives from the islands for more than a thousand years. A voyage made by Orlyg the Old from the Hebrides to Iceland around 900 AD is believed to be the first recorded emigrant voyage from the British Isles.[16] Mass emigrations began in 1772-73 when 831 hopeful souls left Lewis for the eastern seaboard of North America, settling in New York and Pennsylvania. By the 20th century departure for better opportunities in Canada, America and Patagonia, among other destinations, was a well-trodden route, especially for young men. Single emigrations of large numbers were familiar, with ships stopping in at Stornoway specifically to pick up departing emigrants. James A. Smart, Depute Minister for the Canadian Interior, looked for 500 men for the railways in 1906 and 148 men left Lewis on 13th September that year, with 20 more the following week.

The *Canadian Boat-Song* expresses the yearning felt by those exiled from poor, but tight-knit communities with a longstanding, distinctive, and rich culture:

> *"Yet still the blood is strong, the heart is Highland,*
> *And we in dreams behold the Hebrides."*[17]

Not all islanders who went to Canada intended to emigrate permanently. Writing in 1912, Angus L. Macdonald stated: "*Now it is quite common for Lewismen to go to Canada in spring and come home in the beginning of winter with their earnings*".[18]

In this context it is not surprising that many of those connected with the *Iolaire* had far-flung connections – brothers and uncles who served with the Canadian forces, one returning serviceman who had been a shepherd in Punta Arenas, Chile and another who was born in Cape Breton and had already served in the Australian Navy before joining up in Britain. Experience deep sea and time spent working overseas on the fishing or on the land were commonplace experiences for these globally-connected islanders.

While physical mobility by sea was quite common, other forms of communication developed only slowly. Stornoway was joined to the mainland by a subsea cable, which brought a telegraphic extension to the islands in 1880, but the ten country post offices then established did not get extensions immediately, leaving communications between town and country down to the speed of a horse. The communications network was valuable – youngsters breaking the small white porcelain insulators on telegraph poles were harshly treated, with the birch being the strongest deterrent.

When it came to physical communication with the mainland, that was, of course, by sea. Prior to 1897, Lewis was linked by mail steamer sailings from Poolewe or, latterly, from Stromeferry to Stornoway. This was supplemented by weekly cargo sailings from Glasgow. A railhead established in 1897 at Kyle of Lochalsh had a huge impact on travellers, as it meant that islanders could travel from there onto anywhere in the United Kingdom. David MacBrayne Ltd ordered a new Stornoway service steamer and the plucky little *Sheila* came on to the route in 1904. No other vessel served the route until the war, when the *Plover* was occasionally used to assist.

Stornoway as a naval base – The Royal Naval Reserve and RNR (Trawler)

Lewismen's love of the sea starts at an early age, the roaring of the waves being the first sound that breaks on the ears of many island infants. Lewis children of the late 19th and early 20th centuries grew up hearing tales of the sea from fathers, uncles and elder brothers and were inherently aware of the dangers associated with the sea.

The Royal Naval Reserve, a reserve force of volunteer seamen formed by the Naval Reserve Act of 1859, evolved into a naval fighting unit that could quickly supplement regular forces manning ships at sea. The men initially came from the Mercantile Marine and, from 1873 onwards, also included volunteers from among the coastal fishermen of Britain, especially northern Scotland. Lewismen quickly volunteered when fishermen were offered the chance as, apart from the adventure and a free holiday, they were remunerated with an annual retainer. The Customs House in Stornoway was where men from Lewis and Harris were registered and received travel warrants for training.

By 1876 Stornoway was identified as one of six battery and training depots destined to be built in Scotland and, in the two years before the new naval base opened, in 1878, at what became known as Battery Point, HMS *Flirt* was despatched to Stornoway to undertake the training of the men. Early adventures in training featured incidents worthy of a Compton Mackenzie novel. The Hebridean winter hindered training, not least by a lack of daylight. When, in 1891, modern breech-loading rifled guns and quick firers like Maxim machine guns came into use, the ordnance available at training batteries became outdated. In 1894 HM ships

Views of Newton and Inaclete in Stornoway around 1900. Fishermen's cottages faced the sea.

In the second picture the RNR base at Battery Point can be seen in the distance.

South Beach, Stornoway, after 1905. The Imperial Hotel is in the foreground, and to the left herring barrels are piled against the harbour wall.

Superb and *Galatea* were despatched to embark reservists at Stornoway for sea training. The Admiralty, however, forgot to consult locals and, with insufficient notice for the men to muster, only four men boarded – a salutary lesson to the Sea Lords sitting behind desks in Whitehall.

By 1897 matters were improving. The RNR Battery at Stornoway had received small calibre modern guns and the provision of Lee Metford rifles ensured rifle drill and shooting practice was up to date. A morale booster came in 1898 as minor uniform changes meant that, apart from cap tallies, the men of the Royal Navy and RNR wore the same uniform.

In 1901 the battleship HMS *Camperdown* was allocated to embark Lewis ratings on six months' training, returning to Stornoway on the quarter for another 75 men. A similar number of island sailors had to go to the Clyde to train with the battleship HMS *Benbow* and when they returned home another 75 travelled south.

In 1904 came the great naval reform. Under the new system men were expected to embark for three months in their first year of service and afterwards for one month in every alternate year. The new regulations made it quite clear that no applicant would be accepted for enrolment in the RNR unless he were a British subject, able to speak and understand the English language, educated at least enough to sign his name, free from physical defects and was in health, character and every other aspect fully eligible. A man desiring to be entered as a seaman had to prove, among other things, that he had been to sea for at least two years, that he knew enough about seamanship to be able to box the compass, steer, heave the lead, tell the marks and pull a good oar and that he was willing to declare his intention of following the sea for at least five years after enlistment.

Seamen had to go through training in general drills, commission drills, watch evolutions, physical training, signalling, gun drill on all gun types up to six inch and stokers had to undertake physical training, musketry and gun pulling as well as stokehold work.

In January 1910 the Admiralty founded the Trawler Division of the Royal Naval Reserve, which was designed to man requisitioned vessels to be used in minesweeping. The danger of mines had been highlighted in the Russian/Japanese War of 1904 and counter measures were desperately required in order to keep sea lanes open and the Grand Fleet at sea. The uniform of the trawler section consisted of a jersey with RNR over a 'T' in red worsted and a pair of serge trousers. Second hands had a red crown over the RNR/T and enginemen had a peaked cap with no badge.

The minesweeping trawlers were vessels requisitioned from the fishing fleet and soon training in sweeping began in fishing ports around the coast. In April 1913 armed merchant cruisers first appeared, with the *Aragon* carrying two 4.7" guns.

The presence of the naval base in Stornoway was enormously important to the islands. The *Stornoway Gazette's* second editor (son of the founder editor) wrote in 1994:

> "It is impossible to over-estimate the importance of the Battery in the economic and social life of the island. The Crofters Commission in 1901 drew a comparison between conditions in the island then and twenty years before. Referring to the large contribution the island made to the army and navy, the report commented:"Since the establishment of a Royal Naval Reserve station at Stornoway a large proportion of the young men from the islands join that service rather than the militia. They undergo their annual course of training at whatever season of the year is most suitable for them and form a very

King Edward Wharf at the outset of war. MacBraynes sheds, the fish mart and the old Caledonian Hotel dominate the scene.

Zulu fishing boats tied up at Cromwell Street and North Beach quays c.1910.

fine body of men. In the present year 2,500 men have undergone their annual course of training in Stornoway. Of these 2,300 were from Lewis and the remaining 200 from Harris and the Uists."[19]

In a newspaper article published around the same time, W. J. Gibson,[20] who was always precise with his facts, described the Stornoway Naval Reserve station as: "*the largest in the United Kingdom.*"

The value of the Stornoway base to Britain can be reckoned from the fact that in 1916 there were at least 2,348 Lewismen on active service with the Royal Navy, the great majority of them Reservists who had trained at Battery Point."

The last pre-war return of the strength of the Royal Naval Reserve was dated 1st August 1914. It listed the RNR ratings for the whole of Great Britain as: wireless telegraph operators 6, engine room artificers 513, leading seamen 197, seamen 9,793, leading stokers 88, stokers 4,733. Total strength was 15,330. For the trawler section as: skippers 111, second hands 152, enginemen 275, trimmers 119, deckhands 368. Total strength was 1,025 for a grand total of 16,335. Of this number, no less than 2,340 Lewismen would be ready to serve when the call-up came in 1914.

The Home Fleet's torpedo destroyer flotilla came into Stornoway harbour in 1912 as tensions escalated across Europe. They remained for three weeks and were welcomed with civic pomp and hospitality for the crews.

Chapter 1 Footnotes

1. William Henderson Macdonald quoted in *Old Stornoway Revisited*, Stornoway Historical Society, 2001

2. Bothies – small, one-roomed buildings with thatched roofs, used for shelter and not as an abode

3. *Report of Her Majesty's Commissioners of Inquiry into the Condition of the Crofters and Cottars in the Highlands and Islands of Scotland*. Napier and Commissioners. Edinburgh, 1884

4. As above

5. Napier, 1884

6. *Forty-seventh Report of the Board of Supervision* 1891-2, App A14

7. *Public Administration in the Highlands and Islands of Scotland* J. P. Day. University of London Press, 1918

8. *Report to the Local Government Board for Scotland on the Sanitary Condition of the Lews* Frederick Dittmar and Alexander B. Millar, Royal College of Surgeons of England. Glasgow, HMSO 1905

9. *Public Administration in the Highlands and Islands of Scotland* J. P. Day. University of London Press, 1918

10. Ross and Cromarty, the County Authority for Lewis at that time

11. *Report of the Royal Commission on the Housing of the Industrial Population of Scotland, Rural and Urban*. Sir Henry Ballantyne et al. HMSO Edinburgh, 1917

12. *Report of the Committee on Medical Service in the Highlands and Islands*, 1917

13. Ballantyne, 1917

14. *The Spectator* book reviews. 21st December 1918

15. Frank Thompson from Stornoway Historical Society website, 2009

16. Details describing the voyage and settlement can be found in the Icelandic *Landnámabók*

17. *Canadian Boat-Song* Scottish, anonymous. First published in *Blackwoods Edinburgh Magazine*, 1829

18. *Highland News*, 1912

19. James Shaw Grant *In Search of Lewis*. Stornoway Gazette, 21st March 1994

20. W J Gibson was rector (principal) of the Nicolson Institute at the time of the Great War

Chapter 2

Islanders at War

"The mobilisation of the Militias and Territorials, after the Naval Reservists, has practically denuded Lewis of its able-bodied male population. It is safe to say that no other district in the British Isles has contributed of its manhood in such proportion as Lewis."[1]

On Sunday 2nd August 1914 the Customs Office in Stornoway was instructed to mobilise the Royal Naval Reserve. That afternoon, motor cars travelled to all the Lewis villages with notices calling on the men to report to Stornoway. Earlier in the day, church ministers had received telegrams asking them to announce mobilisation from their pulpits. The Sunday call-up created an unusual disturbance and an unheard-of breach of the conventional Lewis Sabbath, but the response was prompt and almost all the men had reported to Stornoway by Monday evening. Their departure left the island, and especially the fishing fleet, with a desolate air – drifters, Zulus[2], sgoths[3] and rowing boats were all beached, moored or tied up in harbours on the Saturday, some to remain unused for four years, others never to be used again.

On Monday 3rd August, 430 men left Stornoway on the steamers *Sheila* and *Claymore*, heading for the naval base at Chatham in Kent, where they would meet hundreds of other Lewis naval reservists who had been fishing out of Fraserburgh, Peterhead and other mainland ports. A huge crowd gathered at Stornoway harbour for the send-off and their cheers were joined by the sirens of herring drifters and other shipping, which kept up the deafening noise until the *Sheila* and *Claymore* had rounded the beacon at Arnish point.

Custom Officers and Police that day visited every fishing boat tied up in Stornoway harbour and instructed all members of crews who were Naval Reservists to report immediately to the Customs Office. That night 50 of those men left on the mail-boat en-route to Chatham. Some 2,340 Lewismen, nearly all seamen or deckhands, responded when the call came in August 1914. This represented around one fifth of the British RNR quota of seamen and deckhands – a proud record for an island with a population in 1911 of 29,603. Before long men from Harris and Barra also were in the ranks.

Men in the 3rd Battalions (Reserve Battalions) of the Seaforth Highlanders, Queen's Own Cameron Highlanders and Gordon Highlanders followed quickly on their heels to Fort George at Ardersier, to Inverness and to Aberdeen. The Ross Mountain Battery also assembled at the Drill Hall on Church Street, Stornoway, before being shipped away to link up with the Battery section based at Lochcarron.

War was officially declared between Britain and Germany on 4th August 1914. The outbreak of hostilities completely paralysed the fishing industry, and hundreds of Lewis fishing girls returned home nightly from the East Coast while the able-bodied men in the island were mobilising. At the outbreak of war the herring fishing season was at its height, but within months the industry was in tatters, the markets gone, mines floating in the herring grounds and boats lying disused. Herring girls and the fish-curing businesses on land were inevitably affected as their season was cut short.

There were many difficult partings. A young herring girl, Catherine Campbell from 54 North Tolsta, Lewis, working in Fraserburgh, waved goodbye to her six brothers, who were all serving on fishing boats in the port and were conscripted on the outbreak of war. As she shook hands with her sixth brother she was overcome with grief, and was comforted by other herring girls in the crowd at the railway station. The brothers were not even allowed to go home to say farewell to their widowed mother.

The impact on the community as a whole was immediate. The land was now peopled by women, children, invalids and the old. Every fit man in the island was on active service – a heavy burden especially for sparsely-populated islands. Not only had the young men rushed to defend their country, but older men in the reserve and the militia had also volunteered, long before the time of their call-up was due. Hardly a fisherman was left in Lewis except men who were too old for conscription, some of whom attempted to sail fishing boats beached when crews left for the war. To those left behind fell the hard task of cultivating the ungenerous lazy beds to provide food and continuing the hard labour of animal husbandry, peat-cutting and the thousand other tasks needed to live.

The situation in the islands was desperate, even in comparison to the hardships experienced elsewhere. A Stornoway correspondent wrote to the national newspapers pleading that starvation would be the lot of the inhabitants of the Island of Lewis unless Government help was forthcoming. Another correspondent appealed through the newspaper columns on behalf of Harris women for people to order hand-knitted socks. The women's outlook for the coming winter was very serious as nearly all their men had left with the Naval Reserve, the herring industry was at a standstill, and there were no visitors to buy the tweeds or to spend money in the Islands. They would make socks of soft wool in a large size for 1s 9d pair.[4]

The *Times* reported:

"DISTRESS IN THE HEBRIDES – LOCHIEL who is raising a special battalion of the Camerons, has appealed to the MACKINTOSH of MACKINTOSH, as Lord Lieutenant of Inverness-shire, to relieve the deplorable conditions prevailing in the OUTER HEBRIDES in consequence of the war. Not a single able-bodied man has been left on the Island of Benbecula and there is no one to gather the crops. Similar conditions also prevail in North Uist, South Uist and Barra."[5]

If the practical situation of the islands was desperate, the emotional strain on those left at home was no less severe. The huge contribution of the islands' menfolk meant that every family had sons, fathers, brothers and uncles away serving at sea or in the trenches. There was desperate worry every day, especially once news began to filter through of men lost, wounded, missing and imprisoned by the enemy.

The infantry regiments in which some islanders served would post casualty lists in the newspapers, naming the dead, missing and wounded of their regiment, perhaps later announcing that someone listed as missing had been found to be a prisoner-of-war. The Admiralty favoured notices in the Post Offices, which would come to Stornoway and be forwarded on to rural Post Offices, where they would be posted up and anxious relatives would come to see what news might have arrived.

Most dreaded was the telegram to the door of the house, sent to tell a family that their boy was missing, his vessel had been sunk, or perhaps that he had died

A YMCA canteen was
opened for servicemen in
Stornoway Town Hall.

Sandwick Bay showing HMS Iolaire, the Stornoway naval base, front right, Holm island top right

The Imperial Hotel was the naval headquarters during the war.

Rear Admiral Boyle, commander of the Stornoway naval base for the majority of the Great War.

The Royal Naval Reserve on parade at Battery Point.

in hospital of wounds. In town and in the populated districts such as Back and Point, these would be delivered by boys on foot, running from the Post Office which had received the message. In the country the Post Mistress or Post Master would bring the message, or it would arrive with the postman. Not long afterwards would come the Minister or the Elders of the church, alerted to a bereavement, to pray with the family as neighbours gathered to give what comfort they could.

These daily blows to small communities came on top of unremitting hard work to keep food on the table and warmth in the home. The strain is eloquently conveyed in this poem by Catherine Macdonald of Portnaguran, thinking continuously of her fair-haired brother out fighting in the trenches:

Saighdear an Fhuilt Bhàin

Nuair a thèid mi chun an dorais,
Nuair a bhios a' ghealach slàn,
Bidh mo smuaintean air na balaich,
Tha a-nochd sgapte air feadh a' bhlàir.

Nuair a thèid mi dhan a' mhòine,
Bidh mo dheòir a' ruith gu làr,
Is ged a lìonadh iad mo bhrògan,
Chan innsinn mo bhròn do chàch.

Nuair a thèid mi dhan an leabaidh,
Nuair tha càch air dhol fo thàmh,
Bidh mo smuaintean air mo bhràthair,
Sin mo ghràdh, an saighdear bàn.

Nuair a thig an cogadh-sa gu deireadh,
Is gum faigh iad às an trainnse ghrànd',
Bidh sinn ag ùrnaigh ris an Tighearna
Gun tig na gaisgich dhachaigh slàn.

The Fair-haired Soldier

When I go to the door
When the moon is full
My thoughts are with the boys
Who are tonight scattered across the field of battle

When I go to the peats
My tears fall to the ground
But, although they would fill my shoes
I would not tell my sorrow to anyone else

When I go to bed,
When everyone else has gone to rest
My thoughts are with my brother
That is my loved one,
the fair-haired soldier

When this war is over
And they get out of the ugly trench
Our prayers will be to the Lord
That the heroes will come home safe and sound[6]

Catherine's brother did come home – wounded, but able to live a long, hard-working life. From island men like him the contribution to the war was astonishing. As H. H. Wilson wrote:

> "Had the proportion of enlistments over the whole British Isles been equal to that of the Lews, the fighting power of the Crown would have numbered 6,500,000, and there would have been no Cabinet crisis. The military value of the contingent from this little surviving area of the old Highland world is not fully represented by numbers, for the casualty and honours lists bore ample testimony to the fighting quality of these crofters and fishers."[7]

In the First War, out of a population of approximately 29,000 on the Isle of Lewis, 6,172 served in the armed services, of whom 3,500 were in the Royal Navy. The figure is actually higher counting the merchant seamen who were not classed as forces of the Crown, and the islanders who fought with Colonial and American forces. At least 560 Lewismen were serving with the Canadian Army.[8]

The first island casualty was Philip MacLeod of Steinish, serving in the Royal Field Artillery, who was killed at the battle of Le Cateau on the 26th August 1914. He was to be the first of a grim toll of island boys and men who would pay the ultimate sacrifice over the next four years. On one day alone – 25th April 1915 – 17 Lewismen, serving with the 2nd Battalion, Seaforth Highlanders, were killed near Ypres at the Battle of St Julien.

Royal Naval Reserve and Mercantile Marine Reserve

Island seafarers were ideal for the roles the Admiralty now urgently required. They were skilled and able in rowing, sailing, fishing, shooting, trapping, knots, strict discipline, suffering austere conditions and many other attributes that made a hardy sailor. To those joining the Navy, enemy minefields, shells and submarines were merely new hazards that had to be overcome at sea during the war. The seafaring people of the Highlands and Islands contributed 4,431 men to the Royal Naval Reserve at the outbreak of the Great War.

It soon became evident that the Trawler Section required expanding beyond all expectations, with men manning drifters as well as trawlers. Initially there were not enough ships, resulting in many RNR men being utilised with the Royal Naval Division as soldiers defending Antwerp. It says much for their training, discipline and attitude that the RNR boys could wield a rifle and bayonet and fight in the trenches before many units of the regular army had crossed the English Channel. At sea, naval engagements took place at Heligoland, Coronel, the Falklands, Dogger Bank and Jutland, but most naval and mercantile casualties were caused by mine and torpedo. From battleship to submarine, Hebridean sailors served in all oceans, all weathers and in all types of action.

War stories – battles and engagements and heroes' tales

With so many men serving with the Navy, it was not long before former fishermen from Lewis, now naval ratings, were in action against the enemy. The first major naval action of the Great War was the Battle of Heligoland Bight, on 28th August 1914, when the newly commissioned light cruiser HMS *Arethusa* was badly damaged. On board this ship were island reservists including the first Lewis sailor to be wounded in the war – Leading Seaman John M MacLean of Battery Park, Stornoway. After a short stay in hospital he rejoined his ship and took part in the action off Cuxhaven, on Christmas Day, 1914 and the Battle of the North Sea on 24th January 1915. For his bravery in the action at Heligoland Bight, MacLean was promoted to First Class Petty Officer. He survived the war.

HMS *Carmania*

News was soon to reach Lewis of the first island naval reservist to die in action. He was 19-year-old Kenneth John MacLeod of 7 Ranish, killed on 14th September 1914 in action on HMS *Carmania. Carmania* was an ex-Cunard liner that had been commissioned as an armed merchant cruiser, within a few days of the outbreak of war. Of her newly assigned naval complement of 62, over a third were Naval Reservists from Lewis, who are described in the Cunard official history as 'Scottish fishermen of the best type.'[9] The *Carmania* was one of a number of cruisers and battleships sent to the South Atlantic to patrol Britain's important trade routes along the coast of South America and to protect merchant ships from a German cruiser squadron deployed to the area. All the British capital ships sent to the South Atlantic to thwart the German Navy and defend the British merchant fleet had naval reservists from the Western Isles in their complements.

On 14th September 1914 the German armed merchant cruiser *Cap Trafalgar* was being coaled off the Brazilian coast near the island of Trinidad when she was spotted by the *Carmania*. A fierce engagement ensued and, although the *Carmania* managed to sink the German cruiser, she was badly damaged and had to be towed by HMS *Macedonia* to Gibraltar for repairs.

Of the seamen wounded on board the *Carmania*, none suffered more grievously than Donald MacLeay (Dan Tee) of Shader, Barvas whose brother, Donald (Dolaidh Tee) also served on the ship. Dan showed conspicuous gallantry in the action in carrying shells to the big guns, despite enemy shells falling all around him. While he was carrying the last shell to his gun, a German round hit the shell in his arms, throwing it to the deck. In the explosion that followed, MacLeay's right arm was torn away above the elbow, his right leg almost cut off and his body pitted with numerous shrapnel wounds.

Bleeding profusely, MacLeay was lying unconscious amongst the debris and wreckage on the deck when the burial party ratings lifted him up. Assuming he was dead, they were about to throw him over the side into the sea, when his brother Dolaidh arrived on the scene. With clenched fists he remonstrated with the ratings and prevented his brother being thrown overboard.[10] Dan MacLeay had to suffer excruciating pain from his injuries for a number of weeks before the ship docked in Gibraltar. He was later transported to England and to hospital, where his right leg was amputated. His recovery was a marvel to the medical staff who tended him. He returned to Lewis, where he lived happily, was twice married and died at a ripe old age.

Also on the *Carmania* was Malcolm Nicolson of Ranish, who was to be drowned on the *Iolaire*, Donald MacLeod of Broker, who was severely wounded later in the war, and Roderick MacRitchie of Eoropie, Ness, who was lost on 8th August 1915, when the armed merchant cruiser HMS *India* was sunk by a submarine off the Norwegian coast. The Navy League presented a silver plate to the *Carmania* for outstanding war service, the only ex-merchant ship so honoured in the First World War. For sinking the *Cap Trafalgar* the crew of the *Carmania* shared a prize bounty of £2,115.

Trawlers and drifters

As well as more regular navy duties, many of the fishermen called up served on the war-time drifters and trawlers, undertaking dangerous and onerous work like mine clearance. Donald J. MacLennan of Carloway was involved in this kind of work when, on 15th May 1915, an Austrian force of light cruisers and destroyers attacked a drifter line in the Adriatic. The drifters had little fire power compared to the Austrian warships and 14 of them were sunk. Donald was among 72 survivors taken prisoner by the Austrians. His brother, Malcolm, was also serving with the RNR (Trawler Section).

Alexander MacLeod of Berneray, Harris, skipper of the ex-Aberdeen trawler *Ben Gulvain* was awarded the Distinguished Service Cross for bravery, for his attempt to save lives when HMT *Fraser* was blown up by a mine, while the two vessels were operating in company near Boulogne. His son, Sgt-Major Malcolm MacLeod, had been awarded the Distinguished Conduct Medal and the

French Croix de Guerre with Laurel Leaf whilst serving with the 1st Life Guards. It is most unusual for a father and son to be decorated during the same war. Sadly, Malcolm was accidentally killed in London in 1919.

HMS *Orama*

The German cruiser SMS *Dresden* was the only German vessel to escape from the British naval victory at the Battle of the Falklands on 8th December 1914. She eluded pursuit for over three months until, on 14th March 1915, she was engaged by HMS *Glasgow*, HMS *Kent* and HMS *Orama*, near the Chilean Juan Fernandez Islands. After five minutes of intense action, the *Dresden* hauled down her colours and the crew that survived, including several who were seriously injured, were rescued by the British ships. The sinking of this notorious German ship, that had been a thorn in the side of British merchant ships, was hailed as a great British victory at sea. It also ended the German plan to raid the British station at Port Stanley in the Falklands.

On board the *Glasgow*, *Kent* and *Orama* were many Lewis naval reservists – but by far the largest number were aboard the auxiliary cruiser *Orama*, with reputedly eighty Lewis naval reservists in her complement. On the *Orama* when action stations sounded, locked in a shuddering gun turret, were Alexander MacIver, his brother Norman and their neighbour Angus MacKay, from Shulishader, Point. Perspiring in the heat, noise and foul air, they must have wondered whether they would ever see home again. They all survived the engagement, but Alexander and Angus were later to die in the wreck of the *Iolaire*.

The *Orama* eventually docked in Sydney, Australia in August 1915, to a rapturous welcome. The ship was visited by Australia's Governor General Viscount Novar, the former MP for Ross and Cromarty. After a general inspection, he inspected the Lewis reservists on their own, since he was well acquainted with the island from his earlier life. In his speech to the crew the viscount said:

> "A few days ago I went into a barber's shop. The barber, as barbers will, began to tell me the news. Had I seen the ship which had come to Sydney, with strange men on board, with blue eyes and teeth like hounds, and speaking a language no one could understand? I didn't tell him who I was. If I had, he would have had a sign next day, 'Patronised by the Governor General.' But before I left, I said to him, 'These men are fellow countrymen of mine. The island they come from has provided some of the best pioneers who ever came to Australia.'"[11]

For nine weeks the *Orama* lay in Sydney and the Lewis seamen got to know many fellow islanders settled in that city. During her stay the *Sydney Sun* reported:

> "There is a big grey ship in the harbour just now, which holds things more terrible than even her grim exterior suggests. She used to be a floating hotel; now she is a ship of war. She numbers among her crew 70 sailors who speak nothing but Gaelic, and 25 of them are MacLeods. ..... The MacLeods all come from Stornoway, and are never content unless there is a fight raging. They love a scrap, and delight in telling the way in which the British guns smashed the *Dresden*. Any number of Germans would be safe in the hands of the MacLeods of Stornoway."[12]

After leaving Sydney the *Orama* patrolled foreign waters for three years, before returning to the UK. Among other islanders who served aboard her were six men from the parish of Uig, Donald Smith, Donald J MacDonald from Valtos, Angus Morrison of Carishader and John Nicolson, Angus MacDonald, John MacKay and John MacDonald, all from Crowlista. Petty Officer Roderick MacLeod of Coll and Stornoway had run away to sea as a boy and, in 1892, served on HMS *Hyacinth* – the last British naval vessel under sail. Incredibly, he survived six wars from Crete in 1896 to the Second World War. It is unlikely that any other man in the navy had been in action in so many wars and survived.

Angus MacDonald of Crowlista, aged 31, another of the *Orama* ratings, was drowned on the *Iolaire* after surviving four years of war at sea.

The fall of Antwerp

The Royal Naval Division was a curious mixed military unit, under the control of the Admiralty. Before any proper methodical military training was carried out, they were transported across the English Channel to defend Antwerp in a reckless effort to save the city from

Donald Murray (left) in the trenches near Antwerp.

43

German occupation, mounted by the First Sea Lord, Winston Churchill. A number of Lewis reservists served with the 1st and 2nd Naval Brigades which, under the command of Churchill, were used in a desperate attempt to plug the gaps in the British Expeditionary Force. The attempt was a fiasco – outnumbered, their supplies diminishing and with little artillery support, the Naval Division had little option but to retreat. Many escaped to reach allied lines, but others had to go into the neutral Netherlands to escape capture by the Germans. Over 100 Lewis sailors were among the Division sailors interned at Gröningen.

Donald Murray, RNR from North Tolsta – later an *Iolaire* survivor – recounted his experience years later:

> "Then we were down to Antwerp. We used to go to the trenches when night fell. . . . Now I was in a machine crew – and the Germans began coming over the top. They were a wild lot – the Belgians had retired into the town – we were between the Germans and the town and we were holding them back – they would come and they would retreat – this went on for a few nights – we were realising they were getting reinforcements – we were getting nothing. We didn't have ammunition either. You see we had plenty of machine guns and plenty of rifles but we didn't have men."[13]

The Rev DM Lamont, writing an article on Lewis reservists interned in Holland, wrote:

> "Our interned Islanders in Holland are neither sanctimonious saints nor male angels. They have their fun, their jokes, their pipe music. But let me say very emphatically that in morality, and as worshippers of the true God, and in all-round manliness, we may proudly compare them with any section of the British Navy."[14]

The Battle of Jutland

Like other island fishermen, Murdo Macleod (Murchadh Gharrabost) of Aird, Point, mobilised at the outbreak of war in 1914 and was on the cruiser HMS *Galatea* along with Kenneth Campbell, North Tolsta, when their ship made initial contact with the German High Seas Fleet at Jutland on 31st May 1916. Murdo and Kenneth survived the battle, but were lost as they travelled homewards on the *Iolaire*. Eleven Lewismen died on one ship, when a German shell detonated inside HMS *Invincible*, the magazine igniting and exploding. Smoke and debris from the *Invincible* shot up hundreds of feet into the air and the ship was no more, taking 1,026 men with her.

Eight other Lewis sailors were lost at Jutland; four on the heavy cruiser HMS *Defence* which exploded with all hands and one on each of the battlecruisers *Indefatigable* and *Queen Mary*, heavy cruiser *Black Prince* and destroyer *Broke*.

News from home

Letters from home were eagerly awaited by all servicemen and kept Lewis men up to date with important matters concerning the croft, the fishing and the well-being of neighbours. 19-year-old Roderick Murray of South Shawbost joined up in March 1918 and was serving on the cruiser HMS *Roxburgh* on convoy duties. His 18-year-old brother Kenneth was a civilian living in Glasgow. Letters passed between them and their family in Lewis to fill them in on home news.

From their father Donald to Roderick, 24th October 1918:

"Dear son, Just a few notes to let you now that we are all well keeping well ..... we are getting on with the work just now at home we have the first start lifting the potatoes we have bad potatoes this year it will be very hard on people to get true (through). Lot of people were home that month and most of them are away. Just now we are all wondering to see you but we think that we see you sometime ...... from your loving Father." [15]

From young brother Donald (then aged 15), 29th August 1918:

"Kenneth is coming home for the harvest. Andrew Mitchell came home last night. He is serving in the Australians. Donald Mitchell's son. And Also Donald Macleod, 'Norman' came home. I heard your father speaking about sending for harvest leave. I hope to God that you've got it too. They are getting some herring. Alex Macleod is keeping well. I think *Kent* is patrolling round Glasgow." [16]

Stornoway naval base in wartime

The Royal Naval Reserve on Battery Point, also known as Inaclete Point from the time before the Battery was founded, was the largest RNR Battery and Training Depot in Great Britain during the 41 years of its existence. Many thousands of men from Lewis, Harris and Wester Ross received their training for service in the Royal Navy during that time. In addition to the training depot, which had regular Royal Navy instructors, the Admiralty took over war accommodation in the Imperial Hotel and the Town Hall.

Until March 1915, when the HMS *Iolaire* base was founded, HMY *Vanessa II* was in Stornoway, followed by the auxiliary patrol depot ship HMS *Manco*. In late 1914 a request was made to the Admiralty for 12 armed trawlers and one yacht to be based at Stornoway, to patrol the east coast of the Hebrides and west coast of Skye and Mull. At West Loch Tarbert in Harris the request was made for six armed trawlers to patrol the west coast of the Hebrides, with 12 armed trawlers and an armed yacht based at Loch Ewe to patrol mainland Scotland. The principal base for Area 1 was quickly switched from Aultbea, near Loch Ewe, to Stornoway, once it was realised that the mainland location was 40 miles away from the nearest railhead.

Auxiliary Patrol Area 1 was the largest of all the 18 areas surrounding the British Isles. It covered the coastline of Scotland from Skerryvore and the Mull of Kintyre in the south to Cape Wrath in the north-east, and the Atlantic as far north and west as was necessary. The reason for the strong naval presence at Stornoway was to protect the north-west of Scotland as enemy U-boats were active off the Outer Hebrides, with over 40 ships sunk, mostly in 1917. The Northern Patrol also played a huge part in the blockade of shipping to Germany, which contributed to victory for the Allies with food, ammunition, fuel and raw materials being denied to the enemy.

The commander of Patrol Area 1 based at Stornoway was Vice-Admiral Reginald Tupper, who had joined the Royal Navy in 1873, and remained in the Senior Service until 1921, a total of 48 years. He was promoted to Rear Admiral in January 1916 and left for a new command at the end of the following month. He was succeeded as commander of the Stornoway naval base in April 1916 by Rear Admiral Robert Francis Boyle, son of the 5th Earl of Shannon, who had been promoted to Rear Admiral on 25th April 1914.

The first HMY Iolaire, which served from the Stornoway base 1915-18. She left the base after HMY Amalthaea arrived in November 1918. Amalthaea then became the new HMY Iolaire.

Vice-Admiral Tupper recalled in his memoirs:

"I went to Area No 1 on the 1st January, 1915, at twenty four hours' notice. I was taken to Stornoway in a yacht called the *Vanessa*, which became my headquarters. I had no staff whatever but I picked up my coxswain at Portsmouth Barracks before I started North, and happened to meet Mr. Norman Craig, K.C., who was serving as Lieutenant in the yacht *Lorna*; and, as I was made Competent Authority of the Hebrides, said to him. 'You know something about the law, if you don't about anything else, so come along and be my Flag Lieutenant and legal adviser and helper'. I had an eighteen-year-old youth as a Secretary to start with, and it took me something like five weeks before things were working efficiently. At the end of six months I had 6 yachts, 36 trawlers, 40 drifters, 8 MLs and 6 of these extraordinary things called whalers to carry out the duties of the Area.

"I spent at least four days a week at sea, visiting my patrols and searching all the fjords and so on. It was well that I did so, for the first time I went afloat I found nearly all my patrol craft in harbour; they said they went in every night because they thought that was the right thing to do! I soon disabused them of that idea, and the result was that they did very good work.

"I claim that my little patrol destroyed three submarines and picked up ninety-five mines; only one merchant ship was torpedoed during my fifteen months in command. Ships of the Grand Fleet used to go down to dock through the Area and nothing happened to any of them."[17]

In March 1915 the Defence of the Realm Act (DORA) was extended by prohibiting civilian procurement of alcohol for men of the Northern Patrol. The penalty imposed on civilians was £10 or 60 days imprisonment. The alcohol ban was strictly adhered to and locals caught supplying naval personnel were dealt with immediately, as evidenced in the pages of the *Highland News* and *Stornoway Gazette*.

On 16th April 1915 HMY *Vanessa II* returned to Stornoway carrying local fishermen from the southern Hebrides, who had taken the King's shilling with the RNR. 32 Eriskay men, 58 from Barra and 10 Vatersay lads enlisted for naval training and so 100 more Hebrideans were added to the King's navy.

A personal picture from the album of telegraphist Leonard Welch shows the 3-inch bow-mounted gun on the Amalthaea, later to become the Iolaire, with a crew member, possibly Welch himself.

The Stornoway base was named HMS *Iolaire*, following a tradition whereby Royal Navy shore bases had a small vessel carrying the same name as the shore establishment. Since the Stornoway base officially opened in March 1915, she took the name *Iolaire* from the yacht that served her at that time. This was the first HMY *Iolaire*, built in 1902, a yacht of 999 gross register tonnage (GRT), built by Beardmore and Company in Glasgow, for the Scottish shipowner Sir Donald Currie. Sir Donald Currie had brought his new yacht to Stornoway soon after she was launched, offering her to Stornoway Town Council in 1902, when the King and Queen (Edward VII and Queen Alexandra) were visitors. The offer was accepted and the *Iolaire* carried the Royals from the royal yacht *Victoria and Albert* to the landing known later as the King Steps at King Edward Wharf.

This elegant yacht was later hired from the widow of Sir Donald by the Admiralty for wartime service. A twin-screw vessel with a speed of 17.5 knots, she was armed with two three-inch guns, mounted fore and aft. A third gun was added later in the war and was an anti-aircraft three-pounder, believed to be mounted amidships. She was also equipped with depth charges, mine ramps and wireless and arrived in Stornoway in May 1915. As the war drew to a close, such requisitioned vessels were being returned to their owners by the Admiralty, so the first *Iolaire* was sent back to Dundee to be decommissioned on 5th November 1918, becoming the *Amalthaea* as she swapped names with the second *Iolaire*. One of the crew who went away to Dundee with her was John Maclennan ('Ain Geal) of Kneep, who was to return after the war's end on board the second *Iolaire*.

The newly-arrived yacht *Amalthaea*, now HMY *Iolaire*, was older, smaller and slower. Built in 1881 and registered at 634 tons, she had three furnaces, an iron hull and was a single screw vessel, which meant she was only able to achieve 10 knots. She was sometimes described as a poor sea-boat, liable to roll and pitch in heavy seas, partly due to the guns which were later added fore and aft and on the promenade deck. The *Iolaire*, like all requisitioned vessels, was not designed for this added weight and it made her top heavy.

After a lifetime as a millionaire's yacht, with a succession of owners and various names, she had been requisitioned by the Admiralty in March 1915, given a new coat of battleship grey paint and newly armed with two three-inch guns, fore and aft, and a three-pounder anti-aircraft gun amidships. As *Amalthaea* she operated in the Portsmouth Area until August 1916 when she was sent north to Area II, Shetland Islands. Lt Cdr Richard G. W. Mason, who was to remain her commander at Stornoway, was appointed to command her in March 1917. He was not shy of battle and engaged a U-boat off Shetland on 7th July 1917, while escorting a Lerwick to Holmengraa convoy. *Amalthaea* moved to Area X, Yarmouth, on 19th December 1917 and from October 1918 came to Area I, Stornoway. She swapped names with the first *Iolaire* on 6th November 1918 and this was the vessel which stranded and sank on 1st January 1919.

Stornoway's excellence as a naval training base was demonstrated not just by the sea-going service record of island men. Many Lewis naval reservists were trained as gunners at the Battery in Stornoway. Some of these men were drafted to merchant ships that had guns mounted for defensive purposes only. A demonstration, specially staged for the King of the Belgians, resulted in a six-inch gun on the super-dreadnought HMS *Queen Elizabeth* setting a record, by firing 28 rounds in 58 seconds. The King was greatly impressed and afterwards the gunners were congratulated by Vice-Admiral Sir David Beatty, commander of the 1st Battlecruiser Squadron. No 3 on the gun was Murdo MacDonald of North Tolsta, an ex-fisherman.

Donald MacLeod (Junior), an ex-fishermen from Garyvard, with two team-mates, won the World Championship for three-inch wire splicing. Another Lewis naval reservist – John MacIver of North Tolsta – obtained his Board of Trade extra skipper's certificate in 1918 and at that time he had the honour of holding the BOT record in chart work for accuracy, neatness and speed.

Stornoway was ideally placed to function as a hub of communication, guarding the north-western approach to Britain from the Atlantic and from further north. After her arrival in January 1915, HMS *Manco* was anchored in Glumaig Bay at Arnish, equipped with wireless telegraphy. From here she kept in touch with ships in the Minch and relayed by signals the latest news to signal boys from the Stornoway Boys' Naval Brigade (later the Sea Cadet Corps). This unit manned a position on number 2 pier and relayed the messages to the naval offices at the Imperial Hotel, which was sited fronting the harbour, where An Lanntair arts centre now stands on South Beach Street. Once wireless telegraphy had been installed in the hotel itself, *Manco* departed.

The Admiralty's port pilot at Stornoway during the war was Captain George Watt of Newmarket. He had gone to sea as a young lad at the end of the 1860s, becoming a Master on sailing ships before transferring to steamships. He retired in 1913 but was soon recalled to service when war was declared, and had a strenuous war berthing and piloting steamers. Large numbers of ships of friendly and neutral nations were taken into Stornoway during the war, after being stopped and searched north and west of Lewis. Sometimes over 40 large vessels were being berthed at one time and Watt supervised all without a hitch or accident. He was made an MBE in April 1920.

A naval canteen located in Stornoway Town Hall was thought to have been the origin of a fire which gutted the building, and endangered large areas of the town centre, on 2nd March 1918. It was reported to the Admiralty in London thus:

Iolaire Sweetheart Badge - given by sailors based in Stornoway to their sweethearts.

"The Stornoway Town Hall, a very fine modern building, was completely gutted by fire. The fire was first found about 5pm in the central hall and appeared due to leaks in gas piping. The Town Hall hoses were fixed by naval officers and men, but there was no water in the hydrants, and the fire quickly gained. The town fire hoses were brought along and fixed to the street hydrants after some delay, but they were unable to do any good and there was not sufficient pressure to reach the roof. Practically all the important documents, furniture, etc., were removed from the various rooms used as offices for naval purposes and civil ones as well – the work being mostly done by naval officers and men. The naval barracks' small fire engine was brought down and proved the most efficient of the hoses.

"Efforts were made to confine the fire to the Town Hall building and to prevent it from spreading, this was successfully accomplished and the naval fire parties were withdrawn about 4am. At one time it appeared that the whole town might be destroyed owing to there being no fire engine, either steam or manual, and the inefficient water service.

"The rooms used by the navy in the Town Hall were Commodore's Office, Commodore's Secretary's Office, Fleet Paymaster's Office and the Ship's Office, the latter a very large room with accommodation also for Lieutenant (G) and Chief Gunner. It is believed that all important papers, etc., were removed and arrangements are now being made to utilise rooms in the Imperial Hotel to replace those lost."[18]

The necessity for the daily presence of navy vessels, personnel and procedures in Stornoway was well-understood by island people, who had their own experiences of the close proximity of hostilities. There were mines in the Minch and, many years later, Malcolm M Johnston (Calum Crotchie) of 17 Benside, Newmarket, recalled a German mine explosion at the cliffs of Holm, a childhood memory of sitting in class in the infant room of the Laxdale public school, when suddenly the school shook violently, and its doors and windows rattled. After school he was told that houses further out in the Newmarket area had panes of glass broken by the force of the explosion.

Also in the Minch were the constantly prowling U-boats, reported frequently by fishing vessels, the mailboat and by Navy vessels. MacBrayne's *Plover*, a regular caller to Stornoway with cargo from Mallaig, had a traumatic encounter on 29th July 1918, as she was sailing from Oban to Castlebay. At 3.45pm she was an hour into the final leg between Tiree and Barra when a U-boat surfaced and began firing with the deck gun. As the shells flew over the tiny vessel, the passengers and some of the crew acted in panic and launched three lifeboats. Admiralty records reveal that the passengers, including around 20 women and a party of Royal Naval Reservists going on leave, rushed the boats. The reservists were said to be in a state of intoxication and had been earlier reprimanded by the Master for their unruly behaviour.

The Master, Neil MacDougall, tried to quell the panic. The davits were almost bent to the water with the people scrambling to board the boats. To avoid swamping the boats the Master chose to stop the *Plover*, left the bridge and the ship began drifting broadside to. According to an eye witness it was Lt Col Finlay MacKenzie, the proprietor of the Lochboisdale Hotel, who mounted the bridge and swung the ship round end-on again. The ship's gunner also deserted his post, but the gunner's mate, Able Seaman Lawless, returned the submarine's fire with such accuracy that the U-boat was forced to submerge.

One of the lifeboats, with passengers and some crew aboard, landed at Rhum during the night and another at Barra the following day. The Inquiry into *Plover's* encounter with the U-boat was still in progress when the war ended. For his act of courage Lawless received the Distinguished Conduct Medal, but the gunner was court-martialled for deserting his post.[19]

Despite all the hardships they endured, islanders' loyalty and unwavering service to their King and country remained undaunted. The young men who came of age while the war was being fought showed enthusiasm to join their older relatives and neighbours in the great fight – often doing so as soon as their 18th birthday made them eligible. It's known that some took on useful roles even before they were old enough to join up – Norman Mackenzie (Kiman) of Garrabost was a telegram boy during the war and Jack Macaskill of Keith Street in Stornoway took a job as a junior clerk in the Harbour Office soon after war broke out, as well as joining Stornoway Boys' Naval Brigade. Both joined up as soon as they were 18, and both were to end their lives when the *Iolaire* went down on 1st January 1919.

The war comes to an end

After more than four long years, islanders finally heard the news they had hoped for on Monday 11th November 1918 – Armistice had been signed, the war was over. General rejoicing was shared quickly around the islands, ships sounding their sirens and school logbooks recording the celebrations:

"11th November 1918 – Foghorns are blowing in Stornoway harbour at this moment (11.30am). I understand this as evidence that the armistice has been signed. Gathered the children into the main room, addressed them on the war, called for cheers for our soldiers and sailors, reminded all present of the fallen, and concluded by singing together 'God save the King'. Hoisted flags outside. Received telegram from Clerk to declare a holiday for tomorrow."[20]

"11th November 1918 – Shortly after 11 o'clock today the signing of the armistice was signalled by the sirens of the patrol fleet in the harbour. A joint-session attendance was completed at 1.30 and school dismissed."[21]

"12th November 1918 – Yesterday there was a telegram from the Clerk of the Board to the effect that, hostilities having ceased yesterday at 11 o'clock, today would be observed as a holiday. The pupils who came were advised to that effect and after singing the National Anthem and giving loud cheer, dispersed to their various homes."[22]

No more daily visits would need to be made to the local Post Office to read the bulletins of the missing and dead and no more would families anxiously watch the postman on his rounds, delivering the dreaded death telegrams. Prayers were offered in island homes and churches, and God was thanked for the complete victory and the safe return of loved ones from the war.

The Highland News reported:

"Tuesday was observed as a public holiday and day of rejoicing at Stornoway on account of the news that the Armistice had been signed. Large detachments of naval men connected with the Stornoway base assembled at No. 1 Wharf at 11am and, headed by several pipers and drummers, marched around the town. Weather conditions were favourable and the lavish display of bunting on the streets and by all the boats in the harbour gave the town a gay and festive appearance. The procession lined up at No. 3 Wharf, where a large crowd had gathered to hear an address to his men by Rear Admiral Boyle."[23]

Rev Roderick Morrison of the High Church was also on the platform and led the gathering in prayer before the Rear Admiral, in a long speech, thanked all units of the Royal Navy including the WRNS and the Mercantile Marine. He also read out a message from King George V, who stated at the end that he was proud to have served in the Royal Navy.

It was a much-needed moment of celebration, but troubles were not over in Lewis. The Spanish Flu pandemic, which had begun in Glasgow in January, had swept towards the islands and many were dying. RNR sailor Roderick Murray of South Shawbost, serving aboard HMS *Roxburgh*, had this news from his father in early December:

"The flu is very bad at Carnan and North Shawbost, but it did not come to South Shawbost yet. All those who were sick got better except the Blacksmith's sister. Chirsty died after a short illness."[24]

The islands' medical authority closed schools to prevent the spread of the disease, Sandwickhill School was closed on 29th November by order of the authority, and The Nicolson Institute, initially closed for three weeks, then had the closure extended twice, each time by two weeks. Achmore School was closed from 8th November 1918 until 4th March 1919, Crowlista School reopened on 28th January 1919 after being closed for 12 weeks and Lemreway School was closed from 18th December 1918 until 5th May 1919 due to flu and whooping cough. This pattern was repeated across the islands, as the disease claimed children, young people and adults with terrifying speed.

Nor were the war losses yet over – on Armistice Day, Donald Maclean RNR of 9 Doune died at Granton Hospital, aged 26. The day before, Lt Donald Macdonald, 10 Holm, commander of the paddle minesweeper HMS *Ascot*, was lost off the Farne Islands. The 25-year-old's brother, John, was lost just weeks later on the *Iolaire*.

Our researches reveal that upwards of 330 men from the Outer Hebrides died serving on over 150 ships lost. In addition, some 140 seamen died serving their country in various other capacities. Considering that a conservative figure of 6,172 Lewismen served, practically all of the men of military age, the percentage was extremely high. These figures do not take into account men serving in the Mercantile Marine – most men serving or lost in the so-called 'Fourth Service' were omitted from the *Loyal Lewis Roll of Honour*. It should also be noted that during the Great War a total of 150 Lewis and Harrismen died serving with the Canadian forces.

The Western Isles probably sustained the heaviest proportional casualty rate of any area of the British Empire. The subsequent impact on the population, as war and emigration took their toll, is eloquently expressed by census figures. In 1911 the population was robust and the fishing industry at its highest. By 1921 the war had wrought its damage and by 1931 emigration had added its drain. The latest census figures are from 2011, showing rural areas at a shadow of their numbers 100 years before, the diminished population centralised in Stornoway.

Population of the Lewis parishes and Harris[25]

	1911	1921	1931	2011
Harris	5449	5276	4468	1264
Barvas	6953	6660	5876	3244
Lochs	4750	4396	3849	1810
Stornoway	13438	13366	12116	13009
Uig	4462	3956	3364	1595

Rear Admiral Boyle on South Beach addressing the crowd on Armistice Day 1918. Provost Murdo Maclean is on the platform with Bailie Roderick Smith to his left. The Imperial Hotel is behind the flagpole.

Armistice Day at South Beach with the assembled crowd surrounding the platform. Holm, Goat Island and Arnish in the background.

Stornoway, Royal Naval Reserve Field Battery at drill.

Chapter 2 Footnotes

1. *Highland News* 8th August, 1914

2. Zulus were two-masted boats with three heavy sails that were fast on the water and invaluable to the herring fishing industry

3. Sgòths – a wooden sailing boat typically associated with Ness in Lewis

4. www.scotlandswar.co.uk. Western Isles Home Front

5. *The Times*, 22nd August 1914

6. Catherine Macdonald of Portnaguran. Contributed and translated by Anna Mairi Martin of Aird for Isles FM's *The Great War: Through the Eyes of Women*, 2015

7. *The Great War, 1914-19* (13 volumes) H. H. Wilson

8. *Loyal Lewis Roll of Honour 1914 and After William Grant. Stornoway Gazette,* 1916

9. *The Ship That Hunted Itself* Colin Simpson. Weidenfeld and Nicolson, 1977

10. *Devil In The Wind* Charles Macleod. Gordon Wright Publishing, 1979

11. *Highland News*, August 1915

12. *Scotland's War.* Western Isles: Gunnery Instructor Roderick Macleod. www.scotlandswar.co.uk

13. Donald Murray, translated from Gaelic by Annie Morrison. *Stornoway Gazette*, 23rd May 1992

14. *Loyal Lewis Roll of Honour. Stornoway Gazette,* 1920

15. Personal letters carried by Roderick Murray, 25 South Shawbost and kept by his family

16. As above

17. *Reminiscences* Admiral Sir Reginald Tupper. London: Jarrolds, 1929

18. Excerpt from letter to Secretary of the Admiralty, received 6th March 1918

19. Recounted in the *Oban Times*, 16th August 1947

20. School logbook entry, Fidigarry school

21. School logbook entry, Nicolson Institute, Stornoway

22. School logbook entry, Bernera School

23. *Highland News*, November 1918

24. Personal letter from Donald Murray, 25 South Shawbost, 7th December 1918. Carried by Roderick Murray

25. Figures extracted from the National Census

Chapter 3

The Boys are Coming Home

"It was not a passenger boat, nor did it resemble one. It was different from any we ever had the pleasure to sail on. It was a beautiful 900-ton steam yacht which belonged to a rich Clyde ship-owner. … I felt rather honoured being conveyed on my last lap homeward on a millionaire's yacht."[1]

As surely as the men had streamed from the island on the day war was declared, now those who survived would return home. Demobilisation would not be immediate, the Admiralty had an enormous logistical task on their hands. The strength of the Navy at the date of the Armistice (including the Mercantile Marine Reserve, but excluding the Royal Naval Division) was 415,162 and many of these men were still needed for a wide range of post-war duties, all outlined in an official Government statement released a year later:

> "Between the 11th November 1918 and the signing of the peace treaty in June, it was necessary to keep the Fleet in Home waters at a very full strength, both on account of operational necessities, especially in the Baltic .....and because active measures might have been necessary to induce the Germans to sign the peace treaty. The services of the Navy were called upon in assisting to enforce the actual terms of the Armistice. Immediately upon its conclusion, the Grand Fleet was engaged in taking over the German ships for internment, and escorting them to Scapa Flow, whilst the Harwich Force took over the surrendered German Submarines. A portion of the main Fleet was constantly employed in watching the ships interned at Scapa Flow up to the 21st June (1919), when the German ships were scuttled by their own crews."[2]

In the Baltic, British ships were operating against Bolshevik forces in an attempt to prevent Estonia and Latvia falling into Communist hands. Russia, Siberia, the Black Sea and the Caspian Sea all saw operations against Bolsheviks, in support of 'the North Russians', and gradual withdrawal of British and Allied forces as the Bolshevik influence spread. Meanwhile, in home waters, Navy ships were involved during unrest in Ireland, strike action in northern England, and reconstruction work on the Belgian coast. This included salvaging wrecked ships that blocked harbours, and reconstructing port hardware such as bridges, cranes and piers.

However, the Government's statement was unequivocal in saying:

> "One of the largest tasks that confronted the Allied Navies after the cessation of hostilities was that of clearing the seas of mines, which had been used in this war on a quite unprecedented scale…. Some idea of the task involved may be gathered from the fact that during the war no less than 1,360 minefields or groups of mines were laid by the Germans in proximity to our coast, totalling some 11,000 mines, in waters abroad to be cleared by the British about 60 fields or groups, totalling some 1,200 mines, while British mines, which had also to be swept up, numbered about 65,000 in home waters and 8,000 in the Mediterranean…….The arrangements for the organisation of the Mine Clearance Service had been worked out in detail before the Armistice, and were brought into force on the 1st December 1918."[3]

The situation in the last few weeks of 1918 was far from normal, and there were absences and difficulties still to be accepted. Naval reservists on minesweepers were offered a higher rate of pay if they would stay in the service and help with minesweeping operations. The work was dangerous and demanding, but these extra duties after the war were viewed as a golden opportunity by some island sailors. Donald Macleod (Dòmhnall Crutch) of 38 South Shawbost wrote to his schoolfriend Roderick Murray:

"I went in for that minesweeping business and I expect to go on another leave this week. We are getting £8 a month extra and 10 days leave before we will start. I expect you heard all about it... Please let me know did (you) join the minesweeping stint yourself."[4]

After the Armistice and up until the end of 1921 (CWGC criteria) over 100 servicemen from Lewis and Harris died – a third of the Spanish Flu that ravaged the world population. Tuberculosis, other illnesses, wounds, gassing and drowning through mines, sinkings and accidents accounted for the rest. Many men were still in service and there were those who had already been lost, gallant local sailors and soldiers who would never again wander on the island's sea-girt shore. Some were now buried in graves in foreign lands, some had no known grave and some found repose in the depths of the ocean, where no gravestone could mark their final resting place. Many were wounded in mind and body or had suffered in prison camps. So, although the guns were silent, there was cause for restraint in the celebrations.

The first peace-time Hogmanay

Nevertheless, the festive season of 1918 could be celebrated at last, as the nation revelled in the coming of peace. Throughout Great Britain, in dance halls, churches and in homes, people celebrated the victory and the end of hostilities. Prime Minister David Lloyd George promised 'a land fit for heroes to live in' and war-weary servicemen and civilians alike looked forward to post-war reunions, prosperity and contentment. The Admiralty reported that:

"Early in December 1918 …. orders were given for a considerable number of ships in Home Waters to proceed to their Home ports and grant their crews the 28 days demobilisation leave that had been specially approved."[5]

The return of service boys for their long New Year leave was eagerly awaited by families in Lewis and Harris. Letters flew to and fro discussing the arrangements for their leave. At HMS *Roxburgh* 19-year-old Roderick Murray heard from his father in South Shawbost, and from his younger brother Kenneth in Glasgow, both eager to confirm arrangements as he headed home:

"Dear Son, Just a short note to let you know that we are all well at home, and also all the surrounding friends and neighbours. We were glad that you arrived quite safe, and that you got your Warrant alright at Stornoway... We are missing you very much, but we hope that you will not be very long in coming home now anyway.... I am Your loving father Donald Murray."[6]

"Dear Brother, Just a few lines to let you know that I am well, so I think I will be leaving for home next Monday on 30th Dec. So let me know at once will you come through Glasgow or will go right on, or will I wait for you so I make up my mind to go off for a wee while any way. If possible let me know before Monday hoping to see you soon. Kenneth Murray."[7]

Roderick had his travel warrant and was ready to depart on December 27th. He put the warrant safely in his pocket, together with letters from his father, brothers and friends, before setting out for home with his fellow Scots from HMS *Roxburgh* at Devonport.

This would not be their final return home, but a good long period of rest and repose with their families, followed by the near-certainty that permanent demobilisation was not long away. The first watch of English and Welshmen would be allowed leave to return home for Christmas and the second, the Scots, for the all-important New Year, the principal celebration of the winter – and indeed of the year – for Scots.

The origins of Hogmanay are unclear, but it may be derived from Norse and Gaelic observances. Customs vary throughout Scotland and in the islands involved visiting the homes of friends and neighbours, with special attention given to the first-foot, the first guest of the new year. It was observed with great enthusiasm in the islands, while Christmas was only celebrated by the exchange of presents and a family dinner. Until as recently as the 1970s, Christmas Day was not considered a holiday in the islands and even the Harris Tweed mills in Stornoway worked on Christmas Day. In Gaelic, New Year's Eve is consistently referred to as Oidhche na Bliadhn' Ùir' – the Night of the New Year.

On this first Hogmanay of peacetime, as the Lewis people watched their clocks ticking out the old year, croft houses were crowded with excited families and friends, preparing to welcome the return home of the sons, brothers and fathers who had won the victory for Britain and had survived many battles and actions. Warm underwear – long johns, vests and shirts – was aired in front of glowing peat fires and new geansaidhan (jumpers) and socks had been knitted from home-grown wool for the sailors. Clootie dumplings (fruit puddings) or duffs were made, pots of broth were prepared and the local Scottish Blackface lamb or beef was simmering on the hearth, ready for a sumptuous meal when the returning heroes arrived home. The welcoming fires in the croft houses were burning brightly with an abundance of peats, and the cows and horses in the barns had been attended to and fed for the night.

Old men had searched out their prized bottle of whisky or rum to welcome in the New Year and give the returning heroes a dram. Grandfathers, fathers and uncles hoped to receive a coil or two of black twist tobacco, Navy-issue cigarettes or maybe a bottle of warming Navy neaters (rum - navy slang). Excited children, some of whom could barely remember their fathers, wondered what gifts might have been brought from distant shores. Older children were desperate to welcome home fathers they had not seen since the beginning of the war. Mothers, wives, sweethearts and sisters donned their finery after the croft work and housework had been completed. Youngsters prepared for the New Year's dances and celebrations, which were to last well into the following day. In the villages and districts great bonfires had been prepared on hilltops to celebrate the New

Year and welcome the heroes home. Happiness and companionship was felt throughout the neighbourhoods and it was a pleasure to be alive after four years of war.

Meanwhile in the town, as midnight approached, the people of Stornoway looked to see the ships enter the harbour. A happy throng gathered on Stornoway's No 1 pier to welcome home the menfolk who had survived the war. In Leurbost, the sister of Murdo Maclean left the house at number 39 to collect her brother from the pier at Stornoway. As she set out, her mother Mòr said merrily: "See and don't come home without Murdo now!" 13-year-old Murdo Crichton of 12 Knock in Point travelled into town to meet his father, Angus, and newlywed Jessie Macdonald of Skigersta, Ness, was at the pier, eager to meet her husband of just two and a half months, Iain. Also waiting, nursing her excitement – and a secret – was herring girl Catherine Wares from Pulteneytown, Wick. Her young man, Herbert William Head, was a private in the Royal Marine Light Infantry and was returning to his posting in Stornoway from his Christmas leave. Only she and he knew that they were to be married that day, and that she was carrying his child.

The long journey home

While all this preparation was occupying the islands, throughout 31st December 1918, island sailors poured into Inverness railway station on the homeward trail. They came from naval stations and ports north and south, including English ports in Chatham, Portland, Devonport, Portsmouth, Shotley, Dover, Falmouth, Immingham, Liverpool and Harwich, the Welsh port of Milford Haven, Larne in

The men were issued with warrants to travel home from their bases. Roderick Murray of South Shawbost used this warrant to travel home from HMS Roxburgh. The final part of his journey would be on the Iolaire.

Northern Ireland, Queenstown (now Cork) in Ireland and, in Scotland, Scapa Flow, Aberdour, Ardrossan and Granton. The London train, travelling daily both north and south between Euston and Thurso via Inverness, was nicknamed the "Jellicoe Express" after Admiral Lord Jellicoe, and had been set up in 1917 to solve the problem of complicated travel arrangements when men serving with the Grand Fleet in Scapa Flow were trying to get home on leave. Now soldiers were also on the trains, coming from depots and barracks all over the country.

Train journeys from the south of England naval bases to the north of Scotland were a tiring and uncomfortable experience. Trains were overcrowded and cold, and one was lucky to even get a seat. The corridors were piled high with kit bags and parcels, the toilet facilities primitive, and on some trains no food was available. These tedious train journeys to the north of Scotland sometimes lasted for nearly a full day. Stornoway man Alexander M. Maciver related that the train he travelled on left Glasgow at 4.45am on the 31st and they got into Kyle at 6.15pm, 13½ hours later. On this occasion, the agonising trek was prolonged when the Highland Railways train from Inverness to Kyle via Dingwall was inexplicably delayed.

Sailors leaving the south coast, from Falmouth to Sheerness, had to travel by rail to London, where the Chatham men joined them. The Jellicoe Special of Southern Railways arrived between 8 and 10pm at Perth, where those aboard got tea and sandwiches on the long platforms. Two trains with about 30 coaches each left Perth at midnight and struggled into Inverness, an hour late, at 8am on Hogmanay. Trains from Thurso and Aberdeen carried yet more service personnel bound for Kyle and, after breakfast, all the men boarded the Highland Railway trains to Kyle. Originally

three trains were expected in Kyle but Inverness reduced that to two. One left Inverness at 11.40am, a 'special' train following on half an hour later.

Arriving at Kyle of Lochalsh, tired, hungry and dishevelled, the men looked forward to boarding the ferry as quickly as possible, dumping their kit bags and parcels and getting their heads down to rest on the passage to Stornoway. Many faced a long trip home even after arriving in Stornoway, where only a handful of them lived. A dram at their home hearth among their loved ones was what they were dreaming of.

By the end of the First World War the railhead village of Kyle of Lochalsh had a population of over 400, mostly English-speakers due to the railway. The Drill Hall in Church Street was fitted out to act as a welcome place of rest for travelling servicemen from Skye, Uist, Harris and Lewis, who would arrive at Kyle and await their boat home. The Red Cross Society, both here and at the connecting station in Dingwall, supplied the weary travellers with hot food, drinks and somewhere to sleep. A brass tablet was later placed inside Kyle hall carrying the inscription:

"This building was used as a rest for soldiers and sailors from 19th April 1916 to 30th April 1919, in connection with the Ross and Cromarty Branch Red Cross Society. During that period 9,821 men were put up for the night, and 32,022 meals were served."[8]

With the station right beside the pier, there was no opportunity for the sailors to obtain bottles of 'ammunition ale' or anything stronger for the trip. Generations of Lewismen went into the Kyle Pharmacy, which had a striking frontage and lay close to the station and pier on the junction of Main Street and Station Road. It opened in 1911 and was a must for a yarn for islanders passing through, as Duncan Macpherson's wife Margaret Maciver was a policeman's daughter from Lewis.

The problem of conveyance

The Admiralty officials were aware that the *Sheila* – the Stornoway to Kyle of Lochalsh mail steamer – was unable to cope with the number of seamen from the islands being released for the New Year. For days before New Year other boats, including the drifter HMD *John Watt*, had been used to convey seamen home to Lewis. The *Stornoway Gazette* reported just days before:

> "Large numbers of leave men are now arriving home nightly. On Tuesday night of last week over 300 service men crossed the Minch, and two drifters had to be detailed to assist the mail steamer *Plover*, which was unable to take them all."[9]

A Lewis soldier who wished to remain anonymous and referred to himself as "Close Shave" years later wrote a letter to a newspaper describing his experience at Kyle of Lochalsh:

> "On the evening of the 30th December, 1918, I with a party of demobilised soldiers, mostly Seaforths, arrived at Kyle….. We were told that only a drifter, called the *John Watt*, was crossing that night, and it was reserved for naval ratings only. However, we walked down the pier, where we were met by a naval officer, who asked us what we wanted. One of the party, who acted as a spokesman, said we wanted to cross to Stornoway in the *John Watt*. The naval officer, who turned out to be the Port Officer, told him in no uncertain voice, that the *John Watt* was for naval ratings only and no soldiers were allowed on that boat.

> "Our spokesman, on recovering his breath, replied, "Are we not as much entitled to cross to-night in that boat as any blue-pencilled naval rating?" or words to that effect. By this time the party were lined along the edge of the pier, looking down on the *John Watt* which appeared, at low tide, too far down below us to jump on board. Just then a voice with a very strong Stornoway accent shouted, "Shove the 'niaff' (fool) over the pier, Jock!" The contemptuous inflection conveyed in the local 'blas' (accent) will remain one of my most cherished memories."

> "As there was no use staying any longer on the pier, I made my way to the Soldiers' Home in the village. Soon afterwards my comrades came in, and from the way they talked I came to the conclusion that, to put it mildly, naval ratings were not popular that night. After a while we all found some place to lie down in and soon, as old Homer has it, 'pleasing sleep had sealed each mortal eye', all except my next bed companion, who regaled me with a description of what he would do with the Port Officer if he had him there for five minutes….

> "Next morning we were told that the *Sheila* would be at Kyle that afternoon. In due course we went on board and staked our claim, determined not to be left in Kyle another night."[10]

Twenty-two naval ratings for Stornoway, who had been unable to get home the night before, also boarded the MacBrayne mailboat, *Sheila*, with the soldiers and civilians. Captain Colin Cameron, aged 59, of Lewis Street, Stornoway was the master of the *Sheila*. He realised that his ship could not accommodate all the extra naval reservists along with soldiers and civilians safely across the Minch. He got in touch with the naval authorities who sent a telegram to the naval base in Stornoway. As a result the *Iolaire* left Stornoway at 9.20am, according to the HMS *Iolaire* base log, and crossed to Kyle of Lochalsh to ferry home some of the naval personnel.

HMY *Iolaire*

His Majesty's Yacht *Iolaire* was the second ship of that name to serve the Stornoway naval base HMS *Iolaire*. Originally built as *Iolanthe*, a pleasure yacht, she had been owned by a succession of wealthy businessmen including shipowner Sir Donald Currie, the Duke of Montrose and the New York Singer family, of sewing machine fame. Before being requisitioned for the Navy in 1914 her latest owner had been the racehorse owner Charles Garden Assheton Smith of Vaynol – an ancient estate in North Wales. He named her *Amalthaea* and made luxurious design changes, including a new smoking room, and hung her walls with commissioned paintings of his three Grand National winning horses.

The yacht had not been at Stornoway long and would have been new to most of the men. She had arrived and taken the name *Iolaire* only in November 1918, to replace the vessel which had served Stornoway since the base opened in 1915. This new vessel would have appeared impressive to the servicemen lining up at Kyle for their passage home, despite her familiar battleship grey paint. Her

Steam Yacht Amalthaea (later Iolaire) in dry dock before she was requisitioned for war service.

lines slender and her fittings finely made, at first sight HMY *Iolaire* seemed a handsome and luxurious transport. Donald Macdonald, of 23 Cromore in South Lochs, was a survivor who later emigrated to Shell Lake in Canada. He recounted:

> "It was not a passenger boat, nor did it resemble one. It was different from any we ever had the pleasure to sail on. It was a beautiful 900-ton steam yacht which

belonged to a rich Clyde ship-owner. It was now commandeered by the Government for patrol and submarine scouting. Here it was with little alteration, with the exception of a coat of slate grey on hull and tall masts, and an 18 pounder on a high stern platform surrounded by numerous depth charges. It was called the *Iolaire*. I felt rather honoured being conveyed on my last lap homeward on a millionaire's yacht."[11]

HMY Iolaire was ordered to Kyle to help transfer the men home to Stornoway.

What the men did not then know was that she compared poorly to her predecessor. Under-powered and with a single-screw engine, her top speed was only 10 knots, by comparison to the former *Iolaire's* 17.5 knots and twin propellors. She was renowned as a poor sea-boat, liable to roll and pitch in heavy seas, which often resulted in crew members suffering from sea-sickness. On one occasion in November 1918, while taking the Chaplain of the Mission to Deep Sea Fishermen from Stornoway to St Kilda to perform a wedding, the *Iolaire* was caught in a force eight gale, resulting in the Chaplain and some members of the crew being violently sick. The rolling was partly due to her having guns mounted fore and aft and a gun on the promenade deck. In common with many requisitioned vessels, she simply was not designed for this added weight and it made her top heavy.

On the night of 31st December, HMY *Iolaire* was under the command of her usual master, Lieutenant Commander Richard Gordon William Mason, with Lieutenant Edmund Cotter as his navigating officer.[12] Lt Cdr Mason was a vastly experienced seaman who had been at sea since 1889 and had trained, before the war, in naval skills and techniques. He remained in the Mercantile Marine on the outbreak of war, but on 7th March 1917 he was called to serve and appointed Lt Commander with HMY *Amalthaea* (later *Iolaire*). He stayed with her as she was attached to various shore bases, finally to HMS *Iolaire* at Stornoway.

Lt Leonard Edmund Dillistone Cotter was a yachtsman and a RNVR officer who had been in the Mercantile Marine at the turn of the century. He was promoted twice in 1916, his recognised ability being navigation, but he was cautioned for an error of judgement after a naval Court of Inquiry was held into the collision of his vessel, HMY *Goissa*, with Granton West Pier – the second collision *Goissa* had that year. From his naval record it would appear that he did not serve again until he was posted to HMY *Amalthaea* (later *Iolaire*) on

Thousands of men were transported north from their military bases on the so-called 'Jellicoe express'. Here a troop train pulls into Kyle of Lochalsh.

The railhead at Kyle of Lochalsh. Ships waited at both sides of the pier to carry the men home.

28th June 1918. He had been on leave for Christmas and had returned to the *Iolaire* four days before New Year. On the night of 31st December he was late reporting for duty at Kyle and the mate on the *Sheila*, John MacLeod (Seonaidh Ruadh Iain Bhàin), from Drinishader in Harris, was alerted that he might have to deputise. However, Cotter appeared in time to navigate the *Iolaire* that night.

Normally the crew of the yacht operating from Stornoway would have numbered about 40. However, 16 members of the crew were on New Year's leave and the men who came off the Christmas leave (the port watch) crewed the vessel, with a couple of men seconded from other vessels based at Stornoway.

Confusion at the pier

Around 4pm on 31st December the *Iolaire* arrived at Kyle and, after a miscalculation between bridge and engine room, she collided with the pier. The collision resulted in ten feet of the *Iolaire*'s gunwale being broken and damage to the pier, caused raised eyebrows and comment and later led to speculation that the officers in command of the *Iolaire* were intoxicated. Some of the island seamen watching the scene from the deck of the *Sheila* and from the pier refused to board the *Iolaire*, thinking the officers or crew lacked the ability to sail the vessel safely across the Minch to Stornoway. Seeing the yacht take such a wide sweep to berth, and then hit the pier at speed, puzzled the experienced island seamen. There are currents which mean the approach has to be made with caution, but Lt Cdr Mason had been with the yacht since 1916 and he was the man on the bridge. Nonetheless, she made fast at the pier-head, where the *Sheila* already occupied the berth on the west side of the pier.

Island soldiers returning home from the war were anxious to board any vessel that would carry them across the Minch. Many of them were angry that they were not allowed to board ships taking naval reservists home, as some aboard were friends, neighbours and relatives. The Lewis soldier who styled himself 'Close Shave' in a later newspaper report was nominated by his small group aboard the *Sheila* as a spokesman, and sent to ask the naval officer whether they could go aboard the *Iolaire*, which was set to depart earlier. He later related:

> "He told me to go back and tell my party to stay on board the *Sheila*, as the *Iolaire* was for naval ratings only. He also made this remark – 'The *Sheila* will be in Stornoway yet before the *Iolaire*.' He little knew how true his words would prove."[13]

This man and his party were far from the only soldiers anxious to get a place on the *Iolaire*. Pte Evander John Mackenzie, Seaforths, of 47 Upper Bayble, aged 21, had been wounded in August 1918 by shrapnel and only lately discharged from a Nottingham hospital. He tried to get on the *Iolaire*, but ended up sailing on the *Sheila*. Pte William "Clod" Finlayson, Canadian Army, of 10 North Tolsta was not allowed to board *Iolaire* as he was a soldier. His Canadian comrade Sgt Major Donald Macleod, newly demobbed from the Canadian Army after being wounded at Ypres in 1916, could not get on the *Iolaire* either, despite wishing to join his cousin Malcolm Macleod of 28 Swainbost.

Some managed to board but were ordered off. 26-year-old Pte Angus Gunn, Lovat Scouts, of 34 Cross, Ness, had seen service in Turkey, Egypt and Greece and had been wounded. He was on the *Iolaire* but was ordered off as soldiers were not allowed on her. Pte William Henderson "Willie Spuds" Macdonald, Seaforths, 19 years old and from 23 Lewis Street in Stornoway, was Captain Cameron's next-door neighbour, and that relationship probably saved his life, as the *Sheila's* master ordered him aboard his vessel.

While soldiers were clamouring for places on the *Iolaire*, officers at Kyle were scratching their heads over space for all the seamen expected to arrive by train. Lt Charles Wayles Hicks RNR, aged 50, was the officer in charge of ascertaining passenger availability on both *Sheila* and *Iolaire*. The Master at Arms at Kyle was 52-year-old CPO William John Wyman from Westbury-on-Severn. He was to meet the train as assistant to Lt Commander Walsh.

The number of naval ratings arriving at Kyle was more than double what the naval authorities had anticipated. At 4.20 pm, the naval base at Kyle received a message from the Divisional Naval Transport Officer at Inverness. 530 naval ratings had left Inverness on the train, originally scheduled to depart at 11.40 am. The train was running three hours late and was in two parts. The numbers far outweighed expectations by Rear Admiral Boyle in Stornoway and the naval authorities receiving them at Kyle. Lt Commander Walsh asked MacBraynes if there was another vessel that could be diverted to take some of the sailors back to Stornoway. He was told not, yet the mail steamer *Plover* was certainly in the vicinity, as she came into Stornoway from Mallaig later on New Year's Day.

Lt Commander Mason, the commanding officer of the *Iolaire*, was asked by a harassed Lt Commander Walsh if he could take 300 men. Mason reportedly replied that he could take that number easily enough. In fact, the *Iolaire* had lifeboat capacity for 100 men, and only 80 lifebelts.

The first part of the delayed train from Inverness arrived at Kyle at 6.15pm and the naval ratings were fallen in on the platform two deep. Those for Stornoway were ordered to form on the right and those for Skye, Harris, the Applecross area and elsewhere on the left. The Stornoway ratings, around 190, were in two files, and walked up the single gangway leading to the *Iolaire*, master at arms William Wyman stamping their liberty tickets and travel warrants. The names of those boarding the vessel were not documented, so no record was made of which men were aboard the yacht.

At 7pm the second part of the train arrived, with around 130 men for Stornoway. A MacBrayne's representative came along and informed the naval officers that the *Sheila* could take 60 ratings. These were marched on board the *Sheila*, and 70 naval ratings were sent to the *Iolaire*. Most of the Isle of Harris ratings were sent to the Red Cross Station and the Skye men were ordered to board the drifter *Jennie Campbell*, which left Kyle at 8.15pm for Broadford, Raasay and Portree with mails.

Changing ships, cheating fate

There was a relaxed and merry atmosphere at the pier. Robert Mackinnon of Tarbert and Malcolm Macinnes of Lemreway were both granted New Year's leave from the cruiser HMS *Dublin* and travelled home together. Donald

Murray of North Tolsta was travelling with his friend John Morrison, with whom he had served the whole length of the war. They boarded the *Iolaire* together, too, and in later years Donald recalled:

> "Now the war had ended and the Englishmen got Christmas leave and when they returned we got New Year's leave, that's why so many of us were coming back to Stornoway at the same time. What joy there had been in Kyle that day when so many village boys met after not seeing each other for years!"[14]

Donald Morrison of Knockaird recalled how happy everybody was coming from the south of England to Scotland for their New Year's leave:

> "The trains were full of people and everybody was jolly because they were getting home for the New Year. There was no drink. I didn't smell drink from Portland till I got home."[15]

John Maclennan of Kneep, returning home after seeing the first *Iolaire* (*Amalthaea*) to her decommissioning port, later remembered:

> "There was a huge crowd coming up. I think there was three trains there, and at the station they were sending us to the *Iolaire*, some to the *Sheila* – the *Sheila* was in at the other side of the quay. There were some people in Kyle the night before who didn't get home at all."[16]

The seamen were under naval command and obeyed the orders they were given to embark, but Lewis and Harris naval reservists were jubilant on meeting so many relations and friends, many they had not seen since 1914 and their happy reunions did result in some questioning of the embarkation orders – even downright insubordination. Men swapped and changed between vessels to be with friends and relatives. Some, caught in the act, were sent back to the ship they were detailed to, or refused permission to board.

James Stewart RNR, of 27 Benside, was prevented by PO Murdo Macaulay RN, DSC, of 10 Lower Sandwick from boarding the *Iolaire* and they sailed together on the *Sheila*. Murdo had himself been urged to join the *Sheila* by his Lower Sandwick neighbour Roderick Mackenzie, known as "Flemon", a crewman on the *Sheila*.

Roderick Mackay Jnr RNR, from Rhenigidale had put his kitbag on the *Iolaire* and then went to see the last portion of the train arriving. On it was his first cousin, Roderick Mackay Snr from the village, who had saved his life in a pre-war boating accident. He saved his life again by persuading him to fetch his kitbag off the *Iolaire* and they boarded in a lodging house in Kyle until they would take the boat to Tarbert the following day.

Donald Nicolson RNR, of 15 Lemreway, initially went aboard the *Iolaire* with his first cousin Neil Nicolson but, as a teetotaller and non-smoker, he preferred the civilian mail boat and switched vessels. 30-year-old Dugald Sinclair Macaulay RNR(T) of 30 Balallan, decided to sail home on the *Sheila* when he noticed a friend aboard her. John Macleod RNR, of 21 Flesherin, heard that the *Iolaire* was to sail first and got aboard her. He was ordered off and told to board the *Sheila*. In attempting to board the yacht a second time with companions, they were told that they would be arrested if they tried once more.

It was not so much fate as a stubborn and rebellious nature that saved Alexander Macleod RNR, of 11 Lower Bayble, Point. He boarded the *Iolaire* on the fateful evening with his uncle Donald Macleod from the same address. They were not long aboard when Alexander saw a girl from Point that he knew boarding the *Sheila*. Perhaps after trying to go ashore via the gangway, he took matters into his own hands and slipped down the mooring ropes of the *Iolaire* to the shore. With no ticket to board the *Sheila*, he then had to climb up her bow ropes and boarded the vessel in this way. His uncle stayed aboard *Iolaire*.

There were others who made the switch in the other direction, and for them the decision was to prove fateful. Roderick Mackenzie of 5 Swordale was asleep on the mailboat and awoke to be told that they were not away yet, but that the *Iolaire* was leaving first. With that, he got up with his bundle and crossed the rails of the *Sheila*, up and onto the *Iolaire*.

Neither did the crew escape their share of fate. They had drawn lots for Christmas and New Year leaves and Ernest Leggett, who was acting quartermaster on the night, had drawn New Year leave, but his crewmate Charlie Dewsbury, knowing that Ernie was a family man with eight children who would wish to spend Christmas at home, got teenager Charles Kingsbury to swap and the youngster's fate was secured.

The *Iolaire* sets sail

The *Iolaire* was eventually commissioned to take some 260 naval ratings – our figures show she took a total of 254. She also had 24 crew and two base sailors coming home from leave which takes the total to 280 men aboard. Once aboard the islanders had to squeeze into any corner they could find. The *Iolaire* had two small saloons and the men headed there for warmth, shelter and rest. John Maclean, from Borrowston, was on the upper deck of the yacht and described how the young ones 'frolicked about', while the older hands slept.

There were insufficient seats for all and not just the saloons but chartroom, galley and the open deck were crammed with men already exhausted after travelling for many hours. Most wanted an undisturbed sleep on the Minch where the wind, the deep swell and the rolling and pitching of the *Iolaire* would not bother seafarers. Melodeon music, Gaelic songs and chat competed with the *Iolaire* engines. There was no food aboard for the passengers and so it was only what they had brought aboard in their kitbags that sustained them. The few that were in the galley and chartroom were provided with a cup of tea.

John Macleod from Portnaguran travelled on the *Sheila* with three other RNR friends and remembered the men on the *Iolaire* shouting as they left Kyle: "Try to catch us now!" The night was dark, with a rising breeze, as at 7.30pm the *Iolaire* took in her mooring ropes. Her single screw churned the Kyle waters and she turned with her valuable human cargo towards home.

The football team and officers from the crew of HMY Amalthaea, prior to her posting to Stornoway in November 1918, when she was renamed HMY Iolaire. Deckhand James MacLean is the tall man at the centre of the back row (see chapters 4 and 6).

Others identified are: Seaman David Ramsay (2nd from left - back row), Deckhand William Stanley (1st from left - middle row) and Lt Cdr Richard Mason (3rd from left - middle row)

Chapter 3 Footnotes

1. Survivor Donald Macdonald, of 23 Cromore writing from Canada, *Stornoway Gazette*, 10th August 1956

2. *Statement of the First Lord of the Admiralty. Explanatory of the Navy estimates, 1919-1920* presented to the House of Commons by Walter H Long, 1st December 1919. HMSO

3. Walter H Long, December 1919

4. Personal letter from Donald Macleod at HMS *Cachalot*, Devonport, 3rd December 1918. Carried by Roderick Murray, 25 South Shawbost and kept by his family

5. Walter H. Long, December 1919

6. Letter from Donald Murray, 25 South Shawbost, to Roderick Murray, 7th December 1918

7. Undated personal letter from Kenneth Murray at Elder Street, Govan to Roderick Murray, HMS *Roxburgh*

8. Commemorative plaque at Drill Hall, Kyle of Lochalsh

9. *Stornoway Gazette*, 27th December 1918

10. Account by 'Close Shave' *Stornoway Gazette*, 7th March 1941

11. Donald Macdonald of 23 Cromore writing from Canada, *Stornoway Gazette*, 1956. Macdonald's description is not factually correct, but does show how the vessel was viewed by those about to board her

12. What is known about the naval career of the two men is given in Appendix 1

13. Account by 'Close Shave' *Stornoway Gazette*, 7th March 1941

14. Interview with Donald Murray, translated from the Gaelic, *Seanchas*, Winter 2006

15. *Stornoway Gazette*, 4th January 1992

16. John Maclennan ('Ain Geal) interviewed on *Dealan-Dè*, BBC Radio nan Gàidheal. Presenter Kenneth Maciver (Coinneach Maciòmhair) 1987

Chapter 4

The Wreck of the Iolaire

"All accounts appear to agree that from some cause or other the vessel made, not straight for the harbour but direct for the lee shore to the north of the harbour entrance. There, under overhanging cliffs of rock, she was literally piled up on a rocky beach, upon which was breaking the thundering sweep of heavy seas with a powerful under current. The rest is a tale of suffering and death."[1]

"But Heavens, when she struck, the sea was wild… Where she now was the sea went up to the upper limits of the shingle… when it came out it swept everything out with it."[2]

The Beasts of Holm seen from the shore in rough weather.

The village of Holm (Tolm in Gaelic) is around three miles by road from Stornoway. The name is derived from the Old Norse word 'Holmi' meaning a low island in the sea near the shore. Two farms are there, Holm Farm near the village and Stoneyfield Farm, closer to the coast in the direction of Stornoway. Just off the shore every passing ferry passenger can still see, at low tide, the sea skerries 'Biastan Thuilm' or the Beasts of Holm. Scoured by the tides, these skerries resemble the black backs of sea mammals – porpoises, seals, or perhaps the 'biast-dhubh', the black beast, as the otter is known in Gaelic.

Though not far from the shore, the Beasts are only just visible above the water at low tide. As if configured for maximum hazard to any vessel, they are obscured below the water at high tide. A great danger to shipping, they are marked by an unlit red beacon. The adjacent coast consists of sharp and chaotic conglomerate rock, shelving steeply down to the sea from the grasslands above. This grassland itself is wet, deep and boggy, cut by ditches often filled with rainwater and with numerous gorse bushes near the farms, very hazardous for anyone walking in the dark.

December 31st 1918 was the dark of the moon, the new moon due on January 2nd, and there was dense cloud cover. High tides in Stornoway were at 6pm the night before, and just after six the following morning, so it was low tide around midnight. Data from the HMS *Iolaire* (naval base) log shows a quickly rising gale at force 8 from the south at midnight, reaching force 10 at 4am. There were frequent sleet showers as the night wore on.

Long before the *Iolaire* reached Holm, men who were awake on board began to recognise the longed-for shore of their home island. Seaman John Montgomery of Ranish, who was familiar with the entrance to Stornoway harbour, described the situation:

> "As we were coming towards Stornoway, I could see Tiumpan Head Light well on the starboard bow and Arnish Light perhaps three points on the port bow. I also saw Cabag Light when we passed it on our port beam. ... I could see the sea breaking on the shore ... The land I saw was the land on the East side of Holm Bay."[3]

Alasdair Mackenzie, from Aird in Point, was known as 'Am Boicean'. Pre-war he had been a fisherman and was as familiar with the Minch as he was with the contour of the land in his native village. 'Am Boicean' boarded the *Iolaire* and met his brother John Mackenzie, whom he had not seen since they were called up in 1914. They found a corner in the saloon and started chatting. Across the room someone was playing Lewis Gaelic tunes on a melodeon and they soon realised that it was another cousin – Alick Mackenzie from Aird. Soon they were joined by a friend from their schooldays, Alick Macleod, of Portnaguran. After midnight 'Am Boicean' and Alick Macleod left the smoky saloon and went out on deck. There they found a number of men peering into the dark looking for landmarks. As experienced fishermen, who since boyhood had been hauling herring nets from the restless waters of the Minch, they readily identified to the north Tiumpan Head light – not far from their homes.

Donald Macdonald from Upper Bayble was on deck and watched the familiar seamarks around his home village come into view:

The land of Holm with the present-day memorial to the wreck of the Iolaire. The men had to scale jagged rock to reach help.

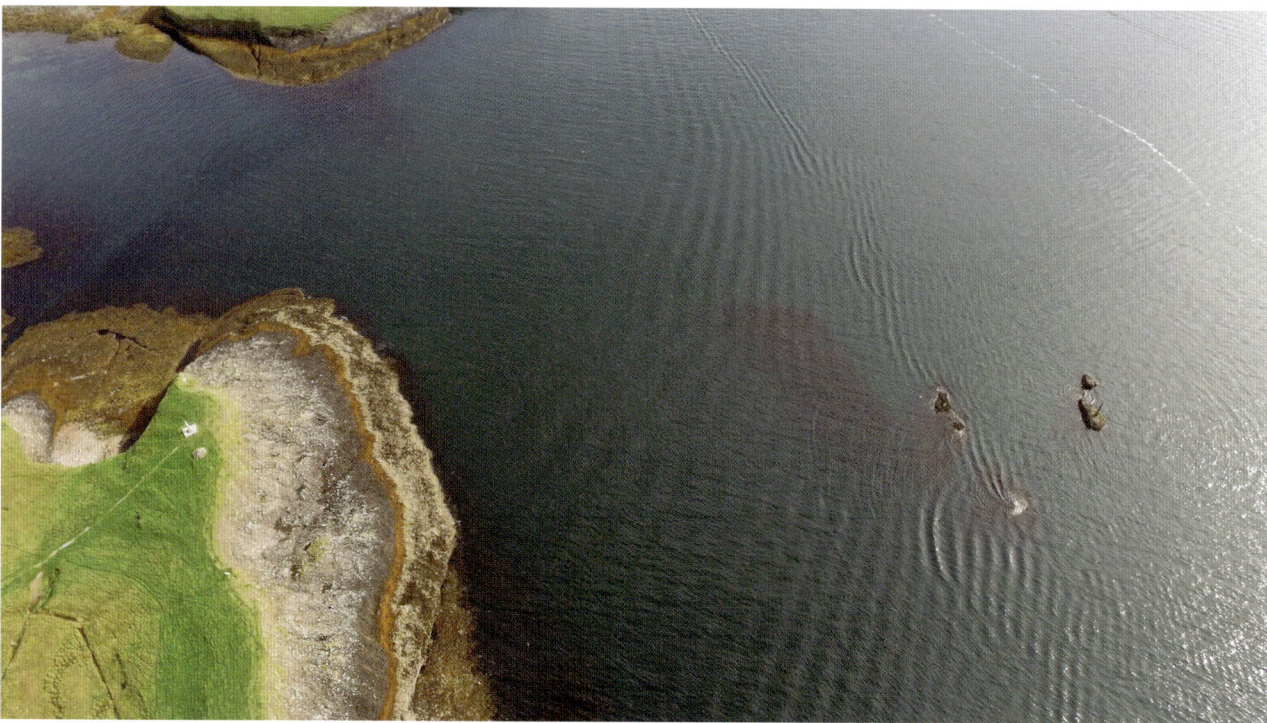

An aerial shot showing the Beasts of Holm concealed just below the surface of the water at high tide.

"When we were approaching Lewis I saw all the lights, Cabback (Kebbock Head), Tiumpan and Arnish – quite clearly... I could not judge how far we were from the Lewis shore, but I think a good mile, or more. I could see the land ... it was not very clear, but I could tell it was land. I know the coast well. From my observation at that time I thought the vessel's course was right for Stornoway.

"Between Cabback and Arnish I noticed a fishing vessel, but I did not know whether it was a motor boat or a drifter. She was on our starboard side. I saw her afterwards on our port side. ... I said to Kenneth, my chum, 'We'll soon be in; there's the land 'of Holm'."[4]

The fishing vessel Donald saw was the east coast fishing boat *Spider*. James Macdonald, an engineer on board, later recounted what he saw:

"When sailing past the mouth of Loch Grimshader on our way back to port, a steamer passed us on the starboard side. I did not identify her and thought she was the *Sheila*. We followed immediately in her wake and when approaching Arnish Light, I noticed that the vessel did not alter course but kept straight on in the direction of the Beasts. I remarked to one of the crew that the vessel would not clear the headland at Holm as it went too far off its course to make the harbour in safety."[5]

James Macdonald was not alone in feeling unease at the course the *Iolaire* was setting. On board the ship, there were those who knew the route into Stornoway well enough to notice even the tiniest deviation from a safe and familiar route.

John Maclennan of Kneep ('Ain Geal) noticed the course:

"Approaching Stornoway Harbour on the *Iolaire* the mistake was made when we changed course. All it required was less than half a point, it just needed to be slightly to the West. The lighthouse was visible, but the man at the wheel didn't alter course when he should have."[6]

Donald Murray of North Tolsta gave his account:

"It wasn't a bad night, but it was rough around Kebbock (Kebbock Head) and it was from the south that it was bad there. Anyway, we thought everything was fine. I remember that when we were about the mouth of Loch Grimshader, that I said to Donald Red (Donald Maciver, New Tolsta) who was with us – there was a crowd of villagers – I said I was going on deck to see how near we were.

"I could see the Stornoway Lighthouse flashing. You'd think there was no possibility of anything going wrong – but now there was a strong breeze – the wind was astern and, my goodness, when the sea hit us, it was fearsome. I went down and I said: 'Lads we are almost there.' We all had kitbags so we took them up on deck when we felt her altering course out to the west – instead of going in --- I didn't understand."[7]

Donald Morrison of Knockaird (Am Patch) was travelling with his brother Angus, after meeting up with him at Kyle. Donald recounted:

"We went up on deck and among those there were my brother and a number of other boys from Ness. There was a gale but the *Iolaire* was sailing straight and steady until she changed course to port. If she had changed four or five minutes earlier, she would have gone right into Stornoway, but she changed too late because the rocks of Holm were right in front of her."[8]

One of the deck crew, acting quartermaster James Maclean, came on duty at the helm at midnight, when the course was north-easterly. At 12.30am the course was changed to north and at 1am, with Commander Mason still on the bridge, he was relieved by Deckhand Ernest Leggett. Maclean went below for a smoke and returned 10 minutes later to find that Mason had gone below and Lieutenant Cotter had taken over. Maclean later told the inquiry that he acted as a lookout when he was on the bridge, but there was no lookout when he went below.

An un-named young Naval Reservist interviewed in the *Ross-shire Journal* said:

"As we were approaching Arnish Lighthouse we commenced getting our kits together, expecting to be safely alongside Stornoway pier in a few minutes. It was about ten minutes to two, and I was in the saloon when there came a great crash, and the vessel heeled heavily to starboard. It was so dark that we could not see the land, which, as afterwards transpired, was only 30 yards distant from the point where we struck. I don't think it was a rock we struck, but just that we ran ashore."[9]

It was 1.55am on January 1st 1919. HMY *Iolaire* had struck the Beasts of Holm, inside the cone marker which still stands at the spot. There was immediate confusion as the yacht rose up and heaved on to her starboard side at an angle of 35 degrees. Around 50 to 60 men jumped into the sea, or slid and fell from the sloping deck as the waves came breaking over the stricken yacht. Survivor testimonies suggest that many thought they had struck a mine or been torpedoed. That and the sloping deck made men jump, as they would have thought that the yacht was going to capsize. Survivors agreed that all of these perished in a cauldron of wicked water between the ship and the shore.

Until the first flare went up, few knew exactly where they were. Men struggled to see what was happening after the glare of the yacht's lights, their eyes unaccustomed to the darkness. It was impossible in the blackness to see the shore which, it later transpired, was less than 20 yards distant. Then rocket lights were fired, illuminating the landscape and vividly showing the precarious position they were in. The *Iolaire* was inside the red marker on the Beasts, on a rising tide, with a southerly gale rising from force 8 to 10 and driving onto the shore.

Lying on her starboard side with the deck tilted, the stricken yacht was pounded by crashing waves with dreadful force and regularity. The vessel disintegrated minute by minute, battered by the mountainous seas – one moment pounded broadside on, the next moment with her stern facing the shore. She appeared to be lifted seawards off the rocks that had snared her, came onto a much more even keel, then came back in closer to the Holm shore. The flares showed that the vessel's stern was only half a dozen yards from a ledge of rocks leading to the safety of the shore.

A dozen or more men summoned up the courage to leap for the rocks or into the sea close to the cliff face. John Mackenzie, 51 Upper Bayble, was about to jump and noticed his cousin 'Am Boicean', standing mesmerised at the rail. "*Siuthad Alasdair!*" ("Come on Alex!") he shouted. "Get your hands out of your pockets and jump with me!" Alexander Mackenzie, 1 Aird, soaked in his Navy greatcoat, replied hopelessly. "It's useless, I cannot swim! It is me that the sea is calling, not you!" John escaped and scrambled up the rocks, but others who made the attempt were swept away as waves sucked between the yacht and the rocks, the undertow pulling some under the yacht herself. Now the *Iolaire* swivelled away from the cliff and lifted her stern onto the reef, where it remained for some time. As she settled down she turned broadside on to the shore, pivoting on more rocks and creating a barrier to the force of the sea.

Later survivor accounts differ when it comes to conduct among the passengers. Some said that there was panic and others that everybody kept calm – possibly some were in shock. Donald Morrison from Knockaird was on deck in the cold night air and recalled, many years later, that people around him jumped overboard immediately. He recalled that Finlay Maclennan from Miavaig, who did not survive, told him it would be suicide to launch the boats, but the two on the starboard side, nearest land, were launched by the passengers. The first waves swamped them both with heavy loss of life. Another survivor, Donald Murray of North Tolsta, said that few got out of the sinking lifeboats and all of these were drowned within a couple of minutes.

Crew member Ernie Adams, one of the firemen who were stoking the boilers, scrambled up the ladder to the deck after the crash as the yacht hit the rocks. He later told the papers:

> "There was a terribly rough sea. The waves were rolling in mountains high, dashing her down on the rocks and we could scarcely stand on the deck. Two boats were lowered, one off the port side and one from starboard, but both were smashed. Before the boats were lowered, and when she heeled heavily to starboard, 50 or 60 men jumped overboard. I think every one of them was drowned or killed by being dashed against the rocks."[10]

In the short period between the time the *Iolaire* struck the rocks and her eventual sinking, some of the passengers showed how their own understanding of the sea, their seamanship and their knowledge of the island shores could save their own lives and those of others. But what of the crew and, especially, of those in command of the vessel, how did they respond?

Crewman James Maclean later reported that he heard no orders given by those in charge to take boat stations and none of the crew reported, to his knowledge. He heard Commander Mason say something about the boats when the yacht was still on a list and Maclean himself later helped to lower the 'midships whaler, which became waterlogged and grounded on rocks. By following the line to that boat Maclean found himself close to the shore and got himself and one passenger ashore.

Ernie Adams also later testified that the officers in command of the *Iolaire* made little attempt to save lives and failed to give any orders to the passengers after the vessel struck the rocks. He himself went on deck and helped to get one of the boats out, before seeing the acting bo'sun, Leading

High tides and strong winds drove the seas over the Beasts.

Men struggling ashore still had the sharp rocks and the strong pull of the tide to contend with.

Deckhand Dewsbury. Adams asked whether he should try and get 'the big boat' out and Dewsbury reportedly replied: "This is terrible," and walked away. Adams heard no orders given at any time.

The ship's master, Commander Mason, was not positively sighted by any of the island survivors, but Telegraphist Leonard Welch did speak to him. Years later he recounted how he and the chief engineer had patched up a broken cable to get the wireless set working. Returning to his wireless cabin, he said:

> "I got back there, and as I reached it, the Commander himself came down with the ship's position and instructions for the distress signals. Just at that moment, the ship gave another terrific lurch, some of the bulkheads came down, and the lights went out once more. I never saw the Commander alive again."[11]

Welch was one crewman who seems to have acted positively to try and remedy the situation. He later told the Inquiry that he could not send any distress signals after the ship struck as the set was 'smashed', but he tried for some time to rig up another set. His wireless cabin was below deck and sea water gushed in after the hull was breached, but he still had power to transmit.

> "I stayed in my cabin for some time, endeavouring to fix some emergency transmitting gear, with the aid of an electric torch and some dry batteries, but as by that time there was about 3 feet of water on my deck, I finally abandoned the attempt and went up top."[12]

Donald Macdonald of Upper Bayble would later recount:

"After she struck I heard no orders from the bridge. There was a good deal of disorder on board – men from the ship shouting to men in the water. Some were shouting in Gaelic and some in English. There was nobody taking charge of the ship's boats. Men were running up and down the deck looking for things. After she struck I waited to see if any orders would be given, and then I went and looked for a lifebelt for myself. I didn't find one. Others were looking for lifebelts too and they could not find them, I went a second time and I saw two of the crew in the galley and I asked if there were any spare lifebelts. They said, 'No'. There was no panic on board. It was the naval ratings themselves that lowered the two boats on the starboard side. The boats on the port side could not be lowered."[13]

As Donald's account illustrates, the island seamen were far from helpless onlookers or passengers awaiting rescue, as many individual acts would later show. Leading Seaman Angus Nicolson, of Battery Park in Stornoway, shouted to the bridge to blow the steam whistle and three or four long blasts were blown for a few minutes. He met a crewman at the engine-room door and suggested to drive the yacht astern, as there was a passage ashore that way, but was told there was engine trouble.

It was John Macinnes of North Tolsta who blew the whistle on the bridge. He also asked Lt Cotter if he had a searchlight and was told that it would not work, as the dynamo was broken. It would have rendered valuable help in lighting up the area, helping those nearing the rocky shore in trying to scale the storm-lashed rocks.

Lieutenant Cotter himself was on the bridge and fired the flares. Leading Deckhand Charles Dewsbury opened the locker containing the flares and Deckhand James Willder took them to the bridge. Willder said he passed on the flares to one of the passengers, thought to be Alexander Maciver, from Shulishader, who was seen trying to fire them. He was later drowned. Survivor Malcolm Macritchie was also on the bridge, having climbed up onto the boat deck. Survivor John Mackay was another who, having escaped the saloon by breaking a window, searched the bridge for rockets. John Macphail from Doune Carloway estimated that well over a dozen rockets were fired and crew member Arthur Topham said he saw 15 rockets.

Despite all these individual attempts to set rescue action in motion, the *Iolaire*, from the moment she struck the Beasts of Holm, seems to have been effectively under no-one's command and without the power or equipment to save lives. Yet, although many survivors reported that they heard no lifesaving orders from those in command, it must also be remembered that there was a howling gale and huge waves were breaking over the ship. Even if orders had been given, few would have heard anything on a yacht nearly 200 feet long. There was no means of communicating in the dark as bewildered men moved about the deck looking for a lifebelt, a boat or any means to escape the predicament they were all in.

The yacht's external lights finally failed, by various accounts, about three quarters of an hour after she struck the Beasts (around 2.40pm). All the flares and rockets had been exhausted by then and the gale was worsening by the minute, building to a force 10 on a night of pitch darkness in midwinter.

On their own resources

It was under these conditions that the returning islanders found themselves literally fighting for their lives – not against a military enemy, but against the raw elements of sea, wind, cold and brutal shore. Naval ratings and fishermen, born to the sea, many were strong swimmers and, when they realised there was no means of rescue, around fifty tried to swim ashore through the swirling swell. Many were lacerated and bruised by fragments of twisted and jagged metal and splintered wood from the ship. Some of those who made it to the rocky shore were fatally dashed against the steep rocks by incessant crashing waves. The sea, even in the short distance they had to cross, was a maelstrom and the desperate sight of failed attempts to reach land made those still aboard fearful and reluctant to try that route of escape.

Donald Macdonald, of 23 Cromore in South Lochs vividly recounted the scene many years later:

"... Mountainous waves relentlessly lashing over towering cliffs with narrow ledges and jagged crags. The waves descended in a mighty cataract into the churning, boiling and spuming depths below. ... The scene was terrible to behold. We were used to mines, torpedoes and shell fire but this struck fear in our hearts. We knew we were trapped, as no life-boat could live in that maelstrom. The most powerful swimmer would be a toy. We would be dashed to pieces, quartered and torn asunder by the piercing knife-like crags....

"I threw my kit-bag down, threw my heavy over-coat away. With the aid of a flash-light I groped my way amidships. By now the lights were out. Rockets were fired from the bridge and ... In the rocket's flare I could see sailors everywhere, single and in groups. Pieces of the life-boats on the wind side were being hurled over our heads. Some sailors were trying to get two boats out on the lee side. Some were climbing the tall masts fearing being washed overboard.

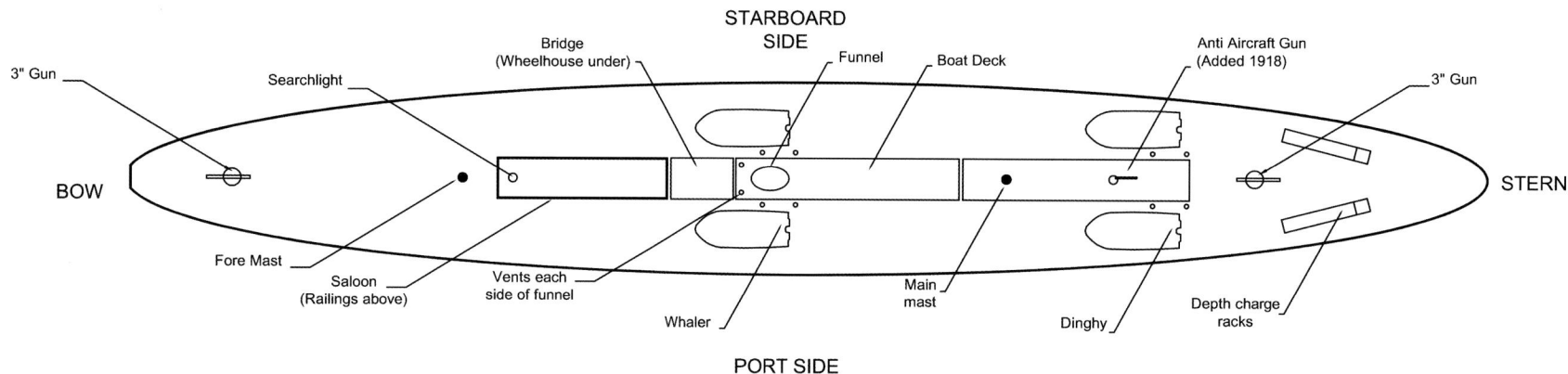

A deck plan of HMY Iolaire showing the position of the lifeboats.

"I .... descended to the bulwarks to jump into one of the boats. Thank goodness I missed it by seconds. It was loaded. I watched it churning and swirling and in an instant down it went. I could see little black specks on the foaming froth. Something determined me from jumping into the second boat. I gazed at it as I shoved off, then a mighty back wash wave seemed to fill the boat. It seemed to glide up to their shoulders, their heads – and then no more. I could not see any survivors from any of the boats…

"I braced myself for a good long leap – a leap of death, I thought….. I jumped and caught the rope. One, two heaves shoreward then my legs went round my head. I felt myself carried forward. I hit the crags. I was numb. I rolled like a football down the jagged rocks. The back wash hurled me outwards. …. It happened that some of the sailors who had managed ashore on the rope had enough strength left to run back and fro with the waves, hauling ashore the dead and the living. One of them hauled me to a ledge."[14]

The flare gun from HMY Iolaire, fired to attract attention as the ship went on the rocks.

John Finlay Macleod and the rope

'The rope' was referred to by many survivors, a symbol of salvation on that night of loss. Undoubtedly the hero of the night was John Finlay Macleod, of Port of Ness, an RNR carpenter coming home on leave, who swam ashore from the stricken ship with the rope and so helped to save the lives of 40 men that night. His son, John Murdo, many years later recounted his father's courageous action:

"Maybe he was fortunate, that he was somewhat familiar with that coastline. He used to come up there on a trading smack that my grandfather had. A flare went up and he identified the area. Having decided on his course of action, he gave the end of a heaving line to a fellow beside him, and told him that he must not let it go.

"My father didn't put the rope round his middle, but two times round his left hand and locked the end of the rope with his thumb. Then he dropped into the water. At the first attempt, the surge carried him away from the shore. With extraordinary presence of mind, he then took stock of the situation. Local knowledge again told him that the 'fath' of seven smaller waves was followed by the 'cliath', three bigger ones. He reckoned that if he could let himself go on the third high wave, with luck he would be carried over the rocks and land on the slope.

"This is what happened. After four had come ashore on the heaving line, he realised it would not hold and the hawser[15] line was sent across. In all 40 lives were saved on the rope and John Finlay Macleod was at the end of it until finally there was nobody else coming ashore."[16]

John Murray (Dell) and Robert Mackinnon of Tarbert were among four men that followed John Finlay ashore, and they helped to secure the hawser that was sent across after the thinner rope. Robert told his own story soon after the events:

> "I went to the starboard side, stripped off my oilskin coat and jumped into the sea. After a great struggle I reached the shore, but was washed out again on the receding wave, but I managed to swim towards a little bay and was lucky to come on a shallow place and so got on to the ledge of rocks and up out of reach of the sea. I looked about to see what I could do for the others, when I saw a man on the shore pulling a rope from the ship. I went to his assistance and we got a stout rope ashore. I could not find any convenient rock to make it properly fast to, so I took a turn of it round a jag of rock standing a few inches out of the ledge. Another chap and I hung on to the rope and the men began to come ashore on it. I am not sure how many got ashore, but all who tried did not manage to hold on."[17]

Now there came another heroic life-saving action. The hawser was first tied to the depth charge rack at the stern of the *Iolaire*, but there it exposed the men on the rope to the full force of the waves and the stern itself was pitching about with the sea's wild motion. John Maclennan of Kneep and others now moved the rope amidships to the after-lifeboat davit[18], to give the men more shelter from the breakers. The yacht herself would act as a breakwater against the waves while the men clung to the line. John later recalled:

> "I remember moving the rope from the stern to the side, but today I don't quite know how I managed it. A lot of those around me had lost their mind, particularly the younger men."[19]

Angus Nicolson estimated that it was a six-inch hawser, the size normally used for towing, and that 35 men used it to get ashore. Remarkable under the circumstances is the fact that men formed an orderly queue for their turn to try and reach the shore on the rope. Some of those watching were dismayed when they saw men swept off the rope by the incoming waves and the undertow sucking at them as the waves receded, straining the rope tight each time the yacht heeled back. Others judged their time and got ashore. John Maclean, from Borrowston, later said that as the ship rocked men on the rope fell off and others were scared when they saw so many being drowned. His cousin tried to dissuade him from going on the rope but he went, after waiting for large waves to pass, and was only wet up to his middle. As the tide ebbed, the distance to shore got longer, but all those men who came off the rope uninjured helped to hold it, maintaining the lifeline for as long as possible.

Another hero of the night, Donald Morrison of Knockaird (Am Patch) had already saved the life of Murdo Morrison of Skigersta, who was in one of the lifeboats that sank. Donald had managed to lower a rope to the stricken lifeboat, enabling Murdo to climb back on board the *Iolaire*. Now Donald recounted seeing the whole operation of the rope unfold:

> "I saw John Macleod from Port of Ness. He was a daring man. He got a rope on deck and said to someone 'Take a hold of that!' He saw the man was a bit shaky and said to him that he wouldn't do, so he gave the rope to another man.

"John jumped into the water with the other end of the rope and swam to the rock and then another wave came and washed him back to sea under the *Iolaire*. I said to myself, 'That's the last of you.' Then I saw him come up again on the crest of a wave and he managed to secure the rope on the rock. He stayed there with the rope and that is how most of the men were saved, although quite a lot of men were lost trying to get ashore on the rope".[20]

Donald Morrison waited his turn on the line and, as he waited, heard the man behind him speaking out loud to his wife: "*Mo ghràdh ort, chan fhaic mi tuilleadh gu bràth thu.*" ("My love, I will never see you again.") Donald's brother-in-law, Alexander Morrison, is believed to have been the last man to come ashore on John Finlay Macleod's rope before it broke.

Donald Murray of North Tolsta managed to get ashore on the rope, having already had a narrow escape when he tried to join one of the doomed lifeboats. That experience made him cautious, so he carefully studied what was happening:

"Now, once you were on the rope you were safe enough, do you see, if you caught the incoming succession of waves. The tragedy was when the waves were coming out one after the other and sweeping the men off the rope. The first ones hadn't studied this. I was watching for so long as I had vowed to myself not to leave the vessel. I began to think that if I did catch the incoming waves I would be borne onto the shingle beach like a fish before the sea returned again. The returning waves were sweeping the rope bare. You can't comprehend the ferocity of that sea. I was still watching – the sea was coming in under the rail.

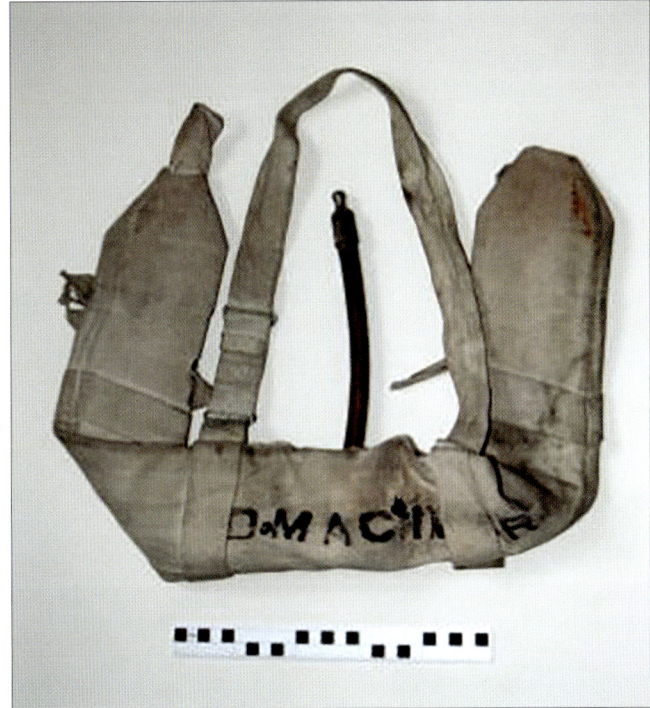

Only a few men were able to find lifebelts and not all who wore them survived.

"Many had now lost heart to go onto the rope as they saw what was happening. I thought I had to take my chance of life or death when the next sea would be going landwards. As the waves hit her side I got onto the rope and with a death grip I clung on. I felt the sea receding and the rope curving with its force but by then I was among the rocks. Clinging to the rope I made my way through the rocks – that's how I got away – my time hadn't yet come."[21]

Donald was hardly ashore when he saw a flash and the yacht sank 'like a stone'. The ship suddenly shifted on the rocks, yanking the hawser tight and catapulting those men that were still on it into the sea. With a great roar the *Iolaire* slipped off the rock and began to sink. There was an explosion and fire as the boiler appeared to blow up and the funnel collapsed, the stays breaking. All those aboard, including Donald Morrison, were plunged under the waves. It was 3.25am, just 90 minutes after the *Iolaire* first struck the Beasts of Holm.

Donald Morrison, Am Patch, vividly recalled the next minutes for the rest of his life:

"I was just getting ready to go for the rope when another wave came in and most of the *Iolaire* went down and I went down with her. I don't know if I went right to the bottom of the sea. I was struggling in the water, as anybody would be if they were drowning. A rope came into my hand and I got to the riggings and then up the mast as far as I could get. I looked behind and there was another chap coming up after me. Then a big wave came rolling in and I never saw him again.

"I didn't think I had a chance of surviving, but you fight for life as long as you can. I was on the main mast and had a wire in each hand and a foot on each side of the mast clinging on... I was squeezing my face to the wires and the mast as the waves came rolling in. This is what kept me alive...

"I heard a crash and the two men on the foremost mast had gone. It broke just like a match. Every wave after that I was waiting for a crash. At one time I was nearly thrown off the mast, when one of the wires came out of my hand and the aerial wires came down on top of me... I thought I was a goner. If there had

been someone else up the mast with me I would have been a goner. It was the weight of the two men on the other mast that caused it to break, with the strength of the waves."[22]

Many of those drowned on the *Iolaire* lost their lives trapped in the lower deck saloon, which had seemed so warm and inviting a spot to tired sailors boarding after their long journey home. The saloon was small and, with not enough seats or benches, many stretched out on the floor to get some sleep, their kit-bags and personal parcels also taking up a lot of room. There was only one narrow stair leading from the saloon to the upper deck. Once the ship hit the rocks, the interior lights went out and sailors were thrown in a heap. Still drowsy and wondering what had happened to the vessel, in the pitch blackness and with some of them injured, it would have been very difficult to find the way out. Those who made it to the top of the stair found that the door to the deck was jammed tight shut, trapping them in the lightless saloon with the sea gushing in. Many drowned where they were and, when some bodies were recovered, their greatcoats were still fastened. Some may have died in the saloon while still asleep.

Donald Maciver, a survivor from North Tolsta, detailed his experiences of the dreadful night in the book *Call na h-Iolaire*[23]. He was in the lower saloon when the vessel struck and told of the ship lying at an angle of 45 degrees, while the saloon door could not be opened. With his boots he managed to smash one of the saloon windows and escape. His shipmate, Donald Murray from Habost, Ness, coming home on leave with him from HMT *Joseph Burgin*, was drowned.

From the age of sixteen, Donald Murray of 46 South Bragar had served on armed trawlers in Icelandic waters.

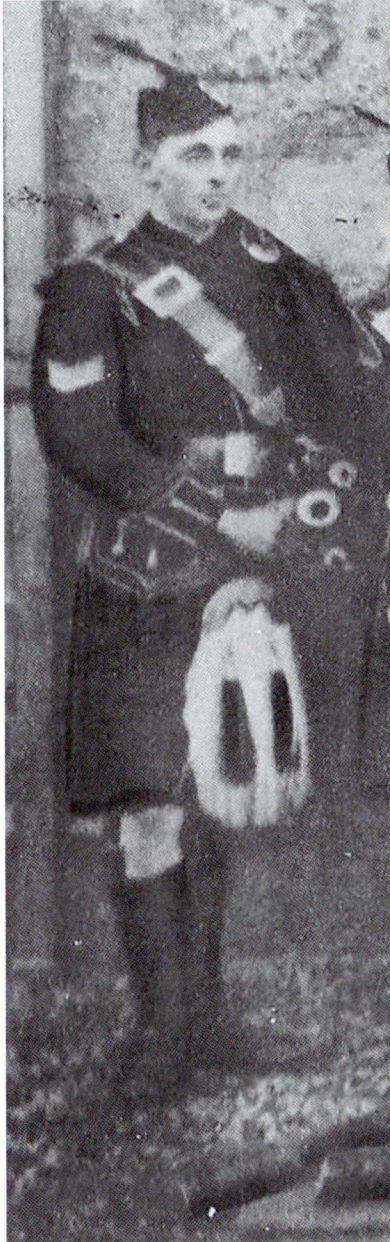

The survivors made their way to Stoneyfield Farm where they were given hot drinks and kept warm. Some men were able to journey onto Stornoway while others were injured and required assistance.

Anderson Young, the farmer at Stoneyfield Farm, where so many men found help on the night of the wreck.

As a 19-year-old he was coming home on the *Iolaire* on leave from HMT *Olympia*. Murray had seen much war service in the Mediterranean despite his youth and, as the *Iolaire* foundered, he was involved in lowering the lifeboats and then escaped from the flooding whaler. He was one of the last to leave the ill-fated ship and was fortunate to get onto the rope that connected the ship to the shore. However, as he came close to the shore he heard cries in the water of "*A Dhòmhnaill, A Dhòmhnaill!*" ("Donald, Donald!") The cries were from a friend in the sea and Donald went to save him. With his friend clinging to his boot, they managed to make the shore through the crashing waves. Earlier he had persuaded another friend to don a lifebelt and try and make it to the shore. He remained another unsung hero of the *Iolaire* disaster.

Many were the deeds of heroism, men seeking to help those struggling alongside them. Especially poignant were the deeds of those who tried, and failed, to save a brother, friend or relative. Donald Macaskill of Shulishader travelled home with older brother Duncan on the *Iolaire*. Donald was one of the few passengers who located a lifejacket but, as he was a stronger swimmer than his older brother, he gave the jacket to him. The family recounted how Duncan swam to the shore with Donald hanging on to his back, but Donald was swept away and his body was never recovered.

Alex Dan Maciver of Church Street Stornoway had been in the upper deck saloon when the vessel grounded. He was a survivor who claimed no heroism, but whose straightforward account of his survival was published in the weeks immediately following the disaster. The reporter recounts:

"Along with several others, he was in the deck saloon when the vessel struck, and they all immediately rushed out to see what had happened. They found that the ship had heeled over very much, but during a lull they managed to get two of the lifeboats lowered. As soon as they reached the water, however, they were swamped, and the occupants, numbering about 20 in each case were drowned.

"The ship then changed her position and drove in towards the shore stern first, then falling heavily broadside on to the shore. Eventually Mr Maciver dropped overboard, and after swimming about in the water for half-an-hour, with the aid of some floating wreckage, managed to reach the shore. He made his way to Stoneyfield Farm, where he and several of the survivors were most hospitably treated by Mr and Mrs Young. Some others reached Holm Farm, and were equally well treated."[24]

Whilst many still battled for survival in the frightful turmoil of wind and waves, those who had made it ashore had still to find a place of aid. The wet, slippery grass, deep bog and clinging whinbushes made progress slow and weary for men soaked with seawater, bruised and injured from the rocks and wreckage. It was dark, a force 10 gale was now blowing and neither light nor buildings could be seen from the shore.

John Maclennan of Kneep had made it ashore barefoot, like many others. He remembered:

"When I got ashore I was shoeless, as I had been resting (on the ship) and as I had taken them off. A lot of the men had taken their shoes off and were lying down, wherever they could get space to rest their head. Reaching the shore I fell into a bog and lost my socks, then I headed for the nearest house, where a huddle of injured people had gathered. I was injured with cuts on my chest, but I never let on to anyone."[25]

Tenant farmer William Anderson Young Jnr (known as Anderson Young) and Mrs Margaret Young at Stoneyfield Farm in Holm would prove to be two more of the quiet heroes of a dreadful night. They were awoken at about 3am on 1st January 1919 by the first survivor, Alex Dan Maciver from Church Street, Stornoway, who stumbled in a dazed condition into the farmhouse.

"He had been over half an hour in the water, which was bitterly cold. Taking his bearings from the light of Stornoway Lighthouse, he walked westward until he came to the farmhouse of Stoneyfield. He aroused the inmates (Mr and Mrs Anderson Young) who bade him welcome and soon had a blazing fire, dry clothes and hot drinks prepared. In short time Maciver was followed by other 20 survivors, some of those injured being helped along by their comrades. Previous to their arrival, their hosts had in readiness hot teas and beds to which the injured were put. Mr Maciver and the other survivors are full of gratitude to Mr and Mrs Young for their great attention and kindness."[26]

Alex Dan's arrival at Stoneyfield brought the first definite information anyone on the island had of the tragedy. Annie Nicolson, a maid at the farm, recalled[27] that they were about to go to bed when the men began to arrive, barefoot, with no boots or stockings. Mrs Young and her maids worked tirelessly through the night, providing food, milk and hot drinks for the growing band of traumatised men

Leonard Welch, Telegraphist on the Iolaire

who started to find the farm as the lights were lit. Mr Young himself went out towards the shore with a light, once he had returned from Stornoway, to guide those still struggling across the boggy ground.

One such was Donald Maciver from New Tolsta:

"I also got on the rope where I was washed ashore among the rocks (and) was helped up by a man, years after I found to be Alex John Macleod, Coll … I slept for a while until I was able to make my way through broom and bogs, so arrived at Stoneyfield house, which was full of naval men lying. As I was in a daze, seeing a basin of eggs on the dresser, I started drinking some, which helped me put up (vomit) all the salt water and then I felt better."[28]

The farmhouse became a refuge for stunned, physically exhausted men who had witnessed terrible scenes and survived an unspeakable ordeal. The worst cases were put to bed, still coughing up sea water, but many stayed for just a short time before setting out on foot for Stornoway.

For those very few survivors who were crew of the *Iolaire*, the confusion of the night was compounded by a total lack of familiarity with their surroundings. Telegraphist Leonard Welch, who had fought his way through the waves to the shore, after abandoning his attempt to make the radio work, later told of his experience:

"It was pitch black, and pouring with rain and sleet, and I could find no one about, I wandered on, but not knowing whether I was on the mainland or some odd island. I had one great desire, and that was to lie down, but something told me, that once I did so, I should never get up again. I fell across one man lying down, and got him to his feet, and together we staggered on, and at last we saw the light in a crofter's cottage, to which we made our way. The man I had gathered up, collapsed altogether just before we reached the farm and I myself, finished the last few yards on my hands and knees.

"I fell into the house as the door opened, and they brought the other fellow in. We did not stay many minutes as they had three other survivors there, and after a hot drink, a farm hand came with a lantern to guide us to the Battery, where we were soon in between blankets with a good tot of rum."[29]

John Maclean of Borrowston told of the last survivors ploughing through gorse and ditches to the farm house, many arriving crawling and vomiting, while Neil Nicolson (Niall Ruadh) from Lemreway spoke of a farmhouse crammed with survivors. Both these men later walked into Stornoway, as did John Maclennan, barefoot and injured.

The hospitality shown to survivors by Mr and Mrs Young at Stoneyfield Farm was praised by one of the first official rescuers to reach the scene, Sub Lt Charles Murray, who later reported:

"The owners[30] of Stoneyfield farm showed the greatest kindness and sympathy to all survivors, and offered all they had in the way of stores and clothing."[31]

And at the official inquiry into the loss of the vessel, the jury also put on record their appreciation of the hospitality shown to the survivors.

The first sight of disaster

Ashore at the RNR base at Battery Point, Stephen Saunders, Yeoman of Signals, saw a blue light between 1.50 and 2am and reported it as a vessel requiring a pilot. He saw another blue light, then a third one, around 2.20am, which was red. He reported that there was a vessel in distress. The yacht fired white flares thereafter.

Tied up in Stornoway harbour was the drifter HMD *Budding Rose*, supposed to meet the *Iolaire* and act as a pilot boat and tender. Her commander, Lieutenant W B Wenlock, could have held the vessel out at sea beyond the Arnish Lighthouse, where he could possibly have guided the yacht in, or signalled by flare or Aldis lamp to warn her off the rocks. His report to Rear Admiral Boyle after the events gives this account:

> "January 1st at 12.30 a.m. I proceeded in accordance with your orders on board HMD *Budding Rose* to await the arrival of HMY *Iolaire*. At about 1.55 when on board *Budding Rose* I saw a rocket and proceeded immediately to investigate. I made for what I considered to be the position from where the rockets were being fired and found a ship in distress on the Beasts of Holm rocks, but was unable to render any assistance owing to the heavy seas running. I approached to the edge of the breakers but found it was impossible to communicate with the ship in any way.

> "I then returned and reported to you and acting under your orders again proceeded to sea and stood by until daylight."

Wenlock continues with a short account of the rescue of a man from the wreck, given in the next chapter, and concludes:

> "This conclusion I beg to bring to your notice that I was on the scene within half an hour of the first rocket being fired and that when the last rocket was fired I was as near to the actual position of the ship as was possible taking into consideration that safety of my ship and the heavy sea running at the time."[32]

Wenlock did not stay close to the scene of the disaster but instead returned to Stornoway. He reported at the Imperial Hotel then returned to sea but both the *Budding Rose* and HM Whaler *Rorqual* thought it unwise to close in on the wreck in the gale.

Aboard the fishing vessel *Spider*, the men saw the *Iolaire* as she ran towards the Beasts of Holm. Engineer James Macdonald reported:

> "Immediately afterwards, we heard loud shouting and knew the vessel was on the rocks. We were passing the Beacon Light at Arnish at that time and could hear the shouting of the men as we were coming into the harbour. The night was very dark and a strong breeze from the South was raging with a heavy sea running. We were unable to give any assistance as we could not rely on our engine to operate in such rough seas."[33]

The little mailboat *Sheila* had left Kyle half an hour after the *Iolaire*, and came to the pier at Stornoway at 2.20am, 25 minutes after the *Iolaire* had stranded. The crew and passengers of the *Sheila* saw the lights of a vessel underneath the rocky shore at Holm and heard the yelling of men. The 300 passengers aboard the little steamer so crowded the starboard rails, that the *Sheila* listed to starboard as she neared the white Arnish Lighthouse beacon. Captain Cameron had to order the passengers to come away from the rails to secure stability. The Captain later told the Public Inquiry into the sinking: "I would say I saw six or seven rockets ... Hundreds saw them on Stornoway pier."

William Henderson Macdonald from Stornoway was a soldier with the Seaforths and a passenger aboard the *Sheila*. He wrote:

"When some miles from the Stornoway Lighthouse we could discern many lights in the vicinity of Holm, but nobody was aware that these lights were from the *Iolaire*. On arriving at No 1 Pier the passengers aboard the *Sheila* were greeted by many questions from anxious and agitated people ashore; "Are you there Kenny?" "Are you there Murdo?" "A bheil thu ann Iain?" ("Are you there John?") etc. It was only hours afterwards that we knew the reason for this display of anxiety. The *Iolaire* had struck Holm with the loss of many brave Lewismen."[34]

A young fishmarket worker, Louis 'Quinn' Macleod, heard the captain of the *Sheila* say that there was a ship on the rocks at Holm. The crowd on the pier thinned but some waited on, peering out to the Arnish Lighthouse and beacon through the sleet, but there was no sign of lights and they slowly dispersed.

In various parts of the island the signs of a tragedy to come were seen and heard, but not understood. Boys celebrating New Year outside in Leurbost saw flashes of light in the sky over Stornoway around 2am, and assumed they were part of Hogmanay celebrations. Similarly at a ceilidh house in Aird, Point, the whistle of a ship was heard in the early hours and thought to be from a drifter that had set its clocks wrongly.

As midnight came and went, the home of Kenneth Macleod at 17 Battery Park was full of celebrations. Kenneth was a crewman on the *Sheila*, originally from 12 Cross, and his home had become a convenient town focal point for Niseachs (people from Ness) waiting to welcome the returning servicemen home. With the gale getting fiercer, the fire was stoked higher, but glimpses down the windswept street showed no sign of any lights of ships at sea. The *Sheila* docked at 2.20pm, and the door burst open not ten minutes later. Donald Morrison of Lionel, who had been waiting for his brother Norman at the quayside, rushed in with the startling news that the *Iolaire* was on the Beasts. The Niseachs emptied the house and rushed in a body up to town, anxiety in their hearts, to get more news.

Inaction and confusion ashore

As soon as the first man had stumbled into the farmhouse kitchen at Stoneyfield Farm, farm tenant W Anderson Young set out for Stornoway on his bicycle to raise the alarm. When he reached naval HQ at the Imperial Hotel the sentries would not let him enter. Once they admitted him, he had difficulty convincing the inebriated naval officers that a disaster had occurred. Around 3.30am, five ratings from the *Iolaire* also reported at the Imperial Hotel. Rear Admiral Boyle later reported that:

"Little information could be obtained from them; they appeared to have been washed on shore or else dropped from the stern when the vessel's stern was swung over the rocky shore at Holm Point – in fact they did not know exactly how they got on shore."[35]

Warrant Officer William Barnes was acting Chief Officer of the Coastguard at Stornoway.[36] At 3am a naval messenger called at his house on Seaview Terrace – just 300 yards from the Battery – with a message from the Rear Admiral that there was a ship in distress at Holm, and that he was to get the Life-Saving Apparatus (LSA) ready at once. Jumping from his bed, he reached the Battery at 3.15am, by his own report, and ordered the apparatus out of its shed.

The LSA in Stornoway contained a rocket-propelled breeches buoy system, which consisted of a pair of 'breeches' (trousers) attached to a lifebuoy and pulled between ship and shore on a rope pulley. The first line would be sent between ship and shore by rocket, the crew attaching it to a strong part of the ship and further ropes and pulleys then being set up by which the 'breeches' could be hauled across. It was capable of carrying one person at a time, and had proved extremely effective in rescues of ships' crew where vessels had run aground, since its introduction early in the 19th century. Many ships carried the equipment, and Coastguard teams around Britain also had the equipment available.

The breeches buoy in Stornoway had been successfully deployed within recent memory. On February 2nd 1915 the schooner *Laura* had gone ashore off Battery Point, entering Stornoway with a heavy sea running. Using the breeches buoy the crew of four were safely hauled through the surf. On that occasion the wreck was right beside the LSA station and so transportation of the equipment was not an issue, but

the apparatus could be moved anywhere in the island.[37] In Stornoway it was designed to be carried on a horse-drawn cart.

The Divisional Chief Officer of Coastguard, Frederick Boxall, arrived at about 3.40am and found that the two horses needed to pull the apparatus had not arrived. The Officer of the Watch at the Battery gave them 19 men and, at 3.50pm, the men harnessed themselves on to the one-ton apparatus by drag ropes and set out for the scene of the wreck by road. Some survivors passed them on the road, walking towards Stornoway. After three and a half miles Barnes left the men and made an attempt to search the beach, with the inadequate oil carriage lamp from the cart. Barnes saw wreckage, but he had no powerful light to sweep the area. At one time he thought he heard shouting, but he saw no small boats and no survivors. Barnes reported:

"By this time the storm was high and there was a heavy sea running. The seas were lashing the cliffs and it was impossible to get on the beach at places."[38]

Meanwhile Boxall and one other man went around the coast. The darkness and boisterous weather made progress slow, but they were aided by a man with a light and entered Stoneyfield Farm where there were several survivors, one of whom told him that he was the last to leave the ship and that she was totally lost.

At 2.45am Sub Lt Charles W Murray RNVR received orders to raise the lifeboat crew and get assistance to Holm. Stornoway had a lifeboat and a lifeboat station, established in 1887 by the Royal National Lifeboat Institution. Then, as now, the lifeboat was manned by volunteers. Sub Lt Murray set out to rouse honorary secretary Duncan Mackenzie at the Royal Hotel. After 20 minutes banging on the hotel's door, Murray forced an entrance at the rear, woke Mackenzie and told him to report to Rear Admiral Boyle. He then went to rouse the caretaker of the lifeboat, who lived opposite the lifeboat station. The caretaker had been ill for several weeks, but he handed over the key and directed Murray to the house of the lifeboat coxswain John "Shonnachan" Maclean. Murray went back to the station to light the lamps and was soon joined by Mackenzie, Maclean and three soldiers. No other men were available to man the lifeboat. Murray went back to the Imperial Hotel to report the unsuccessful exercise at 4.30am.

Next he roused Surgeon Lt Thomas Owen, the naval base surgeon, and set out to try and get a car to take a first aid party down to Holm. A succession of frustrating attempts to waken car-owners involved knocking, kicking at doors and throwing stones at windows, until he came to the private home of garage owner Mr Henderson and managed to wake him. Sub Lt Murray later reported:

> "He opened a small window above the door and asked what I wanted. I replied that I wanted a car at once. He asked where I wanted to go to and I told him Sandwick. He did not seem very agreeable, so I told him there was a ship ashore at Holm Point with 250 men aboard and I must get out to take assistance to any survivors. He then replied that he did not think that I could have a car, as his drivers were at home and probably would not come out on such a night – when I pointed out that men's lives were in great danger and delay might be fatal, he replied that he "didn't know" and that he "would see". I asked him if he could give me the key to the garage so that I could drive the car myself – this he refused, also my offer to buy one of the cars."[39]

Stornoway Post Office around 1910. Sub Lt Charles W Murray was given use of the Post Office car just after 6am by the Postmaster, and took Surgeon Owen and a sick bay attendant to Stoneyfield.

John Maclean, coxswain of the RNLI lifeboat. Not enough men could be found to form a crew and reach the stricken Iolaire.

It was now 6am, and Murray remained tenacious in his quest. He set out again to try and get a motor cycle, but, as he was attempting to wake the owner, he saw a car enter the Post Office.

"I immediately went in and explained the situation to the Postmaster, who promptly placed the car at my disposal and offered any further assistance that was in his power to give. On leaving the Post Office we proceeded direct to the Sick Bay, where we arrived about 6.30 a.m. Left Sick Bay at 6.40 a.m. with Surgeon Owen and Sick Bay Attendant Jones, also stretchers and First Aid Gear."

The small party reached Sandwick about 7.15am, left the driver at the closest point by road and set off to Stoneyfield Farm. They arrived at 7.30am to find several survivors being tended to by the family. Surgeon Owen began to attend to the survivors and one of the women of the house went to show the driver another road by which he could bring the car to the farm. The car arrived at the farm at 7.50am and the first party of survivors were sent off to Stornoway at 8am.

Light began to creep into the sky at 8.30am and Surgeon Owen, coastguard officer Boxall and Sub Lt Murray set out towards the scene of the wreck. On their way they passed a man's body, thought to be that of Alick Macleod of 1 Portnaguran, who had made it ashore but did not survive to reach help, possibly succumbing to a heart attack after his exertion. The small party attempted artificial respiration without success. It was just the first of the day's many grim discoveries, as the bodies of drowned and shattered island men washed up along the shores around Holm and Stornoway.

At 6.10am on 1st January 1919 Rear Admiral Boyle sent the following telegram to the Admiralty in London:

"Regret to report Yacht 056 *IOLAIRE* at 0230 with 260 ratings from Kyle to Stornoway on leave grounded on eastern shore of entrance to Stornoway.

Southerly gale blowing – auxiliary patrol vessels sent to assistance – unable to approach *IOLAIRE*. Several ratings have reported that they swam to shore at very short distance. Rocket apparatus despatched. No further information available at present."[40]

Chapter 4 Footnotes

1. *Ross-shire Journal*, 3rd January 1919

2. Survivor Donald Murray, interviewed for the *Stornoway Gazette*, 23rd May 1992. Translated from Gaelic

3. The National Archive. PRO Admiralty file 116/1869

4. PRO Admiralty file 116/1869

5. PRO Admiralty file 116/1869

6. John Maclennan interviewed by Maga Mackay, translated by Maggie Smith for *Hebridean Connections*, 2005

7. Interview with Donald Murray, *Stornoway Gazette*, 23rd May 1992

8. Donald Morrison (Am Patch) interview, *Stornoway Gazette*, 4th January 1992

9. *Ross-shire Journal*, 3rd January 1919

10. Ernest Adams interviewed in the *Stornoway Gazette*, 10th January 1919

11. *My Amazing Drama - Wrecked on the Beasts of Holm* Leonard Welch. T V Boardman Ltd, 1942

12. As above

13. PRO Admiralty file 116/1869

14. Donald Macdonald of Cromore writing from Canada, *Stornoway Gazette*, 10th August 1956

15. Hawser – a rope or cable thick enough to hold a ship at moorings or when being towed

16. *West Highland Free Press*, 1993

17. Robert Mackinnon interview, *Stornoway Gazette*, 10th January 1919

18. Davit - a small shipboard crane, used for suspending a lifeboat

19. John Maclennan interview by Maga Mackay, translated by Maggie Smith for *Hebridean Connections*, 2005

20. Am Patch interview *Stornoway Gazette*, 4th January 1992

21. Interview with Donald Murray, translated from the Gaelic, *Seanchas*, Winter 2006

22. Am Patch interview *Stornoway Gazette*, 4th January 1992

23. *Call na h-Iolaire*, Tormod Calum Domhnallach, Acair 1978

24. *Highland News,* 11th January 1919

25. Interview with Maga Mackay, translated by Maggie Smith for *Hebridean Connections*, 2005

26. *Inverness Courier: First Ashore*, 3rd January 1919

27. Home At Last Grampian TV, 1989

28. Donald Maciver interviewed on BBC Radio nan Gàidheal, 25th February 1976

29. *My Amazing Adventure: Wrecked on the Beasts of Holm* Leonard Welch. TV Boardman, 1942

30. The Youngs were tenant farmers and not owners

31. Report by Sub Lt Charles W Murray RNVR to Rear Admiral Boyle, January 5th 1919

32. PRO Admiralty file 116/1189

33. PRO Admiralty file 116/1189

34. *Old Stornoway Revisited* Stornoway Historical Society, 2001. From a series of articles by W H Macdonald, *Stornoway Gazette*, 1965-73

35. Letter from Rear Admiral Boyle to The Secretary, Admiralty, 3rd January 1919

36. PRO Admiralty file 116/1869

37. The breeches buoy life-saving apparatus continued to be used in Lewis right up until the 1960s. The largest breeches buoy rescue in history was off the west side of Lewis on 31st January 1953, when 66 crew members and the ship's cat were rescued from the cargo liner Clan MacQuarrie, which ran aground off Borve in winds of over 100 miles per hour

38. PRO Admiralty file 116/1869

39. Report by Sub Lt Charles W Murray RNVR to Rear Admiral Boyle, 5th January 1919

40. Telegram from Rear Admiral Boyle to Admiralty, 6.10am, 1st January 1919. PRO Admiralty file 116/1869

Chapter 5

The Darkest Dawn

"Who of those who saw it will ever forget the little boats working with grappling irons around the rocks at Holm, and the bodies lying in sodden rows on the grass, and the little red and blue country carts coming in from the villages of Barvas, Uig and Lochs, Back and Point, to claim their dead?"[1]

"There's a wail in the wind and a sob in the waves all round our shores in these sad days. The profound gloom cast over the community by the loss of the *Iolaire* on New Year's morning weighs upon one and all like a hideous nightmare which they would fain shake off."[2]

Small boats rowing around the masts of the sunken Iolaire, while the Beasts and their beacon stand sentinel. The Iolaire struck the rocks inside the beacon and sank close to the rocky cliffs at Holm.

No darker dawn was ever known in Lewis, as the first light of New Year 1919 revealed sights and sounds that would not be forgotten for generations. Light revealed bodies floating in the sea, bodies washed up on the shore, shattered men limping barefoot away from the scene of the wreck, so close to the land that it seemed to mock the homecoming hopes of the sailors and their families. The welcoming bonfires would never be lit, the underwear and new sweaters airing at the hearths would never be worn and little of the food prepared for the homecoming was consumed. Mourning and unspeakable grief came with the New Year to Lewis and Harris, on the first peaceful Hogmanay after four years of bloodshed and strife.

It is hard to imagine, in a world where pictures of tragic events can be seen around the world in seconds, how the scale of the *Iolaire* tragedy became gradually known, at the slow speed of human travel, radiating from the scene of the wreck itself to villages and districts all over the islands of Lewis and Harris.

The first civilians to know of the tragedy were friends, relatives and sometimes strangers in the villages of Holm and Sandwick, later in Stornoway, who took in survivors and gave them help. Soaking wet, drained of energy and hollow-eyed, some had managed to walk into Stornoway, wandering around the streets as daylight arrived, barefoot, semi-naked, mud-caked and covered in grease and oil. Nearly all the survivors were those who had the presence of mind to jettison boots, heavy coats and even trousers and tunics to prevent weight drag in the surging sea. They were given refuge, clothes and food in local houses before some were transported to the naval sick bay, or to the naval base where they reported.

One of these men was Donald MacRae (Dòmnhall Bàrnaidh) of Ranish. He and two of his mates knew the area well enough to set out walking for Stornoway, staggering and holding on to one another. On the way they met a boy who had come home on the *Sheila* and were taken to a house in Sandwick, where they were given hot tea. In the morning they went to the Stornoway depot – the people in the house went most of the way into Stornoway with them to see that they would not fall down. At the depot they were given a new uniform and then walked home to bed, carrying to their home village the news of the wreck – five men from Ranish were lost and five survived.

Alex John Macleod of Coll reached Stoneyfield Farm, after dragging himself up the rocks from the wreck. The Young family gave him a hot drink, then he and three others were taken into town by farmer Anderson in his horse and cart. Feeling weak, in wet clothes and 'with feet full of thistles', Alex walked out of the town to an aunt in Laxdale. He knocked the family up and, believing him to be drunk, they took him in and gave him oatmeal and treacle. Exhausted by the fight for survival, he slept for hours before he was woken by the mother of a boy looking for her own son, who had been lost on the *Iolaire*. He then walked home to Coll, unaware that his brother had already searched for him at his digs on Kenneth Street and his father was looking for him with just the same desperate anxiety – he was the only survivor from the Back district.

The trauma experienced by the surviving sailors manifested itself in different ways. Some seemed blank, confused and lost. Murdo Morrison of North Shawbost had no recollection of his escape from the *Iolaire* across the rope, even years later, while John Mackay of Shulishader in Point was thought by his family to have been lost, as he sheltered at a peat bank for three days before walking the six miles home. Calum "Safety" Smith relates:

"Before the news that day in 1919 broke a group of us were standing in front of one of the croft houses in North Shawbost, when a sailor in uniform came trudging wearily along the street with his head down. We recognised him and, as he went past one of the boys called: *"A' Mhurchaidh, an tàinig m' athair-s' raoir?"* (Murdo, did my father come home last night?) We all thought it strange that Murdo did not raise his downcast head, look round or make any response. Later that day we heard what had happened, and that Murdo was one of the survivors, and we understood."[3]

There were people still waiting at Stornoway harbour, hoping against hope that news would come, that the boy they awaited was on another ship, that he was safe somewhere. One young girl on the pier was Johanna Macdonald, the fiancée of Malcolm Macinnes from Lemreway. In 1989 she told of how she was looking for him, when she saw someone she knew had been with him. The sailor told her: *"I am very sorry but I'm afraid he's gone. He was at my back on the rope. The rope broke and I saw him no more!"* Johanna never married after losing her betrothed.[4]

Nearby waited Catherine Wares, a herring girl from Pulteneytown Wick, expecting her lover, the Royal Marine Herbert Head, who was a passenger on the *Iolaire* on his way back to his Stornoway post after visiting his family on leave. Today was to be their wedding day, arranged in haste as Catherine was expecting his child. Now she learnt that he had got ashore from the wreck, but had gone back into the sea to help others and had then been lost.

Young John Campbell of Habost was also there. He was an 18-year-old civilian and had come home on the *Sheila* after being treated for TB on the mainland. How delighted he must have been when he encountered his older brother Alex John (AJ) at Kyle and watched him go aboard the *Iolaire*, due to be reunited in Stornoway and to travel home to their waiting family together. John waited in vain on the quay at Stornoway for his brother, learning of the tragedy early next morning. John's brother's body was never recovered, and he himself was to die at home a year later, aged 19.

For many relatives, though, the certainty of their loss was still hours, or even days away. The lack of a concerted rescue attempt in the earliest hours after the sinking meant many survivors took their own route to help and inadvertently caused confusion, anxiety and grief as relatives tried to find what had happened to their boys. It did not help that there was no manifest of the passengers aboard the *Iolaire* taken at Kyle, so that nobody knew for certain who was and who was not on board the yacht. It was to be years before the location or even the identity of every passenger, living or dead, could be confirmed.

John Mackenzie (Iain 'An Anndra) of Portvoller was blown from the sea by a gust of wind, which filled the oilskin jacket he was wearing and threw him up on the rocks. He was slightly injured, but alive, and walked to his sister's house in Sandwick. John Murray ('An Help) of South Dell went to Kenneth Street where a lady from Ness shouted that there was a man outside who was soaking wet and brought him in. John Macinnes (Iain a' Bhroga) of Tolsta was washed ashore at Holm unrecognisable and somehow stumbled along to the lighted farmhouse from where he was taken to the Sick Bay.

At the home of Mrs Macaulay in Point Street, the early hours of New Year's morning brought thunderous knocking on the door. Mrs Macaulay, her husband away serving in India and with two small children, was naturally frightened and shouted: "Who is it?" The voice on the other side insisted it was an emergency and told her to open the door immediately. When she opened the door, her cousin Alexander Macleod (who served in the Navy as Murdo) from Bragar stood there in his sailor's uniform but without his cap, coat and boots. Beside him was a younger man in naval uniform but with his cap, oilskin and boots on. They were accompanied by Angus Nicolson, who urged Mrs Macaulay to get a fire going and to try and get some dry clothes, which she managed to borrow from neighbours, already wakened by the noise. Mr Nicolson had his New Year bottle with him from which he gave drinks to the men. He had been on his way to Sandwick to first foot[5] when he met the men, on Oliver's Brae[6], and turned back with them to his own home on Point Street. Murdo knew where his cousins stayed and was already making his way there on his stocking soles.

Some survivors were thought drunk as the disjointed account of what had happened came tumbling from trembling lips. George Alexander Morison (Seòras a' Mhinister) of the UF Church Manse at Knock, Carloway, made it to Anderson Young's farm and then walked barefoot to Stornoway, to the Ross family house at Keith Street, where he had lodged when a pupil at The Nicolson Institute. He threw stones at a window to rouse the family and a 10-year-old girl, probably the daughter Ann Christina (known as Ancris) thought he was drunk when she heard how wildly he was talking. George was put to bed beside the father, John, by Mrs Ross after she had taken his soaked clothes off. He remained for several days, exhausted and disorientated.

John ''Ain Geal' Maclennan survived the wreck, having got ashore on the rope. Scratched by the rocks and with no shoes, he lost a sock in the bog and was chilled by frost, feeling the cold intensely. He reached the farmhouse, saw that there were too many already there, so he walked to Stornoway to his relations, the Maclennans of Plantation Road. A girl in the house was crying – having already heard of the wreck, she had thought John was drowned. Now she fetched him hot water and mustard and, after reporting in to the base later that morning, he was sent in a car to Callanish, from where he made his way home to Kneep, in the far west of Lewis.

The thought of home acted as a beacon to minds exhausted and traumatised by the wreck, and some of those who made it ashore set out with dogged determination to their family homes. Alexander Donald Maciver (Alex Dan) walked from Stoneyfield Farm to his Stornoway home at Church Street, surprising his family at 6am. Murdo Stewart of Lower Bayble was so traumatised after surviving that he walked straight home from the shore at Holm, barefoot and wearing just his trousers and a shirt. He climbed into his house through a window rather than through the front door, to be welcomed by his surprised mother and two sisters – sister Dollag remembered it as the most atrocious night in living memory. Donald Macleod (Dòmhnall Mhurchaidh) also of Lower Bayble, walked with his neighbour the eight miles home, barefoot in the dark.

For a few, the single-minded journey home was truly monumental, and speaks of what we would today describe as post-traumatic stress disorder (PTSD). Alexander Campbell (Ailig Mòr) of Plocropool in the Bays of Harris took two days to get home. Alick set off without any rest or treatment, his hands skinned by the hawser as he escaped the broken vessel, to walk home to Harris. When the sun rose on 1st January he realised that he had taken the wrong road and was well to the west of his intended route. He headed south-east, crossing rough, boggy country to Balallan, and sought shelter for the night. Angus Macdonald of Laig in Harris later recollected that Alick called at their home between Drinishader and Plocropool, and was still soaking wet, just before he reached home on the evening of Thursday 2nd January. His widowed mother and his sisters, Maggie Sarah and three-year-old Margaret, would have been at home when he finally reached his hearth to collapse, traumatised, perhaps speechless and certainly exhausted. He was forbidden by the family from ever going to sea again – their father had already been drowned when fishing.

While each survivor followed their unique path to safety and rest, for so many others that moment would never come. The grim toll of the wreck became obvious from the first glimmer of dawn, bodies floating in the sea or washed up on the shore. As so often happens after a sudden, violent storm, the morning was calm, the sea grew gradually more peaceful, but the tranquillity of the day belied a storm of grief and devastation that would unfold as the hours passed.

Angus Macleod of Aird, Point, had returned home on 30th December on the mail steamer *Sheila* with many Lewis servicemen. On New Year's Eve he had been celebrating in the local ceilidh house and went away to sleep early in the morning. Shortly afterwards he was awoken by somebody going around knocking all the doors, telling them what had taken place. Angus's father and others from Aird headed for the Beasts of Holm and got there about daybreak. Even to those hardened by trench warfare, as Angus had been, the sight was one to break the heart. The sea was full of bodies, floating and washing onto the shore, and every second body was someone they knew.

Murdo Macfarlane, the Melbost bard, related[7] that in the morning he was with some herring girls and they went onto Sandwick beach. The girls stopped and one said in Gaelic: *"God of mercy what is this?"* The girls went away from the shore but Macfarlane carried on. The first victim he saw was a sailor with his back to the cemetery wall. It seemed that the sea and the cemetery were competing for him. Another body he saw was that of 23-year-old John Macaskill, who he knew as the son of Mèireag Ailean (Mary Macaskill). Their house was within sight, across the cemetery – he was drowned at his own door. The sights affected Macfarlane deeply, and his song of grief, *Raoir Reubadh an Iolaire*, has an immediacy that could only come from a personal, intense memory of that day.

> *The maiden wept bitterly the following morning when they found her loved one drowned in the seaweed, no shoes on his feet as he had taken to swimming; then she crouched and kissed his cold lips.*

(translated from the original Gaelic version)

Young Alex Macaulay of Stornoway was one of the children inexorably drawn to the horrible scenes at the shore. As an adult he recalled:

"The following day, which was calm, some pals and I walked all the way to Holm to see the wreck. There were men in small boats dragging for bodies and I can still see the face of one sailor whose body they took up, facing the shore where we sat. He still had, in death, a ruddy complexion. He had a moustache. I cannot remember much else of the scene except the calmness of the sea and all the men about talking in low tones."[8]

The impact of such terrible sights on such very young children can only be guessed at, but the way in which the stories were told so many years later speaks of images burnt into young memories. In 1989, Ina Macritchie told her story of visiting the beach as a youngster. *"When we saw sights down there we just ran home. It was terrible."*[9]

At home at Battery Park, young Catherine Macleod (Katie, aged 6), daughter of Kenneth who had seen the wreck from the *Sheila*, had been kept indoors by her mother to look after Kenneth, aged three. Looking from the window, she was transfixed at seeing an exhausted man walking up the road, wearing a naval tunic top, long johns covered with oil, grass and seaweed stains and in his stockinged feet. It was their neighbour Angus Nicolson, returning to his home at number 25 Battery Park, after reporting in at the Imperial Hotel to the naval authorities. It was a vivid memory that she never forgot until she died aged 94.[10]

From Kate's home her sisters Annie (aged 10) and Agnes (aged 8), were allowed down to the Sandwick shore, where they saw the remains of many sailors close to their house. Some corpses looked as if they were asleep, while other faces and hands had been marked and disfigured by the rocks. The wailing of grieving relatives, the waves crashing on the shore, the creaking of cart wheels and snorting of horses were the sounds of that still late morning as more and more rural people came searching for a missing loved one on the shore.

For the news was travelling, from mouth to ear, migrating steadily from Stornoway into the country districts. The mother of 18-year-old Norman Mackenzie of Garrabost, who would never come home, was gripped by fear as daylight brought an eerie phenomenon. Mary Mackenzie went outside early and heard a strange noise in the distance, coming from the direction of Stornoway. The whole family stood outside in the still morning and listened fearfully as the noise grew louder. It was the sound of wailing, as the news of the disaster spread from the Bràighe[11], eastwards down through the villages of Point. 39 of the sons of the district were drowned in the wreck of the *Iolaire*. That wailing, which pierced the air in Stornoway and the villages of Lewis and Harris, haunted those that heard it for the rest of their lives.

Right at the easternmost tip of Point, almost 10 miles from Stornoway in the village of Aird, a young woman would later recollect the events of New Year's night and the terrible day that followed:

"My mother was a young woman on the night that the *Iolaire* was shipwrecked – and she told me that it was a really, really dreadful night, gale force winds and very, very dark. And then of course they heard later the *Iolaire* had gone aground on the rocks and the majority on board, who had come safely through the war and were now on their own doorstep, as it were, and yet so many of them perished. It was very difficult for me, as a young person and even up until this point in time, to listen to some of the stories that unfolded as a result of that terrible tragedy. I think of the parents who were awaiting their loved ones and, as the night wore on and they didn't appear, what their thoughts must have been. And of the children waiting for their father to arrive. And then we were told that from many parts of the island the parent, the father or a relative, would come, with a horse and cart, to lift the body of their loved one. It's just such a horrific story."[12]

National and local papers brought the details of the tragedy to a disbelieving nation.

THE DAILY MIRROR, Wednesday, January 8, 1919.

PREMIER TACKLES DEMOBILISATION TROUBLE

The Daily Mirror

CERTIFIED CIRCULATION LARGER THAN THAT OF ANY OTHER DAILY PICTURE PAPER

No. 4,743. Registered at the G.P.O. as a Newspaper. WEDNESDAY, JANUARY 8, 1919 [16 PAGES.] One Penny.

AFTER THE WRECK OF IOLAIRE ON 'THE BEASTS OF HOLM'

The mizzen-mast and stump of the main-mast of the Iolaire, with a ventilator just showing above the water between them. Beyond are the fatal "Beasts of Holm" rocks, on which the yacht was battered to pieces by the waves. Inset: Late Commander Richard Gordan William Mason, R.D., R.N.R., who commanded Iolaire.

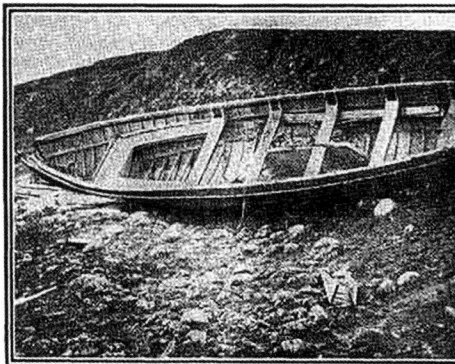

A shattered lifeboat from the wreck driven up on the rocky shore by the waves.

Boats on the scene of the disaster searching for the bodies of those who perished.

Where the ill-fated steam yacht Iolaire was driven on the rocks off Stornoway by the fury of a sudden storm and wrecked, with a loss of some 250 lives. The tragedy was painfully intensified by the fact that many of the men who perished were on the first leave from naval service they had enjoyed for years, and that they went to their deaths when actually in sight of the lights of their home harbour. The whole island of Lewis has been plunged in mourning.—(Exclusive to *The Daily Mirror*.)

NAVAL YACHT ASHORE OFF STORNOWAY.

FEARED HEAVY LOSS OF LIFE.

The steam yacht Iolaire, with about 250 naval seamen on board, was entering the harbour at Stornoway naval base early yesterday morning, when she struck the rocks known as the Beasts of Holm. It is feared that of those on board only about 30 lives were saved.

It appears that some 500 sailors and soldiers were going to Lewis on New Year leave. Their numbers were beyond the capacity of the mail steamer Sheila, and some 250 naval ratings were being conveyed from the Kyle of Lochalsh to Stornoway on board H.M. Yacht Iolaire, which in addition carried a crew of 24. The ship, which was in charge of Commander Mason, left the Kyle about 8 p.m., an hour ahead of the Sheila. She had an excellent passage across the Minch, with a fair wind from the south, freshening as the voyage proceeded. Between 1 a.m. and 2 a.m. she was approaching Stornoway Harbour, the lights on Arfish Point and the beacon off the harbour entrance being quite visible. The passengers were in high spirits, eagerly anticipating their New Year holiday, the first since hostilities began, when the vessel ran ashore at full speed near Holm Head. Accurate figures of the survivors are not available, but the number is put variously at 35 to 50, so that it is feared that the loss is well over 200 men.

SURVIVORS' NARRATIVES.

One of the survivors has given the following account of the accident :—

It was very dark, there being no moon. But the atmosphere was clear, and lights were distinctly visible at a great distance. As we approached [...] lighthouse we began getting our kit together.

January 2, 1919   THE DAILY MIRROR   Page 3

LEAVE BOAT DISASTER—BRITISH PEACE DELEGATES

New Year's Tragedy of Patrol Vessel that Struck Dangerous Rocks at Stornoway.

270 SAILORS LOST AT HOME'S DOOR.

All the Officers and Crew Drowned—30 Lives Saved.

A terrible disaster, which has cast a gloom over Stornoway and Lewis, took place yesterday, when the steam patrol vessel H.M.S. Iolaire, with 800 sailors on board on New Year holiday leave, struck the rugged, dangerous rocks known as the "Beasts of Holm," which are situated to the right of Stornoway Harbour.

Of the 800 on board only about thirty were saved, some being seriously injured in their attempts to reach the shore.

All officers and crew of the Iolaire were lost.—Central News.

A DIFFICULT PASSAGE.

Passengers Were on Their First Leave Since the War.

From Our Own Correspondent.

Invergarven, Wednesday.

The harbour, in a westerly wind and with a heavy sea running, is a difficult one to negotiate, and the Iolaire, caught by wind and a huge wave, was driven on the rocks and wrecked.

A peculiarly poignant feature of the disaster is that the passengers were 550 men of the island, who were mostly all on their first leave [...]

PRIME MINISTER AND THE PROMISES.

Resignation If Government Did Not Do Best to Fulfil Them.

WHEN PARLIAMENT WILL MEET

Mr. Lloyd George broke his journey at Carnarvon yesterday on his way to Criccieth. Speaking in Welsh at the Liberal Club, he said they could rely upon one thing—that he was still in the same place, and was one of the people. It was for them he had worked and would continue to fight.

He had sprung from the people. He was, however, only the people's guardian and trustee, and should he ever betray them they might be certain that something had happened to him which had never happened before.

In the last election, which was among the most momentous in the history of the country, democracy had an opportunity of showing its confidence in the present Government to change the face of the country.

If the Government did not do their best to fulfil the promises made he would no longer be head of the Government, but would go back to the people and ask for the renewal of their confidence. (Cheers.)

Parliament's Opening.—The Daily Mirror understands it has been decided to postpone the meeting of Parliament for a fortnight—from January 21 to February 4.

The New Cabinet.—The Daily Mirror was authoritatively informed last night that the new Cabinet is not likely to be announced until Sunday evening next. The Prime Minister is "thinking out" his selections at Criccieth.

Scene of the disaster to the British leave boat.

"OUR KING AS MODEL FOR PRESIDENT OF GERMANY.

New Constitution To Be Based on Those of Britain and America.

Vorwärts publishes an authorised statement describing the form of the new Constitution which it is proposed to establish in Germany.

The new Government will be a Republic headed by a President, whose power will be between that of an American President and the King of England.

The President will be chosen by the direct votes of the people, and will be assisted by a parliamentary Cabinet similar to that of England.

M. Paderewski, says the Berliner Tageblatt, is probably leading the Poles in the fighting at Posen.

In heavy street fighting over fifty people were killed.—Reuter.

"FIGHT BRITISH ON RHINE WITH GERMAN COMRADES."

Russian Executive Leader's Wild Talk to Spartacus League.

BOLSHEVISTS 18 MILES FROM RIGA.

MEN WHO ARE GOING TO VERSAILLES.

Will Capt. J. O'Grady Be a Labour Delegate?

JANUARY 13 THE DATE.

Lord Hardinge, Sir E. Crowe and Sir L. Mallet Leave on Saturday.

The British delegation to the forthcoming Peace Conference at Versailles, which it is anticipated, will open on January 13, have now been definitely selected.

The British Government will be represented at the Conference table by:—

THE PRIME MINISTER.
MR. BALFOUR.
MR. BONAR LAW.

Permanent officials in attendance will include:—

VISCOUNT HARDINGE, the Permanent Head of the Foreign Office. [He is an ex-Viceroy of India and a former British Ambassador to Russia.]

SIR WILLIAM TYRRELL, Senior Clerk in the Foreign Office. [Has been in Foreign Office twenty-nine years.]

SIR LOUIS MALLET, who will be in charge of all matters relating to Turkey. [Was British Ambassador to Turkey, 1913-14.]

SIR ESME HOWARD, Northern Europe. [Was British Minister to Switzerland, 1911-13; previously Consul-General in Hungary.]

SIR RALPH PAGET, the Balkans, and [Assistant Under-Secretary for Foreign Affairs, 1913-16. Previously British Minister to Serbia.]

SIR EYRE CROWE, Western Europe. [Assistant Under-Secretary for Foreign Affairs since 1912.]

In all the Foreign Office will have about thirty representatives. In addition, there will be large delegations representing the War Office and the [...]

THE OBAN TIMES, SATURDAY, JANUARY 11, 1919.

TERRIBLE DISASTER AT LEWIS.

200 LIVES LOST OFF STORNOWAY HARBOUR.

Stornoway Gazette
and West Coast Advertiser.

STORNOWAY, Friday, January 10, 1919.

LEWIS IN MOURNING.

Heavy and sad as have been her losses during the war, Loyal Lewis has borne them with a quiet fortitude that has been no surprise to those who know anything of the spirit of Lewis men and women. Fathers,

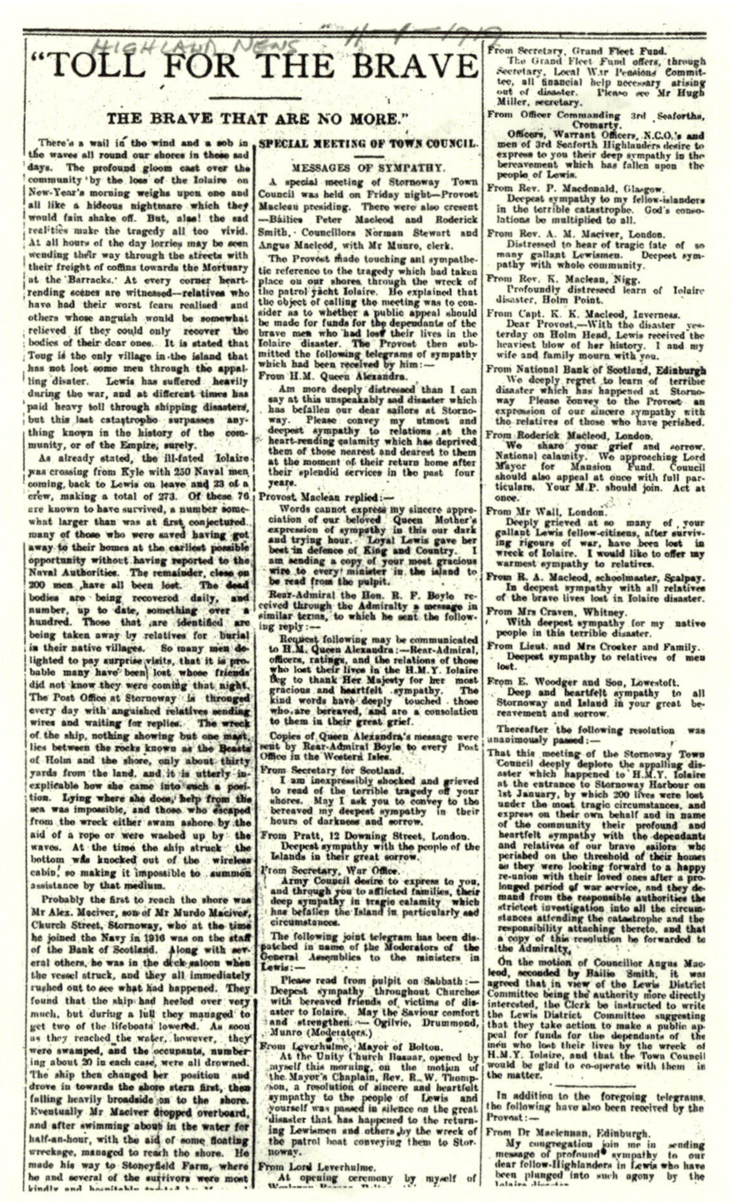

"TOLL FOR THE BRAVE

THE BRAVE THAT ARE NO MORE."

There's a wail in the wind and a sob in the waves all round our shores in these sad days. The profound gloom cast over the community by the loss of the Iolaire on New-Year's morning weighs upon one and all like a hideous nightmare which they would fain shake off. But, alas! the sad realities make the tragedy all too vivid. At all hours of the day lorries may be seen wending their way through the streets with their freight of coffins towards the Mortuary at the Barracks. At every corner heart-rending scenes are witnessed—relatives who have had their worst fears realised and others whose anguish would be somewhat relieved if they could only recover the bodies of their dear ones. It is stated that Toug is the only village in the island that has not lost some men through the appalling disater. Lewis has suffered heavily during the war, and at different times has paid heavy toll through shipping disasters, but this last catastrophe surpasses anything known in the history of the community, or of the Empire, surely.

As already stated, the ill-fated Iolaire was crossing from Kyle with 250 Naval men coming back to Lewis on leave and 23 of a crew, making a total of 273. Of these 76 are known to have survived, a number somewhat larger than was at first conjectured, many of those who were saved having got away to their homes at the earliest possible opportunity without having reported to the Naval Authorities. The remainder, close on 200 men, have all been lost. The dead bodies are being recovered daily, and number, up to date, something over a hundred. Those that are identified are being taken away by relatives for burial in their native villages. So many men delighted to pay surprise visits, that it is probable many have been lost whose friends did not know they were coming that night. The Post Office at Stornoway is thronged every day with anguished relatives sending wires and waiting for replies. The wreck of the ship, nothing showing but one mast, lies between the rocks known as the Beasts of Holm and the shore, only about thirty yards from the land, and it is utterly inexplicable how she came into such a position. Lying where she does, help from the sea was impossible, and those who escaped from the wreck either swam ashore by the aid of a rope or were washed up by the waves. At the time the ship struck the bottom was knocked out of the wireless cabin, so making it impossible to summon assistance by that medium.

Probably the first to reach the shore was Mr Alex. Maciver, son of Mr Murdo Maciver, Church Street, Stornoway, who at the time he joined the Navy in 1916 was on the staff of the Bank of Scotland. Along with several others, he was in the deck saloon when the vessel struck, and they all immediately rushed out to see what had happened. They found that the ship had heeled over very much, but during a lull they managed to get two of the lifeboats lowered. As soon as they reached the water, however, they were swamped, and the occupants, numbering about 20 in each case, were all drowned. The ship then changed her position and drove in towards the shore stern first, then falling heavily broadside on to the shore. Eventually Mr Maciver dropped overboard, and after swimming about in the water for half-an-hour, with the aid of some floating wreckage, managed to reach the shore. He made his way to Stoneyfield Farm, where he and several of the survivors were most

SPECIAL MEETING OF TOWN COUNCIL.

MESSAGES OF SYMPATHY.

A special meeting of Stornoway Town Council was held on Friday night—Provost Maclean presiding. There were also cresent—Bailies Peter Macleod and Roderick Smith, Councillors Norman Stewart and Angus Macleod, with Mr Munro, clerk.

The Provost made touching anl sympathetic reference to the tragedy which had taken place on our shores through the wreck of the patrol yacht Iolaire. He explained that the object of calling the meeting was to consider as to whether a public appeal should be made for funds for the dependants of the brave men who had lost their lives in the Iolaire disaster. The Provost then submitted the following telegrams of sympathy which had been received by him:—

From H.M. Queen Alexandra.

Am more deeply distressed than I can say at this unspeakably and disaster which has befallen our dear sailors at Stornoway. Please convey my utmost and deepest sympathy to relations at the heart-rending calamity which has deprived them of those nearest and dearest to them at the moment of their return home after their splendid services in the past four years.

Provost Maclean replied:—

Words cannot express my sincere appreciation of our beloved Queen Mother's expression of sympathy in this our dark and trying hour. Loyal Lewis gave her best in defence of King and Country. I am sending a copy of your most gracious wire to every minister in the island to be read from the pulpit.

Rear-Admiral the Hon. R. F. Boyle received through the Admiralty a message in similar terms, to which he sent the following reply:—

Request following may be communicated to H.M. Queen Alexandra:—Rear-Admiral, officers, ratings, and the relations of those who lost their lives in the H.M.Y. Iolaire beg to thank Her Majesty for her most gracious and heartfelt sympathy. The kind words have deeply touched those who are bereaved, and are a consolation to them in their great grief.

Copies of Queen Alexandra's message were sent by Rear-Admiral Boyle to every Post Office in the Western Isles.

From Secretary for Scotland.

I am inexpressibly shocked and grieved to read of the terrible tragedy off your shores. May I ask you to convey to the bereaved my deepest sympathy in their hours of darkness and sorrow.

From Pratt, 12 Downing Street, London.

Deepest sympathy with the people of the Islands in their great sorrow.

From Secretary, War Office.

Army Council desire to express to you, and through you to afflicted families, their deep sympathy in tragic calamity which has befallen the Island in particularly sad circumstances.

The following joint telegram has been dispatched in name of the Moderators of the General Assemblies to the ministers in Lewis:—

Please read from pulpit on Sabbath:—Deepest sympathy throughout Churches with bereaved friends of victims of disaster to Iolaire. May the Saviour comfort and strengthen.—Ogilvie, Drummond, Munro (Moderators.)

From Leverhulme, Mayor of Bolton.

At the Unity Church Bazaar, opened by myself this morning, on the motion of the Mayor's Chaplain, Rev. R. W. Thompson, a resolution of sincere and heartfelt sympathy to the people of Lewis and yourself was passed in silence on the great disaster that has happened to the returning Lewismen and others by the wreck of the patrol boat conveying them to Stornoway.

From Lord Leverhulme.

At opening ceremony by myself of

From Secretary, Grand Fleet Fund.

The Grand Fleet Fund offers, through Secretary, Local War Pensions Committee, all financial help necessary arising out of disaster. Please see Mr Hugh Miller, secretary.

From Officer Commanding 3rd Seaforths, Cromarty.

Officers, Warrant Officers, N.C.O.'s and men of 3rd Seaforth Highlanders desire to express to you their deep sympathy in the bereavement which has fallen upon the people of Lewis.

From Rev. P. Macdonald, Glasgow.

Deepest sympathy to my fellow-islanders in the terrible catastrophe. God's consolations be multiplied to all.

From Rev. A. M. Maciver, London.

Distressed to hear of tragic fate of so many gallant Lewismen. Deepest sympathy with whole community.

From Rev. K. Maclean, Nigg.

Profoundly distressed learn of Iolaire disaster, Holm Point.

From Capt. K. K. Macleod, Inverness.

Dear Provost,—With the disaster yesterday on Holm Head, Lewis received the heaviest blow of her history. I and my wife and family mourn with you.

From National Bank of Scotland, Edinburgh

We deeply regret to learn of terrible disaster which has happened at Stornoway Please convey to the Provost an expression of our sincere sympathy with the relatives of those who have perished.

From Roderick Macleod, London.

We share your grief and sorrow. National calamity. We approaching Lord Mayor for Mansion Fund. Council should also appeal at once with full particulars. Your M.P. should join. Act at once.

From Mr Wall, London.

Deeply grieved at so many of your gallant Lewis fellow-citizens, after surviving rigours of war, have been lost in wreck of Iolaire. I would like to offer my warmest sympathy to relatives.

From R. A. Macleod, schoolmaster, Scalpay.

In deepest sympathy with all relatives of the brave lives lost in Iolaire disaster.

From Mrs Craven, Whitney.

With deepest sympathy for my native people in this terrible disaster.

From Lieut. and Mrs Crocker and Family.

Deepest sympathy to relatives of men lost.

From E. Woodger and Son, Lowestoft.

Deep and heartfelt sympathy to all Stornoway and Island in your great bereavement and sorrow.

Thereafter the following resolution was unanimously passed:—

That this meeting of the Stornoway Town Council deeply deplore the appalling disaster which happened to H.M.Y. Iolaire at the entrance to Stornoway Harbour on 1st January, by which 200 lives were lost under the most tragic circumstances, and express on their own behalf and in name of the community their profound and heartfelt sympathy with the dependants and relatives of our brave sailors who perished on the threshold of their homes as they were looking forward to a happy re-union with their loved ones after a prolonged period of war service, and they demand from the responsible authorities the strictest investigation into all the circumstances attending the catastrophe and the responsibility attaching thereto, and that a copy of this resolution be forwarded to the Admiralty.

On the motion of Councillor Angus Macleod, seconded by Bailie Smith, it was agreed that in view of the Lewis District Committee being the authority more directly interested, the Clerk be instructed to write the Lewis District Committee suggesting that they take action to make a public appeal for funds for the dependants of the men who lost their lives by the wreck of H.M.Y. Iolaire, and that the Town Council would be glad to co-operate with them in the matter.

In addition to the foregoing telegrams, the following have also been received by the Provost:—

From Dr Maclennan, Edinburgh.

My congregation join me in sending message of profound sympathy to our dear fellow-Highlanders in Lewis who have been plunged into such agony by the

Point district policeman John Macarthur was summoned to the scene of the tragedy and was immediately faced with the bitter sight of his own brother-in-law Murdo's body, washed up on the shore. 32-year-old Murdo Mackay was a single man, living in Swordale, and was heading home to join his parents, married sister Mary and nephew John. In the drowned man's pocket John senior found a toy that Murdo was taking home for his young nephew – PC Macarthur's own son.

Among the wreckage on the shore, clothes, shoes and kitbags might be all that would ever tell a grieving family that their son or father, brother or uncle, would indeed come home no more. 43-year-old Kenneth Smith's body would never be recovered to return to his parents, wife and children at Earshader, but his belongings were found on the shore and included a silk handkerchief, silk fabric and toys from Gibraltar. Angus Crichton, aged 40, had four sons from two marriages, and his second son Murdo had gone from their home at Knock in Point to meet him off the *Iolaire* at the pier. Angus did not return, neither was his body ever given up by the sea, but a bag with his name on it was washed up, and was found to contain four oranges bought as gifts for his boys.

No less poignant were some of the belongings of those whose remains were recovered – a watch in the pocket of 18-year-old Malcolm Macleod of Grimshader, stopped at eight minutes past one and an engagement ring in the pocket of John Macdonald ('Speed' or Iain Bàn) of Lower Shader. The name of his intended was never made public, but it is said she never married.

The news of the *Iolaire*'s loss continued to spread, gradually reaching villages further and further from Stornoway. In 1969, Murdo Macleod from Leurbost related[13] how he and a group of village boys, out celebrating New Year, dodged the rain and made for a house which had a light burning. It was number 39, where Mòr Maclean, widow of Alasdair, was still

From early in the morning of 1st January rowing boats were searching around the wreck of the Iolaire in a frantic attempt to retrieve the lost sailors.

up awaiting Murdo, her oldest son. Next morning none of the sailors had come home, but nobody was unduly worried as travel then was not dependable and the residents made for church on New Year's morning. The minister gave a sermon of thanksgiving, as the year was opening with peace after four years of a horrific, destructive war.

After the sermon, Murdo went out for buckets of water to the well. He noticed Mòr also coming to the well. Now and again she looked east out to sea watching a ship that was passing northwards. As Murdo filled the buckets for her she said to him, "Do you think that is the ship with the lads?" Murdo did not think it would be as the ship appeared too big and she was not on the course the *Sheila* used to take. "Oh" she said, "Goodness knows when they will arrive".

They walked towards the houses and when they reached Murdo's house, the nearest house in the village, they noticed a car a short distance away on the road and a number of people round it. A car was a rarity in these days and as soon as he got rid of the buckets, Murdo made for the crowd. He saw Mòr walking up the road, her buckets abandoned in the road, which surprised him. He then heard crying, weeping and wailing and, before he reached the car, Mòr herself was crying and people were trying to comfort her. It was people from Stornoway who belonged to Leurbost who were in the car and, though their news was not complete, the substance of their story was that the *Iolaire* had gone down at the Beasts of Holm and that eleven from the village had been lost.

Peggy Macdonald from No 36, widow of Murdo, went to Mòr and said, "Oh! Mòr, my own son's body is also on the sand!" There were others as well as Mòr and Peggy who received the news of the sinking at that spot. The crowd scattered, those mourning to their own homes, and the others to try and comfort and assist those bereaved. Horses were harnessed, attached to traps and taken to Stornoway. Some of the carts returned with men who had been rescued that day.

The body of Roderick, son of Murdo and Peggy Macdonald, was found on a sandy beach, just as his mother said. He was a strong, handsome lad, 27 years of age, who used to play the bagpipes and was very popular with the lads. The boys who had been his friends stood outside Peggy's house at dusk, wondering if they should enter. Peggy heard them outside and called them: "Come in boys. Many a night you came in to be in his company and tonight you will see him for the last time". The lid of the coffin was opened and Peggy sat beside the body of her dead son and started to comb the sand out of his golden blond hair. Later, the lads heard that Roderick had tried to swim ashore and reach the land. He was a strong swimmer and the striving and effort he made to escape the sea was clearly to be seen on his body – his face was speckled black as a result of the waves smashing him against the rocks: his nails and the tips of his fingers were gone with the great exertion he had made to grasp a rock, fighting against the receding waves that were hauling him away from the shore. Murdo wrote: "I will never forget my last sight of you, kind Roderick."

The next day, Saturday, the boys went to the cemetery. The sight of coffins with two brothers, John and Alexander Mackenzie from No 16, side by side in the one grave would never be forgotten. The father of those two boys, Donald, wearing a heavy overcoat, stood at the top of the grave and, when the earth took the coffins out of sight, turned to one side and covered his face with a spotted red handkerchief as he shed his painful, bitter tears. It was sorely memorable to see such a clever, energetic, reliable man hurt to the quick.

For days the village was under a dark cloud. Not a weaver's shuttle went into a loom: no work was performed except what was necessary. The village was so quiet that even a cock crowing or a dog barking gave one a sudden start. Day after day news was received that other bodies had been found. Day after day one could see rows of men in great coats and hats solemnly walking the road to the cemetery. At last the burials ended. Nothing more was to be done and slowly the village returned to normality. People no longer mourned openly and publicly, but the sadness continued and for those that lost their loved ones, the gaps would never heal.

From 51 houses in the village of Leurbost, 32 men were killed or badly wounded in the First World War and a further 11 were lost on HMY *Iolaire*.

Throughout the islands such scenes were replayed. Loss piled upon loss as the bodies came ashore – some brought by the sea itself, others dragged from the water, some not discovered until days or even weeks later. The stories that would be told in the years that followed showed cruel coincidences, harsh decisions made by naval authorities and stoic determination to carry on by bereaved relatives. For now, there was a practical problem of where, and how, to lay out the many men lost, so that relatives could find the remains of their loved ones and carry them home.

The mortuary

The task of what to do in this unprecedented peacetime situation fell to Hull-born Lt Frederick Edward Townend, who had arrived in Stornoway in March 1915 as skipper of a requisitioned Admiralty trawler, on minesweeping and armed patrol duties. He spent nearly all of the war in Stornoway and lived at Croistean House on Church Street. His job in wartime was to make compass adjustments for the armed trawlers and other small naval vessels in Stornoway. Lt Townend was wakened in the middle of the night by the landlord of his billet, shaking him and saying: "Why are you sleeping warmly there, when Lewis seamen are drowning on the Beasts of Holm?" "Talking almost as if it were my fault," said Captain Townend. He went on to recount:

"In the morning the base Commander ordered me to take charge of all the bodies brought in, pending identification and awaiting collection for burial. It was a situation on which there was nothing in the Manual of Seamanship, and with which I simply did not know how to cope. So I approached the Master-at-Arms, told him what I had to do, and said, 'Forget that I am an officer, and from your long service and experience, tell me as man to man, how you would go about this?

"The Master-at-Arms came to attention, saluted and said: 'Whatever you say, sir.'… I hesitated a moment, and then I came to attention and rapped out, 'Clear the ammunition store! That is an order!' While the store was being cleared I was thinking things out.

Small horse-drawn carts like these, pictured in Ness in 1912, were used to bring home the bodies of loved ones.

111

"I requisitioned a supply of strong, brown paper bags from the NAAFI[14] and, as the bodies were brought in and laid out on the floor of the ammunition store, the contents of the pockets, cap tallies, anything that might help with identification, were put into one of the bags, the bag was numbered, and the same number was chalked on the boot-soles of the body – most of them were wearing their boots – or on a tag attached to their clothing.

"Watching the relatives of missing men searching for their dead was the most harrowing experience of my life, especially when an identification was made. For months after it was all over, I saw in my dreams rows of naval-issue boots, with numbers chalked on their soles."[15]

The naval base provided a temporary mortuary in the battery shed, where the bodies were laid out for identification. A total of 24 bodies were recovered by 2nd January 1919, 18 of them on New Year's Day. The base logbook records that all were put in the battery shed.

The deaths of eleven members of the crew were consecutively registered first on 5th January 1919. Their names, together with death registration number, were: 6 Hern, 7 Rankin, 8 Humphrey, 9 George, 10 Stanley, 11 Ramsay, 12 Moore, 13 Leggett, 14 Mason, 15 Henley, 16 Matthews. All deaths are given as due to drowning, between 2am and 4am, at sea, near Holm Point, Stornoway.

No more casualties appear in registration records until 27th March 1919. The cause of death is now given as: *Suffocation due to submersion per verdict of Jury* and certified by Thomas Owen, Surgeon Lt, RN, who saw the body after death. The registrations were made with the information of CG Mackenzie, Procurator Fiscal. Where remains were not recovered, the certificate states: *Body not recovered.* The registrations continued until 29th December

The first burials at Sandwick Cemetery with temporary wooden crosses above the graves.

1919 when Norman Mackay, Obbe was the last casualty recorded. In the confusion caused by the lack of records from the vessel's boarding, 17 men were recorded twice and two men were not registered at all.

Telling the news

While the news of the disaster spread by word of mouth around the islands, the machinery of the press was carrying it further and further afield. The newly established *Stornoway Gazette* was on the scene and able to get immediate access to the news, but she had gone to press before the disaster, and so editor William Grant was prepared to share early reports with other titles. As early as 2nd January London's *Times* newspaper was bringing the terrible events starkly into homes across the nation. Under the headlines '*Naval Yacht A shore off Stornoway: Feared Heavy Loss of Life*' the story featured on page six:

> "The steam yacht *Iolaire*, with about 250 naval seamen on board, was entering the harbour at Stornoway naval base early yesterday morning when she struck the rocks known as the Beasts of Holm. It is feared that, of those on board, only about 30 were saved."[16]

On the same day the *Daily Mirror* carried early reports of the tragedy from various correspondents, together with a map showing the approximate location of the wreck, under the headlines: '*Leave Boat Disaster: New Year's Tragedy of Patrol Vessel That Struck Dangerous Rocks at Stornoway: 270 Sailors Lost at Home's Door: All the Officers and Crew Drowned – 30 Lives Saved.*' They reported:

> "A terrible disaster, which has cast a gloom over Stornoway and Lewis, took place yesterday, when the steam patrol vessel HMS (sic) *Iolaire* with 300 sailors on board on New Year holiday leave, struck the rugged, dangerous rocks known as the 'Beasts of Holm', which are situated to the right of Stornoway Harbour. Of the 300 on board only about 30 were saved, some being seriously injured in their attempts to reach the shore. According to earlier messages: one correspondent stated that 200 lives were lost, another version was that the casualties were small in number….. Several of the crew succeeded in swimming ashore."[17]

A week later the *Iolaire* disaster was front page news in the *Daily Mirror*, which carried pictures of the masts of the *Iolaire*, still sticking up out of the water[18], of small boats searching the wreck site, of a lifeboat washed up on shore and a portrait of Commander Mason. The *Daily Mirror*'s 'exclusive' report stated:

> "The tragedy was painfully intensified by the fact that many of the men who perished were on the first leave from naval service they had enjoyed for years, and that they went to their deaths when actually in sight of the lights of their home harbour."[19]

When the *Gazette*'s first post-disaster edition appeared, it was full of detail. The explicit story of what had happened after the vessel struck was vividly described by an *Iolaire* crew member, fireman Ernest Adams, under the headline '*A Graphic Narrative*':

"The engines were stopped and the wind drove her round, and she fell off the ledge of rock on which she had struck, and then went in stern first, and latterly turned broadside on to the shore. I should say her stern was not more than six or seven yards from a ledge of rocks jutting out from the shore. There was a terribly rough sea. The waves were rolling in mountains high, dashing her down on the rocks and we could scarcely stand on the deck. ......
I was one of the last to leave the deck, and almost as soon as I had reached the land the yacht toppled over to port and disappeared, all but her masts."[20]

The weekly newspapers closest to the islands in geography carried the most emotive reporting of the disaster. In the *Oban Times*:

"A terrible disaster befel (sic) the Island of Lewis on New Year's Day, when nearly 200 sailors returning home on leave lost their lives at the entrance to Stornoway harbour. The tragedy occurred through HM Yacht *Iolaire* (formerly *Amalthaea*), the parent ship of the Stornoway base, running upon the rocks after all but completing the passage from Kyle of Localsh. The *Iolaire* carried a crew of 23 and there were on board 250 bluejackets, all Lewis men, and all eagerly looking forward to spending the New Year furlough with their families and friends. Of this total of 273, only 75 survived the wreck, and an anticipated season of rejoicing was turned into one of grief and mourning."[21]

The *Highland News* on the same date carried a heart-rending account under the headline '*Toll for the Brave*':

"There's a wail in the wind and a sob in the waves all round our shores in these sad days. The profound gloom cast over the community by the loss of the *Iolaire* on New Year's morning weighs upon one and all like a hideous nightmare which they would fain shake off. But, alas! The sad realities make the tragedy all too vivid.... At every corner heart-rending scenes are witnessed – relatives who have had their worst fears realised and others whose anguish would be somewhat relieved if they could only recover the bodies of their dear ones.... Lewis has suffered heavily during the war.... but this last catastrophe surpasses anything known in the history of the community, or of the Empire, surely."[22]

Found and lost –
the bodies of island sons

From first light at Holm, people on the shore sought among the rocks and weed for bodies of their boys, while boats set out for the wreck to see whether anything could be found or anyone saved. Over the days to come, the bodies of victims would be lifted lifeless from the water, some by their own relatives, unable to rest until they could bring home the body of a son or brother. One such was Angus Macphail of Arnol, who sought his brother Kenneth, a strongly-built man who had already survived the wreck of the SS *Cambric* off Algeria in October 1917. He had told his brother Angus that he felt riddled with guilt after that incident, insisting that he 'should have gone down with the boys'. After the sinking of the *Iolaire*, Kenneth's body was not one of those washed up by the tide, so Angus spent days working from a rowing boat over the wreck, using grappling irons in a desperate search for the body of his brother. Eventually Angus recovered Kenneth's corpse and was astonished to find that his hands were stuffed firmly into his pockets. Angus believed that, after the trauma of the *Cambric*, Kenneth made no attempt to save himself from the wreck of the *Iolaire*, but simply resigned himself to his fate.

The sight of small boats coming and going around the wreck was to become familiar over the next few days:

"Seventeen bodies were washed ashore on Wednesday and it was expected that many more would be washed up by last night's tide. The wind, however, changed and only a few bodies were washed ashore. A number of row-boats were taken to the scene and the crews recovered about 30 bodies, by dragging with grappling irons placed around the wreck. The corpses were landed on a ledge of rock and then carried over rocks to the grassland, where the features were eagerly scanned and papers examined in hope of identification."[23]

Bodies quickly accumulated, not just in the temporary mortuary at the battery, but on the shore at Holm and Sandwick, on the grass above the shore and, later, on the pier at Stornoway.

Through the day news was spreading around the Isle of Lewis and anxious islanders converged upon Stornoway to find their boys. On their arrival in the town, they were greeted by serried rows of the lifeless bodies, lying in a makeshift mortuary or on the grassy slope close to the shore at Holm, where they had been placed by the eight naval whalers with grappling irons, who trawled in the vicinity of the wreck. On Wednesday 2nd January an estimated 30 bodies were

recovered in this matter-of-fact way, while 17 more were washed up. Naval ratings carried the recovered bodies back up from a rocky ledge to the grass and later to the mortuary, processing silently and solemnly along the Sandwick shore. Young and old, men and women, walked slowly between the rows of the dead, trying to identify the recovered remains of sons, brothers, fathers, husbands and friends. Those that were identified were handed over and little processions of horse and carts, in twos and threes, passed between the sentry boxes at the barrack gates to carry home their loved ones.

It was here at the mortuary that two men from the village of Aird came seeking Alasdair Mackenzie, 'Am Boicean'. They found 'Am Boicean', wrapped in his greatcoat, with a piece of paper attached to his lapel – 'ALISDAIR MACKENZIE (BOYKEN) – AIRD.' On either side of him lay his cousin, Alick Mackenzie, Aird and schoolfriend Alick Macleod, Portnaguran, three of the four neighbours who, just a few hours earlier, met on the *Iolaire* after four years separated by war. Only 'Am Boiceans' brother, John Mackenzie of Portvoller, had survived the wreck.

Strangely, given that so many sought their relatives so diligently, there did remain some bodies which were not identified. *The Bulletin* stated:

"UNIDENTIFIED BODIES --- Particulars of these bodies were circulated throughout the island, but the relatives were not found, and the bodies were reverently buried yesterday as "unknowns." The only clue to the identification was that in one case the hair was dark and that there was a tattoo mark --- a man's head over the letters D. MacD ---- on the right forearm. In the other case the clothing was marked A.M.L. and these letters were also tattooed on the left forearm."[25]

Day after day the procession of relatives came seeking, and scene after heart-breaking scene was played out. The *Glasgow Herald* reported:

> "An old man sobbing into his handkerchief with a stalwart son in khaki sitting on the cart beside him, the remains of another son in the coffin behind – that was one of the sights seen today as one of the funeral parties emerged from the barrack gate. Another, an elderly woman, well dressed, comes staggering down the roadway and bursts into a paralysis of grief as she tells the sympathisers at the gate that her boy is in the mortuary. Strong men weeping and women wailing or wandering around with blanched, tear stained faces are to be seen in almost every street and there are groups of them at the improvised mortuary."[26]

Daughters, sisters and mothers also undertook the painful search for their own. 20-year-old Angus Morrison from Upper Shader was coming home on leave from HMT *St Ayles*, after serving for three years on the North Sea patrol, when he met his end on the *Iolaire*. His widowed mother would not hear of anyone else going over to Stornoway to collect his remains. She personally took her son's body home on a cart for his last journey. Nor were the very youngest spared from the horrific responsibility of taking a loved one home – 20-year-old George Morrison (Seòras Chèisein) of Brenish was carried to his last rest from Stornoway by horse and cart, the sad task of collecting his body entrusted to his 14-year-old brother John, who took three days to complete the long and lonely journey back to the remote village in the district of Uig.

The man on the mast

As much as the coming of day revealed the tragedy of death, and the pathos and harrowing experience of the saved, it also revealed the most astonishing tale of survival from the wreck, that of Donald Morrison of Knockaird in Ness, who had been about to save himself on John Finlay Macleod's line when the hawser snapped and the ship sank. Better known as 'Am Patch', Donald never saw himself as a hero, but in Lewis he would always be known as the 'Man on the Mast'. The *Iolaire* had sunk around 3.25 in the morning, her plates and bulkheads tearing until her back was broken. From then until the following morning Donald had clung to the mast in desperation. In a newspaper article towards the end of his long life, he recalled:

> "An hour is long enough in that kind of situation, but eight hours was something else… When daylight came, the wind slackened a bit but there was a big sea running.

> "At last I saw a boat coming out and I said, 'I am not going on board that boat, I am safer as I am.' The first boat that came out went back to shore.

> "When the (next) boat came as near as it could, I heard the officer in charge say, 'Can you come down?' I shouted over to him, 'Sir, if you can take the boat between this stay and the mast I will come down.' I held on to the stay until the boat came right underneath me and then I jumped down as fast as I could. He put his hand round me and helped me in – that was all he had to do."

Donald Morrison was quite correct in thinking that a different boat had come back to rescue him. He was taken from the wreck by fellow islanders in an open boat sent out from HM Whaler *Rorqual*. As daylight arrived they saw nothing of the *Iolaire* except her masts. The foremast had been carried away at the hounds,[27] but the mainmast was standing and one survivor was clinging perilously to it. One of the men who volunteered to try and save the man on the mast told the story of the rescue many years later:

> "The rain and the wind. We put on our oilskins and went out, out to where she was. It was so dark, we could just see the two masts but as day broke and it got lighter, we could see only one. ... We could make out that that there was a man in the mainmast.

> "Our old man (Calum an t-Siaraich from Bayble) took the ship so far in that we were within sight of the Battery. He sent a signal that there was a man in the mainmast and got a reply, telling him to attempt to take him off, if he could get volunteers. He already had his volunteers – his crew, all five of us: me (Murdo Macdonald from Hushinish), Malcolm Macleod (Calum an t-Siaraich) from Lower Bayble, William Macleod from Sheshader, Allan Macdonald from Uist and a fellow, (John Maciver) nicknamed the Bird, also from Point (Aignish).

> "Out we went and we lowered our own lifeboat with two buckets of oil on board. All we had on were our slippers, flannel trousers and the lifebelt ... When we were opposite the reef, the PO (Petty Officer), the man from Bayble, asked for one of the buckets to be poured out.

> "We poured the oil out and it calmed the sea to the extent that no white was to be seen. We waited for a while – these Point men were familiar with these waters as they were used to lobstering there – and when they got the opportunity they were waiting for, in they went. They shouted to him to come down, he came down, in they came again, they guided his foot on to the gunwale, got a hold of him and were off out."[28]

Despite his ordeal, Donald tried to help get the small boat back to land:

> "I went for one of the oars to help them go back to the patrol boat, the *Budding Rose*, but the officer said to leave it to them. I got warm clothes aboard the *Budding Rose*. I was still shaking, in fact I thought I would never stop."[29]

In later accounts, the skipper of the *Budding Rose* gave a slightly altered story, in which his instructions and initiative effected the rescue, and the island men's efforts went unmentioned. This kind of dismissive treatment was not unexpected to the island men, who were philosophical about who would take the credit – then and later. As Murdo Macdonald went on to say:

> "Then we saw a boat coming, a trawler, with a small motor boat on tow. The PO said, "We'll hand him over to this small boat that's coming. It won't matter to us if Big John gets all the credit for this, we wouldn't get it anyway but he will, so we'll just give him to them." The boat reached us, we gave them the man and off she went to Stornoway. She would be at the quay in Stornoway long before we would. We then started heaving the lifeboat up, he put her broadside in the

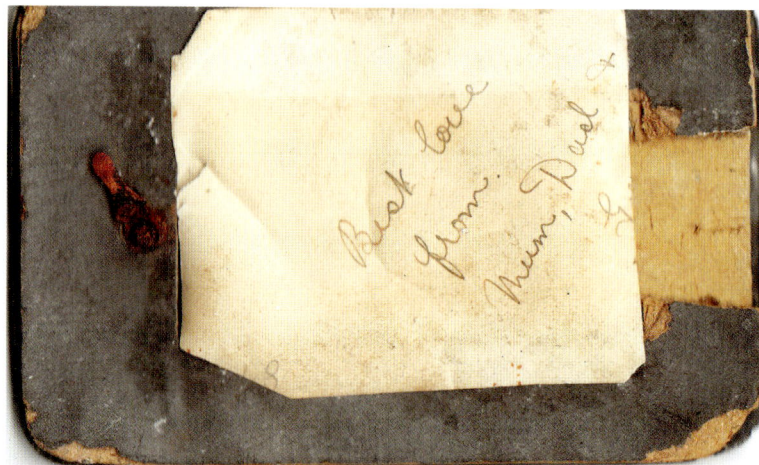

Poignant reminders of individuals came from the pockets of the drowned and their belongings washed up on the shore.

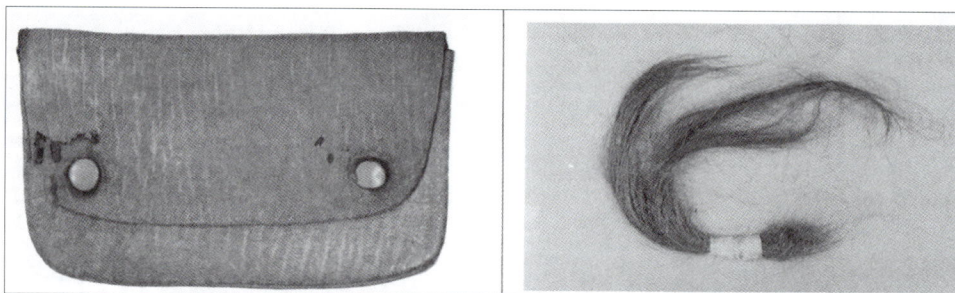

Cigarette tin issued to Alexander Mackenzie, 1 Aird, Point Christmas 1914;

The back and front of a photo frame carried by Alexander Mackenzie, 1 Aird, Point

Tobacco pouch containing a lock of his wife's hair, found in the pocket of Angus Mackinnon, 4 Caversta.

Watch from the pocket of Malcolm Macleod, 3 Grimshader

wind, she rolled and when the boat came in she hit the side, the davit. It broke her. That was how that morning was, a rough morning."[30]

The men's pragmatic suspicions were justified. When it came to reporting on the rescue of the man from the mast, Lt W B Wenlock, commander of the drifter *Budding Rose*, told his superiors:

"On reporting to you at 9am it was reported that a man was still on the mainmast. I immediately returned to the scene of the wreck and with the aid of a small boat which I had secured from one of HM Trawlers succeeded with great difficulty in rescuing him."[31]

Donald's story had a sorrowful footnote, for Rear Admiral Boyle issued the wrong name for the survivor on the mast.[32] The press seized on his information that John Macdonald of Holm had survived and caused further heartbreak to another family because of it. Alexander and Margaret Macdonald, the parents of John, who had drowned at just 18-and-a-half years old, were given false hope on New Year's Day when the *Inverness Courier* reported that he was a survivor. This report proved false and, as other newspapers had repeated it as truth, they had to apologise in the following edition.

Donald himself, once ashore, was taken to the Imperial Hotel:

"I was asked what I would like best, whisky or rum. I said whisky. They sent a car and it was a postman from Swainbost who took me to the hospital. I didn't get a wink of sleep. All the hot water bottles in the hospital were put round me… I remember my two sisters came over from Ness to take me home and the doctor saying that I shouldn't go in case I got pneumonia."[33]

The Matron, Margaret Elizabeth Maclennan, also tried her level best to get him to stay.

Through the eyes of children

As 1st January wore on, more bodies were recovered and the pathetic processions of grieving relatives, limp and soaked corpses and naval ratings worn down by their sad task continued to wind along the shore and the road to Stornoway. Once again, it is from the testimony of those who were children at the time that we learn of scenes becoming all-too-familiar to the island.

Aleen Murray was the eleven-year-old daughter of Dr Donald Murray, newly-elected MP for the Western Isles, who lived at The Cottage, Church Street:

"Throughout New Years Day 1919, Aleen watched from an upstairs window as cart after cart carried its precious cargo to the Drill Hall opposite her home. A temporary mortuary had been set-up there with her father in attendance. The carts in small processions of twos and threes carried coffins from the mortuary, through the streets of Stornoway, to outlying villages where families awaited the final homecoming of their loved ones.

"So great was Dr Murray's concern for the families of the victims that he insisted on accompanying the policeman who brought the official sad news to many of the homes affected. In one of these homes there lived a woman who had lost a husband at the beginning of the war and two sons during it. Her sole surviving son had made the last part of his homeward journey on the *Iolaire*.

"The sheer scale of the tragedy was mind-numbing. Aleen vividly recalled the grey pallor of her father's face as he travelled between the Drill Hall and their home. His professional skills had been the means of delivery for many of these boys into the world, and his professional skills were now called upon, prematurely, to confirm their cruel passing from it.

Dr Donald Murray, newly-elected MP for the Western Isles, attended at the drill hall as men's bodies were laid out.

"As the horrific news swept throughout the Islands, ordinary life froze. Joyful reunions were muted in the face of so devastating a loss. Lord Leverhulme cancelled a party at the castle that night, where Aleen's classmate Duncan Morrison (Major) was due to play. Everything had changed overnight."[34]

Dr Donald Murray also helped supervise the Drill Hall, where bodies of crew members were laid out before being taken to the mainland. He attended the funeral of 19-year-old Norman Macleod, of 10 Portnaguran, as he felt so sorely for the grieving mother, Christina Macleod, who had now lost four sons in the war.

At Holm Farm, next to Stoneyfield Farm, Willie John Macdonald was eleven years old and in bed with influenza on New Year's Day. Seventy years later he described what he saw when he got out of bed:

"The first we knew about it was the following morning when there was a hue and cry – everybody going along the beach looking for their own relations. The mast was still showing – the lorries were down and taking the corpses and carting them up through the village to Sandwick with a tarpaulin over them. It was a gruesome sight. There was a great commotion with people coming back and fore."[35]

William Macleod, Keith Street, heard the news at 8am when his brother Alasdair, who had spent the night at his granny's house at Sandwick, came in breathless. William saw the drifter *Budding Rose*, with bodies lying on the deck, later in the day opposite the mortuary.

Kennedy Cameron was a little boy, not yet five, son of Angus Cameron of the National Bank of Scotland, who lived on Bank Street. He recalled seeing bodies landed at the slant[36] at No 2 Pier and loaded onto lorries to be transported, but he knew not where. Conscious of the gloom at the time, he was taken to Holm by older brother Asti and saw the *Iolaire*'s mast sticking out of the water.

Nearby, on the junction of Point Street and Bank Street, 21-year-old Catherine Mackenzie lived above Charles Morrison and Sons Ltd. At the Bank Street door she saw a horse-drawn cart with covered bodies, laid out alternately head to toe, heading along North Beach to the town mortuary. The mortuary itself, based on Cromwell Street quay, behind Granite House, was considered for use but decided to be inadequate, unable to accommodate more than two dozen bodies. It is believed that it was retained for the use of townsfolk dying of other causes, such as the outbreak of the Spanish Flu.

In the sick bay

In Stornoway naval barracks, the sick bay provided an initial place of treatment for those too ill to continue on their journey home – both the island passengers and the surviving crew members. Naval staff and civilians helped to treat men suffering from cuts and grazes, hypothermia and immersion from swallowing seawater. Later reports give accounts of men with the skin stripped from their palms and fingertips where they had tried to grip the rope or the rocks. Crew member James Maclean had badly scraped hands and knees. Others would have been coughing up or vomiting seawater. Am Patch's uncontrollable shivering would have been common among those who had made it ashore through freezing seas into the sleety weather, though he was the only man taken to Lewis Hospital.

Donald Macdonald of 23 Cromore later recalled:

"Next morning I woke up in Sick Bay in Stornoway, my father was sitting by my bedside. He informed me that over 200 perished below the cliff. Some sailors were washed ashore a few yards from their home cemetery as if to say, 'This is your final resting place.' Only three of the yacht's crew were saved. The Captain was found mangled amongst the rocks. By noon all that was left of HMS *Iolaire* was a fathom of the foremast, pointing like an accusing finger at the cliff. Nobody could throw any light on this mysterious disaster, half a mile from the lighthouse at the harbour's mouth."[37]

In fact, six of the crew were saved, but of these there were three in the sick bay. Firemen Ernie Adams and Duncan Griffiths Ramsey, both from Cardiff and Trimmer Arthur Topham, from Hull had all been in the stokehold and boiler room below and were thought to have escaped by climbing up on the coal heap as the ship flooded. Ernest Adams related later that they heard that the local inhabitants were aggrieved by the loss of the *Iolaire* and he and the other two crew members were aware of it in the sick bay. The three crew survivors were quickly transported away to hospital in Oban and, due to ill-feeling there against them, they were then moved on to hospital in Aberdeen.

There were several islanders in the sick bay on Seaview Terrace. Norman Mackenzie, who lived at the back of the Post Office in Cross, Ness, was quite seriously ill. A young man and a strong swimmer, he had almost reached the rocks time and again, dragged back by the undertow and surge of the yacht in the heaving sea. He was badly injured as his body smashed against the wickedly sharp rocks and he washed up on the shore among the dead bodies in the morning. His sister Chrissie was working in Stornoway and rushed down to Sandwick shore, where she found his near-naked body on the beach. At first she thought he was drowned, but then he moved and quickly she alerted the services and had him taken to the naval sick bay. Norman contracted rheumatic fever but recovered later in Lewis Hospital. He never fully recovered his health, though, and died in middle age.

John Mackenzie of Tobson, Bernera, despite surviving the *Iolaire* disaster, could not cope in peacetime with his experiences. He was awarded a disablement allowance for 'Traumatic Neurasthenia' and had to go into a home in Glasgow in 1930, where he died ten years later.

John Mackinnon of Tarbert was later called to give evidence at the Public Inquiry, but was excused on the basis of a letter from a doctor – he had severe catarrh and a cough. His health never fully recovered, and he died of pernicious anaemia just five years later leaving a widow and young daughter.

The other sickbay room-mates were John Macinnes, 2 Hill Street, North Tolsta, Murdo Morrison, 8 Skigersta, Archibald Ross, 29 Leurbost – the oldest survivor of the *Iolaire* and Roderick Nicolson, 36 Ranish, who was awarded a disability pension for six months and went on to live to be 61.

The mystery of the missing captain

The most enduring mystery of the *Iolaire* disaster surrounds the body of Commander Richard Mason, the man in charge of the doomed vessel on the night that she went on to the rocks. From that day until this, no conclusive evidence has been presented as to whether his body was found, if so whether it was buried on the island, or spirited away to some other grave – and if that was so, why it might have been. Going by Commonwealth Graves Commission records, Mason's name appears on the Portsmouth Naval Memorial, suggesting that his remains were not recovered, but there is strong evidence to the contrary.

There are enough eye-witness accounts of Mason's body being washed ashore on the morning of January 1st for this to be taken as a fact. The Melbost Bard, Murdo Macfarlane was on Sandwick beach that morning and specifically remembered seeing the Captain's body on a green patch there, wearing two lifebelts, but drowned. He recalled another man who had arrived looking down at the corpse and saying. "That did not save you!"

Eleven-year-old Angus Maciver from East Street, Sandwick was down on the shore as dawn broke and remembered seeing Donald Morrison being rescued from the mast. He then recalled: "*I remember the bodies coming* ashore. *I know where the captain came ashore this side of the old churchyard and he had a lifejacket on.*" Other witnesses have the officer's body wearing two lifebelts – two lifebelts would be difficult to wear, but the lifejackets on the *Iolaire* were quite small and two could have been worn.

Lewismen were very familiar with naval uniform and insignia, and those who saw it said that the dead figure on Sandwick shore was a naval officer with naval buttons on his jacket. If it was not Mason who was found, it could only have been the navigating officer Lt Edmund Cotter (body not recovered) or the chief engineer Sub Lt Charles Rankin (body recovered). Cotter's name appears on the Portsmouth Memorial and Rankin was buried at Penzance.

It was after these sightings that Mason's body seemingly disappeared. A rumour exists that the body was beaten up by youngsters on the shore before it was removed to the temporary mortuary. That remains unsubstantiated, as do claims that the body was spirited away so that the sight of the two lifejackets could be hidden.

The *Inverness Courier* reported that Mason's body had been washed up and research for this book shows that there was indeed a death certificate issued for Richard Mason, one of 11 men recorded by the registrar on 5th January 1919, the cause of death given as drowning, between 2am and 4am, at sea, near Holm Point, Stornoway. His death is certified by Lt Thomas Owen MRCS, LRCP, RN. The informant is Robert Y Corbett, Captain, naval depot, Stornoway.

We can safely suppose that the eleven crew members were treated differently from the rest of the many bodies recovered during that period, because they were transported away for burial on the mainland. Other crew members that were recovered were interred at Sandwick. When a body was recovered, the person was invariably interred in a grave. War casualties who were cremated in the war were recorded as such by the Commonwealth War Graves Commission and the crematorium was listed – there is no crematorium in Lewis.

So where did Mason end up? Was his one of the coffins especially commissioned in oak for officers, delivered to Stornoway from Glasgow? Or is his one of the graves in the Sandwick Cemetery, marked 'Known Unto God' in an attempt to protect his last resting place from later hostility?

Reaching home – the survivors' struggle

While families made their fearful way towards the town, to find out whether their sons had been lost, and to bring home their bodies, the survivors were still trickling out of the town towards their homes. Dutiful even in these extreme circumstances, most had reported to the naval base and, in some cases, been given transport to get home.

John Maclennan of Kneep was one of those who wandered, disorientated, into the town centre. In an interview many years later he recalled:

"Seeing a sign for the Post Office, I headed in that direction. I heard a woman crying, it was Maga (nighean Seònaid Chalum Tharmoid). Maga Mackay .... had met two Uig men who had been on the boat, Uilleam Dubh (William Maclennan, 36 Cliff[38])

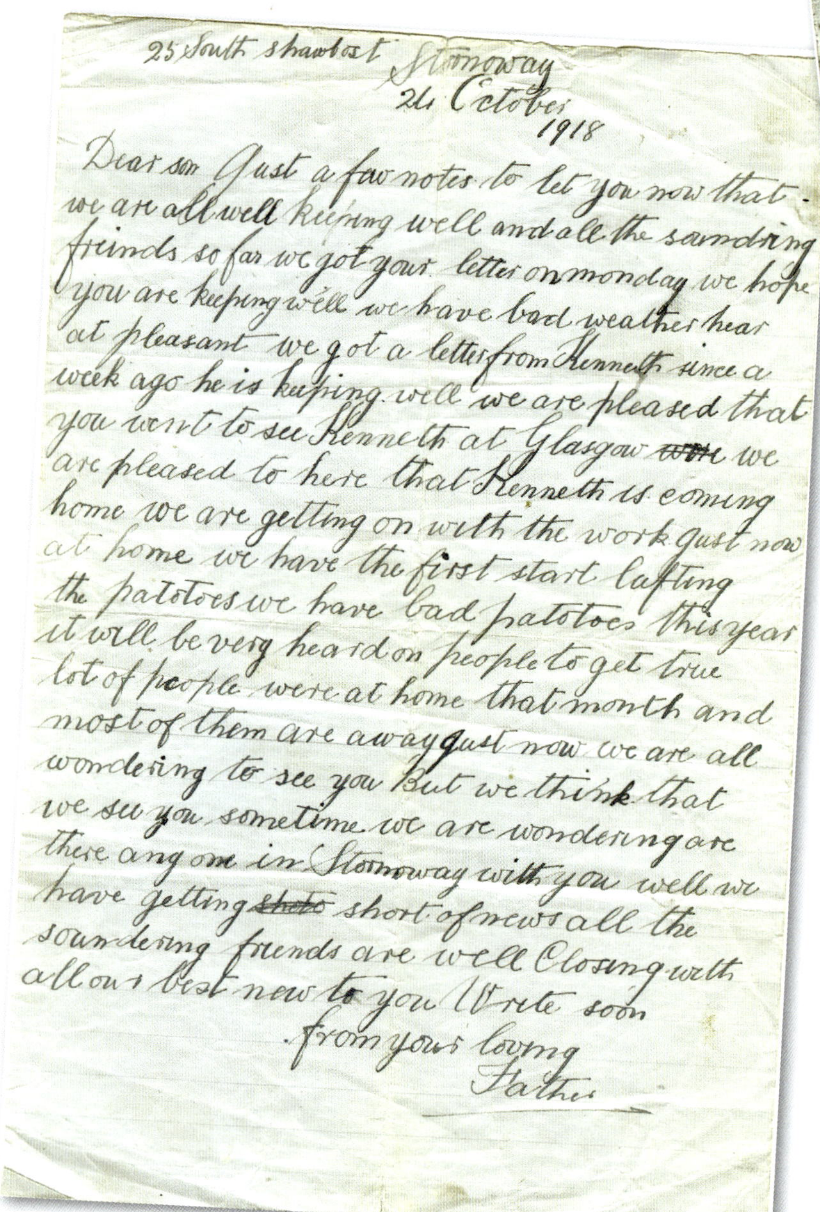

25 South shaw st Stornoway
24 October
1918

Dear son Just a few notes to let you now that
we are all well keeping well and all the sorrounding
friends so far we got your letter on monday we hope
you are keeping well we have bad weather hear
at pleasant we got a letter from Kenneth since a
week ago he is keeping well we are pleased that
you went to see Kenneth at Glasgow we
are pleased to here that Kenneth is coming
home we are getting on with the work just now
at home we have the first start lifting
the patotoes we have bad patotoes this year
it will be very hard on people to get true
lot of people were at home that month and
most of them are away just now we are all
wondering to see you but we think that
we see you sometime we are wondering are
there any one in Stornoway with you well we
have getting short of news all the
sorrounding friends are well Closing with
all our best new to you Write soon
from your loving
Father

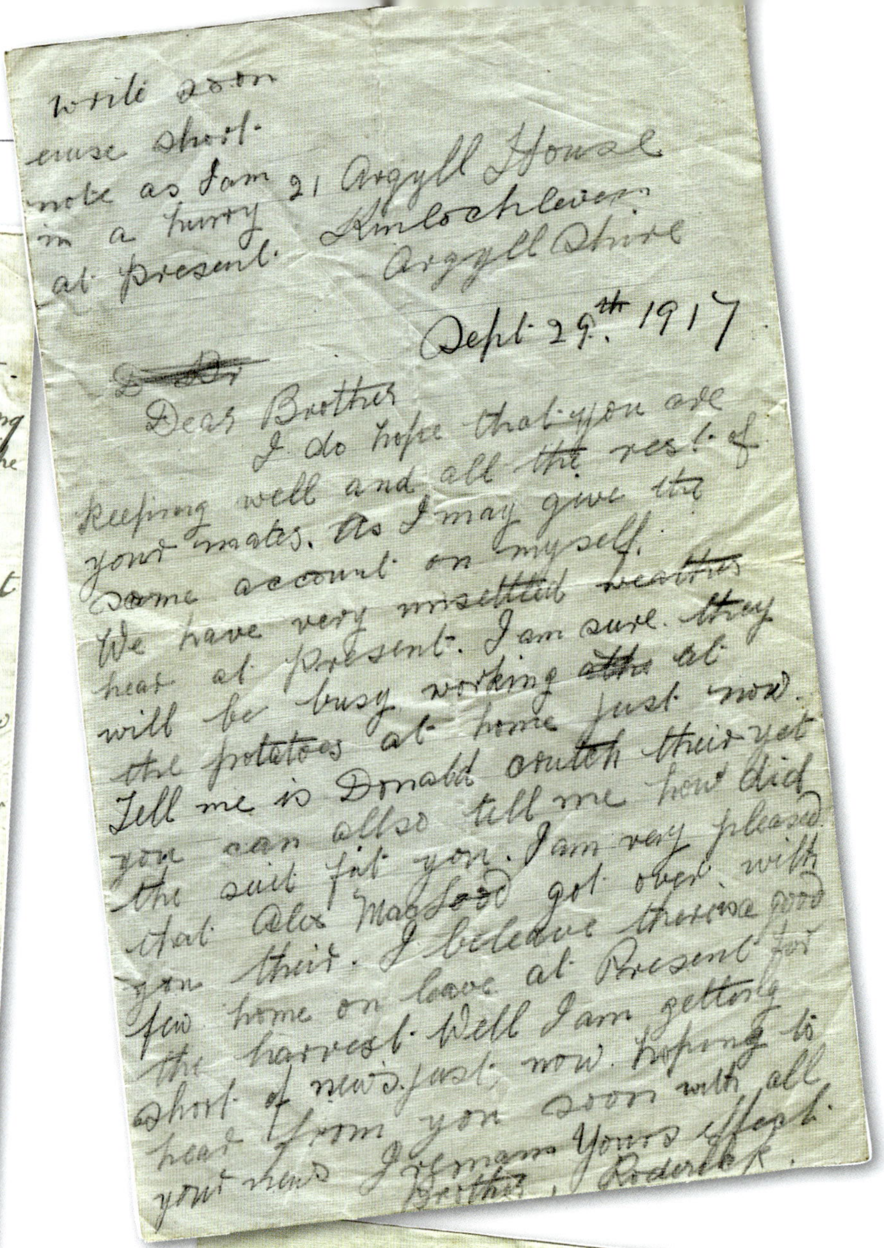

write soon
cause short
note as I am
in a hurry
at present.

21 Argyll House
Kinlochleven
Argyll Shire

Sept 29th 1917

Dear Brother
I do hope that you are
keeping well and all the rest of
your mates. As I may give the
same account on myself.
We have very missettled weather
hear at present. I am sure they
will be busy working at the
the potatoes at home just now.
Tell me is Donald Crutch their yet
you can allso tell me how did
the suit fit you. I am very pleased
that Alex Mac got over with
you their. I beleive there is good
few home on leave at Present for
the harvest. Well I am getting
short of news just now. hoping to
hear from you soon with all
your news Iremam Yours affecth.
Brother Roderick.

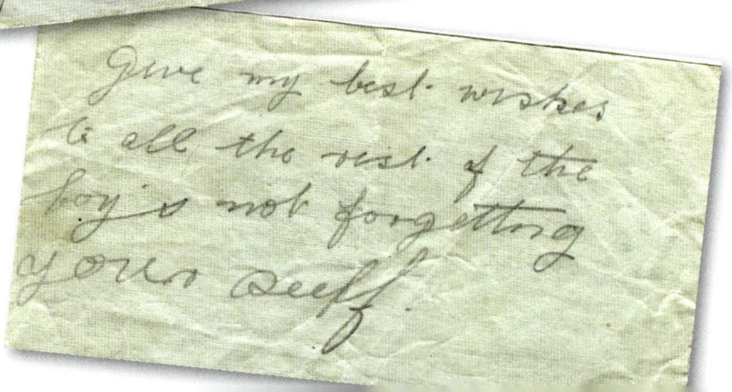

give my best wishes
to all the rest of the
boy's not forgetting
your self.

Letters from the pocket of Roddy Murray.

The agony and grief of those who came seeking, only to find their boys lying lifeless, is vividly evoked in this account by Donald Macphail, recollecting a neighbour finding the body of his son Roddy Murray of Shawbost (translated from the Gaelic):

"There was a man from Shawbost who came over with us, he had a son there, and I remember that he was so beautiful that you could hardly say that he was dead at all; a smile on his face, I remember that, still so beautiful. And his father went on his knees and started to pull out letters from his pocket and money and he was looking at the letters inside his pocket and the tears falling down onto his son's body. I think it's one of the most moving and difficult scenes I've ever witnessed, and that was only one of many."[24]

"Bha fear à Siabost a chaidh a-null còmhla rinne, bha mac ann leis, agus tha cuimhne agam gu robh e cho brèagha is gun canainn nach robh e marbh idir; gàire air aodann, tha cuimhne agam air a sin, cho brèagha fhathast. Is chaidh athair air a ghlùinean ri thaobh agus thòisich e a' toirt litrichean às a phòcaid agus airgead, agus bha e a' coimhead ri litir a bha am broinn a phòcaid, is na deòir a' tuiteam sìos air corp a' ghille. Tha mi smaoineachadh gur e sealladh cho tìomhaidh is cho duilich 's a chunnaic mi a-riamh, is cha robh sin ach aonan de mhòran."

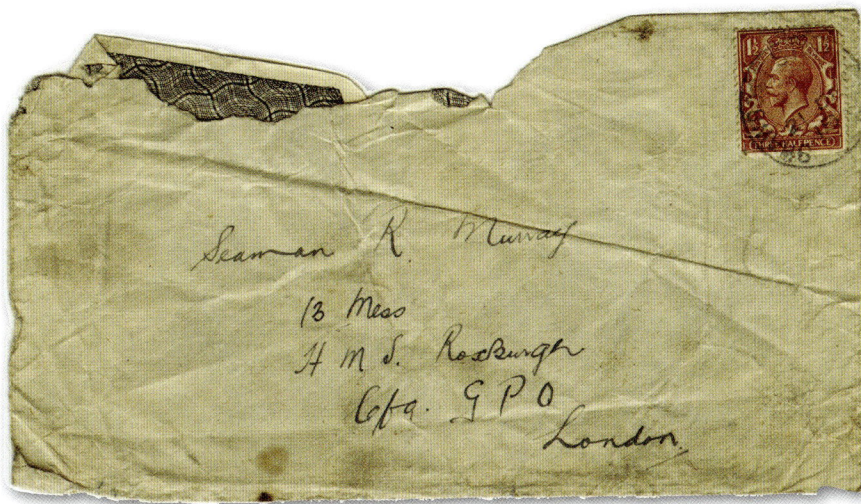

and Tuireag (Malcolm Macritchie, 3b Aird Uig). They had mentioned I was on the ship and, as they hadn't seen me since coming ashore, they had come to the conclusion that I, too, had been lost."[39]

Interviewed in 1989, Maga Mackay added that, when he reached her, John was badly shocked and fell into their arms once inside her house. Two men came into the house afterwards, after trying to identify bodies. The bodies they sought were not there and the men were crying like children. John's account continued:

"I got some 'civvies,' they were clothes belonging to Peter, a brother of Maga. Then went down to the Admiralty building, where a row of us were sitting outside on the wall. Admiral Boyle came and asked me who I was, he didn't know me in the 'civvies.' Then he clapped me on the shoulder and said, 'Thank God you're safe.' He said, 'come back here in quarter of an hour and I'll have the car ready for you.'

"The car took 'Tuireag' and I to Callanish and Duncan Macrae's motor launch took us to Traigh Sheanais (sands) in Reef. Tuireag and I walked back to Kneep and I met my sister Hannah at the top of the hill, she was so happy to see me. I never said anything. I made it home on New Year's Day."

Not all of those who got home were given transport, but the town was full of carts and gigs brought from villages all over the island, as relatives came to meet returning servicemen, sought survivors, or waited to carry home the remains of their loved ones. Donald Murray of North Tolsta was one of only five survivors from that hard-hit village and was taken home by a girl whose brother had been lost:

"I still remember that it was my sister Christina who brought me in from the road. I came down in Coinneach Euadh's gig. It was up in Stornoway meeting his son, Dòmhnall Red (Donald Maciver) (38b Tolsta, aged 26). He was lost and his sister, Ciorstag, who had gone to meet her brother, was returning without him, but she was bringing home the boys who had been saved – five of them."[40]

Of the sixteen seamen from Murray's village of Tolsta, who happily greeted each other at Kyle of Lochalsh, eleven were drowned and five were saved. The tone of grief, tempered by puzzlement, rings down the years as Murray continued with his memories:

"Donald Galson (Donald Macleod, 58 Tolsta) came ashore…they say he went to look for his brother Calum, and that when he didn't find him ashore he went out into the sea to look for him. That's what they said but I can't believe that anyone who got out of that would return… not even for a wife. It would be futile. The two brothers (Donald and Calum Macleod) were buried the same day. John (Morrison, 8 Tolsta) and I had been with each other since we were in the trenches in Antwerp."

Donald Maciver (Am Bèicear) returned home in the same gig, and remembered:

"The four of us from Tolsta was met by relatives and neighbours who expected their men. My Auntie Mary and my next-door neighbour who lost two sons. It was heart-breaking to know they were lost, as none of the boys I left in the saloon was saved and six of them (lived) within sight of my home. But the two Macleod brothers next door I felt more sorry (for)."[41]

The grievous losses suffered by the village of Tolsta on the night of the *Iolaire* compounded existing sorrows. Of only around eighty houses where able-bodied men lived, many had already been wounded and 41 had died in the war, leaving 19 widows, 54 fatherless children and over 150 other dependants. Also lost during the war years were ten schoolchildren, who succumbed to diphtheria between 1914 and March 1919. As an example of the extreme distress experienced in the village, at 3b Tolsta, *Iolaire* victim Donald Macleod's parents had already died before the war and his younger brother, John, had died of TB at Lewis Hospital in December 1914, aged 14. Once Donald senior (Mac Dhòmhnall Iain Saighdeir) was lost on the *Iolaire*, youngest brother Donald Jr was left at home all alone.

The single note of grace for the village came in the fact that, while many *Iolaire* bodies went unrecovered, out of Tolsta's eleven lost men, nine were recovered and identified. The parade of funerals must have seemed unending.

Quiet grief

"By breakfast time on Wednesday morning the news of the terrible disaster to the *Iolaire* had spread all over and the community was plunged into sorrow and gloom. The day was spent in trying to help and console the many stricken hearts in our midst."[42]

Before darkness came again on 1st January, most parts of Lewis were aware of the tragedy, and many knew of their own loss, or that of neighbours. As much as the scenes of the seashore and the mortuary present harrowing images to the mind, there were quiet moments of intense suffering in many a blackhouse, where mothers, grandmothers and aunts sat with uncomprehending children and awaited news, while the younger women and the men went into the town to learn what they could. Calum "Safety" Smith recalled:

"When the news did come through, my recollection is of everything suddenly going quiet, of women talking in hushed voices: it was as if there was a feeling that noise would be an offence to the dead."

"One of my most vivid recollections is of sitting in a neighbouring house the following day as one of the survivors sat on a stool in front of a large peat fire, with his trouser legs rolled up, while his mother knelt at his feet, bathing them in warm water, drying them very gently with a heated towel, and then smearing Vaseline on the cuts and abrasions that he had sustained clambering up the rocks at Holm in his socks."[43]

Mòr Smith was only four years of age when her father, Kenneth Smith from Earshader, was drowned. He had joined up in 1914 before her birth, and had been overseas for nearly the whole war, so Mòr had little recollection of him. He was coming home on New Year's leave from HMS *Cove*. After his body was recovered from the beach at Holm, his suitcase was found to be full of scarves and shawls from Gibraltar that he was bringing home as presents. Mòr remembered in much later life:

"I remember my mother airing his clothes. She had clothes and underwear airing in front of the fire. I don't remember word coming to the house, but I do remember a neighbour coming in and removing all the clothes and vanishing into another room and

I remember thinking: 'That's cheeky!' because it wasn't her house.

"I remember the funeral … . I have never seen so many people. The house was absolutely packed, upstairs and downstairs. When they found his body, my uncle had to go over to identify it."[44]

In a television interview in 2010, Mòr recalled how she had sat, puzzled, on her grandfather's lap as his tears splashed on her face.[45]

In the homes of Tolsta, many such scenes of quiet, domestic suffering were played out. As so often, it is the clear memories of those who were children at the time which paint the most poignant pictures. Young Marion Macdonald lived with her brother and sister for most of the war at the home of grandparents John and Marion Macdonald. Her mother had died of TB in 1915, and father John Macdonald (Seonaidh Mhic Itheach), 1b North Tolsta, was away serving in the RNR. He was due home that day. Marion was eight years old the day her father drowned:

"She recalled the excitement of that New Year's morning when her granny asked her to go to the shop to buy meat for her father's homecoming. On her way up from the Camach[46] she was met by her cousin Iain Mòr and another older member of the family, who enquired of her where she was going. She told him of her errand and was most annoyed when they asked her to turn back with them, as she would not be needing the meat that day. She was having none of this so she kept running up towards the shop.

"Her cousin came after her and took the money from her. They took her by the hand and walked her down to her grandparent's house. It was then that she became aware of the awful tragedy which left her and her brother and her sister orphaned. The memory of that day stayed with Marion into her old age."[47]

A tragic scene unfolded within the home at 35 Leurbost when the death of Donald Maclean (Dòmhnall Sheòrais), aged 50, was reported to his wife Annie and their seven children. His eldest daughter, 19-year-old daughter Catherine, collapsed at the news of the tragedy and died on 6th January. The cause of her death was recorded as influenza. Father and daughter were interred side by side at Crossbost Cemetery.

In the small island of Scalpay another heart was broken. Finlay Morrison (Fionnlagh Dhòmhnaill Fhionnlaigh) was due to be married to Catherine Morrison (Catrìona Tharmoid) from Cuddy Point, Scalpay and, knowing that Catrìona had bought her wedding trousseau, was in a hurry to get home to make preparations for the wedding. It was that which guided his fateful choice of a route home via Stornoway on the *Iolaire* and, for that reason, instead of a wedding, it was his funeral that Catrìona attended. He was interred at Old Luskentyre Burial Ground.

At the home of Alasdair MacKenzie, 'Am Boicean', in Aird in Point, his wife Marion and their six children excitedly awaited the return of the husband and father. A neighbour had told her that the *Iolaire* was scheduled to arrive between two and three in the morning. Marion busied herself preparing broth and a stew, while a clothes horse stood by the fire warming clothes for her returning husband. After midnight she was visited by her cousin and, after wishing her 'Bliadhna Mhath Ùr' (Happy New Year), Marion showed her twenty-seven pounds and seventeen shillings – her war savings, which she was going to use to renovate their house. She remarked: "Alasdair is going to do all the work himself – his first big challenge."

The warm fire made her cousin sleepy. When she awoke, the fire was all but out and the paraffin lamp had been turned down so that the room was in almost complete darkness. Marion was sitting on her milking stool, rocking backwards and forwards and nodding. Her cousin turned up the light. "Has the Boyken arrived?" she asked and in a soft voice, barely audible, Marion replied: "The Boyken will never come home child. I am a widow."

A few hours later, three men dressed in black entered the house. One of them led in prayer and afterwards opened the Bible and read the twenty-third psalm. Her cousin recalled:

> "Within a few minutes the door was opened again and my mother and Uncle 'Shookan' entered. They were followed by four women whose faces were tear-stained. All embraced Marion. There was so much sorrow and weeping that the children were wakened and came down to ask what was the matter."

Later there was consternation in the house when it was learned that Marion was unable to speak. She was struck dumb with the shock of losing her husband, but regained her speech some weeks later. However, for the rest of her life she was similarly struck dumb at the end of each year, a poignant reminder of the disaster.[48]

Some later discoveries were just as tragic, for those unaware that their loved-one even intended to return home aboard the *Iolaire*. 19-year-old John Macleod of Kirivick, near Carloway, (Iain Stuaman), visited his sister in Glasgow on his way home, so the family thought he had rejoined his ship. It was only later that his parents, Malcolm and Mary Macleod, learnt that he was among the recovered bodies. He was interred at Dalmore Cemetery.

To some waiting homes, doubly cruel news was delivered as relatives who had met gladly on the quayside in Kyle perished together on the *Iolaire*. At number 2 Crossbost, 51-year-old Donald Macleod was lost alongside his nephew, 19-year-old Malcolm Macleod. Donald and his wife Mary were childless, but Malcolm had been brought up by them since he was 10 years old, making it still more poignant that he met his uncle, a father-figure to him, in Kyle and joined him on the *Iolaire* to return home. Uncle and nephew drowned together, but only the youngster's remains were recovered. His father, remarried at Keith Street, was also notified by the Admiralty of his loss.

In nearby Leurbost, the address of number 11 was given for two cousins who grew up together. Alexander Mackenzie was 39 and his 25-year-old cousin Allan had been brought up from the age of nine by his Aunt Margaret, after his parents died. Allan was like a wee brother to Alex but, although they both drowned as New Year dawned, they were separated in death. Alex was buried at Crossbost cemetery, but Allan was not found.

Close friends Donald Paterson and Norman Mackillop grew up together on the tiny Isle of Berneray, in the settlement of Borve. Born just a month apart, they had joined up together in September 1918 and served a short war at the same station, HMS *Pembroke* at Chatham. The 18-year-olds were travelling home together on 31st

December when they made the choice to come home on the *Iolaire*, rather than take the more usual route via Skye to Harris and homewards from there. Both were drowned, though the sea gave up only Donald's body for burial.

The comfort of faith

At this time of sore trial in the life of the islands, the people's faith, the words of scripture, the lifting of voices in psalm and the quiet murmur of prayer from others offered essential support to those feeling a grief almost impossible to express. Ministers and elders called on the new-made widows and bereaved parents at their homes to guide them in prayer and to offer what support they could.

Half a century later Murdo Macleod from Leurbost recalled how, on New Year's morning the villagers headed for church, where the sermon was one of thanksgiving by the Minister, on this first New Year of peace after four years of war. It was later that day that the terrible news came, and that night the very same people were gathered again, now in the houses of those mourning.[49] A service of worship was held in each house separately. The scene at the home of Alasdair Mackenzie, 'Am Boicean', in Aird, Point would have been repeated at home after home. Men dressed in black led prayers and read from the bible. The sounds would have been of murmured prayer, muted sobbing and the melancholy sound of Gaelic psalms arising into the darkness.

Prayer was natural to the people it marked the rhythm of life, the seasons of the year and the beginning and end of days. It was associated with work and with fellowship, and it was always part of the ritual of death. The call to serve in the war had been announced from the pulpits of island churches, the great news of peace had been given there. Now, on Sunday January 5th, the first Sunday after the disaster, island ministers rose to the challenge of finding words that could bring any comfort to a population so greatly tried, so utterly bereft. The sermons given were important enough for parts of them to be reproduced entirely in the *Stornoway Gazette*, to be read and re-read as a source of comfort and reflection.

In the Parish Church of St Columba's in Stornoway, Reverend John M Menzies said:

"We are struck dumb by the horror of the awful event which happened at our very doors this past week. What can we say? It came like a meteor across our sky and (at) once we are driven to think deeply and furiously thoughts that are too deep for tears. There are circumstances connected with the awesome tragedy which make it soul-harrowing. It has been my lot, and unfortunately that of too many of us, to give what consolation we could to the friends and relatives of many of those who have fallen in this war. That was hard enough, but they had at least this comfort that their loved ones gave their lives in the cause of their country, so that through their tears they were proud that their beloved made such a noble sacrifice. But what can we say of this? Peace was restored, and we were all looking forward with glad hearts to the home-coming of our loved one. These lads – the flower of our island – were hurled into eternity within a few yards of their homes. After many escapes and hardships, they were looking forward to a glad re-union with their loved ones –and here in sight of home and within a yard or two of the land which they loved so well and suffered so much for and to which they had brought so much honour and renown, they met that grim enemy Death, under circumstances so awful that the heart of the whole country is stirred to its depths."[50]

Rev Roderick Morison, High Church, preaching in the English United Free Church (now Martin's Memorial Church of Scotland), spoke in a forthright manner that demanded answers. After referencing the hand of God, as seen in the catastrophe, he went on to say that they could not lose sight of the fact that man's hand was in it too.

"Indeed the danger was that they might be so occupied with man's part in it as to lose sight of God altogether. It was not for them, meantime at least, to attribute blame or responsibility to individuals. They must reserve all their judgements on the matter until a proper enquiry has been made into it. And, of course, there must be a full, impartial and independent search into every circumstance connected with the case. The people of Lewis were in no mood to tolerate – and no one should ask them to tolerate – any hushing up of facts or shielding of individuals. The whole truth must come out, at whatever cost to the reputation or position of men. Lewis had suffered too deeply to have had her agony added to by any such trifling. Not that he anticipated any such thing. He would say nothing of the contribution of Lewis to the defence of the Empire or of the loyalty and bravery of her sons and daughters. On the simple ground of human rights they should demand sympathy and justice and the most searching scrutiny into this tragic affair. Never in all its previous history had the island suffered such a calamity. They were all bewildered and shocked beyond expression."[51]

Reverend Kenneth Cameron of the Free Church took for his text Psalm 46, verse 10: *"Be still and know that I am God."*

"After pointing out the setting of the words, he said that they could be applied to periods of unusual trial, to times of dark and mysterious happenings in the Providence of God. One says that God's providence are sometimes "deep and unsearchable," sometimes "dark and mysterious," sometimes "humbling and cheering," at other times "prayer-hearing providence." To the second class Mr Cameron said belongs the startling, catastrophic, appalling event of New Year's morning. We are ready to rush to rash conclusions about these tragic occurrences. We seek to solve the mystery in some way that accords with our own mind. We assign the blame now to this party: now to the next. The text comes to us to keep us right in our thinking and in our attitude to the event. It bids us contemplate the majesty of God, bow before His sovereignty, believe in His righteousness, have recourse to His mercy. It calls us very clearly to seek to be related to God through Christ as that "it shall be well with" us in the ordinary experience of life, in the more solemn events of time and forever. Our prayers and sympathy go out to all who have been called upon to drink this heavy cup of unlooked-for sorrow."[52]

Reverend Neil Macintyre of the Free Presbyterian Church said:

"We are meeting today under the darkest and most ominous cloud that ever enveloped the island of Lewis. The whole island from end to end is trembling with grief and sorrow and, like Rachel "weeping for her children, refused to be comforted for her children, for they were not." Our hearts go out today in pity and sympathy to those who are stricken down with grief and whose hearts are rent with sorrow for their fathers, husbands, sons and brothers who had lost their lives so mysteriously within sight of their homes."[53]

What was said in the pulpits in the other churches from Ness down to Berneray was not recorded, but in every community the coming together of villagers, those bereaved, their neighbours and their friends, would have given important spiritual comfort.

The seagoing communities of the islands are religious, but were much more devout at the end of the First World War. Those coming together in the churches reeled at the loss of such a large number of able men on the *Iolaire*, especially as it followed a war that had already reaped a deadly harvest among a generation of islanders. The poignancy was hard to deal with. The further suffering that had struck their congregations so soon after the Armistice made many individuals challenge their beliefs. That is a natural feeling in times of sudden loss in a tragedy, but such was their strength of belief and deep knowledge of the Bible that the families quickly reconciled themselves with God.

Despite the devastating war losses and the *Iolaire* tragedy, the religious communities of the islands strengthened in their faith and their Christian way of life bound them even closer together to survive the coming difficult times. Black clothes worn by women, day in and day out from then onwards, became a feature of the island for decades and church attendance remained at a level hard to imagine today.

To the secular society of today, the unshakeable faith of so many in the islands seems almost unbelievable after the test

to which it was put in January 1919. The Lewis-born poet Iain Crichton Smith put it succinctly in 1989 when he asked:

"What kind of a God could have thought up such a punishment? He must have been a peculiarly sadistic God, and what were they punished for? In some places such a tragedy would have destroyed the credibility of a loving God: in Lewis it only strengthened their faith in him."[54]

Funeral after funeral

It is still the custom in Lewis and Harris for funerals to be held soon after the death of any family member. Funerals were often held from the homes of the lost ones, who would be 'waked' all through the previous night, the house full of friends, relatives and neighbours. Later the men would carry the coffin, entrusting the precious burden from hand to hand and making the journey on foot, whatever the distance, to the cemetery serving their district – these could be some distance from the village, as most cemeteries were located on the sandy land near to beaches.

From the very day of the disaster, the sad trains of carts carrying hastily collected coffins began to make their way to island cemeteries. The *Scotsman* newspaper reported:

"Carts in little processions of twos and threes, each bearing its coffin from the mortuary, pass through the streets of Stornoway on their way to some rural village, and all heads are bared as they pass."[55]

An immediate problem was posed by the huge demand for coffins, not just for the *Iolaire* victims but for island deaths due to Spanish 'flu, which was just taking hold all

Undertakers Archibald Macrae kept a record of coffins made locally and brought from Glasgow, of bodies recovered and the funerals as they happened.

over Britain, Lewis and Harris not escaping. The business record for Archibald Macrae, undertaker, on Keith Street shows that they could only supply 26 coffins immediately and that around 200 coffins were procured from Glasgow. The total bill, including three polished oak coffins which, it is presumed, were required for officers, was settled by the Admiralty at £749 6s 9d.

Poignant record of the island-wide impact of these numerous funerals comes from the school report books around the islands. Despite the long closure of many schools due to the Spanish flu epidemic, some opened as usual on 6th January for the return of pupils after the New Year holiday. At Bernera school a visiting official recorded:

"6th January 1919 – Visited school this day 12 noon. Signed registers; attendance somewhat better today altho' still poor. Weather dry but cold. The funeral of two of the *Iolaire* disaster is passing by to the Bosta Burying ground. This terrible (word missed by writer) is aggravated by the report that it occurred through the indiscretion of the officer-in-charge. Two of the victims from this island are still missing."[56]

At Mangersta school on the same date the teacher wrote:

"Owing to the funerals in the district I thought it best to close the school for the day."[57]

And at Bragar on 9th January:

"Attendance improving but still poor. The naval disaster to HMS (sic) *Iolaire* accounts for most of the absences. Day wet and stormy."[58]

The teacher at Fidigarry school recorded:

"6th January 1919 – School reopened after seven weeks closure. Very poor attendance. Spoke to the senior pupils of the dreadful disaster to the '*Iolaire*' on New Year's morning which involved the deaths of two to three hundred naval ratings."[59]

Funerals predominantly went unreported, but that of the 18-year-old messenger boy Donald Macleod, of 10 Murray's Court, was given in the *Highland News*. His body was recovered on 17th January 1919 and interred the following day. The newspaper reported:

"The cortege arrived at St Peter's Church at 2pm, the gun carriage being followed by the father Mr John Macleod, with his brother and son, after whom came the Stornoway naval Corps and Boys' naval brigade, and then a large number of bluejackets and civilians. When the first part of the burial service was concluded, the procession, headed by Pipe Major Macleod, Gordon Highlanders, proceeded to the cemetery, where the Rev H. Anderson Meaden[60] concluded the service. Bugler Kenneth Macleod, an old comrade, sounded the "Last Post" after which the Pipe Major played "The Flowers of the Forest." The large company of mourners included the Provost of Stornoway, Dr Murray MP, ex-Provost Mackenzie MBE, and other well-known members of the community, while the Navy was well represented by Commander Humphrey RN, Lt Boxall RN, and Lt Allman RNR".[61]

The funerals would continue for weeks, as bodies gradually came to shore, or were found in the rocks and seas around Lewis. Laxay's only *Iolaire* victim, John Macleod, was recovered from the wreck on Wednesday 8th January and brought to Laxay the following day. He was interred at Old Laxay Cemetery. 26-year-old Malcolm Mackay of Crowlista was found on the 14th and was interred the following day at Ardroil Cemetery.

Nineteen-year-old Signalman John Alex (Jack) Macaskill, born in Liverpool but raised in Stornoway, had survived three sinkings during the war – the torpedoing of two ships and a collision. He was buried at Sandwick, hardly a stone's throw from the scene of the sinking, in March 1919. His remains were found there late in February amongst the seaweed on the seashore by his friend, A J Macleod, who had spent weeks consistently searching for him since the day of the disaster.

For some, the agony would continue for months – Ness man Angus Macdonald's remains were eventually spotted in July 1919 by two men from Crossbost from a fishing boat, at Tom an 'Ic Lang near Crossbost cemetery, where he would be buried. The men returned to shore and reported to Stornoway. Arrangements were made to recover the badly decomposed body, his identity disc still around his neck.

But most of the funerals were completed before January was out, and it was the place of local district correspondents in the *Stornoway Gazette* to record the impact on each community. On 24th January 1919 the paper carried a number of local reports:

"Bragar news – In common with the west side villages, Bragar had an extremely sore trial in connection with the *Iolaire* disaster.

"When the war ended we were preparing to have our celebrations of Christmas and New Year when the sudden plague of influenza spread through these villages with such rapidity that in one week the village of Bragar had to record ten deaths as a result of this scourge.

"It was thought the calamities had reached their limit, until on that black New Year morning, a catastrophe that has deprived us of eight Bragar men under such distressing circumstances that all previous disasters have been overshadowed: mothers and children watching the road for their beloved husbands and fathers who were hourly expected; breakfasts fitting for New Year and homecoming prepared, and expectations all round higher than they had been for many years – the tragedy of it.

"There are several cases even more tragic than others. For instance, one case, that of a mother with twins a few weeks old, and the rest of the family being all young children, was made a widow by that dire calamity.

"Tolsta news – Since we have sent in our last report the remains of three of our local men have been recovered and buried in the local cemetery. viz Donald Macleod and Malcolm Macleod, 56 North Tolsta and Evander Murray, 45 North Tolsta. The bodies of Donald Campbell, No 44 and John Maciver No 69 have not been recovered.

"Ness news – The remains of John Murray, 36 Lionel, were removed last Saturday and buried at Ness on Monday. This brings the number of bodies found up to 13, out of a total of 23."[62]

The number of *Iolaire* victims' bodies recovered in Ness eventually reached 16.

The *Stornoway Gazette*, in only its second year of existence, had become the paper of record for the daily impacts and collective grief of an island in deep distress. The same edition in January 1919 carried this searing poetic memorial among the notices of deaths.

"MACKAY. - In memory of William MacKay, 7 Fivepenny Ness, lost in the wreck of HM Yacht "Iolaire" on 1st January 1919.

"Oh my lost friend, and my own, own friend,
And my love that loved me so;
Is there never a chink in the world above
Where they listen for words from below?

"We shall walk no more through the sodden plain
Where the last farewell was said;
But perhaps I shall meet thee and know thee again
When the sea gives up her dead.

(Inserted by his loving friend, Chirsty MacFarlane, Port of Ness)"[63]

Dreams and premonitions

Two of the bodies recovered weeks after the disaster were said to have been found with the help of dreams, which in both cases guided fathers to the site of their son's remains. The two stories have been conflated in the past, and the details have become hazy, but in essence they are these.

Donald Macdonald, Dòmhnall Lisidh, aged 20, of 44 Breasclete, was missing for six weeks after the disaster. His nephew Alex Dan Macdonald recounted the tale of his grandmother's dream, in which she saw Donald lying between two rocks and wearing his naval oilskins. Alex Dan recounted:

"She woke up my grandfather in the middle of the night and told him to get the horse and cart ready as they were going to head off to Stornoway together, as she had seen the exact place he was lying. They made their way there and on arrival she made her way towards the shore and headed directly to a spot on the shoreline where Donald's body was lying between two rocks. I remember in Gaelic it was said: *"Bha e na laighe eadar dà sgor dìreach mar a bhruadair i."*

The *Stornoway Gazette*'s account of the discovery left out the role of the dream, but does not stray far from the tale otherwise:

"Callanish News – Everyone here as well as his own native villagers were deeply grieved to hear that Donald Macdonald, Outend Breasclete, was among the many fine lads who perished in the *Iolaire* Disaster. His father was in Stornoway a week after the disaster, but the boy's remains were not recovered. On Friday 14th inst., his father went again and went to the scene of the wreck alone. It was low tide at the time, and he went out on the rock as far as possible, and saw by the ship's side, what he took to be his son's remains. He informed the authorities, and when the body was recovered it was found to be that of the man's missing son. On Saturday the remains were brought home and buried in Dalmore Cemetery."[64]

The second tale of a dream predicting the location of a drowned son came from Uig, where John Maclennan, ''Ain Geal', recalled that 19-year old Angus Matheson, Aonghas Chàdham, from 18 Uigen, had been found in this way:

"Càdham (Matheson) had a premonition or a dream, because six weeks after the tragedy on New Year's morning, he set off for Stornoway telling the family that he was going to collect his son's body. On approaching the Admiralty base, he demanded a boat and they decided to humour a grieving father and take him to Glumaig Bay as he wished. In the bay there they found the body of his son, Angus Matheson, from Uigen, in the location where his father had seen his body in the dream or premonition."[65]

In an intensely oral culture, the importance attributed to premonitions and dreams is strong, and such reports are taken seriously. After the disaster, there were reports of those who had predicted the tragedy, and other stories of immediate premonitions that told waiting relatives their son or husband would not return.

One such story related to Armistice Day, and a man known to be a seer, who lived in Swordale in Point:

"A man in the village, Donald Mackenzie, was considered a prophet – he was bedridden and blind. This very man, the day someone went up to his bed and told him that peace was declared: 'Oh,' he said, 'Are you sure of that?' 'Yes', they said, 'Word has come round that peace has been declared.' There were no phones then. He said: 'It amazes me, because the biggest loss that the islands have had, hasn't happened yet.' The *Iolaire* disaster."[66]

Another person said to have had foreknowledge of the disaster was the mother of John Maclennan of Kneep. As he recounted in his later interviews:

"I went into the house, my mother was in bed and I went to her bedside. She said, 'Iain, what happened?', 'Nothing happened' I said. 'Something happened, I've known for a long time that something dreadful was going to happen'."[67]

More than one man was said to have known of his own fate, never to return to his home island. On his last leave, John Murray of 36 Lionel had commented that he had a premonition that he would not see 'Mullach Lional' (Lionel) again. On his fatal journey home, Murray met an acquaintance in Glasgow who said: "What about your prophecy now, John?" to which he replied, "I haven't arrived there yet."[68]

Leading Seaman Alexander Macdonald, 28 Lower Bayble, had been a fisherman for most of his working life. Like so many of his island contemporaries he often fished from Peterhead or Fraserburgh and, if he had time in Aberdeen, he used to visit an acquaintance from Lewis, a Mrs Campbell. Shortly after war was declared he was mobilised from a fishing boat and he called on Mrs Campbell and told her that now he was going to war and that he would not survive. When he reached Kyle of Lochalsh on 31st December 1918, he boarded the *Iolaire* and a fellow islander said to him that, contrary to his prediction, he had survived the war. Macdonald replied, "I am not home yet!" He was drowned on the *Iolaire* coming home on leave from HMS *Nairn*.

On the night of the wreck itself, at Northton in Harris, Donald Maclean woke up during the night before 1st January 1919 dawned. "Something has happened to

Kenneth!" His wife Mairi reproached him: "Be quiet you fool, you are having a nightmare!" Their 18-year-old son Kenneth was one of the boys lost, laid to rest at Scarista Cemetery. Mairi's nephew Norman Mackay of Leverburgh was also lost.

James Shaw Grant, who became the second editor of the Stornoway Gazette, related a tale from the night of the wreck. He had heard that one of the crew on board the *Sheila* on the night of the disaster walked round the stern of the ship before she sailed from Kyle. In the gloom he saw a blurred shape on the deck, as if something had been stowed there, but he knew there was nothing. He assumed it was a trick of the light and gave it no further thought. A few days later, when the *Sheila* sailed again from Kyle, there was an unmistakeable black shape on the deck at the stern – a pile of coffins, covered with a tarpaulin. They were being hastily sent to Stornoway, because the local undertaker did not have enough coffins to cope with the bodies recovered from the wreck of the *Iolaire*.[69]

Like the fathers who were able to locate their sons, some widows felt they had communication from lost husbands after the disaster. Peggy Gillies of Lionel was four years of age when her father died on the *Iolaire* and, although she had no clear memories of the events, she did remember a later tale told by her mother:

> "Many years later there was an *Iolaire* programme on the radio and I don't think she quite grasped what it was, but I started talking about it myself. She said, 'The night after I got news of your father's death I saw him in my dream. He came to me and I said to him, 'What am I going to do? I'm so frightened' and he said, '*Cha b' iongnadh mi fhèin nuair a chuala mi an glag?*' ("No wonder, I was frightened when I heard the bell")

> "Years after she died my only brother was home from Glasgow and we got word that the *Iolaire* bell had been found by some divers. The bell was handed over at a ceremony in June 1971 in Stornoway Town Hall. I said, sitting in the Town Hall, 'I wonder if that is the bell that my mother referred to, that my father said to her in a dream'."

These tales were to emerge, some many years later, from an island almost submerged by grief and incomprehension. In the immediate aftermath the practical business of finding, recognising, carrying home and burying their boys occupied almost every village. Yet as wracked with grief as the islanders were, there was also immediate disquiet after the tragedy itself. Very quickly a special meeting of Stornoway Town Council, a gathering of leading citizens, even a call from the pulpit, would add to the clamour for an inquiry to be called into the disaster, so that mistakes could be identified and some sense made of what seemed senseless. Islanders wanted to know how and why their precious boys had been lost within grasping distance of their homes and, most of all, they wanted to know who was responsible.

Chapter 5 Footnotes

1. Foreword to *Sea Sorrow, Stornoway Gazette,* 1960
2. *Toll for the Brave, Highland News,* 11th January 1919
3. *Around the Peat-Fire,* Calum Smith. Birlinn, 2001
4. *Home at Last* Grampian TV, 2nd January 1989
5. First footing – bringing in the New Year by visiting friends and relatives and sharing a drink. This account comes from letters sent to James Shaw Grant, editor of the *Stornoway Gazette,* by Alex Macaulay, at the time
6. Olivers Brae, a street on the main route between Sandwick and Stornoway
7. As told in Children of the Black House by Calum Ferguson. Birlinn, 2003
8. Account taken from letters sent to James Grant Shaw and published in the *Stornoway Gazette,* 1979
9. Ina Macritchie interviewed for *Home At Last* Grampian TV, 1989
10. Personal story told to author by his family
11. The Bràighe, the narrow isthmus which joins Point to the main part of Lewis
12. Anna Mairi Martin, Aird Point, interviewed for *The Great War: Through the Eyes of Women* on Isles FM radio, November 2015
13. Murdo Macleod interviewed in Gaelic in the *Stornoway Gazette,* 4th January 1969
14. NAAFI – Navy, Army and Air Force Institutes, which provided catering and supplies to armed forces
15. Account given in *Around the Peat Fire* by Calum Smith. Birlinn, 2001
16. *The Times,* 2nd January 1919
17. *The Daily Mirror,* 2nd January 1919
18. The wreck broke up in a gale less than two weeks later and the mast finally disappeared from view
19. *The Daily Mirror,* 8th January 1919
20. *Stornoway Gazette,* 10th January 1919
21. *Terrible Disaster at Lewis* reported in the *Oban Times,* 11th January 1919
22. *Toll for the Brave, Highland News,* 11th January 1919
23. *Lewis Disaster* report in the *Inverness Courier,* 3rd January 1919
24. Donald Macphail interviewed by Fred Macaulay. BBC Radio nan Gàidheal, 1961
25. *The Bulletin* (Glasgow), 14th January 1919
26. *Glasgow Herald,* 4th January 1919
27. Hounds – a pair of fore-and-aft braces that serve as supports for a topmast
28. Murdo Macdonald interviewed by the Rev. Donald John Morrison of Kyles Scalpay in 2007 and translated into English by Anna Mackinnon
29. Interview with Donald Morrison (Am Patch) *Stornoway Gazette,* 4th January 1992
30. Murdo Macdonald interviewed by the Rev. Donald John Morrison of Kyles Scalpay in 2007 and translated into English by Anna Mackinnon
31. Report by Lt Wenlock to Rear Admiral Boyle. PRO Admiralty File 116/1869
32. PRO Admiralty file 116/1869
33. Interview with Donald Morrison (Am Patch) *Stornoway Gazette,* 4th January 1992
34. As told by Jean MacDonald, daughter of Aleen Murray. *Criomagan* Vol 4, Issue 1, 1999
35. Willie John Macdonald, Stornoway butcher, relating his memories in 1988
36. The slant – timber piles and slips/steps at the sides of the piers
37. Survivor Donald Macdonald, of 23 Cromore writing from Canada, *Stornoway Gazette,* 10th August 1956
38. William Maclennan was originally thought to be a survivor of the *Iolaire,* but was in fact on the *Sheila*

39. John was interviewed by Maga Mackay, who features in this story. John had been lodging with Maga's parents when serving on the crew of the first HMY Iolaire, based at Stornoway. His interview was translated by Maggie Smith for *Hebridean Connections* in 2005

40. Donald Murray interview, *Seanchas*, No 53, Winter 2006

41. Donald Maciver interviewed on 25th February 1976

42. *Highland News*, 11th January 1919

43. *Around the Peat Fire* Calum Smith. Birlinn, 2001

44. Mòr Smith interview in *Seanchas,* No 53, Winter 2006

45. Mòr Smith interview on TV programme *Coast*. BBC, June 2010

46. Camach – an area of Tolsta village, Tràigh Ghiordail, above the beach where the fishing boats were landed

47. Marion Macdonald's memories recounted in *Seanchas*

48. From *Children of the Black House*, Calum Ferguson, Birlinn 2003

49. Murdo MacLeod, *Stornoway Gazette,* 4th January 1969

50. *Stornoway Gazette,*, 10th January 1919

51. As above

52. As above

53. As above

54. *Home at Last* Grampian TV, 1989

55. *The Scotsman*, 6th January 1919

56. School record book, Bernera school

57. School record book, Mangersta school

58. School record book, Bragar school

59. School record book, Fidigarry school

60. Rev Anderson Meaden also officiated at the memorial service conducted over the wreck site on 14th January 1919. A poem written by him, reflecting on the islands' losses, is included in Chapter 10 "Song, poetry and verse"

61. *Highland News*, 24th January 1919

62. *Stornoway Gazette,* 24th January 1919

63. As above

64. *Stornoway Gazette,* 21st February 1919

65. John Maclennan interviewed by Kenneth Maciver for BBC Radio nan Gàidheal, 1987

66. Morag Morrison, interviewed for *A Memorial of the Airwaves*, Isles FM, November 2014

67. John Maclennan interviewed by Maga Mackay, translated by Maggie Smith for *Hebridean Connections*, 2005

68. Peggy Gillies, *Stornoway Gazette,*, 31st December 1988

69. *In Search of Lewis* by James Shaw Grant. *Stornoway Gazette,* 1989

Roll call of men lost in the wreck of the *Iolaire*

A total of 201 men, 181 islanders, 18 members of the crew of HMY *Iolaire* and two naval passengers returning from leave were lost on 1st January 1919. In this section we name every man who died, with a short summary of their lives and service up until their tragic deaths. The list is given in order of the districts and villages where the men lived, starting from the north of the Isle of Lewis.

Each man's information is given as follows:

> ### Name
> (with Gaelic, familiar and nicknames).
>
> **Date of birth. Age at date of death in the *Iolaire* disaster.**
>
> **Address. Rank and service.**
> **Service number if known. Memorial/s where commemorated.**

Chatham, Plymouth and Portsmouth Naval Memorials were raised by naval authorities and the Commonwealth War Graves Commission as a way to commemorate those lost at sea, who had no known grave. In cases where the bodies of the *Iolaire* victims were recovered, their place of burial is given within their details (WG references War Grave). Where the remains were not recovered, the naval memorial recording their loss is given, together with local memorials.

All the men are listed at the bronze sculpture unveiled at Holm as part of the centenary commemorations. An index to other local memorials can be found at the end of this section.

John Macdonald
(Iain 'An Dh'll Iain Bhreacair)

born 29th October 1889. Age 29.

10 Skigersta. Seaman RNR.
Service number 4490/A. LWM 1/LWM 8

Iain was the son of John and Christina Macdonald (née Maclean) and was a fisherman pre-war. He joined the RNR on 8th October 1912 and served at HMS *Victory* from the first call on 4th August 1914. He then went to HMS *Excellent*, HMS *Attentive*, the Tribal class destroyer HMS *Nubian* and finally HM Tug *Seahorse*, where he served with Angus Gillies, South Dell, who was also lost on the *Iolaire*. Iain was a newlywed, having married Jessie Finlayson from 18 Skigersta on his last leave home, on 18th October 1918. Jessie was initially refused a widow's pension, on the grounds that there was no proof that her marriage was consummated. Her father told the authorities that this was "no business of theirs" and she eventually received her due pension. Jessie's wedding ring is still kept by the family. Iain's sister Peggy was married to John F. Macleod, the man who swam ashore with the line, and his mother was a widow. His remains were interred at Ness (St Peter) Old Churchyard. (WG).

Murdo Campbell
(Murchadh Gheadaidh)

born 28th May 1900. Age 18.

4 Eorodale. Deckhand RNR.
Service number 20536/DA. LWM 1/LWM 8

Son of Donald and Catherine Maclean (née Campbell), Murdo had six sisters and two brothers – Donald (RNR) and Norman (Gordon Highlanders). Murdo was a young victim of the *Iolaire* tragedy, who had just joined the RNR on 11th June 1918. The armed merchant cruiser HMS *Patia* appears on his record, but as this ship was sunk by UC-49 in the Bristol Channel, two days after he enlisted, he may only have been due to join her and never actually reached her before she was lost. Murdo saw brief service at HMS *Pembroke I* and then went to HMS *Attentive III* at Dover. At the war's end he was with the trawler section on HMT *Matthew Flynn*. He was interred at Ness (St Peter) Old Churchyard (WG).

John Macleod
(Iain Thorcail)

born 15th October 1898. Age 20.

13 Eorodale. Deckhand RNR.
Service number 15739/DA. LWM 1/LWM 8

John was the son of Donald and Mary Macleod (née Macdonald) and had served from 17th April 1917. He was at the Dover base HMS *Attentive III* where he spent all his service with the minesweeping trawler HMT *Wren*. He was interred at Ness (St Peter) Old Churchyard (WG).

Angus Macdonald
(Aonghas Chaluim Breabadair)

born 16th August 1895. Age 23.

3 Port of Ness. Deckhand RNR.
Service number 2597/SD. LWM 1/LWM 8

Son of Angus and Margaret Macdonald (née Campbell), at nearly six feet two inches, Angus was one of the tallest Lewis sailors. His brother Malcolm was also a naval reservist. Angus enrolled at Glasgow on 20th September 1915 and trained at HMS *Victory*. He served on the brand-new *Yarrow* (later M-class) destroyer HMS *Sabrina* for a year and a half, then moved to HMS *Dreel Castle* and served from that base with HMD *Primrose II* until Christmas 1918. His body was unrecovered for some time, until observed in July 1919 by two men from Crossbost from a fishing boat, at Tom an 'Ic Lang, near the place he was later buried. The men returned to shore and reported to Stornoway, where arrangements were made to recover the body, his identity disc still around his neck. His remains were interred at Crossbost Cemetery (WG).

Angus Morrison
(Aonghas Dhòmhnaill a' Choire)

born 4th February 1886. Age 32.

7 Knockaird. Petty Officer RNR.
Service number 5306/A. Chatham Naval Memorial and LWM 1/LWM 8

Son of Donald and Jessie Morrison (née Gunn) and brother of 'Am Patch' – Donald Morrison, the man on the mast – Angus joined the RNR on 8th December 1913, serving as John Morrison, with his birth date given as 20th October 1892 in naval records. He was rated a Leading Seaman on 1st April 1914 and was fishing at Peterhead at the outbreak of war. He reported to Devonport and was at HMS *Eclipse*, the Plymouth depot for naval mine and ordnance, from 19th August 1914 until 6th March 1915. He was at HMS *Vivid* at Devonport until 20th May 1915, was posted to the armed boarding steamer HMS *Heroic* from 8th August 1916 until 29th August 1918 and was promoted to Petty Officer from 5th August 1918. Angus was based at HMS *Vivid* when he received his New Year leave pass, and travelled to Kyle to board the *Iolaire*, together with his brother Donald, who famously survived by clinging to the mast through the night. Their father had died on 15th January 1918 but their widowed mother, Jessie, lived to be 99 and was the last of the grieving mothers to die, on 4th February 1961.

John Morrison
(Iain an t-Saighdeir)

born 12th June 1900. Age 18.

12 Knockaird. Deckhand RNR.
Service number 21746/DA. LWM 1/LWM 8

John, the son of Norman and Margaret Morrison (née Smith), had only enrolled on 6th September 1918 and was heading home on his first leave since joining up. Brother Angus also served in the RNR and came home safely. John's base was HMS *Victory* at Portsmouth. He was briefly with HMY *Nairn* and HMS *Research* and was a crew member of the trawler HMT *David Conn*. Like all youngsters who enrolled in the later months of the war, after his death his family was informed that he did not qualify for a War Gratuity. He was interred the day after he was found at Ness (St Peter) Old Churchyard (WG).

Angus Morrison
(Aonghas Iain Buachaill')

born 6th November 1898. Age 20.

10 Eoropie. Leading Deckhand RNR
Service number 14310/DA. Chatham Naval Memorial and LWM 1/LWM 8

The son of John and Catherine Morrison (née Macleod), Angus joined up at HMS *Iolaire* (base) on 9th January 1917. He was posted to HMS *Vivid*, then HMT *Daniel Harrington*, operating out of HMS *Satellite* at Shields, then he was on HMT *Norman II* from HMS *Idaho* at Milford Haven. Angus packed a lot into his naval career and was also on the Hunt class minesweeper HMS *Cotswold* from HMS *Vivid* at Devonport. He served further in 1918 at HMS *Gunner*, HMS *Nairn* and HMS *Venerable* and was on the battleship HMS *Implacable* at the war's end.

Donald Macleod
(Dolaidh na Gruagaich)

born 10th May 1890. Age 28.

5a Fivepenny, Ness. Deckhand RNR.
Service number 10941/A. Chatham Naval Memorial and LWM 1/LWM 8

Donald's parents Angus and Margaret Macleod (née Macleod) saw four sons go away to war – brothers John (Iain na Gruagaich), Kenneth and Allan were also with the RNR. Donald enrolled with the reserve on 11th April 1916 and was obviously considered a competent seaman at Stornoway, as he was posted directly to HMT *Quercia*. After a spell with HM Whaler *Rightwhale*, from 2nd October 1916 to 3rd March 1917 at Stornoway, he returned to the requisitioned minesweeper HMT *Quercia*, then based at HMS *Idaho* at Milford Haven. Donald was one of a large number of Nessmen aboard the *Iolaire* on Hogmanay as she cast off from Kyle.

William Mackay
(Uilleam Màiri Bhàn)

born 26th August 1892. Age 26.

7 Fivepenny, Ness. Signalman RNVR.
Service number Z8218. LWM 1/LWM 8/LWM
19

The only son of William and Mary Mackay
(née Mackay), William was brought up
by his mother on her own, after his father
Uilleam Aonghais' died of peritonitis, aged
26, when William was just six months old.
William was a teacher at Cross School
and signed up for hostilities on 27th June
1916. He served at HMS *Victory VI*, HMS
Vivid I, and was a Signalman based at
HMS *Vivid III* at Devonport from 17th April
1917. He was interred at Ness (St Peter)
Old Churchyard (WG). A tribute to William
was placed in the *Stornoway Gazette* in
January 1919 by 'his loving friend, Chirsty
MacFarlane, Port of Ness'. (See Chapter
5).

Donald Morrison
(Dolaidh Buachaill')

born 9th September 1890. Age 28.

11 Fivepenny, Ness. Deckhand RNR. Service
number 11859/DA. LWM 1/LWM 8

The youngest of eight children born
to Donald and Gormelia Morrison (née
Campbell), Donald was serving with the
2nd Battalion Seaforth Highlanders in 1914,
and was amongst the first batch of soldiers
to go to France. In November 1914 he was
so badly wounded at Ypres that he was
discharged from the army. At home, he
felt his health had improved and he joined
the Navy at HMS *Iolaire* (base) on 14th
August 1916. Donald went to HMS *Victory*
at Portsmouth and, on 2nd November 1916,
he joined HMT *Iceland* at HMS *Halcyon*, the
Auxiliary patrol base at Lowestoft. He was
serving on the minesweeping trawler HMT
Sir Mark Sykes at Lowestoft from 31st March
1917 until he was due home for New Year
1919. He was interred at Ness (St Peter) Old
Churchyard (WG).

Norman Morrison
(Tarmod Dh'll Eachainn)

born 1st June 1898. Age 20.

17 Lionel. Seaman RNR.
Service number 12088/DA. LWM 1/LWM 8

Sons of Donald (Dòmhnaill Eachainn)
and Jessie Morrison (née Campbell),
Norman's brother Donald was in the
trawler section of the RNR and Angus
was wounded fighting with the Seaforths.
Norman enrolled on 20th September 1916
at Stornoway and went to HMS *Pembroke
I*, HMS *Actaeon* and HMS *Gunner*, where
he served on the minesweeper HMS
Hambledon. He later served on the
requisitioned Fleetwood trawler HMT *Urka*
based at HMS *Pekin*, HMS *Venerable* and
HMS *Implacable*. Norman was interred
at Ness (St Peter) Old Churchyard (WG).
Brother Donald, who had been at the pier
to meet Norman, died of TB in 1922, aged
22.

Roll call of the lost

Angus Campbell
(Ila)

born 1st March 1880. Age 38.

31 Lionel. Seaman RNR.

Service number 3590/C. Chatham Naval Memorial and LWM 1/LWM 8.

Angus was the only son of Donald and Catherine Campbell (née Campbell) and the husband of Susan Ann Campbell (née Morrison). He married at Govan on 21st October 1908, when he was a merchant seaman on the SS *Laurentian* and his bride was a domestic servant at 31 White Street. She was from Lochmaddy and they had three children. Angus had enrolled in the RNR on 1st April 1904 and, after three months on battleships, was a gunnery rating at HMS *Excellent* (Whale Island) where a large number of islanders were gunners. He served during the war with HMS *Victory II*, HMS *Vernon*, HMT *Thrush II*, HMS *Excellent*, HMS *Victory I*, HMS *President III*, HMS *Cormorant*, and *Excellent* again.

John Murray
(Am Bogha)

born 29th November 1873. Age 45.

36 Lionel. Seaman RNR.
Service number 2061/C. LWM 1/LWM 8

One of the oldest servicemen lost on the *Iolaire*, John was the son of Norman and Mary Murray (née Gunn) and husband of Annie Murray (née Morrison). They had married at 8 Plantation Road, Stornoway on 7th November 1906 and had three sons and a daughter. John signed up to the RNR on 31st March 1901 and was fishing out of Stornoway and Fraserburgh pre-war. When the call came as war started, he travelled from Fraserburgh to Chatham and ten days later was posted to the Royal Naval Division from HMS *Pembroke I*. He was sent back two months later after the fall of Antwerp. He later sailed on the mine carrier HMS *John Sanderson*, at HMS *Actaeon* and HMS *Pembroke I*. His date of birth is given as 13th January 1876 in naval records and he is interred at Ness (St Peter) Old Churchyard (WG).

Roderick Morrison
(Ruairidh Chaluim Ruairidh)

born 8th April 1874. Age 44.

2 Habost, Ness. Seaman RNR.
Service number 1750/C. LWM 1/LWM 8

Another of the *Iolaire*'s veteran victims, Roddie had enrolled on 18th April 1900, when Queen Victoria still reigned. The son of Malcolm and Margaret Morrison (née Morrison), he married Gormelia Morrison (née Morrison) at the Temperance Hotel, Barvas on 8th January 1901. They had eight children. He was a fisherman at Stornoway and Peterhead pre-war and travelled from Stornoway on 12th August 1914. For the duration of the war he was based at HMS *Ganges* at Shotley, a boys' training establishment where Roddie, like John Finlay Macleod, was chosen to impart his skills to the students. Apart from their nautical studies and practice, the boys and staff completed 600 miles of anti-submarine nets during the war. The base was not left unscathed by war action, as it was bombed by a Zeppelin in 1916 and suffered food rationing shortages. Roddie was lost on his journey home on leave and his remains were interred at Ness (St Peter) Old Churchyard (WG).

Donald Murray
(Dòmhnall 'An Chailein)

born 5th October 1896. Age 22.

11 Habost, Ness. Deckhand RNR.
Service number 19804/DA. LWM 1/LWM 8

Donald was the son of John and Margaret Murray (née Mackenzie) and was single when he decided to serve his country from 19th February 1918, when at Rochester, Kent. He went to HMS *Pembroke* and then to HMY *Nairn* and was with the trawler HMT *Joseph Burgin* at the Northern Patrol depot ship HMS *Implacable* from 18th March 1918. He was interred at Ness (St Peter) Old Churchyard (WG).

Donald Macritchie
(Dòmhnall Fhionnlaigh Tharmoid Sheonaidh)

born 1st July 1898. Age 20.

34 Habost, Ness. Deckhand RNR.
Service number 13258/DA. LWM 1/LWM 8

Son of Finlay and Catherine Macritchie (née Morrison), Donald was a strapping 18-year-old of 5 feet 10 inches when, on 15th November 1916 he joined the RNR. The youth joined at Stornoway and went immediately to HMT *Scarborough*, where he remained for the duration of the war. He was interred at Ness (St Peter) Old Churchyard (WG).

Alexander John Campbell
(Ailig John 'An Duibh)

born 24th March 1898. Age 20.

41b Habost, Ness. Deckhand RNR.
Service number 11999/DA. Chatham Naval Memorial and LWM 1/LWM 8

Naval rating AJ Campbell was the one of four sons of John and Isabella Campbell (née Mackay) to die prematurely, three as war casualties. AJ enrolled in the RNR on 8th September 1916, brother Norman having died on 23rd March that year, serving with the Army. AJ was initially at Stornoway at HMS *Iolaire*, then in November 1916 he was posted to HMS *Gunner* and from that base to HMT *Royallieu*, where he served until March 1918. He then served on HMT *William Fall* and HMD *City of Perth* before HMS *Venerable* at the war's end. He was the third son to perish, as brother Murdo had also died on 19th April 1917, serving with the Army. A fourth brother, John was being treated for TB on the mainland and had a brief, bittersweet reunion with Alex John at Kyle. As a civilian, John travelled home that night on the *Sheila* and waited on the quay at Stornoway for his brother, learning of the tragedy early next morning. Sadly, young John became the fourth son to die, at home on 18th March 1920, aged 19.

Donald Macdonald
(Dòmhnall Iain Mhurchaidh Òig)
born 1st April 1891. Age 27.
13 Swainbost. Seaman RNR.
Service number 5351/A. Chatham Naval Memorial and LWM 1/LWM LWM 8

Donald was the son of John and Mary Macdonald (née Murray) and brother Murdo Snr was also serving in the RNR, and travelling with him on the *Iolaire*. Donald was fishing at Fraserburgh on the *Swallow* (INS 235) when war was declared and he

reached Chatham on 12th August 1914. He served with HMS *Arrogant*, the monitor HMS *Severn*, SS *Stamfordham*, HMS *Brilliant*, HMS *Pembroke*, HMS *Europa*, HMS *President III*, and HMS *Hannibal*. After a spell on a transport, in late 1917, he served as a naval gunner and the following year left his gun on the merchantman SS *Mandala* to return to his native island. A story handed down through the generations relates how Donald, a strong swimmer, reached the rocks but, finding that his brother was not ashore, he plunged back into the waves to try and save Murdo. Both the brothers were lost and Donald's body was not recovered.

Murdo Macdonald
(Murchadh Iain Mhurchaidh Òig)
born 15th April 1898. Age 20.
13 Swainbost. Deckhand RNR. LWM 1/LWM 8

Murdo served from 8th September 1916 and was initially stationed at HMS *Iolaire* (base) then HMS *Ganges II*, the battleship HMS *Orion* and then HMS *Wallington* from which he was in the crew of the drifter HMD *Aspire*. He sailed for home from Kyle on the *Iolaire* with his elder brother Donald, who is said to have returned into the water to try and save his brother, after making the shore himself. Neither of the men survived. Murdo's body was returned for burial but Donald's was not recovered. Their father was an Elder in the United Free Church. Murdo was interred at Ness (St Peter) Old Churchyard.

battleship HMS *Redoubtable* based at Portsmouth was his last posting. It is said that he boarded the *Sheila*, but saw his neighbour Donald Macdonald from No 13 aboard the *Iolaire* and switched vessels to join him. He had not seen him since 1914. His widowed mother and girlfriend were left to bear the news of his loss, while their neighbours mourned the loss of two sons. Calum was interred at Ness (St Peter) Old Churchyard (WG).

Malcolm Thomson

(Calum 'Mob')

born 3rd November 1890. Age 28.

14 Swainbost. Seaman RNR.
Service number 4557/A. LWM 1/LWM 8

Son of John and Christina Thomson (née Maclean), Malcolm placed his signature on the RNR recruiting form on 18th October 1912 when he was fishing out of Stornoway. He was an AB on SS *Tiger* and then SS *Princess Louise* in 1913 and 1914. When war was declared, he travelled from Glasgow to report to HMS *Excellent* then HMS *Victory I* and the armed merchant cruiser HMS *Celtic*. Before 1914 was out he was serving on HMT *Oceanic II* and after a year on her was on the minesweeping trawler HMT *Horace Stroud*. He left the trawler for a course at HMS *Excellent*, followed by DAMS training at HMS *President III* on 7th June 1917. He was at HMS *Victory I* thereafter and the old

Malcolm Macleod Jnr

(Crud)

born 26 April 1897. Age 21.

28 Swainbost. Ordinary Seaman Royal Navy.
Service number J/65506. Plymouth Naval Memorial and LWM 1/LWM 8

One of four sons of of Murdo and Christina Macleod (née Macleod), all of whom served in the war, Malcolm was not a peacetime reservist, but had been a motor driver when he originally volunteered on 28th January 1917 into the RNVR. He later became a regular sailor in the Royal Navy, for hostilities only. After training at HMS *Vivid I*, he joined the submarine depot ship HMS *Maidstone* at Harwich on 15th June 1917. His father was with the 3rd Camerons and the four brothers were all in the thick of the action. Sgt John Macleod, 2nd Seaforth Highlanders, was killed at Arras on 28th March 1918, brother Malcolm Senior survived the sinking of the depot ship *Fisgard* in 1914 and Donald was gassed while serving with the Seaforths at Ypres.

Angus Macritchie
(Aonghas Dh'll Màiri)

born 21st February 1899. Age 19.

38 Swainbost. Deckhand RNR.
Service number 16522/DA. LWM 1/LWM 8

Son of Donald and Henrietta Macritchie (née Mackenzie), Angus enrolled on 12th June 1917 and served at the RN barracks at HMS *Pembroke* in Chatham. He switched base to HMS *Attentive III* and was on the minesweeping trawler HMT *Hero* from 23rd June 1917 until his departure for New Year leave. His war had not been uneventful – on the trawler, he received a lacerated hand when the sweep wire caught him and he had also fractured his wrist on 15th December 1917, undertaking dangerous work on the wet deck. His brother John was held at Gröningen after the fall of Antwerp in 1914. Angus was interred at Ness (St Peter) Old Churchyard (WG).

Angus Gillies
(Aonghas Alasdair Iain Ghilis)

born 11th April 1889. Age 29.

35 South Dell. Seaman RNR.
Service number 4502/A. LWM 1/LWM 8

Angus was the son of Alexander and Isabella Gillies (née Mackenzie) and had two brothers in service – Donald was wounded fighting with the Seaforths and Allan was with the RNR. Angus had been fishing at Stornoway, Buckie and Macduff in the three years leading up to the war. He had enrolled with the RNR on 10th October 1912 and during the war served at the land bases HMS *Ganges*, HMS *Pembroke I*, HMS *Victory*. He was then on HMY *Verona* for three months before HM Tug *Seahorse*, where he served from 27th June 1915 with John Macdonald of Skigersta, who was also lost on the *Iolaire*. Angus was interred at Ness (St Peter) Old Churchyard (WG).

BARVAS PARISH – Borve to Shawbost: 28 men lost

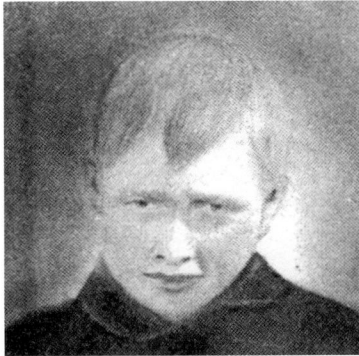

Murdo Macdonald
(Murchadh Aonghais Cùdhail, Murchadh a' Bhrot)

born 2nd October 1900. Age 18.

15 Borve. Seaman RNR
Service number 9534/A. Chatham Naval Memorial and LWM 1/LWM 9

The son of Murdo and Mary Ann Macdonald (née Graham), Murdo was one of the youngest *Iolaire* victims, having enrolled for service just after his 18th birthday on 5th October 1918. He was at Chatham, at HMS *Pembroke*, at Christmas. With several other islanders Murdo headed north in the crowded train for Inverness for his first leave. His record stated that his conduct in the RNR was 'Very Good', but it also registers a claim for money which does not seem to have been paid to the family, despite an ink stamp being placed on the record for figures to be recorded. His father Murdo also served in the RNR in the First World War. Young Murdo's body was not recovered.

Malcolm Matheson
(Calum Chaluim Dhòmhnaill)

born 10th February 1890. Age 28.

10 Upper Shader. Leading Deckhand RNR.
Service number 11907/DA. LWM 1/LWM 9

Malcolm was a son of Malcolm and Catherine Matheson (née Maciver) and his brother Alex was also in the RNR. Calum had been with the 3rd (Reserve) Battalion, but was posted to the 1st Battalion Seaforth Highlanders in France from the outset, and from December 1915 was in Mesopotamia, where he was shot in the left forearm. He had already been mentioned in despatches at Ypres and was now honourably discharged from the Persian Gulf and sent home. Malcolm did not have to join up again, but obviously felt fit to serve and joined the Royal Naval Reserve at the RNR Barracks at Stornoway on 21st August 1916. Four days later he was at HMS *Victory* and on 15th November 1916 he was posted to HMT *Iceland*. He

was a gunner on the armed trawler, which was credited with shooting down two Zeppelins in the North Sea as they headed for the English coast. He received a commendation for his actions in downing the airships and was promoted on 10th November 1917. He became a casualty of the *Iolaire* tragedy and his widowed mother was left to mourn a hero who opted to serve twice. He was interred at Barvas (St Mary) Old Churchyard (WG).

Angus Morrison

(Aonghas Chaluim Bhàin)

born 24th March 1898. Age 20.

31 Upper Shader. Deckhand RNR.
Service number 12126/DA. LWM 1/LWM 9

Angus was the son of Malcolm and
Christina Morrison (née Macdonald)
and enrolled on 26th September 1916
at the naval barracks at HMS *Iolaire*. He
reported to HMS *Pembroke* on 6th October
1916 and served at HMS *Wallington*, the
Auxiliary Patrol base at Immingham, from
11th August 1917 until the end of 1918,
sailing on HMT *St Ayles*. Brother Donald
Murdo fought with the Seaforths but
came through the ordeal on land. Angus
was interred at Barvas (St Mary) Old
Churchyard (WG).

Norman Martin

(Tormod 'An Màrtainn)

born 17 March 1876. Age 42.

8 Lower Shader. Seaman RNR.
Service number 3397/C. LWM 1/LWM 9

Norman, son of John and Margaret Martin
(née Martin), was in the war at sea from
1914. He had enrolled on 1st January
1904 as a fisherman. Six weeks later he
married Annie Smith and they had three
children when he left for Portsmouth
and HMS *Excellent* on 14th August 1914.
He served at HMS *Victory*, HMS *Colleen*,
and in the crew of HMD *Magnet II* at
HMS *Victory* in Portsmouth. Brother John
fought at the Falkland Islands and brother
Roderick was invalided home from the
RNR. Norman was interred at Barvas (St
Mary's) Churchyard (WG)

John Macdonald

('Speed' Iain Bhàin)

born 20th November 1887. Age 31.

25a Lower Shader. Deckhand RNR.
Service number 19654/DA. LWM 1/LWM9

John was the son of John and Mary (Màiri)
Macdonald (née Macleod). He enrolled in
the Royal Naval Reserve on 29th January
1918 and, after service at HMS *Vivid III*,
he was at HMS *Wallington* on the
Humber, serving on HMT *By George III*.
John was returning to the widowed mother
and an un-named girlfriend when he was
lost on 1st Januray 1919. When his body
was recovered, an engagement ring was
found in his pocket — so a poor girl wept
for him and, it is said, never married.
John was interred at Barvas (St Mary's)
Churchyard (WG).

Angus Macleay
(Aonghas Puth)

born 6th September 1880. Age 38.

38 Lower Shader. Seaman RNR.
Service number 3689/B. LWM 1/LWM 9

Angus was the son of John and Annie Macleay (née Macdonald) and first put on the RNR uniform on 1st July 1905. He married Katie Ann Martin at Barvas on 15th February 1912 and was fishing out of Stornoway pre-war and out of Peterhead in 1913. He was briefly at HMS *Excellent* before being posted for the duration of the war to the modern battleship HMS *Emperor of India*, on which several Lewismen served. Brother Donald was discharged from the RNR and brother John died while an internee at Gröningen. Angus was interred at Barvas (St Mary's) Churchyard (WG).

Donald Macleod
(Dòmhnall mac Mhurchaidh 'Ic Alasdair Ruaidh)

born 8th July 1885. Age 33.

20 Lower Barvas. Seaman RNR.
Service number 3553/B. LWM 1/LWM 24

Donald was the son of Murdo and Catherine Macleod (née Murray), and was single. He entered into the RNR on 9th July 1905 and continued to fish out of Stornoway until war was declared, when he reported to HMS *Pembroke* at Chatham. A naval gunner, he was posted to the armed merchant cruiser HMS *Orama* on 17th August 1914 and he remained with her for three years. After a brief spell back at *Pembroke* he was posted to HMS *President III*, which was a gunnery holding base for gunners on merchantmen. He was on the troopship SS *Saxonia* (a requisitioned Cunarder) at the end of the war. Donald was interred at Barvas (St Mary's) Churchyard (WG).

Norman Macleod
(Tarmod Tharmoid Choinnich)

born 7th February 1882. Age 36

13 Arnol. Seaman RNR.
Service number 3343/C. LWM 1/LWM 22

Norman was the son of Norman and Margaret (Peggie) Macleod (née Macleod), his birthdate given as February 1892 in naval records. He was married to Christina, née Murray, from 37 Arnol and they had two sons, Norman, who later emigrated to Canada, and John, who became a minister and a bard. Norman enrolled in the RNR on 1st January 1904 and was on the fishing boat *Oceans Gift* (FR 863) when war was declared. He left Fraserburgh and joined the armoured cruiser HMS *Kent*, seeing action very quickly when, on 8th December that year, she sank the German cruiser *Nurnberg* during the Battle of the Falkland Islands. On 19th March 1915 his ship took part in the destruction of the German cruiser *Dresden*, which had escaped into the

Pacific at Juan Fernandez island. Norman continued to serve on the *Kent* until 11th January 1917. He then went from HMS *Victory* to HMS *Excellent* and finished his war with HMY *Seahorse II*. His older brother John was killed on 7th October 1918, aged 40, while serving as a Corporal with the Machine Gun Corps. After the wreck of the *Iolaire*, Norman's body was found at the Braighe and he was interred in Bragar Old Churchyard and Extension (WG). His parents died in 1921 and 1925, having lost both their sons to war, and Norman's wife Christina is said to have been driven mad by grief, eventually dying at Craig Dunain Hospital, Inverness District Asylum, on 8th September 1933 aged 49.

Kenneth Macphail
(Coinneach Maois, Coinneach Chaluim Dhòmhnaill Shiaboist)

born 26th February 1891. Age 27.

24 Arnol. Seaman RNR.
Service number 3320/A. LWM 1/LWM 22

Kenneth was the son of Malcolm and Catherine Macphail (née Macleod) and enrolled in the RNR at Stornoway on 4th February 1911. He was a fisherman pre-war out of Stornoway and Fraserburgh and left the north-east port for HMS *Victory* at the call on 3rd August 1914. He was at Walmer Naval Camp by the end of the month. He served at HMS *Excellent*, then HMS *Victory* until 3rd February 1915. He was at the Dardanelles and Gallipoli landings with the pre-dreadnought battleship HMS *Prince of Wales* and was with her until 5th May 1916. After a spell at HMS *Pembroke*, he was at

HMS *President III*, attached to merchant ships as a gunner. Kenneth miraculously survived the sinking of the SS *Cambric* in the Mediterranean Sea on 31st October 1917, spending 36 hours in the water before reaching shore at Tunisia. According to villagers, Kenneth insisted that it was only 34 hours he had endured. He was originally thought to be the sole survivor, but it later transpired that four others were rescued by U-35 and became prisoners of war in Germany. Kenneth was admitted to the military hospital at Cherchell in Algeria, suffering from exposure then, on 25th November 1917, he transferred to the British Hospital at Algiers. He was last based at HMS *Pembroke* in Chatham before heading for home on what would be his last voyage, on HMY *Iolaire*. Kenneth was interred at Bragar Old Churchyard and Extension (WG). His was the last of many losses his sorrowing father had to bear – daughter Catherine died in infancy in 1894, eldest son John died of measles in 1897, aged 26, Peggy died of typhoid in 1899, aged 14, and daughter Ann died of tuberculosis in 1900, aged 21. His mother was spared the further tragedy of losing Kenneth, having died in 1917, but the father bore it all before his own death in 1922.

Donald Macdonald
(Dòmhnall Dhòmhnaill Mòr, Dhòmhnaill Tharmoid Mhurchaidh Tàilleir)

born 2nd June 1895. Age 23.

35 Arnol. Seaman RNR.
Service number 5296/A. Chatham Naval Memorial and LWM 1/LWM 22

Donald was the eldest son of Donald and Henrietta (Effie) Macdonald (née Macleod). He enrolled with the RNR on 6th December 1913 while fishing on the *Reliance* (FR646) out of Stornoway. When war became a reality, he went as a rating to HMS *Dolphin* (Gosport) and HMS *Victory* (Portsmouth). He was latterly a sailor at HMS *Vernon*, the home of the Royal Navy's Torpedo Branch at Portchester Creek near Chatham. Brother Murdo also joined the RNR, though another brother was too young to serve.

Angus Maciver
(Sùrdaidh, Aonghas Tharmoid Dhòmhnaill Tharmoid)

born 4th July 1881. Age 37.

45 Arnol. Seaman, RNR.
Service number 1855/C. LWM 1/LWM 22

Angus was the son of Norman and Catherine Maciver (née Macleod) and had married Catherine Macphail in Stornoway on 3rd March 1904. They had five children. Angus enrolled in the RNR in September 1900, when his birthdate was given as February 1880, and he re-enrolled after lapsing on 26th October 1910. He was fishing out of Stornoway pre-war. He served with HMS *Pembroke*, HMT *Agatha II*, HMS *Actaeon*, HMS *Victory*, Portland naval base, Gibraltar. Angus was hospitalised at Chatham on 6th December 1915 with seasickness and an ear infection, but recovered and served at HMS *Pembroke* for the remainder of the war. He left HMS *Pembroke* to travel for home, by rail and sea, and had his kitbag ready to disembark when the armed yacht *Iolaire* reached Stornoway. The five children were made fatherless by his drowning. He was interred at Bragar Old Churchyard and Extension (WG).

Murdo Mackay
(Murchadh Tharmoid Chaluim Fìdhleir)

born 27th December 1897. Age 21.

7 North Bragar. Deckhand RNR.
Service number 16652/DA. LWM 1/LWM 22

The middle son of Norman (An King) and Peggy Mackay (née Nicolson), Murdo was another of the young, single men stripped from the island by the loss of the *Iolaire*. Elder brother Malcolm was wounded at La Bassée with the Gordon Highlanders and the youngest brother, Angus, was in the RNR. He left for Canada post-war. Murdo enrolled, for hostilities only, on 27th June 1917 from an address at 7 Blackburn Street, Glasgow. He went to HMS *Pactolus*, then served at the Swansea auxiliary patrol base HMS *Shikari II* on HMT *Houbara* and HMD *All's Well* for the rest of the war. He was interred at Bragar Old Churchyard and Extension (WG).

Murdo Macdonald

(Murchadh Mhurchaidh Dhòmhnaill Fhìbhig)

born 21st May 1900. Age 18.

3 (Fevig) South Bragar. Deckhand RNR. Service number 20516/DA. Listed as Malcolm on the Lewis War Memorial. LWM 1/LWM 22

Son of Murdo and Annie Macdonald (née Macleod), Murdo was also young and single when he enrolled on 6th June 1918, to serve just six months before he was drowned on the shores of his home island. Murdo served at HMS *Pembroke*, HMS *Kingfisher* and HMT *Charles Chappell* when at Portsmouth, attached to HMS *Venerable*. He had four younger brothers and a sister and was interred at Bragar Old Churchyard and Extension (WG).

Murdo Maclean

(Murchadh Aonghais Iain)

born 16th January 1876. Age 42.

6a South Bragar. Seaman RNR. Service number 1903/D. LWM 1/LWM 22

Murdo was a veteran of the RNR, having enrolled on 20th July 1898. He reported for duty from Fraserburgh to HMS *Victory* on 2nd August 1914. He served on the armed merchant cruiser HMS *Carmania* until 5th June 1916, with many other Lewis Reservists, seeing action in the duel with *Cap Trafalgar*, where the German ship was sunk and the British one severely damaged. He then spent part of the war at the land bases HMS *Victory*, *Excellent* and *President III*. At the latter he became a DAMS gunner and served as a gunner on SS *Inverbervie*. On 14th September 1916, the steamer was on a voyage from Cardiff and Messina to Taranto, with a cargo of coal and three motor launches for the Royal Navy. She was torpedoed and sunk by the Austrian submarine KUK U-4, 17 miles south by west of Cape Rizuttu at the toe of Italy. Six men were lost but Murdo survived, only to be lost at war's end when the *Iolaire* foundered. Originally from 17 South Bragar, his brother John was also lost on the yacht. The son of Angus and Annie (née Macleod), he married Effie Campbell in Bragar on 31st January 1905 and they had four sons and a daughter. When Murdo's wife died, on 24th March 1971 aged 91, she had been a widow for 52 years. Murdo was interred at Bragar Old Churchyard and Extension (WG).

Malcolm Maclean
(Calum Mhurchaidh Aonghais)

born 16th November 1870. Age 48.

10 South Bragar. Seaman RNR.
Service number 2679/C. Chatham Memorial
and LWM 1/LWM 22

Malcolm's naval records give his birthdate
as 13th December 1871. Son of Murdo
and Catherine MacLean (née Macaulay),
he had four sisters and a brother, was
single and trained on HMS *Benbow* before
enrolling in the RNR on 1st October 1902.
He was fishing at Stornoway when war
broke out and he served from 2nd August
1914 at HMS *Victory*, HMS *Excellent*, HMS
Dolphin, HM Tug *Magpie* and HMS *Vernon*.
From these postings he would appear
to have been experienced in mines and
torpedoes. He received the RNR Medal for
Long Service and Good Conduct on 19th
March 1917. After his loss in the *Iolaire*
disaster, his remains were never found.

John Maclean
(Iain Aonghais Iain)

born 31st August 1881. Age 37.

17 South Bragar. Seaman RNR.
Service number 4280/B. LWM 1/LWM 22.

Son of Angus and Annie Maclean (née
Macleod), John was the husband of
Murdina, née Macleod. His birthdate
is given as 28th November 1882 when
he enrolled on 1st April 1906 and he
also had a previous record of over two
years service. He served in the RNR as
Malcolm, for reasons unknown. He was
fishing in Stornoway in the years before
war was declared and went to war from
Fraserburgh. He served at HMS *Excellent*
from 4th August 1914, HMS *Victory*, HMS
Attentive, the destroyers HMS *Nugent* and
HMS *Crusader*, and finally he was at HMS
Excellent. He was qualified in gunnery
and was mentioned in despatches on 29th
April 1915, when he was also awarded

the Italian Bronze Medal for Valour while
serving on the Tribal class destroyer
Crusader of the 6th Destroyer Flotilla
off the Belgian coast. He was interred
at Bragar Old Churchyard and Extension
(WG).

John Murray
(Iain Dhòmhnaill Mhurchaidh Dhòmhnaill
Gobha)

born 28th December 1892. Age 26.

30 South Bragar. Deckhand RNR.
Service number 4689/SD. Chatham Naval
Memorial and (LWM 1/LWM LWM 22)

Son of Donald (Breidean) and Henrietta
"Effie" Murray (née Smith), John had a
twin brother Norman who died in 1910
aged just 17. The family included five boys
and two girls, brother Angus also died at
home after serving in the war with the
RNR, on 7th May 1916, aged 26. John had
joined up on 10th April 1916 and was at
the Devonport barracks of HMS *Vivid*, his
first and only vessel HMML 461, a launch
attached to HMS *Research*, HMS *Vivid*
and HMS *Onyx*, all in the south-west of
England.

Malcolm Mackay
(Calum Dhòmhnaill Dhòmhnaill Chaluim Chaoidh)

born 10th January 1881. Age 38.

36 South Bragar. Seaman RNR.
Service number 2613/C. LWM 1/LWM 2

Calum's birthdate was given as October 1881 when he enrolled on 1st April 1902. Son of Donald (Domhnall Arnoil) and Catherine Mackay (née Campbell), he had three brothers and four sisters — sister Christina died at 22 in 1897 and 24-year-old Donald in 1903. Calum was a fisherman and worked out of Stornoway, but reported direct from Peterhead to Portsmouth on 3rd August 1914. He served at HMS *Hermione*, HMS *Excellent*, HMS *Eoropa III*, HMS *Victory I*, HM Monitor M12. Latterly he served at HMS *Imperieuse* which was an old ironclad warship, based at Scapa Flow as a receiving ship. He was married to Katie Ann, née Macleod, with whom he had five children. Katie Ann suffered further tragedy when their eldest son, Donald Malcolm, died of rheumatic fever on 29th December 1924, aged 14. Malcolm was interred at Bragar Old Churchyard and Extension (WG).

Malcolm Macdonald
(Calum Aonghais Bheàrnaraigh)

born 23rd June 1873. Age 45.

57 South Bragar. Seaman RNR.
Service number 1874/C. Chatham Naval Memorial and LWM 1/LWM 22

Malcolm's father Angus was a fisherman from Tobson, Isle of Great Bernera, who married Ann Macaulay in Bragar. Malcolm had known a life with sorrows — he was married and had two sons and a daughter to Mary, née Macdonald. She and the daughter both died in 1911. Malcolm remarried to Isabella Smith and they had a daughter, born in 1913. His mother had died in 1907 and his father also passed away in 1918. Malcolm's naval record gives 1st July 1876 as his birth date. A veteran of the RNR, he first joined on 20th September 1900 and re-enrolled on 17th November 1910. He was fishing out of Stornoway and North Shields before the war. As war became imminent he was summoned to HMS *Victory* at Portsmouth, on 2nd August 1914, then served at HMS *Excellent*, the armed merchant cruiser HMS *Celtic* off Central and South America, HMS *Victory* and the armed merchant cruiser HMS *Calgarian*. He was awarded the RNR Long Service and Good Conduct Medal aboard *Calgarian* on 27th June 1917. He survived the horrendous Halifax explosion of 6th December 1917, when the Nova Scotian town was ripped asunder by an ammunition ship explosion, and his ship *Calgarian* helped in the rescue and medical relief. He then survived *Calgarian*'s torpedoing on 1st March 1918 off Rathlin Island, when 49 men died. Malcolm ended the war on HM Tug *Magnet*, attached to HMS *Victory,* and the sea claimed him at last during his last voyage home on the *Iolaire*. His body was never found.

Donald Nicolson
(Dòmhnall an Teine, Dòmhnall Choinnich Neacail)

born 11th November 1869. Age 49.

10 North Shawbost. Deckhand RNR.
Service number 8955/DA. LWM 1/LWM 22

Donald was another veteran aboard the *Iolaire*, his birthdate given as November 1868 in naval records, which also spell his surname Nicholson. He was the son of Kenneth and Peggy Nicolson (née Macphail) and was married to Catherine, née Maclean. They had seven of a family. He enrolled in the RNR on 5th October 1910 and, when war came, travelled to HMS *Pekin*, the Auxiliary Patrol base at Grimsby. He served on HMT *Yokohama* from 30th March 1916 and on 15th January 1917 the trawler operated out of HMS *Iolaire* at Stornoway. He moved to HMS *Dreel Castle* at Falmouth and served on HMT *Walwyns Castle*. On 27th April 1918 he was at Gibraltar and was then posted to HMS *Gunner* at Granton on 6th August serving on HMY *Thomas Henrix* there. He was at HMS *Venerable* and HMS *Vivid* at Devonport where he served on HMT *Calera* before his final journey towards home on 31st December 1918. Donald was interred at Bragar Old Churchyard and Extension (WG).

Malcolm Macleod
(Calum Mhurchaidh Phàdraig Choinnich)

born 23rd June 1900. Age 18.

32 (sometimes given as 29)
North Shawbost. Seaman RNR.
Service number 20774/DA. LWM 1/LWM 22

Malcolm was the son of Murdo (Murchadh Phàdraig, Murchadh Moilean) and Catherine Macleod (née Maclean). His father was married three times and Malcolm was one of ten sons and four daughters. Malcolm's mother died in 1907 and step mother Margaret (née Maclean) in 1913. Malcolm joined the Royal Naval Reserve soon after his 18th birthday, on 9th July 1918 at Stornoway and went to HMS *Pembroke I*. After training he went to HMS *Attentive III*, from where he served on HMT *Sabreur* before departing for that last journey home. His stepmother Catherine was the person notified of Malcolm's death and, like those of other very young servicemen, his family did not receive any war gratuity or prize money. He was interred at Bragar Old Churchyard and Extension (WG). His father died in 1958. Malcolm's half brothers Roddie M and Peter were well known in political terms throughout the island and the last-born (John Murdo) was a loved traffic warden in Stornoway before his death in 2010.

Donald Macleod
(Dòmhnall Phàdraig Dhòmhnaill Choinnich)

born 14th September 1896. Age 22.

38 North Shawbost. Deckhand RNR.
Service number 4125/SD. LWM 1/LWM 22

Donald was the son of Peter Angus (Pàidean) and Christina Macleod (née Gillies). The mother had died in 1914 and he had two sisters, Katie Bell and Chrissie Mary and a brother, Peter Angus. He had enrolled on 11th February 1916 and was at HMS *Pembroke* and HMS *Actaeon* until 7th November 1916. He sailed on HMD *Beatrice* which had HMD *City of Perth* as her base ship. Donald's remains were recovered and interred at Bragar Old Churchyard and Extension (WG). His father died in 1944 in his 85th year.

Donald Macleod
(Dòmhnall Tharmoid 'An 'Ic Dhòmhnaill Bhig)

born 18th July 1898. Age 20.

5 South Shawbost. Deckhand RNR. Service number 4944/SD. LWM 1/LWM 22

Son of Norman and Effie Macleod (née Smith), Donald was one of a family of nine — younger brother Murdo John was well known as a local Gaelic bard. Donald enrolled on 11th February 1916 and reported at HMS *Pembroke*. He went to sea on HMT *Harvest Moon* on 23rd April 1916 when based with HMS *Actaeon* at Sheerness. He then was in the crew of HMT *Beatrice II*, followed by HMT *City of Perth* and his last vessel, the minesweeper HMT *Sesostris*, a requisitioned Grimsby trawler. His elder brother John was wounded in the left arm when serving in Mesopotamia as a Corporal with the 1st Seaforths. Donald was interred at Bragar Old Churchyard and Extension (WG).

Angus Macleod
(Aonghas Phàdraig Aonghais Phàdraig)

born 12th November 1866. Age 52.

11 South Shawbost. Seaman RNR. Service number 2020/D. Chatham Naval Memorial and LWM 1/LWM 22

Son of Peter and Catherine Macleod (née Macaulay), Angus was one of the oldest men aboard the *Iolaire*, and was a single man. His parents predeceased him in 1914 and 1895. His naval record gives his birthdate as 1st November 1873. He first enrolled on 11th August 1898 and was a fisherman before the war at Stornoway and at the north-east ports of Peterhead, Buckie, Macduff and Aberdeen. When war began he served at HMS *Victory* at Portsmouth until 24th November 1914. He moved to HMS *Halcyon* at Lowestoft for two weeks, then HMS *Columbine* at Rosyth. From the same base he served on the store carrier HMS *Stephen Furness* and then moved to HMS *Thalia* at Cromarty, an armed boarding steamer. Angus served on her there until 30th April 1917 and, in December, was at the training school at HMS *Vernon*, from where he headed for home. His body was never recovered from the seas of his home island after his death in the *Iolaire* tragedy.

John Smith
(Iain 'An Fhionnlaigh)

born 14th April 1881. Age 37.

11 South Shawbost. Seaman RNR. Service number 3516/B. LWM 1/LWM 22

John was a fisherman at Buckie, Fraserburgh and Stornoway prior to the war. His parents were John and Mary Smith (née Campbell) from 14 North Bragar and he was the husband of Catherine Marion (Kate), née Macleod. They had four children. From Fraserburgh he reported to HMS *Pembroke* and HMS *Ganges* in the early months of the war. The armed boarding steamer HMS *Duchess of Devonshire* was his first and only posting — he served with her from 18th November 1914 for the length of the conflict. His wife lived nearly 50 years as a widow before her death in 1967. John was an uncle of the "Safety" family who had a huge academic, public service and footballing reputation on the island in the years that followed. He was interred at Bragar Old Churchyard and Extension (WG).

Roderick Murray
(Ruaraidh Dhòmhnaill Ruaridh)

born 25th April 1899. Age 19.

25 South Shawbost. Ordinary Seaman
Royal Navy.
Service number J/86329. LWM 1/LWM 22

An Ordinary Seaman, Roddie was not a
reservist and enlisted on 4th March 1918
for hostilities only, as a regular sailor. Son
of Donald (Gusaidh) and Mary Murray (née
Macleod). Roddie was a furnaceman when
he volunteered. He served at HMS *Vivid I* at
Devonport, then from 18th August he was
one of 655 crewmen with the Devonshire
class cruiser HMS *Roxburgh*. He was interred
at Bragar Old Churchyard and Extension
(WG). His father died in 1922 and his mother
passed away in 1940. Roddie's brother
Donald married a daughter of the Harris
Tweed firm of Kenneth Macleod, Shawbost
and their two sons continued with the mill,
now run by Harris Tweed Hebrides. Donald
was in command of the local Home Guard in
the Second World War.

Donald William Gillies
(Dòmhnall Uilleam Aonghais Aonghais
Ghiolais)

born 24th November 1888. Age 30.

30 South Shawbost. Seaman RNR.
Service number 3309/A. LWM 1/LWM 22

Donald was the youngest son of Angus
and Mary Gillies (née Morrison), who
had a family of six boys and three girls.
Brother Malcolm was an RNR Petty
Officer and later became a minister.
Donald enrolled with the RNR on 2nd
February 1911 and was fishing out of
Stornoway between that time and the
outbreak of war. After fighting with the
Hawke Battalion of the RN Division, he
was at the Crystal Palace Depot, from
where he served with HMS *Vivid*, HMS
Caribbean, HMS *Orama*, HMS *Victorian*,
HMS *President*, HMS *Pembroke* and
then was aboard the aircraft carrier
HMS *Campania*. He was among the
rescued crew on 5th November 1918 off
Burntisland, near Rosyth, when a Force
10 squall forced her to drag anchor and
collide with the battleship HMS *Royal Oak*.
Her hull was damaged and flooded and
the converted liner sank five hours later.
After that experience Donald finished the
war at Chatham at HMS *Pembroke*. He
was interred at Bragar Old Churchyard
and Extension (WG). Donald's father
received his 1914 Star on his behalf on
3rd December 1919. His mother died the
following year.

Donald John Murray
(Dòmhnall Iain Iain Choinnich)

born 12th June 1878. Age 40.

43a South Shawbost. Petty Officer, RNR.
Service number 2811/B. LWM 1/LWM 22

Donald was the son of John and Mary
Murray (née Maclennan) and had four
brothers and a sister. Husband of Murdina,
née Maclean, Donald had four children
living when he went away to war. The
couple had lost three sons in early
childhood between 1911 and 1915 – They
were Angus Senior (27th February 1911),
aged 8, Angus Junior (26th February
1914), aged 2 and Kenneth John (24th
March 1915) aged 13 months. Donald
John enrolled in the RNR on 1st January
1905, after being in the service briefly
in 1901. He went to work in Canada for
about a year, returning to the island in
1911. He fished out of Stornoway and
Fraserburgh and reported to Stornoway
immediately on 4th August 1914. Five days
later he was at Scapa Flow and served
there on fleet repair ships, including at
HMS *Imperieuse* for much of the war. He
became a Leading Seaman on 22nd June
1917 and a Petty Officer on 29th November
1917. Brother Kenneth John died on 20th
December 1915, also aged 40, serving with
the 2nd Battalion Seaforth Highlanders.
Donald John was interred at Bragar Old
Churchyard and Extension (WG).

UIG PARISH – East Uig: 9 men lost

John Macaskill
(Iain a' Bhucaich)

born 7th February 1899. Age 19.

3 Kirvick. Deckhand RNR.
Service number 14567/DA. LWM 1/LWM 10

Son of Donald and Maggie Macaskill
(née Maclean), John was born at Kirvick
and enrolled with the RNR on 8th
February 1917. He served with HMS *Iolaire*
(base) initially, then HMS *Pembroke*,
HMS *Halcyon II*, HMD *Maggie Jessie*,
HMS *Thalia*, HMT *Sir John French*, HMS
Kingfisher and, in his last months, on the
new non-standard Strath Class trawler
HMT *Sir John Fitzgerald*. Brother Donald
was wounded in France fighting with the
Seaforths and was also in Greece. John
was interred at Dalmore Cemetery (WG).

John Macleod
(Iain Stuaman)

born 7th March 1899. Age 19.

6 Kirvick. Deckhand RNR.
Service number 19980/DA. LWM 1/LWM 10

Young John lived his life in parallel with
his neighbour and schoolfriend John
Macaskill, born just one month before him
in the last year of the 19th century and
lost in the wreck of the *Iolaire* on the same
night in 1919. He was the son of Malcolm
and Mary Macleod (née Macarthur), joined
the forces six weeks after his neighbour
on 19th March 1918 and went, like him,
to HMS *Pembroke I*. He then went to HMS
Gunner and served on the Hunt class
minesweeper HMS *Hambledon*. He also
served on the brand-new HMT *Henry
Butcher* from HMS *Implacable*. After the
wreck of the *Iolaire*, his family did not
immediately realise he had been lost, as
he had visited his sister in Glasgow on
the way home and the family thought he
had rejoined his ship. He was interred at
Dalmore Cemetery (WG).

Donald Macarthur
(Dòmhnall Bell)

born 12th November 1884. Age 34.

12 Kirvick. Deckhand RNR.
Service number 4443/SD. Chatham Naval
Memorial and LWM 1/LWM 10

Son of Malcolm and Isabella Macarthur
(née Mackay), Donald was married to
Jane, née Maclean. Donald enrolled
on 13th March 1916 and served at HMS
Attentive, HMS *Vivid*, HMS *Attentive
III*, HMS *Thalia* and with HMT *Thomas
Bird*, joining the trawler on 29th August
1917. Like John Macleod at No 6, he saw
latter service with HMS *Implacable*, a
pre-dreadnought battleship. As his body
was not recovered, his widowed mother
and wife had no grave to visit.

Norman Macphail
(Tarmod Boyce)

born 19th December 1881. Age 37.

32b Knock Carloway. Deckhand RNR.
Service number 14663/DA. LWM 1/LWM 10

Son of Norman and Ann Macphail (née
Macleod) of 13 Doune, Norman was
married to Maggie (née Macleod, 4 Park
Carloway.) His birthdate was given as
December 1886 when he enrolled to
serve at sea on 14th February 1917 at
the RNR Barracks at Stornoway. He left
there for HMS *Pembroke* and was posted
to HMS *Thalia* at Cromarty. He was at
HMS *Victory* until 12th September 1917,
then went aboard HMT *James Berry* and
HMT *James Bentole* during 1918. He left
HMS *Venerable* at Portsmouth to travel
home with his two brothers, John and
Angus from 13 Doune, who both survived
the tragedy that was the *Iolaire*. He was
interred at Dalmore Cemetery (WG).

Donald Macphail
(Dòmhnall Beag)

born 5th December 1874. Age 44.

11 Borrowston. Seaman RNR.
Service number 2222/D. LWM 1/LWM 10

The son of Donald and Marion Macphail
(née Macleod), Donald was married to
Mary, (née Mackay) and they had five
children. Naval records give his birth date
as January 1874. Donald had enrolled in
the RNR on 29th March 1899 and had
nearly 20 years service. He reported
to HMS *Pembroke* from Peterhead via
Stornoway, on 14th August 1914, and eight
months later joined the aircraft carrier
HMS *Campania*, staying with her until she
was sunk in a collision on 6th November
1918. Donald left the Chatham barracks
at HMS *Pembroke* for his first New Year of
peacetime and never reached his home.
He was interred at Dalmore Cemetery
(WG).

Murdo Mackenzie
(Murchadh Shuigeart)

born 20th April 1880. Age 38.

15 Garenin. Seaman RNR.
Service number 2793/C. LWM 1/LWM 10

Murdo joined HMS *Benbow* for training on 2nd
October 1902, and his date of enrolment in the
RNR is given as 1st January 1903. Son of John
and Christina Mackenzie (née Macdonald)
and married to Christina, he also had three
brothers in the RNR – Norman, John and
Donald. Donald fought at Antwerp and was
interned at Gröningen. Murdo left Stornoway
on 2nd August 1914 and was serving on the
armed merchant cruiser HMS *Macedonia* five
days later. He moved to the armed merchant
cruiser HMS *Princess*, a German prize taken
in 1914, on 7th August 1917 and served on her
off South and East Africa. He served with HMS
Pembroke thereafter and *President III* from 8th
May 1918, after qualifying as a naval gunner
on three pounders and Vickers machine guns.
He was returning home from SS *Carena* for
the New Year when the sinking of the *Iolaire*
ended his life. He was interred at Dalmore
Cemetery (WG).

Alexander Angus Macleod
(Ailig Angaidh a' Bhuanna)

born 22nd June 1898. Age 20.

28 Tolsta Chaolais. Deckhand RNR.
Service number number 3455/SD.
Chatham Naval Memorial and LWM 1/
LWM 11

Alex Angus was the son of Alexander and
Annie Macleod (née Macleod) and lived
with his parents and brother Norman at
Tealabhal, Tolsta Chaolais before they
settled in Stornoway. His birthdate was
given as 4th June 1896 when he enrolled
on 23rd November 1915. He served on HMY
Sabrina and had been serving at Milford
Haven, at the auxiliary patrol base HMS
Idaho, when he was amongst those lost on
the Iolaire. His body was never recovered.
Their mother was spared the tragedy of his
loss as she had died in February 1917.

Malcolm Maciver
(Calum Nèill Chaluim)

born 19th January 1885. Age 33.

40 Breasclete. Seaman RNR.
Service number 2778/A. LWM 1/LWM 23

Malcolm was the son of Neil and Chirsty
Maciver (née Macaulay) and was single.
He enrolled on 11th July 1910, his address
then 7 Garden Road, Stornoway and his
birth date given as 19th January 1889.
He fished out of Peterhead, Kirkwall,
Stornoway, Fraserburgh and Blyth
pre-war, all on Banff and Peterhead
boats. During the war he served with HMS
Excellent, HMS Victory, HMS Zaria, HMS
Hermione, the armed merchant cruiser
HMS Carmania, and he had just left the
armed merchant cruiser HMS Kildonan
Castle to be posted to HMS Victory at
Portsmouth on 28th December 1918 when
his leave was due. He was interred at
Dalmore Cemetery (WG).

Donald Macdonald
(Dòmhnall Lisidh Alasdair Iain)

born 29th April 1898. Age 20.

44 Breasclete. Leading Deckhand RNR.
Service number 12453/DA. LWM 1/LWM 23

Donald was the son of Alexander and
Effie Macdonald (née Maclean). On 9th
October 1916, Donald enrolled with the
RNR and served on the drifters HMD
Sunbeam II and HMD White Oak based
at HMS Kingfisher. He also served and
qualified as a DAMS gunner at HMS
Victory, HMS Excellent and HMS Gunner.
He had already survived one sinking
during the war, as a gunner on SS
Dartmoor, sailing from Bone to Garston,
Liverpool via Gibraltar when she was
sunk by UC-50 on 17th May 1917. The
Dartmooor, laden with iron ore, went
down 35 miles south-east of Fastnet.
A total of 25 crew, including four Barra
seamen, died but Donald was among the

UIG PARISH – West Uig: 14 men lost

survivors. HMS *Pembroke* was the last base for young Dòmhnall Lisidh, who was lost as he headed for home on the *Iolaire*. He is said to have been seen by a Macphail boy from Tolsta Chaolais on the rope, but he lost his grip and went under. Donald was interred at Dalmore Cemetery (WG).

John Mackenzie Snr
(An t-Olach)

born 15th March 1879. Age 39.

8 Breacleit, Isle of Great Bernera.
Seaman RNR.
Service number 2038/C. Chatham Naval Memorial and LWM 1/LWM 12

John was born at Croir in Bernera, the son of Malcolm and Annie Mackenzie (née Macphail), He was the husband of Mary, née Macdonald and they had one daughter, Catherine. He was a fisherman on SY378 pre-war. He first served as a reservist on 2nd April 1901, when his birthdate was recorded as 15th April 1880 in naval records. He went from Stornoway to HMS *Pembroke* on 2nd August 1914, then was with HMT *Olivine*, and HMS *Actaeon*, before serving at HMS *Victory* at Chatham when he received his last New Year leave. His brother John Jnr was a prisoner in Germany after fighting in Seaforths colours. John's body was not recovered.

Donald Macaulay
(Dòmhnall 'An Sheòrais)

born 27th May 1897. Age 21.

4 Hacklete, Isle of Great Bernera.
Deckhand RNR.
Service number 2658/SD. LWM 1/LWM 12

Donald was the third son of John and Christina Macaulay (née Macdonald), his mother already a widow. Donald enrolled on 24th August 1915 and served with HMS *Sir Redvers Buller*, HMS *Pembroke I*, HMS *President*, HMS *Gunner*, HMS *Ganges*, HMT *Nellie Dodds*, HMT *John Bell* and HMS *Implacable*. He had also served on the requisitioned trawler HMT *Max Pemberton*, (H563), before his journey towards home began. His remains were interred at Bosta Cemetery (WG). Of his three brothers, John was killed with the 2nd Battalion, Seaforth Highlanders at St Julien on 25th April 1915 aged 23, Neil was wounded in France, then served in Mesopotamia and was wounded again at Basra, but returned home and lived to be 80. George, another brother of Donald, also served with the RNR.

Donald Macdonald Snr
(Dòmhnall Ruadh)

born 14th October 1882. Age 36.

13 Tobson, Isle of Great Bernera.
Leading Seaman RNR.
Service number 2688/B. Chatham Naval
Memorial and LWM 1/LWM 12

Son of Angus and Mary Macdonald (née Macdonald) and husband of Catherine, née Macdonald, from 4 Tobson, Donald had a young son and a daughter. He enrolled with the RNR on New Year's Day 1905, fished out of Stornoway pre-war and was called to duty on 3rd August 1914. Donald served at HMS *Pembroke* from 5th August 1914, was promoted on 20th January 1915 and then was with HMT *Island Prince*, before spending the majority of the war at Shotley with HMS *Ganges*. Donald had four brothers serving in the Great War, one was torpedoed, one wounded and one (Donald Junior) interned. Donald's loss on HMY *Iolaire* was doubly tragic – his wife Catherine had passed away from TB on 4th April 1914 aged 32, so his death in the wreck of the *Iolaire* left his two children orphans. His mother and sister Mary were able to bring them up, but daughter Mary herself died on 29th January 1921. Donald's son Angus was only 30 when he, too, drowned in the North Atlantic, as minesweeper HMT *Northern Princess* was torpedoed on 7th March 1942.

Kenneth Smith
(Coinneach Iain Mhoireach Mhurchaidh)

born 6th September 1875. Age 43.

1 Earshader. Seaman RNR.
Service number 1620/C. LWM 1/LWM 12

Kenneth was the son of John and Marion Smith (née Smith), husband of Christina, née Mackay, and left a son and daughter. He joined the RNR on 29th March 1900 and left for Chatham, with so many other islanders, on 3rd August 1914. He was at HMS *Pembroke* until 14th December 1915, then he was posted to HMS *Iolaire* where he remained until 16th December 1917. He returned to *Pembroke* for four months, then was posted to the Chatham base until 9th June 1918. His last few months were spent with the mine carrier HMS *Cove*. After his loss on the *Iolaire*, his belongings were recovered from the debris-strewn shore and found to include presents for his family – a silk handkerchief, silk cloth and toys from Gibraltar. Kenneth was interred at Bosta Cemetery on the Isle of Great Bernera (WG). Kenneth's death cast a shadow over his family which lasted over 90 years. His son Kenneth, who served in the RNR in the second war, wrote a poem about the sinking, *Fir Threin na h'Iolaire* (1978). Daughter Mòr was the last survivor of the children left fatherless by the disaster. She attended the 90th Anniversary Service at the *Iolaire* monument in 2009. Kenneth's wife Christina, who died on 15th October 1980 aged 92, was also believed to be the last of the *Iolaire* widows.

John Macleod
(Seocan a' Ghobha)

born 7th May 1898. Age 20.

17 Uigen. Deckhand RNR.
Service number 44351/SD. LWM 1/LWM 13

John was the son of Murdo and Ann Macleod (née Smith) and enrolled on 11th March 1916. He travelled from Stornoway to HMS *Victory* and was transferred to the trawler section on 1st October 1916. He served on the 37-ton launch HMML 502, doing coastal minesweeping and anti-submarine duties. He spent all his war days with her, as she was moved around from HMS *Eaglet* (Liverpool), to HMS *Nesmar II* (Oban) and then HMS *Vivid* (Devonport). He was interred at Old Valtos Burial Ground (WG).

Angus Matheson
(Aonghas Chàdham)

born 11th September 1899. Age 19.

18 Uigen. Deckhand RNR.
Service number 18694/DA. LWM 1/LWM 13

Angus was the son of Malcolm and Catherine Matheson (née Morrison) and was single when he joined the service soon after his 18th birthday, on 24th October 1917 at HMS *Iolaire* (Depot). He went to HMS *Brilliant* on 18th November 1917 and served on the trawler *Beluga*, which moved base to HMS *Attentive III* at Dover on 8th March 1918. He also served on HMD *Winner* before returning for his New Year Leave. Aonghas Chàdham was lost to the tiny village, along with his neighbour John Macleod, when the yacht *Iolaire* foundered. Both were interred at Old Valtos Burial Ground, Angus at (WG).

Murdo Nicolson Jnr
(Murchadh Beag Dhòmhnaill 'Ic Mhurchaidh)

born 7th June 1897. Age 21.

1 Crowlista. Deckhand RNR.
Service number 4258/SD. Chatham Naval Memorial and LWM 1/LWM 13

Murdo was one of a family of eight boys and four girls born to Donald and Catherine Nicolson (née Macaulay). He was a younger brother of Donald Nicolson, Seaforth Highlanders, who was wounded in action and died in hospital in France on 8th August 1917 aged 26. Of his other brothers, Murdo Snr was also in the RNR, Kenneth was interned in Holland and Norman was with the Royal Engineers. Murdo Jr served on HMML 10, before his final leave took him to the *Iolaire*. Sister Marion was at home when news of his loss came. In 2017 Murdo's war medals were sold by a dealer in Wales, were bought by one of the authors of this book and returned home to the island for good. They must have reached Wales with Murdo's elder sister, Chirsty Anna Scott, who lived in Wales and had no surviving children.

Angus Macdonald

(Aonghas 'Ain Dhuibh)

born 16th October 1887. Age 31.

6 Crowlista. Seaman RNR.
Service number 4554/A. LWM 1/LWM 13

Angus was the son of John and Annie Macdonald (née Macleod) and served with the RNR from 15th October 1912. He fished out of Stornoway and Peterhead pre-war. He served with HMS *Victory*, HMS *Excellent* and in 1918 was in the crew of the cruiser HMS *Kent*. His last posting before Christmas 1918 was at HMS *Excellent*. Brother Hector was severely wounded with the Seaforths but Roderick (RNR) and Donald (RAMC) came through unscathed. Angus was interred at Ardroil Cemetery (WG).

Ewen Macdonald

(Eoghain Sheorais)

born 8th March 1900. Age 18.

13 Crowlista. Deckhand RNR.
Service number 19896/DA. LWM 1/LWM 13

Ewen was born to Christina Ann (Chirsty) Macdonald at Callanish and she later moved to Islivig, but Ewen was brought up by his uncle Malcolm and aunt Dolina Macleod at Crowlista. They had five daughters and four sons of their own. He enrolled as soon as he was 18, on 26th March 1918, and was drowned on the *Iolaire* before he reached the age of 19. He had served at HMS *Pembroke* and HMS *Pactolus* and was part of an 18-man crew on the new Strath Class trawler HMT *John Gray*. He was interred at Ardroil Cemetery (WG).

Malcolm Mackay

(Calum Ruadh Dhòmhnaill Nèill)

born 4th November 1892. Age 26.

14b Crowlista. Seaman RNR.
Service number 7699/A. LWM 1/LWM 13

Son of Donald and Margaret Mackay (née Maclean), Malcolm signed up on 1st February 1915 and reported to HMS *Pembroke*. He was posted to the aircraft carrier/seaplane tender HMS *Campania* when she was commissioned on 17th April 1915 and was still with her five days before the Armistice when, on 5th November 1918, she dragged her anchor during a squall in the Firth of Forth, hit the bow of the battleship HMS *Royal Oak* and sank five hours later. All the crew were taken off safely. Malcolm moved to HMS *Pembroke* at Chatham, from where he set out for home on 31st December. After the sinking of the *Iolaire*, it was two weeks before his body was recovered. He was interred at Ardroil Cemetery (WG). His medals are with his great-nephew in Fortrose.

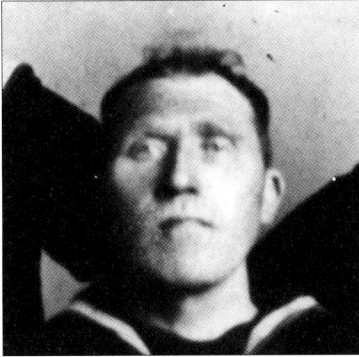

John Macdonald
(Iain Aonghais Mhòir)

born 3rd December 1873. Age 45.

16 Crowlista. Leading Seaman RNR.
Service number 2554/C. Chatham Naval
Memorial and LWM 1/LWM 13

John was the son of Angus and Flora
Macdonald (née Maciver) and married to
Rachel, née Nicolson. His parents died
before the war, on 6th January 1913 and
13th January 1910. John had enrolled with
the RNR at Stornoway on 1st April 1902
and he was called to war from fishing at
Stornoway, on 12th August 1914. He was
at HMS *Pembroke* for a fortnight, then
spent the entire war at Dover based at
HMS *Arrogant*, an old cruiser, converted
as a depot ship for motor launches and
submarines of the Dover patrol. John
was promoted to Leading Seaman on
31st December 1917 and worked on motor
launches operating from the cruiser. His
last launch before leaving for home was
HMML 10. His wife Rachel was doubly
bereaved, becoming a widow and losing

her brother Murdo (1 Crowlista) on that
dreadful night. Their daughter Joanna was
born on 10th February 1919, six weeks
after her father's death.

Peter Buchanan
(Pàdraig Dhòmhnaill Chaoil)

born 23rd January 1886. Age 32.

23 Crowlista. Seaman RNR.
Service number 7700/A. Chatham Naval
Memorial and LWM 1/LWM 13

Peter was the son of Donald and Chirsty
Buchanan (née Mackay) and was a single
man. A fisherman, he enrolled in the
RNR on 1st February 1915 and served at
HMS *Arrogant*, then the battleship HMS
Hindustan with the Grand Fleet before
becoming a gunner attached to HMS
President III during the war. He was lost
on the *Iolaire* after leaving the Chatham
base of HMS *Pembroke*. Kenneth, his
brother, also gave the RNR his service.

Murdo Mackinnon
(Murchadh Cheidhein)

born 26th July 1900. Age 18.

18 Breanish. Deckhand RNR.
Service number 21209/DA. LWM 13

Son of Cain and Christina Mackinnon (née
Buchanan), Murdo had been working at
Mangersta Farm for John Mitchell until
he enrolled on 13th August 1918. After
initial training at HMS *Pembroke I*, he was
serving on HMD *Eddy* at the war's end.
His body and that of his fellow villager
were taken home by George's brother John
on a horse and cart. Murdo was one of
the *Iolaire*'s youngest victims at just 18
years and six months old, single and now
interred at Ardroil Cemetery (WG). His
father and brother Angus were among four
fishermen drowned off Mealasta in 1932.

Roll call of the lost

George Morrison
(Seòras Chèisein)

born 6th November 1898. Age 20.

20 Breanish. Deckhand RNR.
Service number 3499/SD. LWM 1/LWM 13

Son of John and Marion Morrison (née Macleod), George's birthdate was given as 27th September 1895 in naval records, meaning he seemed old enough when he joined the RNR on 25th November 1915, aged just 17. He went from Inverness to HMS *Victory* and on 1st October 1916 transferred into the Trawler Section. He was serving aboard HMMLs 121 and 119 at HMS *Actaeon* and at HMS *Thames* until 22nd February 1917. He was with HMMLs 119 and 250 at HMS *Victory*, HMS *Actaeon* and HMS *Pembroke*. On 13th October 1918 he was with HMML 260 at HMS *Hermione* and was at HMS *Victory* serving on HMML 307 before he packed his kitbag for the last time. He was interred at Ardroil Cemetery. His commanding officer wrote to his parents, expressing the esteem George was held in and offering the condolences of all the crew.

John Macdonald
(Seonaidh MhicGeoch)

born 17th September 1879. Age 39.

1b North Tolsta. Seaman RNR.
Service number 3339/B. LWM 1/LWM 14

John was the son of John and Marion Macdonald (née Mackay), and a widower after his wife Catherine died of tuberculosis on 9th May 1915, aged 33. A daughter, Catherine, had just been born at the time and John's own death on HMY *Iolaire* left her and three other children orphaned. John was from No 16 originally and had already served with the 3rd Battalion Seaforth Highlanders, doing garrison duty in Cairo during the Boer War, where he was one of 26 Tolstonians serving in a battalion made up almost entirely of Lewismen. He enrolled with the RNR on 1st April 1905 and fished out of Stornoway for several years before the war. He went to HMS *Excellent* on mobilisation and served on the battleship HMS *Emperor of India* from 10th October

1916 until war's end. He was interred at Tolsta Cemetery (WG). His children spent the war with their grandparents, who also suffered the grief of losing six-year-old daughter Mary to tuberculosis, a month after her father's death.

Donald Macleod
(Mac Dhòmhnaill Iain Saighdeir)

born 1st July 1897. Age 21.

3b North Tolsta. Deckhand RNR.
Service number 3968/SD. LWM 1/LWM 14

Eldest son of Donald and Ann Macleod (née Macleod), who died young before the war began, Donald had also lost a younger brother John, who had died of TB at Lewis Hospital in December 1914, aged 14. Donald served for nearly three years after enrolling on 17th January 1916. He was at the bases at Chatham and Portsmouth (HMS *Pembroke* and HMS *Victory*) before serving on HMML 180 then HMML 148. He was with HMS *Osiris I*, HMS *Eoropa*, HMY *Valhalla II*, HMY *St George* and finally HMS *Victory I*. He was interred at Tolsta Cemetery (WG). Youngest brother Norman (known locally as Tormod Peigi) was left without parents or brothers.

11 men lost

John Morrison
(Iain Choinnich Iain Moireasdain)

born 19th June 1892. Age 26.

8 North Tolsta. Seaman RNR.
Service number 4645/A. LWM 1/LWM 14

John was the only son of Kenneth and Mary Morrison (née Macleod) and had five sisters. He showed his willingness to serve when he signed up on 2nd December 1912 as a fisherman at Stornoway and Wick. At the outset of the war John travelled from Banff to HMS *Victory*, then served with the Drake Battalion of the RN Division from 16th September until 27th October 1914, when he was discharged back to serve at sea from Portsmouth. His first ship was the armed boarding steamer HMS *Partridge* and he served on her until 18th March 1918. She was used as a fleet messenger originally and became *Partridge II* in 1916. When the transatlantic passenger ship *Lusitania* was sunk, in May 1915, the *Partridge* was signalled to help and, while they were lowering a lifeboat,

John fell out and was almost drowned. His fellow villager Donald Murray, who served together with him throughout the war and who survived the *Iolaire*, recounted that event and recalled that they did not save any of the *Lusitania*'s survivors. John's last posting was HMS *Venerable* on 19th March 1918. He was interred at Tolsta Cemetery (WG) and his medals, including the 1914 Star, were presented to his father on 6th February 1920.

Donald Maciver
(Dòmhnall Red)

born 13th April 1892. Age 26.

38b North Tolsta. Deckhand RNR.
Service number 18720/DA. LWM 1/LWM 14

Son of Kenneth (Coinneach Ruadh) and Annie Maciver (née Macdonald), Donald's brother Murdo also served with the RNR and they had five sisters. Donald enrolled for hostilities only on 9th October 1917

and served at HMS *Pembroke*, HMT *Glen Boyne*, and lastly on the requisitioned trawler HMT *Iranian*, which was based at HMS *Attentive III* at Dover. Donald was interred at Tolsta Cemetery (WG). Murdo wrote to the naval authorities towards the end of 1919 to tell them that his brother's War Gratuity had not been paid — it was paid on 27th February 1920. Donald was interred at Tolsta Cemetery.

Donald Campbell
(Dòmhnall Eachainn)

born 15th June 1872. Age 46.

44a North Tolsta. Seaman RNR.
Service number 3356/B. Chatham Naval Memorial and LWM 1/LWM 14

Donald's date of birth is also given as December 1873 and 20th June 1873 in naval records. He was the son of Hector and Catherine Campbell (née Macrae), and husband of Catherine (Catriona). A veteran RNR man, he had enlisted on 1st January 1905. He served during the war with the battleship HMS *Triumph*, HMS *Tamar* at Hong Kong, the sloop HMS *Cadmus*, HMS *Victory* and HMS *Excellent* at Portsmouth and as a DAMS gunner attached to HMS *President III*, before going back to *Victory*. His remains were not recovered.

Kenny was a fisherman pre-war, sailing from Stornoway and Lowestoft. He enrolled at Stornoway on 7th January 1913 and was called to Portsmouth on 2nd August 1914. He served briefly at the shore bases HMS *Dolphin* and HMS *Victory*, then he was for four years on the light cruiser HMS *Galatea*, which was the first ship to see action at Jutland. Kenneth was interred at Tolsta Cemetery (WG).

Evander Murray
(Ìomhair Iain Sheòrais)

born 12th August 1873. Age 45.

45a North Tolsta. Seaman RNR.
Service number 1829/D. LWM 1/LWM 14

Eldest son of John and Margaret Murray (née Maciver) Evander was the husband of Margaret, née Morrison. He joined the RNR on 20th November 1897 and fished out of Stornoway before the war. He arrived at HMS *Victory* on 4th August 1914 and went to Fort Blockhouse, at HMS *Dolphin* in Portsmouth, on 18th August. He was there until 8th October 1918, after which he served on the submarine depot ship HMS *Thames*, an old cruiser stationed at Harwich. He was awarded the RNR Long Service and Good Conduct Medal on 27th January 1917. His brothers Murdo and George also gave service to the Admiralty as naval reserves. Evander had previously been married to Margaret, née Macleod, who died of cancer on 7th May 1914 aged 38, so daughter Catherine, aged 18, was orphaned when her father drowned on the *Iolaire*. He was interred at Tolsta Cemetery (WG).

Kenneth Campbell
(Coinneach Iain Iain Bhàin, Peatair)

born 28th January 1889. Age 29.

54 North Tolsta. Seaman RNR.
Service number 4804/A. LWM 1/LWM 14

Son of John and Isabella Campbell (née Graham), Kenny was one of the Campbell brothers of No. 54 who held a record, in that all seven served with the Royal Naval Reserve during the war. Their mother was asked to choose a son to keep at home, but could not choose between them – and so all seven went away. King George V sent a personal letter to the widowed mother for the contribution being made by her family to the war. Murdo 'Crùbaidh', Torquil Mòr, John 'Horrigan' and John 'Dodds' survived, but Donald 'Sùill' was lost on 22nd July 1917, Angus 'Schlang' was lost on 29th May 1918 and Kenny perished on January 1st 1919 on the *Iolaire*. Kenny was married to Mary Campbell (née Murray) from number 30, where they lived with their children. A strapping six-footer,

Donald Macleod
(Dòmhnall Ghabhsainn)

born 20th October 1887. Age 31.

58 North Tolsta. Seaman RNR.
Service number 3329A. LWM 1/LWM 14

Tragedy was doubled at No 58, where parents Malcolm and Mary Macleod (née Maciver) learnt that they had lost two sons on the night the *Iolaire* went down. Donald enrolled on 6th February 1911 and fished out of Buckie, Stornoway,

Lossiemouth, Great Yarmouth, Fraserburgh and Wick before the war. He became a Christian just before the war commenced. He reported to HMS *Victory* on 2nd August 1914 and was among the boys of the naval division sent to try and protect Antwerp, where he was at the end of a bridge when a German shell blew up the other end, trapping many of his colleagues in Holland. Returning to England, he had a spell at Devonport where he was at HMS *Vernon*. He crewed the trawlers, HMT *Loch Assater* and HMT *Loch Assalet* until 4th July 1915. The bases HMS *Vivid*, HMS *Dreel Castle* and HMS *Egmont* followed. He was then based on the old battleship HMS *Queen*, latterly a depot ship at Chatham, and for his last two months he was at HMS *Vivid* at Devonport, from which he was demobilised with effect from 31st December 1918. When the armed yacht *Iolaire* was lost many bodies went unrecovered, but of Tolsta's eleven lost men, nine were recovered and identified. It is said that Donald swam ashore but on finding that his younger brother, Malcolm, had not made it, he turned back into the sea and went to look for him. Sadly, both perished. Donald was interred at Tolsta Cemetery (WG).

Malcolm Macleod
(Calum Ghabhsainn)

born 17th September 1893. Age 25.

58 North Tolsta. Leading Seaman RNR.
Service number 5478/A. LWM 1/LWM 14

The second son lost from the same address, Malcolm enrolled with the RNR at Stornoway on 3rd January 1914. A pre-war fisherman on *Gray Dawn* (A579) sailing out of Lerwick, he reported to HMS *Victory* on 2nd August 1914 from Peterhead. He was posted to HMS *Hermione*, HMS *Excellent*, HMS *Victory* and HM Tug *Eagle*. He then went to the gunnery school at HMS *President III* and was a gunner on merchant ships from Alfred Holt and Company, known as the Blue Funnel Line, for the duration of the war. Like his brother Donald, Malcolm was interred at Tolsta Cemetery (WG).

John Maciver
(Iain Mhurchaidh Bhig)

born 28th November 1870. Age 48.

69a North Tolsta. Seaman RNR.
Service number 2619/C. Chatham Naval Memorial and LWM 1/LWM 4

John was the son of Murdo and Isabella Maciver (née Campbell) and had two children by his first wife Margaret, née Mackay, who died in 1904. By the time of the war he had remarried to Catherine, née Macleod. His naval record gives his birth date as 10th February 1875 when he enrolled on 10th April 1902. Just before the war he had fished out of Yarmouth and Stornoway. He served at HMS *Victory*, HMS *Dolphin* and in the latter stages of the war was based at Portsmouth again with HMS *Victory*. It was from there that he travelled north by crowded train to Inverness and then onto the railhead at Kyle of Lochalsh. His remains were not recovered.

Roll call of the lost

173

accident on board the minesweeper HMT *Fishergate*, when both his hands were caught in deck equipment, leaving him with wounds all over his hands and a broken finger. He was never to rejoin his new bride and, when Dolina died in 1956, she was interred with John at Tolsta Cemetery (WG).

John Maciver
(Iain mac Iain Mhic Aonghais Ruaidh)

born 20th December 1886. Age 32.

Hill Street, North Tolsta. Seaman RNR.
Service number 2496/A. LWM 1/LWM 14

John was the son of John and Isabella Maciver (née Murray), 33 North Tolsta, and the new husband of Donaldina (Dollag) née Macleod, whom he had married on his last leave before the war ended. The couple had no family. John's father, from No 33, had died in 1909 having outlived two wives, and leaving an extended family of eight children. John enrolled with the RNR on 28th January 1910 and fished out of Fraserburgh and Stornoway pre-war. On 1st June 1913 he received 12 months leave from the Reserve to fish in Canada, on Lake Winnipeg. During his war service, he was on HMT *Letterfourie* and at bases to which trawlers were attached – HMS *Pembroke*, HMS *Satellite*, HMS *Victory* and HMS *Eaglet*. On 3rd September 1918 he had an

Donald Macdonald
(Cabar)

born 14th August 1899. Age 19.

11 Back. Deckhand RNR.
Service number 17809/DA. LWM 1/LWM 15

Donald was the son of Murdo and Catherine Macdonald (née Mackenzie) and had seen his two older brothers invalided and discharged from the services. He enrolled soon after his 18th birthday, on 22nd August 1917 at Stornoway, and served from there on HMT *Lord Landsdowne*. He then served on HMT *Santora* from HMS *Idaho*, based at Milford Haven. Donald was interred at Gress Old Churchyard (WG).

– Back to Tong: 9 men lost

William John Murray
(Robert mac Aonghais Duinn)

born 26th May 1897. Age 21.

Well Cottage, Lighthill, Back.
Deckhand RNR.
Service number 11935/DA. LWM 1/LWM 15

Robert was the son of Angus 'Duinn' and Agnes Murray (née Burns). It is believed that he was known as Robert on account of his mother's maiden name. He enrolled on 28th August 1916 at HMS *Iolaire* (base). He went to HMS *Victory I* at Portsmouth, then was posted to the submarine depot ship (former *Pelorus* class light cruiser) HMS *Pactolus*, based at Ardrossan. Brothers Angus (RNR), Duncan (Canadians) and Alex (Sgt, RMB) also served the cause well. Robert was interred at Gress Old Churchyard (WG).

John Macaskill
(Mac Bhraoididh)

born 10th January 1892. Age 26.

Lighthill, Back. Seaman RNR.
Service number 3397/A. LWM 1/LWM 15

John was the son of Murdo and Ann Macaskill (née Macdonald), the only other son and sole support for his widowed mother after his younger brother Pte Alexander Macaskill, 1st Battalion Gordon Highlanders, was killed on 7th May 1915, aged 19. He had enrolled into the RNR on 20th February 1911, when fishing out of Stornoway, and was in Fraserburgh on 2nd August 1914 when the RNR was called to service. He served with HMS *Excellent*, HMS *Armadale Castle* and HMS *Victory*. Before his last journey, John was with HMS *Redoubtable*. He was interred at Gress Old Churchyard (WG).

Donald Campbell
(Am Pad)

born 15th June 1870. Age 48.

3 Vatisker. Leading Seaman RNR.
Service number 2058/C. LWM 1/LWM 15

An experienced seaman, having enrolled on 12th April 1901, Donald's naval record gives October 1887 for his birth, but his death certificate lists him as aged 50. Son of Norman and Margaret Campbell (née Chisholm), he was married to Catherine, née Macrae. He was reported to be a brother of Alexander (No 8) in the *Stornoway Gazette* in January 1919. His relations have confirmed that he was indeed a half brother, his father having remarried after his mother died in 1874. He was a fisherman who had sailed on Lake Superior before the war. He served on the requisitioned packet steamer, HMS *Prince Edward*, at HMS *Ganges* and had been posted at HMS *Pembroke* as 1918 ended. Donald was interred at Gress Old Churchyard (WG).

and Vivid during the war. For the first three and a half years he was on a trawler in the Mediterranean Sea. He had been home shortly before the war ended and was expecting a discharge. His remains were not given up by the sea and a wife, a mother, a sister and two children were left without their breadwinner.

Alexander Campbell
(Mac Òrd)

born 22nd June 1876. Age 42.

8 Vatisker. Leading Seaman RNR.
Service number 2999/C. Chatham Naval
Memorial and LWM 1/LWM 15

The half-brother of Donald at No 3, who was also lost, Alex was the son of Norman and Annie Campbell (née Macdonald). He was married to Jessie, née Graham, had a family of two and also cared for an aged mother and a sister for whom he was the sole support. He had joined the RNR on 1st April 1903, his birthdate given as 20th January 1878. He was promoted to Leading Seaman on 2nd May 1916 and had been "approved to be rated Petty Officer" according to his record. He was drowned on HMY Iolaire after completing his war service at the Portsmouth base HMS Victory, having also served with HMS Halcyon, Hannibal

William Macleod
(Mac Iain na Pilleag)

born 19th January 1899. Age 19.

8 Coll. Deckhand RNR.
Service number 14603/DA. Chatham Naval
Memorial and LWM 1/LWM 15

William was born at Vatisker, son of Angus and Margaret Macleod (née Macrae). He had a brother, John, in the RNR and had two step-brothers and a step-sister, after his mother remarried to John Macleod following the death of his father on 11th November 1899 when he died of leukaemia, aged 30. He enrolled 10 days before his 18th birthday, on 9th January 1917, and was at HMS Iolaire (base) then went to HMS Pembroke at Chatham on 3rd May 1917. He had served at HMS Dreel Castle, the auxiliary patrol base at Falmouth, when the war ended. His body was not recovered.

gunnery on three- to 15-pounders. He was then with HMS *President III*, which provided naval gunners for merchant ships. He was a gunner on the passenger/cargo coaster SS *Norwood* – sunk by a torpedo by UC-29 off Aberdeen on 11th February 1917. John was a survivor of that sinking, but lost his life less than two years later on his way home. He was interred at Gress Old Churchyard (WG). His wife Kate also lost two brothers in the war. She died on 26th April 1926 aged 48.

John Morrison
(Iain 'An Nis)

born 14th August 1874. Age 44.

10 Coll. Leading Seaman RNR.
Service number 3026/C. LWM 1/LWM 15

John was the son of John and Catherine Morrison (née Maciver), and married Catherine 'Kate', née Finlayson, on 21st November 1899. The couple had eight children under 18 at the time John was drowned. John had decided to join the reserves on 1st April 1903, his birth date given as 24th August 1875 in naval documents. When war was declared, he travelled from Peterhead to HMS *Victory* and moved to HMS *Excellent*, also in Portsmouth. He served on the armed merchant cruiser HMS *Patuca* from 30th November 1914 until 20th December 1916 – she converted to a balloon ship in 1915. He served at HMS *Excellent*, where he was an acting Leading Seaman after qualifying in

Murdo Macleod
(mac Mhurchaidh Tàilleir)

born 7th May 1881. Age 37.

30 Coll. Able Seaman Royal Navy.
Service number J76479. Plymouth Naval Memorial and LWM 1/LWM 15

Murdo was the son of Murdo and Catherine Macleod (née Stewart) and was a widower, after his wife Ann died of acute peritonitis on 28th June 1915 aged 30. He decided, on 21st August 1917, to sign up with the Royal Navy for hostilities only. He was at HMS *Vivid I* at Portsmouth and HMS *Diligence* at Scapa Flow, and served on the modern oil-fired battleship HMS *Revenge* from 24th March 1918. His drowning in the *Iolaire* tragedy left his 4-year-old daughter Angusina orphaned. She was raised by his mother-in-law, Catherine Macleod, at 33 Aird Tong.

Alexander Beaton
(Mac Sheumais Alasdair)

born 10th March 1891. Age 27.

40 Coll. Able Seaman,
Mercantile Marine Reserve.
MMR number 968068. LWM 1/LWM 15

Alexander was the son of James and Isabella Beaton (née Maciver). An older brother, George, had died aged 24 in 1909 and brother Murdo served in the RNR in the war. A sister was left at home. Alexander served on the armed drifter HMD *Rose III*, 81 tons, in the mercantile service which pre-figured the Merchant Navy. (In essence a Merchant Seaman requisitioned to serve with the Royal Navy). He was interred at Gress Old Churchyard (WG).

Roll call of the lost

LOCHS PARISH – North Lochs: 21 men lost

Malcolm Macleod
(Calum Iain Chaluim)

born January 25th 1900. Age 18.

3 Grimshader. Able Seaman, Mercantile Marine Reserve. MMR number 973382. LWM1/LWM 17

Malcolm was the youngest son of John and Mary Macleod (née Macrae). His brother Donald died in 1911, aged 18 and he had three older sisters, all brought up by their fisherman father, since the mother died in 1903. Serving on HMT *Agnes Nutten*, Malcolm was under Royal Navy jurisdiction on T124X rates of pay. Despite his youth he had fishing experience and this led to him being at sea with the Royal Navy from the time he was made available to serve. When his body was recovered his fob watch was on him, stopped at eight minutes past one. He was interred at Crossbost Cemetery (WG).

John Macaulay
(Iain Aonghais Mhurchaidh Bhàin)

born 26th January 1871. Age 47.

11b Grimshader. Seaman RNR. Service number 1567/C. LWM 1/LWM 17

When John first enrolled in the RNR, on 13th March 1900, Queen Victoria was on the throne and dreadnoughts were unheard of. He was a fisherman, drawing his quarterly retainer of thirty shillings whilst working from Stornoway. John was the youngest son of Angus and Annabella Macaulay (née Mackenzie) and was married to Alexina, née Mackinnon of 8 Ranish. They had five children. John served with the Royal Naval Division and was an internée at Gröningen during most of the war. Based latterly at Scapa Flow at HMS *Imperieuse*, John must have been in good spirits as he travelled to the railhead at Kyle of Lochalsh. He was interred at Crossbost Cemetery (WG).

Malcolm Nicolson Jnr
(Calum Beag Iain Dhòmhnaill)

born 15th September 1895. Age 23.

20 Ranish. Seaman RNR. Service number 5396/A. Chatham Naval Memorial and LWM 1/LWM 17

Malcolm was the son of John and Marion Nicolson (née Mackinnon) and was single, a fisherman who enrolled for the RNR on 18th December 1913. He went to HMS *Excellent* on 4th August 1914 and joined HMS *Carmania*, where he served from 10th August 1914 for nearly two years. He was one of the crew when she sank the German raider *Cap Trafalgar* in the South Atlantic. After a brief spell at HMS *Victory* in 1916, Malcolm was a seaman on HMS *Cordova*, a boom gate vessel, based at HMS *Magpie* at the war's end. His brother Donald was drowned when his ship, SS *Portloe*, was torpedoed on 20th April 1917.

Alexander Macleod

(Alasdair Alasdair Iain Ruairidh)

born 10th March 1879. Age 39.

21 Ranish. Seaman RNR.
Service number 2745/A. Chatham Naval
Memorial and LWM 1/LWM 17

Alex was the son of Alexander and Isabella
Macleod (née Mackenzie) and husband of
Marion, née Mackinnon, who later lived
at 18 Grimshader. He enrolled to serve
the King on 1st February 1910 and was a
fisherman in the waters off Peterhead and
Stornoway in the years up until the war.
He served at the repair ship HMS *Cyclops*
at Scapa Flow, until 27th October 1914,
and thereafter he remained at Scapa Flow
with the repair ship HMS *Imperieuse*. He
had a spell in between serving with the
Boadicea-class cruiser HMS *Bellona*, which
was based at Scapa Flow with the Home
Fleet. Alex was an experienced hand, yet
his was another body never recovered from
the seas around his home.

Donald Macdonald

(Dòmhnall a' Chuligich, Dòmhnall Iain
Dhòmhnaill)

born 24th April 1890. Age 27.

23 Ranish. Leading Deckhand RNR.
Service number 3516/SD. LWM 1/LWM 17

Eldest son of John and Margaret
Macdonald (née Macsween), Donald had
two younger brothers, Murdo and Angus,
in the RNR and five older sisters. He
served from 26th November 1915 and was
promoted to a Leading Deckhand on 13th
March 1917. He served with HMS *Vivid III*,
before joining HM paddle minesweeper
Kylemore, on which he was wounded
on 3rd May 1916, when a mine exploded
aboard the ship. He was then at HMS
Victory, HMD *White Oak*, HMD *Mara Smith*
at Falmouth, with the Auxiliary Patrol
at HMS *Dreel Castle*. He was interred
at Crossbost Cemetery (WG). Donald's
record reveals that his naval effects
were sold on 13th January 1920 and the
proceeds passed to his next of kin, while
his personal effects remained at the RN
base at Devonport. His father was to be
asked what he wanted done with them.

John Macleod

(Iain Uilleam Aonghais Cuithir)

born 19th June 1879. Age 39.

31 Ranish. Mate, Mercantile Marine.
LWM 1/LWM 17

John was the second son of William and
Catherine Macleod (née Macdonald),
but six of his seven brothers and sisters
predeceased him between 1892 and 1904.
His mother had died on 10th March 1910,
aged 58. Only Angusina, the youngest
daughter, survived. John and his wife
Maggie, née Maclean, had four children.
He was a vastly experienced seaman
serving on the naval trawler HMT *Cornrig*
as a merchant seaman under Royal Navy
discipline. As a Mate, he was effectively
an officer and wore a peaked cap. On
deck on the stricken *Iolaire*, John had just
watched his neighbour Donald Macrae get
to the shore on the rope, and was due
to go himself, when it snapped. John's
remains were recovered and interred at
Crossbost Cemetery (WG).

Donald Macaulay
(Dòmhnall Chaluim Iain)

born 13 October 1886. Age 32.

41 Ranish. Seaman RNR.

Service number 2576/A. Chatham Naval Memorial and LWM 1/LWM 17

Donald was the eldest son of Malcolm and Margaret Macaulay (née Maciver) and his brothers, Norman and Neil, were also naval reservists. He was single and an experienced seaman when he enrolled on 11th February 1910. He was a fisherman on Inverness, Peterhead and Stornoway boats pre-war and reported to HMS *Victory* in August 1914. He served with HMS *Triumph*, the troop ship SS *Malwa*, HMS *Andes*, HMS *Excellent*, HMT *Rose IV* and HMS *Pekin* at Grimsby. At the end of the war he was a temporary deckhand on a trawler working from HMS *Gunner* at Granton. His remains were never recovered.

Donald Macleod
(Dòmhnall Chaluim Ruairidh)

born 4th June 1867. Age 51.

2 Crossbost. Deckhand RNR.
Service number 1427/SD. Chatham Naval Memorial. LWM 1/LWM 7/ LWM 9

Donald was the youngest son of Malcolm and Annie Macleod (née Macleod) and was married to Henrietta (Effie), née Macdonald. They had no family. One of the oldest men aboard the *Iolaire*, his naval records give December as his birth month when he enrolled in the RNR on 5th June 1915. He reported to HMS *Pembroke*, then joined the newly requisitioned paddle minesweeper HMS *Waverley*. Based at HMS *Actaeon*, then HMS *Pembroke II*, he went to sea on HMT *Hero II*, then HMT *Braemar* which acted as a boom defence vessel. He reported to HMS *Thalia* on 12th January 1918. He was briefly at HMS *Victory I* and had been based with HMS *Dreel Castle*, the auxiliary patrol base at Falmouth, before he was lost in the *Iolaire* disaster. His remains were not recovered and he was lost together with his nephew Malcolm (see below).

Malcolm Macleod
(Calum Chaluim Chaluim Ruairidh)

born 10th December 1899. Age 19.

2 Crossbost. Deckhand RNR.
Service number 12081/DA. LWM 1

Recorded as born at 51 Keith Street in Stornoway, Malcolm was the son of Malcolm and Donaldina (Doldina) Macleod (née Macaskill). His parents had married in Fraserburgh on 26th August 1898 and lived at 42 Keith Street, but Malcolm's naval record has him born at Crossbost on 1st February 1898 and the same record gives his Aunt Mary at 2 Crossbost as next of kin. Malcolm joined up on 19th September 1916 at Stornoway and was at HMS *Pembroke* for six weeks. HMS *Wallington*, the Auxiliary Patrol base at Immingham covering the Humber basin, was his next posting. He was brought up by his uncle and aunts at 2 Crossbost from about ten years of age, making it still more poignant that he met his uncle in Kyle and joined him on the *Iolaire* to return home. Uncle and nephew drowned together, but Malcolm's remains were recovered and he was interred at New Sandwick Cemetery (WG). The record states on 10th March 1919 that 'Mr Malcolm Macleod (father), 42 Keith Street, be suitably informed re death of Macleod'.

John Macleod
(Mogaidh, Iain Chaluim Ruaidh)

born 6th January 1898. Age 20.

13 Crossbost. Able Seaman Mercantile Marine Reserve.
MMR number 974908. LWM 1/LWM 17

Youngest son of Malcolm and Lilias Macleod (née Nicolson) John had two older sisters and two brothers – Roddie was in the RNR and half-brother Angus was serving his new country, Canada. Their mother was widowed in 1917. John was in an agreement to serve with the Royal Navy as a member of the MMR and sailed on HMD *Rose* before leaving to travel home on the *Iolaire*. John was interred at Crossbost Cemetery (WG).

Allan Macleod
(Ailean Leòd Mhurchaidh)

born 22nd February 1894. Age 25.

11 Leurbost. Seaman RNR.
Service number 4661/A. Chatham Naval Memorial and LWM 1/LWM 17

Born at 43 Ranish, son of Leod and Johanna Macleod (née Macleod), Allan was brought up from the age of nine by his Aunt Margaret at 11 Leurbost, after his parents died. Allan would have been like a wee brother to Alex (above) and they were lost together as New Year dawned. Allan's older brother Angus had already been killed on 25th April 1915, aged 25, fighting with the 2nd Seaforths at St Julien. On 4th December 1912 Allan put his name down to serve in the RNR, fishing out of Stornoway until the war. After serving as an AB with the Anson Battalion of the Royal Naval Division in Belgium he rejoined HMS *Vivid* in October 1914.

He was at Gibraltar before joining the old battleship HMS *Victorious*, a dockyard repair ship, on 31st December 1917. After a spell at HMS *Gunner*, he served with the armed boarding steamer HMS *Duke of Cornwall*, then at HMS *Vivid* at Devonport and at HMS *President III*, a London accountancy office for naval gunners based on merchant vessels, as the war concluded. Allan drowned together with his cousin Alex, but the younger boy's remains were never found. He appears on the North Lochs War Memorial twice, under Ranish and Leurbost.

Alexander Mackenzie
(Alasdair Alasdair Dhòmhnaill Ailein)

born 31st December 1879. Age 39.

11 Leurbost. Seaman RNR.
Service number 1663/C. LWM 1/LWM 17

Alex's birthdate is given in RNR records as November 1878 when he signed up for RNR service on 5th April 1900 as a fisherman. Third son of Alexander and Isabella Mackenzie (née Macdonald), he was single and his youngest brother John was in the Seaforth uniform. He fished out of Stornoway on the *Orient* (SY848) before the outbreak of war. He was at HMS *Pembroke* (Chatham), HMS *Ilex* (Kingstown and Holyhead), HMS *Boadicea II* (Kingstown/Holyhead) and HMS *Dreel Castle* at Falmouth. He trained as a naval gunner and served on HMD *Roman Empire* out of Falmouth before being lost from the *Iolaire* together with his cousin Allan (see below) who had grown up with him at 11 Leurbost. Alex was interred at Crossbost Cemetery (WG).

Alexander Mackenzie
(Alasdair Dhòmhnaill Alasdair)

born 1st July 1898. Age 20.

16 Leurbost. Deckhand RNR.
Service number 12080/DA. LWM 1/LWM 17

Two brothers were lost from 16 Leurbost, a double tragedy for parents Donald and Mary Mackenzie (née Smith). Alexander served from 19th September 1916 at the HMS *Iolaire* (base) at Stornoway. Three weeks later he was at HMS *Pembroke I*, followed by HMS *Kingfisher*. He continued service at HMS *Satellite* where he was on drifter HMD *Triumph II*. His next posting was to HMS *Attentive III* at Dover where he served aboard HMD *Mary Stephen* in the period up until Christmas 1918 and the trip home on leave, joining his brother John on the doomed *Iolaire*. He was interred at Crossbost Cemetery (WG).

John Mackenzie
(Seonaidh Dhòmhnaill Alasdair)

born 20th July 1888. Age 30.

16 Leurbost. Seaman RNR.
Service number 3274/A. LWM 1/LWM 17

Son of Donald and Mary Mackenzie (née Smith) and older brother of Alex (above), John signed up for the RNR on 24th January 1911. He was a fisherman sailing out of Peterhead, Stornoway and Kirkwall pre-war. It was from Peterhead that he reported to HMS *Excellent* at Portsmouth on 2nd August 1914, serving for the rest of the war on the modern battleship HMS *Emperor of India*, before being lost with his brother on the *Iolaire*. Like his brother, John was interred at Crossbost Cemetery (WG).

Kenneth Smith Jnr
(Kenny Beag, Coinneach Mhurchaidh Choinnich Alasdair)

born 4th December 1877. Age 41.

28a Leurbost. Seaman RNR.
Service number 1956/D. Chatham Naval Memorial and LWM 1/LWM 17

Son of Murdo and Mary Smith (née Smith), Kenny was the husband of Annie, née Macleod of 19 Ranish, and left two daughters fatherless. His elder brother 'Kenny Mòr' was also in the RNR. Born in August, according to naval records, he served at HMS *Pembroke*, then HMT *Bengal*, HMS *Ilex*, HMY *Boadicea II*, HMS *Hannibal*, HMT *King Egbert*, HMS *Egmont II*, HMT *Macduff* and finally back at HMS *Pembroke* at the end of the war. He received the RNR Medal for Long Service and Good Conduct on 24th March 1918, 10 months before his tragic death aboard the *Iolaire*. His body was not recovered. His wife died in 1955.

Donald Smith
(Dòmhnall Ruairidh Dhàidh)

born 26th June 1891. Age 27.

34a Leurbost. Seaman RNR.
Service number 2972/A. LWM 1/LWM 17

Donald was the son of Roderick and Catherine Smith (née Mackenzie) and was single when he signed up to train as a reserve sailor on 1st November 1910. He was fishing out of Stornoway and Wick, then went deep sea on the SS *Sardinian*, SS *Columbia* and SS *Hesperian* and was back fishing on the *Noblesse* (PD285) when the war came in August 1914. He reported to HMS *Excellent* from Stornoway on 11th August and two months later he was posted to the new battleship HMS *Emperor of India*, on which ship he served for the duration. He was interred at Crossbost Cemetery (WG). His family became dispersed, many of his siblings emigrating to Australia and the United States.

Donald Maclean
(Dòmhnall Sheòrais)

born 5th March 1868. Age 50.

35 Leurbost. Seaman RNR.
Service number 2820/B. LWM 1/LWM 17

A senior serviceman in the RNR, Donald's birthdate was given as 17th March 1880 when he enrolled on 1st January 1905. Son of George and Isabella Maclean (née Macdonald); he was the husband of Annie, née Macaulay, and had seven children, the eldest of whom barely outlived him. He was fishing at Stornoway, Wick and was at Fraserburgh when called to serve on 4th August 1914. He went directly by train to Devonport, then HMS *Pembroke*. His war was served with the cruiser HMS *Sutlej*, HMS *Pembroke* (at Chatham) and in Gibraltar. The armed merchant cruiser HMS *Almanzora* was his home for six months and from May 1916 he was a sailor at HMS *Colleen* at Queenstown (Cork). He was one of the oldest casualties of the ill-fated *Iolaire* and was buried together with his 19-year-old daughter Catherine, who collapsed at the news of the tragedy and died on 6th January. Her death certificate gives her cause of death as pneumonia. They were interred side by side at Crossbost Cemetery (WG).

then HMY *St George* with the auxiliary patrol base HMS *Wallington* at Immingham. He was interred at Crossbost Cemetery (WG).

Roderick John Macdonald
(Ruairidh Iain Mhurchaidh Mhurchaidh)

born 13th June 1891. Age 27.

36 Leurbost. Seaman RNR.
Service number 2966/A. LWM 1/LWM 17

Roddie was the son of Murdo and Margaret (Peggy) Macdonald (née Morrison); he was single and his brother Murdo was also an RNR seaman. Roddie enrolled with the RNR on 1st November 1910 and was fishing out of Fraserburgh and Stornoway until 1913, when he joined the Mercantile Marine and sailed on SS *Cameronia*, SS *Grampian*, SS *Carthaginian* and SS *Mongolian* before resuming fishing at Fraserburgh. He served at HMS *Dolphin*, HMS *Victory I*, HMS *Vernon*, HMS *Manco* and HMY *Hersilia* at Stornoway,

Murdo Maclean
(Murchadh Alasdair Alasdair)

born 10th January 1887. Age 31.

39 Leurbost. Deckhand MMR.
MMR number 974252. LWM 1/LWM 17

Eldest son of Alexander and Marion (Mor) Maclean (née Macleod), Murdo was single and had a younger brother Alex who also wore a naval uniform. Murdo had been sailing with the Royal Navy on HMT *Snipe*, a requisitioned Hull trawler, before he became another victim of New Year 1919. His sister had gone to meet him and, as she left the house, her mother jokingly said to her: "See and don't come home without Murdo now!" He was interred at Crossbost Cemetery (WG).

Angus Macdonald
(Aonghas Ailean)

born 7th November 1873. Age 45.

Caberfeidh, 42 Leurbost. Seaman RNR.
Service number 1830/D. LWM 1/LWM 17

Angus was the son of Allan and Mary Macdonald (née Macleod) and was from a family of eight. He was married to Mary, née Mackenzie, and they had five children. An experienced seaman who had served with the RNR from 19th November 1897, he was working ashore in Stornoway in the years immediately before the war. He served at HMS *Cyclops*, HMS *Imperieuse* (both at Scapa Flow) and at HMS *Iolaire* (Depot). His brother, Murchadh Ailein was one of the longest serving soldiers in the British Army, enlisting in the Seaforth Highlanders at Fort George in 1887 and rising to the rank of Colour Sergeant. He served in the Indian Frontier War, the

Egyptian Campaign and the Boer War and retired in 1908 after 21 years service. Angus was back at Scapa Flow with HMS *Imperieuse* when he set out for his first peace-time leave. He was interred at Crossbost Cemetery (WG).

Angus Macleod
(Aonghas Aonghais Iain)

born 2nd May 1891. Age 27.

46 Leurbost. Deckhand MMR.
MMR number 973997. LWM 1/LWM 17

Angus was the son of Angus and Marion Macleod (née Maciver). He was single and, like his neighbour Murdo Maclean at number 39, had been serving on HMT *Snipe*, a boom defence vessel. The two neighbours served together, travelled home together and died together on HMY *Iolaire*. Like Murdo, Angus was interred at Crossbost Cemetery (WG).

Donald Smith
(Dòmhnall Iain Aonghais)

born 10th May 1891. Age 27.

5b Achmore. Leading Seaman RNR.
Service number 4173/A. Chatham Naval Memorial and LWM 1/LWM 17

Donald was the single son of John and Christina Smith (née Mackenzie) and a fisherman at Stornoway and Wick after enrolling on 8th February 1912. He travelled from Fraserburgh to HMS *Excellent* on 2nd August 1914 and served at HMS *Victory* before he was posted to the armed merchant cruiser HMS *Himalaya*, operating in the South Atlantic and round the Cape of Good Hope. He next became a DAMS gunner at HMS *President III* and served on SS *Highland Watch* on the River Plate run, into Buenos Aires from Liverpool and then to Brazil and the Mediterranean on the same ship. After spells at HMS *Excellent* and HMS *Victory* he was with the armed merchant cruiser HMS *Orama* at Dakar. On 14th December 1917 he

was a gunner on SS *Riverdale* and his record shows him at HMS *Excellent* and HMS *Victory* again in 1918, still attached to HMS *President III*. Donald was heading home after serving all the years of the war in seas around the world, when the sea of his home island took him and refused to yield up his body.

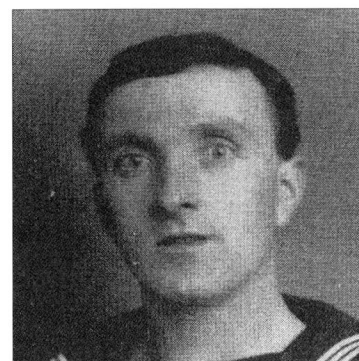

John Macleod
(Iain Chailein Aonghais)

born 2nd January 1894. Age 24.

25 Laxay. Seaman RNR.
Service number 3607/SD. LWM 1/LWM 21

One of nine children of Colin (Cailean Aonghas) and Catherine Macleod (née Mackay), John was lost on HMY *Iolaire* a day before his 25th birthday. He had served with the Cameron Highlanders and, after being discharged through ill health, he joined the

Trawler Section of the Royal Navy on 4th December 1915. He went to Portsmouth and was on HMML 104 until 7th November 1918, then was with the armed launch HMML 411, operating from HMS *Victory* at Portsmouth. His record suggests that he had been posted to HMD *White Oak* on the day he was travelling up to Kyle. Unusually, he had already been home on leave in early December 1918, yet he was to lose his life travelling home for a second spell of leave with his family. John's body was recovered from the wreck on Wednesday 8th January and brought to Laxay the following day. He was interred at Old Laxay Cemetery (WG). His brother Malcolm was wounded serving with the Camerons and brother Roddie was wounded in a Canadian uniform.

Malcolm Macleod

(Calum Chaluim Alasdair an t-Saoir)

born 19th September 1898. Age 20.

18 Balallan. Seaman RNR.
Service number 14384/DA. Chatham Naval Memorial and LWM 1/LWM 21

Son of Malcolm and Joan Macleod (née Mackenzie), Malcolm joined the RNR on 29th January 1917, at the barracks in Stornoway. He served at the HMS *Vivid* barracks at Devonport and then moved to HMS *Colleen* at Queenstown (now Cork). He had latterly served on HMT *Thomas Cago* based at HMS *Idaho* in Milford Haven. His body was not found. His brother Alex John was wounded in France with the 1st Seaforths and endured a fever in Mesopotamia.

Malcolm Martin

born 4th August 1879. Age 39.

21a Balallan. Seaman RNR.
Service number 12067/DA. LWM 1/LWM 21

Malcolm was one of six sons and five daughters born to Donald and Christine Martin (née Macaulay). A single man, he had been working as a shepherd at Punta Arenas in Chile, but was home when the war broke out. He volunteered his services but, as the war lasted longer than anyone expected, he applied for exemption from service in March 1916 on the grounds that he faced serious hardship, as he had horses and property in Chile that required his personal attention. He was refused the exemption at a Military Service Tribunal held on the 16th. He enrolled on 15th September 1916 at Stornoway, giving his birthdate as 12th August 1880. Two weeks later he was in the crew of the

LOCHS PARISH – Pàirc: 8 men lost

minesweeping trawler HMT *Swan*, then served at HMS *Pembroke* before serving on HMT *Treasure Trove* from HMS *Zaria* and HMS *Pembroke*. His body was said to have been one of the first to be recovered after the sinking of the *Iolaire*, and he was interred at Old Laxay Cemetery (WG). The family had to bear sorrow upon sorrow, as news had reached them just days earlier that brother Murdo had been mistakenly shot in Argentina on 9th September 1918, aged 29. Brother Finlay also served with the Royal Naval Air Service, as an air mechanic attached to the Royal Flying Corps, and was invalided home after being wounded in the Somme offensive.

Angus Mackinnon
(Aonghas Ghibidh)

born 14th April 1894. Age 24.

4 Caversta. Deckhand RNR.
Service number 2615/SD. Portsmouth Naval Memorial and LWM/LWM 18)

Son of Donald and Margaret Mackinnon (née Macleod), Angus enrolled on 24th August 1915 at Glasgow and went to HMS *Victory*, where he joined the crew of HMT *Night Hawk*. He served at HMS *Arrogant*, HMS *Pembroke I*, then with the Racecourse-class paddle minesweeper HMS *Sandown*. He later served at the Dover base, HMS *Attentive III*, on convoy duties with the new Anchusa-class sloop HMS *Chrysanthemum*. He married Ethel May Mackinnon (née Ratcliff) of 22 Minerva Avenue, Dover, while on service on 1st June 1918 and left his pregnant wife to visit his parents in Lewis at New Year. His body was not recovered but his greatcoat was found, and in its pocket a tobacco pouch containing a lock of Ethel's hair. The tin was kept in Lewis and is now on display at the local history museum at Ravenspoint, Kershader, South Lochs. Ethel named her daughter Nellie Iolaire May, and later remarried and had two sons and a daughter who grew up with Nellie.

Alexander Macleod
(Alasdair a' Ghàrraidh, Dosan)

born 7th January 1893. Age 25.

1a Garyvard. Deckhand RNR.
Service number 17041/DA. Chatham Naval Memorial and LWM 1/ LWM 18

Son of John and Annabelle (née Macleod), Alexander's body was not recovered. He had joined up on 4th July 1917 at HMS *Iolaire* base, then went to HMS *Zaria* and HMS *Vivid*, where he served on HMT *Iceland*. Brothers Malcolm and Donald Junior were also in uniform.

Angus Montgomery
(Aonghas Choinnich Bhàin, Maois)

born 25th June 1872. Age 46.

2 Garyvard. Deckhand RNR.
Service number 1445/SD. LWM 1/LWM 18

Angus was the son of Kenneth and Margaret Montgomery (née Morrison) and married to Mary Ann, née Macdonald. A veteran serviceman, Angus had been a Boer War soldier, awarded several medals. His brothers also served – Torquil in the RNR and Alex in the KOSB. Angus's birthdate was given as July 1874 when he enrolled in the RNR on 7th June 1915 at HMS *Iolaire* (base). He transferred to the Trawler Section on 1st October 1916 and went to HMS *Vivid III* from HMS *Cormorant* a month later. On 1st August 1917 he was based at HMS *Idaho* and served with the crew of HMD *Unity II*. He was interred at Old Laxay Cemetery (WG).

John Mackenzie
(Iain Alasdair Mhurchaidh)

born 28th September 1890. Age 28.

13 Marvig. Seaman RNR.
Service number 5937/A. Chatham Naval Memorial and LWM 1/LWM 18

John was the son of Alexander and Maggie Mackenzie (née Macleod) and served with the RNR from 2nd December 1909 when pursuing the fishing at Stornoway. He spent 1912 at Aberdeen, forfeiting his four retainers for the year. He reported to HMS *Vivid* on 2nd August 1914 and by 18th September he was with the Anson Battalion of the RN Division. He was among those who were neither captured nor interned following the fall of Antwerp, going on to serve with the armed merchant cruisers HMS *Cedric* and HMS *Macedonia*. The former patrolled off the Faroes and the latter was in the Southern Atlantic. John was then at HMS *Vivid III* and served at the war's end on the pre-dreadnought battleship HMS *Albemarle*. His body was not recovered.

Donald Macaskill
(Dòmhnall Beag Dhòmhnaill Òg)

born 14th March 1883. Age 36.

9 Gravir. Deckhand RNR.
Service number 21143/DA. Chatham Naval Memorial and LWM 1/LWM 18

Donald was the son of Donald and Margaret Macaskill (née Maclennan) and was on his father's fishing boat *Mary* (SY 150) in the 1902 Coronation Cup race. He was a fisherman pre-war. He enlisted on 22nd July 1918 and, after HMS *Pembroke*, served at Granton at HMS *Gunner*. His was on board *Iolaire* with his younger brother Allan, who survived the tragedy. Donald's body was not recovered.

Malcolm Macinnes
(Chalum Mhurchaidh Dhòmhnaill Nèill)

born 16th February 1893. Age 26.

2 Lemreway. Seaman RNR.
Service number 8896/A. Chatham Naval
Memorial and LWM 1/ LWM 18

Malcolm was the son of Murdo and Mary
Macinnes (née Macritchie) and had served
from 21st February 1916, his birthdate given
as July 1895 in naval records. He was
posted to the Town class light cruiser HMS
Dublin on 27th March 1916 and served on
her for the rest of the war, including at
the Battle of Jutland, where she attacked
and sank a destroyer. After his loss on the
Iolaire, Malcolm's body was not recovered.
His girlfriend Johanna Macdonald never
married and his parents moved in 1922 to 6
Orinsay with their other seven offspring.

David Macinnes
(Daibhidh Phàdraig Dhòmhnaill Nèill)

born 25th December 1899. Age 19.

2b Lemreway. Deckhand RNR.
Service number 19531/DA. LWM 1/LWM 18

David was the son of Peter and Ann
Macinnes (née Nicolson) and enrolled
on 12th February 1918. He served at HMS
Pembroke and HMS *Halcyon* and latterly on
the Castle-type trawler HMT *Daniel Henley*,
which had HMS *Implacable* as base ship.
Lost on the *Iolaire* just a week after his
19th birthday, David was interred at Gravir
Cemetery (WG).

Murdo Ferguson
(Murchadh Mhurchaidh Aonghais Iain)

born 3rd December 1871. Age 47.

3 Lemreway. Seaman RNR.
Service number 258/SD. LWM 1/LWM 18

Murdo was the son of Murdo and Christina
Ferguson (née Macmillan) and was married
to Betsy, née Chisholm. They had a family
of four sons and two daughters. Murdo
enlisted in the RNR on 26th April 1915 and
was mobilised before undergoing training.
He was at various ships and bases –
HMS *Pembroke*, HM Paddle Minesweeper
Balmoral, HMS *Eoropa*, HMY *St George*, RN
Depot Port Said, the fleet messenger HMS
River Fisher, HMS *Hannibal*, HMS *Vivid*, HMS
Actaeon and had served on HMT *Morgan
Jones* from *Hannibal* before losing his life in
the *Iolaire* disaster. Murdo was interred at
Gravir Cemetery (WG).

Alexander Macleod
(Alick)

born 11th April 1877. Age 41.

1 Portnaguran. Seaman RNR.
Service number 2808/C. LWM 1/LWM 20

Alick was the son of Matthew and Maggie Macleod and husband of Margaret, born at Garrabost. He was a fisherman at Stornoway, Buckie and Peterhead before the war and joined the naval reserve on 1st January 1903 – he was listed as Angus Macleod by the naval authorities. He reported to HMS *Excellent* from Fraserburgh, without going home, on 3rd August 1914. He was quickly sent to crew SS *Lake Manitoba* from Montreal to Liverpool, as she was being requisitioned by the Royal Navy. He had a varied war and served with HMS *President III*, HMS *Colleen*, HMT *Setter*, HMS *Victory I*, HMS *Excellent*, HMS *Alert*, the Royal Naval Division (Benbow Battalion), HMS *Dalhousie*, HMS *Sapphire*, SS *City of Cologne* (as a gunner), and was at HMS *Excellent* again when he headed for home. Alick was known to have got ashore from the *Iolaire*, but succumbed just past the rocks at Holm. He was found by a small party of rescuers, as day broke, near Stoneyfield Farm. They attempted resuscitation, without success – it was thought that he had suffered a heart attack. He was interred at Aignish Burial Ground (WG).

Norman Macleod

born 14th March 1899. Age 19.

10 Portnaguran. Trimmer/Cook RNR.
Service number 1186/TC. LWM 1/LWM 20

Son of Donald and Johanna Macleod (née Macleod), Norman came from a family that suffered greatly in the cause of war, with four sons lost. Norman was just 15 when his brother Alexander was lost, on 14th December 1914, fighting with the Gordon Highlanders in France. Less than a year later brother William was drowned when HMT *Lydian* was sunk by a mine off South Foreland, on 18th September 1915. The third brother, Angus, had been interned at Gröningen, serving with the Royal Naval Division after the defence of Antwerp. He was released home on medical grounds by the Dutch authorities, only to die at home on 26th June 1916. It must have been against his parents' pleas that Norman joined up as a Trimmer/Cook in the RNR on 24th September 1918, to serve just three months before his death. He was at HMS *Pembroke* from Stornoway from 26th September and joined HMY *Helvetia* a month later. His parents were heartbroken beyond description to see their fourth son lost in the wreck of the *Iolaire*. He was interred at Aignish Burial Ground (WG).

Alexander John Macleod
(Alasdair Iain Mhurchaidh Dhòmhnaill Tharmoid)

born 16th April 1900. Age 18.

3 Broker. Deckhand RNR.
Service number 20422/DA. LWM 1/LWM 20

Son of Murdo and Mary Macleod (née Murray), Alex John was a young, single man who had only enrolled as he became old enough, on 28th May 1918. He travelled to HMS *Pembroke I*, then was based at HMS *Attentive III* at Dover, from which he served aboard HMT *Matthew Flynn*. He disembarked there to head home for the first New Year since the war had ended. His loss at Holm was a grievous blow to a family who already cared for another son, Donald, severely wounded on the armed merchant cruiser HMS *Carmania* very early in the war. Alex John was interred at Aignish Burial Ground (WG).

Alexander Mackenzie

(Am Boicean, 'The Boyken' Alasdair Uilleam Alasdair Uilleam)

born 1st April 1876. Age 42.

1 Aird, Point. Seaman RNR.
Service number 3360/C. LWM 1/LWM 20

Am Boicean was the son of William and Mary Mackenzie (née Nicolson) and was married to Marion, née Macdonald, of 6 Portvoller. He had joined the RNR on 1st January 1904 and served continuously as a reservist, joining HMS *Victory* from Fraserburgh at the outset of war and serving at HMS *Dolphin* for most of the war before he left HMS *Victory*, the base at Portsmouth, for the last time and never saw home. His brother John, married at 8 Portvoller, was a survivor. Alex was interred at Aignish Burial Ground (WG).

Alexander Mackenzie

(Alick Dai, Alasdair Dhòmhnaill Dhòmhnaill Uilleam)

born 1st January 1877. Age 42.

5 Aird, Point. Seaman RNR.
Service number 3892/B. LWM 1/LWM 20

Alick lost his life on his 42nd birthday, having registered his name with the RNR on his 29th birthday, 1st January 1906. Son of Donald and Catherine Mackenzie (née Maciver), Alick was married to Margaret and was a Deacon at Knock Free Church. He was fishing out of Fraserburgh, Scrabster and Stornoway before the war, on boats such as the *Star of Hope* and *Girl May* of Fraserburgh and *Clan Macleod* of Stornoway. During the war he was at HMS *Cyclops*, a repair and depot ship, and served latterly at Scapa Flow on HMS *Imperieuse*. He was interred at Aignish Burial Ground (WG).

Murdo Macleod

(Murchadh Mhurchaidh Aonghais)

born 17th June 1876. Age 42.

10a Aird, Point. Seaman RNR.
Service number 4219/B. LWM 1/LWM 20

Murdo was the son of Murdo and Margaret Macleod (née Murray), born at Garrabost and married at Aird to Ann Macleod. He joined the RNR on 1st April 1906 in Stornoway and re-enrolled on 22nd May 1911. He was a fisherman and served on Stornoway, Methil, Banff and Fraserburgh boats, including one of the most famous Stornoway fishing boats, *Muirneag* (SY486). He served during the war at HMS *Excellent*, from 8th August until 11th November 1914. He had just four days at HMS *Victory*, then from 19th November 1914 until his last departure for leave on 31st December 1918, he was in the crew of the modern light cruiser HMS *Galatea*. He was aboard her when, on 4th May 1916, the *Galatea* took part in the shooting-down of the German Zeppelin L7. Soon afterwards she was the first ship of the Home Fleet to sight the Germans at the Battle of Jutland, and the first British ship to receive a hit in the battle. A shell from the German light cruiser SMS *Elbing* hit her but it did not explode. Murdo survived all this, but did not survive his peacetime journey home. He was interred at Aignish Burial Ground (WG).

Norman Montgomery
(Tarmod Chaluim Alasdair)

born 22 January 1881. Age 37

3 Sheshader. Seaman RNR.
Service number 3391/C. Chatham Naval Memorial and LWM 1/LWM 20

Son of Malcolm and Isabella Montgomery (née Campbell), Norman was the husband of Isabella and enrolled with the RNR on New Year's Day 1904. He was a fisherman pre-war, sailing on Britannia (FR153) in July 1914 as war approached. During the war he served with HMS *Excellent*, where he qualified as a gunner, then from the bases *Zaria*, *Brilliant*, *Attentive III* and *Research* on the trawler HMT *Ariel II* from 26th September 1914 until war's end. His remains were never recovered.

Donald Macdonald
(Mac Iain Dhòmhnaill Dhòmhnaill Phortair)

born 24th October 1877. Age 41.

5 Sheshader. Seaman RNR.
Service number 2373/C. LWM 1/LWM 20

Son of John and Christina Macdonald (née Macaulay), Donald was single and enrolled on 1st January 1902 – April 1876 is stated as his birth date in his naval records. He was fishing out of Stornoway when the Reserves were mobilised for war. His first posting was as a qualified gunner from HMS *Excellent* and he then served with HMS *Victory*, HMY *Ombra* operating from HMS *Colleen* at Queenstown, and the Hunt class minesweeper HMS *Muskerry*. He had seen action against enemy U-boats off the Belgian coast before he left to return to Lewis. He was interred at Aignish Burial Ground (WG).

Murdo Macaulay
(Mac Uilleam Mhurchaidh Iain Duinn)

born 1st October 1885. Age 33.

7 Sheshader. Deckhand RNR.
Service number 4004/SD. LWM 1/LWM 20

Murdo was the son of William and Kate Macaulay (née Macdonald), and was single, his birthdate given as 12th October 1887 when he enrolled in the RNR on 21st January 1916. He was transferred that year to the Trawler Section and served with HMS *Pembroke*, HMS *Gunner*, HM paddle minesweeper *Epsom*, HMS *Iolaire* (base) and, from 3rd April 1917, on the drifter HMD *Violet II* which was based with HMS *Attentive III*. Like all the homecoming Sheshader men on HMY *Iolaire*, he would never reach his home. He was interred at Aignish Burial Ground (WG).

William Murray
(Uilleam Moraidh)

born 4th May 1896. Age 22.

11 Sheshader. Seaman RNR.
Service number 6772/A. Chatham Naval
Memorial and LWM 1/LWM 20

William was the son of John and Matilda
Murray (née Macdonald) and was single,
with four brothers serving. Brother Duncan
was decorated by the Russians while in
the RNR, Kenneth and Donald were in the
Canadians and John was torpedoed twice
in the Transport Service. William enrolled
on 17th November 1914 and served on
the armed merchant cruiser HMS *Orotava*
from 21st December 1914 for nearly three
years. He left her at Glasgow in November
1917, having been down to South America
on the last voyage. He went from HMS
Pembroke I and became a DAMS gunner
attached to HMS *President III*. He also
served on SS *Thistle* of the Laird Line. He
left Chatham Barracks for New Year leave
with a large group of other islanders,
but he and others would never see their
homes. His body was not recovered.

Donald Murdo Macaulay
(Dòmhnaill Iain 'An Mholaich)

born 1st January 1898. Age 21.

13 Sheshader. Deckhand RNR.
Service number 4363/SD. LWM 1/LWM 20

Donald was the son of John and Christina
Macaulay (née Mackenzie), who had
already known the heartache of war. His
older brother, Peter, was killed on 23rd
April 1917, aged 24, while fighting with the
Seaforths in France and another brother,
Murdo, was gassed serving with the same
regiment. Donald enrolled on 4th March
1916 and transferred to the Trawler Section
seven months later. From HMS *Victory* he
was posted to HMML 857 on 22nd November
1916 and later to HMML 372. His depot
when he set out for his last leave on 31st
December 1918 was HMS *Idaho* at Milford
Haven. He should have been celebrating his
21st birthday, but instead he was interred at
Aignish Burial Ground (WG).

Murdo Mackenzie
(Murchadh Choinnich Mhurchaidh)

born 23rd March 1873. Age 45.

15 Sheshader. Seaman RNR.
Service number 3122/B. Chatham Naval
Memorial and LWM 1/LWM 20

Murdo was the son of Kenneth and Anne
(Nancy) Mackenzie (née Mackay) and
he was married to Dolina, née Macleod.
He became a Reservist on 1st April 1905
and was fishing pre-war at Stornoway
when called on 3rd August 1914 to HMS
Pembroke. He served briefly on the armed
merchant cruiser (AMC) HMS *Marmora*
then, from 15th September 1914 until 6th
January 1918, he was with the AMC HMS
Edinburgh Castle. For most of 1918 he was
at Chatham with AMC HMS *Morea* and it
was from there that he set out for home.
His body was never recovered.

John Macdonald Snr

(Iain Mòr)

born 2nd October 1888. Age 30.

20 Sheshader. Seaman RNR.
Service number 2558/A. LWM 1/LWM 20

Two brothers died from the same
household on January 1st 1919, and both
were called John, the elder two inches
taller at 5ft 10ins (hence Iain Mòr – Big
John). They were sons of Kenneth and
Catherine Macdonald (née Macaulay)
and were both single. Iain Mòr enrolled
on 8th February 1910 and was fishing at
Stornoway, Fraserburgh and Yarmouth
pre-war. He was mobilised in August 1914
and went to HMS *Victory* at Portsmouth.
Early in the war he served with the Drake
Battalion of the Royal Naval Division, then
in 1918 he was with the armed boarding
vessel HMS *Partridge II* and his last posting
was at HMS *Venerable*. He and his brother
were together on their last voyage. They
were both interred at Aignish Burial Ground
(WG).

John Macdonald Jnr

(Iain Beag)

born 7th December 1892. Age 26.

20 Sheshader. Seaman RNR.
Service number 3074/A. LWM 1/LWM 20

Iain Beag (Little John) enrolled later in
the same year as his brother, on 12th
December 1910 and was fishing out of
Stornoway, sometimes on Fraserburgh
boats fishing from the port. He reported
at HMS *Excellent* in August 1914 and from
10th October 1914 served on the new
dreadnought battleship HMS *Emperor of
India*. He left the battleship, after over four
years service, with his travel warrant for a
homeward journey. The brothers were laid
to rest beside each other at Aignish Burial
Ground (WG).

Donald Mackay

(Dòmhnall 'An Chailein)

born 21st July 1898. Age 20.

22 Sheshader. Deckhand RNR.
Service number 12090/DA. LWM 1/LWM 20

Donald was the son of John and Matilda
Mackay (née Macleod). His elder brother
Colin, a Sergeant in the 1st Battalion,
Seaforth Highlanders, died of wounds in
Mesopotamia (Iraq) on 14th December
1917, aged 27. Brother Norman also served
in the RNR. Donald had served latterly
on the Formidable-class battleship HMS
Implacable when he set out for the home
he would never reach. His body was
recovered and interred at Aignish Burial
Ground (WG).

Norman Macleod

(Tarmod Chaluim Uilleam)

born 9th September 1890. Age 28.

23 Sheshader. Leading Seaman RNR.
Service number 4803/A. LWM 1/LWM 20

Norman was the son of Malcolm and
Annie Macleod (née Macaulay) and his
brothers Donald and William also wore
naval uniform. He enrolled with the RNR
on 7th January 1913 (his birthdate given
as August) and was one of many Point
seafarers sailing out of Stornoway pre-war
to pursue the fishing. He served at HMS
Pembroke from 3rd August 1915, went
to HMS *Arrogant* shortly afterwards and
was there until 15th June 1918. He served
thereafter as a gunner, attached to HMS
President III. He was interred at Aignish
Burial Ground (WG).

Donald Macaulay

born 24th December 1880. Age 38.

1 Shulishader. Seaman RNR.
Service number 2065/C. Chatham Naval
Memorial and LWM 1/LWM 20

Donald was the son of John and Annie
Macaulay (née Murray) and was
married to Rachel, née Macmillan.
He enrolled on 22nd March 1901, when a
fisherman operating out of Stornoway and
Fraserburgh. He served at HMS *Excellent*
from 2nd August 1914, joining the base
from Fraserburgh, then went on, with
many other Lewismen, to HMS *Emperor of
India*. Donald was lost when sailing home,
compounding his family's grief after
brother Murdo was killed serving with the
28th Battalion Canadian Infantry on 26th
June 1918, aged 29. Donald's body was
never recovered.

Kenneth Mackenzie

born 29th May 1892. Age 26.

4 Shulishader. Seaman RNR.
Service number 3046/A. LWM 1/LWM 20

Kenny was the son of Donald and Isabella
Mackenzie (née Morrison) and had three
brothers in the navy, one of them a Petty Officer
with the Australians. Kenny served from 22nd
November 1910, at a time that he fished out of
Stornoway on Banff and Stornoway boats. He left
Peterhead to join HMS *Excellent* on 3rd August
1914 and was on the cruiser HMS *Kent* from 2nd
October 1914 until 10th June 1918. During his
service he was in the Battle of the Falklands
on 8th December 1914, in which HMS *Kent* sunk
the German light cruiser SMS *Nurnberg*. On 14th
March 1915, along with the cruiser HMS *Glasgow*,
the *Kent* tracked down and sank the sole survivor
of the German Pacific Squadron, the light cruiser
SMS *Dresden* at Mas a Fuera, Chile. The cruiser
was mostly employed on convoy duties later.
Kenny was at HMS *Ganges* towards the end
of 1918 and, when he set out for leave in late
December, was at HMS *Victory*. He was interred
at Aignish Burial Ground (WG).

Roll call of the lost

Angus Mackay

born 16th May 1875. Age 43.

Hillside, Shulishader. Second Hand RNR. Service number 2258/D. LWM 1/LWM 20

Angus was a fisherman and enrolled with the RNR on 16th March 1899. Son of Murdo and Catherine Mackay (née Mackenzie), he was married to Annie and was a member of Knock Free Church. He served with HMS *Pembroke* from the outset and was one of many *Iolaire* victims who saw action on the armed merchant cruiser HMS *Orama*. He was with her from 10th September 1914 until 17th August 1917, including at the Battle of the Falklands. Angus was then at HMS *Pekin* and HMS *Attentive III*. He was awarded the DSM, for services in minesweeping operations at Ostend, on 14th February 1918. Angus served for a short time at HMS *Iolaire* at home, in the crew of the trawler HMT *Walwyns Castle*. He participated in the attempt to trap German U-boats in port at the Zeebrugge Raid, defined as 'hazardous

service' by the Admiralty, on 23rd April 1918. In December 1919, Angus's widow Annie was presented with his Distinguished Service Medal. MacKay's award recognised service on the minesweeper HMS *Plumpton*, leader of the minesweeping flotilla that entered Ostend Harbour after it had been evacuated by the Germans. The ship had struck a mine and the whole of the forepart as far as the bridge was blown up. All the occupants of the bridge were killed or hurled into the water by the force of the explosion — nine of the crew were lost and eleven badly injured. With all the officers killed or incapacitated, MacKay assumed command of the ship and directed the launching of lifeboats to rescue men struggling in the water. He then oversaw the removal of the dead and wounded from the sinking ship. He personally went to the engine-room and carried to the deck three sailors — two who were dead and one seriously wounded. The Commander of the flotilla came alongside and his launch was taken in tow and safely beached. The Commander personally complimented MacKay on his coolness and resourcefulness, whereby the lives of many were saved. In appreciation of his conduct he gave MacKay the honour of hoisting the White Ensign on the wreck of the famous HMS *Vindictive* at Zeebrugge. He was also given the honour of hoisting the flag over Ostend, as the King and Queen of the Belgians re-entered the city after its liberation. His courageous service through the whole length of the war ended in tragedy in home waters, and he was interred at Aignish Burial Ground (WG).

Donald Macaskill

born 26th June 1898. Age 20.

14 Shulishader. Seaman RNR. Service number 7041/A. Chatham Naval Memorial and LWM 1/LWM 20

Donald was the son of Donald and Margaret Macaskill (née Macleod) and enrolled on 10th December 1914, when he was just 16, adding two years to his age with the birthdate September 1896. His brother Hugh served with the Ross Mountain Battery and brother Angus was also in the RNR, as was older brother Duncan, who travelled home with Donald on the *Iolaire*. Donald served with HMS *Brazen*, HMS *Pembroke*, HMS *Actaeon*, HMY *Ceto* and HMY *Sigismund*. On the fateful homeward journey, he was one of the few *Iolaire* passengers who located a lifejacket but, as he was a stronger swimmer than his older brother Duncan, he gave the jacket to him. The family recounted how Duncan swam to the shore with Donald hanging on to his back, but he was swept away and his body was never recovered.

Alexander Maciver
(Ali)

born 26th January 1876. Age 42.

19 Shulishader. Leading Seaman RNR. Service number 1691/C. LWM 1/LWM 20

Son of Angus and Mary Maciver (née Macsween) and husband of Mary, née Macdonald, Alex enrolled with the RNR on 30th March 1900 and was sailing on the fishing boat *Bloom* (SY182) when the war was declared. During the war he served at HMS *Pembroke*, then HMS *Orama* for three years, some of it with his brother Norman. He was awarded the DSM while serving on

the *Orama*. He went on to HMS *Pactolus*, HMS *Colleen*, HMS *Venerable* and finally HMS *Implacable*, where he was serving on the Castle Class trawler HMT *Joseph Connell* and had been promoted to Second Hand, though this promotion was not implemented due to his death. He was also a qualified gunner. As he returned home on the *Iolaire*, he was said to have been the sailor who fired distress rockets and, while not substantiated during the Public Inquiry, this is an action clearly attributed to him in the Loyal Lewis Roll of Honour. Alex was interred at Aignish Burial Ground (WG).

John Macleod

born 7th March 1879. Age 39.

30 Lower Garrabost. Deckhand MMR. MMR number 968097. LWM 1/LWM 20

Son of Alexander and Catherine Macleod (née Campbell), John was the husband of Maggie and had two sons, both called Sandy. Like so many others, he was a peacetime fisherman who entered the Mercantile Marine Reserve under naval orders. He spent two of the war years at St Margaret's Hope, South Ronaldsay, as part of Scapa Flow operations. He returned home with fellow villager Norman Mackenzie (below) from Portsmouth, where they had both been based at HMS *Victory*. Both he and Norman were victims of the *Iolaire* and both now lie at Aignish Burial Ground (WG). Norman's elder son, Sandy Mòr, was a little boy when his father was lost and always remembered hearing someone say: "They found Iain." Iain's wife Maggie never again went to Stornoway after the disaster as she would have had to pass the cemetery to do so. She also disposed of all his naval memorabilia, including photographs. Iain's Gaelic bible, embossed John Macleod, was returned to family members from Canada in July 2015. Two of Maggie's sisters had emigrated to Vancouver and one of them may have taken it with her.

of the youngest aboard the *Iolaire*. He began his naval career at HMS *Pembroke I*, then served on HMT *Lothian* and left HMS *Victory* at Portsmouth for his New Year's leave. Early in the morning of 1st January 1919 John's mother went outside and heard a strange noise, the sound of wailing as the news of the disaster spread through Point – her son was one of those lost. Norman was the only one of the *Iolaire* lost to be interred at Eye Old Churchyard (WG).

Norman Mackenzie
(Kiman)

born 2nd April 1900. Age 18.

1 Church Street, Garrabost. Deckhand RNR.
Service number 20072/DA. LWM 1/LWM 20

Norman was the eldest son of John and Mary Mackenzie (née Campbell). John was from Bayble and was born deaf and dumb, as was his brother Donald. Both were enrolled at Donaldson's School for the Deaf in Edinburgh, where Donald trained as a tailor and John as a shoemaker – he became a master in that trade. Norman was nicknamed Kiman and carved that name on the back pew of the Church of Scotland in Garrabost, where it can still be seen. He worked as a telegram boy for most of the war, delivering the news of men wounded, missing and lost in the great conflict to households around Point. He himself enrolled as soon as he was old enough, on 16th April 1918, and was one

John Maciver
(Iain Iain Mhòir Dhòmhnaill Mhurchaidh)

born 12th August 1871. Age 47.

19 Lower Bayble. Mate MMR.
Chatham Naval Memorial and LWM 1/ LWM 20

John was the son of John and Margaret Maciver (née Maciver), and was married to Margaret, née Mackenzie. A devout man, he had been a fisherman pre-war and, when war came, served as a Mate on small naval vessels, a merchant seaman under naval orders. His eldest son Murdo was a naval reservist. John sailed for home on HMY *Iolaire*, but was never to rejoin his wife Margaret, who lived a widow until she passed away aged 90 in 1964. John's body was not recovered.

Alexander Macdonald

(Alasdair Iain Dhòmhnaill Tàilleir)

born 27th October 1877. Age 41.

32 Lower Bayble. Leading Seaman RNR. Service number 2046/C. Chatham Naval Memorial and LWM 1/LWM 20

Alex was the son of John and Isabella Macdonald (née Macleod) and husband of Margaret. A veteran of the sea, he had enrolled with the RNR on 26th April 1901, but lapsed before re-enrolling on 11th May 1911. He was a fisherman at Stornoway in the years leading up to the war. He served with HMS *Pembroke* and HMS *Natal* and was endorsed as a Leading Seaman at Chatham on 13th July 1915. He was with the cruiser *Natal* when she was sunk by an internal explosion at Invergordon on 30th December 1915. Nearly 400 were killed, including women and children. Later postings were at HMS *Stephen Furness* and HMS *Thalia* and his last service before his fateful leave was at HMY *Nairn*, an armed yacht. She was at Peterhead when Alexander left her and his commanding officer later reported that he had not returned from leave. In fact, he had perished in the wreck of the *Iolaire* and his remains were never recovered.

Murdo Maciver

(Murchadh Aonghais Dhòmhnaill Mhurchaidh)

born 14th July 1868. Age 50.

36 Lower Bayble. Deckhand RNR. Service number 775/SD. Chatham Naval Memorial and LWM 1/LWM 20

Murdo was the son of Angus and Isabella Maciver of No 29 Garrabost and married to Annie (née Graham). At the age of 50, he was old enough to be a father to some of his fellow passengers on the *Iolaire* and indeed sons Colin and Murdo were also RNR men who had survived the war. Murdo enrolled on 17th May 1915 and served at HMS *Pembroke*, then the armed boarding vessel HMS *Mona's Isle* operating out of HMS *Iolaire* and then HMS *Vivid*. On 25th August 1918 he went to the requisitioned minesweeping trawler HMT *Zena Dare*, attached to HMS *Vernon* and left her to return to his family. He never reached home and his remains were not relinquished by the sea.

William Macdonald

(Uilleam Dhòmhnaill Iain Dhòmhnaill Ruaidh)

born 2nd September 1897. Age 21.

44 Lower Bayble. Deckhand RNR. Service number 14360/A. LWM 1/LWM 20

The son of Donald and Catherine Macdonald (née Macleod), William's birthdate was given as July 1896 when he enrolled on 15th December 1916, joining up at Stornoway. He served throughout on the Auxiliary Patrol yacht HMY *Surf* and was the third war casualty in his family. Brother Donald (RNR) had drowned off the *Euphoric* on 1st December 1917 and brother Alexander was wounded in action with the Gordon Highlanders. William was interred at Aignish Burial Ground (WG).

John Smith

(Iain Aonghas Gobha)

born 6th September 1874. Age 44.

17 Upper Bayble. Seaman RNR. Service number 8055/A. Chatham Naval Memorial and LWM 1/LWM 20

Son of Angus and Isabella Smith (née Macleod), John was a fisherman and had lost his first wife Catherine, née Maciver, on 27th August 1914. He was already remarried to Annie Smith (née Smith) when he decided to offer his services at Stornoway on 15th April 1915, his birthdate then recorded as February 1876. He served on HMS *Polmont*, a captured Hungarian vessel used by the Royal Fleet Auxiliary (manned by the Royal Navy) as a store carrier. He later served at HMS *Theseus* and HMS *Pembroke*. His remains were never recovered after his drowning in the wreck of the *Iolaire* and he left his widow with two children. One, born 19 days after the disaster, died three months later.

Donald Mackenzie

(Dòmhnall Ruairidh Dhòmhnaill Alasdair)

born 2nd July 1863. Age 55.

22b Upper Bayble. Deckhand MMR. MMR number 967820. Plymouth Naval Memorial and LWM 1/LWM 20

The oldest man lost from the *Iolaire*, Donald was the son of Roderick and Catherine Mackenzie (née Maciver) and was married to Peggy (née Macleod). He was serving on HM Tug *Wickstead* as the war ended. The tug had been called *Wyvern* but was renamed in July 1918 as a new destroyer was allocated that name. Donald was homeward bound when his life was ended on the *Iolaire*. His remains were never recovered.

John Macleod

(Iain Mhurchaidh Chaluim)

born 15th April 1878. Age 40.

43 Upper Bayble. Seaman RNR. Service number 2736/B. LWM 1/LWM 20

Born at Portvoller, John was the son of Murdo and Hannah Macleod (née Macleod) and husband of Catherine, née Macdonald. He signed up for service as a naval reservist on 1st January 1905 and was a fisherman sailing out of Fraserburgh and Stornoway in the immediate pre-war days. He was a gunner based at HMS *Excellent* but was posted on 7th August 1914 to a requisitioned liner, which became the armed merchant cruiser HMS *Aquitania*. Two months later he was with another of the same class, HMS *Teutonic*. In 1916, he joined HMS *Moldavia* and was still aboard her when, on 23rd May 1918, she was sunk off Beachy Head by a single torpedo from

UB-57. Of her passenger complement of US troops a total of 56 American soldiers were drowned, but John survived and served thereafter at HMS *Victory I* and HMS *Excellent*. His life came to an end on the Beasts of Holm and he was interred at New Sandwick Cemetery (WG). By a tragic coincidence his son, Donald John 'Am Bleeb' Macleod, also drowned at the Beasts of Holm on 25th March 1977, aged 60, when the fishing vessel *Ivy Rose* [SY347] struck the rocks coming home from Lochinver.

Malcolm Macmillan

(Calum Chalum Chaluim)

born 14th July 1871. Age 47.

51 Upper Bayble. Seaman RNR.
Service number 1848/D. LWM 1/LWM 20

Son of Malcolm and Christina Macmillan (née Macleod), Malcolm was married to Catherine, née Mackenzie. He had both 18th January 1870 and 29th December 1870 recorded as dates of birth on his naval record. He enrolled on 13th November 1897 and fished out of Stornoway, before reporting to the repair ship HMS *Cyclops* at Scapa Flow on 3rd August 1914. On 28th October he was posted to HMS *Imperieuse*, also at Scapa Flow. Waiting for the *Iolaire* in Stornoway on January 1st 1919 was his 19 year-old son Malcolm, who was himself in the Gordon Highlanders and had obtained leave for New Year. Malcolm was interred at Aignish Burial Ground (WG).

Roderick Mackenzie

born 27th March 1887. Age 31.

5 Swordale. Second Hand RNR.
Service number 7246/DA. Chatham Naval Memorial and LWM 1/LWM 20

Roddy was the son of Murdo and Anne Mackenzie (née Macleod) and was married to Mary, née Macdonald. He enrolled on 10th May 1915 and was promoted to Second Hand on 6th November the same year. He served on HMT *Cardiff Castle* and HMT *Dragoon* from his home base, HMS *Iolaire*. On 3rd May 1917 he was posted away to HMS *Vivid II*, then he returned on 1st June 1917 to *Iolaire* with HMT *Romilly* and HMD *John Watt*. On 15th August 1918 he received a posting to HMS *Vigorous* and he served on HMD *Bellona II* and HMT *Romilly* again before his final trip home. According to John Macleod, a passenger on the *Sheila*, Roddy was asleep on the mailboat at the harbour in Kyle and awoke to be told that they were

not away yet, but that the *Iolaire* was leaving first. With that, he got up with his bundle and crossed from the *Sheila*, over the rails and onto the *Iolaire*, a fateful decision. His family still have his Death Penny Medal, but his body was never recovered.

Murdo Mackay

born 16th July 1886. Age 32.

16 Swordale. Seaman RNR.
Service number 4511/B. LWM 1/LWM 20

Son of Angus and Christina Mackay (née Macaulay) Murdo was single and enrolled on 5th March 1907. He fished out of Stornoway, Macduff and Peterhead pre-war and was called in August 1914, arriving at HMS *Dolphin* from Peterhead. He served with HMS *Victory I*, HMS *Columbine*,

HMS *Gunner*, HMT *Ratapiko*, the Q-ship HMS *Alma*, HMT *WS Bailey*, the anti-submarine gunboat HMS *Kildwick* (with dazzle camouflage), then HMS *Idaho* at Milford Haven. His last posting had been with the Mersey-class auxiliary patrol trawler HMT *George Fenwick*. When Murdo's body was found by his brother-in-law, the policeman John Macarthur, he was found to be carrying in his pocket a toy for his young nephew, the son of Murdo's sister Mary, who was John Macarthur's wife. He was interred at Aignish Burial Ground (WG).

Angus Crichton

born 3rd January 1878. Age 40.

12 Knock. Seaman RNR.
Service number 2687/B. Chatham Naval Memorial and LWM 1/LWM 20

Son of Colin and Jessie Crichton (née Macdonald), Angus was the husband of Mary, née Macleod, from Garrabost. His first wife Jane, née Macleod, from North Shawbost, had died on 25th March 1907 leaving him with two young sons, and he had two more sons with Mary. Angus enrolled on 1st January 1905, his birthdate given as December 1875. He fished out of Stornoway, Peterhead and Wick pre-war. He was posted to the armed merchant cruiser HMS *Edinburgh Castle* on 11th September 1914 and remained with her until 6th January 1918. He then served on the HMS *Morea* on passage as she was being decommissioned. He was also at HMS *Pembroke I*, HMS *Vulcan* (a depot ship for torpedo boats which was at Stornoway in early December 1918), HMY *Boadicea II*, HMS *Actaeon*, HMS *Ganges II*

and was posted to HMS *Ganges* at Shotley with effect from 1st January 1919, a posting he would never serve. It was said that a bag with his name containing four oranges for his children was recovered after the tragedy. His second son Murdo, aged 13, had travelled to Stornoway on New Year's Eve 1918 to meet him at the steamer pier and he and his elder brother Hugh were made orphans. Their half-brothers, Donald Angus 'Beaver' and Hugh (Uisdean), moved later to live at Scotland Street in Stornoway. Angus's body was never recovered.

Alexander Campbell

born 5th October 1898. Age 20.

26 Swordale. Deckhand RNR.
Service number 13353/DA. Chatham Naval Memorial and LWM 1/LWM 20

Alex was the only son of James and Mary Campbell (née Maciver) and enrolled on 21st November 1916. He was first based at HMS *Venerable*, from where he served on the minesweeping trawlers HMT *Miranda* and HMT *Sesostris*, then for most of the war on armed motor launches in the North Sea. From Swordale and Knock, Holm Point is in view and was a constant reminder to the bereaved from these villages, three men lost from Swordale alone. Alex's body was never recovered.

Donald Crichton

born 24th June 1895. Age 23.

15 Knock. Seaman RNR.
Service number 9066/A. Chatham Naval Memorial and LWM 1/LWM 20

Donald was the son of Alexander and Mary Crichton (née Macleod). He had enlisted with the RNR on 10th June 1916 and served at HMS *Pembroke I*, HMS *Queen Victoria*, HMS *Europa*, HMS *Hannibal* and then *Pembroke*. Apart from serving with the netlayer, HMS *Queen Victoria*, he was at land bases for the majority of the war. He packed his kitbag to return home in the barracks at Chatham, where he was based with HMS *Pembroke*, and travelled home with neighbour Angus Macleod (below), separated as death gripped them both. His wife Mary, née Maclean, was left without a gravestone to tend, as his body remained in the deep.

HMS *Arrogant* for HMML 422, then HMS *Victory* for HMML 419 and HMML 197. From 6th October 1918 he served at HMS *Victory*, HMS *Attentive III*, HMS *Arrogant* and HMS *Hermione*. He left HMS *Pembroke* with his neighbour Donald Crichton and they were together on the *Iolaire*. The sea gave up Angus's body, thus parting the two friends. He was interred at Aignish Burial Ground (WG) and his father soon joined him, dying on 17th February 1919, aged 76.

Angus Macleod

born 28th December 1896. Age 22.

18 Knock. Seaman RNR.
Service number 4548/SD. LWM 1/LWM 20

Angus was the youngest son of Torquil and Mary Macleod (née Macleod). He was single and one of a family of four brothers and a sister, Catherine, who had taught at Knock School and was a nurse at the Military Isolation Hospital in Aldershot. Brother Donald was already home on leave from the RNR at New Year 1919, Angus Senior was also a naval reservist and Alexander had died in 1901 aged 22. Angus Jr served from 10th March 1916, heading for Chatham with HMS *Pembroke* via Stornoway. He was then posted with the RNR (T) to HMS *Victory* at Portsmouth before moving to HMS *Gunner* at Granton, where he served with HMML 296. He continued on motor launches, serving at

Malcolm Macleod

born 5th February 1898. Age 19.

5 Aignish. Leading Deckhand RNR.
Service number 4793/SD. Chatham Naval Memorial and LWM 1/LWM 20

The eldest son of Donald and Catherine MacLeod (née Munro), Malcolm had a youngest brother he would never meet, born on 14th October 1918. Malcolm enrolled on 27th April 1916 at Stornoway with seven others from the district. He went to Portsmouth and HMS *Victory* and served with HMML 575. After six weeks he moved to HMS *Idaho* and served on the motor launch HMML 485 for two years, during which he was promoted quickly to Leading Deckhand. He received New Year leave and was expecting to see his fisherman father, who also served, but was home on leave when the *Iolaire* was lost. Instead the family were left to grieve without even his remains to lay to rest in home soil.

Roll call of the lost

203

STORNOWAY PARISH –

Malcolm Maciver

born 20th December 1881. Age 37.

28 Aignish. Deckhand RNR.
Service number LWM 1/LWM 20

Malcolm was a single man, son of
Malcolm and Catherine Maciver (née
Nicolson) and a teacher, who had
apprenticed at Knock School and was
assistant master at the John Neilson
Institute, Paisley, before the war. His
mother had died on 7th August 1913.
Malcolm joined the RNR on 8th January
1916 and served in the Irish Sea and in
the Atlantic, plagued by U-boats and
mines. He served at HMS *Iolaire* (base),
HMS *Pembroke*, then at Gibraltar with
HMT *Rushcoe* from 6th February 1917.
With the trawler he did service in the
Atlantic and the Irish Sea. HMD *Vigorous*
was his last posting, on 8th December
1918. He was interred at Aignish Burial
Ground (WG). His substantial headstone
was provided by the Neilson Academy,
Paisley and the Teacher Training College,
Dundee. His widowed father Malcolm
died in 1920, aged 77.

John Macdonald

born 11th July 1900. Age 18.

10 Holm. Deckhand RNR.
Service number 21078/DA. LWM 1/LWM 9

John was born at Burghead in Morayshire,
youngest son of Alexander and Margaret
Macdonald (née Maciver). John's father was
born in one of several crofts which were
removed to create Holm and Stoneyfield
Farms, where so many found succour on the
terrible night of the *Iolaire* disaster. Alexander
and five of his sons all served during the war,
two of the sons — 25-year-old Donald and
18-year-old John — never to come home.
John attended The Nicolson Institute from 1st
September 1915 until 22nd June 1917, after
which he helped at home before going into
uniform on 6th August 1918, almost as soon
as he was old enough. His record shows nine
shillings in recompense, for his trip from Kyle
to Glasgow on 7th August 1918. He served on
HMD *Genia* from 30th August 1918 and was
expected home at New Year, but became the
second son lost in seven weeks, when the
Iolaire came to grief on the rocks of his home
village. Elder brother Lt Commander Donald
Macdonald was lost seven weeks earlier
when HMS *Ascot* was sunk by UB-67 off the
Farne Islands, the day before the Armistice.
Sadly, John's parents were given false hope
on New Year's Day when the *Inverness
Courier* reported that he was a survivor, found
clinging to a mast. This proved false and, as
other newspapers followed suit, they had to
apologise in the following edition. John was
interred at Old Sandwick Cemetery (WG).

John Macaskill

born 16th January 1895. Age 23.

12 Lower Sandwick. Leading Deckhand RNR.
Service number 9635/DA. LWM 1/LWM 9

John was the son of Kenneth and Mary
Macaskill (née Macleod) and was single.
He had joined up with the RNR on 30th
September 1915 and was promoted to
Leading Deckhand on 7th June 1917. He
began service at HMS *Iolaire* (base), then
served on HMT *Donna Nook*, HMS *Victory*,
HMT *Chalcedony* and finally HMT *Thomas
Booth*. He had been home on leave in
October 1918 and his home shore exerted
what seemed a mystical pull even after
death — he was washed up on Sandwick
beach, almost outside his own front door,
and was interred equally close to home
in the Old Sandwick Cemetery, next to the
beach and the street on which he lived,
(WG).

Burgh and District of Stornoway: 8 men lost

Angus Macleod

born 20th March 1900 Age 18.
1 Newvalley. Deckhand RNR.
Service number 19972/DA. LWM 1

Born at Ranish to Alexander and Henrietta (or Euphemia) Macleod (née Maclean), Angus volunteered for naval duties on his 18th birthday, 20th March 1918. He was serving on HMT *Sir Mark Sykes* out of HMS *Nairn* in the north-east of Scotland, then switched trawlers to HMT *Transvaal*. He moved bases to HMS *Venerable* and was on the requisitioned trawler HMT *Resmilo*, which was acting as a minesweeper and equipped with hydrophones. Angus was interred at Crossbost Cemetery (WG).

Alexander Macdonald

born 9th August 1887. Age 31.
7 Newvalley. Second Hand RNR.
Service number 11708/DA.
Chatham Naval Memorial and LWM 1

Son of Donald and Margaret Macdonald (née Maclean), Alex was born at Sydney, Cape Breton and had two brothers, Angus and Malcolm who also served. He gave the Seamans' Mission, West Hartlepool as his address when he registered with the RNR at North Shields on 26th July 1916. In 1914 he was already a master mariner in the Australian Mercantile Marine and served with the Royal Australian Navy as a signaller at the Dardanelles until he returned to Britain in 1916. He served on HMD *Good Tidings* from HMS *Brilliant* then he went to HMS *Zaria* at Longhope. There followed HMT *Halcyon II*, HMT *Cleopatra II*, HMS *Victory I*, HMCS *Niobe* and finally HMD *Inchbroom*. He was promoted to Second Hand on 23rd May 1917 and was believed to have received an award for lifesaving during the Halifax, Nova Scotia, explosion on 6th December 1917, when 2,000 died and 9,000 were injured. At that time he was on the Canadian cruiser *Niobe*, which remained operational despite losing all her funnels, ventilators and masts. Alex had hoped to return to Australia after the war, but was drowned while returning from HMS *Pembroke* to see his widowed mother, who lived at Newvalley. His body was not recovered.

Donald Macleod

born 4th July 1900. Age 18.
10 Murray's Court. Ordinary Seaman RNVR.
Service number Z/9964. LWM 1/LWM 9

Donald was born to John and Mary Ann Macleod (née Morrison) at 7 Marvig, then the family lived at 10 Church Street before moving to Murray's Court, which was a close off Cromwell Street which is no longer a thoroughfare. He had two other brothers, Allan and Alexander and two sisters, Margaret and Dolly. Donald had been a member of the Boys' Naval Brigade attached to St Peter's Church pre-war. He served as a messenger at the Royal Navy depot at Crystal Palace and had trained as a gunner. He volunteered on 6th August 1918 but, despite his evident record of enthusiasm for service, he was adjudged to be ineligible for a war gratuity. Donald was interred at New Sandwick Cemetery (WG), where he is beside Alfred S Taylor, the *Iolaire* Steward.

Malcolm Macleod
42 Keith Street – See 2 Crossbost.

Donald Macritchie

born 24th January 1889. Age 29.

46 Keith Street. Cooper 4th Class, RN.
Service number M/23855. LWM 1

Donald was born in Leurbost, son of
Christina Macritchie who subsequently
married Finlay Maclean. He lived at 37
South Beach in Stornoway before he
married Jeanie Maciver on 12th August
1915 in Glasgow. The family lived at 10
Newton Street, where daughter Davidina
(known as Dina) was born, then they
moved to Keith Street. He was a member
of the Loyal Lewis Lodge of Oddfellows,
which met at Lodge Fortrose, a street
away on Kenneth Street. A Cooper 4th
Class, his trade was useful in the service
at a time when barrels were still used for
storing foodstuffs. He joined the service
on 30th March 1917 and was based at
HMS *Pembroke* at Chatham when New
Year leave promised the comfort of home
with his young wife and daughter. Donald
was interred at New Sandwick Cemetery
(WG). The headstone carries the Gaelic
inscription: '*Gus am bris an latha san teich
na sgàilean – Dina Macritchie*' ('Until the
day breaks and the shadows flee away')

John Alexander Macaskill
(Jack)

born 7th March 1899. Age 19.

75 Keith Street. Signalman RNVR.
Service number Z/8453. LWM 1/LWM 9

Born in Liverpool to Hugh and Chrissie
"Teens" Macaskill (née Maclean), Jack
Macaskill was their only son and had just
one sister, Maggie 'Teens'. Jack was well
known in the town as a junior clerk in the
Harbour Office, from soon after war broke
out. He was a member of the Stornoway
Boys' Naval Brigade and volunteered his
services as soon as he reached an age to
enlist. His signalling skills were quickly
spotted and he was engaged by the
RNVR to serve from 1st April 1917 until the
cessation of hostilities. He served at HMS
Victory VI, HMS *Victory I* and HMS *Vivid
III* and saw plenty of action, including
being torpedoed twice. He left HMS
Vivid at Devonport to rejoin his family in

Stornoway but was never to see them again. His body was not recovered until late February 1919 and he was then interred at Old Sandwick Cemetery (WG). A memorial tablet to his memory is in St Peter's Church, Stornoway.

William Kirk Wilson

born 27 August 1879. Age 39.

36 Beach House, South Beach Street. ERA4 RN.
Service number M/14184. Chatham Naval Memorial

Born at Coatbridge to James and Elizabeth Wilson (née Crawford), William had married Mary Angusina (née Nicolson) from 12 Gravir on 4th November 1916, while serving from the Stornoway base. He had been in the Mercantile Marine and was engaged for the duration of hostilities from 28th June 1915, when his birth year was given as 1890. After training at HMS *Pembroke*, he was posted to HMS *Manco* at Stornoway from 4th August 1915 to 30th September 1915. William was posted to HMY *Iolaire* on 1st October 1915 and was at Stornoway on the yacht until 27th March 1918. He was posted away for a month at HMS *Pembroke II* before going out to Gibraltar on 22nd April 1918 to join HMS *Mistletoe*, a modern sloop which was disguised as a 'Q' ship to attract U-boats. When in Stornoway William lived at 56 Keith Street with his wife and they had two daughters before moving to South Beach. They had intended moving to Glasgow once the war ended, but Mary was at home in Gravir when William got his unexpected New Year leave. He planned to surprise her and would probably not have seen his second-born daughter. It was heartbreaking for survivors who knew him to tell his wife that William had been aboard the *Iolaire*.

ISLE OF SCALPAY – 1 man lost

Finlay Morrison
(Fionnlagh Dhòmhnaill Fhionnlaigh)

born 10th March 1893. Age 25.

Ardhanasaig. Deckhand RNR.
Service number 4515/SD. LWM 2

Born at Kyles, Scalpay, Finlay was the son of Donald and Mary Morrison (née Macdermid), of Ardhanasaig. He enrolled on 11th April 1912 and left Stornoway for HMS *Victory* on 12th May 1916. He served throughout the war on the armed motor launches 278, 280 and 250 and was with HMML 560 when sent home on New Year leave. He was due to be married to Catherine Morrison (Catriona Tharmoid) from Cuddy Point, Scalpay and, like a number of Harris sailors, opted to cross the Minch with the Lewis contingent rather than wait until the following day for a connection to Tarbert via Skye. Finlay knew that Catriona had bought her wedding trousseau and he was in a hurry to get home to make preparations for the imminent wedding. Instead of a wedding, it was a funeral that Catriona attended after his remains were found and brought for interment at Old Luskentyre Burial Ground (WG). Finlay's brother Donald, who travelled with him as far as Kyle, had waited for the Harris transport and got home safely.

ISLE OF HARRIS –

Finlay Maclennan
(Frank)

born 27th June 1897. Age 21.

Meavaig South. Deckhand RNR.
Service number 18771/DA. LWM 2

Son of Christina Maclennan (née Morrison), Finlay joined up on 14th November 1917 from Glasgow. After six weeks training at HMS *Vivid I*, the RN Barracks at Devonport, he joined the battleship HMS *Queen* on 1st January 1918. His next posting was the HMD *Primevere*, then he sailed with HMT *Loch Hourn*. He was listed as being with HMS *Imperieuse* at Scapa Flow in December 1918. His naval records show two addresses, one at 84 Plantation Street, Glasgow and the other was his parents' home in Harris. For some sad reason, his war gratuity payment was not paid to his next of kin, but instead went to the Exchequer at Edinburgh, administrator of estates of deceased persons. Finlay's body was interred at Old Luskentyre Burial Ground (WG).

4 men lost

Farquhar Morrison
(Fearchar Dhòmhnaill 'Ic Chaluim)

born 11th September 1883. Age 35.

Scrott, Stockinish. Seaman RNR.
Service number 3161/B. LWM 2

Farquhar was the son of Donald and Rachael Morrison (née Macdonald). He had been married to Rachel, née Mackinnon, but her death on 27th November 1909 left Farquhar to bring up daughter Rachael, a year old at the time. He enrolled with the RNR on 1st April 1905 and was a merchant seaman at Greenock and Ardrossan pre-war. He served on the paddle steamers *Duchess of Argyll* and *Duchess of Montrose* as well as SS *Torch*, SS *Spinel*, SS *Gyp* and SS *Hebridean*. He became an AB in the Mercantile Marine in 1912. He was at Newcastle when the war began and after HMS *Pembroke* he was at HMS *Halcyon* for armed trawler duties. He was briefly with HMS *Illustrious*, then he was aboard HMT *Settsu* at HMS *Cyclops*, followed by HMY *Vanessa* and HMS *Manco* in Stornoway, until HMS *Iolaire* was established in 1915. HMS *Dreel Castle* was his next base, then HMS *Hannibal* and he was with HMY *Valhalla II* at HMS *Pembroke* when given his final New Year leave.

Farquhar would have been expected on the boat coming into Tarbert from Kyle and so, as was the custom in Stockinish, a boat from the village rowed out to meet the passenger steamer. Youngsters gathered on the shore at Stockinish to welcome Farquhar home. Noticing that he was not in the returning rowing boat, they called out, "Nach d' thainig Fearchar?" ('Did Farquhar not come?') Farquhar's father, who was sitting in the stern of the boat, with a bowed head, said solemnly: "Cha d' thainig 's cha tig." ('He didn't arrive and never will'.) The naval authorities formally notified Miss Johanna Morrison (guardian) of the loss, which made young Rachael an orphan at the age of 10. Farquhar was interred at Old Luskentyre Burial Ground (WG).

Kenneth Maclean

born 8th July 1900. Age 18.

12 Northton. Deckhand RNR.
Service number 20994/DA. LWM 2

Born at Bayhead, Lingerabay, Kenneth and his parents Donald and Mary Maclean (née Mackay) moved to Northton with his eight siblings when he was two. He enrolled on 12th July 1918 and went from Aberdeen to the HMS *Satellite* base on the Tyne. He served on HMD *Consolation* and HMT *William Browning*, then served on the London class pre-dreadnought battleship HMS *Venerable* in the latter months of 1918. His mother Mary lost not only a son but a nephew in Norman Mackay of Leverburgh. Kenneth was interred at New Scarista Cemetery (WG).

Norman Mackay

born 26th May 1900. Age 18.

Leverburgh (Obbe). Seaman RNR.
Service number 9494/A.
Chatham Naval Memorial and LWM 2

Norman was the son of Neil and Flora Mackay (née Macmillan). He was single and had only just enrolled on 9th July 1918, sent to the base at HMS *Pembroke* at Chatham. Intending to walk over 60 miles from Stornoway to his home, he joined the small group of Harrismen who made the journey over the Minch on the *Iolaire*. Like relatives of many another very young man, his family received nothing by way of gratuity from the Admiralty. The headstone of his parents at Rodel Churchyard records their son's loss.

ISLE OF BERNERAY – 2 men lost

Donald Paterson
(Dòmhnall Raonaid Dhòmhnaill Mhòir)

born 3rd May 1900. Age 18.

5 Borve. Seaman RNR.
Service number 9521/A. LWM 3

The son of a merchant, John, and Rachel Macleod, Donald was a herdsman at Middlequarter, North Uist, before serving. He was sometimes referred to as Macleod on his native island. He enrolled on 25th September 1918 and was with lifelong friend Norman Mackillop when they left HMS *Pembroke* at Chatham together, for a New Year back on their home island. Together they took the fateful decision to seek passage to Stornoway rather than await the boat for Tarbert later the following day and together they drowned, though only Donald's body was yielded up by the sea. He was interred at Berneray Burial Ground (WG). His father John was drowned at Broadbay just over 10 years later, on 2nd March 1929, aged 52.

Norman Mackillop
(Tarmod Mhàiri Nèill)

born 7th June 1900. Age 18.

11 Borve. Seaman RNR.
Service number 9522/A.
Chatham Naval Memorial and LWM 3

Norman was the son of Mary Mackillop and stepson of Donald Maclean. He and his pal Donald Paterson went to the local school together in 1906 and then joined up together in September 1918, with consecutive service numbers. They had not been in the service for long and were still in training as they left from the barracks of HMS *Pembroke* for New Year leave at home. Their families did not receive a War Service Gratuity as they were reckoned not to have seen any war service, despite losing their lives in returning on leave. Norman's body was not recovered.

REST OF THE UNITED KINGDOM – *Iolaire* crew 18 men lost

Ernest Ainsworth Brown
born 16th November 1895. Age 23.

Grimsby. Trimmer/Cook RNR.
Service number 902/TC. Grimsby Roll of Honour 1914-19 and Chatham Naval Memorial.

Ernest was born at Grimsby, the son of William and Martha Brown (née Stocks), and had four brothers and three sisters. In the 1911 census he was described as an 18-year-old house boy. He enrolled into the RNR on 29th November 1916 and served with several small vessels. He received 42 days detention for deserting HMT *Robert Betson* on 29th August 1917. He was posted to HMS *Iolaire* and served on HMT *William Jones* from 3rd December 1918. Due to the *Iolaire*'s crew shortage he was loaned from the trawler to the yacht. He was single and his mother (also referred to as Ellen) had remarried to Stephen Kendall after his father's decease. Ernest's body was not recovered.

Leonard Edmund D. Cotter
born 8th April 1869. Age 49.

Cowes, Isle of Wight. Lieutenant RNR. Portsmouth Naval Memorial, St Mary's Church, Cowes and Cowes War Memorial.

Leonard Edmund Dillistone Cotter was born to Edmund Dennis and (Emily) Pamela Cotter (née Back) at Great Yarmouth. His father was a lamplighter with Trinity House (Lighthouse) service but went on to be a seaman. Leonard is believed to have had six brothers and sisters. By 1901 he was married to a Welsh woman, Margaret Mayall, at Bridgend and was listed as a Master Mariner. He was master of the steam yacht *Christabel* in America pre-war. During the war Cotter was on the bridge of HMY *Goissa* when she collided with the battlecruiser HMS *Invincible*, during the return home from a search for enemy craft off Yarmouth and Lowestoft. *Invincible* was rammed by the *Goissa*, which left her bow broken off and embedded in *Invincible*'s starboard side. *Invincible* was forced to haul out of line and go to Rosyth for repairs in drydock. Four men (including a Lewisman) were killed in the yacht and one sailor died on the larger vessel. The same yacht, under Cotter's navigation, was in collision with Granton West Pier, which led to an inquiry. Cotter's record states 'Committed error of judgement – cautioned'. He did not go to sea again for some time, but was posted to HMY *Amalthaea* on 26th August 1918, shortly before she became *Iolaire*. His body was not recovered from the *Iolaire*'s wreck on 1st January 1919. Cotter's wife died three months after him, of influenza and other complications, leaving their four children as orphans.

Charles Dewsbury
born 30th May 1889. Age 29.

Great Yarmouth. Leading Deckhand MMR. Brighton War Memorial

Charles was reported to be an American married in England, but was definitely the son of Sergeant Major William John and Caroline Sarah Dewsbury (née Fuller) who, at the time of the 1891 census, were living at 12 Warne Street, Kingston-Upon-Hull – son Charles is listed as born 1889 in Knightsbridge. It appears they went overseas sometime thereafter, possibly to Canada or the USA which could have led to the American story. Charles joined the MMR in 1909 and was the husband of Emily Matilda Dewsbury of 1 Rodney Road, Great Yarmouth. He was interred at New Sandwick Cemetery (WG).

Frank Humphry
born 10th March 1877. Age 41.

Southampton. Steward MMR.

Frank grew up at the Retreat Hotel in Poole, run by his father Adolphus and Scottish mother Elizabeth Humphrey (née Hutchinson). Frank had an elder and younger brother and was married to Annie Humphrey (née Dadswell) of 188 Derby Road, Southampton. His remains were transported home and he was interred at Southampton Cemetery (WG).

Thomas Harris
born 1st January 1892. Age 27.

Portsmouth. Greaser MMR.

Born at Landport, Portsmouth, Thomas Edward Henry Harris was the son of Samuel and Emma Harris (née Roberts) and had an older brother. His father was a baker in Portsmouth Dockyard. Thomas was single and drowned in the engine room of the *Iolaire* on his 27th birthday. He was interred at Portsmouth (Kingston) Cemetery (WG).

Alfred William Henley
born 1st June 1873. Age 45.

Ryde, Isle of Wight. Chief Petty Officer MMR. MFA 2932.

A Chief Petty Officer Cook, Alf was lost in the New Year's Day tragedy four days after being home on leave. He was the son of Richard and Urania Ann Henley (née Toogood) and was married to Elizabeth Jane Oates (Janie) Henley (née Cundy) of Newlands, St Helens, Isle of Wight. He and his brothers were noted footballers and he was Secretary of the Blue Star club of St Helens in his younger days. In peace-time he had been a chef, then joined the Royal Navy with brother Ernest, who was a seaman. He had left the Navy and was Chief Cook on Lord Howard de Walden's yacht *Callista* pre-war, then rejoined the Navy when hostilities broke out. After his loss on the *Iolaire*, Alfred's body arrived home on the 6th January and was interred the following day, after a service at the Parish Church held by Rev JH Pearson. He is buried at St Helens Churchyard, Ryde, Isle of Wight (WG).

John Hern
born 26th January 1892. Age 26.

Sunderland. Second Engineer MMR.

John was born at Monkwearmouth, only son of John and Anne Elizabeth Hern (née Lamb). He had three sisters, was single and his father, his grandfather and three uncles were all master mariners. John became an engineer serving under naval discipline on T-124X rates. After the loss of the *Iolaire*, his remains were recovered and he was interred at Sunderland (Mere Knolls) Cemetery (WG). His father refused to claim from the *Iolaire* Fund as he felt that: "There are more urgent cases than ours on your island." But, he added "Would you kindly let me know if you are having a Public Inquiry?"

Joseph William George

born 30th July 1876. Age 42.

Newcastle. Fireman MMR.

Son of Samuel and Margrite George (née Turnbull) and born at Consett, Durham, Joe worked in the stokehold of the *Iolaire*. At the turn of the century he worked in a factory as a boring machine man, while his father was an iron worker. In the 1911 census he was away at sea. He married Jane, née Archer, of Byker, in 1909 and had four step-children. He was interred at Newcastle-on-Tyne (Byker and Heaton) Cemetery (WG).

Ernest John Leggett

born 8th September 1879. Age 41.

Emsworth, Hampshire. Deckhand MMR. MMR number 69521 and MRA 2935.

Born at Portsea, son of James and Jane Leggett (née Sheppard), Ernie was the husband of Maud Ethel, née Matthews, who died before him after having eight children. He was acting quartermaster on the night the *Iolaire* struck the rocks, having been a fisherman and at sea for most of his life. His crewmate Charles Kingsbury, later claimed that Leggett reached land after the *Iolaire*'s wreck, but died of exposure in the bitter darkness. He was interred at Havant and Waterloo (Warblington) Cemetery (WG) and eight children were left orphans. Two sons, Ernest and Fred, aged 13 and eight, had an application to the *Iolaire* Fund made on their behalf through All Saints Orphanage in Lewisham, where they were living on 8th June 1921. Ten-year-old daughter Dolly was with an aunt and little Willie, aged six, was in Devonport Children's Home. The family also included four older children, two boys aged 18 and 17 and two girls aged 18 and 15.

David Macdonald

born 10th June 1901. Age 17.

Aberdeen. Signal Boy RNR. Service number 1265/SB. Aberdeen City War Memorial.

Son of John and Mary Macdonald (née Duff), David was the youngest casualty of the *Iolaire* disaster and had been a crew member only since October 1918. The son of a coal carrier, he had enrolled on 3rd October 1917 when he was just five feet one inch tall, but had already served with HMS *Victory*, HMT *Foss*, HMS *Dreel Castle* and HMS *Kingfisher*. He had Christmas leave at home at 53 Virginia Street and was coming back with the Lewis boys for the New Year. He was interred at New Sandwick Cemetery (WG) and the foot of his headstone is inscribed 'Thy Will Be Done'.

Henry Orley Mariner

born 29th June 1894. Age 23.

Portsmouth. Deckhand MMR. MMR number 821982. Portsmouth Naval Memorial.

Born at Portsea Island, Henry lived in peacetime with his parents, Charles and Minnie Elizabeth Mariner (née Orley) at 217 Queens Road, Buckland, Portsmouth. In 1911 'Harry' was listed as an errand boy and his father was a wholesale grocer. His body was never recovered from the wreck of the *Iolaire*.

REST OF THE UNITED KINGDOM – *Iolaire* crew

Richard Gordon William Mason
born 23rd April 1874. Age 44.

Sheffield. Commander RNR.
Portsmouth Naval Memorial.

Son of Robert G.S. and Julia C. Mason (née Lambert) and born in Newry, Ireland, Mason was a career seaman and had served in the in the RNR and Mercantile Marine all his working life. His four-year apprenticeship was under sail with A and J H Carmichael of Greenock and he had sailed with the White Star Line as a qualified Master from 6th July 1901. His first wife, Alice, née Carr-Ellison, died just a year after their marriage in Liverpool in 1915, but he soon remarried, to Lucy Lavinia Gough of 75 Main Road, Handsworth, Sheffield. On 20th January 1917 he served with the Royal Naval Reserve. Mason's last command would prove to be a tragic one, but the mystery of what happened on that night also leaves a question about the eventual resting place of his remains. After the wreck of the *Iolaire* his body was recovered, according to registrar records and to an early report in the *Inverness Courier*, but there is no record of an interment.

Frederick Charles McCarthy
born 9th August 1885. Age 33.

Hartlepool. Carpenter MMR.
Plymouth Naval Memorial.
Newcastle Cathedral (plaque).

Fred was the son of John Joseph and Jane McCarthy (née Sleightholm) of 14 Hope Street, West Hartlepool. He was single and worked as the ship's carpenter on the yacht, responsible for electrical, wooden and metal fittings. His first job after school had been as an ironmonger's assistant. His mother died young and the father and his two sons lived with an older married daughter. Fred had been a bell-ringer at Stranton Church in Hartlepool and a member of Durham and Newcastle Association of Bell-ringers. He is commemorated on a plaque in Newcastle Cathedral. His body was not recovered from the wreck of the *Iolaire*.

David Bisset Ramsay
born 6th September 1868. Age 50.

Auchterarder. Seaman RNR.
Service number 1350/D.
Auchterarder War Memorial.

Born at Westhaven, Carnoustie, to David and Mary Ramsay (née Bisset – her name is also given as Ann), David was the husband of Martha Robertson Nicol, née Buchan, who he married on 22nd February 1907. David had long-term seafaring experience as a whale harpooner on the *Morning* (Captain Adamson) at the outbreak of hostilities. He had enrolled into the RNR on 6th November 1894 and was in the mercantile marine pre-war. His ships included *Eveline*, *Scotia*, *Aberfoyle*, *Glitra*, *Alexa* and *Patunia*. He was awarded the RNR Medal for Long Service and Good Conduct on 27th November 1911. As soon as war came, he was called to serve on the store carrier RFA *Intaba* until 19th

July 1915. He then served briefly on HMY *Amalthaea* with spells at HMS *Victory*, HMS *Brilliant*, HMS *Zaria* and HMS *Kingfisher* before returning to the yacht, now named HMY *Iolaire*, on 15th October 1918. He went home for his Christmas leave in 1918 and left on the 27th to return to Stornoway. After his remains were recovered from the wreck he was returned to his home town and his coffin, draped with the Union flag, was carried by a bearer party of seamen and servicemen to be interred to the sound of the Last Post at Auchterarder Cemetery (WG). His death left four children fatherless.

Harold James Moore
born 31st December 1888. Age 30.

Southend. Deckhand MMR.
Southend-on-Sea
County Borough War Memorial.

Son of John Frederick and Elizabeth Moore (née Cosgrove), Harold had just passed his 30th birthday and was to die in the first hours of his 31st year. A Deckhand on the *Iolaire*, Harold was, like many of the crew, a merchant seaman sailing under naval discipline. Before the war he worked as a waterman and he had two brothers and two sisters at home, a widowed mother and a wife, Mary. His remains were brought back to them and he was interred at Southend-on-Sea (John the Baptist) Churchyard (WG).

Charles Ritchie Niven Rankin
born 10th October 1887. Age 31.

Penzance. Sub Lieutenant RNR.
Roll of Honour, St Marys Church Cowes, Isle of Wight; Cowes Town Memorial and the Court Foresters Isle (No 1822) Memorial, now also held at St Mary's Church, Cowes.

The Sub Lieutenant (Engineer) on the ill-fated yacht, Charles was born at 13 Copeland Road, Govan, Glasgow to John and Annie Campbell Rankin (née Niven) and became an apprentice fitter at 14 years old in Cowes, Isle of Wight – his parents had moved there as his father was a marine engineer. By 1911 he was an engine fitter living in digs at Portsmouth and working in HM dockyard. On 26th April 1915 he was with the yacht *Rovenska* and in February 1916 he became a Sub Lieutenant (Engineer). He married Gladys Wood in 1918, when their address was 4 Movabe Lee, Penzance. He joined HMY *Amalthaea* (*Iolaire*) from HMS *Kingfisher* on 26th March 1918 and she would be the cause of his untimely end. Charles was interred at Penzance Cemetery (WG).

William Joseph John Stanley
born 6th July 1899. Age 19.

Greenwich, London. Deckhand MMR.

William was the son of William and Lucy Maria Stanley (née Prior) and lived at 75 Calvert Road in East Greenwich. He had an elder sister but was motherless, Lucy dying shortly after his birth. William attended Calvert Street County Council school. His father worked on the river which bounded their world, as a waterman and lighterman for the Thames Conservancy – William followed him into the job on leaving school. He joined up on 23rd July 1917 and joined *Amalthaea* just three months later, in October 1917. She would be his only posting. William perished in the salt waters off Holm and was brought back to the riverside to be interred at Greenwich (Shooter's Hill) Cemetery (WG). A relation, Dorothy Waring, came to Stornoway in 2015, visited the *Iolaire* monument at Holm and gave some of this biographical detail.

Roll call of the lost

215

Passengers returning to HMS *Iolaire* base from Christmas leave – 2 men lost

Alfred Samuel Edwin Taylor

born 2nd July 1885. Age 33.

Hyde Park, London.
Assistant Steward MMR.

The *Iolaire*'s assistant steward was born in Landport, Portsmouth to Alfred John and Jane Louisa Taylor (née Samphier). His father was a shipwright in HM dockyard at Portsmouth and there were four children. By 1911 Alfred was living with his younger brother, Albert, at 173 Cleveland Street, when he was described as a weaver, braid maker and silk spinner. It's not known when Alfred joined up or where he had served, but he was by that time living at the same address as an aunt, Miss M. Allen, at Gloucester Lodge, 205 Gloucester Terrace, Hyde Park, London. His life ended on the *Iolaire* and he was interred on 3rd January 1919 at New Sandwick Cemetery in Stornoway (WG), following a service conducted by Rev S. Morris Crow, chaplain of the Missions to Seamen. Alfred's coffin was conveyed on a gun carriage to St Peter's Episcopal Church, and thence to the cemetery. The carriage was drawn by a contingent of 18 sailors under the charge of Lieutenant Boxall, RN Divisional Coastguard. His parents had passed away before his loss, the father in 1915, and his sister Cecilia Taylor is given as next of kin in 1919.

Herbert William Head

born 10th December 1883. Age 37.

Ipswich. Private RMLI.
Service number PO/11997.
Portsmouth Naval Memorial.

Herbert was born at Lavenham, Suffolk, to George William and Catherine Sophia Head (née Lewis) of Church Hill, Monks Eleigh, Ipswich. He was the son of a farm labourer and became a Royal Marine, enlisting on 23rd October 1901 and giving his birthdate as 12th December 1881. He was probably a gunner at sea. Herbert had served on the pre-dreadnought battleship HMS *Queen* for much of the war and most of his service ashore was spent at Portsmouth and HMS *Victory*. He was a single man but Catherine Wares from Pulteneytown, Wick was waiting for him at the pier in Stornoway – New Year's Day was to be their wedding day. Catherine was expecting a baby, something which may not have been known to Herbert's family. She believed that Herbert, a strong swimmer, had got ashore from the wreck, but went back to help others. He was then lost and his body was not recovered. Catherine returned to Pulteneytown and worked as a herring gutter, her daughter born on 13th June 1919 and christened Elizabeth (Betty) Head.

Albert Richard Matthews

born 16 October 1896. Age 22.

Chiswick, London.
Leading Victualling Assistant RN.
Service number M/15986.

Born at Islington to William Thomas and Annie Matthews of 19 Whitehall Park Road, Chiswick, Albert was a clerk before he was engaged by the Royal Navy on 25th October 1915 for hostilities only. He served at HMS *Vivid I* until he was posted to HMS *Iolaire* base as a Ships Steward Assistant (SSA). He became a Leading Victualling Assistant at HMS *Iolaire* base on 26th October 1918 and his job ashore was as a storekeeper for navy rum rations and other liquor on the base. Albert was returning from Christmas leave as a passenger on the *Iolaire* to continue his service at Stornoway when he was lost. His remains were interred at Islington Cemetery and Crematorium (WG).

Casualty Statistics

At the time of the *Iolaire* Disaster, the media reported that approximately 205 souls had been lost, but no formal listing of all of the men was made at the time, apart from one containing 195 names by the *Times*. In separate tallies of *Iolaire* casualties, authors Norman Malcolm Macdonald, John Macleod, Donald J MacLeod, Malcolm Macdonald and Don Kindell have each concluded that the number lost was 201. In preparing the material for this book, the authors found that the evidence given to the Public Inquiry accords exactly with this figure, but was then unrecorded in the findings, and the erroneous casualty figure of 205 used from that point onwards.

The following five sailors have, in the past, been in various lists of those lost on the *Iolaire*, but were not aboard the vessel. Two were drowned elsewhere, one was on the mailboat, Morrison was not on board and the other appears to have not existed.

Badcock, Frank Smn RNR 3374/C HMS *President III* – Clovelly, Devon – died 1st January 1919

Marshall, Albert AB RN 208745 HMS *Landrail* – Nottingham – died 1st January 1919

MacLennan, William Smn RNR, 18336/DA HMS *Satellite* – 36 Cliff, Uig – was on board the *Sheila*

Morrison, Colin DH RNR, 20569/DA HMS *Pembroke* – 21 Breanish, Uig – was listed as a casualty by the Clan Morrison Society. He was not aboard and died at Edinburgh on 30th March 1960.

Maclellan, John AB MM, T-124Y Rates – it is believed this name has appeared due to confusion with survivor John Maclennan, who had been in the crew of the original HMY *Iolaire*.

To correct other errors repeated at different times: Kenneth Nicolson, one of the *Men of Lewis* in the book of that name, was listed as a casualty in the *Oban Times*. No sailor of that name existed, but the father of Donald Nicolson, 10 North Shawbost, was named Kenneth. A Norman Maclean of 13 Doune Carloway was listed as one of those drowned in the 1960 book *Sea Sorrow*. No man of that name existed, but Norman Macphail, listed as lost from his married address at Knock, Carloway, had grown up at 13 Doune Carloway and was brother to two survivors who still lived there. It was formerly believed that 175 Lewismen were lost, but it is now known that 174 Lewismen and 7 Harrismen were lost. 18 crew and 2 passengers also drowned, adding to a total of 201.

Local War Memorials as referred to above

LWM 1 Lewis (Stornoway)

LWM 2 Harris (Tarbert)

LWM 3 Isle of Berneray (quay)

LWM 4 North Uist (Clachan)

LWM 5 Benbecula (Griminish)

LWM 6 South Uist (Bornish)

LWM 7 Barra (Nask)

LWM 8 North Lewis (Cross)

LWM 9 North Lewis (Borve)

LWM 10 Carloway

LWM 11 Tolsta Chaolais

LWM 12 Isle of Great Bernera (Breaclet)

LWM 13 Uig (Baile na Cille)

LWM 14 Tolsta (North Tolsta)

LWM 15 Back (Back)

LWM 16 Branahuie/Melbost

LWM 17 North Lochs (Crossbost)

LWM 18 Pairc (Kershader)

LWM 19 Nicolson Institute (main entrance eSgoil)

LWM 20 Point (Garrabost)

LWM 21 Kinloch (Laxay)

LWM 22 Arnol/Bragar/Shawbost (Bragar)

LWM 23 Loch Roag (Callanish)

LWM 24 Barvas and Brue (Barvas)

Chapter 6

Rumours, Questions and Inquiries

"The people of Lewis were in no mood to tolerate – and no one should ask them to tolerate – any hushing up of facts or shielding of individuals. The whole truth must come out, at whatever cost to the reputation or position of men. Lewis had suffered too deeply to have had her agony added to by any such trifling. …… On the simple ground of human rights they should demand sympathy and justice and the most searching scrutiny into this tragic affair."[1]

Amidst the grief and desolation at loss of loved ones, questions about how such a disaster could have happened soon began to circulate in the islands. Allegations about the primary causes of the disaster were made by survivors and civilians and caused deep unrest and pain, increasing the demand for a full and impartial inquiry. Among the rumours, the assertion of drink playing a part became folklore. At least one survivor talked of bottles of liquor on the bridge and, given the time of year, the suspicion that drink was involved was natural. Fuelling the rumour were survivors' accounts of the *Iolaire*'s collision with Kyle pier as she arrived, vocal and persistent enough to lead to this swift exchange of telegrams between Rear Admiral Boyle and the Port Office at Kyle on the Sunday following the disaster:

> "**From**: Rear Admiral, Stornoway ….Rumours have reached me that the Officers in "*Iolaire*" on 31st December were not in a fit state to take charge. Request your opinion."

> "**From**: Port, Kyle…… Your 1315, from personal knowledge and from information received can state Commanding Officer and Navigating Officer fit state to take charge, have no reason to suppose other officers were not equally fit."[2]

The assertion was probably given an added impetus by the political background. Prohibition was a live and emotive issue at the time. A year later Stornoway was to vote to go dry and remained so for six years.

Another unpleasant rumour alleged high words between the *Iolaire*'s master, Commander Mason, and some of his Lewis passengers at Kyle. Before the vessel sailed Mason was supposedly heard to threaten, "I'll dip their heels before we get to port!"

These and other causes for grievance, especially given the huge number of people bereaved, led to swift public declamations by island representatives, including at least one minister, the town council and other leading citizens. Stornoway Town Council met on Friday 3rd January and approved a letter to be sent to the Admiralty in London:

> "This Town Council deeply deplores the appalling disaster which happened to HMY *Iolaire* at the entrance of Stornoway Harbour on 1st January, by which over 200 lives were lost under the most tragic circumstances, and express on their behalf and in the name of the community their profound sympathy with the dependants and relatives of our brave sailors who perished on the threshold of their homes as they were looking forward to a happy reunion with their loved ones after a prolonged period of war service, and they demand of the responsible authority the strictest investigation into all the circumstances attending the catastrophe and the responsibility attached thereto."[3]

Even the widow of Commander Mason, who might have been implicated in the *Iolaire*'s loss, wrote to the *Daily Telegraph* to express her satisfaction that resolutions have been passed demanding the Admiralty pursue the "strictest investigations into all the circumstances attending the catastrophe," as she was extremely anxious that her late husband should bear no dishonour with regard to the loss. She continued:

> "Having been 31 years at sea, he was a most capable navigator and seaman, and I feel sure there is something as yet unaccounted for which ought to be discovered, so that unnecessary blame should not

be attached to the names of those who so unhappily lost their lives in the performance of their duty, and for the satisfaction of the relatives bereaved, as well as to prevent any further such awful disasters taking place in the future."[4]

Where ships of the Royal Navy foundered or were involved in a collision, it was the normal peace-time procedure for the Admiralty to hold a court martial as an in-depth investigation into the occurrence. During the Second World War, in response to a question about 'the old-established custom of holding naval courts-martial following the loss of ships of the Royal Navy in order to determine the circumstances of such loss,' the then First Lord of the Admiralty, Albert Alexander MP, explained:

"It is true that up to 1914 it was not the invariable rule but a very general direction to have courts-martial, mostly in peace-time, with regard to the loss of ships, but during the first two years of the Great War it became necessary not to follow that practice, and even in the last two years of the Great War courts-martial were not excessive in number having regard to the heavy losses of ships. In regard to the procedure, it means, of course, that, if you have a court-martial, all the evidence is in public."[5]

A court martial would have been the highest level of investigation, with the potential for attributing responsibility to members of the crew, or to naval authorities responsible for sending the men to sea on the *Iolaire*. Rear Admiral Boyle, in command of the Stornoway naval base, certainly felt that a court martial could be held, judging by his telegram to the Admiralty on 3rd January 1919:

"Received 2.12 pm. 610: REQUEST INSTRUCTIONS AS TO WHETHER COURT MARTIAL SHOULD BE HELD ON THE LOSS OF YACHT *IOLAIRE*. (Noted by hand) – Hold Court of Enquiry. H.I.K. 3/1/19."[6]

Admiral Boyle had himself been the subject of a court martial only eight years earlier, when he was severely reprimanded after the vessel he commanded, HMS *Duke of Edinburgh*, ran aground. His service record for September 1910 states:

"Court Martial found the charge of negligence proved against this officer."[7]

Again, during wartime in 1915, as an operational Rear Admiral, he was reprimanded for 'omissions of a very serious nature' during gunnery tests, and told:

"in future the necessary precautions to be rigidly adhered to."[8]

He was perhaps anxious on this occasion to ensure that everything was done by the book.

If so, he might have been surprised by the response the next day from the Admiralty:

"Sent 12.35 4.1.19. 999: Your 610. COURT OF ENQUIRY IS TO BE HELD. RICHARD WALTON FOR HEAD OF N.D."[9]

The Admiralty's decision to refuse a Court Martial, and to hold instead a Court of Inquiry, seems in this peace-time context to be curious – unless we assume that it showed

The Admiralty map of 1911 showing the approaches to Stornoway Harbour with Arnish Lighthouse, the Beasts of Holm and Stoneyfield Farm at Holm clearly marked.

concern over the possible findings of a Court Martial. But the clamour for an inquiry continued. On 6th January The *Scotsman* reported on the Stornoway Town Council meeting of 3rd January and a public meeting on Saturday 4th:

> "Statements of survivors, as to the primary cause of the disaster, and the allegations made by them are causing deep unrest in the minds of the bereaved.
>
> "At a special meeting of Stornoway Town Council on Friday night Provost MacLean referred to the tragic happening, and a resolution was unanimously passed deploring the disaster, expressing sympathy with dependents and relatives, and demanding of the responsible authorities the strictest investigation into all the circumstances attending the catastrophe and the responsibility attached thereto.
>
> "An informal gathering, attended by a number of the leading citizens, was held in the Parish Church Hall on Saturday night, when it was unanimously resolved to request the Lewis District Committee and the Stornoway Town Council to convene a public meeting of the inhabitants to voice the feelings of the community, and to demand a full and impartial inquiry, free from all red tape and gold lace[10], into the whole circumstances before, during and after the disaster, less than which, it was asserted, would not allay the rumours in circulation nor satisfy the public conscience."[11]

Not everyone agreed that an inquiry would satisfy the craving of a bereaved island population. The *Stornoway Gazette* published this reflective editorial note:

> "There is an agitation being worked up certain parties for what they call "a public and independent inquiry" into the disaster. Such an inquiry will be forthcoming regardless of any public demand. Any person who could possibly be responsible for the loss of the *Iolaire* has already paid the supreme penalty and from personal observation, I cannot help thinking that the atmosphere, even in such tragic circumstances, is not altogether what it ought to be."[12]

Naval Court of Inquiry

All the *Iolaire* survivors were summoned to attend an inquiry in Stornoway by a telegram, sent to village post offices before 7th January 1919. The Inquiry papers state:

> "All survivors were informed that their presence was required at the base on the 7th of January with a view to weeding out those whose evidence is of no value. Each man was interrogated and those required in court were informed that they were required on 8th January to attend a court of enquiry. This amounted to 25. Those not required were allowed to return to their homes."[13]

Feelings were running very high in Lewis at this time and the public were angry at the way in which survivors were treated. Such haste in proceeding to a quick investigation was insensitive to the feelings of traumatised survivors and the decision as to which evidence was 'of value' was not explained, either then or for the historical record.

Those men who received the notification in time proceeded to Stornoway by boat from distant villages, by horse-drawn cart, a few by car and the majority on foot. How many attended is not recorded and records of the first interrogations of January 7th do not survive. We therefore do not know what each individual contributed towards the Royal Navy's understanding, or lack of understanding, of what had happened on that dreadful night. Only the interrogations of the 25 individuals selected were kept. More than 50 men were dismissed and we have no knowledge of how those who gave evidence were selected. Were these 25 sailors more likely to corroborate the Admiralty's preferred view? Did some of those dismissed see things differently, were their statements simply duplicate accounts, or could they not be relied upon in Court?

The Court of Naval Inquiry which met in Stornoway on Wednesday 8th January consisted of William Bradley, Commander RNR, DSO, aged 52, who had been at Stornoway since 28th March 1918; Ivan Gordon Humphreys, Commander RNR, who was posted to HMS *Iolaire* on 3rd January 1917 and Lt William Armstrong Westgarth, RNR, who was married in Stornoway to Isabella, a daughter of the banker Ebenezer Ross, in January 1917. A holder of the DSC, William served at the Stornoway naval base for the last three years of the Great War, commanding the minesweeper HMS *Pavlova*, which was based there.

The following 17 islanders were called as witnesses: Neil Nicolson (Lemreway), Alexander Maciver (Stornoway), Archibald Ross (Leurbost), John Finlay Macleod (Port of Ness), Murdo Macfarlane (Cross), Donald Maciver (New Tolsta), Norman Maciver (Arnol), Donald Macrae (Ranish), John Montgomery (Ranish), Alexander John Macleod (Coll), Murdo Macdonald (North Tolsta), John Macinnes (North Tolsta), Kenneth Macleod (Swordale), Angus Macdonald (Stornoway), Angus Nicolson (Stornoway) John Maclennan

(Kneep), Malcolm Macritchie (Kneep) and John Mackinnon (Tarbert) who presented written evidence. All six crew survivors were witnesses and they were recalled to the stand for cross-questioning, as were Alexander Maciver and Angus Nicolson. Precognitions[14] were received from John Mackay, John Smith, John Mackenzie (5 Portvoller) and James Macdonald of the fishing vessel *Avoca*, who was on the night a crewman on the fishing vessel *Spider*. A written statement from James Maclean (crew) was available, although he was also in attendance on the day.

All of those men who gave evidence were in the room within a week of their traumatic experience, while still in the throes of grief for lost comrades and family members, and while still suffering physical ill-effects. John Mackinnon of Tarbert was excused attendance due to ill-health suffered following his escape from the *Iolaire*. A note to this effect was signed by Doctor K C Crosbie in Tarbert on 8th January 1919. Mackinnon made a statement at a later date to Commander Humphreys. John Maclennan ('Ain Geal, Kneep) also later revealed that he had not attended due to injuries.

Lt William Westgarth, RNR, one of the men who conducted the naval inquiry in January 1919.

The report of the Naval Inquiry was not released until 50 years afterwards, but it was sent to the Admiralty via Admiral Boyle in January 1919. A full transcription of the evidence was then sent to the Admiralty in London by Thomas Carmichael, Solicitor in Scotland to the Admiralty, on 19th March 1919. The report stated:

"Sir, We have the honour to report that in compliance with your referendum No.19/13 of 7th January, we have held a strict and careful inquiry into the circumstances attending the loss of H.M.Yacht 056 "*Iolaire*" stranded on the Biastan Rocks at approximately 0150 on Wednesday 1st of January, and then drifter (sic) to the shore to the Northward of the rocks and became a total wreck.

"There is no evidence to explain how the accident occurred as none of the Officers on board, or the helmsman or lookouts who were on deck at the time are among the survivors, and no opinion can be given as to whether blame is attributable to anyone in the matter.

"The Court is further of the opinion that no adequate or properly organised attempt was made to save the lives of those on board; the only steps were to fire rockets, burn blue lights and blow the whistle to attract attention. The boats appear to have been lowered without orders or guidance, and a hawser was got ashor (sic) from the stern: Orders from the bridge were subsequently given to bring the hawser amidships to gain a better lea........

"We have the honour to be, Sir, Your obedient Servants, (Signed) I. G. Humphreys, Commander; W. Bradley, Commander, RNR; W. A. Westgarth, Lieutenant, RNR."[15]

At the time, the Admiralty refused to release the finding of the Naval Inquiry, leaving islanders dissatisfied with the situation. The community and survivors had anyway expected that a naval inquiry would be a whitewash, aimed at exonerating the officers involved and the naval authorities. For those still alive when the Inquiry report was released, 50 years later, there was evidence enough that they were right – as a single example, the claim that the life-saving rope or

John Norrie Anderson represented the widows and children of the Iolaire victims at the Public Inquiry.

hawser was moved amidships on 'orders from the bridge' was simply untrue, and credited the yacht's officers with actions which were, in fact, undertaken entirely on their own initiative by passengers.

An inquiry into the stranding and sinking was also held under Captain John Alexander Webster CBE MVO, Director of Navigation at the Royal Navy Hydrographic Department 1916-1919. He reported on 23rd January 1919:

"The evidence is very indefinite and in parts contradictory... The cause of the accident seems to have been finding himself to the Eastward of his intended position the Commanding Officer altered course to pass close to Arnish beacon light but, owing to the angle at which he was approaching the harbour, this track led him close to Holm Point; being further from Arnish Point light than he estimated (the brightness was probably affected by the drizzling rain) instead of clearing Holm Point the ship ran on to the Biastan Holm Reef. Owing to the contradictory nature of the evidence as to the final alteration of course, it is impossible to say with certainty if this is what actually happened, but it appears to be the most probable explanation".[16]

The Admiralty's man closest to the scene of the tragedy was Stornoway's naval base commander, Rear Admiral Boyle. There is evidence that local feeling was becoming vociferous and assertive enough to make him uncomfortable, since on 14th January he sent memos marked 'Confidential' to the Secretary of the Admiralty in Whitehall reporting:

"*Ill-favoured rumours are circulating*" and "*Feelings are still running high.*"[17] It may have been this popular pressure which forced the Lord Advocate, James Avon Clyde, later Lord Clyde, Scotland's most senior law officer, to hold the subsequent Public Inquiry into the sinking. Extraordinarily for a supposedly civilian procedure, the Lord Advocate first consulted the Admiralty and asked if they would agree to an Inquiry.

The Public Inquiry that had been called for was held at Stornoway Sheriff Courthouse, Lewis Street, on Monday and Tuesday, 10th and 11th February 1919. John MacIntosh of Inverness was Sheriff Principal and the Sheriff Depute was William Dunbar of Stornoway. Presenting the Admiralty case were James Campbell Pitman (Counsel), a vastly experienced Edinburgh Advocate, supported by William Alexander Ross, a practicing solicitor and former Stornoway Town Councillor with offices at 50 Kenneth Street, Stornoway. Thomas Carmichael was Solicitor in Scotland to the Admiralty and later received reports from the Inquiry. Under his instructions Pitman and Ross received, by the First Sea Lord's approval, a full set of Court of Inquiry papers.

The case for the Crown was conducted by Advocate John Charles Fenton from Edinburgh, supported by Stornoway Procurator Fiscal Colin George Mackenzie.[18] Representing the widows and children was John Norrie Anderson, said to be the ablest Lewisman of his time, founding partner in the Stornoway law firm Anderson, Macarthur & Co, which is still in existence.

The light from Arnish Lighthouse is seen on the approach to Stornoway Harbour. Beacon to the right.

Seven Stornoway residents were on the Jury. They were Malcolm Maclean (baker), Alexander Roderick Murray (draper), George Morrison (merchant), John Ross (clerk of works), Malcolm Ross (grocer), Kenneth Mackenzie (painter) and Angus Macleod (contractor). Women had just received the vote in 1918 and were not permitted to sit on a Scottish Jury until 1920.

Also present were William Grant, editor of the *Stornoway Gazette*, who took shorthand of the proceedings, Sheriff Clerk Depute William John Clarke and Archibald Munro, Town Clerk of Stornoway, familiar to all locals at the time due to his quaint, old-fashioned attire.

The 34 witnesses called at this Inquiry included members of the crew at Stornoway naval base (HMS *Iolaire*) including Lt Robert Robinson Ansdell RN, who was Officer of the Watch until 9am on January 1st and Sub Lt Charles W Murray RNVR, the man who was sent on his own to call out the lifeboat and to arrange transport to Holm. Surgeon Lt Thomas Owen RN was called, as was Lt Frederick Edward Townend RNR, who was in charge of the temporary mortuary at the RNR Battery. Lt Walter Benjamin Wenlock RN was undertaking naval harbourmaster duties at Stornoway.

Of those active at Kyle of Lochalsh, CPO William John Wyman RN, Master at Arms was called, as was Lt Charles Wayles Hicks RNR, who had ascertained the passenger availability on both *Sheila* and *Iolaire*. Two railway porters at Kyle were also called as witnesses.

Coastguard officers called were Divisional Commanding Officer Frederick Boxall, who had been based at Stornoway for one month and Chief Officer William Barnes, who was depute to Boxall and lived on Seaview Terrace. Three other Coastguard volunteers were called, all of whom lived locally.

Only 13 survivors were called to testify. They were Angus Nicolson (Stornoway), Kenneth Macleod (Swordale), John Montgomery (Ranish), John Mackay (Shulishader), Alexander Maciver (Stornoway), John Macinnes (North Tolsta), John Smith (Leurbost), John Mackenzie (Portvoller), James MacLean (crew, Campbeltown), Archibald Ross (Leurbost). Norman Maciver (Arnol), Donald Macdonald (Upper Bayble) and John Macphail (Doune Carloway).

There were some surprising witness omissions. The naval base commander himself, Rear Admiral Boyle, who was in charge of the onshore response, was not summoned and neither was any written testimony from him presented. Lt Fawcett Shinner was the officer in charge of the *Iolaire* when she made the same journey, taking liberty sailors home from Kyle of Lochalsh to Stornoway, on 29th December 1918. He was not called upon to explain which course he had navigated.

Frank Pierre Carnegie, manager of the Imperial Hotel, could have testified as to the Admiralty response and general sobriety of those present there, especially as the first news of the disaster was reported at the hotel by Lt Wenlock and by Anderson Young of Stoneyfield Farm.

Crew member James Macdonald, at the time on the fishing vessel *Spider*, was called, but the un-named skipper of the fishing vessel was not. This was the one boat which was physically present as the *Iolaire* approached the rocks at Holm. James Macdonald's age was given as 44 but his origins were not recorded by the court, so it is not known if he was an islander or an east coast man. He is the only witness who cannot be positively identified, as even the railway porters from Kyle have their ages and home villages listed. He was listed as being on the crew of MFV *Avoca* by the time of the Inquiry, having left the *Spider*.

The men who crewed the boat from HM Whaler *Rorqual* and brought Donald Morrison (Am Patch) from the mast on 1st January were not called or even mentioned by name. The bouquet for this remarkable rescue was handed to Lieutenant Wenlock of the *Budding Rose* who was called as a witness by the Admiralty. After being sworn in, Wenlock referred to the man on the mast, and said in his evidence: "*I succeeded in rescuing the man with some difficulty.*" He makes no mention that it was islanders in a lifeboat from HM Whaler *Rorqual* who actually rescued Morrison.

A full list of the witnesses who appeared is given in Appendix 1.

Evidence is given

The proceedings opened with an address to those present by Sheriff MacIntosh, who said that:

"He desired to take the first opportunity he had of expressing his deep sympathy with those who had been bereaved by the terrible tragedy which had taken place almost at their very doors in the opening hours of the present year. It had sent a thrill of horror through the whole country. All the circumstances were so sad and the tragedy involved the loss of so many who had served their King and country. He wished to express his deep sympathy for the many homes scattered throughout the Island of Lewis and those elsewhere that had been desolated by bereavement and grief.

"Reading the directions to jurors, he said the purpose of their meeting together that day was for the painful duty of enquiring into and pronouncing upon the circumstances and cause of this calamity in so far as these were discoverable. The public authorities had directed that inquiry to be held, and as they might have gathered from the reports submitted, the Admiralty had given every assistance and facility to ensure a searching and complete Inquiry. He further emphasised the fact that the jurors were to fix their attention upon the facts proved in evidence. It was inevitable that the tongues of rumour should have been busy about such an accident, but it was their duty to purge their mind of all preconceived ideas, of all they had heard or read, and fix their attention exclusively upon the facts proved in evidence. The main point now was prevention. They must try, if possible, to discover the cause of the disaster and take steps to make a recurrence of such a tragedy impossible."[19]

The first witness, Lt Cdr Arthur Hepburn Walsh, was liaison officer for the US Navy in Kyle and was responsible for organising the boarding of the men returning to Stornoway on the night of the disaster. He gave the following testimony:

"On 31st December last I paraded the naval ratings who came off the train leaving Inverness at 11.40am. The train arrived in two portions and I paraded the ratings on both occasions. The 11.40 was due at 3.30pm but did not arrive until about 6.15. In the first portion there were about 190 naval ratings for Stornoway and a certain number for Harris and Skye. In the second portion there were 130 for Stornoway and also men for Harris and Skye. I had received a telegram from a senior naval officer in Inverness after 4pm, telling me to expect 530 men from the 11.40 train. Knowing at that point that the *Iolaire* had arrived, I instructed Lt Hicks to ascertain from MacBrayne's representative on how many men the

Sheila could take. The first train portion of 190 men were marched to the *Iolaire* and ultimately there were 260 naval ratings on the yacht.

"Before the train came I talked to the Captain about the accommodation of the ship's boats. He told me, I think, that his four boats would carry roughly something like 100, but I think that was a little optimistic. It would require calm weather to hold the whole hundred. I asked him how many lifebelts he had got on board, and, to my recollection, he said about 80. The boats a ship carries are arranged according to the ship's complement, and passengers are not taken into account, because these are not passenger ships. The same is true as regards lifebelts.... I was also asked if rafts could have been placed on the *Iolaire*. I agreed that they could but were not available."

Questioned, he added information on Commander Mason:

"**Q** Was Commander Mason perfectly sober?

A Perfectly.

Q You had a conversation with him and you would have noticed if there had been the slightest hint of intoxication?

A Yes."[20]

Lt Charles Wayles Hicks assisted Walsh with the boarding of passengers onto the vessels. He also testified to the sobriety of the officers:

"On the evening of 31st December last I went on board the *Iolaire* when she arrived at Kyle. I saw Commander Mason and the Navigation Officer,

Lieut Cotter. I spoke to them both. They were both at that time perfectly sober. As far as I know they showed not the slightest sign of drink at all. I went on board again just before she left and on that occasion I saw the Navigating Officer and spoke to him. I also spoke to Commander Mason (on the bridge) just as they were leaving. Both at that time were perfectly sober."[21]

As Lt Commander Mason (captain), Lt Cotter (navigating officer) and Acting Quartermaster Leggett (coxswain) all drowned, it was impossible for the Public Inquiry to clarify the mystery of the *Iolaire*'s position when making for the entrance to Stornoway harbour. The most significant witness was therefore 39-year-old assistant quartermaster James Maclean, the only survivor of the *Iolaire* disaster who had any real knowledge pertaining to the officers, crew and course steered. He not only gave his statement but was questioned closely.

A former fisherman, James 'Creel' Maclean joined the patrol service of the RNR in July 1915 and was posted as a deckhand to HMY *Iolaire* (then *Amalthaea*) in February 1916. He was therefore knowledgeable about the yacht herself and came to Stornoway with her when she arrived on 22nd October 1918. The following is a summary of Maclean's story:

"On 31st December our vessel got instructions to proceed to Kyle. We left Stornoway in the forenoon, and when we got to Kyle we went alongside the Pier. We went round the island outside of Kyle and came alongside with our head facing out to the harbour mouth. We had no difficulty in turning our vessel. As we came alongside we struck the Pier.

"We had a crew of 17 or 19, and our Commander was Commander Mason and the Lieutenant, Lt. Cotter. She carried four boats. These boats could accommodate 60 men. We had at least a dozen lifebuoys. I could not say whether there would be as many as 80 lifebelts and lifebuoys. I was caterer and quartermaster, taking the wheel, looking out occasionally, and catering for the boat in Harbour.

"The damage to the Pier was not serious and there was nothing that affected the seaworthiness of the ship. In my opinion it was the tide. Leggett was on the wheel. He is drowned. Commander Mason was on the bridge. That day we took a number of naval ratings on board – 260, I believe. Before we left Kyle I saw Commander Mason and Lieut. Cotter. Lieut. Cotter was on the gangway, but I did not see Commander Mason at that time. I cannot say that I saw Commander Mason before leaving Kyle. Lieut. Cotter was Navigating Officer."[22]

On being questioned, Maclean denied that Cotter or himself were the worse for drink and stated that nobody could have got ashore to get drink. Maclean was questioned twice in relation to Mason's sobriety and repeated that he saw no sign of drink.

"I turned in somewhere between 9 and 10 o'clock. The ship by that time was on her way. I was called out before 12 and took the wheel at 12 o'clock exactly. I was relieved at 1 o'clock. When I took the wheel at 12 it was a dark night. The wind was fresh – the first of a Southerly gale – and increasing. There was no fog and lights were quite visible. When I took the wheel the vessel was on a North Easterly course. She was no points to the East of North – she might be a degree, or 2 degrees. That was the compass bearing. I cannot say what our ship's deviation was. I don't know what is the variation between magnetic North and true North. The course was always taken off the standard compass. At half-past 12 the course was changed to North, magnetic. No bearings were taken while I was at the wheel. Commander Mason was on the bridge the whole time from 12-1 while I was at the wheel."

Asked if the view from the bridge was obscured Maclean replied:

"No, there was nothing to obscure the view, and that night I could see all the lights[23] clearly. I was looking at the compass all the time. Commander Mason gave me instructions as to the course. I was relieved at 1 o'clock by Leggett. Commander Mason was still on the bridge when I was relieved. I went down and had a smoke. I was down for about 10 minutes. I came on deck again and stopped there a few minutes and then went up to the bridge. I was keeping a look-out. I was the only one keeping a look-out. There was no one stationed at the boat's head – not during this voyage at all. I don't know the lights. I know Arnish light and Arnish beacon. I cannot say I know Tiumpan Head or Cabback Head lights, but I know Stornoway harbour lights. I saw Arnish light when I was on the look-out but when I was on the wheel I did not pay any heed to the lights. I went on the look-out at 10 or 15 minutes past 1. Lieut. Cotter was on the bridge then; he had relieved Commander Mason."

Under questioning Maclean added:

"I remember telling them about the light. I said "That's the light" and they said "That's all right!" Lieut. Cotter told me to go down and call the hands, and to get the anchor ready; that we would soon be in the Harbour.

Q How long was that before the vessel struck?

A From a quarter of an hour to 25 minutes.....
I went down again to see that the men were coming (I was down) about 10 minutes. As I came on deck again the vessel struck."

With regard to the *Iolaire*'s handling capabilities, Maclean stated:

"I have often steered the *Iolaire*. She was not difficult to steer. She was a little slow at turning. I think her build would be the cause of it."

Maclean was questioned by all sides about his role as a lookout, and about the whereabouts of the vessel's Commander when she struck:

"**Q** Who put you on look-out?

A Nobody.

Q You were just looking out on your own?

A No, not on my own: it was a rule to have a look-out.

Q How did you come to go on look-out?

A It was the hands' duty, but the vessel was shorthanded on that voyage.

Q As a rule did you always have a look-out?

A As a rule."

Q It is correct to say that Commander Mason had left the bridge before the ship struck?

A Lt. Cotter was on the bridge when I went up to look-out and Commander Mason was not there I was not on the look-out when the ship struck. There was no look-out when the ship struck. When I went down to call the hands I did not make any provision for anyone to take my place as look-out. I was away about 10 minutes each time, and during these times there was no look-out that I know of.

Q Who placed you on look-out?

A I went there myself.

Q On your own initiative?

A Yes."[24]

Captain Cameron of the *Sheila* stated later in the Inquiry that it was normal procedure when approaching the harbour to have two lookouts.

In answer to a series of questions Maclean revealed that the vessel remained in the same place, on a terrible list, for 10 to 15 minutes after she struck the Beasts. The siren was sounded, non-explosive rockets were fired. No flares were burnt to give the men a light to see and the searchlight was not used but Maclean did not know why. None of the three guns were fired. She then righted herself, and practically got off the rock. Her stern swung round from east to North, and ultimately the seas were coming over her port quarter. He also thought that the vessel was driven in stern first towards the shore and after her stern struck she came round again until she was practically broadside on.

Maclean admitted being allocated to the dinghy on the port quarter but did not go there although he claimed he 'was about there'. No orders were given by those in charge to take boat stations and none of the crew reported that Maclean was aware of. He heard Mason say something about the boats when the yacht was still on a list.

Maclean then gave a most confusing account about the midships whaler which he helped to lower. Thereafter the questioner asked him about his later escape which was via the same waterlogged whaler. Maclean revealed that it was attached to the yacht and was out to the full extent of the painter (a rope six to nine fathoms long). He heard Lt Cotter at the last saying "*Pull that boat alongside, she cannot sink, she is full of tanks*" (Flotation tanks). He and another young sailor ran forward to try and pull the boat alongside, but the boat's keel was on the rock and she was full of water, so they could not do it. The sailor was also said to be a witness in court – identified by witness Archibald Ross as Norman Maciver, Arnol. Maclean asked Maciver to go on the painter but he refused so Maclean went. He found the boat hard and fast about three yards from the shore. Maciver followed and got ashore with him.

Under questioning Maclean stated all the other men were waiting in line or manning the rope and he attested that both Mason and Cotter were on the bridge at this stage. Maclean had a lifejacket which he kept under his bunk, where all the crew kept their lifejackets. There were one or two spares in the boats but he could not say he saw others in lifejackets.

It was three quarters of an hour to an hour before he got ashore and there were a lot of men on the beach when he landed. He waited, but nobody appeared to have followed the two of them on the painter. He shouted, but was uncertain if anybody on the yacht heard him as the gale was increasing. They helped a man in the rocks to the farmhouse. He heard the farmer's wife say it was 20 minutes past three. There was one survivor there before them, Alexander Maciver.

The master of the MacBrayne mailboat *Sheila*, which followed the same path as the *Iolaire* and came into Stornoway harbour safely at 2.20am, was called as a witness to the Inquiry. Captain Colin Cameron had seen little of the incident itself, but he was clearly an expert witness on what may have happened in terms of navigation, being a regular

Captain Cameron of the MacBrayne's vessel Sheila had often sailed the route between Kyle and Stornoway and was a key witness at the inquiry.

on the route from Kyle to Stornoway, and a local to the town. He was questioned, in part based on the information Maclean had given about the navigation he witnessed. The following is an edited excerpt from his testimony:

"There is a strong current at times at Kyle and it varies in different parts of the channel and it is quite possible that a ship might bump the pier even with a careful and experienced navigator, particularly one who had not berthed his ship alongside the pier before. I saw several of the officers and crew … and there was nothing to indicate that any of them were under the influence of drink … I saw Iolaire leave in a seamanlike manner. We left at 8.45, about an hour after the Iolaire.

During our passage to Stornoway I saw several lights but I cannot say they were the *Iolaire*'s lights.

"**Q** Is Stornoway a difficult harbour to enter at night?

A Well, it is for the man that does not know it, a man who has not actually taken a vessel in – and in many cases they stand out all night until they get a Pilot to take them in. …. *Iolaire* is longer than *Sheila* … there might be difficulty if he was too close on the land before trying to turn, but he would turn quite safely half a mile off shore or less…

Q When you came up to Stornoway Harbour did you have a lookout?

A I always have a lookout…

Q Am I right in saying that your evidence is that the usual course to Stornoway from Kyle is Northerly, at any rate after you pass the Shiants?

A From South Rona.

Q Keeping the Shiants on the port, you steer for Arnish light as near as you can.

A Yes.

Q And when you are coming in you have to make a slight deviation to get round the Arnish beacon and having got round Goat Island you head up for the Quay – that is, two slight deviations in the course.

A Yes.

Q Do you think it is a difficulty to a stranger in these waters not to have a light on the Holm side of the harbour?

A I don't miss it myself; I keep closer to the lighthouse side.

Q Take the case of a stranger, and he has to make Stornoway in the dark, with the lights visible but the land not very visible?

A It would be a big help to have a light on the Holm side, he would then see he had only to enter between the two lights.

Q About a lookout. If it was said that the rule or custom on a ship was to have a lookout only when at sea, and when it is distinctly dark, or foggy, or otherwise a bad night, do you think this is good navigation?

A On a dark night it is necessary to have a lookout, but the case may be that you cannot keep man at the ship's head in bad weather … there is need for a good lookout at all times … I don't know anything about the course the vessel took but it doesn't take a man very much to be off his course to land where he did …

Q If you were steering a North easterly course, where would you take the ship to before changing course?

A I would take her within half a mile of the Chicken and then come in safely.

Q Even with the wind that was in it that night?

A Yes.

Q Would it have been possible on that night for the *Iolaire* to have come up as far as the Chicken and then from the Chicken down to Holm Head?

A It is quite probable but North East in my opinion would take him further out.

Q Would it clear the land?

A Yes but he would turn and come into Holm."[25]

The evidence given by Ernest Reginald Adams, fireman[26] on the *Iolaire* that night, substantiates the statements given by others that the officers in command of the *Iolaire* made little attempt to save lives and failed to give any orders to the passengers after the vessel struck the rocks. Adams had been in the stokehold, but was in the engine-room with the Chief Engineer, Sub Lt Charles Rankin, RNR:

"**Q** When the ship struck, did the telegraph ring?

A Just after she struck, almost immediately they rung down "Stop".

Q Between 12 o'clock and the time the ship struck, was there any other alteration in the speed of the engines?

A No…

Q What did you do then after you stopped the engines?

A We waited down there for about five minutes. Then the Chief sent me down to the stokehold to see what it was like, and she was making water (filling with water). I reported that to the Chief Engineer and he and myself then went on deck. We remained on deck until the ship began to break up….

Q When you got on deck what did you do?

A I helped to get one of the boats out…

Q What happened then?

A I went to the boat deck and I saw the leading hand – Dewsbury – and I asked him if he could try to get the big boat out – the whaler, port side.

Q What did Dewsbury say?

A He said, "This is terrible", I said, "Yes", and he went away……

Q When you were on board at any time did you hear any orders given by anybody?

A None at all…

Q When you spoke to Dewsbury on the deck, was he in the act of doing anything?

A No.

Q Did he not take steps to control the passengers?

A No.

Q Where was he at the time you spoke to him?

A On the promenade deck near the port whaler.

Q You could hear any orders from the bridge quite distinctly from that position?

A Yes, if there had been any given; but I did not hear any…"[27]

Donald Macdonald from Upper Bayble was on deck as the vessel approached the harbour:

"When we were approaching Lewis I saw all the lights, Cabback (Kebbock Head), Tiumpan and Arnish – quite clearly. When we passed Cabback light I took a bearing on the standard compass on deck. The Cabback light was bearing West by South, one point abaft the port beam. I did not take the bearing of Arnish light, but I think it was half a point on the port bow. I did not take notice of Tiumpan Head at that time, but when I did notice it I think it was on the starboard bow. The vessel at that time was steering North, a quarter West. I could not judge how far we were from the Lewis shore, but I think a good mile, or more. I could see the land; …. It was not very clear, but I could tell it was land. I know the coast well. From my observation at that time I thought the vessel's course was right for Stornoway.

"Between Cabback and Arnish I noticed a fishing vessel…. She was on our starboard side. I saw her afterwards on our port side. I don't know whether we passed across her, or if we gave way to her. I don't know whether we passed her ultimately or not. I noticed the land on the Cabback side before we came to Cabback light, and I could see it all the time as we came past it. The wind at the time was blowing from the South – right astern of the vessel. I remained on deck until the vessel struck."[28]

Macdonald was questioned:

"Before the vessel struck I noticed land on the starboard.

Q   How long before?

A   I should say it was five minutes anyway.

Q   Was the land in any way distinct?

A   It was.

Q   It wasn't simply the loom of the land?

A   No, it was distinct. I said to Kenneth, my chum, 'We'll soon be in; there's the land 'of Holm'. .....

Q   Between the time you first saw the land and the time the vessel struck did the '*Iolaire*' alter course?

A   Not to my knowledge – after I took the bearing I never went to the compass again. Before the vessel struck I did not notice Arnish light or Arnish beacon. After I said to Kenneth 'She'll soon be in' I took no further notice of the lights."[29]

Seaman John Montgomery of Ranish, who survived and was familiar with the entrance to Stornoway harbour, described the situation:

"As we were coming towards Stornoway, I could see Tiumpan Head Light well on the starboard bow and Arnish Light perhaps three points on the port bow. I also saw Cabag Light when we passed it on our port beam. After we came to the land and the ship

Witnesses were questioned about the visibility of the Arnish light

altered course, I saw a light. She altered course five or six minutes before she struck. I cannot say exactly how Arnish Light was bearing just before she altered course. I saw both Arnish lights before she changed course and they were something like three points on the port bow. After she altered course, the Beacon light at Arnish was right ahead and the Arnish Light would be one point to port. I could see the sea breaking on the shore about five minutes before she struck. The land I saw was the land on the East side of Holm Bay. This was about five minutes before she struck and at the time the Arnish Beacon light was right ahead. We had closed down[30] Tiumpan Head Light altogether."[31]

The evidence given by Warrant Officer William Barnes at the enquiry is informative of the situation with regard to the life-saving equipment available on-shore:

"On 1st January I got a message that there was a ship in distress at Holm. That message came from the Rear Admiral, Stornoway. It was brought by a messenger, a naval man, James Pearson. That was the first intimation I received of any kind that there was a ship in distress. I was directed by the messenger from the Rear Admiral to get the life-saving apparatus ready at once. I got the message at 3 o'clock exact.

The lighthouse at Tiumpan was mentioned by several witnesses who saw the light fall away behind the ship.

" ...I went to the Battery. It was 3.15 when I got to the Battery. The apparatus was still in the shed, I gave orders to get it out at once. It was got out at once...

"...I borrowed men from the Battery. I got 19 men. They harnessed themselves on to the drag ropes and we took the apparatus out to the scene of the wreck. We stopped at the crossroads at the Sandwick Road for two or three minutes waiting to see if the Divisional Officer was coming along, as I was afraid he might take the wrong turning, being a stranger just arrived. I saw some survivors from the wreck there and I spoke to them...

"I saw no sign of any ship. Then I turned and searched the beach and I found wreckage. The light I had was a carriage lamp with a candle inside it, which forms part of the rocket apparatus. I had nothing in the nature of a powerful light. At one time I did think I heard someone shouting and I met two men. I concluded it was these men who had been shouting. They belonged to Sandwick. I asked them if they had been shouting. They said they had been talking but not shouting...

"...I searched along the beach for the wreckage. I saw wreckage and a lot of woodwork. I saw no small boats and I saw no survivors. By this time the storm was high and there was a heavy sea running. The seas were lashing the cliffs and it was impossible to get on the beach at places. I waited on the beach about an hour and forty minutes. That is from the time I left the cart till I got back to the cart again. I was called at 3 o'clock. When I got to the spot where I left the men with the cart it was 4.40. The distance from the Battery to where I left the cart, is, I think, three and a half miles..."[32]

Coastguard Divisional Commanding Officer Frederick Boxall added:

"I waited some time intending as soon as the man could find his way to send for medical assistance and myself search round the scene of the wreck, but before any sign of daylight a Medical Officer with Sick Berth Attendant and another officer arrived at the farm from the base, attendin (sic) to the survivors and sending some on by Car. As soon as we could see at all the two officers from the base and myself proceeded to search towards the wreck. I came across the body of a man who had apparently tried to reach the farm, the Surgeon attended to him at once but the man was already dead. I then went on towards the wreck still searching, nothing but wreckage was found in the vicinity. The Rocket party returned having found nothing. At daylight a man was seen clinging to mast and was taken off by a service boat. I am of the opinion that the man could not have been got off any other way and I consider it was a good piece of work by the Officer and Boats Crew. I remained at the wreck until this man was rescued and then returned to Station."[33]

The man sent to fetch the horses was John Macsween, a Life-Saving Apparatus (LSA) team member. He said he had been called at 3am by the Wireless Operator at the Battery and 10 minutes later by WO Barnes. When he got to the Battery he saw the cart with the LSA apparatus at the gate ready to go. He went to two carters to get their horses. At about 3.30 he called the first carter on South Beach, John "Blue" Macdonald and five minutes later Alex Neal, the other carter. The horses were actually kept in a stable 400 yards from the Battery. When Macsween got back to the Battery the naval men had hauled the cart to Sandwick crossroads. It would appear that they waited for the horses to appear but only one did eventually. Macsween agreed, when questioned by John Norrie Anderson, that if they had not waited for the horse they could have been at the wreck an hour sooner (4am). As it was, the sailors dragged the cart the whole way and the horse hauled it back. The road at that time only went as far as the two farms and so the equipment had to be hauled quite a distance in the dark, in a gale, over rough undulating land with whins (gorse) and stones. After that there were gulleys and crags as one approached the scene on slippery grass. In any case the rescue party was too late as the ship had sunk at 3.25am.

Macsween led Barnes to the wreck using one oil lamp (a carriage lantern with a candle inside which was LSA property and which would have been useless in the conditions, but no other light was available). They did not have rockets or flares. They saw wreckage but no men at all. They heard the shouting from the mast but could do nothing and returned at 5.30am. Macsween stated that the weight of the cart and equipment was fully one ton and that twelve men were supposed to be able to take the cart anywhere on an ordinary road.

Reading the statements taken relating to those responsible for the life-saving effort on shore it is obvious that there was a lack of organisation, cohesion and efficiency. If it was chaotic aboard the *Iolaire*, it was little better onshore.

What does not appear to have been taken into account in all the questioning about the Life Saving Apparatus is that the vessel had already sunk, as survivors told the men ashore as soon as they met. A huge amount of the Inquiry places emphasis on the time taken to reach the site, but the time the company left was 3.50am, 25 minutes after the *Iolaire* had actually gone under. All the talk of horses, men, darkness, terrain and why there was only nominal Coastguard presence in wartime was mere talk – probably to keep the focus of the Inquiry away from the Admiralty's own failings.

Those witnesses who had been aboard the *Iolaire* would have expected aid from land to come more quickly. Donald Macdonald of Bayble estimated that he had reached the shore about half an hour after the *Iolaire* struck – although allowance must be made for the confusion of the scene, it could have been much longer or shorter a time. He told the Inquiry:

> "I did not wait long on the shore – not more than five minutes – I was sent for assistance. I went first to Stoneyfield and stayed there half an hour. Mr. Young, the farmer, guided us with a lamp. When I left the vessel her lights were on, but after I got ashore they went out. After that there were no rockets sent up as far as I know. Owing to the position of the vessel it was not possible to render any assistance from the sea. Assistance would be possible from the shore. I was expecting myself before I left the ship to see some help coming."[34]

What did the Inquiry reveal?

As the Inquiry drew to a close, the advocates made their summing up. Mr Pitman, for the Admiralty, said that:

> "An over-running of the course for a few minutes, a mere error of judgment, was sufficient to account for what had happened, and to say on account of that error of judgment that the navigating officer was incapable or incompetent was unfair to his memory."[35]

John Norrie Anderson, representing the bereaved relatives, referred to press reports that some of the confusion on board was due to naval ratings not understanding orders given in English. He said:

> "No one who heard the witnesses give their evidence could say that they were unable to understand orders given in English. In fact, there were no orders given."[36]

He called for a verdict of gross negligence.

Sheriff Principal MacIntosh closed the evidence by saying:

> "...It was an unfortunate circumstance that the accident had taken place at a season traditionally associated with conviviality, and he was glad that some of the lying rumours reflecting on the officers in this connection had been effectively dispelled by the evidence. It had been proved that there was no truth in these rumours, and he thought it proper to remove this painful reflection from the memory of those dead men and from the minds of their surviving relatives. The jury, he said, would be chary in assuming the position of censors and distributing blame, because it would be in their experience that a great many casualties at sea must for ever remain enigmas."[37]

The jury retired for over an hour. When they returned to the expectant room they presented a unanimous verdict:

- That the *Iolaire* went ashore, and was wrecked on the rocks inside the Beasts of Holm, about 1.55 am on the morning of 1st January, resulting in the deaths of 205 men.
- That the officer in charge did not exercise sufficient prudence in approaching the harbour.
- That the boat did not slow down.
- That a look-out was not on duty at the time of the accident.
- That the number of lifebelts, boats and rafts was insufficient for the number of people carried.
- That no orders were given by the officers with a view to saving life.
- That there was a loss of valuable time between the signals of distress and the arrival of the life-saving apparatus in the vicinity of the wreck.

They recommended:

1. That drastic improvements should be made immediately for conveying the life-saving apparatus in the case of ships in distress.
2. That the Lighthouse Commissioners take into consideration the question of putting up a light on the Holm side of the harbour.
3. That the Government should in future provide adequate and safe travelling facilities for naval ratings and soldiers.

The jury felt that they could not know the absolute truth about what had happened, so no blame was attached to the officers and crew. They stated there had been a loss of valuable time between the signals of distress and the arrival of the life-saving equipment in the vicinity of the wreck, and added that they were satisfied no one aboard was under the influence of intoxicating liquor, and also that there was no panic on board after the vessel struck.

As a rider to their verdict the jury recommended to the Carnegie Trust and Royal Humane Society Seaman J. F. Macleod, suggesting some token of appreciation of his conduct in swimming ashore with a line, by means of which the hawser was brought ashore, and many lives were saved. They also extended their sincerest sympathy to those who had lost relatives in this regrettable disaster, and expressed appreciation of the hospitality shown to the survivors by Mr and Mrs Anderson Young, Stoneyfield Farm.

The Public Inquiry was severely hampered by the fact that the men who should have been the principal players in the court drama were among those lost in the tragedy. It was further compromised by missing witnesses still living, some of them pivotal to the events of the night, who were not called and by shortcomings in the questioning, which failed to uncover significant information. As an example of the Inquiry's failings, deckhand James Willder, who survived the wreck, escaped any searching questions on his actions and responsibilities by claiming to be the acting cook. In fact, CPO Henley, who drowned, was the cook on board and the lawyers asking the questions should have noted this and questioned Willder further about his role as one of the deck crew. This role included lookout duties and the anchoring of the yacht. Our examination of the effect of these deficiencies can be found in Chapter 11.

Local and national newspapers reported the outcome of the inquiry.

THE "IOLAIRE" DISASTER.

PUBLIC ENQUIRY AT STORNOWAY.

JURY RETURN UNANIMOUS VERDICT

THE appalling disaster which occurred at the entrance to Stornoway harbour in the early hours of New Year's Day morning, involving the loss of over 200 lives, formed the subject of an inquiry, which opened at Stornoway on Monday and occupied the whole of two days. Sheriff-Principal Mackintosh presided, and the following jury was empannelled:— Messrs Malcolm Maclean, Point Street; A. R. Murray, Cromwell Street; Malcolm Ross, Francis Street; John Ross, Bayhead; Kenneth Mackenzie, Keith Street; and Angus Macleod, Keith Street.

Mr J. C. Fenton, advocate, and Mr C. G. Mackenzie, Procurator Fiscal, Stornoway, conducted the case for the Crown. Mr J. C. Pitman, advocate, Edinburgh, and Mr W. A. Ross, solicitor, Stornoway, appeared for the Admiralty; and Mr J. N. Anderson, solicitor, Stornoway,

THRILLING EXPERIENCES

Angus Nicolson, leading seaman (32), 25 Battery Park, Stornoway, was the next witness. He deponed that the Iolaire left Kyle about 20 minutes to 8 o'clock. The only officer he saw was a Lieut-Commander whom he took to be the captain of the ship. He took several of the men into the charthouse, and told them to make themselves comfortable there. He asked them if they were on New Year leave and said that about one-half of his crew were on leave so that they were short-handed. There were four or five men in the charthouse. Witness saw no signs of drink about the officer who spoke to them. He appeared quite normal. He (Nicolson) remained in the Charthouse until they had passed Rona Light. He returned to the charthouse until they were about seven miles east of the Shiant Lights. When he next emerged he saw

---

HIGHLAND   N

"IOLAIRE" DISASTER INQUIRY CONCLUDED.

No Foundation for Cruel Rumours.

DRASTIC IMPROVEMENTS RECOMMENDED.

On Monday and Tuesday last a public inquiry was held at Stornoway into the loss of H.M.Y. Iolaire. Sheriff Mackintosh presided, while the advocate for the Crown was Mr Fenton, and for the Admiralty Mr Pitman, with Mr W. A. Ross, solicitor, and Mr J. N. Anderson, solicitor, appearing on behalf of relatives and survivors. After the seven jurors had been chosen by ballot, Mr Pitman explained that he was there as representing the Admiralty, whose attitude throughout had been one of the utmost sympathy with bereaved relatives. An official inquiry had already been held, and the whole of the evidence secured there had been placed at the disposal of the

of the Sheila for lifebelts because the Sheila herself was absolutely full up. He was not on the pier when the Iolaire left, but was speaking to the Commander within five minutes of their leaving. There was no accident as the Iolaire was leaving Kyle Pier. There had been an accident as she was coming in—a bit of blundering as she was coming alongside. The tides there were peculiar, and unless one had local knowledge it was very difficult to say which way the tide was running. He had heard it said that the Iolaire was not a good turning ship. The damage done to the pier was not serious.

Angus Nicolson, leading seaman (32), 25 Battery Park, Stornoway, was the next

thereafter she struck. tive evidence as to vessel after she struck the rockets, and the He made an effort to g but was washed off it, washed ashore by the hausted condition. have been procured fr the darkness of the n lifeboat capsized and water.

Cross-examined by life-saving would have before the vessel struc ing vessel he saw to the height of the li After observing the had no time to warn t ship struck. He did there was a look-out

Questioned by the notice any slackening before she struck.

John Montgomery (27 Ranish, said he spe in the galley, but was borative evidence of ha of Tiumpan, Cabag Iolaire altered her cou minutes before she str

---

THE STORNOWAY DISASTER.

Inquiry Concludes.

VERDICT AGAINST THE COMMANDER.

VESSEL FAILED TO SLOW DOWN : NO LOOK-OUT.

The inquiry into the wreck of the Iolaire off Stornoway Harbour on New Year's Day was concluded at Stornoway yesterday.

The jury, in their verdict, found that the officer in charge did not exercise sufficient prudence in approaching the harbour; that no orders were given from the bridge, and that there was a loss of valuable time before the arrival of the life-saving apparatus.

They recommended several improvements which, in their opinion, were necessary for the safety of ships entering the harbour, and commended the gallantry of Seaman J. F. Macleod, who swam ashore with a life-line.

STATEMENT BY MASTER OF THE S.S. SHEILA.

CALLING OUT OF RESCUE APPARATUS.
(From Our Own Correspondent.)

Stornoway, Tuesday.

At the resumed inquiry into the circumstances attending the loss of H.M. yacht Iolaire off Stornoway Harbour to-day, several witnesses gave evidence to the effect that the officers and crew of the Iolaire were perfectly sober on leaving Kyle.

Capt. Cameron, master of the s.s. Sheila, said the route followed was quite a proper one. Less than five minutes' delay in turning the ship could quite easily cause her to land on the rocks where she did. The Iolaire left Kyle about an hour before the Sheila, and so far as he knew they never saw her lights until after she had struck the rocks. He reported immediately he reached the pier, that there was a ship on Holm Head. He saw absolutely nothing wrong with any person or thing about the Iolaire.

Rear Admiral Boyle – the missing witness

One man who absolutely should have appeared at the Inquiry was Rear Admiral Robert Francis Boyle MVO RN. There were countless questions that could have been asked of Admiral Boyle if he had been a witness. How many men were normally at his disposal? How many were on leave, how many were demobbed, how many were available on the night to raise the call for help, for the Coastguards, or to crew the lifeboat? How many naval ships were in the harbour and how many were crewed and ready to help with any recovery of survivors? He should have been asked to answer questions on inadequate transport planning for service personnel. Most especially, he should have been asked why he failed to adequately respond to such an emergency.

Rear Admiral Boyle was, arguably, the man with the most immediate authority over events as they unfolded on the night. He would have approved arrangements for HMY *Iolaire* to cross to Kyle and help bring the men home, and he was certainly the man reported to as the first flares were sighted when the *Iolaire* ran aground. He personally gave orders to despatch the life-saving apparatus, and he received reports from the first survivors ashore, and from the commander of the *Budding Rose*, after he had seen the *Iolaire* on the rocks.

Why was Admiral Boyle not called to the Inquiry? Could it have been because the Admiralty were unsure what he might say? His service record shows he had been at sea all his life, and his promotion record was steady, if unspectacular. But he had asked the Admiralty on 3rd January whether a Court Martial should be held on the

sinking, a move which could have made them worry that he was perhaps too conscientious and could be too truthful about naval shortcomings during the Inquiry.

On the day that the Public Inquiry ended, 10th February 1919, Boyle was promoted to Vice Admiral and the next day placed on the retired list. Was this recognition by the Navy that his actions on the night of the *Iolaire* had been flawed? Did they, without public admissions, withdraw from him his operational status? Or was he becoming troublesome because of his close personal contact with the traumatised community of the islands? That possibility is given some credibility because of Admiral Boyle's suggestion to the Admiralty that they make a statement to the press after the Inquiry closed. He received the following reply:

> "Their Lordships do not consider it desirable to re-open this matter and no statement will therefore be published in the Press."[38]

Correspondence between Admiralty staff, now open to examination at the National Archives, evidences a strong feeling in the immediate aftermath of the Inquiry that it was best not to carry on with any public release of information. Removing Rear Admiral Boyle from Stornoway may have been part of an agreed plan to reduce speculation and possible negative press reporting. The feeling was that the Admiralty wished to brush the matter under the carpet and that, with war over, enough was enough.

Public response to the Inquiry

The Admiralty could not completely subdue appetite for news of one of the most sensational and tragic events to happen after the war's end. Immediate press reactions to the Public Inquiry findings were split between straight reports without opinion, those who found the crew blameless and those who saw blame apportioned. While the *Highland News* had '*No Foundation for Cruel Rumours*' they also added '*Drastic Improvements Recommended.*' The *Aberdeen Daily Journal* had the headlines: '*The Stornoway Disaster: Inquiry Concludes: Verdict against the Commander: Vessel Failed to Slow Down: No Look Out.*' The unemotional headline in *The Times* was '*Lifesaving plans criticised.*'

In fact, British national newspapers gave little prominence to the findings of the *Iolaire* Inquiry. Journalists from the national newspapers did not question the findings of the Inquiry or quiz the Admiralty. Britain was still celebrating a glorious victory, after four years of a bloody war, and there were other pressing concerns to be reported – the spread of Bolshevism and civil unrest in Poland shared the front page of the *Times* on 2nd January with news of the loss of the *Iolaire*.

Some of the reports which did appear during and after the Inquiry carried claims which islanders found fallacious, unjust or insulting. Claims that sailors could not understand English were untrue, even though the *Inverness Courier* suggested confusion over orders and that orders in Gaelic may have saved lives. Other newspapers picked up on this without examining any facts. The claim originated from an era before state education, which from 1872 was delivered in English. The oldest *Iolaire* sailor was 55 (born in 1863) so, from the age of nine, he would have been speaking English at school every day.

To compound that sense of injustice, the only islanders singled out for praise in a night of extremes were John Finlay Macleod and the farmer Anderson Young, with his wife. Telegraphist Leonard Welch much later recalled that:

> "many were the acts of heroism that night, and I shall always cherish the memories of the amazing bravery and courage of so many who passed over on New Year's Eve, 1918."[39]

None of these acts of heroism were recorded or placed before the jury at the Inquiry. In the case of the boat crew who rescued Donald Morrison from the mast, they were specifically overlooked in the part that they played. Even at the time, many were of the opinion that one reason for ignoring the bravery of the island seamen was to prevent them from getting any praise for their gallantry and seafaring expertise. Many felt that it was galling that the Royal Navy did not make any awards for gallantry on the night.

The palpable hostility to the Admiralty and the way in which it had responded and handled the evidence of survivors did not go unnoticed by the legal representatives for the authorities. The advocate who had represented the Admiralty at the Inquiry was James Campbell Pitman, and he wrote to the Scottish Solicitor General the next day:

> "It may interest you to know that I am satisfied it was just as well that the Admiralty was represented. From the talk in the place and questions put by individual Jurymen, it became clear to me that the latter would be only too ready to give a verdict which would reflect seriously on the Admiralty as responsible for the officers and crew, the taking of so many liberty men on board with half a crew, and

no lifebelts, &c., and in being someway responsible for providing men for the life-saving apparatus and the lifeboat. ..... The whole Inquiry seemed almost like a criminal trial with the Admiralty in the dock – and the difficulty that any questions put by me were looked upon as an attempt to shift blame off official shoulders. I hope that the Jury's verdict will now be accepted by the population as being the worst that can be said in regard to the responsibility of the naval authorities, but I doubt whether it will."[40]

Mr Pitman was absolutely right. The island community had yearned for the Inquiry to yield a satisfactory explanation and to conclude where the fault lay. The inconclusive findings generated much ill-feeling. The Inquiry apportioned no blame to the Admiralty for their reaction in Stornoway, yet they seemed to blame the local coastguard, lifeboat and owners of motor vehicles, admitting no responsibility themselves.

Many years later, Stornoway fishing skipper John "Jackie" Morrison was quoted as saying:

"It is obvious that the Admiralty Inquiry was a whitewash exercise to deflect blame from their Lordships and their officers. It is astonishing that the captain and officers of a ship that was wrecked with such appalling loss of life should have been found blameless. Yet that was in fact the conclusion of the Admiralty Inquiry. Indeed, the only people their Lordships found reason to criticise were a couple of civilian taxi drivers. Also the remark by one of their lawyers 'there were enough fishermen available to man the lifeboat twice over' was a quite deliberate attempt to apportion blame to men who were sleeping in their bunks, wholly ignorant of the disaster.

"The loss of the *Iolaire*, and the deaths of over 200 men was the fault of the Captain and his officers. There is no evidence that after the ship struck any action or attempt was made by the Captain or his officers to save lives. Ashore, there were no facilities provided by the Navy for saving life from a stranded vessel, and no action by the Commander or his staff at the naval base at Stornoway saved life.....

"No mention was made in the Admiralty Inquiry of the body of the Captain of the *Iolaire* being found on Sandwick Beach wearing two lifebelts. There are reliable witnesses still living who can testify to this shameful act".[41]

This is, of course, a public response some time after the disaster, from a skipper in the fishing community who, though well-respected, may or may not have studied all aspects of the various inquiries into the tragedy. Yet the strength of his words more than sixty years after the tragedy shows the lasting bitterness left in the minds of island people at the failings of the Public Inquiry.

It may be purely coincidental that two main players in the Public Inquiry departed Lewis shortly afterwards. John Norrie Anderson represented some of the families and William Alexander Ross acted for the Admiralty. Both left the island within two years of the Inquiry. Anderson was born in Lewis and had lost his wife. It is believed that his only drafts for a book about the history of Lewis, advertised in the local press as being near completion, were lost in the Town Hall fire of March 1918 and the book was lost as a result. Ross had been thirty years in Stornoway and lost a son in a tragic accident in the harbour in 1917. Although these personal tragedies and setbacks could have led to their departure, one must wonder whether these men also felt public scorn, whether they knew that the Inquiry was viewed as a travesty of justice, rightly or wrongly, by a large percentage of the local population. Were they hounded out by the reaction of the public, who considered that they had not represented the island adequately?

How the *Iolaire* disaster slipped from view

"Up to this day you will still see that bitterness when people talk of this loss, and how small the impact was felt in London, in Westminster. If this had happened in the south of England there would have been a great deal more noise made about it and there would have been a lot more stir."[42]

Their Lordships of the Admiralty hoped the *Iolaire* disaster would soon be forgotten and were pleased that they had escaped national condemnation. However, within a very short time the Islands' first MP, Dr Donald Murray,[43] was vocal in the House of Commons on the subject of the *Iolaire*. The House met for the first time since the 1918 General Election on 4th February 1919, and Dr Murray was not sworn in as an MP until March, but on 26th February he asked this question in the House:

"To ask the First Lord of the Admiralty, whether his attention has been called to the finding of the fatal accidents inquiry into the loss of HMY *Iolaire*, in which a strong recommendation is made that proper provision should be made for the safe transit of naval ratings on leave to the Western Isles; whether he intends to act upon this recommendation; and, if so, what steps he proposes to take."[44]

The Admiralty was disturbed by the question and wondered what other queries might follow. The question was passed around senior naval officers to find a formula that would give a safe answer. The First Lord of the Admiralty, Walter Long (MP for Westminster St George's) took the opportunity of expressing:

"The profound regret of the Board of Admiralty at the loss of over 200 gallant lives and of tendering their deepest sympathy to the relatives of the men who were lost in such tragic circumstances,"

but added:

"A copy of the findings of the jury has been received, and these findings and the recommendations accompanying them, including that referred to by my Hon. Friend, will of course receive the very fullest consideration by the Admiralty. No statement can be made at the present moment except that the very exceptional circumstances under which a large number of naval ratings required to travel to Stornoway on the same day are not likely to be repeated."[45]

If their lordships thought that Dr Murray would be prepared to let the tragedy fade from public consciousness they would be disappointed. In his maiden speech on 10th March 1919, Dr Murray pleaded for the right of returned servicemen to have smallholdings (crofts) from which they could make a living. He said:

"In the first week of the War going through the whole of the Western Isles, which I have the honour to represent, and especially through the Island of Lewis, you could hardly find a man capable of bearing arms. Every man, I should say, between nineteen and forty-one or forty-two was either in the Army or the Navy fighting on land or sea. We have had from the beginning of the War the long shadow cast by the setting sun of many a young life, darkening many a home in Lewis and the Western Isles. These sacrifices have continued throughout the War, and these sacrifices were crowned, as the House knows, when at their very door two hundred of our gallant sailors lost their lives while returning home to their families. These are the men for whom I plead here before the High Court of Parliament this evening."[46]

On 12th March he asked the First Lord of the Admiralty:

"Whether the Board of Admiralty proposes to sell, or has already sold, to salvage contractors the wreck of His Majesty's ship "*Iolaire*"; whether he is aware that among the friends of the large number of victims of the disaster whose bodies have not been recovered there exists a strong feeling against disturbing the wreck, and especially against, any blasting operations thereon; and whether he can see his way to respect the local sentiment in this matter?"[47]

And in May he drew attention to the continuing deficiencies of steamer transport to the islands, which had led to food shortages in Stornoway. At that time he again referred to the *Iolaire* disaster, saying:

"The only thing that excited our indignation during the War was the way our soldiers and sailors were treated when they came from France and then had to travel seventy miles by sea in an open, shelterless boat. It was a disgrace to our country that that should have occurred. A terrible thing occurred also at the mouth of Stornoway Harbour, when 200 of these gallant seamen were drowned. I do not cast any blame, but these things throw a lurid light upon the defective character of the steamer communication with the mainland."[48]

Dr Murray was fighting a rearguard action. The tragedy of the *Iolaire* was no longer front page news and it would be left to those within the islands to pull together over the years and decades to come, in an attempt to rebuild their shattered strength after a blow which affected every family in Lewis and Harris.

Dr Donald Murray (far right) welcomes a party of Stornoway politicians outside the Liberal Club, London.

Chapter 6 Footnotes

1. Rev Roderick Morrison quoted in the *Stornoway Gazette*, 10th January 1919

2. Telegrams between Rear Admiral Boyle and Kyle Port Office, 5th January 1919. PRO Admiralty 116/1869

3. Letter from Stornoway Town Council to *The Scotsman*, 4th January 1919

4. Letter from Mrs L Mason to the *Daily Telegraph*, January 1919

5. *Hansard*, 31st July 1940 vol 363 cc1221-3

6. Telegram from Rear Admiral Boyle, Stornoway, 3rd January 1919

7. Service record Rear Admiral Boyle, 1910. PRO file Admiralty 196/88/28

8. As above, 1915

9. Telegram from Admiralty to Rear Admiral Boyle, Stornoway, 4th January 1919

10. Gold Lace - a reference to the controlling authority of the Royal Navy, the Admiralty, who were seen locally to be at fault

11. *The Scotsman*, 6th January 1919

12. Random Notes, *Stornoway Gazette*, 14th January 1919

13. Admiralty File 116/1869 HMY Yacht *Iolaire*, Court of Inquiry, PRO

14. Precognitions Scots Law practice of taking a factual statement from witnesses before a trial

15. Pro Admiralty File 116/1869

16. As above

17. Rear Admiral Boyle to Secretary of Admiralty PRO Admiralty file 116/1869

18. Colin George Mackenzie was succeeded as Procurator Fiscal in Stornoway by his son Colin Scott Snr (1936-1971) and grandson Colin Scott Jnr (1971-1989). The family between them held the position for 90 years

19. *Highland News*, 15th February 1919

20. Evidence of Lt Cdr Walsh, PRO Admiralty 116/1869

21. Evidence of Lt Hicks, PRO Admiralty 116/1869

22. Evidence of Deckhand James Maclean, PRO Admiralty 116/1869

23. Maclean was referring to the lighthouses and harbour lights

24. Evidence of Deckhand James Maclean, PRO Admiralty 116/1869

25. Captain Cameron's testimony. PRO Admiralty file 118/1869 PRO

26. Mercantile Marine rating for a stoker, in which position he would have been below stoking boilers

27. Evidence of Fireman Adams, PRO Admiralty 116/1869

28. Evidence of Donald Macdonald, PRO Admiralty 116/1869

29. As above

30. 'Closed down' indicates that ship's position meant the land now obscured the light at Tiumpan

31. Evidence of John Montgomery, PRO Admiralty 116/1869

32. Evidence of Warrant Officer Barnes, PRO Admiralty 116/1869

33. Evidence of Coastguard DCO Boxall, PRO Admiralty 116/1869

34. Evidence of Donald Macdonald, PRO Admiralty 116/1869

35. *Highland News*, 15th February 1919

36. As above

37. As above

38. Memo in PRO Admiralty file 116/1869

39. *My Amazing Drama - Wrecked on the Beasts of Holm Leonard Welch*. TV Boardman Ltd, 1942

40. Letter from J. C. Pitman to Thomas Carmichael SSG. 13th February 1919. From PRO Admiralty file 116/1869

41. *Stornoway Gazette*, 18th December 1981

42. Peigi Gillies interviewed for An Iolaire, BBC Radio nan Gàidheal, 1999

43. Dr Donald Murray was elected as Liberal MP for the Western Isles in the post-war General Election, December 1918

44. Hansard, House of Commons Debate 26th February 1919 vol 112 cc1715-6

45. As above

46. Hansard, House of Commons Debate 10th March 1919 vol 113 cc945-1052 Par 1037

47. Hansard, House of Commons Debate 12th March 1919 vol 113 cc1260

48. Hansard, House of Commons Debate 19th May 1919 vol 116 cc79-162 Par 146

Chapter 7

The Long Shadow of the Iolaire

"We grew up under this dark cloud. Although we were so young when it happened and we had such little understanding of it, as we were growing older we were beginning to understand this more, and it was as if we were growing up under this dark sorrow."[1]

"I have thought of it every day of my life. You couldn't do otherwise. It is as clear today as when it happened."[2]

The wreck of the *Iolaire* marked a pivotal moment in the history of the Isles of Lewis and Harris. From the very day of the tragedy, when concerts due to be held on New Year's Day were cancelled, the atmosphere, character and future course of events in the islands were forever changed. A darkness came into the islands which was reflected in the sombre clothing of those bereaved, while those who survived the wreck struggled to make peace with their own good fortune, in the face of so much loss.

The Public Inquiry did little to help the bereaved come to terms with their loss, or to help survivors adjust to the trauma of the night and the shaken feelings they were left with. The whole island of Lewis was plunged into a deep gloom that took decades to pass and is still discernible to this day.

The Inquiry took place against a background of other activity – press reporting locally and nationally was feverish, civic meetings were held and resolutions passed, ministers sought to comfort their congregations through prayer and reflection. And for months, bodies were found and recovered – by relatives, friends and strangers. Funerals became an everyday occurrence, in villages from Port of Ness to Borve in Berneray.

In the midst of all of this, the naval authorities signally failed to give the lead and reassurance the people needed. Despite the fact that many of those lost had passed through the Stornoway naval base, or were based there, a sense of detachment prevailed. At best, this was disappointing, but at worst it seemed to signal a lack of concern, a dismissiveness of the fierce human emotions which seethed below the dignified surface of stoical suffering.

The Admiralty response

From the first hours after the tragedy, the naval base seems to have been gripped by an inability to respond feelingly or to acknowledge the scale of the tragedy. Even the base log of the *Iolaire* naval base gives a strangely incomplete account of what, by any measure, was a monumental event in maritime history. In the entry for 1st January 1919 the loss of the yacht *Iolaire* is not mentioned at all, although there is an entry: '*18 bodies placed in battery shed*', and again: '*Body of Roderick Macdonald RNR taken away by brother Malcolm Macdonald, 26 Leurbost, Lochs*'. On that day '*a .303 rifle was found on the beach; left in charge of Chief gunner, Mr Taylor RN*'. There is no related entry on 2nd January, but just after midnight on 3rd January:

'the body of AR Matthews, ASE, conveyed to mail steamer.'

On 4th January 1919 at 2.40pm:

'*Body of late Fred Taylor, Asst Stew, HMY Iolaire, accompanied by funeral party left for burial at Sandwick cemetery*' and on several days from 1st January onwards the log notes that '*Lt Ansdell and search party have left in the morning*'.[3]

Just once, on New Year's Day, it was noted that they had a stretcher. From the point of view of the naval base HMS *Iolaire*, that is the sum total of the activity related to the disaster.

At the same time, it should be noted, Stornoway-based naval ratings and officers were in the front line of the early activity surrounding the recovery, identification and burial of those drowned. It was Hull-born Lt Frederick Edward Townend who was charged with establishment of the mortuary and who, by common sense and with apparent sensitivity, made it possible for relatives to find and carry away their sons, brothers and husbands. Lt Townend was later haunted by the sight of row upon row of bodies laid out for identification, their boot-soles chalked with numbers. For the most part, naval ratings carried the bodies found on the shore along to Battery Point with solemnity and respect, and burials of crew members were carried out quietly and reverently.

But, despite being the first to learn of the tragedy, Stornoway's naval base commander Rear-Admiral Boyle seemed slow to respond. It was not until the day before the public inquiry, 7th January, as evidence was already being taken from survivors, that he sent his expression of regret to Provost Maclean, speaking to the town and community on behalf of the Admiralty:

> "I should be obliged if you would promulgate through the islands of Lewis and Harris my gratitude to the relatives of those who lost their lives in the recent terrible calamity which overtook the gallant men of the Hebrides. The relatives, by their courteous patience and assistance, have won the respect and appreciation of myself, all the officers, and ratings who have had heartrending duties to perform. The fact that nearly 100 remains were transported to their last resting place is a feat which could not have been achieved without the kindly help so graciously given by those who are left to mourn. The messages of condolence from Their Majesties, The King and Queen and from the Queen Mother Alexandra may be taken as the feeling shared by the whole Navy, of which all those connected with the Stornoway base are a unit."[4]

Rear Admiral Boyle's words, even if they had not been so restrained in their mention of 'gratitude' and 'appreciation', could not undo some of the poorly-judged actions of the naval commander in the immediate aftermath of the loss of the *Iolaire*. With the populace desperate for a compassionate and humane response to incomprehensible loss, the search continuing day after day and many bodies unrecovered, the Admiralty alienated local feeling again and again.

On the day of the wreck, 1st January 1919, naval diver Victor George Gusterson was given the uncomfortable task of searching the wreck. He found that the *Iolaire* saloon and the surrounding sea was full of bodies and, after opening the saloon, he refused to go down again. His wife's uncle, Kenneth Smith, who left a widow and two children, was one of eleven men from the village of Leurbost who was drowned on the *Iolaire*.

Admiral Boyle's telegram report to the Admiralty says:

> "Divers report Yacht *IOLAIRE* completely broken in two abaft foremast. After part completely wrecked apart from skin of ship. Divers think boiler blew up this is not borne out by evidence of Surveyors and mainmast is still standing."[5]

And the next day he adds:

> 631. My 618★. Divers report is unreliable. By using waterglass at LWS with smooth water it appears that the sheer deck aft is intact. Back is broken as

Royal Navy Diver Victor Gusterson was sent down to the wreck and reported the saloon full of bodies.

previously reported. There is no indication that boiler exploded bridge and engine room skylight glass appear to be undamaged."[6]

Gusterson's report of the boiler having exploded is, however, supported by several of the survivors, who reported a flash and explosion as the *Iolaire* sank, some describing it as the boiler exploding.

Naval authorities nearly caused a riot in Stornoway by sending a salvage crew on an east coast drifter out to the wreck – it was seen hoisting bodies in nets, using the derrick and sling. These bodies were then unceremoniously dumped on the quayside like dead fish.

Meanwhile a wave of squally weather was working on the wreck itself, until then still visible above the waves. In a newspaper report just two weeks after the tragedy it was reported that the *Iolaire* was fast breaking up[7] and immediately the Admiralty pounced. Their announcement that the wreck was up for sale to ship-breakers, with over 80 bodies still unaccounted for, caused universal dismay and horror. A ledger held by the Naval Historical Branch reveals that the authority for sale of the wreck was dated 14th January, the purchaser Jas (James) A. White of the East Coast Wrecking Co Ltd, and gross proceeds £125.[8] The ledger also records:

'In view of local feeling against blasting operations, work was suspended by request of Admty. Purchase price refunded plus out of pocket expenses (£2133.0.4) plus £425.16.0 as loss of profit."

The matter was later discussed in Westminster, as the *Stornoway Gazette* reported:

"Dr Murray asked a question in the House of Commons regarding the wreck of the *Iolaire* and was told that it had been sold in January and that, following representations that operations should not be proceeded with so long as any bodies remained unrecovered, the purchasers had suspended the salvage work."[9]

Dr Murray had, on 12th March in the House of Commons, forcibly expressed the 'strong feeling against disturbing the wreck' that existed in the islands, and specifically counselled against blasting operations at the site.

Despite this, a powerful salvage boat was brought to begin work on the wreck in February,[10] and divers today (2018) report that the wreck was destroyed, very likely with explosives and cutting equipment, by salvage crews commissioned by the Admiralty in the late 1920s. So far from considering the wreck as a grave site, Admiralty officials seem to have sanctioned the destruction of the ship and retrieval of artefacts while widows and children still mourned within sight of the wreck.[11] It was little wonder that the community was enraged.

The trauma of survivors

The very first impacts of the wreck were felt by those who had survived the sinking. It is well-understood today that those who survive a traumatic event are likely to be damaged by the experience. Some of the survivors were later both candid and articulate about the feelings they experienced as they returned home safely, when neighbours, relatives and friends had perished. Donald Morrison of Knockaird in Ness, Am Patch, was the man who endured a night clinging to the mast of the sunken yacht. He was sent home from hospital after being rescued, and later told of his mixed feelings about getting home:

"I would have rather stayed in the hospital because I knew what was waiting for me because I had lost my brother. I didn't want to face that. Anyway, I went with them… The car took us to Lionel and we had to walk home from there. My father had died a year earlier so staying in the home were my mother and two sisters. My married brother was in our home that night and they were all mourning the loss of my brother. They were glad to see me, but the crying was just the same. The fact that the men had come through the war and had been drowned so close to home was awful."

Donald's story gives a first hint of the wrenching, complex emotions felt by those who survived the *Iolaire*'s wreck. From some of the contemporary reactions it is clear that it affected some men immediately, and badly. Not only did Donald not want to go home, but when he did reach home, he was afraid to come out of the house:

"I was afraid at first after losing my brother and the others I knew. It was terrible."

John Maclennan,''Ain Geal', had the same harrowing sense of guilt after arriving back in his home village of Kneep:

"Somehow word must have got back to Uig, because Càdham (Malcolm Matheson) and An Gobha (Murdo Macleod) came to the house and, as I had not seen either of their sons since coming ashore, I feared the worst. I went to hide at the other end of the house and wished I hadn't come home so soon. Going to face those men knowing their sons were drowned, but I couldn't tell them that."[12]

Like so many other young men of the islands, John was drawn away from his home after the war and spent a spell of 14 years in Australia, as he could not settle in Lewis after the disaster.

Morag Morrison of Swordale recounted:

"My uncle was on the *Iolaire* – he swam ashore and he went up, his aunt was married in Sandwick and he managed to go up to the home and stayed a while there, until they got some conveyance to take him home. Another man used to say: "Did you see our Murdo?" And he didn't want to say that he saw him, because he knew if he hadn't come home that he must be lost. "Oh," he said, "there were so many on the *Iolaire* you could hardly see many." He didn't want to say that he did see him, because he had seen him, and he had spoken to him. He had come off the *Sheila*, which was the boat that came into Stornoway, because he noticed a friend of his he hadn't seen all during the war."[13]

Murdo Stewart of 9 Lower Bayble also found it difficult to cope with survivor's guilt after being questioned by relatives of those lost. He emigrated for Montreal, Canada in June 1922 on the Canadian Pacific liner *Melita*. He was at Fort William, Ontario, then married in British Columbia,

settling at Gibsons, where he became a fisherman. When his niece, Donna Macleod, visited his wife and twin daughters in Canada in 1991 she took with her from Lewis the booklet *Sea Sorrow*, an account of the *Iolaire*'s loss, and found that her uncle had not told his family anything about the ordeal he had endured.

One survivor, Malcolm Macdonald from Ness, went to Canada and his relatives could not make contact with him after his departure. A fitter to trade when he enlisted, it is thought that he is the 27-year-old fitter who emigrated on the Canadian Pacific Railways liner *Marburn* on 9th May 1924. It is not known where he went subsequently, or whether he married, and his date of death is unknown – he remains the only survivor definitively untraceable.

14 of those who survived emigrated to Australia, Canada or New Zealand. Emigration was a common recourse for young men seeking a better life, so the significance of this should not be overstated, but it is fair to conjecture that escaping the sense of guilt, and the all-pervading gloom of the decades after the Great War, would have added to their motivation for leaving. Many survivors also left the island to settle in Glasgow or other parts of Scotland.

For the survivors there was no counselling as there is today. The emotional, cognitive and physical effects of such trauma were as little understood in 1919 as shell shock had been in 1914, when cowardice or, at its kindest, hysteria were given as reasons for survivor behaviour after intense combat stress.

Post-Traumatic Stress Disorder (PTSD) is now understood to bring with it a wide range of symptoms. Murdo Stewart (Lower Bayble) left his family bemused

Survivor guilt was one of the drivers for emigration. Many young men and women left the islands in the 1920's.
Here crowds see off an emigration vessel leaving Stornoway.

when he entered his own croft house by the window rather than the door, immediately after walking home barefoot from the site of the *Iolaire* tragedy at Holm. Others reportedly could not speak for a time.

> "A man who lived next door, he had come across the moor, I think. How he got to shore, I just don't know, but it was as if he had gone crazy. The ones who had lost their family in the village, mothers and women, they were coming in to ask if there had been any sight of Donald or Angus or John and he could only look at them, with the tears coming down his cheeks. He had two words that he would repeat over and over: 'Good God, Good God!' It was as if he had grabbed hold of those words on board and they were following him and they were the only words he could say."[14]

John Mackenzie, Doonie, of 8 Tobson was awarded a disablement allowance of five shillings and sixpence a week from July 1919 to August 1920, due to what was defined as 'Traumatic Neurasthenia' which in 1911 was defined as nervous weakness arising from shock or injury. He later returned to fishing, and re-enrolled in the Reserves. After his term of enrolment expired, on 23rd April 1927, his health again deteriorated and he had to go into a home in Glasgow in 1930, where he died. His brother recalled taking him fresh clothes shortly after he was admitted, but when he visited the following day he noticed other patients were wearing them.

For some of those who survived the events of 1st January, the impacts were upon their physical health. Alexander John Macleod was said to be the second last man ashore on John Finlay Macleod's life-saving rope before it broke. His health suffered after the war and he spent time in the Lewis Sanatorium. Alexander Maciver

from Stornoway was found drowned in Stornoway harbour during the Second World War. Who knows what went through his mind and how he came to be in the water close to Battery Point, where the dead had been laid out in the makeshift morgue in January 1919?

The longer-term consequences for *Iolaire* survivors are hard to evaluate as they, like so many of the Great War generation, did not easily talk about their experiences. It's probable that many survivors found solace spending time with their colleagues, especially at New Year and on occasions when the anniversary was marked in some way – by a memorial or event.

Of the 73 island survivors of the disaster, 16 died prematurely, some within a short time of the wreck, of causes which included tuberculosis – rampant in the islands at that time – heart problems and tubercular meningitis. At least two men were excused from giving evidence at the Inquiry due to symptoms following their traumatic experience. Many of the men were awarded a disablement pension for a short time either immediately after the wreck, or in some cases within a few years. Several of the survivors were also demobilised on compassionate grounds soon after the event.

As the allotted leave period drew to a close, the Admiralty appeared to recognise the extreme strain placed on *Iolaire* survivors. On 18th January 1919 it was announced that:

> "The Admiralty have granted a fortnight's extension of leave to all survivors of the *Iolaire* Disaster. Their shaken nerves will need as long a rest as is possible."[15]

Survivor Donald Maciver from Tolsta attributed this concession to the intervention of Western Isles MP Dr Donald Murray.

Tributes and reports – the news spreads

By contrast to the dispassionate, some would say callous, response from local naval authorities, the island community was soon inundated with expressions of sympathy and condolence from further afield. The press were efficient in mobilising the sympathies of the nation and internal communications within the navy were still swifter. The men of Lewis and Harris already enjoyed enormous respect around the fleet as shipmates and serving men, their seamanship second to none. As news of the disaster spread through the fleet, there was shock, sorrow and disbelief. There were Western Islanders amongst the crews on most of the ships of the Royal Navy and Mercantile Marine and, when shipmates learned of the *Iolaire* disaster, it was hard for them to fathom how so many of those drowned had been lost in home waters. Shortly after the disaster, letters of condolence from officers, shipmates and friends began to arrive in Lewis, some addressed to the populace as a whole, but many personal letters of sympathy sent by shipmates to the grieving families.

Mrs Henrietta (Euphemia) Macleod of Newvalley, received the following letter after the loss of 18-year-old Angus.

"I am writing on behalf of myself and the crew of the *Resmilo* to express to you our deepest sympathy for the loss of your son Angus on HMY *Iolaire*. His loss was a great shock to us all, especially at such a time when most of us were so happy among our loved ones at home.

"Your son has been under my command since July last, and I have always considered him as one of my best men. He was so jolly and willing under any circumstances, and was a great favourite among the rest of his shipmates, who greatly feel his loss, and all join with me in sending this note to you, which is but poor comfort for your sad loss. I am enclosing a letter which I found written by him to you, which he evidently meant to post before going on leave. All his belongings will be sent to you by the naval authorities, as I have no power to send them myself. If there is anything you would like to know or anyway I can assist you, please accept my services."[16]

The body of the young signalman, John Alex (Jack) Macaskill, was not found on the shore until late February 1919, but his widowed mother had already known that he was lost, without the comfort of a body to lay to rest. Perhaps the warm regard he inspired in his friends brought her some comfort, when this letter arrived at her Keith Street home just a week after the tragedy:

"Allow me to intrude upon your most sacred thoughts of your son. We received the news of Jack's death with sorrow-stricken hearts, and we feel more deeply grieved when we realise how near he was to the home he loved, and how little we can do to mitigate the grief which you have to bear. Your son, Jack, as he was popularly known, was loved by all he came in contact with, as the nice dispositioned lad he was. He had only been in this hut with us a month, yet during that brief period he had won our hearts by his unselfish and noble demeanour. We feel grieved more excessively knowing that the loss of a son of such intrinsic value must be overwhelming, but in our most sincere and deep-felt sympathy all we can do is to commend you to the mercy of God. He comforts everybody.

"The cheery manner in which your son compassed all the difficulties and misfortunes which beset him will never be forgotten by us, and we know how proud you must feel to have mothered such a man.

"Assuring you, Mrs Macaskill, of the earnest and devotional sympathy of all us boys in this hut, not to mention numerous friends he possessed among the other Convoy Signalmen. I am, Madam, on behalf of the boys, yours very sincerely."[17]

Jessie Campbell of 8 Vatisker lost her husband, Alexander (Mac Òrd), who had been home on leave and expected his discharge imminently. He left not just his wife but two children, an ageing mother and a sister for whom he was the main support. Jessie evidently informed his captain, who must have also been a good friend, that he would not return to service, for she received this at Vatisker:

"I got your letter this morning with the terrible news of your dear husband's sad end. You know you have my deepest sympathy, for you have lost a good man; no better ever sailed under my command. He was several years with me, and I always knew when he was on the helm the ship was safe. Time alone can soften this blow for you, though it can never cause you to forget. I have several letters from him which he sent during the war. He was always cheerful and optimistic about the result. He came in to see me the last time he was in Glasgow, and gave me his photograph. This I shall always keep among my treasures. I will write you again. In the meantime try and bear up, remembering that he would have wished you to do so, and may the Almighty in His mercy comfort you and the many others bereaved by this sad calamity.[18]

Mr and Mrs John Morrison of Breanish, Uig, lost their eldest son George, Seòras a' Chèisean, aged 20 years, in the disaster. He had eagerly joined the Navy at the age of 17 and was coming home on leave when he died on the *Iolaire*. His father received the following letter from his commanding officer:

"Your son was one of the very best boys it has been my privilege to have under my care, and his loss has shocked me very deeply. Just previous to going on leave he was granted his first good conduct badge. In extending you my sincerest sympathies I can just realise what has been your anxiety. Your son was a general favourite aboard because of his cheerful disposition and his willingness at all times to bear a hand when a job of work was in hand. All the members of the crew have asked me to express their deepest sympathies with you in your sad bereavement."[19]

Provost Murdo Maclean, representing the town of Stornoway, and the Commander of the naval base, Rear-Admiral Boyle, were natural recipients for more generic messages of sympathy. Day after day, telegrams, letters and press reports of sympathies minuted in meetings around the country poured in. In Glasgow, where so many citizens were islanders or of Western Isles descent, the bereavement felt was real and tangible, expressed forcefully at a meeting of the Lewis and Harris Association of Glasgow, which recorded:

"The resolution of sympathy which was moved by the Chairman was in the following terms: "The Lewis and Harris Association desire to place on record their sense of profound sorrow at the overwhelming disaster whereby so many gallant Lewis sailors have lost their lives, and which has plunged the whole island in grief, and they tender their heartfelt sympathy to the stricken relatives so suddenly and cruelly bereaved." Mr John Mackay, who seconded, confessed to having been stunned by the news of the disaster – the horror, and, as the Chairman had said, by the apparent needlessness of so great a loss of life. He could not bear to speak of it, and would simply second the resolution, which was thereupon declared: Carried."

There were other forms of solidarity, from services, civic bodies and those with Scottish connections. From the army:

"Army Council desire to express to you, and through you, to affected families, their deep sympathy in tragic calamity which has befallen the island in particularly sad circumstances."[20]

"Officers, Warrant Officers, N.C.O's and men of the 3rd Seaforth Highlanders desire to express to you their deep sympathy in the bereavement which has fallen upon the people of Lewis."[21]

From representatives of the government:

"I am inexpressibly shocked and grieved to read of the terrible tragedy off your shore. May I ask to convey to the bereaved my deepest sympathy in their hour of darkness and sorrow."[22]

And from representatives of the church to the ministers in Lewis:

"Please read from the pulpit on Sabbath – Deepest sympathy throughout Churches with bereaved friends of victims of disaster to *Iolaire*. May the Saviour comfort and strengthen. – Ogilvie, Drummond, Munro (Moderators)."[23]

Of course, in January 1919 as now, the news of a horrific loss of life on home shores was to command acres of column inches in newsprint. The first reports of the tragedy appeared in print on the day itself, when the *Inverness Courier* made its erroneous claim that a second man had survived by clinging to the mast, and from then a constant stream of information – more or less accurate – went out to the nation.

Until the public inquiry was held, much of the reporting was emotive, trying to capture the atmosphere of the islands. As might be expected, the local newspaper, the *Stornoway Gazette*, published its first report as soon as it appeared after the tragedy. In a deeply personal tone the founding editor, William Grant, wrote:

"No one now alive in Lewis can ever forget the 1st January 1919, and future generations will speak of it as the blackest day in the history of the island, for on it 200 of our bravest and best perished on the very threshold of their homes under the most tragic circumstances. The terrible disaster at Holm on New Year's morning has plunged every house and every heart in Lewis into grief unutterable. Language cannot express the anguish, the desolation, the despair which this awful catastrophe has inflicted. One thinks of the wide circle of blood relations affected by the loss of even one of the gallant lads, and imagination sees those circles multiplied by the number of the dead, overlapping and overlapping each other till the whole island – every hearth and home in it is shrouded in deepest gloom."[24]

The following day the *Scotsman* reported:

"The appalling catastrophe at Stornoway still monopolises all thoughts on the island. The villages of Lewis are like places of the dead. No one goes about except on duties that cannot be left undone. The homes of the island are full of lamentation – grief that cannot be comforted. …. Scarcely a family has escaped the loss of some near blood relation. Many have had sorrow heaped on sorrow. Messages of sympathy and offers of what help is possible continue to pour in from all quarters."[25]

The *Stornoway Gazette* later had the following report from Glasgow:

"Appalling. Even to those of us who have been smitten by the war in the loss of our dear ones, the terrible calamity which overtook the Island of Lewis on the eve of the New Year is so overwhelming that one feels stunned even at the thought of it. Language lamentably fails in giving expression to one's grief. We are simply dumb in amazement and wonder whether it is not all a dream. That over two hundred brave Lewismen who have weathered – many of them – five winters on the vigil of the ocean, should, after warfare ceased, be done to sudden and violent death, as one may say, at their own door, seems altogether too terrible. Lewis suffered in the war

– on the battlefield and on the high seas – but this appalling disaster, not so much its extent as its circumstances, puts even that loss into a secondary position. The loss on the battlefield is partly reckoned on from the start and not unexpected, as we eagerly scanned the casualty lists from time to time in search of names familiar to us and associated with our families. But this is a calamity totally unforeseen and wholly unexpected. The heartfelt sympathy of the nation – of the world – is with gallant little Lewis today in its hour of travail and sorrow.

"In the Highlanders' Memorial Church last Sabbath, at all diets of worship, special prayers were offered on behalf of all stricken with grief in Lewis. In the other Highland Churches throughout the City touching references were also made, and keen sympathy expressed with the islanders in this their hour of sorrow".[26]

Clubs and societies with connections to the islands wrote from all over the world, offering condolences, expressing profound shock and sadness, and sending money for bereaved relatives. Similar messages came from places with no express connection to the islands, simply from working and serving people who felt a sense of solidarity with the islanders as they struggled with their loss. At Peterhead Town Council on January 6th Provost James Hutchison Catto, who was a herring exporter by trade, moved an expression of sympathy from 'a community (that) had been so closely associated with many of the inhabitants of the Island of Lewis, in interests allied to each other for long years'. The motion was unanimously agreed.

The messages came from north and south, from the North Camberwell Unionist Association and from the people of Bolton in Lancashire, where the Lewis landowner, Lord Leverhulme,[27] was mayor:

"The Mayor, Aldermen, and Burgesses of the County Borough of Bolton in Council assembled at their meeting this morning have in silence passed the following resolution: "That this Council with feelings of profound grief deplore the appalling disaster which occurred during the early hours of the 1st January instant, just outside the harbour of Stornoway, occasioned by the wreck of the patrol boat conveying to their island homes for New Year's leave Lewismen and others who were serving in His Majesty's Forces, as a result of which it is feared over 200 lives have been lost, and in tendering their heartfelt sympathies to the relatives and dependants of the loyal and brave men who have lost their lives, pray that they may receive Divine comfort and consolation in their sorrow. Bolton people would in any case have felt keenly the sorrow that has overtaken the people of the Island of Lewis, but at the present moment, in view of the fact that I am directly connected with the island, they feel a closer intimacy and have the keener sympathy with all those who are weighed down with sorrow."[28]

Within a short time the terrible news had reached Gaels all over the world, and island emigrants and descendants were discussing the terrible blow to their home islands:

"The members of the Gaelic Society of Vancouver, B.C., were shocked to see by the daily papers news of the death by drowning of 270 (sic) Royal Naval Reservists of H.M. Steam Yacht *Iolaire* on January, 1st. As these were all residents of the Island of Lewis, and safe to say, all Gaelic speakers, we, as Highlanders, deeply deplore such a calamity and feel that not only has the Gaelic cause, but the Empire as a whole, suffered a loss through their death. As its heroic defenders, they have fearlessly carried out their duties in different parts of the world and endured the perils and privations inseparable from such a life, and to be cut off in their prime on the shores of their native island and on the eve of a joyous reunion with their loved ones, after an absence of four long and anxious years, makes it still more sad. A considerable proportion of the members of our Society are natives of North Uist, Harris and Lewis, and we know full well that the Island of Lewis has given more than its quota to the noble cause for which our Empire and her Allies have fought and won. At a regular meeting of the Society held on the evening of the 2nd inst., it was unanimously resolved: – "That the Provost of Stornoway be asked to convey through the press, or by any other means at his disposal, the Society's deepest sympathy with the dependants and relatives of these brave men in their bereavement.""[29]

Back in Britain, news of the grievous loss in the Western Isles swept through the country, and reached the very highest in the land. The following telegram was received from King George V and Queen Mary by Rear-Admiral the Hon. RF Boyle, through the Admiralty:

"For the Rear Admiral, officers, ratings, and relatives of those who lost their lives on H.M.Y. *Iolaire*. Their Majesties The King and Queen were shocked to hear of the disaster which has overtaken the naval Leave boat returning to Stornoway and send their deepest sympathy to all the bereaved families."[30]

To which the reply was sent:

"Request following may be communicated to H.M. The King. – The Rear-Admiral, officers, ratings and relatives beg to thank their Majesties for their gracious message of sympathy which will greatly assist those who are bereaved to bear their grief."[31]

The Queen Mother, Queen Alexandra, added more personal condolences when she contacted Stornoway's Provost, Murdo Maclean by telegram:

"Am more deeply distressed than I can say at this… sad disaster which has befallen our dear sailors at Stornoway. Please convey my utmost and deepest sympathy to relations at the heartrending calamity which has deprived them of their nearest and dearest to them at the moment of their return home after all their splendid services in the past four years. Alexandra."[32]

Provost Maclean replied:

"Words cannot express my sincere appreciation of our beloved Queen Mother's expression of sympathy in this our dark and trying hour. Loyal Lewis gave her best in defence of King and Country. I am sending a copy of your most gracious words to every minister in the island to be read from the pulpit."[33]

Copies of Queen Alexandra's message were also sent by Rear Admiral Boyle to every Post-Office in the Western Isles.

The *Iolaire* Disaster Fund

The urge to contribute something to the relief of suffering was as strong in 1919 as it is today and, from the very first, the letters which brought expressions of sympathy also carried with them donations of money to give practical form to the sorrow of the senders.

On 2nd January the Provost of Stornoway received this message from a former captain of the *Majestic*, where many Lewismen had served:

"During the war it has become my good fortune to become acquainted with many men from Lewis, and better men I don't want to meet anywhere. I fear that some of them may have been amongst those who lost their lives in the recent disaster. I know very well what this will mean to their families. No doubt the Admiralty will deal liberally with them, but Government Departments are always slow to act, and some sort of fund will probably be opened for immediate relief. I therefore venture to enclose the sum of £5 5s, which I hope you will employ in any way you may consider desirable. I wish that it were a hundred times as much, and that would not square the debt I owe to the gallant Bluejackets from the Western Islands who have helped me in many a tight place. I hope that some of them may remember their old skipper not unkindly."[34]

Vice Admiral Seymour Erskine was commodore-in-command at the Royal Naval barracks at Chatham, from where many *Iolaire* boys had made their final departure on 31st December. He wrote:

"During the three years I served in Chatham I got to admire your islanders for their many noble qualities, and our hearts go out to the patient folks at home waiting for the time of re-union which, alas! is postponed to many. Allow us to send a very small cheque, which we hope you will devote as you think best to any relief cases where the bread-winner has been taken. We pray that the Almighty will send His comfort which alone can heal."

The Provost of Stornoway was inundated with promises of money, including £500 from the Grand Fleet Fund[35]. At a meeting on 7th January, a body was convened to receive these monies and administrate the funds so that they could be dispersed fairly.

The *Inverness Courier* reported:

"For the assistance of dependents, it has been decided to set up a fund known as the "*Iolaire Disaster Fund*," and a large committee registered under the War Charities Act, has been formed for its administration. Gratifying offers of help have been received. Subscriptions will be received by Provost Murdo Maclean (Merchant), the Chairman; ex-Provost John Mackenzie (Fishcurer), Vice-Chairman; Baillie Peter Macleod (Baker), Vice-Chairman; Councillor Angus Macleod (Harbour Collector), Secretary; and Mr Angus Cameron (National Bank of Scotland, Stornoway), Treasurer."[36]

The other principal office bearer from the meeting was ex-Provost John Norrie Anderson (notary public) as joint chairman. The rest of the committee comprised Dr Donald Murray MP, Baillie Roderick Smith (chemist), ex-Councillor John Macritchie Morrison (fish salesman), Councillor Norman Stewart (merchant), Councillor Alexander R Murray (draper), Rev George Macleod (UF Church, Garrabost), Rev Roderick Macleod (Free Church, Knock), and Mr John Mackenzie (school board clerk, Tarbert). The remit was to draw up a public appeal and to make any necessary arrangements in connection with it. Rev George Macleod saw war service as chaplain to Gaelic speaking naval personnel at Portsmouth and was from Lochs, Rev Roderick Macleod from Harris, Roderick Smith from Bragar, Norman Stewart from Back and Alexander R Murray from Ness.

These men gave of their time and acted quickly in order that relief be provided to the families. Some of the town councillors also represented rural communities as district councillors and all the committee members and officers were experienced in handling public affairs and monies. Stornoway had the only banks in Lewis and treasurer Angus Cameron was with the National Bank of Scotland in Stornoway from 1893 until 1925.

One of the first to donate was the owner of the Isle of Lewis, Lord Leverhulme, who had already sent the sympathies of his home town of Bolton in his capacity as Mayor of that borough. Now he wrote:

"To Provost Maclean – Your telegram arrived. Am pleased to hear Council and District Committee decided to open subscription list behalf distress caused by last week's disaster. Please enter me £1000, and I will telegraph National Bank tomorrow to have this immediately at your disposal. Let all possible be done to prevent or alleviate distress and suffering. – Leverhulme."[37]

News of the fund spread quickly. An appeal was made in the *Highland News*:

Form A (left)

No. 61

"Iolaire" Disaster.

The Committee of the "Iolaire" Disaster Fund will be pleased if you fill in the information asked for in this Form and return the Form, as soon as possible, in this enclosed addressed envelope.

Late ...... _Malcolm Mackay 36 South Bragar_

Name of Dependant ...... _Kate M. Mackay_

Address ...... _36 South Bragar Stornoway_

Relationship to Sailor ...... _Wife_

Official Number of Deceased ...... _2613_ ...... Rating ...... _Seaman R.N.R._

PARTICULARS OF MEMBERS OF HOUSEHOLD.

Relationship to Deceased.	Name.	Age.	Occupation or School.	If in Employment Wages earned.
Wife (a)	Kate M. Mackay	35	Housewife	
Sister (b)	Margaret	32	housework	
Son (c)	Donald Malcolm	8	Bragar School	
Son (d)	Donald	6	do. do.	
Son (e)	Murdo	4	4 years	
Son (f)	Malcolm	3 mos		
Daughter (g)	Mary	3 months		

INCOME.

Total Amount of Allotment and Separation Allowance received in respect of Deceased... _£2-7-6 weekly_

Total Amount of Allotment and Seperation Allowance received in respect of any other member or members of household ... ... _none_

Total of other source of Income ... ... _none_

I certify that the above statement is true to the best of my knowledge and belief.

(Signature of Dependant) _Kate M. MacKay_

Date... _February 8th_ 1919.

Form B (right)

No. 173

"Iolaire" Disaster.

The Committee of the "Iolaire" Disaster Fund will be pleased if you fill in the information asked for in this Form and return the Form, as soon as possible, in this enclosed addressed envelope.

Late ...... _Norman Macleod Portnaguran_

Name of Dependant ...... _Donald Macleod_

Address ...... _10 Portnaguran Stornoway_

Relationship to Sailor ...... _Father_

Official Number of Deceased ...... _1186_ ...... Rating ...... _P.N.R.B.J.C._

PARTICULARS OF MEMBERS OF HOUSEHOLD.

Relationship to Deceased.	Name.	Age.	Occupation or School.	If in Employment Wages earned.
Father (a)	Donald Macleod	60	—	
Mother (b)	Catherine			
Son (c)	John			
Daughter (d)	Christina			

all sons lost in the war

INCOME.

Total Amount of Allotment and Separation Allowance received in respect of Deceased... _3/- weekly_

Total Amount of Allotment and Seperation Allowance received in respect of any other member or members of household ... _nil_ ... ...

Total of other source of Income ... _nil_ ... ...

I certify that the above statement is true to the best of my knowledge and belief.

(Signature of Dependant) _Donald Macleod_

Date... _8 ... ?_ ...1919.

The Iolaire Disaster Fund Committee received hundreds of applications and letters of appeal for support.

No. 192

"Iolaire" Disaster.

The Committee of the "Iolaire" Disaster Fund will be pleased if you fill in the information asked for in this Form and return the Form, as soon as possible, in this enclosed addressed envelope.

Late .... Ernest Leggett, Emsworth, Hants

Name of Dependants ... Ernest, Fred, Dorothy, Willie, Children of the late Ernest Leggett.

Address ... Ernest & Fred c/o Mr Parham, 27 Queen St, Millin c/o Mrs W Ramsey

South St, Dorothy c/o Mr Ackerman, Battersea Fire Station

Relationship to Sailor ... Major J M Robinson, Guardian of Children, Western House, Emsworth, Hants

Official Number of Deceased ... M.T.A. 2935 ... Rating ....

PARTICULARS OF MEMBERS OF HOUSEHOLD.

Relationship to Deceased	Name.	Age.	Occupation or School.	If in Employment Wages earned.
Guardian of children	Major J M Robinson designated above		Rev'd C H Blofield All Saints Orphanage Lewisham	
4/4/08 Son	(a) Ernest	11	School	Birth 4/4/05
15/1/11 Daughter	(b) Dorothy	8	Mrs Ackerman 21 Cherry Garden Rd Bermondsey	15/1/11
18/2/13 Son	(c) Fred	6	All Saints Orphanage Lewisham	12/2/12
12/3/15 Son	(d) Willie	4	tender age Miss Giles Alexandra Children Home Stoke Devonport	12/3/15

INCOME.

Total Amount of Allotment and Separation Allowance received in respect of Deceased ... 23/a week Ernest & Fred / 12/- Dorothy / 12/- Willie

Total Amount of Allotment and Separation Allowance received in respect of any other member or members of household ...

Total of other source of Income ... Leggett some allowance for John as allowed by Pension Committee

I certify that the above statement is true to the best of my knowledge and belief.

The representative

(Signature of Dependant) ... Ellen Jewell

Date ... Feb 17 1919.

J M Robinson Major
Lieut Sec & Asst Havant District

SOLDIERS AND SAILORS' HELP SOCIETY.

Havant District.

Major T. M. Robinson,
Hon. Sec. & Treas.

Western House
Emsworth,
Hants.

30th March 1919

To Angus Macleod Esqre
Iolaire Disaster Fund
Stornoway

Dear Sir, I am taking up the case of the 4 orphan children of the late Ernest Leggett who lost his life on board "The Iolaire" and has left his children alone in the world his wife having predeceased him a year. Can you give me the name of the owners of the "Iolaire" or who ever paid the crew as I want a certificate that he was serving on the yacht at the time of the disaster. I find it very difficult to get information from the relations, but I gather that Leggett had served on board for some years and at the time of his death was one of the quarter masters. I propose applying to the Admiralty for pensions for the children and therefore with them as full information as possible I shall be very glad for any you can give me or of putting me in the way of getting it. You were good enough to send £5 was is there any chance of getting more. I keep the children till the question of pension is settled. Yrs faithfully

J M Robinson Major

Major T M Robinson acted as guardian for the four orphaned children of acting quartermaster Ernest Leggett and appealed for their support. Three of the children were already in orphanages.

263

"We are glad to learn that steps are being taken to obtain contributions in Inverness and surrounding districts for the relief of the widows, children and other relatives of the gallant Lewis and Harris men who perished so tragically within a mile of Stornoway pier on the first day of the year.

"At the desire of Provost Macdonald, acting on the authority of the Committee in Stornoway, Mr James Maxwell, Town Chamberlain, has kindly agreed to receive subscriptions in his office in the Town Hall, and remit them to the Treasurer of the Fund.

"There is profound sympathy with the Lewis people, especially throughout the North of Scotland, but practical help is better. Inverness, the Capital of the Highlands, and the surrounding districts, now so prosperous, should, notwithstanding many other calls, contribute liberally to the "*Iolaire* Disaster Fund."[38]

The next day the *Stornoway Gazette* had the following report from Glasgow:

"The Magistrates of Glasgow recommended that on Saturday the 22nd of March 1919, a "Lewis Flag Day" be held in the city. The Magistrates said the object was well worthy of making the 22nd a red-letter day in the history of flag days in Glasgow. Flag sellers were allocated stations most suitable to themselves. The Flag Day was organised by Mrs. Hourston, An Comunn Gaidhealach Offices, 108 Hope Street and Mr R.M. Montgomery, secretary, Lewis and Harris Association, 26 Montague Street, Kelvinbridge."[39]

In May 1919, the Glasgow Committee formed by the Lewis and Harris Association deposited £2,902 19s 7d in the account. The money had been raised by the flag day (£1,277) and a collection at the picture house (£999 10s 9d).[40] Food parcels from Glasgow were also received by families, bringing exotic delights unfamiliar after war-time shortages – it was some time later that young Maggie Campbell at 8 Vatisker realised that what she had eaten as sweets was in fact jelly!

Meanwhile, at home in Stornoway in the weeks following the disaster, the harbour had become so congested with fishing boats from all over the UK that a meeting was called to discuss the matter. The meeting was held in the Stornoway Fishmarket on Wednesday 15th January 1919 and was presided over by ex-Provost John MacKenzie. He said that, before dealing with the subject of congestion, he was sure the meeting would wish him to make reference to the sad disaster that took place outside the Stornoway harbour mouth on New Year's morning:

"By the loss of the 'Iolaire' over 200 brave men perished, many of them on the very threshold of their homes. As to the cause of the disaster, that was being enquired into, and until the enquiry was completed it was best to be silent, and not to be led away by anything they might have heard or might hear.

"The terrible disaster had plunged over forty villages in Lewis, as well as a number of homes in Harris and other parts of the kingdom, into grief and sorrow. Many of these brave lads were coming home after four years' service to King and Country, and longing to be joined to their loved ones who were waiting for them".

Mackenzie was well aware that the fishermen present sympathised with the friends and the relatives of the departed. Many were fishermen just as they were themselves, and he knew their brotherly feeling would go out to the loved ones left behind. With their consent he moved the following resolution:

"That this meeting of fishermen, fish salesmen and fish buyers extend their deepest sympathy to the friends and relatives of the brave men who perished in the *Iolaire* disaster of 1st January, 1919, and hope that the sympathy thus extended will help to ease and comfort the hearts of those who mourn the loss of their dear ones. The resolution was seconded by Mr Donald Macleod, skipper of the steam-drifter "*Bure*" and supported by John McR. Morrison, fish salesman, and unanimously carried."[41]

The chairman moved on to the more practical aspect of showing sympathy with the bereaved. In view of the appeal made to the public, and which he was glad to say was meeting with a generous response, he was sure that all fishermen fishing out of the Port of Stornoway during the season would be glad to do their part by contributing to the fund. He suggested that their sympathy should take the form that every boat landing herring at the port this season would give one cran[42] of herring per boat towards the fund, that the salesmen sell the cran and hand the proceeds to the treasurer of the fund, Mr Angus Cameron, National Bank. The top shot[43] of herring landed at Stornoway the following week was 100 crans by the Lewis drifter *Stornoway Castle*. The *Hopeful* (Duncan Maciver, Stornoway) grossed £1033 for a single shot of herring, giving an idea of the wealth created by the fishing industry in the ports around the coast.

Elsewhere in Gaeldom, Comunn Gàidhlig Lunnainn (London Gaelic Society) unanimously agreed that all the cash in the Prisoner of War Fund be transferred to the *Iolaire* Disaster Fund. There was a kinship, too, between islanders and the city of Liverpool, from where many of those lost on the *Iolaire* had sailed as merchant seamen before and during the war, on naval and merchant vessels. Many Lewis seamen had shipmates from the city. The following report from Liverpool appeared in the *Stornoway Gazette*:

"The Liverpool Gaelic Society held a social gathering in St Andrew Church Hall, Rodney Street, on the 15th inst – the Rev. James Hamilton, M.A., minister of the church, in the chair. Mr Donald Smith, a native of Lochs, Lewis, addressed the meeting and spoke feelingly of the Lewis naval disaster. Piper James Scott played a lament on the bagpipes, the audience standing in sympathy, after which a collection was taken, which resulted in a handsome sum, which we trust to augment by a further sum raised by friends and well-wishers in Liverpool, to be forwarded to the Provost of Stornoway in due course."[44]

Around the world, the Lewis diaspora did not forget the hurt their kith and kin at home were suffering and organised support for the bereaved families in many ways. The letter below is a good example:

"Port Arthur and Fort William, Ontario, Canada.

On hearing of the fatal disaster, the Lewismen of both cities considered it their duty to assist in some way, and called a meeting, with the Rev. N. MacLeod, Port Arthur, as chairman. Collectors were appointed, and, needless to say, the results were satisfactory. Although the amount will not make up for the loss of the brave men who perished on the threshold of their homes while in defence of our country, we all felt it our duty to assist the dependants who lost their dearest, and we sincerely hope that the amount, although small, will help to meet some of their needs."[45]

A letter from Kenneth Campbell of Ontario, with a draft to the value of £319 5s 3d and a list of contributors was enclosed with the letter.

Even a year after the *Iolaire* disaster ex-pat islanders were still sending money to the *Iolaire* Disaster Fund. In the *Stornoway Gazette* of 9th January 1920, Ex-Provost Maclean acknowledged with thanks the receipt of a draft from Alexander A. Stewart of Graniteville, Vermont, USA, on behalf of a large number of subscribers, all of whom were named by reference to their native Lewis villages.

Not all of the fundraising efforts made on behalf of islanders were fully appreciated. During January 1919, when hurt was still so raw in the islands, the naval authorities added insult to injury by proposing that a concert be held on a Sunday in Inverness Music Hall, in aid of the *Iolaire* Disaster Fund. Whilst they may have been oblivious to any unintended offence, the magistrates asked to grant permission for the concert were not. The Inverness Dean of Guild, John Fraser, said that all sympathised with the object in view, but he strongly objected to a concert on the Lord's day, and especially on the evening of communion Sabbath. He was quite sure the very people whom it was desired to assist would resent collecting money in this way. Baillie McAllan said that the Lewis people were strict sabbatarians and he questioned very much whether they would thank those responsible for anything they could do for them by giving a Sunday concert. However, by a slight majority the magistrates agreed to grant permission.

When it was learned in Lewis that the concert was to be held, the following telegram was sent to the town clerk of Inverness:

"*Iolaire* Disaster Fund Committee learn with dismay that it is proposed to hold a concert at Inverness on Sabbath evening in aid of that Fund. My Committee whole-heartedly disapprove of such action. Apart from it being a flagrant breach of the sanctity of the Lord's Day, they regard the proposal as dishonouring the memory of the gallant dead and an outrage upon the feelings of the bereaved. Kindly make this known. – Honorary Secretary."[46]

But another concert attracted no such controversy, and brought with it a tribute from no less a personage than the Secretary of State for Scotland, Robert Munro.

"The Right Honourable Robert Munro the Secretary for Scotland, presided at a concert in the Usher Hall, Edinburgh, last week, under the auspices of the Association of Highland Societies of Edinburgh. The concert which was in aid of the Lewis Disaster Fund, was attended by a gathering which completely filled the hall.

"Mr Munro, in the course of his remarks, referred to the fact that he was no longer representing a Highland constituency in the House of Commons. … But he might add that nothing and no one could rob him of his birthright as a Highlander and of the affection which he had for the Highlands and the people who lived there, or of his desire and determination that, in so far as in him lay, he would consult and promote their best interests."[47]

Contributions great and small also arrived from individuals. Commander John Teignmouth, Inspecting Officer for the Royal Naval Reserve between 1881-86, enclosed a donation of £1 and stated:

"their efficiency was always remarked on and commended by the Admiral Superintendent of Naval Reserves." And Maria Wisely, the wife of Captain E Wisely (she was also the daughter of the late Sir Donald Currie, the Scottish shipping magnate, who at one time owned the *Iolaire*) sent a cheque for £500, *"to be used in the prompt relief of the more urgent cases of distress which may come to your knowledge as a result of this tragic event."*

By 31st January 1919 the *Iolaire* Disaster Fund's treasurer, Angus Cameron, was able to record dozens of donations ranging from £2,000 to numerous donations of £5. Donors included Orkney trawlermen, the servants at Eisken Lodge in Lewis and Messrs David MacBrayne Ltd, the ferry operators. Many were the sums in single figures, and even in shillings, representing no less a contribution from those who put their hands in their own pocket. In the first year's accounts, the amount in the *Iolaire* Disaster Fund (split between money held at the bank and Victory Bonds purchased) stood at over £94,000. Of this, £2,198 11s 4d had been distributed to dependents.[48]

The immediate need of the families left bereaved was great. A gratuity of £5 was given to each family by the Navy League at the time of the disaster, afterwards refunded to the Navy League by the Disaster Fund. Other support from the authorities was slow in coming – for some families it was four years before the Royal Navy paid out the gratuities and prize monies due.

The case of 44-year-old Donald Macphail of 11 Borrowston illustrates the somewhat piecemeal nature of awards from the Navy to those who had served during the war. Donald was a Seaman RNR, married to Mary and father of five children. An experienced sailor, he had received an RNR Gratuity of £50 in September 1918, before his death on the *Iolaire*. A War Gratuity of £25 10s was paid to his widow after a claim on 11th December 1919 – by this time Mary had raised her children alone for nearly a year. Over three years then passed before a payment of £18 15s was paid as naval Prize money on 28th March 1923 and an Interim Award of £2 10s was paid almost a year after that, in February 1924.

Families of the younger, single lads were even less fortunate – regardless of whether they left unsupported aged parents, siblings or other family needs. The family of Norman Macleod of 10 Portnaguran, one of four boys lost to that family during the war, received a £5 War Gratuity while some other single lads lost on the *Iolaire*, after joining in the latter weeks of the war, were denied such a payment.

Many families, therefore, suffered financially until the *Iolaire* Fund started to make payouts. The fund committee agreed that the scale of payments would be £5 to each senior dependant and £1 to each child under 16. By the time of their meeting on 20th June 1920 they had made two payments based on those figures and hoped to establish a permanent scheme of distribution.

But the fund and its management was not without critics, and by June 1920 the committee was faced with considering a number of issues beyond the allocation of funds. Letters from Aird, Shulishader, Sheshader, Knock and Swordale tabled on 20th June 1920 opposed the annuity scheme and asked for immediate distribution of the available money. The letters were reported to have been left to lie on the table. At the same meeting the committee also rebuffed allegations that they were being remunerated for their services. The complaints were perhaps triggered by a job advertised earlier that year by the Ross and Cromarty Local War Pensions Committee, which offered a salary of £120 per annum for a secretary/treasurer of the Lewis Sub-Committee based at Stornoway. In fact the Disaster Fund secretary was not receiving any payment by the time of these allegations, though the secretary who administered the fund was later salaried at £52 per annum. Another source of discontent arose from the very specific remit of the *Iolaire* Disaster Fund. For other families bereaved during the war, the *Iolaire* families were felt to have been given a privilege.

If there was any criticism due of the administrators, it was that they were too stringent in maintaining funds and not favourable with generous disbursement of the monies accrued. In the 20 years the fund was in operation, payments to dependants amounted to £43,854 14s 5d. Funeral expenses totalling £345 were paid and administrative expenses amounted to £2159 17s 5d. There were also court expenses of £314 18s 10d.

As well as disbursing monies to dependants for general subsistence, the fund also supported the children of men lost to have a better life. In November 1921, 10-year-old Malina Maclean from 6 South Bragar was sent away for an operation to her left hand – her thumb and little finger were contracted after a burn in infancy. Much later a young Mòr Smith of Earshader, having proved bright and capable at school, set out for Edinburgh with financial assistance from the fund. She trained for nursing and in 1937 was appointed District Nurse/Midwife for Barvas and Brue. Other youngsters were similarly helped.

As donations began to flood in a flag day was organised in Glasgow.

Over the years that the fund was in operation the financial office-holders changed. The original secretary, Angus Macleod, resigned in 1920 and died in 1922. Donald "Danny Caidh" Mackay, Burgh treasurer, from 21 Lewis Street, was the treasurer for over a decade. He had become the secretary of the *Iolaire* Fund as well before 1928. The first auditors were Hugh Macleod, factor of the Lewis estate and Colin George Mackenzie, Procurator Fiscal. Auditor William McNab, from Evanton, arrived at the National Bank in Stornoway in 1927 from the head office. The last auditor, Donald J McIver was also the branch manager of the National Bank where the funds were lodged.

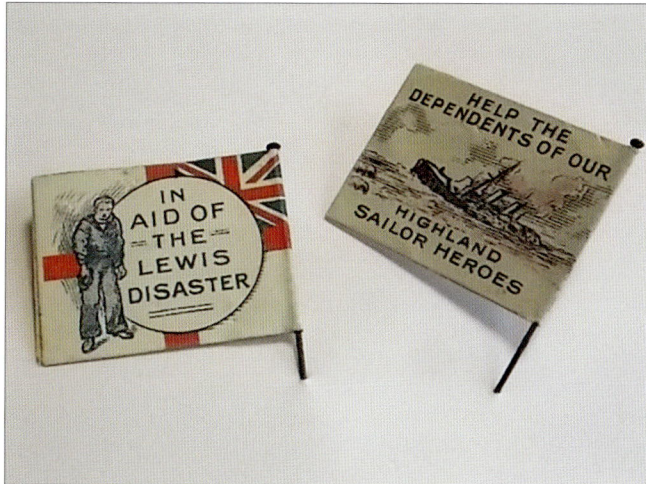

in January 1938 was handed over to the Lewis Hospital. The *Iolaire* Disaster Fund had operated for nearly 20 years and been available for the orphans and fatherless children of the lost servicemen until almost all of them would have reached their legal age of adulthood at 21.

Widows and orphans – a lifetime of grieving

While the *Iolaire* Disaster Fund would help to alleviate some of the practical concerns of bereaved families, there was little it could do to bring any emotional comfort to families left without a father, husband, son or much-loved uncle. Dependent elderly relatives, forlorn widows and fatherless children had to rely on the support of their communities to reshape their lives after 1st January 1919.

The disaster left over 250 children without a father. Some *Iolaire* widows had large families to fend for. The widow of Alexander Macleod of Portnaguran, Margaret, had seven children, as did Annie, widow of Murdo Maciver of Lower Bayble and Catherine Nicolson of North Shawbost, who lost her husband Donald and was left to bring up seven children. Still larger families of eight children each were left to Kate, widow of John Morrison from Coll, to Gormelia, widow of Roderick Morrison, Habost, Ness and to the widow of Angus Montgomery of Garyvard, Mary Ann. Among the *Iolaire* crew, Ernest Leggett left eight children orphaned, three of whom were later homed in an orphanage.

Many widows were left with three, four, five or six children. The two children of Donald Macdonald, Tobson, four children of John Macdonald, North Tolsta,

In 1931 the committee was: Chairman, Murdo Maclean, the former Provost; Sheriff John George Burns; Archibald Munro, town clerk; Hugh Miller, district council clerk; George Macleod, Lewis public assistance joint committee clerk; John Macritchie Morrison, fish salesman; Provost Alexander Maclennan; Angus Smith, chairman of Lewis District Council and Rev Murdoch Macrae, chairman, Lewis public assistance joint committee.

The final meeting of the trustees of the *Iolaire* Disaster Fund was held towards the end of 1938, when the activities of the Trustees were wound up and it was decided to hand over the records for preservation in the Town Council Chambers in Stornoway. The balance of £33 4s 7d remaining when the last payments were made the daughter of Murdo Macleod, Coll and the daughter of Farquhar Morrison, Stockinish were all orphaned. The two eldest sons of Angus Crichton, Knock and those of Malcolm Macdonald, South Bragar, were also orphaned when their father died, but in both cases the father had remarried and there were offspring from these marriages, so a stepmother and half-siblings were also left bereaved.

A definitive number of children affected by the tragedy cannot be given, as children were born and died both immediately before and after the disaster. 40-year-old Donald John Murray, of 43a South Shawbost, and his wife Murdina had already lost three children in early childhood between 1911 and 1914 – Angus Maclean Murray to whooping cough and bronchial pneumonia aged six, his brother Angus with measles and bronchial pneumonia aged two and Kenneth John to bronchial pneumonia aged 13 months. That left Murdina with four children living when she heard the news that her husband had been on the *Iolaire* and would never come home.

It was the nature of the time that infant mortality was to be expected, and with Spanish 'flu, tuberculosis and other illnesses already raging through the islands, children died while their fathers were away at war and would continue to do so in the early years of their lives immediately after the war years. As an example, twins were born to Jessie, the widow of Alexander Campbell (Mac Òrd), Vatisker, after the disaster. The boy lived but the little girl died barely seven days after being born. Jessie already had two young children and Alexander's aged mother and unmarried sister were also dependent on him.

The passengers on the *Iolaire*, all of them returning servicemen, left a total of 217 children plus four adopted children fatherless. Another four children had died shortly before the *Iolaire* disaster. Nine children born after the disaster are included in above totals, as are eight children who died shortly after the disaster. The crewmen lost from the *Iolaire* left 21 children plus four adopted children. One child was born after the disaster. In total there were 255 children.

The children of those lost on the *Iolaire* were deprived not only of a father, but in some cases even of memories. Some of them were born after their father was lost and others were yet too young to remember their father. Older children experienced the psychological trauma of knowing the man who, so eagerly awaited on New Year's Eve, would now never come home. Added to this, many were left, like other war families, to grow up with a heartbroken mother. Some families had difficulties staying together – some indeed were torn apart by the need to find a future. There was also jealousy shown towards some by war-ravaged families within their villages, aggrieved at the preferential treatment shown to the *Iolaire* dependents as money was distributed from the Disaster Fund.

For some of those left behind, the loss of the father, husband or only son was detrimental to their health and mental well-being. Christina Macleod of 13 Arnol lost her husband Norman at the age of 36. Grief-stricken, Christina took out her husband's uniform every summer and washed it, hanging it outside on a wall, a ritual which haunted her children. The trauma of losing her husband drove Christina insane and she died at Craig Dunain asylum, near Inverness, on September 8th 1933, aged just 49.

Marion Macdonald of Aird, widow of Alasdair – 'Am Boicean' – was unable to speak for several weeks after her loss. It was reported that, at New Year each year, she would once again lose her power of speech for a short time.

The five fatherless children of Iolaire cook Alfred Henley of Ryde, Isle of Wight

Lives were irrevocably altered for families left bereaved after the disaster.

William Wilson of South Beach with his wife and daughter

Kenneth Smith and family, Leurbost

271

Alexander and Margaret Macleod, 1 Portnaguran

Angus Mackinnon's parents Donald and Margaret Mackinnon are pictured here outside their home at 4 Caversta.

The widow of John Macleod, Maggie, at 30 Lower Garrabost died in 1952 – having never gone to Stornoway after the disaster. She would have had to pass the cemetery at Aignish, on the Braighe, where her husband was buried, to reach the town. She also disposed of all his naval memorabilia, including photographs. Her elder son, Sandy Mòr, was the second last of the *Iolaire* children to die.

Alick Macleod of 1 Portnaguran had got ashore from the *Iolaire*, but succumbed either to a heart attack or to exposure before he reached the farm at Stoneyfield. His son Matthew was nine years old at the time of his father's death – perhaps that childhood trauma contributed to his subsequent ill-health. He was to die at Craig Dunain, the Inverness County Asylum, on 22nd August 1936 at the age of just 27.

For other children who recalled the loss of a father, uncle or brother, there was certainly buried pain, trauma and damage from the events. Mòr Smith, later Macleod, was born on 23rd December 1914, and had only just turned four years of age when her father, Kenneth Smith from Earshader, was drowned. He had joined up before her birth and had been overseas for nearly the whole war, so Mòr had little recollection of him. She later related in an interview:

"I had an understanding that something awful had come upon the home. My grandfather, who used to do so much with me indoors and out, teaching me morals and things like that that were suitable for a four-year-old to be learning. I remember him sitting, the tears running down his cheeks, and everyone that was coming into the house, they were crying. I realised that something awful had happened but I didn't understand what. And I can say, from that day on, thoughts that would have been natural for a four-year-old to think – they went. And in their place was worry, a feeling of burden. But I didn't understand why. What I did understand though, was that something awful had happened, with how upset the home was, in a place that used to be so peaceful and happy, and my grandfather who used to spend so much time with me, he was just sitting with the tears rolling down his cheeks, it was as though he didn't notice me – I missed that more than anything – the attention that my grandfather paid me and all the talking he would do with me, he didn't say a word."[49]

Silence compounded the trauma felt by the children of those lost. Most of the children did not talk about the tragedy and, even in later life, they found it hard to speak about the events of that night in 1919 and the aftermath of it. They had bottled up deep emotions in order that they did not upset one another, following the example of mothers, brothers, sisters, uncles, aunts, grandparents and neighbours in pretending it had not even happened. The bereaved women wore black, but so did the majority of the female population who had also lost fathers, brothers, sons, husbands and fiancées in the Great War. Some of them coped in their grief by pretending that the *Iolaire* men had died during that war – a half-truth that was, in a sense, much easier for them to bear.

For many of these children and widows, the most immediate help came from family members, the very closeness of the small village communities providing the safety net that could not be expected from the naval authorities or the state. The islanders have always been, whatever their innermost suffering, resilient and able to endure on islands where survival depends on being resolute in trying times. Hebrideans come from a hardy, seafaring breed that has had to endure losses at sea for generations, including many heart-rending fishing tragedies in the Minch and in the Atlantic. As a result, the custom of turning their hands to support those left bereft is well-entrenched. For example, at least two cases are known, in Crossbost and Crowlista, where the locals helped to build a small house for *Iolaire* families living in poor conditions. This kind of undemanding, quiet help was continuously offered – neighbouring women helping widows with chores, men helping with peats, feeding animals and providing fish for the pot.

Norman Maclean's father, Murdo Maclean from Bragar, was drowned in the *Iolaire*, together with his brother, John, and first cousin, Malcolm. Norman would much later write a letter to the local newspaper:

"We were a family of five all under twelve years of age. My father and one of my uncles were drowned, while another uncle, who happened to be on the regular mail-boat the *Sheila*, was safe. I only have a dim recollection of my father, as I was five when he was called up on the outbreak of war. His stay at home was short while on leave.

"Very little has been written on how families of those who were drowned fared later. In our case help was immediately at hand. A maiden aunt took over most of the household work from my mother, who was grief-stricken and unwell at the time. My uncle, with other relatives and friends, organised the croft work, vital at that time. In fact we were overwhelmed with kindness and consideration. I well remember a near neighbour of ours who, when he dropped in for a chat, used to inspect our tackety[50] school boots and when necessary used his stock phrase, 'that his pockets were full of thanks and little else.'"[51]

As well as the fatherless children, many of those black-clad women left without sons and husbands suffered prolonged mental trauma after the disaster. The wife of seaman John Macdonald, Skigersta, was Jessie Finlayson, who had married her boy on October 18th 1918 – three weeks before the end of the war, when he was home on leave. After his leave was over he returned to his ship. A few weeks later, on Hogmanay 1918, the young wife travelled to Stornoway to welcome her new husband home. Her happiness was short-lived – her husband had drowned on the *Iolaire*.

Later, Jessie applied for a widow's pension and was rebuffed by the authorities, denying her claim because she had no issue. Fortunately, her astute father intervened and challenged the bureaucrats to prove there would be no issue from the marriage. Eventually they relented and she received the pension that was due to her.

The longest surviving bereaved mother was Jessie, mother of Angus (John) Morrison of Knockaird, who drowned and his brother Donald, Am Patch, the survivor who clung to the mast. Jessie lived to be 99 and was the last of the grieving mothers to die, on 4th February 1961. Mòr Macleod (nee Smith) survived longer than any other child left fatherless by the tragedy. She was the last of the *Iolaire* children when she died on 7th January 2012 aged 97. Three years earlier she had attended the 90th anniversary service held at the memorial at Holm, when some 300 people gathered on a cold morning as 2009 dawned. Sandy Macleod from Garrabost, the second last of the children, had also attended that New Year's Day.

Mor's mother died in 1980 at the ripe old age of ninety-two and is buried beside her husband in a cemetery by the sea at Bosta in Bernera. An *Iolaire* widow for sixty-one years, she never got over her loss the night the *Iolaire* sank.

The silence

With the silence that descended on the island the word *Iolaire* was scarcely heard and nobody talked about the night itself. There was a blank. Even John Finlay Macleod took 20 years to be able to speak about his role in securing the rope ashore to his son John Murdo, who only heard his father speak of the disaster twice – once at the outbreak of the Second World War in 1939 and again in 1965 when John Finlay, with John "Iain Help" Murray, revisited the scene of the disaster for the first time.

The children of the survivors felt the silence about the disaster, their many school friends without fathers were permanent reminders of a dark, unforgettable night.

> "I think that left a pall, a dark cloud over the whole island for generations really, even to this day. A relative (in the village) lost his life that night and I remember his wife, from that day forth, dressed in black … she remained like that for the rest of her life. And there were many others in these villages who lost their loved ones, who lost a father, many children lost a parent. It just is so tragic to think that they had come through these four terrible years of war, and then they were lost on the doorstep of their own homeland."[52]

Mor Smith recalled:

> "The *Iolaire* was a subject that was not discussed in the house when we were growing up. It was taboo. It was so unreal, and I suppose there was this feeling that there were really no answers."[53]

Nobody dared to mention anything about the disaster, in croft houses or in public. It became a taboo subject. The reticence to talk was island-wide. The image of the empty horse-drawn cart aroused painful memories for the families of those not recovered from the sea. Visiting the local cemetery to mourn after any death was dreaded, with so many loved ones lying in fresh graves. Women welcomed the tradition that it was only men who went in funeral corteges.

The wall of silence descended on the community island-wide on the very day of the disaster and endured for decades. A trawl through the logbooks of 30 Lewis schools shows that only Fidigarry, Bernera and Bragar schools mention the loss of the *Iolaire*, the headteachers left stunned and speechless at a disaster which affected every community and its children. Schools physically close to the disaster, like the Nicolson Institute and Sandwickhill, made no remark – perhaps they did not have words for it. Armistice Day on 11th November 1918 was penned in with delight, but 1st January 1919 remained a blank page.

In 1994 Roddy Murray, artistic director of An Lanntair arts centre, wrote about the silence:

> "That it was not widely spoken of is in no doubt. Why, is a matter of conjecture. A silent consensus of respect for the dead and the next of kin. Or possibly that it was simply beyond mere words. Too serious and too sensitive for discussion and certainly not a topic for the dinner table."[54]

It was only after the *Iolaire* memorial was erected in 1960 that there was any talk at all on the subject. The *Stornoway Gazette* book *Sea Sorrow* was published in 1960 and on a BBC radio programme in 1961 Fred Macaulay interviewed survivors. In this way people born years later heard of the disaster for the first time, some previously unaware that a grandfather or granduncle had been lost in such tragic circumstances.

The long shadow

For their fine response in the defence of Britain, its Empire and Allies, the crofting villages of Lewis had paid a heavy price between 1914 and 1919. From North Tolsta, which had around eighty houses with able-bodied men, 52 made the supreme sacrifice. In this village some families lost three sons. After a joyful reunion on the pier at Kyle, 16 Tolsta men boarded the *Iolaire* on the night of New Year 1919. Five survived. Duncan Macdonald, Schoolhouse, North Tolsta wrote in the Loyal Lewis Roll of Honour 1914-18:

> "If Tolsta has responded nobly she has suffered severely. Of the sixteen Tolsta men on H.M.S. *Iolaire* on her ill-starred trip, only five were saved."[55]

Leurbost was another village which suffered harshly on the night of the *Iolaire*. 16 men from the village in North Lochs travelled together on the yacht – 11 were drowned in the wreck, and the bodies of two of these were never recovered. Tiny Crowlista lost six men on the *Iolaire* – not one of the men who stepped aboard the yacht from that village survived the wreck. And from the small village of Sheshader in Point, less than 30 households bore a grim tally of losses, with almost half the homes bereft. Village neighbours had greeted each other gladly at Kyle and would have seen familiar land looming in the darkness as they passed their home district. None of those Sheshader boys who set out on the *Iolaire* would make it home. 10 men were drowned, and the bodies of three were never yielded up by the sea.

With so many young and fit men lost, the difficulties experienced in the islands after the war were not just emotional, but practical. Even a year after the war was over, many men had not been demobilised and the loss of so many working men had a debilitating effect on sparsely populated villages. No longer were there sufficient men to work the land or crew the local fishing boats. Many boats were hauled up on the beaches, where they eventually rotted into the shore – in Lewis, the sad remains of disused fishing boats were a familiar sight right up until the 1970s. The fine, strong hulls of abandoned boats were turned upside down and used as hen coops or storage sheds. The island's fishing industry was decimated.

A letter in the *Stornoway Gazette* from a Lewis skipper, more than a year after Armistice, shows the urgent need to get men back home from the services to man the fishing boats.

"Sir – I would esteem it a favour if you would insert the following in your paper for the information of men in His Majesty's service desirous of release:

"Skippers desirous of the release at once of all members of crew or part-owners of boats should apply immediately by letter (see copy below). The letter to be stamped by the Local Advisory Committee and then posted to the man himself.

"*Copy of Letter*:

"Sir, – I herewith make application for No. 2000 Pte. Jones, A Coy., Hut 30 (giving the regiment and battalion), who, previous to the outbreak of war, was employed by me, and will be re-engaged on his immediate release from the Army. (The same applies to men in the Navy).

"Also please state the direct address of the Local Advisory Committee in Stornoway, where certificates may be stamped. Yours, etc. A.McL"[56]

The loss of so many young men in the war left a cavernous void in the population of the Western Isles. The majority of the younger men who had died were single and their deaths deprived the islands of a generation of young children to follow in their footsteps. A number of those drowned on the *Iolaire* were engaged to be married or planned to get engaged when they arrived home. Many of the young women left behind ended up living out their days as spinsters, their young men having been killed in the war and few men left for them to marry.

The shortage of young men – to marry, to work the land or to crew the fishing boats – came in part from the growing swell of emigration from the islands, especially by working age young men. Emigration schemes were being put forward as one solution to the problem of out-of-work servicemen returning to their homes all over Britain. Between 1919 and 1922 the Overseas Settlement Scheme offered ex-servicemen and women, and their dependents, free passage to the Dominions and the chance to start a new life in Canada, Australia, New Zealand, South or East Africa. Over 3,000 Lewismen, mostly ex-servicemen, left for Canada in the years after the First World War. Many others emigrated to the USA, Australia and New Zealand. Several *Iolaire* survivors were in their ranks. So, in a few years after the First War, the Western Isles through emigration had lost more men than in the war:

> "Out of every hundred people of the island, old and young, to the four young men who went forth to death were to be added a further ten that went forth to exile. The loss did not end there. The withdrawal from the island's population of so many potential husbands denied the opportunity of marriage to hundreds of the younger women, and with peace began a steep decline in the population of the island."[57]

The impact of emigration on the economic and social health of the islands was well-understood at the time. The county regiment for Lewis was the Seaforth Highlanders. An editorial in an early edition of their regimental magazine had this critique on the emigration from Lewis:

> "What is Canada's gain is unfortunately our loss. We have the men and yet nothing is done. Our huge cities are already over-populated, and what is required in the interests of the physical well-being of our race, if nothing else, is for suitable inducements to be held out to those already on the land to remain there. If none are forthcoming it is only natural that the most high-spirited of our countrymen will go elsewhere. We neglect the encouraging of developments, which would make all the difference between success and failure to those already on the land, and we do nothing to ensure profitable employment for an increased population. Millions upon millions are sunk for the development of the Empire in all parts of the earth, but here at home we look in vain for even a small share of those monies, which if properly spent, would transform the Highlands and Islands and provide suitable occupations for the population."[58]

As James Shaw Grant put it:

> "The most significant fact for Lewis about this contribution to Imperial development, as settlers and soldiers, is that it has brought no direct benefit to the Island, economic or social. Individual settlers may have amassed riches in the colonies, individual soldiers may have risen to rank, or won fame, on the field of battle, but the Island has gained no such permanent increment of wealth as it would have done had the same energy gone to the exploitation of the native resources of sea and soil, or the development of the artistic heritage of the race. Two centuries of honourable service for the British Empire has not added to the material or cultural wealth of the Island as much as a single song."[59]

The darkness and the light – long memories

The shadow of the *Iolaire* disaster fell not only across the islands, but reached far across the United Kingdom and the world. There was a persistent feeling amongst islanders that the Admiralty, the Public Inquiry process and perhaps even the crew of the yacht themselves had contributed to the distress of those now suffering from the tragedy. For the six surviving crew members the hostility was unwarranted, for none of them were involved in the decisions which took the vessel to its doom. But the three crew members in sick bay had already seen the accusing glances of island survivors and were not surprised to be moved – first to Oban and later to Aberdeen – in the hope of getting them away from ill-feeling.

One man who was acutely aware of that feeling was John Maclennan, ''Ain Geal', who was in the unusual position of being an island survivor wearing an *Iolaire* uniform. He was coxswain of the first yacht *Iolaire*, crewing her away from the island on 6th November 1918 when she was replaced, and he had left her in Glasgow to come home for New Year. He had survived the wreck with distinction, helping to save the lives of some of his fellows. But although the vessel where he served was now called *Amalthaea*, he still wore the cap tally (ribbon) embroidered with the name *Iolaire* and he was acutely conscious that this could make him a target as he returned to the mainland some weeks later.

John later told how he and a shipmate tried to escape unwelcome attention from people who might think them to blame when they returned to service:

> "My shipmate from Shader (Donald Martin), who emigrated after the war, was also on the *Iolaire* that fated night. When we met to travel to join the ship *Iolaire* in Bowling, Glasgow, we turned the ribbons on our cap so they just showed HMS on them. But people still knew who we were, even when we got to the headquarters in Glasgow. The ship's crew had to go to Portsmouth to be demobbed. One of the officers told me to stay behind until he travelled to Portsmouth with me. I spent a fortnight in Glasgow where he put a car driven by a Wren at my disposal. When I got to Portsmouth I got my demob papers after only four days and the rest of the crew were still there waiting for theirs."[60]

A story was also told of Annie Mary Macphail, niece of Donald Macphail, who was lost on the *Iolaire*. She was married in Cardiff to Albert R. Jarman in the summer of 1940 and coincidentally became a close neighbour of *Iolaire* fireman Ernie Adams, who had escaped the sinking and been

Johanna and Ethel May Mackinnon, sister and wife of Angus Mackinnon of Caversta.

Nellie Iolaire Mackinnon

During the research for this book, the authors have been vividly reminded that it is not just in Lewis and Harris that families suffered the loss of a loved one. Memories both painful and precious have been preserved elsewhere. A child called Nellie Iolaire was born in Dover, months after her father, Angus Mackinnon of Caversta, had been drowned. Even as we completed this manuscript we heard from the grand-daughter of Herbert William Head, the Suffolk man who was serving as a private in the Royal Marine Light Infantry when he was lost, returning from leave to his service base in Stornoway, on the *Iolaire*.

Herbert left, waiting at the quayside, his bride-to-be, herring-girl Catherine Wares from Pulteneytown, Wick. They were to be married on 1st January, and Catherine was already expecting a child. Once she knew of the loss of her man, she returned to Pulteneytown and continued to work as a herring gutter, bearing a daughter – Elizabeth (Betty) Head – on 13th June 1919. Elizabeth's daughter wrote:

> "Life was very hard for mother and daughter as they were not always made welcome in the community. My mother only found out about her father from others.

> "We have no photographs or artefacts about this tragedy – only memories of two lives blighted by the tragic event. The *Iolaire* disaster affected not only those originating from Stornoway, but also families from elsewhere."[61]

Catherine Wares

Baby Elizabeth Head

transferred to a mainland hospital. Her first words to Ernie Junior when he told her about his father were: "I shouldn't be talking to you."[62]

But Telegraphist Leonard Welch, many years later, described a scene which could not have taken place if the Isle of Lewis was, as has been assumed, riven with resentment against the crew of the *Iolaire*:

> "A few days after I recovered I went into a shop in Stornoway to buy some shaving kit. The pound note I tendered was sodden wet, having been in my life-jacket pocket on the *Iolaire*. The lady in the shop would not accept any money and said, 'If the Lord God pulled you out of that wreck I couldn't take it.'"[63]

The six crew members who had dispersed back to their homes around Britain were as thankful for their salvation as any one of the island survivors, judging by the behaviour of both the men themselves, and their families in later years.

Deckhand James 'Creel' Maclean, who was a key witness at the Public Inquiry, had certainly suffered alongside the islanders, both during the sinking and for many years afterwards. Although he himself did not speak of the tragedy, his granddaughter Fiona Maccallum recalled that her mother said he had no skin on his palms after the accident and that he was still uncertain, years later, whether a young lad that he had hauled onto the rocks beside him was dead or alive.[64] After the Second World War, he and his son Neil had fishing boats called the *Amalthea* and the *Mary Maclean*, and they fished briefly out of Stornoway post-war. When he visited Stornoway, around 1948, he was chary of going ashore, but somehow local men heard that he was at the harbour, came along the pier and invited him to join them. How they knew about him he did not know, but he called them all gentlemen.[65]

Dorothy Waring, a relation of Greenwich deckhand William Stanley, who died on the *Iolaire* at the age of 19, visited the memorial as recently as 2015 and other descendants were among those anxious to participate in anniversary events as the centenary came closer in 2018. Ernie Adams' grandson, David Adams, a Royal Naval Reservist, travelled to Lewis in 2004, making a special trip to lay flowers on the site of the sinking. David said then:

> "I will be laying a bunch of flowers on behalf of my family, to say thanks for my grandfather's survival – if he had not survived I would not be here today. This is my fifth trip to the island. I have been to the memorial before but my grandfather's sons and daughters have expressed a wish, that if any of the family get a chance to go to the memorial again – if the opportunity came up – that it was too good to miss and that flowers should be laid there. My father is 81, and he thought, if one of us was in the area, it would be nice for the family to lay some flowers on the memorial in sympathy for the tragic loss of life".[66]

Long indeed was the shadow the *Iolaire* tragedy cast in Lewis and Harris, but in that shadow there were such glimpses of light – humanity, compassion, sincere admiration for heroism from survivors and descendants. And as the years passed the silence began to break, with memories captured in broadcast and written interviews, and with a growing desire to memorialise, to ensure that the story of the events of 1st January 1919 would persist beyond the lifetimes of those who had been there to witness the horrific night, when island boys drowned in island waters, close to their home shore and to those they loved.

Chapter 7 Footnotes

1. Marion Macleod (Mòr Bhrù), interviewed on *An Iolaire*, BBC Radio nan Gàidheal. Presenter Annella Macleod, 1999

2. Donald Morrison (Am Patch), Knockaird interviewed in the *Stornoway Gazette*, 31st December 1988

3. Stornoway Naval Base log book, January 1919

4. Letter received by Provost MacLean from Rear Admiral R.F. Boyle, Stornoway, 7th January 1919

5. Telegram from Stornoway Naval Base (Admiral Boyle) to Admiralty, 4th January 1919

6. Telegram from Rear Admiral Boyle to Admiralty, PRO Admiralty 116/1869

7. *Inverness Courier*, 14th January 1919

8. Op Branch 8A Sales Ledger 1916-1939

9. *Stornoway Gazette*, 15th March 1919

10. Reported in the *Stornoway Gazette*, 21st February 1919

11. The wreck was not designated as a War Grave, and Great War shipwrecks did not receive protection from destructive salvage until the 1986 Protection of Military Remains Act

12. John Maclennan interviewed by Maga Mackay and translated by Maggie Smith for *Hebridean Connections*, 2005

13. Morag Morrison interviewed for Isles FM's *Memorial of the Airwaves*, November 2014

14. Donald Macphail interviewed by Fred Macaulay, BBC Radio nan Gàidheal, 1961

15. *Highland News*, 18th January 1919

16. Letter from Lt. J.O. Dunn, HMT *Resmilo*, Portland. *Stornoway Gazette*, 18th January 1919

17. Letter from Wyndham J James, RNVR, Withnoe Camp, Cornwall, 6th January 1919

18. Letter from Captain Francis H. Wadsworth, SS *Columbia* (Anchor Line, Glasgow) *Stornoway Gazette*, 31st January 1919

19. Letter from commander of HMML 307. *Stornoway Gazette*, 18th January 1919

20. Message from the Secretary for War, *Stornoway Gazette*, 18th January 1919

21. Telegram from Officer Commanding 3rd Seaforths – Cromarty. *Stornoway Gazette*, 18th January 1919

22. Message from the Secretary for Scotland Robert Munro, *Stornoway Gazette*, 18th January 1919

23. Joint telegram in the name of the Moderators of the General Assemblies *Stornoway Gazette*, 18th January 1919

24. *Stornoway Gazette*, 5th January 1919

25. *The Scotsman*, 6th January 1919

26. *Stornoway Gazette*, 18th January 1919

27. William Hesketh Lever, 1st Viscount Leverhulme, was the co-founder (with his brother James) of the Lever Brothers soap empire. A philanthropist as well as an industrialist, Lord Leverhulme had bought the Isle of Lewis in May 1918 and sought to establish industry and employment in the islands. In September 1923 he offered the islands to their people, but only Stornoway accepted the gift, establishing the Stornoway Trust, a community land owner, which still exists to this day

28. Message from Lord Leverhulme to the Provost, reproduced in the *Stornoway Gazette*, 11th January 1919

29. Letter from Lachlan MacLean, Chief and John MacDonald, Secretary. The Gaelic Society of Vancouver, British Columbia

30. *Stornoway Gazette*, 10th January 1919

31. As above

32. As above

33. As above

34. Letter from Rear Admiral B.M. Chambers, late Captain *Majestic*. London. 2nd January 1919

35. The Grand Fleet had been formed in 1915 by Lord Jellicoe, to alleviate distress among men disabled in war, and to help dependents of those killed while in service. By the end of the Great War, it had £33,000 available for distribution, and it was re-named the Royal Naval Benevolent Trust in 1922. It is now the major naval benevolence society

36. *Inverness Courier,* 10th January 1919

37. Report in *Stornoway Gazette*, 10th January 1919

38. Appeal To Invernessians, *Highland News*, 18th January 1919

39. *Stornoway Gazette*, 18th January 1919

40. *Highland News*, 10th May 1919

41. *Stornoway Gazette*, 24th January 1919

42. Cran – defined as 37.5 imperial gallons and 1,200 fish but, because of the varying size of fish, can be between 700 and 2,500 fish. In Scots fishing, quarter-cran baskets were used to carry the fish

43. Shot – the amount of fish caught by one vessel in one trip

44. *Stornoway Gazette*, 24th January 1919

45. *Stornoway Gazette*, 2nd May 1919

46. *People's Journal*, 25th January 1919

47. *Oban Times*, 22nd February 1919

48. Sample figures from the *Iolaire* Disaster Fund accounts are given in Appendix 2

49. *An Iolaire*, BBC Alba, 1st January 2009

50. Tackety boots – boots with metal tacks and heel taps/segs, to prolong the life of the leather soles

51. Letter to *Stornoway Gazette* (date unknown)

52. Anna Mairi Martin, Aird, Point, interviewed on Isles FM radio for *The Great War: Through the Eyes of Women,* November 2015

53. Interview with Mòr Macleod (née Smith) in *Seanchas*, No 53, Winter 2006

54. *Stornoway Gazette* 11th January 1994

55. *Loyal Lewis Roll of Honour, Stornoway Gazette*, 1920

56. Letters page of *Stornoway Gazette*, 21st December 1919

57. *Scotland's War Losses* by Duncan Duff: Scottish Secretariat, 1947

58. Seaforth Highlanders regimental magazine *Cabarfeidh* Vol 1. No 7

59. James Shaw Grant writing in *The Scots Magazine*, January 1943

60. John Maclennan interview by Maga Mackay translated by Maggie Smith for *Hebridean Connections*, 2005

61. Personal correspondence from Elizabeth Wood (descendant) with authors, 2018

62. As told by Ernie Adams Jr in correspondence with the authors, 2000

63. *My Amazing Adventure* by Leonard Welch. TV Boardman Ltd, 1942

64. Fiona Maccallum, correspondence with the authors

65. Told by Malcolm Speed, *Campbeltown Journal,* 18th October 1954

66. David Adams interviewed in the *Stornoway Gazette* 22nd July 2004

Roll call of the Survivors

These men went aboard the *Iolaire* on the night of 31st December 1918, and survived the wreck — 73 men from the islands and 6 crew members. Some gave evidence at the inquiries, or spoke to newspapers and radio/TV programmes later in life. Extracts of their interviews are quoted in this book, with longer versions in Chapter 8 'In Their Own Words'. A short summary of their lives both before and after the *Iolaire* tragedy is given here. The names are listed in order of the districts and villages where they originated, starting from the north of the Isle of Lewis.

Each man's information is given as follows:

Name
(with Gaelic, familiar and nicknames).

Date of birth and death (where known).

Address. Rank and service.
Service number if known.

BARVAS PARISH – Ness

Murdo Morrison

(Murchadh Iain Bhig)

25th May 1899 - 21st January 1947
(age 47)

8 Skigersta. Deckhand RNR.
Service number 16322/DA.

Murdo was the son of John and Margaret Morrison (née Mackenzie) and was born at Skigersta. He enrolled at HMS *Iolaire* (Depot) on 25th May 1917, his 18th birthday. He served at HMS *Pembroke* at Chatham, HMS *Wallington* at Immingham, then HMS *Pekin* at Grimsby, from which bases he was a deckhand on the minesweeping trawlers HMT *Thomas Jarvis*, then HMT *Horatio*. During the wreck of the *Iolaire* on January 1st 1919 he got aboard one of the swamped lifeboats, but hauled himself back aboard the *Iolaire* on a rope lowered by Donald "Patch" Morrison. After surviving the wreck of the *Iolaire*, he was demobilised on 4th February 1919, but re-enrolled afresh with a new service number, 11002/A, and returned to service on HMS *Research*. Once he was finally discharged he received a War Gratuity and went on to work as a labourer. Sadly Murdo died in middle age, of metastatic sarcoma of the spine and ribs, having outlived his wife, Mary Morrison (née Mackay) who died of chronic asthma on 29th May 1943 aged 42.

Malcolm Macdonald

1st January 1896 - unknown date of death.

1 Eorodale. Engine Room Artificer, RNR.
Service number M/33442.

Malcolm was the son of master baker John Macdonald, and his wife Margaret (née Macdonald) who died in 1900. Malcolm's father remarried to Eliza (née Murray) and Malcolm had three older sisters and three younger half-sisters. He was a fitter to trade, and joined up on 14th August 1918 for hostilities only. He was a 22-year-old Engine Room Artificer at HMS *Vivid II* in Devonport when his leave pass for the New Year of 1918/19 was issued, and got all the way home to his fireside for his 23rd birthday, when so many others were lost. He was demobilised on 11th March 1919 and it is believed that he emigrated to Canada on the Canadian Pacific Railway liner *Marburn* on 9th May

1924. A 27-year-old with the same name certainly sailed on that voyage to Quebec and Montreal and his trade was given as a fitter. Malcolm soon lost touch with his relations and it is believed that he died in Canada. At the time that the last known survivor of the *Iolaire* died, the press reported a rumour of an unnamed survivor living in Los Angeles and Malcolm is the only candidate if the rumour was true. Los Angeles death records do not show anyone of that name, but people entering the United States from Canada often altered birth dates or names if they had entered illegally.

John Finlay Macleod
(Iain Mhurdo)

17th June 1888 - 21st December 1978
(age 90)

4 Port of Ness. Carpenter RNR.
Service number 16774/DA.

John Finlay, son of Murdo and Catherine
Macleod (née Mackay), was a carpenter
to trade, who had originally sought
permission not to serve as he was needed
in the community. He enrolled on 28th
June 1917. He reported to HMS *Victory* at
Portsmouth and served on the drifter HMD
Christina Craig from HMS *Satellite* at North
Shields until 26th November 1917. He was
then based at HMS *Ganges II*, a boys'
training establishment, where he was an
instructor – his ability as a carpenter was
obviously recognised. The 30-year-old
became the undoubted hero of the night
of the wreck, swimming ashore from the
yacht to the rocks to secure a rope, by
which 40 men escaped. After the wreck
he was posted from HMS *Ganges* to the
HMS *Iolaire* depot and demobilised on
5th April 1919. John continued to build
his reputation as an accomplished
and versatile tradesman, possessing a
range of skills in woodworking that few
could equal. A perfectionist, he was a
pioneer coach builder, general joiner and
a famous boat builder, like his father
and grandfather at Port. Even after his
eyesight failed, he could feel the grain
in the wood and build small boats,
especially the distinctive Ness sailboat,
the 'Sgoth Niseach'. He met the Queen
during her visit to the island in 1956 and
was awarded the Queen's Silver Jubilee
medal in 1977. John Finlay married Peggy
Macleod (née Finlayson) in January 1920.
His wife died on 4th May 1957 aged 65.
Their son, John Murdo, also became a
renowned boat builder.

Donald Morrison
(Am Patch)

21st November 1898 - 16th July 1990
(age 91).

7 Knockaird. Deckhand, RNR.
Service number 17296/DA

Donald was the son of Donald and Jessie
Morrison (née Gunn), and will always be
remembered as the young sailor rescued
after clinging to the sunken yacht's mast
all night. His birth date is given as 12th
March 1899 in naval records. He was a
younger brother of Angus and John. He
enrolled in the RNR on 31st July 1917 and
reported to HMS *Victory* on 1st August
1917. He served with the Trawler Section
on HMD *Premier II* and HMD *Bracoden* at
Portsmouth and Poole (HMS *White Oak*).
During that time he qualified as a naval
gunner at Whale Island, Portsmouth. He
then served on HMT *Vidonia* and, from
8th November 1918, he served on HMT

William Doak. He was also briefly on HMS *Research*. After the night of the *Iolaire*, he was at HMS *Venerable* and finally HMS *Iolaire* Depot until he was discharged. He re-enrolled afresh as 11414/A. He married late, in 1937, to Catherine (née Morrison), sister of *Iolaire* survivor Alex "Tiger" Morrison from 4 Cross. Catherine died of heart problems on 9th April 1939, aged 41, just over two years after they married. Donald was a mason/builder in his working life. He died at his grand-niece's home at No 9 Knockaird and was interred at Ness (Habost) Cemetery.

Alexander Morrison
(An Tìgear)

14th September 1873 - 24th May 1962 (age 88)

4 Cross. Seaman RNR.
Service number 3297/C.

Alex was the son of John and Effie Morrison (née Maclennan), a seasoned seaman who had enrolled in the RNR on 1st January 1904 and was at Banff when war was declared. He reported to HMS *Pembroke* on 12th August 1914, then served with the seaplane carrier HMS *Hermes*. He survived her sinking in the Straits of Dover on 31st October 1914, when she was hit by the German submarine U-27 after leaving Dunkirk to load another flight of aircraft for France.

He then served with the armed merchant cruiser HMS *Digby*, the armed merchant cruiser HMS *Osiris II*, HMY *Valhalla II*, HMS *Actaeon* (the Auxiliary patrol base at Sheerness), HMS *Pembroke I*, HMS *Satellite* (North and South Shields), HM Tug *Velmar* and finally he was serving at HMS *Pembroke* at Chatham when the war ended. He was demobbed on 4th February 1919 from *Pembroke* and was presented his RNR Medal for Long Service and Good Conduct in Stornoway on 4th January 1921. He remained a single crofter all his life.

Murdo Macfarlane
(Murchadh Chraig)

9th May 1894 - 24th June 1977 (age 83)

24 Cross. Engine Room Artificer, Royal Navy.

Murdo was the son of Murdo, a general merchant in Cross, and Elizabeth (née Macpherson). He was in the Royal Navy as an Engine Room Artificer on the new battleship HMS *Royal Sovereign*. After surviving the sinking of the *Iolaire* and leaving the service he emigrated to Canada in 1920 aboard the Canadian Pacific Railway liner *Minnedosa* from Liverpool to Quebec, where his intention of being a farmer is listed. He married Elizabeth (née Urquhart) and had three sons and a daughter – Angus, John, Donald and Cathie. Murdo certainly returned to Scotland at least once – the Cunard liner *Sylvania* sailed from Liverpool to Montreal on 26th September 1958 carrying Mr Murdo Macfarlane (Engineer) and his wife Elizabeth, who had been residing at 19 Gleniffer Avenue, Knightswood, Glasgow. They were listed as Canadian residents and must have been returning from a visit to the homeland. He died in Vancouver.

Norman Mackenzie
(Làrag, Tarmod Dh'll 'An Bhàin)

27th March 1900 - 14th July 1954 (age 54)

25 Cross, Back of Cross Post Office.
Deckhand RNR.
Service number 20010/DA.

Norman, son of Donald and Margaret
Mackenzie (née Macfarlane), joined the
RNR on 16th April 1918 and served at HMS
Pembroke I, then HMS *Actaeon*. He served
on HMT *Plym*, the Milford Haven base HMS
Idaho and then HMS *Comway*, a wooden
training ship at Liverpool. He survived the
wreck of the *Iolaire* in 1919 but suffered
ill-health all his life. He left HMS *Idaho* on
21st June 1919 and became a bus driver, but
remained single and died in middle age. He
was interred at Ness (Habost) Cemetery.

John Murray
(Iain Help)

**26th December 1886 - 23rd January 1966
(age 79)**

6 South Dell. Seaman RNR.
Service number 4534/A.

John's birth date is also given as 16th
May 1888 in naval records, which list
him as John Macdonald. He was the son
of Norman and Catherine Murray (née
Mackenzie), one of six brothers who fought
and who all returned to their parents
and two sisters. Before the war he was a
fisherman at Stornoway, Wick and Buckie.
He travelled to Chatham and boarded the
armed merchant cruiser HMS *Victorian*
on 21st August 1914, remaining with her
until 31st March 1915. He was then at
HMS *Pembroke II* for six weeks before
joining the monitor HMS *Admiral Farragut*,
immediately renamed HMS *Abercrombie*,
on which he served in the Dardanelles

and the Aegean Sea. He also served with
the armed merchant cruiser HMS *Morea*,
HMS *Pembroke* and HMS *Osiris II*. He was at
Pembroke when demobbed on 4th February
1919.

On the night of the *Iolaire*'s sinking he was
the first man to come ashore by the rope.
He had a present of tobacco for his father
and as he struggled towards the shore,
he had the presence of mind to grasp the
tobacco in his teeth and brought the present
ashore dry although he was saturated in
sea water. John married Catherine (née
Stewart), and they later lived at 43 Vatisker
and had two sons and two daughters. He
was a road labourer during his working life.
A photograph of the early 1960s shows
him and John F. Macleod sitting at the
Iolaire memorial, capturing their emotional
memories.

BARVAS PARISH – Borve to Shawbost

Murdo Graham
(Murchadh Dhòmhnaill a' Bhìodain)

2nd December 1898 – 27th November 1972 (age 73)

8 Borve. Deckhand RNR.
Service number 13739/DA.

Murdo was the son of Donald and Margaret Graham (née Morrison) and enrolled on 7th December 1916, serving at HMS *Pembroke*, HMD *Highland Leader* and HMS *Victory* until he was demobilised on 7th March 1919. He emigrated in the late 20s or early 30s and married Ruth Elizabeth Cook, from Stirling, at Wellington, New Zealand in 1931. Their home became a welcome haven for Lewis sailors calling into Wellington for many years. It is believed that he must be the Murdo Graham, a Scots pelt worker, who died at the Men's Quarters at Borthwicks Freezing Works, Waitara near New Plymouth, New Zealand in 1972. Registration records have no other details for a Murdo Graham that fits with the *Iolaire* sailor. He was interred at Waitara Cemetery.

Angus Macdonald
(Aonghas Theàrlaich)

17 and 32 Borve
(see 51 Bayhead Street, Stornoway).

Roderick Graham
(Ruaraidh Ruaraidh Mhurchaidh)

2nd July 1900 – 27th June 1937 (age 36)

29 Borve. Deckhand RNR.
Service number 20930/DA.

Roddie was the son of Roderick and Gormelia Graham (née Morrison) and had enrolled in the RNR on 16th July 1918. He was serving on HMT *Dinas* of the auxiliary patrol at the war's end and was only 18 when he escaped the clutches of death at Holm after leaving HMS *Attentive III* at Dover for New Year. He later served with the RNR, re-enrolling on 28th February 1925 as 12305/A. He also served with the Seaforth Highlanders, but was a labourer when he died at a young age of pulmonary tuberculosis.

Angus Morrison
(Aonghas Aonghais Dhòmhnaill)

18th July 1887 – 16th August 1975 (age 88)

41 Borve. Seaman RNR.
Service number 3363/A.

Angus was the son of Angus and Marion Morrison (née Smith) and had enrolled in the RNR on 9th February 1911, as the naval arms race was building between Britain and Germany. He was a fisherman pursuing the herring around the coast at Peterhead and Stornoway and joined HMS *Victory* at the first call, on 4th August 1914. He was posted to the Royal Naval Division briefly before moving to HMS *Vernon*. He was later posted to HMS *Vivid* at Devonport and joined HMT *Mary Wetherley*. That trawler went to HMS *Dreel Castle* at Falmouth and then to HMS *Egmont* at Chatham. On 8th March 1918 Angus moved to Taranto in southern Italy, to serve on HMD *Favourite* based at HMS *Queen*. He was posted to HMS *Vivid III* on 3rd August 1918 and finally to HMS *Pembroke*. He was aboard the decommissioned battleship HMS *Canopus*, an accommodation ship at HMS *Pembroke*, when he received his ticket of leave for New Year 1919. He remained single and was a labourer throughout his working life. At the age of 83, in August 1971, he was the oldest man in the village and selected to meet the newly created Baroness Macleod of Borve.

Donald Martin
(Dontal, Mac Sgodaidh)

12th February 1898 – 30th June 1975 (age 77)

33a Lower Shader. Deckhand RNR.
Service number 16806/DA.

Born at 50 Coll on 12th February 1898, Donald was the son of Roderick (Sgodaidh) and Anne Martin (née Macdonald) who had married at Fraserburgh on 27th August 1895. Donald had an older brother, Alexander, who was twice wounded serving with the Seaforths in the war. In the family were also two younger brothers, John and Roderick, and two sisters, Kate and Anne. The family moved to 33 Lower Shader, Roderick (Sgodaidh)'s home village, after mother Anne died in 1909 and he remarried Annie Macleod of 27 Lower Shader. She had a son, Kenneth Macleod, before her marriage. Sgodaidh and Anne had a son, Alexander, who lived in South Galson. Donald served with trawlers and drifters in the trawler section of the RNR during the war. His uncle, Alexander Martin, died when serving with HMS Rugby on 27th November 1918, aged 30.

The family moved to Galson after the war but Donald left for Glasgow and served as a policeman. He later emigrated to Canada settling in Vancouver. Donald was a fisherman on the Pacific coast and had a salmon fishing boat called Barbara Ann. His brother John also emigrated to Canada and ended his days in Trail BC aged 45. Sister Anne also went to Vancouver, Canada to live and married a Macsween from Sandwick.

When Donald was 52 years of age he married a 26-year-old American citizen, Ruth Patricia Hegan, from whom he was later divorced. She was the informant at the time of his death in 1975. He suffered ill-health for the last ten years of his life and died of broncho-pneumonia at St Paul's Hospital, Vancouver BC. He was cremated on 3rd July 1975 at the North Shore Crematorium, North Vancouver.

Norman Maciver
(Tarmod Dhòmhnaill Ruairidh)

2nd July 1895 – 2nd April 1961 (age 65)

21 Arnol. Leading Deckhand RNR.
Service number 2621/SD.

Son of Donald and Margaret Maciver (née Maclean), Norman's birthdate was also given as July 13th in naval records. He enrolled in the RNR on 24th August 1915 and transferred to the Trawler Section after promotion to leading deckhand, on 1st October 1916. His brother Malcolm, known in Stornoway as "Goosey Eye", also served in the RNR and they had six sisters. Norman served with HMS *Vernon*, HMML 4, HMS *Victory I*, HMS *Victory II*, HMS *Gunner*, HMS *Columbine*, HMML 6, and finally HMD *Magnet III*. He was a powerful man, the equivalent of a boatswain on a merchant ship and his sea craft must have aided him in extricating himself from the sinking *Iolaire*. Norman always maintained that the Public Inquiry was a total whitewash. He was demobilised from HMS *Victory* in 1919. He married Catherine (née Smith) from Habost, Ness at Hope Street Free Church in Glasgow on 14th January 1927 and made a career as a policeman. He was living at 14 Limeside Avenue, Rutherglen when he died.

Roll call of the survivors

Murdo Mackay
(Murchadh Iain Dhòmhnaill Mhurchaidh Saighdeir)

23rd November 1899 – 7th May 1972 (age 72)

29a Arnol. Deckhand RNR.
Service number 18856/DA.

Murdo was the son of John and Ann Mackay (née Mackay) and had a twin sister Margaret. He signed up to serve on his 18th birthday, 23rd November 1917, and was based at HMS *Iolaire* from then until 7th January 1918. From Lewis he was posted to HMS *Tarlair* at Hawkcraig Point, Aberdour, the Navy's main hydrophone research and training station, where Murdo's aptitude saw him selected to become an operator. He was one of the lucky survivors that made it to Stoneyfield Farmhouse on that fatal night. Murdo was demobilised from *Tarlair* on 27th March 1919, then moved to Glasgow post-war and was a hopper mate with the Clyde Trust, living at 6 George Drive. He married an Arnol girl, Christina (née Maclennan) on 18th December 1931. Murdo's address at the time of his death was 8 Skipness Drive, Glasgow.

Norman Macleod
(Tarmod Mhurchaidh Aonghais Òig)

21st August 1895 – 24th July 1963 (age 67)

16 South Bragar. Deckhand RNR.
Service number 3556/SD.

Norman was the youngest in a family of three boys and two girls, son of Murdo and Mary Macleod (née Macaskill). He enrolled on 30th November 1915 and served at HMS *Vivid* and HMS *Victory*. On 3rd April 1916 he did a naval cookery course, probably designed to serve vessels not large enough to warrant a full-time cook. He was a deckhand on the armed launch HMML 214 and, after going on leave from her, became a survivor of the wreck of the *Iolaire*. After his survivor's leave he was posted to HMS *Research*, and then back to the Stornoway base at HMS *Iolaire*. Following his demobilisation on 6th February 1919, he emigrated to Dalwallin in Western Australia. He remained single throughout his life and died at Nyamup. He is interred in the Methodist portion of Manjimup Cemetery.

Murdo Macleod
(Alasdair Choinnich an Iarainn)

16th May 1893 – 28th October 1947 (age 54)

22 South Bragar. Seaman RNR.
Service number 4154/A.

Murdo was born at North Shawbost, the son of Kenneth and Christina Macleod (née Smith). He was christened Alexander, but opted for Murdo when serving in the RNR and his date of birth is given as 19th October 1890 in naval records. A pre-war fisherman, Murdo had fished out of Stornoway and Fraserburgh and among his wartime ships and bases were the armed boarding vessel HMS *Snaefell* in the Mediterranean and HMS *Hannibal* at Scapa Flow. He set out for his home leave from Teeside, where he was based at the Adams Depot in Middlesbrough, and he survived the *Iolaire* disaster on his way home. He was demobilised from HMS *Iolaire* (base) on 14th February 1919 but re-enrolled (4624/C) and served until 1922. He lost two brothers in the war, John on 30th September 1918 aged 33, when HMS *Seagull* was sunk, and Murdo as a 25-year-old merchant seaman on SS *Swift Wings*, lost to U-38 on 1st September 1916. Murdo married under his chosen name at 18 Point Street on 12th July 1917 to Johanna Morrison and they lived for a short time at 22 South Bragar. Murdo went to Glasgow in 1921 and tried his hand as a glazier, but by early 1922 was fishing out of Stornoway on the boat registered as SY69. He and his wife emigrated to

Australia in 1923 and had a family of five daughters and three sons. His naval record shows that on 21st October 1939 he was living at 64 Chester Street, Fremantle, Western Australia, so he very likely attended the Gaelic concert held there in mid-September 1939. At his death he was recorded as Alexander Murdo and he was interred at the Presbyterian Cemetery, Freemantle.

Donald Murray
(Dòmhnall Mhurchaidh an Gobha)

25th July 1899 – 26th October 1981 (age 82)

46 South Bragar. Deckhand RNR. Service number 17442/DA.

Son of Murdo and Isabella Murray (née Macleod), Donald took up arms with the RNR on 31st July 1917. He was at HMS *Iolaire* (base) and served there on HMT *Lansdowne* and then HMS *Offa II* based at HMS *Nesmar II* (Oban). He was then posted to Larne and served on HMD *Vigorous*, before serving on HMD *Alfred*. Donald was posted to HMS *Vivid* then HMS *Queen* on 29th April 1918. He saw service as far afield as Iceland and the Mediterranean Sea. His final vessel was the minesweeper HMT *Olympia*, a requisitioned Grimsby trawler, based at HMS *Venerable*. He was demobilised from

that base at Portland with effect from 4th February 1919. He moved to Glasgow before October 1920 and lived latterly at 12 Percy Street, Glasgow, where he was a retired Sergeant of Police who later worked as an insurance salesman. He married Christina Murray Maclean, who he outlived. He was present in Stornoway in June 1971 when the *Iolaire*'s bell and nameplate were handed over to Stornoway Town Council for safe keeping. (The artefacts are now with Museum nan Eilean).

Murdo Morrison
(Murchadh Ruaraidh Tàgaidh)

28th September 1900 – 25th November 1964 (age 64)

31 North Shawbost. Seaman RNR. Service number 9523/A.

Murdo was the son of Roderick and Christina Morrison (née Macleod) and had four sisters and four brothers, including Norman who was lost, aged 30, when HMT *Dirk* was torpedoed on 28th May 1918. Murdo was a raw 18-year-old at the Chatham Barracks of HMS *Pembroke* when the war ended. He travelled back to his island by train and boat, talking to his fellow villagers about the days ahead. His escape from the *Iolaire* was via John Finlay's rope, though afterwards he had no recollection of how he escaped. He was demobilised at Chatham on 11th February 1919 but did not qualify for a War Gratuity. Murdo married Margaret Macleod and they moved to Glasgow, where he was a household gas clerk, living at 43 Holmhead Crescent. He died, over 45 years after the disaster, in the Victoria Hospital, Glasgow.

Roll call of the survivors

Peter Angus Morrison
(Pàdraig Aonghais, Am Muillear)

22nd September 1893 – 6th March 1941
(age 47)

46 North Shawbost. Seaman RNR.
Service number 4586/A.

Peter was the son of Donald and
Helen Morrison (née Copland), born at
Stornoway at 1 Murray's Court. He had
three sisters and three brothers. Peter
enrolled in the RNR on 30th October 1912
and fished out of Stornoway pre-war.
He joined HMS *Excellent* on call-up day,
4th August 1914, after travelling from
Peterhead. He served at HMS *Vernon*, the
mine school at Portsmouth, and returned
to HMS *Excellent*. He served on HMD
Confier when at these establishments.
From 6th May 1917 he served with HMS
President III. He served on HMT *William
Jones* and returned to HMS *Vernon* prior to
his New Year leave. He was demobilised
from HMS *Iolaire* (base) on 11th March

1919. His record shows that he was
medically rejected for re-enrolment and
he was awarded a disablement pension
from 5th September 1919 to 6 July 1920.
He remained a single crofter until his
early death in the dark days of another
war. His youngest brother John succeeded
to the croft.

Murdo Macleod
(Murchadh Phàdraig Mhurchaidh)

9th August 1877 – 10th November 1956
(age 79)

13 South Shawbost. Seaman RNR.
Service number 3316/C

His birthdate given as June 1880 in naval
records, Murdo was the son of Peter and
Annie Macleod (née Macleod). By the
outbreak of the Great War, he was an
experienced campaigner, having enrolled
on 1st January 1904. He was fishing on the
fishing boat *Ruby* (KY 448) and left Methil
to report to HMS *Victory* on 2nd August
1914. He moved to HMS *Columbine* at
Rosyth and the armed boarding vessel HMS
Stephen Furness on which he sailed for 14
months. He then served at HMS *Excellent*,
HMS *Thalia* and HMS *President III*, where
he qualified as a gunner for merchant
vessels. He was an Acting Leading Seaman
thereafter. The minesweeper HMT *Grouse*
was Murdo's last naval posting and he
left the requisitioned Hull trawler looking
forward to home. He was demobilised at
Glasgow on 30th December 1918 but it was
not effective until the end of the following
month, so he was technically still in
service when he survived the sinking of the
Iolaire. He rejoined the RNR post-war and
served until 17th January 1924, by which
time his occupation was as a crofter. The
croft history written by Comunn Eachdraidh
an Taobh Siar (West Side Historical
Society) relates that he was one of the
post-war Dalbeg land raiders. He was the
husband of Annie Macleod (née Macleod).

UIG PARISH – East Uig

George Alexander Morison
(Seòras a' Mhinisteir)

26th July 1898 – 15th August 1980
(age 82)

United Free Church Manse, Knock, Carloway. Stoker 2nd Class Royal Navy. Service number K/54883.

George's father was Rev Neil Maclean Morison, the United Free Church of Scotland minister at Knock Carloway, having also served at Crossbost, Gravir and Barvas. George's mother was Isabel Morison (née Macphail) and he had two sisters, Nessie and Betty. He was said to be a cool lad, even laid back in temperament and was an apprentice fitter when he volunteered his services, for hostilities only, as a Stoker (Class 2) on 30th October 1918 at HMS *Pembroke II*. He was demobilised on 4th March 1919. After surviving the *Iolaire* in a traumatised condition, he later became a marine engineer at sea with the Clan Line before marrying Skye girl Jessie Ann Macmillan.

They settled in Partick, latterly at 5 Caird Drive. He sailed on the India route before his retirement. George's wife predeceased him and, as both had been cremated, the skipper of the Caledonian MacBrayne ferry MV *Hebrides* kindly stopped the ferry for a brief service, so that the couple's ashes could be scattered on the Minch between Skye and Lewis. George had survived over sixty years before the Minch finally claimed his remains.

John Maclean
(Knox)

3rd January 1896 – 23rd February 1983
(age 87)

12 Borrowston. Seaman RNR.

John, the son of Angus and Margaret Maclean (née Macdonald), enrolled on 14th February 1916 and reported to HMS *Pembroke*, then HMS *Victory*. He transferred to the Trawler Section and served with HMML 139 before serving at HMS *Actaeon*.

He was briefly at HMS *Hermione* then left the small naval armed launch HMML 511, based at HMS *Victory*, and headed for home surrounded by Carloway boys. John was demobilised on 21st February 1919 and lived as a crofter to a good age, remaining single. In the 1968 BBC Radio pre-interview notes, Bill Carrocher, of the *Stornoway Gazette*, stated that he had pure Gaelic and was fluent in English. He was well known locally as a 'village bard'.

Malcolm Macleod
(Calum Òg)

13th May 1870 – 4th July 1952 (age 82)

16 Borrowston. Seaman RNR. Service number 2410/C.

His date of birth given as November 1874 in naval records, Calum Òg was the son of Donald and Euphemia (Effie) Macleod (née Macarthur). He enrolled in the RNR on 1st April 1902 and fished out of Blyth, Stornoway, Wick, Peterhead and Buckie pre-war. He joined HMS *Victory* from

Peterhead on 2nd August 1914 and two months later went to HMS *Vernon* where he qualified in modified mine sweeping. He was posted to HMT *Lucknow*, based at Yarmouth, and later from HMS *Victory* at Portsmouth. The *Lucknow* was sunk by a mine shortly after he left her. Malcolm served on the Hunt class minesweeper (Belvoir type) HMS *Tedworth*, based at HMS *Victorious*, for the remainder of the war. He was demobilised from HMS *Gunner* at Granton on 10th February 1919. He was married to Annie Maclean and was a crofter for the rest of his life.

buoy. After a month at HMS *Pembroke* he was on the water carrier *Blossom* at Gibraltar, then HMY *Amethyst III* of the Auxiliary Patrol out of Devonport and HMS *Vivid*. On 11th January 1917 he was posted to HMT *Good Hope II* from HMS *Idaho* at Milford Haven until moving to Falmouth, at another Auxiliary Patrol base, HMS *Dreel Castle*, from 13th June 1917 on the *Good Hope II* – he stayed with her until the war's end. He was demobilised from *Dreel Castle* on 20th February 1919. He married Mary Macleod from 22 Upper Carloway and spent his working life as a fisherman.

26th November 1915. He then joined the recommissioned pre-dreadnought battleship HMS *Vengeance*. She served off the Cape of Good Hope and took part in the capture of Dar es Salaam in 1916. John left her on 5th March 1917 and went to HMS *Leander*, a depot ship for torpedo boat destroyers at Scapa Flow. He served on the B Class destroyer HMS *Arab* at Scapa Flow. After surviving the *Iolaire*, John was demobilised from HMS *Wallington* at Immingham on 11th February 1919. He received a disability pension of 5/6 (five shillings and sixpence) a week from 20th March 1919 until 16th September 1919, but his record shows that the Crown made a claim to recover all or part of this money at a later date. John declined to re-enrol in the RNR post-war. Angus and John's brother Norman (Knock, Carloway) was lost on the *Iolaire*.

Angus Macphail
(Aonghas Boyce/Ixon)

**21st June 1886 – 1st February 1965
(age 79)**

13 Doune Carloway. Deckhand RNR. Service number 3167/SD.

Angus was born to Norman and Anne Macphail (née Macleod) and was a crofter/fisherman's son. He enrolled in the RNR on 9th November 1915 at Stornoway and was at HMS *Pembroke* from 18th November 1915 until 9th May 1916. He served on the requisitioned HMD *Girl Eva* at HMS *Actaeon*, the Auxiliary Patrol base at Sheerness, until 2nd October 1916, when he survived her sinking by a mine off the Elbow light

John Macphail
('An Boyce)

**21st July 1878 – 15th September 1952
(age 74)**

13 Doune Carloway. Seaman RNR. Service number 3428/B.

Brother of Angus (above), John was born to Norman and Anne Macphail (née Macleod) and married to Margaret Macphail, 11 Borrowston, their married home being 7 Doune. He enrolled on 1st April 1905 and was a fisherman at Stornoway, serving on local and Banff boats, from 1910 until war was declared. He reported to HMS *Vivid* at Devonport, then the guard ship HMS *Illustrious* until

UIG PARISH – West Uig

Alexander Macphail
(Alasdair Ruadh)

9th December 1886 - 7th December 1971
(age 85)

18 Tolsta Chaolais. Seaman RNR.
Service number 3364/A.

Alasdair Ruadh, son of fisherman Duncan and his wife Isabella Macphail (née Macdonald), enrolled to the RNR on 9th February 1911. He was fishing out of Stornoway, Fraserburgh and Kirkwall pre-war. He reported with all haste from Fraserburgh to HMS *Pembroke* on 2nd August 1914 and was posted in succession to HMS *Arrogant*, HMS *Attentive III*, HMS *Pembroke I* and the mine carrier HMS *Cove*. As a 32-year-old seaman, he was at HMS *Victory* in Portsmouth when he headed up with a contingent of leave sailors from that base, bound for their beloved isles in the north-west. Alex was among the fortunate sailors to escape the tragedy with his life and continued as a crofter into his eighties. He had married Annie, née Macdonald on 22nd January 1918 and she outlived him.

John Mackenzie
(Doonie)

17th October 1898 - 26th May 1940
(age 42)

8 Tobson. Deckhand RNR.
Service number 14658/DA

Son of Murdo and Mary Mackenzie (née Maciver), John enrolled in the Naval Reserve for hostilities on 12th February 1917 at HMS *Iolaire* (base). He then moved to HMS *Pembroke* and served at HMS *Dreel Castle* and HMS *Gunner*. He left HMD *Concord II* attached to HMS *Implacable* at Portland. Despite surviving the *Iolaire* disaster initially, he could not cope in peacetime with his experiences. He was a fisherman after being demobilised at Stornoway on 27th March 1919, He was awarded a disablement allowance of 5s 6d a week from 18th July 1919 to 14th August 1920, the record stating 'Traumatic Neurasthenia'. Despite this he re-enrolled on 24th April 1922 and was fishing from 1922 to 1924. After his term of enrolment

expired on 23rd April 1927, his health deteriorated, he had to go into a home in Glasgow in 1930 and he died there ten years later.

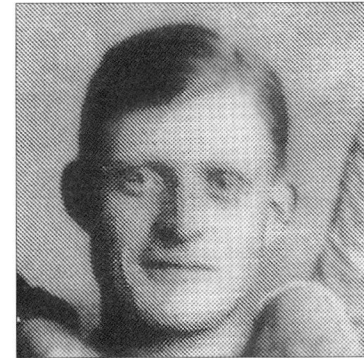

John Maclennan
('Ain Geal, Iain 'ain Seonaid)

11th December 1896 - 17th December 1987
(age 91)

15 Kneep. Able Seaman Mercantile Marine.

The son of John and Henrietta Maclennan (née Macdonald), John was a sailor engaged on T-124Y rates on HMY *Iolaire*, the base yacht before the fated vessel which sank on 1st January 1919. He had been coxswain aboard her and had left Portsmouth, returning home on her replacement, now the *Iolaire* but originally *Amalthaea*. John survived the wreck and then walked home. Shock set in later. A witness at the Public Inquiry, John then spent 14 years in Australia, as he felt he could not settle in Lewis after the disaster. He and his wife, Maggie Mary Macritchie, lived at 4 Aird Uig and he was a crofter/Harris Tweed weaver after his Australian adventure. They had married at Sydney, New South Wales, on 23rd November 1929. His poignant footnote to the *Iolaire* tragedy was: "A child could have brought her into harbour that night." He attended the ceremony in June 1971 when the bell from the *Iolaire* and the engine plate were presented to Stornoway Town Council.

Malcolm Macritchie
(Tuireag)

17th April 1879 – 6th June 1962 (age 83)

3b Aird Uig. Seaman RNR.
Service number 3312/B.

Malcolm was the son of Donald and Margaret Macritchie (née Matheson), his date of birth given as November 1879 in naval records. He became a man the Admiralty could call on at short notice in times of strife. A seaman fishing out of the ports of Stornoway, Peterhead and Fraserburgh pre-war, Malcolm became a reservist with HMS *Kinfauns Castle*, HMS *Victory*, HMS *Zaria* in Orkney during the time of war and he was at HMS *Iolaire* (base) after New Year 1919. He sailed for home and survived the wreck, to reach his eighties living as a crofter at 11 Ardroil, always thinking of those lost. He was the brother-in-law of John Maclennan, who stated that Malcolm had somehow got ashore hardly wet. He was married to Mary, née Maclennan, from 15 Kneep and they had three sons and three daughters.

STORNOWAY PARISH – Tolsta to Tong

survived the wreck of the *Iolaire*, when many powerful swimmers didn't. Murdo was demobilised on 7th February 1919 but re-enrolled as 4580/C and continued his occupation, fishing out of Peterhead and Stornoway for the rest of his life. He married Annie Maciver and their married home was at Lochside, North Tolsta where two girls and two boys were brought up. He was laid to rest in Tolsta Cemetery.

Murdo Macdonald
(Claoid Iain Uilleam)

16th August 1888 – 11th February 1950 (age 61)

1 North Tolsta. Leading Seaman RNR. Service number 3971/A

Murdo was the son of John and Mary Macdonald (née Maclennan). He was fishing out of Peterhead, Stornoway, Wick and Lerwick before the war, after having enrolled for the RNR on 18th December 1911. He reported to HMS *Excellent* on 2nd August 1914 and, on 10th October 1914, he was posted to the battleship HMS *Emperor of India*, on which he served throughout the war. He was promoted to Leading Seaman on 31st August 1918. He was a 30-year-old veteran of the whole duration of the war when he left HMS *Emperor of India* and headed home with fellow villagers. Like all the survivors, he pondered in later years on how he

Roderick Macdonald
(Ruagan)

23rd June 1878 – 29th October 1965 (age 87)

23 North Tolsta. Seaman RNR. Service number 6632/A

Roddie was the son of Murdo and Ann Macdonald (née Maciver), a typical RNR islander with experience of small boats from boyhood. He enrolled on 4th November 1914 and his record is stamped in three places with 'NO TRAINING REQUIRED'. He served with HMS *Pembroke*, HMS *Halcyon*, HMT *Gardenia*, HMS *Columbine*, HMS *Gunner*, HMT *Delphinius* and was with HMS *Pembroke* at Chatham. He was demobilised on 7th February 1919, married Mary Mackenzie and had a long retirement after his working life as a fisherman ended.

Donald Murray
(Dòmhnall Brus)

11th July 1895 – 3rd May 1992 (age 96)

37 North Tolsta. Seaman RNR. Service number 5575/A.

Son of Kenneth and Christina (Cairistìona) Murray (née Maciver), Donald had been in the 3rd Battalion Seaforth Highlanders as a young man before he enrolled with the RNR on 19th January 1914. He was with HMS *Victory I* until he joined the Royal Naval Division on 16th September 1914. He fought in the trenches as an AB with the Drake Battalion of the RND, and recalled the men being addressed by the First Sea Lord, Winston Churchill, who told them that there was three Germans to every one of them before they entered the trenches at Antwerp. They held for some time but the German shelling set fire to the oil tanks in the city. They retired and escaped internment in Holland by getting

Roll call of the survivors

297

across a bridge made from joined up floating lighters, before it was blown up. On 27th October 1914 he was discharged at Portsmouth and received the 1914 Star. He remained with the RNR and served with the armed boarding vessel HMS *Partridge* as a sailor from the end of 1917. He was with the cruiser HMS *Diadem* in March 1918 and latterly was attached to the elderly pre-dreadnought battleship HMS *Venerable*, which was a depot ship. His friend and neighbour John Morrison, from No 8 North Tolsta, was with him throughout the war until they were parted on the *Iolaire*, when John died. Donald married John's fiancée, Maggie Murray (née Macleod) after the tragedy.

Despite his experience of tragedy at sea, Donald Murray made fishing his livelihood. (He also later survived the sinking of a fishing boat). After the war he had part share of the fishing boats *Elspeth Smith* (SY838) and the *Comrade* (SY525). He and Maggie had sons, one of whom, John (Iain) was tragically drowned at Gob an t-Seabhaig on 12th August 1943, aged 13. Donald died in North Tolsta in 1992 at the age of 96, 73 years after the *Iolaire* disaster. He was the second last *Iolaire* survivor to die and lived to the greatest age. Since the 1960s, his sons Iain Angus and Donald and his grandson Iain have skippered the *Comrade* and *Comrade III* (both SY337).

John Macinnes
(Iain a' Bhroga)

21st November 1884 - 26th April 1964 (age 79)

2 Hill Street Tolsta. Seaman RNR. Service number 3403/B

Son of Murdo and Margaret Macinnes (née Maclean), John enrolled with the RNR on 1st April 1905 and fished out of Stornoway, Lerwick, Buckie and Fraserburgh before the call up of late July 1914. He served at HMS *Excellent*, HMS *Halcyon*, HMS *Columbine*, HMS *Imperieuse* and on the trawler *Othello*, attached to HMS *Zaria* (the auxiliary patrol base for the Orkneys and Shetland). On 6th April 1918, his name had appeared in the London Gazette when he was mentioned in despatches for bravery, distinguishing himself in saving the life of a shipmate who had fallen overboard during a dangerous operation when the ship was laying mines.

He was with HMS *Iolaire* depot when he was demobilised on 17th February 1919 and was part of the group of land raiders that broke up Gress Farm to form crofts after the First World War. A fisherman, he settled with his wife Lily Macinnes (née Mackay) at 4 Gress and they raised a family, but war would cast a long shadow over their household. He served in the Second World War and survived the huge explosion on the mine carrier *Port Napier*, at Kyle of Lochalsh on 27th November 1940, and also served on HMS *Newfoundland*. Two sons, Donald Junior and Norman, served in the RNR in the Second World War and a daughter Jessie in the WRNS. One Donald died at Liverpool on war service on 13th October 1940 aged 27. Daughter Bella and an infant son died between the wars.

Donald Maciver

(Am Bèicear)

25th June 1899 - 20th April 1986 (age 86)

14 New Tolsta. Deckhand, RNR.
Service number 19616/A

Donald's date of birth is given as 27th December 1898 in naval records and his address is given as 57 New Street, North Tolsta. The eldest of six boys and three girls, Donald was the son of Alexander and Jessie Maciver (née Graham). He enrolled in the RNR on 29th January 1918 and, from HMS *Pembroke*, he went to HMS *Venerable*, where he served on the Hall Russell-built Strath Class trawler HMT *Joseph Burgin*. Donald served after the *Iolaire* disaster at HMS *Implacable* and HMS *Idaho* before being demobilised on 7th February 1919. He re-enrolled later as 9735/A and worked at Kinlochleven, then the Merchant Navy and was with the Cunard Line before he served in the Royal

Navy again in the Second World War. He later moved to Inverness and had jobs on Caledonian canal locks, as pilot on the canal and finally at a boat slip. He was married to Christina, née Macleod. The lifebelt that Donald wore as he escaped the sinking ship is in the keeping of Museum nan Eilean at Lews Castle.

Alexander John Macleod

(mac Dhòmhnaill Dholaidh)

8th October 1898 - 8th January 1973 (age 74)

63 Coll. Deckhand RNR.
Service number 11991/D

Alex John was the son of Donald and Ann Macleod (née Macleod) and enrolled on 4th September 1916, a month short of his true 18th birthday – his naval record shows his birth date as 2nd September, the slight adjustment allowing him to enlist. He was at HMS *Iolaire* (base) and went on to HMS *Pembroke* and HMT *Lord Lansdowne* before being posted to Gibraltar on 31st August 1917, but two months later was back on the armed trawler. He then served on HMT *Rushcoe* before a spell at HMS *Pembroke I* and left the armed drifter HMD *Scotsman*, for New Year's leave in 1918. He was demobilised on 5th February 1919 from HMS *Pactolus* but re-enrolled afresh as 9803/A. He was

said to be the second last man ashore before the rescue rope broke sending those following him into the raging surf. Alex John's health suffered after the disaster and he spent time in the Lewis Sanatorium which opened after the war. He later emigrated and worked as a coachbuilder on the railways in Chicago. On his return to Lewis he began building bodies for pre-manufactured bus chassis, working with his one of his brothers, who not only painted the finished articles but painted their owner's livery. Alex John was interred at Gress many years after his two fellow villagers above. His wife Catherine (née Stewart) died on 28th June 1989 aged 91.

Roll call of the survivors

299

LOCHS PARISH – North Lochs

Colin Macdonald
(Cailean Ruairidh Iain)

31st July 1899 – 19th July 1970 (age 70)

3 Ranish. Deckhand RNR.
Service number 12785/DA

The middle son of three in a family of nine born to Roderick and Mary Macdonald (née Macleod), Colin enrolled on 30th October 1916 and served at HMS *Iolaire* (base), HMS *Pembroke* and HMS *Gunner* at Granton. He was a teenage deckhand on HMT *Etrurian*, a requisitioned Boston trawler used as a minesweeper and operating out of Granton. Colin survived the trauma of the *Iolaire*'s wreck in 1919 and was demobilised at Granton on 25th February 1919. His sister Christina married *Iolaire* survivor Roderick Nicolson, 36 Ranish. Colin emigrated to Australia and died at Newton near Sydney in 1970, still single.

John Mackinnon
(Iain Rochaidh, Iain Mhurchaidh Dhòmhnaill Iain)

17th July 1887 – 13th June 1924 (age 36)

9 Ranish. Seaman RNR.
Service number 2676/A

Youngest son of Murdo and Margaret Mackinnon (née Macaulay), John registered with the RNR on 13th April 1910 and fished out of Stornoway, Fraserburgh and Peterhead pre-war. He served on the Monmouth class armoured cruiser HMS *Donegal* throughout the war and was demobilised from her on 31st January 1919. The cruiser did duties at Sierra Leone, Atlantic convoys, Archangel convoys, Home Fleet duties and was on the North America and West Indies station. After the war, John re-enrolled with the RNR while continuing to be a fisherman and his service number changed to 4170/C. His father's first wife

Mary (nee Macleod) died in 1875 leaving two infants. John was the last of the five born in the second marriage. His own mother died in 1917. He was the husband of Christina, née Mackinnon, at 15b Ranish but sadly his fate mirrored that of the other John Mackinnon, from Tarbert, who also survived the *Iolaire*. Both men died in 1924, well before their time, John of tuberculosis, the scourge of the isles until the 1950s. John married in 1918 and had five children.

Angus Nicolson
(Aonghas Mhurchaidh Bhig)

17th April 1885 – 5th July 1958 (age 73)

24 Ranish. Leading Seaman RNR.
Service number 5136/B – See under Stornoway district, 25 Battery Park

John Montgomery
(Iain Tharmoid Iain Ruairidh)

27th August 1886 – 25th March 1952 (age 66)

27 Ranish. Seaman RNR.
Service number 3708/B

The son of Norman and Margaret Montgomery (née Montgomery), his father drowned off the Butt of Lewis in 1899. John signed up for the RNR on 27th August 1905. A fisherman out of

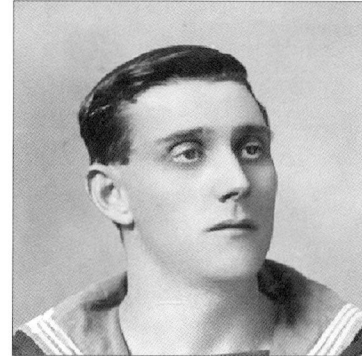

Stornoway and Peterhead pre-war, he travelled from Peterhead to HMS *Dolphin* and moved on to HMS *Victory*. He served on HMT *Cuckoo* (later renamed *Nightjar*), then HMT *Neath Castle* operating from HMS *Zaria* (Orkneys) and HMS *Victory* (Portsmouth). On 2nd November 1916 he moved to the considerably larger armed merchant cruiser HMS *Arlanza*, but returned to smaller vessels on 11th January 1918 and served with the armed launch HMML 74. He left her moorings to join the great homeward move north. On board the sinking *Iolaire*, John watched John Finlay MacLeod swim ashore and helped him to hold the line and then secure the rope paid out to John on the rocks. For survivors like John, with five sailors dead in his village, it was a nightmare return to the bosom of his family. John was demobilised from HMS *Victory* on 1st March 1919 but re-enrolled with a new service number of 3182/D and married Margaret Macleod from 12 Tong

the same year. Their married home was at 18 Tong, which his wife's father had acquired in 1917. He was a fisherman in peacetime. Margaret had lost her brother Angus, killed aged 18 while serving with the Seaforth Highlanders at the Battle of Loos on 9th May 1915. Margaret died at Raigmore Hospital, Inverness in 1949, aged 62, and John was still living at 18 Tong when he died three years later.

Donald Macrae
(Dhòmhnall Bhàrnaidh)

27th June 1891 - 19th May 1977 (age 85)

35 Ranish. Leading Seaman RNR.
Service number 4979/A

Donald was the son of Alexander and Dolina Macrae (née Macdonald) and fished out of Peterhead, Stornoway and Fraserburgh after signing up as a reservist on 29th January 1910. He reported from Peterhead via Stornoway, to HMS *Dolphin* on 14th August 1914. He then went to HMS *Victory*, after being at HMS *Columbine* and HMS *Gunner*. He was at HMS *Iolaire* (base) from 18th May 1916 until 11th June 1917 and, in the last three months there, sailed on HMT *Pavlova*, HMT *Remo* and HMT *Leys*. He then switched between HMS *Victory*, HMS *Excellent* and HMS *President III* during the remainder of 1917. As a gunner he was serving on the

large troopship *Justica*, which was struck by four torpedoes from UB-64 south of Skerryvore. She floated and was being towed to Lough Swilly the following day, 20th July 1918, when two more torpedoes from UB-124 sent her to the bottom north of Malin Head. Donald was then stationed at HMS *Victory* at Portsmouth and was serving on HMT *William Jones* on 31st December 1918 as he was heading home on leave. He was one of the survivors that escaped the *Iolaire* via the rope and was said to be the last man off, with a neighbour behind him on the rope being lost. He was demobilised on 11th February 1919 at the naval depot, Stornoway and later re-enrolled with the new service number of 3962/A. He worked as a labourer, crofter and fisherman for the rest of his life and was the husband of Ann Macrae (née Macleod). Donald settled with his wife at their croft at 2/48 Leurbost and had three children. He was interred at Crossbost Cemetery.

Roderick Nicolson

(Ruairidh Iain Iain)

15th October 1890 – 29th October 1951
(age 61)

36 Ranish. Seaman RNR.
Service number 3160/A

Roddie was born into a fishing family, son of John and Isabella Nicolson (née Montgomery). He enrolled in the RNR on 14th December 1910 and fished out of Stornoway, Peterhead and Fraserburgh. He reported at HMS *Victory* from Fraserburgh on 2nd August 1914 and moved after eight days to HMS *Vernon*. By 9th November 1914 he was aboard the new dreadnought HMS *Erin*. He returned to *Victory* at Portsmouth for nearly a year and then was posted for the remainder of the war to HMS *Zaria*, the Auxiliary Patrol base at Longhope, Orkney. After the *Iolaire* disaster he was posted to HMS *Iolaire* (Depot) and was demobilised from there on 14th February 1919. He re re-enrolled as 11229/C after receiving a disability pension of 8s 3d a week from 15th March 1919 to 16th September 1919. He was the husband of Christina (née MacDonald), remained fishing for the remainder of his life and died of a coronary a few months before his cousin John Montgomery, with whom each New Year he had shared memories of that shattering morning years earlier. Roderick's wife Christina was a sister of survivor Colin Macdonald. The couple made their home at 50 Ranish and had 3 children, the eldest dying in infancy.

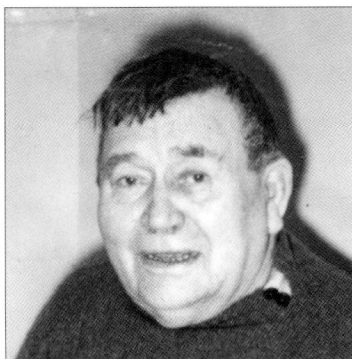

Murdo Mackenzie

(Leigean)

31st October 1879 – 11th May 1962 (age 82)

18 Crossbost. Seaman RNR.
Service number 2939/B

The second son of four, together with a daughter, born to John and Jane Mackenzie (née Macdonald), Murdo was 39 on the night of the disaster and managed to swim ashore. The year 1919 still brought death to his home, as the father died that year, aged 76. Murdo's three brothers went to Canada and youngest brother John was killed with the Canadian forces on 28th June 1916. Murdo had first donned his navy uniform on 1st January 1905 when a fisherman. He sailed out of Macduff, Stornoway and Lowestoft before going deep sea on the SS *Cameronia* and SS *Carmarthenshire*, the latter trip to China and Japan. At the start of the war he travelled from Aberdeen to HMS *Kinfauns Castle* on 3rd August 1914, later serving with HMS *Victory II*, HMS *Excellent*, the troopship HMS *Cardiganshire* and HMS *President III*.

He was demobilised on 26th February 1919 at Stornoway and received a six months disability pension of eight shillings and threepence a week. He was married to Margaret, née Maclean, who predeceased him. They had lived at 22b Crossbost and Murdo had been a fisherman during his working life.

John Macdonald

(Iain Fhionnlaigh Dhòmhnaill Iain)

29th June 1874 – 27th February 1926
(age 51)

3 Leurbost. Seaman RNR.
Service number 4952/B

John was the son of Finlay and Ann Macdonald (née Montgomery), his birth year given as 1875 in naval records. John had served in the RNR from 1st January 1908 under the service number 1477/A, but left before re-enrolling on 27th March 1913. He was a pre-war fisherman and served at HMS *Dolphin*, HMS *Victory* and HMS *Magpie* in the war. He was demobilised from HMS *Magpie*, Isle of Wight, on 29th January 1919. His life was marked by tragedy – he had lost his parents in 1893 and 1901 and his wife, Mary (née Maclean) died of cerebral apoplexy on 20th June 1916, aged 48. John himself was one of several *Iolaire* survivors who died in the years immediately following the disaster. He was working as a labourer prior to his death from pyloric carcinoma, leaving four children orphaned.

Alexander Mackenzie

(Alasdair Ailein Ailein)

1st September 1899 – 10th November 1982 (age 83)

10 Leurbost. Deckhand RNR.
Service number 18017/DA

Alex was the eldest son of Allan and Ann Mackenzie (née Nicolson) and enrolled on 3rd September 1917. He served with HMS *Iolaire* (base), HMS *Thalia*, HMT *Elsie*, HMT *Richard Bennett*, Gibraltar and HMS *Pekin* and was latterly a 19-year-old sailor at HMS *Vigorous*. After surviving the *Iolaire* disaster, he was demobilised on 18th February 1919 from HMS *Vigorous* at Larne, but re-enrolled afresh post-war as 9777/A. He emigrated from London to Melbourne, Australia on 4th May 1922 on the SS *Barrapool*. He married Barbara Gunn Macleod from Helmsdale in 1928 and Alex's brother Donald also emigrated to Australia the same year. Alexander's brother Murdo died in 1926. His brother Allan had also served in the RNR. Alex served with the Royal Australian Navy in the Second World War. He had intended to farm in his new land, but ended his working life still following the sea after 41 years as Captain Mackenzie of the Melbourne Harbor Trust. When he retired on 1st September 1964, his 65th birthday, pipers played *Bonnie Dundee* at No 6 berth on north wharf. Alex lived latterly at 31 Stanhope Street, Daylesford, Victoria and he was interred at Daylesford Cemetery.

Neil Mackenzie

(Neilan Dhòmhnaill Dhòmhnaill)

28th July 1887 – 29th November 1965 (age 78)

14 Leurbost. Deckhand RNR.
Service number 4138/SD

Eldest son of Donald and Margaret (Peggy) Mackenzie (née Maclean), Neil joined the service on 14th February 1916. He left his home at Millburn, Leurbost and arrived at HMS *Victory I*. He was with HMML 322, HMS *Wallington*, HMS *Vivid I*, HMS *Onyx* and HMS *Vivid III*. He was 31 at New Year 1919 and was one of about 20 men that got ashore by swimming alone, until he was able to secure a hold on rocks and clambered to safety, hands and knees scraped from the rocks. Many men perished in the attempt. Neil was not recorded as an *Iolaire* survivor in some records but his daughter, one mainland newspaper and his naval record all confirm that he was indeed on board and had survived that fatal night. He was demobilised on 7th February 1919 and lived as a crofter, married to Kirsty Ann Mackenzie (née Macleod) of 15 Leurbost. Neil and his wife had six children together.

Archibald Ross

23rd August 1864 – 17th February 1947 (age 82)

29 Leurbost. Deckhand RNR.
Service number 4174/SD

Born at Kilmorack, near Beauly, to Alexander and Janet (Jessie) Ross (née Dingwall), Archie's date of birth is given as 4th August 1875 in naval records, and he obviously wished to serve when over age. He had already been discharged from 2/8th Battalion Argyll and Sutherland Highlanders (Reg. No. 2302) on 17th February 1916, but was so keen to serve that he enrolled with the RNR the following day. He was at HMS *Victory* until 21st July 1916, when he was posted to the torpedo training base at HMS *Vernon*, then made up of floating hulks linked together, rather than a concrete shore establishment. Archie was the oldest survivor of HMY *Iolaire*, at 54 years old. He was demobilised from HMS *Vernon* on 12th February 1919 and was awarded a disability pension of eight shillings and three pence a week from 5th March until 2nd September 1919. He worked as a crofter and his wife was Marion Ross (née Maclean).

LOCHS PARISH – Kinloch

John Smith

(An Sionnach)

23rd December 1890 - 21st February 1964 (age 73)

53 Leurbost. Leading Seaman RNR. Service number 3269/A

John was the son of Donald and Marion Smith (née Maclean), 27 years old, and serving at the Auxiliary Patrol naval base at Granton, HMS *Gunner*. His brothers Alexander and Malcolm were serving with the Seaforths. John joined the sea of blue uniforms heading northwards at Waverley Station in Edinburgh on 31st December. He worked as a crofter/fisherman in the years following his service and he and his wife Catherine, née Mackenzie, of 24 Crossbost, had no family.

Allan Mackay

(Ailean Iain Earainn Iain Mhòir)

22nd November 1899 - 4th June 1987 (age 87)

1 Achmore. Deckhand RNR. Service number 18865/DA

Allan came from the only inland village in Lewis, without a seashore to any of the crofts. He was the son of John and Ann Mackay (née Morrison), his father a crofter who lost older son Norman, serving with the Cameron Highlanders, in December 1914. Allan enrolled on 26th November 1917 and was at HMS *Iolaire* (base) then HMS *Wallington* and from that base he served on HMT *Richard Bulkeley*. After his providential survival on 1st January 1919, Allan was demobilised on 7th March and received a disability pension of five shillings and sixpence a week for six months. He later emigrated and by 1924 he was at Nipigan, Ontario, then by 1936 in Vancouver and his address in August 1952 was 445 Main Street, Vancouver.

Malcolm Macleod

20th February 1869 - 27th October 1953 (age 83)

16b Laxay. Leading Seaman RNR. Service number 2331/D

Malcolm was the son of Malcolm and Catherine Macleod (née Maciver). He enrolled on 11th April 1899, shaving a few years off his age with a stated birth date of

10th March 1872 in naval records. He married Effie Macinnes from 11 Lemreway on 20th February 1902 and they had five daughters and two sons — one daughter died in 1912. Malcolm reported to HMS *Pembroke* at the first call on 3rd August 1914 and after six weeks was posted to the armed merchant cruiser HMS *Orama*, which sailed to the Pacific. After a six-week spell at HMS *Vindictive* in 1916, when he had varicose vein problems, he served on the armed merchant cruiser HMS *Edinburgh Castle*. He was at HMS *Pembroke* at Chatham for a good spell and came home on leave from there. He was the second oldest survivor of the *Iolaire*. After he jumped into the small starboard side lifeboat, he realised it was likely to be swamped, so he re-boarded the yacht and was one of the fortunate men to get ashore via the rope. After returning to Chatham he was posted to HMS *Iolaire* (base) on 8th February 1919 and was demobilised from there on 11th March. He received a disablement pension of eight shillings a week from 20th May 1920 until 31st October 1922 and thereafter spent his working life at sea, fishing in the Minch.

LOCHS PARISH – Pàirc

George Macarthur

(Seòras Alastair Mhurchaidh Ruaidh)

27th February 1892 – 9th July 1923 (age 31)

10 Cromore. Seaman RNR.
Service number 3353/A

George was the son of Alexander and Anne Macarthur (née Mackenzie) and husband of Mary, née Macleod, he had enrolled on 8th February 1911 and at the start of the war was with 13th Platoon in "D" Company of the Anson Battalion of the Royal Naval Division at Antwerp. He then moved from Devonport to the armed boarding steamer HMS *Duke of Albany*. She was sunk by UB-27 east of the Pentland Skerries and took with her to their watery graves two Lewis naval reservists. George served at HMS *Vivid*, HMS *Excellent* and HMS *President III* before HMS *Victory*. He also spent a short time on the submarine depot ship HMS *Sandhurst* in July 1917. George was demobilised on 3rd February 1919 but was the first of the *Iolaire* survivors to die, at his home, having contracted tuberculosis, possibly in service.

Murdo Macarthur

(Murchadh Alastair Mhurchaidh Ruaidh)

13th December 1884 – 25th October 1959 (age 74)

10 Cromore. Seaman RNR.
Service number 3186/B

Brother of George, Murdo was a fisherman in peacetime, sailing with George on SY 217. Murdo enlisted with the RNR on 1st April 1905 and was at HMS *Pembroke* throughout the war, apart from five months with the Apollo-class cruiser HMS *Sirius* early in 1918 and two weeks at HMS *President III* in late December 1918. He served at Chatham at HMS *Pembroke* before his demobilisation on 8th March 1919, had passed 2nd Hand and was also a DAMS gunner. His other brothers John (Gordons) and Angus, a Lance Corporal in the Seaforths, were both wounded. Murdo married Mary Kennedy and died of a coronary in 1959.

Donald Macdonald

July 6th 1900 – 16th July 1959 (age 59)

23 Cromore. Deckhand RNR
Service number 18832/A

Donald was the son of Alexander and Margaret Macdonald (née Kennedy) and enrolled, possibly before he was 18, on 31st May 1917. He served originally at HMS *Iolaire* (base) and sailed on HM Whaler *Finwhale*. The whaler was sent to HMS *Zaria*, Longhope (South Walls), Orkney on 1st October 1917 and he remained with that vessel when she moved from there down to HMS *Attentive III* at Dover. He was demobilised from Dover on 15th February 1919. Donald stayed in Edinburgh for a short spell post-war, then emigrated to Canada, married Mary Ann Fontana and settled at Shell Lake, Saskatchewan. He became a teacher there and was the anonymous writer of the story that appeared in the *Stornoway Gazette* in 1956 recounting his experience of the sinking. He died of a blood clot at Saskatoon City Hospital, following a cancer operation, and his grave is in the Veterans' Section of Woodlawn Cemetery, Saskatoon, the stone inscribed Donald Macdonald RNR.

Roderick Finlayson
(Ruairidh Sheonaidh Ruairidh)

6th November 1894 – 11th May 1962 (age 67)

8 Marvig. Able seaman Mercantile Marine Reserve.

Roddie was born to a fishing couple, John and Catherine Finlayson (née Macfarlane), who had married in Peterhead six years earlier. He was a merchant seaman serving on T124Y rates at HMS *Eaglet*, an RNR ship establishment at Liverpool during the war. He was 24 years old when he survived that dark night at Holm. He emigrated to Canada and settled in Vancouver where he died over 40 years later. His wife, Jean Munro was from Melvaig.

Allan Macaskill
(Ailean Dhòmhnaill Òig)

6th March 1898 – 6th April 1987 (age 89)

9 Gravir. Deckhand RNR.

The son of fisherman Donald and his wife Margaret Macaskill (née Maclennan), Allan enrolled on 8th December 1916. He served at HMS *Iolaire*, HMS *Pembroke I*, HMS *Halcyon*, HMT *Dorinda*, HMS *Idaho*, HMT *Gladys Rose*, HMS *Eaglet*, HMD *Letterfourie* and, just before the disaster, on the drifter HMD *Boy Scout*. He was demobilised on 26th February 1919 and lived at Partick for a spell. His home thereafter was at the Old Nurse's Cottage in his home village of Gravir. He was interred at Gravir Cemetery.

Neil Nicolson
(Niall Ruadh)

23rd April 1897 – 27th June 1992 (age 95)

20 Lemreway. Able seaman RNR.
Service number 8895/A

Neil was the last survivor of HMY *Iolaire* to die, just outliving Donald Murray of Tolsta. The son of Isabella Nicolson, Neil was raised by her parents, Malcolm and Catherine Nicolson. His mother had married Donald Montgomery, a widower with three children, in 1901 and settled

nearby at 1 Orinsay where she had two more children. Neil enrolled on 21st February 1916 and survived the sinking of three vessels within three years. He was posted first to HMS *Vivid*, then became a survivor from the armed merchant cruiser HMS *Avenger*, which was torpedoed by U-69 west of Scapa Flow on 14th June 1917. After another brief spell at *Vivid* he served on the armed merchant cruiser HMS *Champagne*, until she was torpedoed by U-96 off the Isle of Man, on 15th October 1917. He last served on HMT *Returdo*, at HMS *Idaho*, Milford Haven. After his third survival, from the *Iolaire*, it was from Milford Haven that he was demobilised on 11th February 1919. He re-enrolled with the number 6234/B and continued in fishing, then served again in the Second World War. He remained a single man throughout his long life.

STORNOWAY PARISH – Point

John Mackenzie

(Iain 'An Anndra)

29th November 1883 - 13th January 1961
(age 77)

5 Portvoller. Seaman RNR.
Service number 4508/B

Son of John and Christina Mackenzie (née Murray), "Iain 'An Anndra" served with the Seaforth Highlanders just before and during the Boer War. From No 5 Portvoller, he set up his home at No 8 after marrying Isabella Macrae on 20th September 1910. They had three sons and two daughters. He had re-enrolled on 4th March 1907 and was a fisherman pre-war at Fraserburgh and Stornoway, before he was called up on 3rd August 1914 from Fraserburgh to HMS *Excellent*. He was posted to the armed merchant cruiser HMS *Calgarian* on 21st September 1914 and was aboard her when, at Halifax, Nova Scotia, several of her crew were casualties of a huge ammunition explosion. SS *Imo* had collided with the

French ammunition ship SS *Mont Blanc* and the ammunition exploded in catastrophic fashion with hardly a building left standing in Halifax. Five sailors from Barra were killed on SS *Curaca*. Iain remained on the *Calgarian* until she was sunk by U-19 in March 1918. He survived that sinking and spent several hours on a drifting raft with Malcolm Macdonald, 57 South Bragar, before being rescued. (Malcolm was later lost on the *Iolaire*). Iain was then posted at Portsmouth with HMS *Victory* from where he was demobbed on 4th February 1919. He re-enrolled and remained in the RNR until 2nd March 1922. He fished post-war and later worked for 15 years as a waterman with the Stornoway Pier and Harbour Commission before he retired. He and his wife moved to live at Portvoller House, 7 Marybank in 1936. John was well known in church circles and was a Free Church elder for 18 years prior to his death. His wife died on 22nd April 1968 aged 83. John was interred at Aignish Burial Ground.

John Mackenzie

(Iain Uilleam Alasdair Uilleim)

16th February 1881 - 12th February 1946
(age 65)

8 Portvoller. Seaman RNR.
Service number 7501/A

John was born at 1 Aird, his birth date given as 1886 in naval records. He was the son of William and Mary Mackenzie (née Nicolson)

and a younger brother of "Am Boicean" who was lost on the *Iolaire*. John had married Portvoller girl Annie Macrae, sister of Isabella above, on 27th December 1910 and they lived with her parents, Evander and Annie Macrae. John enrolled in the RNR on 11th January 1915 and after training at HMS *Victory* in Portsmouth he served on the *Empress of Japan* for a day before being posted to the armed boarding ship HMS *Lama*, a requisitioned British India Steam Navigation ship. John served out in the Far East, including a spell at the Royal Naval Depot at Bombay and a time in hospital at Bombay in July 1916, when the *Lama* was in Bombay in drydock. John recovered and returned to HMS *Victory I* on 1st December 1917. He received a Good Conduct award and was posted to HMS *Excellent* on 23rd May 1918. He had just returned to *Victory* before his New Year leave. Rumours circulated immediately after the *Iolaire*'s sinking that he had been a victim of the tragedy but, like his brother-in-law Iain an Anndra, he survived. After being demobilised on 11th March 1919, John re-enrolled while doing inshore fishing and was given 12 months leave from the RNR to undertake a voyage to Australasia, on the *Hororata* to Wellington, in 1925/26. He stayed at Port Chalmers when in New Zealand. He was still in the RNR until 1930. He died at 8 Portvoller of a cerebral embolism shortly after the end of the second war.

Roll call of the survivors

Malcolm Martin

(alum 'An Màrtainn)

29th September 1873 – 22nd August 1942
(age 69)
13 Portvoller. Seaman RNR.
Service number 2336/C

Born at 13 Portvoller, Malcolm was
the son of John and Mary Martin (née
Macleod) and first donned his naval tunic
on 1st January 1902. He was married to
Annie Smith of Garrabost and lived at
13 Portvoller. Malcolm was a fisherman
at Lerwick, Stornoway and Peterhead
pre-war and reported to HMS *Excellent*
from Peterhead on 3rd August 1914. From
there he joined the armed merchant
cruiser HMS *Celtic*, before going to HMS
Victory on 4th January 1916. He served
on trawlers at HMS *Colleen* and was on
the Q-ship (decoy vessel) HMS *Zylpha*,
which sank in tow four days after being
torpedoed by U-82 on 15th June 1917,
southwest of Ireland. He then served on
the purpose-built Q-ship HMS *Hyderabad*
and was afterwards listed as a 45-year
old-seaman on the old pre-dreadnought
battleship HMS *Redoubtable*. During
1917 he received the RNR medal for long
service and good conduct. Malcolm was
demobilised from HMS *Iolaire* naval depot
on 11th February 1919. He was interred at
Aignish Burial Ground.

John Mackay

12th October 1870 – 6th March 1935
(age 64)
7 Shulishader. Leading Seaman RNR.
Service number 1473/C

John was the son of Donald and Isabella
Mackay (née Macdonald) and had
enrolled into the reserves of the Senior
Service on 13th March 1900. He had
already received the RNR medal for Long
Service and Good Conduct well before war
broke out, on 4th October 1911. Being a
Leading Seaman he was paid ten shillings
more per quarter than an ordinary rating.
Before the war he pursued the fishing all
over the north at Fraserburgh, Stornoway,
Peterhead and Kirkwall. After 1914, he
served first at HMS *Excellent*, then was
one of the several Lewismen who manned
the modern battleship HMS *Emperor of
India*. Eight men from Lewis travelled from
that battleship to Kyle on 31st December
1918, but only two survived. It is said by
his family that he was thought lost, as
he did not come home until three days
later, after sheltering at a peat bank. John
reported back to HMS *Iolaire* (base) on
23rd February 1919 and was demobilised
on 29th March 1919. He was married to
Mary Mackay (nee Murray), was a general
labourer and died at Lewis Hospital of
pancreatic problems.

Duncan Macaskill

10th September 1889 – 8th October 1935
(age 46)
14 Shulishader. Petty Officer, Royal
Canadian Naval Volunteer Reserve.
Service number 2809

The son of Donald and Margaret Macaskill
(née Macleod), Duncan was seven years
older than his brother Donald, who did not
make it to safety. Duncan enrolled with
the RNR on 2nd December 1909 when
fishing out of Fraserburgh and Stornoway.
He was fishing at Lake Winnipeg in 1911
and was declared as 'time expired'
through non-compliance with RNR
Regulations on 14th December 1914, but
wrote stating that he was with the Royal
Canadian Volunteer Reserve and served
back in the UK from 4th November 1916
at HMS *Niobe*, HMS *Victory*, HMS *Patia*,
HMS *Halcyon II* and HMS *Vivid*. He married

Catherine Macphail and lived at Moor View, Upper Carloway. He was listed as a naval pensioner on his death certificate which was signed by his father-in-law, Malcolm Macphail, 39 Upper Carloway, when Duncan died in 1935 of a cerebral haemorrhage.

Angus Macaulay

1st March 1878 - 22nd June 1970 (age 92)
Newlands. Seaman RNR.
Service number 4060/B

Son of John and Anne Macaulay (née Crichton), Angus was a strapping figure at almost six feet, with a 41-inch chest, when he enrolled on 1st January 1906. He had married at Wick on 17 August 1908 and was fishing at Stornoway and Wick until the war started, then served at HMS *Cyclops*, HMS *Hecla*, HMS *Fisgard* and HMS *Imperieuse*. He left HMS *Zaria*, the naval base ship at Longhope in Orkney, and travelled by train to Inverness, where he met up with friends and neighbours for the trip to Kyle on 31st December 1918. He had been recommended for promotion to Leading Seaman and, although demobilised on 20th January 1919, he rejoined the RNR and served until 1923. He was married to Catherine, née Macleod, and his later years were spent at 72 Seaforth Road, Stornoway.

Murdo Stewart
(Murchadh Iain Dhòmhnaill Iain)

27th June 1894 - 10th June 1969 (age 74)
9 Lower Bayble. Seaman RNR.
Service number 4437/A

Son of John and Chirsty Stewart (née Murray), Murdo had donned the RNR uniform on 17th September 1912, as the arms race in Europe escalated. He fished out of Peterhead and Stornoway and reported to HMS *Vivid* at Devonport on 2nd August 1914. He joined HMY *Rhouma* at HMS *Cyclops* two months later and was at HMS *Manco* (Stornoway) shortly after, from where he served on the yachts *Rhouma* and *Vanessa*. Late in 1915 he moved to HMS *Proserpine* (Lyness) and then to the cruiser HMS *Philomel* from 29th December 1915 until 4th September 1917. Murdo returned to serve at HMS *Victory* and HMS *Excellent* at Portsmouth. He then served at HMS *President III* and HMS *Vivid*. He

was demobilised from Devonport on 30th January 1919 and declined re-enrolment, after being seriously traumatised in the aftermath of the *Iolaire*'s sinking. Finding it difficult to cope with survivor's guilt after being questioned by relatives of those lost, he emigrated for Montreal, Canada on 17th June 1922 on the Canadian Pacific liner *Melita*. He found employment at Fort William, Ontario as a railwayman. He then married Bessie Thelia Carter in British Columbia in 1932 and they had twin daughters, Dorothy and Christina. He settled at Gibsons, where he became a fisherman.

Donald Macleod
(Dòmhnall Mhurchaidh Alasdair Iain Ruaidh)

11th August 1880 - 18th July 1961 (age 80)
11 Lower Bayble. Leading Seaman RNR.
Service number 2775/D.

Donald was the son of Murdo and Mary Macleod (née Macleod) and had enrolled in the RNR on 1st January 1905. He was rated Leading Seaman on 1st February 1917. He served throughout the war with HMS *Research*, an Admiralty survey vessel. In 1915 she was stationed at Portland, to be used as a depot ship for armed trawlers and she remained there throughout the war until paid off in August 1919. Donald was demobilised but re-enrolled with the same service number after 4th April 1919 and on 3rd November 1925 he received the RNR Medal for Long Service and Good Conduct. He had continued fishing out of Stornoway in this period and re-enrolled for a further period thereafter. He was a crofter fisherman, living at 8 Eagleton and married to Christina Macleod (née Macleod). He was interred at Aignish Cemetery.

Donald Macdonald

(Dòmhnall Rangach)

11th January 1881 – 14th December 1958 (age 77)

30 Upper Bayble. Seaman RNR.
Service number 16012/DA

Another veteran serviceman, Donald's date of birth is given as 28th December 1880 in naval records. He was the son of Norman and Mary Macdonald (née Mackay) and enrolled on 14th May 1917 at the RN Barracks in Stornoway. He served on HMT *Gloria* from HMS *Iolaire* (base) until his posting, on 15th January 1918, to HMS *Vigorous*, from where he was demobilised at Larne on 2nd February 1919. He was a fisherman who lost his wife Catherine, née Macleod, to peritonitis on 29th June 1934, when she was 41. Donald survived his wife by 24 years and was interred at Aignish Cemetery.

John Mackenzie

(Iain Chaluim Alasdair Uilleim)

28th October 1875 – 11th November 1955 (age 80)

51 Upper Bayble. Deckhand RNR.
Service number 3297/B

Born at 12 Back to Malcolm and Marion Mackenzie (née Macleod), John was a first cousin of 'Am Boicean'. His parents settled at 1 Aird and John married Chirsty Mackenzie on 30th January 1906. He was a full-time fisherman out of Stornoway, enrolling in the RNR on 1st April 1905. From the start of the war on 2nd August 1914 he was based at HMS *Pembroke* and he then left Chatham for the armed merchant cruiser HMS *Edinburgh Castle*, on which he served until 6th January 1918. Between then and the end of the war he served on HMS *Pembroke*, HMS *Hindustan*, HMS *Vulcan*, HMY *Boadicea II* and was at HMS *Pembroke* when he set out for leave on 31st December 1918. He was demobilised on 4th February 1919 from *Pembroke* and was later awarded the RNR Long Service and Good Conduct Medal. Post-war he was a merchant seaman and had three sons and two daughters, his wife sadly dying on 12th May 1928 aged 48. His son Alex was lost at sea in 1947. Later in life he moved to 60 Upper Bayble where he died in 1955.

Kenneth Macleod

22nd November 1878 – 19th March 1934 (age 55)

28 Swordale. Leading Seaman RNR.
Service number 3138/B

Son of George and Isabella Macleod (née Mackay), Kenneth joined up on 1st April 1905 and was promoted to Leading Seaman sometime after 1913. He fished out of Stornoway on various vessels and reported to HMS *Victory* from Fraserburgh at the first call on 4th August 1914. He served on HMS *Glory* for 18 months, first off the Canadian coast before escorting a convoy to the UK. She then went to Gallipoli and saw action there, then served off the Suez Canal before returning home for a refit. He was a naval gunner on the merchant vessel SS *Dalton* after training at HMS *President III* for three months. His base when he left for his New Year leave was HMS *Satellite*. A witness at the Public Inquiry, he described how he had been washed off the hawser when the *Iolaire* was stern first to the shore, but he was able to get ashore himself. He was demobilised on 30th January 1919 but re-enrolled in the RNR with service number 3013/D. He was the husband of Christina, née Macmillan, a general labourer through his working life, and died of heart problems only 15 years after the events at Holm.

STORNOWAY PARISH – Burgh and District

Norman Buchanan
(Tarmod Tharmoid Iain Tharmoid)

18th June 1898 – 12th July 1940 (age 42)

7 Branahuie. Signalman RNR.
Service number 14737/DA

Norman was the youngest of six sons of Norman and Mary Buchanan (née Morrison) and also had a sister. He entered service on 19th February 1917 and was a Signalman serving at HMS *Sphinx II*. He was serving on HMS *City of Perth* before and after the *Iolaire* disaster and was demobilised in February 1919. During the wreck Norman was swept out to sea, but fought back and came ashore at Newton. Norman died of tuberculosis at the Lewis Sanatorium. Three of his brothers emigrated to Canada.

Angus Macdonald
(Aonghas Theàrlaich)

6th November 1886 – 25th October 1942 (age 55)

51 Bayhead Street. Able Seaman RNR.
Service number 2712/A

Angus was born at Fivepenny, Borve, son of Charles and Chirsty Macdonald (née Smith). He moved to Stornoway from 17 Borve as a young man. He enrolled on 17th May 1910 and fished out of Stornoway. When war broke out he served initially at HMS *Pembroke*, then HMS *Ganges* and, from 18th November 1914 to the war's end, on the armed boarding steamer HMS *Duchess of Devonshire*. He was demobilised on 24th January 1919. The husband of Mary Macdonald (née Maciver), his full address was at 5 Mackenzie Buildings, in a close which was part of 51 Bayhead. He worked as a painter with Donald John Mackenzie, of 53

Bayhead Street, who owned that property. In 1939 he and his family moved to the then 21 Manor Park, later addressed as 36 Macaulay Road. Angus had two sons and three daughters. His grandson, Angus, son of Charlie Macdonald (Painter), became a master mariner.

Alexander Donald Maciver
(Alex Dan)

2nd January 1895 – 15th October 1941 (age 47)

42 Church Street. Deckhand RNR.
Service number 12120/DA

Alex Dan was a son of John and Catherine Maciver (née Macleod) and brother of Rev Malcolm Maciver (Crossbost). They also had two sisters. His father was a docker and had previously been a shoemaker. Alex Dan was on the staff of the Bank of Scotland when he joined up on 25th September 1916 and served at HMS *Iolaire* (base), HMS *Pembroke* from 21st October 1916, then he was at Gibraltar from 6th February until 27th May 1917. He then served at the west coast bases, HMS *Idaho* and HMS *Colleen* and survived the loss of the *Iolaire* after serving aboard HMD *Golden Effort* during the latter stages of the war. He was demobilised at Stornoway on 25th January 1919 and returned to civilian life, remaining single. He was living at 11 Garden Road in the town in 1941 when he was noticed missing since tea-time on Monday 13th October. Workmen recovered his remains on Wednesday 15th October at Battery Point — it was assumed he had fallen into the harbour in darkness and drowned. He had survived the *Iolaire* disaster but still succumbed to the fate of so many of his comrades, his body lying close to where they had been laid out for identification in January 1919. His death certificate does not reveal an occupation. His aged mother outlived him.

Angus Nicolson
(Aonghas Mhurchaidh Bhig)

17th April 1885 – 5th July 1958 (age 73)

25 Battery Park. Leading Seaman RNR. Service number 5136/B

Angus was the son of Murdo and Marion Nicolson (nee Macdonald), born at 24 Ranish, the eldest in a family of six — the family have his date of birth as 4th June 1884. He was a fisherman pre-war on the *Remembrance* (SY51) and others and settled, like many from Ranish, at the Battery in fishermen's holdings. The Battery area was part of Sandwick until it was subsumed into the Burgh in the 1930s. Angus enrolled on 14th November 1907 and was promoted to Leading Seaman 10 years later, on 12th November 1917. He left Stornoway for HMS *Cyclops* on 2nd August 1914. He went to HMS *Hecla*, then HMS *Fisgard* on 18th October 1914 and then reported to

HMS *Imperieuse* at Scapa Flow, a repair and training ship (ex-HMS *Audacious*). He remained there for the entire war. Coming home on leave on the *Iolaire*, he was able to survive partly because he knew the Holm rocks like the back of his hand and knew exactly where he was, while others struggled with the gale and darkness. Angus was the third or fourth man off the yacht and helped John F Macleod with the rope before directing others to the Stoneyfield farmhouse. He remained firm friends with John after the war. He walked home across Sandwick beach to the Battery at 5am, arriving home in his long-johns and a vest to where his wife Christina was nursing their fortnight-old daughter by the fire. He was demobilised at Thurso from HMS *Imperieuse* on 14th February 1919 but re-enrolled with the new service number 3619/D. Angus was a member of Lodge St Colm, No 1022, while in service at Longhope and affiliated at home in Stornoway to Lodge Fortrose, No 108, in the spring of 1919. After the war Angus fished with his vessels, the *White Rose* (SY413) and the *Handy* (SY2, scrapped in 1938), then survived the waters again as skipper of the *Lews Castle* (SY213), which sank near the Beasts of Holm on 4th January 1946. He later had the *Fountain* (SY563) before retiring from the sea. He was married to Christina, née Macleod, from Cromore, they lost two sons (Murdo and Angus) at sea in 1940 with the Merchant and Royal Navies.

ISLE OF HARRIS

John Mackinnon

24th April 1886 – 31st August 1924 (age 38)

Smithy Cottage, Tarbert.
Ordinary Seaman Royal Navy.
Service number J/75902

John was the son of Murdo and Flora MacKinnon (née Macphee) and was a law clerk at Lochmaddy when he married Christina Ann Ferguson, from Berneray, on 16th December 1913. He enlisted in the Royal Navy on 15th August 1917 for hostilities only, served at HMS *Vivid I* and was a crew member from 19th August 1918 on the cruiser HMS *Edgar*. He was 32 when he survived the wreck of the *Iolaire*, making it to the rocks alone thanks to his strong swimming skills. He then walked home from Stornoway, but the effort of survival badly affected his health — he was hospitalised and was too unwell to attend the Inquiry the following month. John was demobilised on 6th March 1919. He then moved with his wife to Uig in Skye and later became assistant to the factor of the estate there. His health never fully recovered and he died of pernicious anaemia just a few years later, leaving his widow and a daughter, Flora.

Robert Mackinnon

21st January 1881 – 23rd July 1967 (age 86)

Caw. Able Seaman Royal Navy.
Service number J/79050

Robert's birth date was given as 19th May 1882 in naval records. The son of Ann MacKinnon, he had been a fisherman and was with the RNVR before being engaged in the Royal Navy for hostilities only on 6th October 1917. After a spell at HMS *Vivid I*, he served to the end of the war with the Town Class light cruiser HMS *Dublin*. He was promoted to AB on 7th December 1917. During the traumatic night of New Year 1919, Robert helped John F Macleod to secure the rope at the rocks at Holm. He then had to endure the long trek home to Harris with John MacCuish and Alex Campbell after their survival. Robert was demobilised on compassionate grounds shortly afterwards. His later life was spent as a gardener at the Harris Hotel. He was married to Maggie, née Matheson and lived to a ripe old age.

Alexander Campbell
(Alaig Mòr)

2nd December 1892 – 6th December 1970 (age 78)

Plocropool. Able Seaman Royal Navy.
Service number J/57596

Son of Alexander and Marion Campbell (née Mackinnon) Alick was single and his birth date given as 3rd December 1893 in naval records. There were seven sons and four daughters in the family, plus an elder son by the father's first wife and the family included Marion Campbell, the noted traditional Harris Tweed hand weaver, dyer and spinner. Alick was in the Mercantile Marine pre-war and on a drifter with the RNVR when he volunteered for the Royal Navy, for hostilities only, on 26th August 1916. After HMS *Vivid I* he served on the modern battleship HMS *Royal Sovereign* from 29th January 1917 and was promoted to AB on 2nd November 1917. He was returning home on New Year leave when he decided, with a few

ISLE OF HARRIS

Harris men, to take the longer route via Stornoway rather than waiting for the next day's crossing to Harris — his brother John was on the *Sheila*, quite oblivious that his brother was on the *Iolaire*. Alick took two days to get home, having set off without any rest or treatment to walk home to Harris. He arrived home on the evening of Thursday 2nd January. His widowed mother and his sisters, Maggie Sarah and little Margaret (just three years old), would have been at home. Alick requested and received demobilisation on special compassionate grounds in February 1919. He was forbidden by the family from going to sea again. He lived in Glasgow for a spell post-war and then came home and rebuilt the family home with the help of his younger brothers. Thereafter, Alick helped in house building, worked as a fisherman, carpenter, and later a boat builder and repairer, which he continued until his health began to fail in the late sixties. He died at the County Hospital, Stornoway, and was interred at New Scarista Cemetery.

John MacCuish

13th May 1898 – 29th October 1934 (age 36)
17 Northton. Ordinary Seaman Royal Navy. Service number J/57555

John was the son of John and Catherine MacCuish (née Morrison). His birth date was given as 20th August 1898 in the naval records. He was an Ordinary Seaman in the Royal Navy after signing up on 23rd August 1916 for hostilities only. He served at HMS *Vivid I* at Devonport, then on the battleship HMS *Marlborough* for seven months, then back to HMS *Vivid I*. He joined the drifter HMD *Duthias* on 19th December 1917. She was based at HMS *Thetis*, then HMS *Vigorous*, and he left the drifter to go home, one of the Harris contingent who took the decision to travel home via Stornoway rather than wait a day in Kyle. He faced another 62 miles of road after reaching Stornoway straight from the wreck of the *Iolaire*. He could have left the service on compassionate grounds in February 1919, but served on at HMS *Vigorous* until his demobilisation on 25th March 1919, on special compassionate grounds. He was single and died at a very young age of tubercular meningitis.

MAINLAND – *Iolaire* crew members [listed alphabetically]

Ernest Reginald Adams
(Ernie)

17th January 1899 – 15th July 1974 (age 75)
Cardiff. Fireman Mercantile Marine Reserve.

Born at Sculcoates, Hull, Ernie was the son of Frederick James and Margaret Adams (née Mugridge). He had an elder sister and two younger brothers. He went to sea on a Hull trawler aged 13. His father was lost on a trawler and his mother died before the war, so he went to live with his married sister Isobel Jennings in Cardiff. He was one of the last to leave the stricken yacht *Iolaire* with Ramsay, climbing over the coal before getting onto deck. They leaped onto rocks, an unidentified island Petty Officer with them, as the yacht slewed round and made the leap possible. Ernie married Beatrice Morris in 1928 and worked as a furnace worker in a brickworks. He died at St David's Hospital, Cardiff. Ernie's son Ernest George passed on his father's account of the disaster and his son David visited Stornoway during his Royal Navy service.

James Smith MacLean
(Creel)

18th December 1879 – 23rd April 1961 (age 81)
Campbeltown. Deckhand Mercantile Marine Reserve.

James was the son of Neil and Sarah MacLean (née Smith). He was known as "Creel" in Campbeltown after he carried a creel as a wee boy for his mother as she gathered shellfish on the shore. His father died when he was just 14 and he was married on 23rd December 1904 to Euphemia, née Macaulay. He was a key witness at the Public Inquiry, having served on the *Iolaire*, when she was HMY *Amalthaea*, from 8th February 1916. Like the islanders, he did not like to talk about the tragedy at all, but his granddaughter Fiona McCallum recalled that her mother said he had no skin on his palms after the accident and that he was still uncertain, years later, whether a young lad that he had hauled onto the rocks beside him

was dead or alive. After the Second World War, he and his son Neil had a fishing boat called the *Amalthea* and they fished briefly out of Stornoway post-war. James also had shares in another boat, the *Mary MacLean*. When he visited Stornoway, around 1948, he was chary of going ashore, but somehow local men heard that he was at the harbour, came along the pier and invited him to join them. How they knew about him he did not know, but he called them all gentlemen. James was interred at Kilkerran Cemetery.

Duncan Griffiths Ramsay
(Griffiths)

24th May 1899 – 24th January 1981 (age 82)
Aberavon. Fireman Mercantile Marine Reserve.

Son of Duncan McTavish and Selena Margaret Ramsay (née Lindsay), Duncan's father was a master tailor from Stirling who had married a girl from Wrexham in North Wales. Duncan was born at Wrexham and had at least three brothers and three sisters. In the 1911 census he was listed as a barber assistant/schoolboy of 28 Marsh Street, Aberavon. He escaped from the wrecked *Iolaire* with the other fireman, Ernie Adams and lived for over 60 years after the disaster. He married at Portsmouth in 1922 to Florence Nightingale, then worked as a salesman and died at Shotton, near Wrexham.

MAINLAND – *Iolaire* crew members

Arthur Topham

2nd March 1892 - 6th January 1951
(age 58)

Kingston-upon-Hull. Trimmer RNR.
Service number 4165/TS.

Born at Newington, Hessle, to John
William (Jack) and Ruth Topham (née
Davison), Arthur was one of a family of
at least nine children. His father was a
railway fireman who later became a driver
and in 1911 young Arthur was working
as a dock labourer at Hull. He enrolled
to the RNR on 6th September 1915 and
became a coal trimmer, redistributing
the heaps of coal to keep the vessel trim
and supplying the firemen who shovelled
the coal to the boilers. After service at
HMS *Victory*, Arthur had been posted to
HMS *Iolaire* (base) and served on HMT
Armageddon from 28th April 1916. On the
night of the wreck Arthur had been loaned
to the *Iolaire* in Stornoway, as she was
under-crewed. He was demobilised from
Stornoway on 30th January 1919 and did
not serve again. He married a widow,
Bess Thompson, née Burton, in 1921 and
they had seven children. He was a fish
dock worker when he died at Hull.

Leonard Radford Welch

15th May 1894 - 23rd July 1969 (age 75)

Tapstay, Hereford. Telegraphist RNVR.
Service number 3577/Z.

Born at Lichfield to Henry and Ellen Welch
(née Thomson) of Glen View, Tapstay,
Leonard's father was a fishmonger,
poulterer and fruiterer. He had three
older brothers and, in 1911, was listed as
an apprentice ironmonger, but he was
an accountant when he enlisted, for
hostilities only, on 12th December 1915.
He became a naval telegraphist during
the war, serving at the bases HMS *Victory
VI*, HMS *Lady Blanche* (Tobermory), HMS
Pembroke and HMS *Brilliant*. He had
served at sea on HMY *Sabrina II* at HMS
Lady Blanche and on the Q-ship (decoy),
HMS *Barranca*, for a month in the summer
of 1916. He was posted to HMY *Amalthaea*
(*Iolaire*) on 1st February 1917. Married at

Hereford in 1923, his wife was Dorothy
Welch (née Perkins). He wrote an account
of his survival of the sinking of the *Iolaire*
in 1942. He was a travelling salesman in
his latter working life, living at 115 West
Malvern Road, Malvern and he died in the
Royal Infirmary, Ronkswood, Worcester.

James Edward Willder

5th October 1879 - 6th December 1945
(age 66)

Queenborough, Kent. Deckhand Mercantile
Marine Reserve.

James was the son of Frederick and Mary
Ann Willder (née Cole) and his father
was a fisherman on the census of 1901,
when the family lived at 29 High Street,
Queenborough. James married Florence
Jane Willder (née Eastman) at Milton,
Kent on 31st January 1914 when he was a
stevedore. He died at 1 Somerset Terrace,
Queenborough.

Chapter 8
In Their Own Words

"Ach an fheadhainn a chaill an cuid ann, lean e riutha.
Mar a bhithinn a' cluinntinnn aig m' athair, 'Cha d' fhuair mi
a-riamh air a dhol a chadal, oidhche le gaoth mhòr no muir
mòr ann, gun a bhith ag ùrnaigh airson luchd na mara'."[1]

"Then everything went upside down and there was nothing
but every man for himself.... I kept on swimming until I
reached the shore .... I couldn't get a grip or anything."[2]

AIR BÒRD

'S e Dòmhnall Macìomhair am fear a b' òige a shàbhail air an *Iolaire*. Rugadh agus thogadh e an Tolastadh bho Thuath. Cha robh e air a bhith anns a' Chogadh ach bliadhna gu leth. Fhuair e gu tìr, mar a fhuair a' chuid bu mhotha a shàbhail, air a' ròp a thug Iain Fionnlagh Macleòid ('An Mhurdo), à Nis, gu tìr.

Dòmhnall Macìomhair (Am Bèicear)

Uill, bha an turas math, ged a bha a' ghaoth mòr. An *Chief Officer* thug e dhuinn an saloon airson sìneadh ann; *first class saloon*. Bha ceathrar eile de bhalaich Tholastaidh còmhla riumsa nar sìneadh ann an sin – dà bhràthair, chaidh

ON BOARD

Donald MacIver was one of the youngest survivors of the *Iolaire*. He was born and raised in New Tolsta and had served in the war for only a year and a half. He reached the shore, like so many others who survived, on the rope that John Finlay Macleod ('An Mhurdo), from Ness, brought ashore.

Donald Maciver (Am Bèicear)

"Well, the journey was fine, although there was a strong wind. The Chief Officer gave us the saloon to rest in, the first-class saloon. There were four other boys from Tolsta resting with me there – two

an dithis a chall. Am fear a b' aosta dhe na bràithrean, 's iongantach mar do dh'èirich e, agus chaidh e a shealltainn dud a bha dol. Thàinig e agus thuirt e, 'Èirichibh! Èirichibh! Cuiribh oirbh ur brògan. Tha i gu bhith staigh', agus *bang*, bhuail i 's chaidh a h-uile càil *upside down*, chaidh a h-uile càil *flat*. Chaidh i aig *angle '45 degrees'*, agus fhuair mise chun an dorais, agus ged a fhuair mi grèim air an doras ach chan fhaighinn air fhosgladh. Bha càch a' breith air mo dhruim, h-uile duine ag iarraidh a-mach. Fhuair mi suas a-rithist agus chaidh mi tron uinneag. Chuir mi mo chasan romham agus chaidh mi a-mach, agus sin mar a fhuair mise air deic.

Nuair a fhuair mi air deic bha a h-uile càil a bh' ann a' dol an uair sin. Bha ròp aca air a deireadh, 's cha robh duine ga shàbhaladh, bha an *gap* cho beag, *gap* an deiridh. Nuair a bhuail ise chaidh i a-steach. Fhuair daoine aiste len casan tioram, fear Nis agus *crowd* eile. Thòisich i a-nise a' dol a-mach, agus bha a' muir a bha a' tighinn a-steach eadar i 's a' chreag, bha e na bu mhios' na bha e a-riamh. Thòisich iad a' 'minigeadh' gun 'sibhteadh' iad a' ròp *midships*. Bha mi fhìn dhan cuideachadh leis a' rop. Bha a' ròp shuas aig a' ghunna 's bha e air a chuibhligeadh ann a shin agus bha mi dha leigeil sìos thuc'. Thàinig aon, dhà, trì droch mhuirean, agus chaidh e seachad air a h-uile càil a bh' ann. Bhàth e daoine air deic, agus bha an deic an uair sin làn chuirp a-mach 's a-steach. Chrom mise sìos far an robh a' ròp, is cò bha sin ach fear à Tolastadh, Kenny Campbell, agus sheall e rium, agus dh'aithnich e mi. Ars' esan 'Fuirich gus am faigh sinn a' ròp air a chur ceart!' 'Chan fhuirich,' arsa mise, 'thoir dhòmhsa a' ròp, tha mi falbh'. Agus dh'fhalbh mi. Chaidh mi sìos agus bha mi an uair sin air tìr *right away*. Bhuail mi air tìr agus cha d' fhuair mi grèim, a-mach a-rithist. Chaidh mi a-steach, 's bha mi cantainn

sets of brothers, both were lost. The eldest of the brothers, he must have risen to see what was going on. He came and he said: "Get up! Get up! Put on your shoes. She's almost in." Then bang, she hit and everything went upside down, everything went flat. She went at a 45-degree angle and I got down to the door and, although I got a hold of the door, I couldn't get it open. The others were grabbing at my back, everybody wanting out. I got up again and got through the window. I put my feet before me and slid out, and that's how I got to deck.

"When I got to deck everything was happening there. They had a rope at the back, although no-one was being saved by it, the gap was too small, the gap at the back. When she hit she went inwards. Some got off with their feet dry, the one from Ness and a few others. She then started to slide out and the sea started to come in between the rocks and it was far worse than before. Then they started to plan on moving the rope 'midships. I was helping them with the rope. The rope was up at the gun and it was coiled there and I was passing it down to them. Then came one, two, three bad waves, and it went over everything. This drowned people on deck and then the deck was full of bodies washing in and out. I climbed down to where the rope was and who was there but Kenny Campbell from Tolsta and he looked at me and recognised me. He said: "Wait until I get the rope put right!" "I will not," I said. "Give me the rope, I'm away." And I left. I then went down and was on shore straight away. I hit the shore and I

rium fhèin, 'Uill, mur a faigh thu grèim tha thu dheth'. Chaidh mi steach a-rithist is fhuair mi grèim an uair sin agus thog cuideigin an-àirde mi, agus thuirt mi ris, 'An ruig am muir orm ann an seo?' agus thuirt e 'Cha ruig'. 'S e mac Dhòmhnaill Dholaidh à Col a bh' ann. Fhuair mise gu bàrr na creig agus 's iongantach mar do chaidil mi greiseag.

Dh'fhalbh mi à sin 's bha an *Iolaire* air 'blothaigeadh' suas nuair a dh'fhalbh mise. Ach nam biodh daoine air a thighinn leth-uair a thìde ron a siud bha iad air sàbhaladh tòrr. Ach an oidhche bh' ann, 's e bh' ann oidhche na Bliadhn' Ùire agus cha tug iad gèill dha duda bha a' dol air adhart.

Ghabh mise air adhart 's chunnaic mi solas. Cha robh fios agams' càite robh mi no càil eile, 's e bh' unnam ach balach òg. Cha robh mi a-riamh an taobh ud. Is chaidh mi suas is 's e taigh a bh' ann is bha a' ghaoth air aghaidh an dorais, 's thàinig dà nighean a-mach. Chaidh mi steach a sin is bha *crowd* nan sìneadh air an làr.

Thuirt mi ris a' bhoireannach, 'Cà' 'm beil sinn?' 'Tha,' ars' is', 'ann an Tolm'. 'Cà' bheil Tolm?' arsa mis'. 'Tha, air an rathad chun an Rubha'. 'Uill', arsa mise, 'ma sheallas sibh a' rathad dhòmhs' tha mis' a' falbh'. 'Chan eil', ars' ise, 'chan eil thu falbh idir. Cha dèan thu a' chùis'. 'Dè an ùine tha e?' 'Tha,' ars' ise, 'dà mhìle'. 'Cuir thusa nighean còmhla riumsa chun an rathaid'. Bha mi faireachdainn cho math. Chuir i chun an rathaid mi 's chuir mi dhìom mo dhà bhròig, 's e a' reothadh – cha robh mi fada gun a chuir mi orm iad!

Ghabh mi air adhart gus na thachair an '*life-saving*' rium; 's e eich a bh' aca. 'S thuirt am fear a bha ann an *charge* ris na balaich, bha balaich an Nèibhidh còmhla ris, *stretcher* fhaighinn, agus thuirt e riutha, 'Cuir air an *stretcher* e. *Take him to the depot*'. 'Oh' arsa mise '*you're going to no depot*

didn't have a grip and went back out again. I then went in again and I was saying to myself: 'Well if you have a grip, you're off.' I then went in again and had a good grip and somebody picked me up and I said to him: "Will the sea catch me here?" And he said: "It won't." That was Dòmhnall Dholaidh from Coll's son.

"I then got to the top of the cliff and I must have slept there for a little while. I left there and the *Iolaire* was blowing upwards by this time. But if people had come half an hour before this they would have saved many people. But the night it was, it was New Year's Eve and no one was taking any notice of what was going on.

"I went ahead and I saw a light. I had no idea where I was or anything else. I was only a young lad, I had never been this way. And I went up and it was a house and the wind was blowing on the door and two girls came outside. I went in the house and there was a crowd lying there on the floor.

"I said to the woman: "Where are we?" "You're in Holm." "Where is Holm?" I asked. "It's on the road to Point." "Well," I said, "if you show me to the road, I'm leaving." "You're not!" she said, "You're not leaving at all. You won't make it." "How long will it take me?" "It's two miles" she said. "You send a girl with me to show me to the road." I was feeling so well. She sent me to the road and I put off both my shoes. But the frost! It wasn't long until I put them back on!

"I continued until I met the life-saving. It was horses they had. And the one who was in charge of the boys said – the boys from the Navy were with him and he said: "Put him on the stretcher. Take him to the depot." "Oh!" I said *with me!' 'Where are you going*?' *'I'm going to Kenneth Street'*. Bha tè às a' bhaile againn fhìn a' fuireach a sin.

Nuair a dh'èirich mi làirne-mhàireach, thàinig fear an Nèibhidh, fear a bh' ann a *charge*, 's thuirt e gu feumadh sinn a dhol dhan *depot*; gu faigheadh sinn *duffle coats* agus aodach tioram mus deigheadh sinn dhachaigh. Bha aodach aig na daoine bha timcheall air a chuir a-steach thugainn. *'Alright,'* ars' esan ri fear eile, 'thig a-mach gu Anderson[3] is can ris a thighinn ann an seo le càr ann am mionaid'. Chaidh e a-mach gu Anderson agus thill e 's thuirt e gu robh na *'Cars booked for the New Year'*. Chaidh am fear mòr às a chiall agus thuirt e rinne *'Come on,'* ars' esan, agus dh'fhalbh e agus thug e do mhac Anderson e, 's thuirt e, *'It's not a request, it's an order! Take the car out and get them to Tolsta as soon as possible!'* B' fheudar dha a thoirt a-mach co-dhiù 's dh'fhalbh an càr leinne. 'S aig Griais bhris e sìos, na bheachd fhèin, agus bha sinne a-muigh a' coiseachd gus a slànaicheadh e an càr, agus dh'fhaighnich fear, 'Eil an càr briste?' 'Tha,' ars' esan, 'feumaidh meacanaig a thighinn à Steòrnabhagh'. 'Carson a chùm thu sinn?' Dh'fhalbh sinne, 's cha robh sinn càil ach air falbh nuair a bha e a' tionndadh. Seo rud a bha eadar e fhèin agus Anderson, *'Dump them on the road!'* Choisich sinn a Tholastadh ma-thà.

Bha sinne nar cadal, dòigheil gu leòr sa *first class saloon* nar sìneadh air a' làr ach an fheadhainn a bha an-àirde, an fheadhainn a bha *experienced*, daoine aosta, bu chòir dhaibh a bhith a' faicinn gu robh i ceàrr. Mo sheòrs-sa, cha robh *experience* againn a bhith a-mach 's a-steach à Steòrnabhagh. Nach e na daoine a b' aosta a chaill am beatha, daoine *experienced* a' smaoineachadh gun tigeadh rudeigin, ach an seòrsa agams' cha robh càil ach a' faicinn

"You're going to no depot with me!" "Where are you going?" "I'm going to Kenneth Street." There was a girl from our own village living there.

"When I woke up the next morning a man from the Navy, the one who was in charge, said that we had to go to the depot; that we would get duffle coats and dry clothes there before we went home. There had been clothes donated by the people around. "Alright," he said to someone, "go out to Anderson[3] and tell him to come here with a car in a minute." He went out to Anderson and he returned saying: "The cars are booked for the New Year." The boss was furious and he said to us: "Come on!" and he took him to Anderson's son and said to him: "It's not a request, it's an order! Take the car out and get them to Tolsta as soon as possible!" So he took the car out and left with us. And at Gress it broke down, or so it seemed and we were out walking until the car could be repaired and someone asked: "Is the car broken?" "Yes," he said, "I'm going to have to get a mechanic to come from Stornoway." "Why did you keep us?" We then left and we had only just gone before we saw him turning the car. This had been between himself and Anderson; "Dump them on the road!" And so we walked to Tolsta.

"We had been asleep, happy enough in the first-class saloon lying on the floor, but the ones who were higher up, the ones who were experienced, the older ones, they should have seen that she was off-course. My own kind, we had no experience coming in and out of Stornoway. Was it not the older ones who lost their lives, the experienced ones who thought that something would an cunnart mar a bha e agus faighinn às. Sin mar a tha mi a' smaoineachadh a chaill tòrr dha na daoine aost' am beatha…

Cha robh *panic* idir ann. Bha feadhainn eile a-nis 's bha iad a' *launchadh* an eathair. Bha fear à Tolastadh, Dòmhnall a' Bhrusaich, is bha e anns an eathar, agus dh'èigh an sgiobair, '*Don't launch that boat! I might get off. I'm going astern*'. Uill, 's e mise an aon duine thug an cunntas sin, gun tàinig facal bhon drochaid. Chaidh an t-eathar, chaidh i ceàrr, agus cha do shàbhail na daoine sin idir. Shàbhail Dòmhnall, fhuair e air ais…

Chaidh mise air ais an ceann cola-deug, fhuair sinn cola-deug *leave*, no deich latha. Agus nuair a chaidh mise air ais, bha iad an dèidh reic mo chuid aodaich agus a h-uile càil eile; bha mise air mo bhàthadh co-dhiù. Is thuirt mi ris an duine, 'Uill,' arsa mise, 'gheibh mi air ais.' '*Oh*, chan fhaigh. *There's a lot to be done now, there's a mix-up. You'll have to go to the Sailors' Home*'. Chaidh mise dhan an *Sailors' Home* agus bha mi ann dha na trì làithean, agus bhiodh an sgiobair, sean sgiobair a bh' orm, a' tighinn a choimhead orm a h-uile latha….

Càil san Amharc *BBC Radio nan Gàidheal.*
Preasantair Coinneach Macìomhair, 1986

come to save them? But my kind did not see anything but the danger as it was and to get out of it. That's why I think many of the older ones lost their lives.

"There was no panic at all. There were others now and they were launching the boats. There was one from Tolsta, Dòmhnall a' Bhrusaich, and he was in the boat, and the captain shouted: "Don't launch that boat! I might get off. I'm going astern." Well, I was the only one who heard this command, that any word came from the bridge. The boat, she went wrong, and those people didn't survive at all. Donald survived, he got back.

"I went back after two weeks – we had two weeks leave, or ten days. And when I got back they had sold my clothes along with everything else. I had been drowned anyway. And I said to a man: "Well!" I said, "I'll get them back!" "Oh, no you won't. There's a lot to be done now, there's a mix-up. You'll have to go to the Sailors' Home." I then went to the Sailors' Home and I was there two or three days and the captain, this old captain who was there, would come and check on me every day."

Càil san Amharc *BBC Radio nan Gàidheal.*
Presenter Kenneth Maciver, 1986

Iain Macillfhinnein ('Ain Geal)

'S ann às a' Chnìp an Ùig a bha Iain McIllFhinnein. Bha esan air a bhith air eathar eile air a robh an Iolaire, a bha stèidhichte a Steòrnabhagh 's a bha ri faire airson bàtaichean-aigeil timcheall air na h-Eileanan an Iar tron chogadh.

'S e a chaidh fodha tè ris an canadh iad an *Amalthaea*. Ach nuair a thàinig ise a Steòrnabhagh, chaidh sinne sìos gu Dundee, 's ghabh ise an t-ainm againn agus ghabh sinne an t-ainm aicese. Bha sinn ann an Dundee nuair a sguir an Cogadh. À Dundee chaidh sinn sìos a Phortsmouth, agus bha sinn aig acair aig deireadh an *Victory* ann an sin. Sin nuair a chaidh mise dhachaigh.

Bha leithid de shluagh a' tighinn a-nuas. Cha chreid mi nach robh trì treànaichean ann, agus aig an stèisean bha iad gar cur chun an *Iolaire*, beagan chun an *Sheila* – bha an *Sheila* a-staigh an taobh eile dhan a' chidhe. Bha feadhainn anns a' Chaol an oidhche ron a siud nach d' fhuair dhachaigh

John Maclennan ('Ain Geal)

John MacLennan was from Kneep, Uig. He had previously been a member of the crew on the first HMY Iolaire, which was based at Stornoway until 1918 and was hunting submarines around the Western Isles throughout the war.

"The boat that sank was originally called the *Amalthaea*. But when she came to Stornoway, we went down to Dundee and she took our name and we took her name. We were in Dundee when the war finished. From Dundee we went down to Portsmouth and we were at anchor there at the end of the *Victory*. That's when I went home.

"There was a huge crowd coming up. I think there was three trains there, and at the station they were sending us to the *Iolaire*, some to the *Sheila* – the *Sheila* was in at the other side of the quay. There were some people in Kyle the night before who didn't get idir. Bha i a' tighinn a-nall am Minch agus bha a h-uile càil *alright*, agus bha a' ghaoth air ar cothrom a-nall. 'S ged a bha an oidhche a' fàs fiadhaich, bha i a' dèanamh oidhche mhath dheth. Agus bha h-uile duine nan sìneadh anns a h-uile àite as an faigheadh iad, gus na bhuail i air na Biastan, Biastan Thuilm.

Nuair a bhuail i dh'aithneachadh a h-uile duine gun robh i air bualadh, agus cha robh càil an uair sin ach a h-uile duine a-mach air a shon fhèin. Chaidh tòrr dhan an òigridh às an rathad.

Bha na h-eathraichean a' dol nam pìosan cho luath. Cha robh innte ach rud beag, is cha robh eathraichean innte a bheireadh leatha an ceathramh cuid dhe na bh' innte, ged a b' e oidhche mhath a bhiodh ann.

Fhuair mise dhi air a' ròp, nuair a cheangal mi a' ròp ris an *davit* air a meadhan. Cha do rinn mi càil ach leum a-mach air a' mhuir. Cha robh brògan orm, càil ach cas-ruisgt'. Bha tòrr aca air a' ròp nuair a bha mise ann, ach nuair a bha iad a' tighinn chun an t-snaim bha e mar gum biodh iad a' 'missigeadh' a' ròp dòigh air choreigin, leis an t-snaim a bh' air a' ròp. Bha an dà ròp air a cheangal ri chèile. Chaidh a' chiad fhear, chaidh a cheangal ro ghoirid, agus chaidh ròp eile a cheangal, agus bha iad gan call fhèin ann an sin. Cha d' fhuair mòran air tìr air a' ròp ud, air a meadhan idir, bha i dìreach a' dol fodha.

Mar a bha tuinn na mara, chitheadh tu iad nam bàthadh anns na tuinn. Bha balach còmhla riumsa à Siadar. Tha mi creids' gur e snàmhaiche cho math 's a bha ann an Eilean Leòdhais. Chaidh e a-mach air a' mhuir trì turais agus thàinig air tilleadh. Chan shnàmhadh duin' ann, bha an fhairge na cùis-eagail. Balach à Càrlabhagh, bha e ag ràdh gun rug e air a bhràthair agus gun chaill e e, gun tug an fhairge bhuaithe e. Sin am

home at all. Coming along the Minch everything was alright, and the wind was on our tail on the way over. And although the evening was windy, she was making a fine night of it. And people were lying down wherever they could, until she hit the Beasts, the Beasts of Holm.

"When she hit everyone realised she had struck and there was nothing then but every man for himself. A lot of the young perished.

"The boats were breaking apart so quickly. She was only a small yacht and the boats could only take about a quarter of those on board, even if it were a good night.

"(I got off) on the rope, when I tied the rope to the davit in the middle. I just leapt out onto the sea. I had no shoes on, nothing but bare feet. There were a lot of them on the rope when I was there, but when they were coming to the knot it was like they were missing the rope in some way, with the kind of knot that was on the rope. The two ropes were tied together. The first one was tied too short, and so another rope was tied to it, and they were losing themselves on that. Not many came ashore on that rope, she was just sinking.

"The way the waves were, you could see them drowning in the waves. There was a boy with me from Shader. I'm sure he was the best swimmer on the Isle of Lewis. He went out onto the sea three times and had to return. No one could swim in it, the waves were terrifying. There was a boy from Carloway, he was saying that he grabbed onto his brother and that he lost him, that the waves pulled him away. That's the balach a bha còmhla rium s' a' tighinn. Nis ma bha i air 'slipigeadh' a-steach an taobh eile bha i air a bhith *alright*.

Bha e duilich coiseachd bho far an deach i às an rathad gu taigh Thuilm. Bha e làn bruthaichean 's conasg. Bha nàdar reothaidh ann is bha bonn mo chasan air am milleadh agus bha mo bhroilleach air a mhilleadh a' dol air tìr. Uill, sin nuair a chaidh an Court of Enquiry a chuir air ais. Bha tòrr dha na survivors leòint' agus cha b' urrainn dhaibh a bhith aig a' Chourt of Enquiry.

'S e am Post Office a' chiad àite a dh'aithnich mi ann an Steòrnabhagh. Nuair a ràinig mi am Post Office chuala mi nighean a' gal shìos an t-sràid, agus chaidh mi às a dèidh is dh'aithnich mi cò a bh' ann. 'S e nighean às an taigh anns am bithinn a' fuireach ann an Steòrnabhagh a bh' ann, tè Maga MacKay, agus làirne-mhàireach 's e aodach a bràthair a bh' orm.

Bha *crowd* againn nar suidhe aig gàrradh mu choinneamh an Imperial, 's ann ann a bha staff an Nèibhidh an uair sin. Thàinig an Admiral Boyle gar coimhead, agus stad e dha mo choimhead agus dh'fhaighnich e dhomh '*Do I know you?*'. '*Oh*,' arsa mise, '*You should*'. Dh'fhaighnich e dhomh cò a bh' ann agus thuirt mi ris gur e *coxswain* an *Iolaire* bh' ann. '*Oh*,' ars' esan '*Thank God you're saved for one. Wait there. I'll send a car over in a quarter of an hour, send you home.*' Rinn e sin, agus chuir e a Chalanais sinn, agus chuir e *launch* à Calanais gu àite ris an can iad Tràigh Theinish air an Riof, agus choisich sinn às a sin dhachaigh chun a' Chnìp. Agus choinnich piuthair dhomh mi os cionn an taigh, agus bha i cho *cheery* is cho toilichte airson gun tàinig sinn is a h-uile càil, agus bha mi ag ràdh rium fhèin, 'Cha d' fhuair iad a-mach càil'. Agus chaidh mi a-steach, is bha mo mhàthair anns a' leabaidh, agus chaidh mi suas far an robh i agus dh'fhaighnich

boy who was with me coming. Now if she had slipped in the other way she would have been alright.

"It was a difficult walk from where she struck to the house in Holm. It was rough and full of hillocks in gorse. There had been a frost and my feet were injured and my chest had been injured coming ashore. Well, that's when the Court of Enquiry was put back. Many of the survivors had been injured and they couldn't attend the Court of Enquiry.

"The Post Office was the first place in Stornoway I recognised. When I reached the Post Office I heard a girl crying down the road and I went after her and recognised who it was. It was a girl from the house where I had been living in Stornoway, Maga MacKay, and the next day it was her brother's clothes I was wearing.

"A crowd of us were sitting at the garden in front of the Imperial Hotel, that's where the Navy staff were at the time. Then Admiral Boyle came to see us, and he stood watching me and asked: "Do I know you?" "Oh," I said, "you should." He then asked who it was and I said to him it was the coxswain of the *Iolaire*. "Oh!" he said, "thank God you're saved for one! Wait there. I'll send a car over in a quarter of an hour, send you home." He did that and he sent us to Callanish and the launch sent us to a place they call Theinish Beach at Reef and from there we walked home to Kneep. And one of my sisters met me at the house and she was as cheery and as happy that we had come home and everything and I was saying to myself: "They haven't found anything out." And I went inside and my mother was in bed and I went up to where she was and she asked me: "Iain," i dhomh, 'Iain,' ars' is', 'Dud a thachair?' 'Och,' arsa mis', 'Cha do thachair càil'. 'Thachair,' ars' ise, 'Bha fhios agams' air bho chionn bhliadhnaichean gu robh e a' dol a thachairt.'

Thàinig fios chun a' Post Oifis a Mhiabhag ach cha do chuir e an-àird' e idir. Cha do chuir e air an uinneag no càil e, is cha robh fhios aca air chun a' làirne-mhàireach. Sin nuair a thòisich iad a' tighinn a-steach thugamsa. Is bha fear às na h-Ùigean, fear ris an canadh iad Càdham, is bha mhac, chaidh a bhàthadh ann an Steòrnabhagh. Is an ceann sia seachdainean chaidh e a Steòrnabhagh agus feumaidh gur e bruadarachadh a rinn e, agus chaidh e far an robh an Nèibhidh ann an Steòrnabhagh ach am faigheadh e a-null gu leithid seo a loch air na Lochan, ach am faigheadh e corp a mhic. Is bha dùil aig an Nèibhidh gur ann às a chiall a bha e. Co-dhiù, dh'fhalbh iad leis agus fhuair e corp a mhic far an robh e ag ràdh, an ceann sia seachdainean an dèidh dhan an *Iolaire* a dhol às an rathad.

Bha e duilich a-rithist ann an Steòrnabhagh a' làirne-mhàireach. Bha e dona, dona. Bha Steòrnabhagh dìreach uabhasach; cuirp a' tighinn a-nuas air na cairtean is na làraidhean leis a h-uile càil.

Thàinig mi fhèin is bràthair-cèile dhomh a-mach aiste, ach chaidh deichnear a bhàthadh. Chaidh sianar a bhàthadh à Crabhlasta, dithis à Breànais, dithis às na h-Ùigean, sin na chaidh a bhàthadh.

B' fheàrr leam gu robh mi air tilleadh air ais an taobh às an tàinig mi, a bharrachd air a bhith dhan coimhead, a' ceasnachadh mun deidhinn, is bha fhios agam glè mhath gu robh iad bàthte ach cha b' urrainn mi sin a ràdh riuthasan.

Dealan-Dè *BBC Radio nan Gàidheal.*
Preasantair Coinneach Macìomhair, 1987

she said, "what has happened?" "Oh," I said, "nothing has happened." "Something has," she said, "I knew this was going to happen years before it did."

"News came to the Post Office in Miavaig but he never put it up, he didn't put it in the window or anything and no one knew about it until the next day. That's when people started to come to talk to me. And there was a man from Uigean, a man they called Càdham and he had a son, he was drowned in Stornoway. And after six weeks he went to Stornoway and he must have had a vision and he went to the naval base in Stornoway so he could get over to this specific place in Lochs so he could collect his son. And the Navy thought he was mad. Anyway, they went with him and they found his son's body exactly where he said it would be, six weeks after the *Iolaire* sunk.

"It was difficult in Stornoway the next day. It was terrible, terrible. Stornoway was just awful – bodies coming up on the carts and lorries.

"Myself and my brother-in-law survived, but ten were lost. Six were drowned from Crowlista, two from Breanish, two from Uigean, those were who were lost.

"I wish I could have gone back to where I had come from, instead of having to watch them, being asked questions, and I knew fine well that they had drowned but I could not say that to them."

Dealan-Dè *BBC Radio nan Gàidheal.*
Presenter Kenneth Maciver, 1987

Iain Fionnlagh Macleòid ('An Mhurdo)

'S ann à Port Nis a bha Iain Fionnlagh Macleòid ('An Mhurdo). Esan a' chiad duine a fhuair gu tìr le ròp, agus a shàbhail a' chuid bu mhotha a fhuair aiste. Mar chomharra air a ghaisgeachd air an oidhche ud chaidh duais Comann Rìoghail Daonnachd, Bonn Lloyd agus Sgrìobhainn Carnegie a bhuileachadh air le Urrasairean Maoin Ghaisgich Carnegie ann an 1921.

Bha an rud cho duilich. Feagal orm duine sam bith a ghoirteachadh timcheall air an rud, a bhith ag ùrachadh nì a chaidh seachad, air dhòigh, ged nach deach e seachad do chuid. Mar a thachair, mar a tha fios aig a h-uile duine air an eachdraidh, bha an oidhche rudeigin fiadhaich.

Theàrr i i fhèin suas air a' chreig, is thiormaich i i fhèin 's cho luath 's a chaill ise 'buoyancy', mar a chanas iad, chaidh i air a cliathaich às spot, agus thuit mòran de rudan a-mach aiste aig an àm a bh' ann an sin.

Chanainn gun tug i cairteal na h-uaireach, mar sin. Air mo shon-sa dheth, cha robh càil a dh'fhios agam càite robh i, gus na thurchair dhomh a dhol suas dhan toiseach, is chaidh 'rocket' a

John Finlay Macleod ('An Mhurdo)

John Finlay Macleod ('An Mhurdo) was from Port of Ness. He was the first person to reach the shore with a rope, and he saved half of those who survived. He was awarded the Royal Humane Society award, Lloyd's Medal and the Carnegie Parchment, presented by the Trustees of the Carnegie Hero Fund In 1921, for his heroic efforts that night.

"The situation was so difficult. I was scared of hurting anyone, with every new thing that passed, in a way, although it did not pass for some. As it happened, as many who know the history, the evening was quite windy.

"The *Iolaire* raised herself onto the rock and she dried herself so quickly that she lost buoyancy, as they say, she went on her side straight away, and many things fell out of her then.

"I would say she took about a quarter of an hour like that. Speaking for myself, I had no idea where she was, until I happened to go to the front, and a rocket was sent up.

chuir an-àirde. Chunnaic mi am *beacon*, agus bha mi eòlach gu leòr air a' *bheacon*, agus dh'aithnich mi gur e Biastan Thuilm a bh' ann, agus bha fhios agam leis a sin, nach robh an tìr fad às, ged a bha i doirbh, agus an fhairge dona.

Ann an ceann ùine ghabh i a-steach air a cliathaich ann an sin, gun a theann i gabhail dhi fhèin mu na creagan mu dheireadh.

Thòisich an ùpraid an uair sin, is tha mòran de nithean an sin nach urrainn do dhuine sam bith a chuimhneachadh, gu h-iomlan, cionnas a bha e. Is bha an oidhche cho doirbh agus cho dorch is nach fhaiceadh duine nì sam bith. Bha h-uile duine a' feuchainn an nì a b' fheàrr a b' urrainn 's a b' aithne dha. Bha freastal air cùl an nì, dha na shàbhail co-dhiù.

Cha robh càil de dh'ùpraid ann, rud a bhiodh nàdarrach gu leòr, a h-uile duine coimhead a-mach air a shon fhèin, 's airson chàich. Airson rud sam bith a b' fheàrr a b' urrainn dhaibh a dhèanamh.

Thurchair dhòmhsa nam inntinn an loidhne, a' *'heaving line'*, mar a chanas iad, a thoirt leam na mo làimh, agus leum mi a-mach air a deireadh, airson feuchainn am faighinn air tìr. Cha robh dùil 'am gu robh a' chreag cho doirbh 's a bha i. Ach nuair a ràinig mi an toiseach bha a' chreag bhos mo chionn, agus thug sùthadh na mara a-mach air ais mi, ach nam bithinn air bualadh air aghaidh na creig sin, cha robh càil air mo shon. 'S chaidh mi an uair sin na b' fhaide air falbh ann an sùthadh na mara na bha mi bho thoiseach. 'S nuair a chaidh trì suailichean mòra seachad, an tritheamh tè, dh'fhalbh mi roimhpe, agus bha mi na bàrr, gus na chrìochnaich i mi air uachdar a' stalla gun deach mi bho thoiseach, agus chaidh mo bhroilleach a bhualadh suas air ann an sin. Sin mar a fhuair mise air tìr, agus ghlèidh mi an loidhne fad na tìde. Agus nuair a fhuair mi suas ann an sin agus am muir seachad, shuidh mi ann an sin, gus an tàinig aon cheathrar air tìr air an loidhne chaol sin, gus na dh'èigh mi gu robh i ro ghoirid 's ro chaol is nach dèanadh i a' chùis, iad ròpa garbh a chuir oirre. Chaidh ròpa garbh a chuir oirre an uair sin. Thàinig an còir air tìr air a' ròpa sin.

I then saw the beacon, and I was familiar enough with the beacon, and I recognised that they were the Beasts of Holm, and I knew from that that the shore was not far off, although it was difficult, and the sea was bad.

"After a while she slipped onto her side there, until she eventually tightened herself there onto the rocks.

"Then the uproar began and there are many situations at this time that people completely don't remember how they were. And the evening was so difficult and so dark that no one could see a thing. Everyone was trying their absolute utmost. There was providence behind it all, for those who were saved anyway.

"I made up my mind to take the heaving line in my hand and I jumped out of the back with it, to try and get to the shore. I didn't expect the rock to be as difficult as it was. But when I reached the bow the rock was above me, and the current pulled me back, but if I had struck that rock there would have been nothing for me. I was then pulled further back with the current than I had been before. And when three large waves went over me, the third one, I went ahead of that one, and I was on top, until I ended up on the steep rock that I initially went for, and I was thrown on my chest up onto there. That's how I got to shore, and I held onto the line the entire time. And when I got up there and the sea subsided I sat there, until four people crossed to shore on that thin line, until I shouted that the line was too short and too thin and that she wouldn't make it, that they had to attach a thicker rope. Then a thick rope was attached. The rest came ashore on that rope.

A' chiad duine a thàinig air tìr air an loidhne, 's e fear Iain Murray 's tha e a' fuireach air a' Bhac, ris an can iad 'An Help. Tha cuimhne agam glè mhath nuair a thàinig e air tìr an toiseach, chuir e a dhà làimh mu m' amhaich is mi na mo shuidhe.

BBC Radio nan Gàidheal
Riochdaire Fred Macamhlaigh, 1961

"The first man who came ashore on that line, it was a man called Iain Murray who lives in Back, a man they call 'an Help'. I remember very well when he came ashore first, he put two hands around my neck as I was sitting down."

BBC Radio nan Gàidheal
Producer Fred Macaulay, 1961

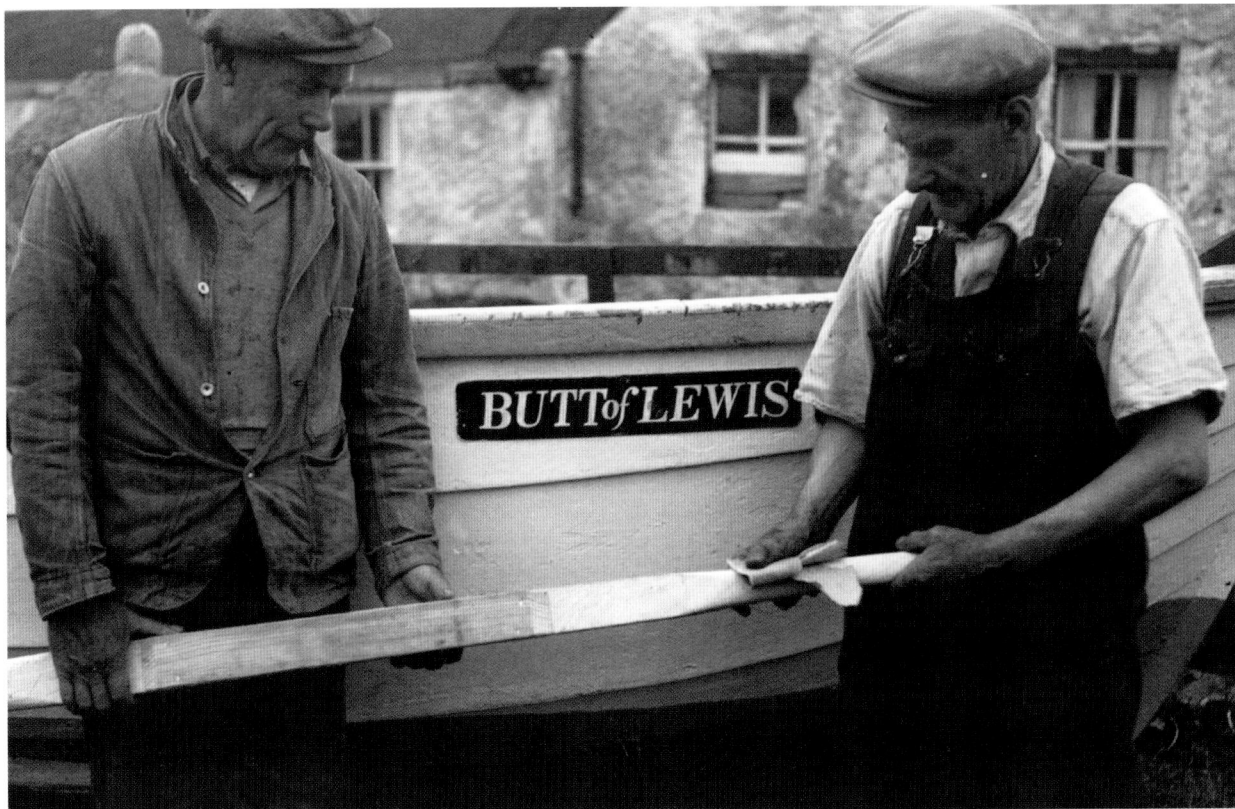

Am Patch (Donald Morrison) and Iain Mhurdo (John Finlay Macleod) pictured in the 1970s.

Dòmhnall Moireasdan (Am Patch)

Bha Dòmhnall Moireasdan (Am Patch), às a' Chnoc Àrd ann an Nis, fichead bliadhna agus mìos nuair a bha e a' tilleadh dhachaigh air an Iolaire. Fhuair Dòmhnall aiste beò às dèidh dha an oidhche a chuir seachad ann an crann-deiridh an Iolaire, agus an còrr dhen t-soitheach air a dhol fodha. B' e an aon duine a thàinig air tìr air a' chidhe ann an Steòrnabhagh.

Cha robh panic idir ann. Cha robh mòran de rud sam bith ann. Chaidh rocaid suas agus sin a' chiad uair a chunnaic mise an talamh, mi fhìn. 'S e oifigear a chur suas i. Chaidh na solais, a' chuid bu mhotha dhiubh, às ach nuair a chaidh a' rocaid suas chunnaic mi e agus dh'aithnich mi gur e deise oifigear a bh' air. Chan eil fhios agam cia mheud a chaidh suas – chaidh dhà na trì, ach cha robh sin a' dol a dhèanamh feum. Bha e do-dhèanta faighinn thuic' far a robh i. Bha an fhairge uabhasach. 'S ann bu mhotha a dh'fhàs a' ghaoth a h-uile car agus chaidh i dìreach uabhasach mu dheireadh. Chaidh i alongside agus a toiseach

Donald Morrison (Am Patch)

Donald Morrison (Am Patch), from Knockaird in Ness, was 20 years and a month old when he was returning home on the Iolaire. Donald survived having spent the night on the mast of the Iolaire, with the rest of the vessel having sunk. He was the only one who came ashore at the harbour in Stornoway.

"There was no panic at all. There wasn't much of anything. A rocket was launched and that was the first time I saw ground, myself. It was an officer who launched it. The lights, most of them, went out when the rocket was launched, and I saw and recognised that it was an officer's uniform he was wearing. I'm not sure how many were launched – three or four anyway, but they were going to be of no help. It was impossible getting to them where she was. The sea

dìreach taobh an taigh-sholais. 'S bha a' chreag mar gum biodh a' falbh bhuat agus ag èirigh, agus nuair a thigeadh na suailichean mòra bha iad ga togail suas air a' chreig. Bha i an uair sin a' tuiteam sìos le fuaim a shaoilinn-s' a chluinneadh tu ann an Steòrnabhagh.

Chunnaic mi fear a thug air tìr a' ròp, cha robh càil a dh'fhios agam cò bh' ann an uair sin. Chunnaic mi e agus bha mi ag aithneachadh gu robh rudeigin aige, eil fhios agad. Cha robh mi coimhead a' ròp idir ach bha mi ag aithneachadh air an t-snàmh aige. Chaidh e suas ann am bàrr suaile ri aghaidh na creige, gu math fada, agus nuair a chaidh a' muir a-mach a-rithist thuit e sìos agus chaidh e a-mach fon a' *stern* aice. Cha robh dùil agams gu faicinn e tuilleadh co-dhiù. Ann am mullach an ath shuaile mhòr a thàinig chun an deireadh aice chunnaic mi e a' tighinn a-steach a-rithist, agus 's ann an uair sin a dh'aithnich mi gur e ròp a bh' aig an duine bh' ann, ròpa caol air choireigin, agus 's e Iain Macleòid às a' Phort a bh' ann. Fhuair e grèim air a' chreig an uair sin, agus tharraing e suas a' ròp, agus dh'èigh e riutha air ais. 'S e ròpa caol a bh' ann, 's mathaid gur e '*heaving line*' a bh' ann. Dh'èigh e riutha ròpa trom a chuir air agus 's ann air a' ròp a fhuair a h-uile duine b' aithne dhòmhs' air tìr.

Mu dheireadh bha sinn ag èigheachd a' ròpa thoirt a-nuas mu meadhan, eil fhios agad, gu robh i a' dèanamh rudeigin de '*bhreakwater*' shuas mu meadhan, ach thàinig mi a-nuas agus bha parsail agam ann an sin ga ghleidheadh, chan eil fhios carson. Ach sheall mi sìos air an deic 's chunnaic mi muir a' tighinn tron an deic aice 's dh'fhàg mi am parsail, dol a dhèanamh air a' ròp.

Thàinig dà mhuir uabhasach a-steach an dèidh a chèile air an deireadh aice, agus chuir mise mo làmh air a' *bhoat-deck* mun a' rèile. Uill, 's e duine a dh'fhalbh le mo bhonaid; chaidh duine seachad air mullach mo chinn 's cha robh mi air càil ach m' anail a tharraing ceart nuair a thàinig an ath thè às a dèidh is chan

was terrible. The wind was getting stronger all the time and she just went horrendous by the end. She went alongside and her front was just directly towards the lighthouse. And the rock felt like it was receding and rising and when the big waves came they were lifting her up onto the rock. She was then crashing down with a noise you would hear in Stornoway.

"I saw the man who took ashore the rope, I had no idea who it was at that time. I saw him and noticed that he had something, you know. I wasn't seeing the rope at all but I could recognise from his swimming. He was thrown up by the wave onto the rock, quite far in, but when the sea receded he fell in again and went underneath her stern. I didn't think I would see him again anyway. On top of the next large wave that came to her stern I saw him coming up again, and it was then that I realised it was a rope he had, a thin rope of sorts, and he pulled up the rope, and shouted back to them. It was a thin rope, perhaps a heaving line. He shouted to them to attach a heavier rope and it was on this rope that everyone I know who survived came ashore.

"By the end we were shouting to take the rope up towards the centre, you know, that she was acting as a kind of breakwater in the middle, but I came along and I had a parcel I was keeping, I don't know why. But I looked down on the deck and I saw the sea coming through the deck, and I left the parcel and made for the rope.

eil cuimhne agams' air càil tuilleadh gus an tàinig mi air uachdar faisg air a' chrann-deiridh aic'. Ach tha cuimhne agam nuair a bha mi 'struggligeadh' anns a' mhuir gun tàinig ròpa caol na mo làimh, agus bha mi smaoineachadh a-riamh gur e tè dhe na *flag halyards* a bh' ann. Thòisich mi a' tarraing air agus thug e chun a' chrainn mi, agus fhuair mi grèim air na '*riggings*', 's ghabh mi suas ann. Nuair a chaidh mi suas pìos sheall mi air mo chùlaibh – bha i an uair sin a' listeadh a-mach chun a' *phort side* – agus bha a h-uile duine a bh' innte a' 'struggligeadh' a sin dìreach air uachdar na mara. Thàinig balach a-nuas às mo dhèidh fhìn cuideachd agus chunnaic mi suaile mhòr a' tighinn agus ghreas mi orm mas beireadh i air, agus nuair a sheall mi air mo chùlaibh a-rithist bha e fhèin an dèidh falbh cuideachd. Cha robh duine agam an uair sin ach mi fhìn. Ach ann an ceann greis, fhuair mi mo fhradharc, eil fhios agad. Sheall mi taobh an toisich aic' agus bha dithis anns a' chrann-toisich feidhir mar a bha mi fhèin; an dàrna fear cho fad 's a gheibheadh e agus am fear eile aig a chasan. Chan urrainnn dhòmhsa innse a-nis dè an ùine a bha iad ann. Bha ise a-nis, ged a bha i an dèidh a dhol sìos, nuair a thigeadh an t-suaile mhòr a-steach, bha e ga sadadh suas air a druim, 's bha i an uair sin a' dol sìos a-rithist air aon taobh, 's bha e a' breith oirre mar sin a h-uile trup.

'S ann mar sin, a' breith air an t-suaile sin nuair a thàinig i, a chuala mi brag uabhasach agus thàinig na h-*ariels* – 's ann gu h-àrd a bha na h-*ariels* – thàinig iad a-nuas air mo cheann. Agus bha job agam a' faighinn às na uèirichean sin. Agus nuair a sheall mise a-rithist chun an toisich bha an crann an dèidh falbh, is na daoine. Chan fhaca mise càil tuilleadh.

'S ann timcheall air uair sa mhadainn a chaidh i sìos. Bha mi a' cuimhneachadh air mo mhàthair 's rudan mar sin. Bha mi ag èibheachd ainm mo bhràthair greis mus deach i

"Two bad seas came in one after the other at the stern and I put my hand on the rail on the boat deck. Well, a man took away my bonnet. A man flew over my head and I had only just managed to take a breath when another came after him and I have no memory of anything else after that until I reached the deck at the stern mast. But I do remember struggling in the sea until a thin rope came into my hand and I was always thinking that it was one of the flag halyards. I started to pull and it took me to the mast and I got a hold of the riggings and I lifted myself up there. When I had climbed a bit I looked behind me – she was then listing out to the port side – and everybody was struggling there on the sea. A boy came up after me and I saw a large wave rushing towards us so I hurried up before the wave caught him, but when I looked behind me again he had gone. I had no one there then but myself. But after a little while I got my sight, you know. I looked towards the front and there were two on the forward mast just as I was; one of them as high as he could go and the other at his feet. I can't now tell you how long they were there for. She was now, although most of her had sunk, when a large wave came, she was thrown up on her back and she was then going down again on the same side and that was catching people every time.

"It was like that, catching that large wave when she came, that I heard this awful bang and the aerials – the aerials were above us – they came down on my head. And I had difficulty getting out of those wires. And when I looked again towards the front the mast had disappeared and the people. I didn't see anything else.

sìos, an dèidh dha falbh sìos dhan an deireadh, 's cha d' fhuair mi *answer*. Bha mi cinnteach às gu robh e air fear dhan feadhainn a leum a-mach. Chan urrainn dhut a bhith smaoineachadh air mòran ann ach dìreach gu bheil thu caillt.

Bha staoidh agam as gach làimh agus bha àit' eile ann anns an robh *ring* timcheall air agus bha cas agam air gach taobh dheth. Agus 's e an aon rud a bha dha mo chumail gun mi tachdadh, nuair a chithinn an t-suaile mhòr a' tighinn bha mi a' cur m' aghaidh air a' chrann 's grèim agam air a' staoidh. Bha e a' cur seachad na h-uimhir orm. Sin uireas a bh' agams de dhìon.

Tha cuimhn' agam, 's bidh, air a bhith ann gu latha – cha robh mi smaoineachadh gu faighinn às beò an dèidh sin, ged a bha mi ann – ach bha thàinig an latha 's a chunna mi tìr bha muir tòrr na b' fheàrr – fhuair mi beagan de chofhurtachd bhon uair sin. Chunna mi 'trawler' 's soitheach beag a' tighinn le dà eathair, tè slaoda'ris gach tè. Smaoinich mi gur ann a' coimhead air mo shon, gu robhas an dèidh fios chur gu robh mi ann co-dhiù, ach bha muir cho dona 'n uair sin 's gu robh mi cantainn rium fhìn, gu robh e cunnartach gun deigheadh iad às an rathad. Bha muir a' briseadh air na sgeirean, agus bha e briseadh dona an uair sin – beul an latha – ach timcheall eadar sin agus deich uairean, thòisich e dol sìos – a' chiad eathar a thàinig, thill i mas do ràinig i mis'. Bha mise ag ràdh rium fhìn gu robh mi na bu shàbhailt' far an robh mi, ged a thigeadh i. Thàinig fear eile a-steach air mo làimh cheàrr – chun taobh deas dhiom – dh'èigh e rium am b' urrainn dhomh thighinn a-nuas – bha 'stay' os mo chionn, 's sìos air mo bheulaibh – cha b' ann sin bha grèim agams' idir. Thuirt mi ris nan tugadh e an t-eathar eadar a' 'stay' 's an crann, gun tiginn a-nuas. Thàinig iad a-nall leath, 's thug iad timcheall i 's bhacaig iad a-steach i, 's nuair a chunna mi i fèir tighinn fodham, leum mi air a' 'stay' 's ann am broinn

"It was around one o' clock in the morning that she sunk. I was remembering my mother and things like that. I was shouting my brother's name before she went down, after he went down to the back and I didn't get an answer. I'm certain he was one of the ones who jumped out. You can't be thinking about much except that you are lost.

"I had a stay in each hand and there was another place where there was a ring and I had a foot on each side. And the one thing that was keeping me from choking, when I would see a large wave coming I was pressing my face against the mast and grabbed a hold of the stem. This was passing most of it by me. That's all the protection I had.

"When the day broke, I began to see the land; the sea had subsided and was a lot calmer. I felt my hopes rising again. Then I saw a trawler and two small boats approaching, but the sea was still not calm enough for them to get near and I remember thinking it was too dangerous and that they would also sink. The sea was pretty rough at daybreak, but between then and 10 a.m. it seemed to subside a bit. The first boat attempted to come near when I hung on, but it had to turn back. I then thought I was safer where I was, than trying to get to that boat. Then the other boat tried and came nearer to my left side. They shouted to me "Can you clamber down?". I said, "If you can manage to get the boat between the mast, where I am and a stay that protrudes further out, I will try". They came round and then backed her in and when I just saw her coming near, I jumped on to the stay and mionaid, bha mise na broinn, 's chuir e làmh timcheall orm. Fhuair sinn fàth mhath dhà-rìreabh – chaidh mo thoirt dhan t-soitheach a thàinig a-mach leis an eathar – Lieutenant Wenlock.

Thug iad air tìr a Steòrnabhagh mi agus tha cuimhne agam fhathast gur ann air Number 2 a thàinig mi air tìr. Cha robh càil ann ach gun dhìrich mi an staidhre. Cha do dhìrich mi i gun beagan cuideachadh. Thug iad an uair sin dhan an Imperial Hotel mi, is bha mi ann an *state* a bha garbh. Cha robh càil annam ach dìreach an deò agus chuir iad a dh'iarraidh an dotair. Thuirt e, 'Tha thu dol suas dhan an ospadal as spot!' agus am b' fheàrr leam branndaidh no uisge-beatha. Cha robh dragh agamsa. Chan eil cuimhne agam dè thug iad dhomh. Thàinig fear às a' sgìr' againn fhìn, fear dha na postan a bh' ann à Suainebost agus thug e suas dhan ospadal mi. Bha mi ann an sin timcheall air dà latha. Cha robh iad airson mo leigeil às idir ach thàinig mo pheathraichean a-nall agus chan fhalbhadh iad às m' aonais. Cha robh càr fhèin ann an uair sin ach ablaichean. Cha do ràinig e leams' ach Lionail co-dhiù agus 's ann air èiginn a choisich mi dhachaigh.

Dealan-Dè *BBC Radio nan Gàidheal*
Preasantair Coinneach Macìomhair 1987 agus 'The Going Down of the Sun / Dol Fodha na Grèine', Acair 2014

in a moment of time I was aboard and they were so glad, that I was embraced in their arms. The Skipper was called Lieutenant Wenlock.

"I remember still that they took me ashore in Stornoway on the Number 2 pier. I had nothing left but to climb the stairs. I needed some help to climb them. They then took me to the Imperial Hotel and I was in a terrible state. I had nothing left in me and then they sent for the doctor. He said: 'You're going up to the hospital straight away!' and what would I prefer, brandy or whisky? I didn't care. I don't remember what they gave me. A man from my own district then came, one of the post men from Swainbost, and he took me to hospital. I was there for around two days. They didn't want to discharge me at all but my sisters came over and they didn't want to leave without me. There were no cars around then except wrecks. We got to Lionel anyway and it was with great difficulty that I walked home."

Dealan-Dè *BBC Radio nan Gàidheal.*
Presenter Kenneth Maciver 1987 and 'The Going Down of the Sun / Dol Fodha na Grèine', Acair 2014

Raibeart Macfhionghain (Na Hearadh)

Thuirt mise ri Calum, thuirt mi ris, "Oh,' arsa mise, 'tha sinn gu bhith a-steach". 'S chuir sinn umainn, oillsgin, 's bha sinn nar suidhe shuas, as an toiseach, deiseil airson steapadh aist', agus thionndaidh mi agus arsa mise, 'A Chalum,' – bhithinn a' spòrs an còmhnaidh ris – 'tha sinn gu bhith air a' chladach ann a seo'. 'Ach,' ars' esan, ' 's ann tha thus' do mhuinntir na Hearadh…" Bhiodh e a' spòrs an còmhnaidh rium…

Chaidh a h-uile càil a bh' ann *upside down* 's cha robh càil ach a h-uile duine a' dèanamh air a shon fhèin. Sheall mi gach taobh dhìom agus cha robh sgeul agam air Calum, agus rinn mi suas. Cha do ràinig mi an drochaid idir, ach bha *lifebelt* ann a sin. Thug mi leam e 's bha e agam. Thòisich na geòlaichean dha lowereadh 's thòisich an fhairge dham bristeadh.

Robert Mackinnon (Harris)

"I said to Calum, I said "Oh, we're almost in!" And I put on my oilskins and we were sitting up at the front, ready to step out and I turned to Calum and I said: "Calum" – I was always teasing him – "We're almost on the shore here!" "Ach," he said, "You just come from Harris!" He was always joking with me...

"Then everything went upside down and there was nothing but every man for himself. I looked to each side but I couldn't see Calum and I made to go up. I didn't reach the bridge at all, but there was a lifebelt there. I took it with me and I had it. Then they started to lower the lifeboats but the waves were breaking

Na geòlaichean ri taobh 's thòisich iad a' tighinn às na h-eathraichean.

Agus nuair a thug mi sùil, bha fear ann an sin is e ag èigheachd. A-nis cha robh sgeul agam air a' bheag an uair sin ach am fear sin agus, 'Seo,' arsa mise, 'siud.' Thilg mi a' *lifebelt* bhuam 's chuir mi dhìom na b' urrainn mi agus sheas mi air a' rèile, agus bha mi faicinn a' chladaich ceart gu leòr, a' muir a' bristeadh air. Bha mi smaoineachadh gum buannachainn co-dhiù gu tìr, ach cha dèanainn mòran ma tha, an taca ri feadhainn eile. Bha snàmh agam gun teagamh agus leig mi mi fhìn a-mach an uair sin ann a sin agus chùm mi chun a' chladaich 's b' fheudar dhomh tilleadh air falbh. Cha robh mi faighinn grèim no càil. Thill mi air falbh agus chuir mi m' aghaidh sìos seachad, agus nuair a ràinig mi an cladach bha mi ann an sin, *stuck*.

BBC Radio nan Gàidheal.
Riochdaire Fred Macaulay ,1961

them apart. The lifeboats were beside us and people were coming out of them.

"And when I had a look there was a man there and he was shouting. I couldn't see the wee one then so I said to myself 'That's that.' I threw the lifebelt off me and threw off all that I could and I stood on the rail and I could see the shore quite well, the sea breaking off it. I thought to myself that I could reach the shore anyway, but I couldn't do much, compared to the others. No doubt I could swim and so I leapt out there and I kept on swimming until I reached the shore, until I had to return back. I couldn't get a grip or anything. I receded and I put my head down, and when I reached the shore I was there, stuck."

BBC Radio nan Gàidheal.
Producer Fred Macaulay, 1961

AIR TÌR
ON SHORE

Katie Watt (née Nicleòid)

Cha robh Katie Watt ach sia bliadhna a dh'aois nuair a chaidh an Iolaire *air na creagan. Bha i a' fuireach air a' Bhataraidh ann an Steòrnabhagh, agus bha h-athair a' tilleadh air oidhche na Bliadhn' Ùir 's e ag obair air an* Sheila. *Chunnaic ise na cuirp a' tighinn air tìr thairis air na làithean às dèidh sgrios an Iolaire.*

Bha mi sia bliadhna is rugadh 's thogadh mi aig a' Bhataraidh agus bha fhios againn gu robh an *Iolaire* a' tighinn a-steach. An oidhche sin thàinig *cousin* dhuinn à Nis, mac le m' antaidh, Dòmhnall Bàn Dhòmhnaill Eachainn, à Lional, agus thàinig e a-null a choinneachadh a bhràthair, Tarmod, a bha gu bhith air an *Iolaire*. Thàinig e sìos thugainn mar a b' àbhaist is ghabh e a shuipear còmhla rinn, is bha sinne nar cloinn is chaidh an oidhche seachad. Thuirt e gu robh an *Iolaire* a' tighinn a-steach 's chaidh mo mhàthair a-mach chun an dorais leis. Oh mo chreach an oidhche a bh' ann, cho fiadhaich, gaoth mhòr is uisge. Co-dhiù chaidh sinne dhan a' leabaidh, agus chaidil sinn. Ach ann an ceann ùine dhùisg sinn is grogadh uabhasach aig an doras, is bha mo mhàthair an-àirde – bha

Katie Watt (née Macleod)

Katie Watt was only six years old when the Iolaire *struck. She was living at the Battery in Stornoway, and her father was returning home on New Year's Eve on the* Sheila. *She saw the bodies being washed up on shore in the days after the* Iolaire *tragedy.*

"I was six years old and I was born and raised on the Battery and I knew that the *Iolaire* was coming in. That night a cousin of mine from Ness, a son of my auntie's, Dòmhnall Bàn Dòmhnall Eachainn, from Lionel, came over to meet his brother Norman, who was to be on the *Iolaire*. He came to our house as usual and he had his supper with us and we were just children and the evening passed. He said that the *Iolaire* was coming in and my mother went to the door with him. Oh my, the night was awful! So windy and a heavy rain. Anyway, we went to bed and slept. But after a while we woke with a terrible knocking at the door, and my mother was up – my father was on the *Sheila*, and she wouldn't be going to bed until m' athair air an *Sheila*, agus cha bhiodh i a' dol dhan an leabaidh gun tigeadh e. Chuala sinn i a' dol chun an dorais is cò bha seo ach Dòmhnall Bàn is e ri gal is ri èigheachd, is cha robh i dèanamh '*head no tail*' dha dè bha e a' feuchainn ri innse dhi. Co-dhiù thàinig e a-steach is cha robh càil aige ach an *Iolaire* is chaidh i às an rathad. Co-dhiù thàinig sinne a-nuas a' staidhre, is bha fhios againn gu robh rudeigin a' dol air adhart, ach cha robh fhios againn dè a bh' ann, ach bha fhios againn gur e rudeigin uabhasach a bh' ann.

Anns a' mhadainn thuirt mo mhàthair rinn, nuair a bha sinn a' gabhail ar bracaist, 'Nise, fuirichibh timcheall air an taigh an-diugh. Na teirigibh air àrainn a' chladaich oir chì sibh rud ann nach còrd ribh'. 'S ann air a' chladach a bhiodh sinn a' cluich, clann a' Bhataraidh gu lèir. Bha gainmheach àlainn shìos an siud, 's ann ann a bhiodh a h-uile duine a' dèanamh a's a' mhadainn. Is nuair a fhuair sinne a-mach, bha a h-uile duine a' dèanamh air a' chladach, is dh'fhalbh sinn sìos a sin gu lèir. Ach nuair a ràinig sinn, mo chreach, cha tèid an sealladh tha siud..., cha deach e a-riamh às mo chuimhne.

Bha bho chladach a' Bhataraidh a-null a Shanndabhaig dubh le cuirp dhaoine, is bha na suailichean a bha a' tighinn a-steach, bha iad a' sadail nan cuirp suas air a' chladach air muin na bha sin de chuirp. Agus bha bonaidean a' seòladh air a' chladach, is bha daoine a shnàmh air tìr 's a bh' air am brògan a chuir dhiubh agus pàirt dhen aodach. Nise, shnàmh tòrr air tìr a-null a Shanndabhaig agus chaidh iad a-steach a thaighean an sin, ach bha iad a' tighinn air tìr aig a' Bhataraidh agus, oh mo chreach, thòisich mo bhràthair- cha robh e ach trì bliadhna is mise sealltainn às a dhèidh – thòisich e 'Mammy! Mammy! Mammy!' agus thòisich sinne a' sgreuchail, agus chaidh sinn dhachaigh.

Cha robh facal aig duine, cha robh gàire, is bha na boireannaich a' falbh bho thaigh gu taigh. Bha plaid' air a h-uile boireannach, feidhir mar gum biodh iad a' dol gu

he arrived. We heard her going to the door and who was there but Donald 'Bàn' and he was crying and wailing, and she wasn't making heads nor tails of what he was trying to tell her. Anyway, he came in and all he could say was the *Iolaire* and that she had struck the rocks. Anyway, we then came down the stairs and we knew that something was going on, but we had no idea what it was, but we knew that it was something terrible.

"In the morning my mother said to us, when we were having our breakfast: "Now, you stay around the house today. Don't go near the shore because you will see something there that you will not like." It was on the shore that we always played, all the children around the Battery. There was beautiful sand down there, it's where everyone made for in the morning. And when we got out of the house everybody was making for the shore and so we all went down there together. But when we arrived, my goodness, that sight, it never went out of my memory.

"From the shore at the Battery all the way over to Sandwick was black with bodies, and the waves that were coming in, they were throwing the bodies up onto the shore on top of all of these bodies. And there were caps floating on the shore and the people who had swam to shore and had thrown off their shoes and part of their clothes. Now, many swam over to Sandwick and went into houses there, but they were coming ashore at the Battery and my goodness, my brother – he was only three years old at the time and I was looking after him – he started "Mammy! Mammy! Mammy!" And then we started screaming, and we went home.

"No one had a word to say, there was no laughter and the women were going from house to house. Every woman taigh-fhaire. 'S thàinig m' athair dhachaigh an oidhche sin, ach thuirt e nuair a dh'fhàg iadsan an Caol gun dh'fhàg an *Iolaire* romhpa. 'S ann nuair a thàinig iad a-steach a' chaladh Steòrnabhaigh – chuir iad na *passengers* air tìr – 's ann an uair sin a chuala iad gu robh an *Iolaire* air a dhol air Biastan Thuilm. Agus thill iad a-mach an uair sin agus rinn iad cobhair cho math 's a b' urrainn dhaibh. Thàinig tòrr air tìr air a' *Sheila*, agus cha chreid mi nach robh dà latha mus tàinig m' athair dhachaigh. Thòisich an uair sin na daoine leis an robh na seòladairean, thòisich an cuideachd a' tighinn dhan iarraidh. Bha iad shìos air a' chladach, agus thòisich iad gan toirt suas chun a' Bhataraidh, chun na *Barracks*, agus 's ann anns na Barracks ann an sin a bhiodh balaich a' Nèibhidh a' cur a-steach drill RNVR airson na bliadhna. 'S ann a sin a bha am *mortuary*, is thug iad na bha sin de sheòladairean suas. Agus nuair a chaidh an 'identifyigeadh' bha na h-athraichean is na bràithrean is na teaghlaichean a' tighinn dhan iarraidh. 'S e each is cairt a bh' aig a h-uile duine, is bha sinne nar seasamh aig geat a' Bhataraidh a' coimhead am *parade* a bha seo a' dol sìos a h-uile latha, chanainn gu robh cola-deug no trì seachdainean. Agus an latha seo chunnacas m' uncail a' dol seachad is Tarmod aige sa chairt, is bha *Union Jack* air a h-uile cist. Is chaidh sinn dhachaigh agus dh'innis sinn dha mo mhàthair gu faca sinn Dòmhnall Eachainn a' dol dhachaigh le Tarmod. Is bha i ri gal is thuirt i cho taingeil 's a bha i gun d' fhuair iad a chorp. Nise, sin a' chuimhne a tha agamsa air an *Iolaire*, 's ann tro shùilean leanabh, ach tha e cho ùr nam inntinn an-diugh 's a bha e an latha ud. Is am feagal a chuir e orm an uair sin, is am bròn a bha air a h-uile duine timcheall. Am bròn, bha e dìreach feagalach.

An Iolaire BBC Radio nan Gàidheal.
Riochdaire Annella Nicleòid, 1999

had a blanket around her, just as if she was going to a wake. And my own father came home that night, but he said by the time they had left Kyle the *Iolaire* had left before them. It was when they got into the harbour in Stornoway – they put the passengers ashore – that was when they heard that the *Iolaire* had struck the Beasts of Holm. And then they returned again and tried as best they could to help. Many people came ashore on the *Sheila* and I believe there was two days before my father came home.

"Then the relatives of the sailors started to come. They were down on the shore and they started to take them up to the Battery, to the barracks and it was in the barracks there that the Navy boys would put in an RNVR drill for the year. That was where the mortuary was and they took all of those sailors up there. And when they were identified the fathers and the brothers and the families would come and collect them. It was a horse and cart that everyone had and we would stand at the Battery gate watching this parade every day, I would say for two or three weeks. And one of those days I saw my uncle going past and Norman with him in the cart and there was a Union Jack on every coffin. And we went home and told our mother that we saw Donald 'Eachainn' going home with Norman. And she was weeping and said how grateful she was that they had found his body. Now, those are my memories of the *Iolaire*, through the eyes of a child, but it is still so new in my mind today as it was then. And the fear it put through me then, and the sadness that everyone around us felt. The sadness, it was just terrifying."

An Iolaire BBC Radio nan Gàidheal.
Producer Annella Macleod, 1999

Mòr Nicleòid (Mòr Bhrù)
(née Nic a' Ghobhainn)

'S ann à Iarsiadar am Beàrnaraigh a bha Mòr Nicleòid (Mòr Bhrù). Bha i ceithir bliadhna a dh'aois nuair a chaill i a h-athair, Coinneach Mac a' Ghobhainn, air an Iolaire. *Thuirt i gu robh i a' faireachdainn gu robh sgòth mhòr dhubh a' leantainn airson bliadhnaichean às dèidh an sgrios. 'S i màthair Mòr a' bhanntrach mu dheireadh dhan an* Iolaire *a bha beò.*

Bha mise glè bheag. 'S e aon uair tha cuimhne agam air m' athair fhaicinn. Bha e aig an taigh air *leave* goirid mus do dh' èigheadh an t-sìth agus bho nach robh e aig an taigh ach an aon uair sin, ri mo chuimhne-sa, 's e strainnsear a bh' agam air. Cha robh mi, mar gum biodh, a' gabhail ris mar gur e m' athair a bh' ann idir.

Ach a-nise an t-àm a chaidh an *Iolaire* air creagan Thuilm, chan eil cuimhne agam air an fheadhainn a thàinig leis an naidheachd idir. Ach tha cuimhne agam air banàbaidh a

Marion MacLeod (Mòr Bhrù)
(née Smith)

Marion Macleod (Mòr Bhrù) was from Earshader, Bernera. She was four years old when she lost her father, Kenneth Smith, on the Iolaire. *She said that she felt that there was a great dark cloud over the community for many years after the tragedy. Marion's mother was the last surviving widow of the* Iolaire *disaster.*

"I was quite small. I only remember seeing my father once. He was at home on leave shortly before he was called to war and since he wasn't at the house but that one time, to my memory, I saw him as a stranger. I wasn't, in a way, seeing him as my father at all.

"Now at the time the *Iolaire* struck the rocks at Holm, I have no memory of the ones who came with the news at all. But I remember a neighbour coming into the house and the clothes that my mother had laid out for

thighinn a-steach, agus an t-aodach a bh' aig mo mhàthair airson gun cuireadh e uime e nuair a thigeadh agus thog i leatha a h-uile pìos aodaich a bha sin agus chaidh i suas leis do rùm eile. Bha sin a-nise dà latha às dèidh dhan an Iolaire a dhol air na creagan. An dàrna latha dhen a' Bhliadhn' Ùir 's ann a ràinig am fios sinne. Cha robh an uairsin *telephones* no càraichean ann, agus thug fios an ùine sin na bailtean, na b' fhaide a-muigh co-dhiù bho Steòrnabhagh, a ruighinn. Agus thòisich an uair sin daoine a' tighinn a-steach agus cha robh mise aig aois gun tuiginn dè bha air tachairt no carson a bha iad a' tighinn a-steach. Agus chaidh corp m' athair fhaighinn agus aithneachadh, agus tha cuimhne agam air latha an tiodhlacaidh, nach fhaca mi uimhir de dhaoine cruinn a-riamh aig an taigh 's a chunnaic mi an latha sin. Ach bha mi cho òg is nach robh mi a' tuigsinn dè an t-adhbhar a bh' air na bha seo de dhaoine a bhith ann.

Bha an duilgheadas cho mòr, agus an call cho mòr, agus bha e mar gum biodh e air tadhal air a h-uile baile, agus 's e daoine òg a bhiodh ann gu lèir. Dh'fhàs sinn suas anns an sgòth dhubh a bha seo. Ged a bha sinn cho òg nuair a thachair e agus nach robh tòrr tuigs' againn dhà, mar a bha sinn a' fàs aosta 's ann bu mhotha a bha sinn ga thuigsinn, agus bha sinn, mar gum biodh, ag èirigh suas fon an doilgheas a bha seo.

Cha d' fhuair iad seachad air a-riamh, agus bha mi mothachadh nuair a bha mi fàs suas gu robh ceangal aca ri chèile, na banntraichean sin, ged nach aithneachadh iad a chèile ron a sin, is ged a bha iad à sgìrean eadar-dhealaichte. Bha an uair sin na sgìreachan, mar gum biodh Ùig is Nis, na h-àiteachan sin, Taobh Thall nan Loch, bha iad fada bho chèile agus bha, mar gum biodh, an t-uabhas a bha seo air tachairt, cheangal e na sgìrean sin ri chèile, gu h-àraid na

my father, that he would have put on as soon as he arrived, she gathered them all up and put them up into another room. This was now two days after the *Iolaire* had struck the rocks. It was the second day of the New Year that the news reached us. At that time there were no telephones or cars and it took that long for the news to reach these villages, the ones that were quite far out of Stornoway. Then people started to come into the house and I wasn't at an age where I could understand what had happened or why these people were coming in. And my father's body was found and identified and I remember the day of the funeral, that I had never before seen as many people together at the house as I saw that day. But I was so young that I couldn't understand what the reason was for this, that there were so many people.

"The struggle was huge and the loss was so big and it was as if it were having an impact on every village and it was all young people. We grew up under this dark cloud. Although we were so young when it happened and we had such little understanding of it, as we were growing older we were beginning to understand this more and it was as if we were growing up under this dark sorrow.

"They never got over it and as I was growing up I began to understand that they each had a connection to one another, these widows, although they had not known each other before this, even though they lived in different districts. At this time the districts, such as Uig and Ness, those places, South Lochs, they were so far from one and other, and this tragedy was, in a way, bringing these districts together, especially the young

banntraichean òga, – agus 's e banntraichean òga a bh' annta – cheangal e ri chèile iad, ann an dàimh air choireigin a bha sònraichte dhan tubaist sin fhèin.

Agus bhithinn a' cluinntinn bho dh'fhàs mi na bu mhotha 's bho thàinig tuigse thugam gur h-iongantach gu robh duin' innt' – 's e seòladairean a bh' innt' gu lèir – nach stiùireadh a-steach gu Steòrnabhagh i sàbhailt' nam biodh sin air fhàgail an urra riutha. G' e bi dè a chaidh ceàrr an oidhche sin.

Agus nuair a chuimhnicheas mi air ais 's ann a shaoileas mi gur ann a bhathas a' fuireach bho bhith bruidhinn air; bha e cho duilich a bhith bruidhinn air. Bha an cogadh air sguir is bha an aoibhneas cho mòr gu robh sìth ann agus gu robh na daoine a' tighinn dhachaigh agus gun tàinig sin orra, mar gum biodh, mar chlach às an adhair, gun dùil ris.

'S ann a dh' fhèumas sinn a ràdh, 'Thachair e, agus feumaidh sinn gabhail leis'. Aig amannan bidh e glè ùr dhomh fhathast. A h-uile Bliadhn' Ùr a bha a' tighinn timcheall cha robh sinn a-riamh mar dachaighean eile, a bha a' dèanamh subhachas aig a' Bhliadhn' Ùr, bhon 's e a bha a' tachairt cuimhneachan air bàs m' athair, agus cha robh subhachas na chois, 's e bha na chois bròn.

An Iolaire BBC Radio nan Gàidheal.
Riochdaire Annella Nicleòid, 1999

widows – and they were indeed young widows – it tied them together in a relationship that was special to that tragedy.

"And I would hear from when I was growing up that it's extraordinary that there were so many there – they were all sailors – that could have safely steered her into Stornoway had it been left to them. Whatever went wrong that night.

"And when I remember back I do think people were hesitant to speak about it; it was so difficult to discuss it. The war was over and there was such joy that there was peace and that everyone was returning home and then this happened to them, so to speak, like a rock from the sky, without expecting it.

"What we have to say is: 'It happened, and we have to accept it.' At times it can be still quite raw for me. Every New Year that came around we were never like the other houses, who would be celebrating the New Year, because we would be remembering our father's death, and there was no celebration around it, but only sadness."

An Iolaire BBC Radio nan Gàidheal.
Producer Annella Macleod, 1999

Peigi Nicillìosa (née Moireach)

*'S ann à Lìonal a Nis, a bha Peigi Nicillìosa. Bha i na nighean
bheag nuair a chaill i a h-athair air an* Iolaire. *Bha cuimhne
mhath aice air an ullachadh a bha a màthair a' dèanamh anns
an dachaigh airson fàilte a chuir air an athair, agus mar a bha
i fhèin agus a bràithrean cho mòr a' coimhead air adhart ris.*

A' chiad chuimhne a th' agams air m' athair 's ann na mo
shuidhe air stòl beag agus a' leughadh, a' gabhail an Leabhair,
agus bha e a' cur ìompaidh orm a bhith còir is a bhith solt. An
ath chuimhne a tha agam 's e na mo sheasamh air beulaibh
an taigh againn fhìn agus e ann an deis ann. Tha mi creids'
gur e an t-aodach a bh' air cho annasach, gun rinn sin fhèin
làrach air m' inntinn. Ach chan eil cuimhne agams air a' chòrr
mu dheidhinn, gu pearsanta, fhaicinn. Ach an ath chuimhne
a th' agam 's ann an oidhche a bha e a' tighinn dhachaigh.
Bha triùir bhràithrean agam; bha dithis na bu shine, is am
fear a b' òige cha robh e ach dà bhliadhna, is bha mise

Peigi Gillies (née Murray)

*Peigi Gillies was from Lionel, Ness. She was a young
girl when she lost her father on the* Iolaire. *She
remembered well the preparation her mother made
to welcome her father back and how she and her
brothers were so looking forward to his return.*

"The first memory I have of my father was when I was
sitting on a small stool and reading, taking the books
[family worship] and he was telling me to be quiet
and to sit still. The next memory I have is of myself
standing at the door of our own house and my father
in a suit. I'm sure it was how strange his clothes were
to me, that that left a mark in my memory. But I have
no more personal memories of him after that. But
the next memory I have is of the night he was due to
return. I had three brothers; two were older, and the
youngest was only two years old, and I was between

eadar 3 agus 4. 'S chaidh leigeil dhuinn a bhith an-àirde gun tigeadh m' athair. Bha duine às dèidh duine againn a' dol a-mach a shealltainn aig ceann an starain ach am faiceadh sinn an robh solas càr a' tighinn a-nuas mullach Thàboist agus dh'fheumainns' mo *thurn* fhaighinn còmhla ri càch. Agus tha cuimhne agam air a sin, nuair a bha an *turna* agam a' tighinn, cho luath 's a bha mi a' ruith a-mach, a' coimhead 's a' coimhead is cha robh càil a' tighinn. Chan eil cuimhne agam air a' chòrr dhen oidhche sin.

Anns a' mhadainn làirne-mhàireach bha sinn an-àirde agus mo mhàthair a' dèanamh ar bracaist dhuinn agus bha balach beag an ath-dhoras, co-aoisean ri mo bhràthair Tarmod, an dàrna balach againn, fear mu 7 bliadhna, agus bha iad an còmhnaidh còmhla, is 's e Tarmod a bh' air fhèin, Tarmod Morrison, Tarmod Plò bhiodh ac' air. Agus thàinig Tarmod, is bha taigh a' Phoilis dìreach trì taighean sìos taobh eile an rathaid is bha e a' coimhead *crowd* dhe na fireannaich ann a sin is bha e gan cluinntinn a' bruidhinn. Bha fhios aige gu robh ar n-athair a' tighinn, agus bha e a' cluinntinn rud dha na bha na fireannaich ag ràdh. Agus ruith e mar a bheatha suas dhan an taigh againne agus thàinig e a-steach, agus thuirt e, 'Tha na fireannaich aig ceann na sràide ag ràdh gun tàinig fios gun deach an t-soitheach anns an robh Iain a' tighinn air na creagan a-raoir agus gun deach na daoine a bhàthadh'. Nise, tha cuimhne agam am balach ag innse seo, ach dè bha e a' ciallachadh anns an àm, cha do thuig mi.

Bha bràthair-màthar agam thall ann an Stèinis, Murdo Morrison, agus bha esan, tha e coltach, a' lorg nan cladaichean mar a bha iomadach fear dha leithid, agus thathas ag innse dhomh gu robh trì seachdainean. Nise, fhuair m' uncail corp m' athar, agus rinn e na gnothaichean a dh'fheumadh e dhèanamh agus thug e dhachaigh e. Tha dealbh nam inntinn air dust m' athar a bhith am broinn

three and four. And we were allowed to stay up until our father came home. We were taking turn about going outside to the end of the path to look up the road for the lights of the car coming up over Habost and I had to take my turn like everybody else. And I remember that, when my turn came, how quickly I would run outside, looking and looking to see if anything was coming. I don't remember the rest of the night.

"The next morning we were up and our mother was preparing our breakfast and a wee boy from next door, the same age as my brother Norman, the second of our boys, about seven years old and they were always together and he was also called Tormod, Tormod Morrison, Tormod Plò they would call him. And Norman came and the police house was just three houses down the other side of the road and he was seeing a crowd of men there and hearing them speak. He knew that our father was coming and he was hearing some of what the men were saying. And he ran for his life up to our house and came in and he said: 'The men at the end of the street are saying that news has arrived that the ship Iain was on went on the rocks last night and that people were drowned.' Now, I remember that boy telling us that, but what it meant at the time, I did not understand.

"My mother's brother lived over in Steinish, Murdo Morrison and he was, it seems, walking the shore like many others were and they tell me that they were doing this for three weeks. Now, my uncle found my father's body and he did all the preparation he had to do and he took him home. I have an image in my head of my father's remains inside the house; it wasn't

an taigh; chan ann anns a' chidsin, ach sìos taobh shìos am *partition* ann an sin, 's ann ann a bhiodh am bùrn 's a' mhòine 's rudan mar sin. 'S ann ann a sin a bha e, air dà stòl. Bha *tarpaulin* timcheall air, agus bha e a' dèanamh *puzzle* eagalach dhomh gu dè an ceangal a bh' eadar an corp a bha seo, agus m' athair. Bha e fhathast nam inntinn gu robh m' athair a' dol a thighinn ach bha iad ag ràdh riumsa gur e m' athair a bha siud.

Bliadhnaichean mòr às dèidh sin bha mi dol dhan a' cholaiste. Cha robh mi a-riamh air a bhith air tìr-mòr. Bha sinn a' seòladh latha brèagha samhraidh a-mach Loch Steòrnabhaigh, agus chunnaic mi post mòr a sin an-àirde – tha mi a' smaoineachadh gur e dearg an dath a bh' air – agus thuirt mi, 'Ach gu dè am post a tha siud, an-àirde anns a' mhuir?' Agus 's e cuideigin a bha a' dol seachad oirnn, a thuirt, 'Sin an spot anns an deach an Iolaire sìos', is shaoil mi gun dh'fhairich mi gaoir a' dol sìos tromham. Dh'fhalbh a' chlann-nighean, tè às dèidh tè, ach sheas mi ann a siud. Bha mi a' cuimhneachadh air mo mhàthair 's air m' athair agus bha mi 'g ràdh, uill, siud an aon rud as urrainn dhomh a dhèanamh aig an spot tha siud.

Bliadhnaichean mòra às dèidh sin 's mi na mo bhean-phòsta, fhuair sinn fios gun deach lorg an glag a bha air an *Iolaire*. Fhuair daibhearan i, agus thugadh an-àird' i agus a glanadh agus chuireadh i dhan an *Town Hall*. Chuir iad a-mach fios gu robh leithid seo a sheirbheis gu bhith anns an *Town Hall* air leithid seo a latha. Is chaidh mo bhràthair, mi fhìn is e fhèin agus an duine agam ann. Bha mi na mo shuidhe ann a sin agus thuirt mi ri mo bhràthair, 'Iain, an dùil an e seo an glag a bhiodh mo mhàthair a' bruidhinn air?', is thuirt e, 'Cha chuala mise a-riamh i a' bruidhinn air glag'. 'Uill', arsa mise, 'an oidhche an dèidh m' athair a chall, chunnaic i e às a cadal'. Chan eil fhios agam dud a thuirt i ris, an e feagal a bh' oirre,

in the kitchen, but down by the partition there, it's where we kept the water and the peats and things like that. That's where he was, on two stools. There was tarpaulin around him, and it was puzzling me what connection there was between this body here and my father. It was still in my mind that my father was going to come home but they were telling me that that was my father.

"Many years after that I was going to college. I had never been to the mainland. We were sailing on this fine summer's day out of Stornoway and I saw this large post sticking out – I think it was red – and I said: 'What's this post, sticking out of the sea?' And it was someone in the passing who said 'That's where the *Iolaire* sank' and I felt a chill go through me. The other girls went in after a while, but I stood there. I was remembering my father and my mother and I was saying to myself, well, this is the one thing I can do here at this spot.

"Many years after this I was now married, we heard news that they had found the bell of the *Iolaire*. Divers had found it and they had taken it up, cleaned it and it was displayed in the Town Hall. They sent out news that there was to be a service in the Town Hall one day. Myself, my brother and my husband all went down. As I was sitting there I asked my brother: 'Iain, do you think that is the bell my mother used to speak of?' and he said 'I never heard her talking about any bell.' 'Well,' I said 'the night after my father was drowned, she saw it in her sleep.' I'm not sure what she said to him, was she scared, or did she get air neo feagal a ghabh i, ach siud am freagairt a thug e dhi as a cadal, 'Cha b' iongnadh mi fhèin nuair a chuala mi an glag'.

Agus bha iad mar gum biodh a' lorg a chèile air feadh an eilein. Bhiodh i a' dol gu òrdaighean; bha iad, mar a tha daoine an-diugh, ann an club. Bha ceangal aca ri chèile. Cha do chuir mo mhàthair oirre càil a-riamh ach aodach dubh. Agus tha cuimhne agam an oidhche a bhàsaich i, nuair a bha mo bhràthair aig an taigh à Glaschu agus chaidh mise steach dhan an rùm is e gal, caoidh mo mhàthair bha mi creidsinn. 'S e tha toirt gal ormsa, carson nach do dhreasaig sinn i ann an aodach soilleir, aon uair, gus am faiceadh sinn cò ris a bhiodh i coltach.

Ach tha mi smaoineachadh gu robh a' chuid as motha againn gur e searbhadas a bha againn ri fàs suas. Bha thu faicinn na rudan a bha a dhìth oirnn a thaobh is nach robh athair againn, ach chaill feadhainn eile an athair. Tha mi creids nan deigheadh tu a dh'fhaighneachd dha leithid mo mhàthair, nam bithist air tòiseachadh air na boireannaich sin a chaill an companaich, chan eil fhios agam cionnas a bhithinns air a bhith, nam bithinn na h-àite. Tha mi creids' gum biodh gu math searbh – ach dè bha thu dol a dhèanamh dheth? Gus an latha an-diugh gheibh thu an searbhadas sin nuair a bhios daoine a' bruidhinn air a' chall a bha ann a sin, agus cho beag làrach 's a rinn e ann an Lunnainn, ann an Westminster. Nam b' ann ann an ceann a deas Shasainn a bha siud air tachairt bha tòrr a bharrachd fuaim air a dhèanamh mu dheidhinn agus tòrr a bharrachd strì air a dhèanamh mu dheidhinn.

An Iolaire BBC Radio nan Gàidheal.
Riochdaire Annella Nicleòid, 1999

a fright, but that's the response that she gave him in her sleep, 'I wasn't surprised when I heard the bell.'

"And it was as if they were finding each other all over the island. She would go to communions; they were, like some people are today, in a club. They had a connection. My mother never wore anything except black clothes. And I remember the night that she died, when my brother was home from Glasgow and I went into the room and he was crying, mourning my mother I believed. 'The reason I'm crying, why did we not dress her in something light coloured, for once, so that we could see what she looked like?'

"But I think most of us were growing up with a very bitter feeling. We were seeing the things that were missing because we didn't have a father, but others also lost their fathers. I suppose if you had gone and asked the likes of my mother, if we were to speak to those women who lost their companions, I'm not sure how I would have been, if I were in their place. I suppose I would be very bitter – but what can you make of it? Up to this day you will still see that bitterness when people talk of this loss, and how small the impact was felt in London, in Westminster. If this had happened in the south of England there would have been a great deal more noise made about it and there would have been a lot more stir."

An Iolaire BBC Radio nan Gàidheal.
Producer Annella Macleod, 1999

Dòmhnall Macphàil

Bha mi seachd-bliadhna-deug, anns an àrd-sgoil an Steòrnabhagh, agus tha cuimhne mhath agam madainn latha na Bliadhn' Ùire. Fear a bh' anns an ath thaigh, thàinig e a-null tarsainn na mòintich, tha mi smaoineachadh. Cionnas a fhuair e air tìr chan aithne dhomh, ach bha e mar gum biodh e às a rian. An fheadhainn a chaill an cuid anns a' bhaile, màthraichean agus nam mnathan, bha iad a' tighinn a-staigh a dh'fhaighneachd am fac' e sealladh air Dòmhnall no air Aonghas no air Iain, agus cha robh e ach gan coimhead, agus na deòir a' tighinn a-nuas air na gruaidhean aige. Bha dà fhacal aige, bha e gan canntainn tric, 'Good God, Good God'; mar gum biodh e air grèim fhaighinn air na faclan sin air bòrd agus lean iad ris an inntinn aige is cha robh facal aige ach sin fhèin.

Ach 's e gnothaich duilich a bh' ann dhan fheadhainn a bha a' feitheamh, mar a bha am bàrd a' cantainn, 'Bha an dachaigh a' feitheamh riutha blàth, is gach nì mar a b' fheàrr air dòigh'. A h-uile dad air ullachadh airson biadh agus aodach airson an fheadhainn a bha a' tighinn. Carthannas agus blàths nan dàimhean a bh' aig an dachaigh, agus naidheachd thùrsach a' tighinn, nach ruigeadh iad tuilleadh. Dh'fhalbh mise Steòrnabhagh le cairt is each, mi fhìn is gille òg eile, agus athair fear dha na gillean a chaidh a chall agus chaidh sinn sìos chun a' Bhataraidh far a robh na cuirp air an cur a-mach far an aithnicheadh daoine iad agus tha cuimhne agam gu robh tiogaid orra – Liùrbost, Siabost is Tolastadh. Bha fear à Siabost a chaidh a-null còmhla rinne, bha mac ann leis, agus tha cuimhne agam gu robh e cho brèagha is gun canainn nach robh e marbh idir; gàire air aodann, tha cuimhne agam air a sin, cho brèagha fhathast. Is chaidh athair air a ghlùinean ri thaobh agus thòisich e a' toirt litrichean às a phòcaid agus

Donald Macphail

"I was seventeen years old, in the high-school in Stornoway, and I remember well New Year's morning. A man who lived next door, he had come across the moor, I think. How he got to shore, I just don't know, but it was as if he had gone crazy. The ones who had lost their family in the village, mothers and women, they were coming in to ask if there had been any sight of Donald or Angus or John and he could only look at them, with the tears coming down his cheeks. He had two words that he would repeat over and over: 'Good God, Good God!' It was as if he had grabbed hold of those words on board and they were following him and they were the only words he could say.

"But it was a difficult situation for those who were waiting, like the poet has said: 'The warm home was waiting for them, and everything was just perfect'. Everything had been prepared for food and clothes for those who were coming home. Compassion and warmth from the ones who were at home and this terrible news coming, that they weren't going to reach. I went to Stornoway with a horse and cart, myself and another young man and the father of one of the boys who had been lost and we went down to the Battery where the bodies were being identified by people and I remember that they were labelled – Leurbost, Shawbost and Tolsta. There was a man from Shawbost who came over with us, he had a son there, and I remember that he was so beautiful that you could hardly say that he was dead at all; a smile on his face, I remember that, still so beautiful. And his father went on his knees and started to pull out

airgead, agus bha e a' coimhead ri litir a bha am broinn a phòcaid, is na deòir a' tuiteam sìos air corp a' ghille. Tha mi smaoineachadh gur e sealladh cho tìomhaidh is cho duilich 's a chunnaic mi a-riamh, is cha robh sin ach aonan de mhòran.

BBC Radio nan Gàidheal.
Riochdaire Fred Macamhlaigh, 1961

letters from his pocket and money and he was looking at the letters inside his pocket and the tears falling down onto his son's body. I think it's one of the most moving and difficult scenes I've ever witnessed, and that was only one of many."

BBC Radio nan Gàidheal.
Producer Fred Macaulay, 1961

Màiri Nicchoinnich (née Nicleòid)

Bha mi cuideachadh mo mhàthair, ag ullachadh airson m' athair. Fhuair i litir bhuaithe làithean ron a sin gu robh dùil aige ri leave, agus gu robh e an dòchas gu faigheadh e leave na Bliadhn' Ùire is gum baisteadh e an leanabh – cha robh an duine a b' òige ach sia mìosan. Bha sinn an-àirde gu dà uair sa mhadainn agus thàinig Iain, bràthair mo mhàthar a-steach agus thuirt e gu robh e a' cluinntinn nan conacagan, agus thuirt mo mhàthair, 'Tha, tha conacagan na Bliadhn' Ùire tha mi creids''. 'Cha b' e,' ars' esan, ''s e bha siud ach conacag èiginneach'. Nis tha cuimhne agam air a sin, ged a b' ann a-raoir a bh' ann.

Agus làirne-mhàireach thòisich mo mhàthair a' nigheadaireachd – cha tàinig m' athair. 'S thàinig searbhant a chuideachadh mo mhàthair 's bha mi a' gabhail iongantas gun thachair sin. 'S chunnaic mi m' antaidh a' tighinn a-nuas an rathad agus chaidh i a thaigh Dhòmhnaill a' Phìobaire, Dòmhnall a' Phìobaire thàinig e an oidhche sin. Bha mi a' cumail aire rithe, agus chunnaic mi gun deach i a-mach an lot gu taigh Iain, bràthair mo mhàthar, agus 's ann anns an tighinn a-steach dhi, 's ann a thàinig i a-steach. 'S sheas i anns an doras 's nuair a chunnaic mo mhàthair i dh'aithnich i anns an spot dud a bh' ann. 'S bha m' antaidh deiseil an

Mairi Mackenzie (née Macleod)

"I was helping my mother, preparing for my father. She had received a letter some days before this that he was expecting leave and that he was hoping to get the New Year's leave and that he could christen the baby – the youngest was only six months old. We were up until two o' clock in the morning and Iain, my mother's brother, came in to say that he was hearing hooters, and my mother said: 'Yes, they'll be the hooters for the New Year, I bet.' 'Oh, no', he said 'that was a distress hooter.' Now I remember that as if it were only last night.

"And the next day my mother started the washing – my father had not come. And a servant came to help my mother and I was thinking that that was strange. And I saw my auntie coming down the road and she went to Dòmhnall a' Phìobaire's house, Dòmhnall had come home that night. I was keeping an eye on her and I saw that she went out the croft to Iain's house, my mother's brother and it was then that she came to our house. And she stood in the door and when my mother saw her she realised straight away what it was. And my auntie was ready after putting on her Sunday clothes, ready to go to the service.

dèidh a cuid aodaich Sàbaid a chuir oirre, agus i a' falbh dhan t-searmon. An àite dhol dhan t-searmon thàinig i a-nuas, agus chaidh i gu piuthair eile a bha an ceann a-muigh a' bhaile. Nuair a sheas i as an doras thuirt i rithe, 'Eil lorg agad air do bhràthair?' Sin mar a fhuair sinne sgeul air m' athair. Cha tàinig fios bho dhuine. Bha iad mar gum biodh a' teiche bhuainn. Cha tàinig bràthair màthar na eile dha innse dhuinn. Cha robh mi ga chreids idir gun thachair e, gun tàinig iad a-steach dhan taigh-fhaire.

Agus nuair a thàinig piuthar m' athar a-steach, sheas i as an doras – bha an còignear againn timcheall air mo mhàthair, cha robh mise ach deich, an duine b' òige sia mìosan – agus thuirt i, 'Taing dhan a' Chruithear, gur e sgiath ur màthar a th' agaibh a-nochd, ged a 's e mo bhràthair a th' ann.'

Bha e greis gun aithneachadh, gun fhaighinn, is 's e aon ghàirdean a bh' air, ach an gàirdean a bh' air bha JML Port Mholair, PV, sgrìobhte air agus 's ann mar sin a dh'aithnich iad gur e a bh' ann.

Cha do dh'èigh iad a-riamh air ar n-athair sinn, ach air ar màthair, agus bha sin a' dèanamh tòrr cron oirnn. Dh'fhàg sin sinn lethoireach 'S e duine ainneamh, fìor sheann duine, a dh'èigh sinne air ar n-athair. 'S tha cuimhne agam aon latha, agus mi air a dhol a shealltainn air tè, Ishbel Iain Chaluim Ruaidh – chan fhaca mi i bho dh'fhàg iad Pabail ann an *November* 1918, mìos mus deach an *Iolaire* às an rathad – 's nuair a sheas mi anns an doras, thuirt i, 'Oh mo chreach, Màiri Iain Mhurchaidh Chaluim!' 'S chan aithne dhomh gun cuala mi a-riamh cho còmhnard ri siud mi gam ainmeachadh air m' athair. Is *bha* sinn ga fhaireachdainn lethoireach, nach robhas gar h-ainmeachadh air ar n-athair, uill bha athair againn.

Call na h-Iolaire *BBC Radio nan Gàidheal.*
Riochdaire Jo Nicdhòmhnaill, 1989

But instead of going to the service she came down and she went to another sister who was at the other end of the village. When she stood in the door she asked: 'Have you found your brother?' That's how we heard the story of our father. No news came from anyone. It was as if they were hiding from us. Neither my father's brother, nor anyone, came to tell us. I didn't believe that it had happened, until they came into the wake.

"And when my father's sister came in, she stood in the door – the five of us were gathered around my mother, I was only ten years old, the youngest only six months – and she said 'Thank God that you're under your mother's wing tonight, even though he was my own brother.'

"It took some time to identify him, to find him and it was only the one arm he had, but the arm he did have had JML Portvoller, PV, written on it, and that's how they identified him.

"They never called us by our father, but by our mother and that was doing us a great deal of harm. That left us diffident. It was a very rare occasion when someone, usually an older person, called us by our father's name. And I remember when one day I went to visit a girl, Ishbel Iain Chaluim Ruaidh – I had not seen her since she left Bayble in November 1918, a month before the *Iolaire* sank – and when I stood in the door, she said, 'Oh my! Mairi 'Iain Mhurchaidh Chaluim!' And I don't think I had ever heard anyone naming me by my father in such a direct way. And it was leaving us diffident, that we were not being named after our father, for we did have a father."

Call na h-Iolaire *BBC Radio nan Gàidheal.*
Producer Jo Macdonald, 1989

Katie Bell Stiùbhart (née Nicdhòmhnaill)

'S ann an coinneamh *cousin* dhomh a bha mis'; Iain Beag, mac piuthar mo mhàthair, a bha na phrìosanach anns a' Ghearmailt aig an àm. 'S ann air mhuinntearas a bha mis' anns a' *Waverley Hotel* ann an Steòrnabhagh agus bha i air a gabhail a-null aig an *Admiralty*, agus dh'fheumainn a bhith staigh aig an uair, agus cha b' urrainnn dhomh feitheamh gus an tàinig a' *Sheila* idir, b' fheudar dhomh tilleadh a-steach. Cha chuala sinne an còir mu dheidhinn càil gu sia uairean sa mhadainn. Thàinig *message-boy* chun an dorais, agus 's e a chuir an-àirde a h-uile duine a bh' ann, a dh'innse gu robh an *Iolaire* air a dhol às an rathad. Bha aig feadhainn a bha a' fuireach ann a sin ri dhol sìos a Tholm airson 'watchigeadh' na cuirp a bha a' tighinn air tìr. Is bidh cuimhne agam a chaoidh cho diombach 's a bha iad, na Sasannaich sin, 's a' ghràin a bh' againn orra, a' smaoineachadh nach robh iad dha ghabhail a-steach. Làirne-mhàireach, na cuirp, na làraidhean a' tighinn le na cuirp, chithinn a-mach air an uinneag àrd iad. Na cuirp mar gum biodh làraidh air a pacaigeach le truisg, a-null 's a-null ann a sin air a' làraidh, agus cha robh *cover* orra, tha cuimhne mhath agam nach robh *cover* orra, ach bha iad diombach airson sin às dèidh làimh, gun thachair a leithid de rud. Agus nuair a chaidh mi a-mach tron latha bha na làraidhean gar coinneachadh le na cistichean *piled up* le ròpan orra dol sìos a Tholm. Oh! Cha tèid sin às mo chuimhne a chaoidh, an seòrsa sealladh a bh' ann is an seòrsa faireachdainn a bh' againn, faireachdainn uabhasach.

Iolaire BBC Radio nan Gàidheal.
Preasantair Nan S. Nicleòid, 2008

Katie Bell Stewart (née Macdonald)

"I was meeting my cousin, Iain Beag, my mother's sister's son, who was a prisoner of war in Germany at the time. I was in service at the Waverley Hotel in Stornoway and it had been taken over by the Admiralty and I had to be in on the hour and I couldn't wait until the *Sheila* had arrived at all, I had to go back in. We didn't hear another thing until six o' clock in the morning. A message-boy came to the door and he awoke everybody who was there, telling everyone that the *Iolaire* had sunk. Some of those who were staying there were to go down to Holm to keep a watch for the bodies being washed ashore. And I'll always remember how annoyed they were, the English and the loathing we had for them, thinking that they weren't taking this all in. The next day, the bodies, the lorries with the bodies, I could see them out of the top window. The bodies were like cod piled up on the lorry, laid out back and forth there on the lorry and they didn't have a cover, I remember very well that there was no cover on them and they were annoyed about that afterwards, that that had happened. And when I went out during the day the lorries were meeting us with the coffins piled up with ropes on them going down to Holm. Oh, that will never leave my memory, that sight and those feelings, terrible feelings."

Iolaire BBC Radio nan Gàidheal.
Presenter Nan S. Macleod, 2008

Mòr Nicleòid
(Mòr Chaluim Bàin à Borgh)
(née Nicamhlaigh)

Tha cuimhn' agam gu h-àraid latha an tiodhlaicidh, a' faicinn sia tiodhlacaidhean a' tighinn seachad air a' sgoil ann an Siabost, air sia cairtean. Cha robh mise a-nis glè aost' aig an àm ach bha dorchadas mòr air a' latha a bh' ann. Clann 's mnathan agus *girlfriends* gu leòr, *broken-hearted*.

Iolaire BBC Radio nan Gàidheal.
Preasantair Nan S. Nicleòid, 2008

Alasdair Macìomhair (Bràgar)

Tha fios agam nach robh sinn fhìn a' saoilsinn mòran dhan a' chùis bhon a bha sinn cho òg, ach tha cuimhn' agam a h-uile uair a thigeadh a' Bhliadhn' Ùr a-steach, 's ann a' gal a bhiodh mo mhàthair.

Call na h-Iolaire BBC Radio nan Gàidheal.
Riochdaire Jo Nicdhòmhnaill, 1989

Catrìona Nicdhòmhnaill

Ach an fheadhainn a chaill an cuid ann, lean e riutha. Mar a bhithinn a' cluinntinnn aig m' athair, 'Cha d' fhuair mi a-riamh air a dhol a chadal, oidhche le gaoth mhòr no muir mòr ann, gun a bhith ag ùrnaigh airson luchd na mara'. Bha daoine tapaidh, a bha air a thighinn tron a' chogadh

Marion Macleod
(Mòr Chaluim Bàin from Borve)
(née Macaulay)

"I especially remember the day of the funeral, seeing six funerals going past the school in Shawbost, on six carts. Now, I wasn't very old at the time but there was a great darkness that day. Children and women and plenty of girlfriends, all broken-hearted."

Iolaire BBC Radio nan Gàidheal.
Presenter Nan S. Macleod, 2008

Alasdair Maciver (Bragar)

"I know that we weren't thinking much about that matter because we were so young, but I remember every time the New Year would come around my mother would be crying."

Call na h-Iolaire BBC Radio nan Gàidheal.
Producer Jo Macdonald, 1989

Catriona Macdonald

"For those who lost their own family, it never left them. As I would hear from my father: 'I never once got to sleep, if there was ever a strong wind or a wild sea, without first praying for those at sea.' They were healthy people, who had made it through the war a' tighinn dhachaigh, agus fhuair iad briseadh-dùil 's fhuair na bha romhp' brìseadh dùil. Bha rud mar gum biodh e ùr dhaibh a h-uile Bliadhn' Ùr. Nuair a bha sinn an-àirde ri fichead bliadhna, bha sinn a' tòiseachadh a' dèanamh fealla-dhà dhuinn fhèin, ach cha robh na pàrantan againn. 'S ann a shaoileadh tu gu robh dubhachas a' tighinn orr' aig àm na Bliadhn' Ùire, agus cha robh iongnadh a sin.

Call na h-Iolaire *BBC Radio nan Gàidheal.*
Riochdaire Jo Nicdhòmhnaill, 1989

and were now coming home and they had such tragedy and those who were waiting for them had such tragedy. It was as if the tragedy was new to them every New Year. When we were in our twenties, we then started to enjoy ourselves, but our parents couldn't. It was almost as if a great sorrow came over them around the time of the New Year and that was completely understandable."

Call na h-Iolaire *BBC Radio nan Gàidheal.*
Producer Jo Macdonald, 1989

Sùil-fhianais

Bha aon duine anns a' bhail' againne agus bhiodh e an còmhnaidh a' cumail a-mach nuair a chaidh a thogail dhan a' chogadh gu robh esan dol a chall a bheatha anns a' chogadh. Co-dhiù, bhiodh na balaich a' magadh air a h-uile trup a thilleadh e air *leave*, 'Oh, cha do chaill thu do bheatha fhathast'. 'Oh, chan eil an cogadh deiseil fhathast'. Ach co-dhiù, bha e air an *Iolaire* an oidhche-sa, agus chunnacas e na sheasamh air na '*casings*', agus chaidh èigheach ris, carson nach robh e a' feuchainn faighinn às mar a bha càch? Is bha a làmhan na phòcaid. 'Cha leig mise a leas,' arsa esan, 'tha m' àm-sa deiseil. Cha tèid mise à seo, ach an aon taobh'. Nise, 's e na daoine a bha a' bruidhinn ris a dh'aithris seo, gu robh creideamh aige gu robh e a' dol a chall a bheatha, gun tuirt an Cruithear ris gu robh e dol a chall a bheatha, agus bha e a' greimeachadh ris a sin.

Call na h-Iolaire *BBC Radio nan Gàidheal.*
Riochdaire Jo Nicdhòmhnaill, 1989

Eye-witness

"There was one man in our own village and he was always stating from when he was called to serve in the war that he was going to lose his life. Anyway, the boys would tease him every time he came home on leave: 'Oh, you haven't lost your life yet!' 'Oh, the war isn't over yet!' Anyway, he was on the *Iolaire* on this night and he was seen standing on the casings and they were shouting at him – why was he not trying to save himself like everyone else? And his hands were in his pockets. 'I needn't bother,' he said 'my time has come. I won't leave here but the one way.' Now, it was the people who spoke to him who recall this, that he had such a belief that he was going to lose his life, that the Lord had said that he was going to lose his life and this had taken a grip of him."

Call na h-Iolaire *BBC Radio nan Gàidheal.*
Producer Jo Macdonald, 1989

Chapter 8 Footnotes

1. Catriona Macdonald speaking to Jo Macdonald, BBC Radio nan Gàidheal, 1989

2. Robert Mackinnon speaking to Fred Macaulay, BBC Radio nan Gàidheal, 1961

3. Anderson - the name of the car-hirer on Bayhead was, in fact, Henderson

Chapter 9

Keeping the Memory Alive

"Ultimately, it is not possible to fully understand the
history of Lewis in the 20th Century without recognising
the scale and impact of the *Iolaire* disaster."[1]

Silence haunted the Isles of Lewis and Harris after the *Iolaire* disaster, but this did not mean that memories were quickly erased. There were many individual acts of commemoration, memorials were raised and gradually, as time passed, there was an increasingly urgent drive to honour the memories of those who had died, and to record the stories of those living.

In fact, the natural urge to remember, to mark the event and to honour both survivors and victims was evident even from first light on 1st January 1919. People were drawn to the cliff tops and shores around Holm, from which, on that day, the mast of the *Iolaire* herself was still clearly visible, showing where the ship had gone down. This single seamark remained as relatives searched the shore for the bodies of their loved ones. Some stood – mute, weeping or wailing their grief – at the spot where the wreck could be seen. At this vantage point a cairn of stones grew, people marking the site and laying their tribute, each single stone a memory and permanent testimonial to a loss that could never be eased.

At 10.45am on Tuesday 14th January 1919, at the conclusion of diving operations round the *Iolaire* wreck, a joint service was held on board HMT *Kimberley*, which was anchored as close to the wreck as possible. The mourners aboard the trawler included Mr and Mrs Macaskill, parents of the popular lad, Jack, whose body was the only one of the Stornoway victims still unrecovered at that date – he was found in February that year. Also present at the service were Lord Leverhulme, Rear Admiral Boyle, Provost Murdo Maclean, ex-Provost John Norrie Anderson, Dr Donald Murray MP, Baillie Roderick Smith, Superintendent and Mrs Robert Alexander, Mr James William Macgilvray and one of his sisters (Margaret or Elizabeth Macgilvray), Mr Ranald Macdonald (Carloway), Mr Aulay Macdonald and others. A party of mourners had also assembled on the shore at Holm, though the time of the service, governed by tidal conditions, was convenient only for those living in town.

The service opened with the hymn "Jesus lover of my soul," and a reading from holy scripture, after which prayers were offered by Rev George A Mills (United Free Church) and Rev John M Menzies (Established Church), who sought divine comfort for the sorrowing homes of Lewis bereaved by the great disaster. Rev Henry A. Meaden (Episcopalian Church) then read the last half of Revelations VII, after which, turning towards the wreck, he committed the bodies to the deep, "looking for the resurrection of the body when the sea shall give up her dead." The service was brought to a close with the hymn "Let saints on earth in concert sing with those whose work be done".[2]

At this time there still remained many bodies of *Iolaire* men missing, some of whom would never be found. But for those whose bodies were lifted from the sea or the shore, the first enduring memorial would be raised at their place of rest, each of which is designated as a war grave – the gravestone supplied, maintained and replaced if necessary by the Commonwealth War Graves Commission (CWGC). The Admiralty took charge of some of the first of the burials at Sandwick cemetery near Stornoway, where there is a row of eleven CWGC Royal Navy headstones in the top half of the 1910 division of Sandwick New Cemetery. Number three is crewman David Macdonald and number ten is his colleague Charles Dewsbury. Number eleven marks John Macleod, 2736/B, from 43 Upper Bayble. For a reason unknown to his family he was interred there without their permission and it was said that the Admiralty had tried to charge them for the funeral – the family would have chosen the cemetery at Aignish to lay him to rest. The other eight graves are marked simply 'A Sailor' and 'HMY *Iolaire*' with the foot of the stone inscribed 'Known Unto God'. A few yards behind the start of this grouping, crew member Alfred S. Taylor is interred with the same type of headstone. A private headstone for Donald

Macleod, 10 Murray's Court, is maintained by the CWGC and is in an adjoining lair to Taylor.

Headstones for other crew members are scattered throughout the country, their remains having been returned to their own families, as far away as Penzance and the Isle of Wight. Nearly every cemetery on the Isle of Lewis has graves of local men who were drowned on the *Iolaire*. Many grey granite headstones are carved with an oblique anchor and the words "HMY *Iolaire*, 1.1.1919." Family headstones also bear the names of sons and husbands whose bodies were not recovered and have no known grave but the sea. Some of the headstones do not mention the *Iolaire*, instead showing the vessel or base where the seaman had served previously – HMS *Attentive*, HMS *Dreel Castle*, HMS *Emperor of India* and so on – but each stone is inevitably connected with the *Iolaire* disaster by the date of death on the headstone, 1st January 1919.

The following cemeteries have First World War graves looked after by the Commonwealth War Graves Commission, including graves of *Iolaire* casualties. There are some cemeteries where there are no *Iolaire* victims and other cemeteries in the islands also have graves from the Second World War.

In the district of Ness, St Peter's cemetery at Swainbost machair has 21 Great War graves, of which 15 are of men lost on the *Iolaire*. On the Westside of Lewis, St Mary's cemetery at Barvas has 11 graves, of which 6 are of men lost on the *Iolaire*, Bragar's 30 First World War graves include 15 *Iolaire* casualties and the cemetery above the beach at Dalmore has 15 Great War graves, 7 of men lost on the *Iolaire*. In the district of Uig, 5 of the 7 Great War graves at Ardroil are from the *Iolaire*, as are two of the three graves at Valtos Old Cemetery. The nearby island of Great Bernera has 3 Great War graves, at Bosta – two are of *Iolaire* victims.

Eleven headstones placed at the graves of Iolaire victims at Sandwick cemetery, to replace the white wooden crosses originally used to mark the graves (see chapter 5). Eight of these graves are of a sailor 'known unto God'.

In Lochs, 16 of the 22 Great War graves in Crossbost are of *Iolaire* men, two of the four at Gravir and three of the four at Laxay old cemetery. The Isle of Harris has three *Iolaire* graves in the old cemetery at Luskentyre and one at Scarista. One of Berneray's four Great War graves is of an *Iolaire* victim.

In Broadbay there are eight *Iolaire* graves among the 13 from the First War at North Tolsta. Six *Iolaire* men are buried at Gress, among 15 Great War graves there. Point has a single *Iolaire* victim, the only Great War casualty buried at the old Eye Church, and 22 more among the 45 Great War graves in Aignish cemetery on the Braighe. Sandwick Old Cemetery near Stornoway has 10 named *Iolaire* casualties, plus eight unknown victims of the tragedy. There are 27 other Great War graves here.

64 bodies were never recovered. Of these, 55 men are commemorated on the Chatham Naval Memorial, five at Plymouth and four at Portsmouth. This is in addition to their commemoration on local memorials as detailed below.

Memorials large and small

As in so many other parts of the country, the sacrifice of local men in the Great War generated a passionate desire to honour and commemorate lives laid down in war – even where there was no local grave to mark their passing. Before the Armistice, Lewis's first memorial had been unveiled at St Moluag's Church in Eoropie, Ness. The Celtic cross, dedicated to all the fallen men of Lewis, was unveiled in August 1918 by Lord Leverhulme – it listed no names, and no-one could have known how much greater the loss still to come would be. The memorial was restored and cleaned in 2002.

Once the war was over, the urge to commemorate in stone the islanders' great sacrifice generated energetic fundraising and activity. The village of Tolsta Chaolais erected an obelisk-type memorial in the village in 1921, after villagers at home and away raised over £200. In 1922 a monument was unveiled in Pairc, at Kershader and the people of Harris raised money to erect a substantial memorial at Main Street, Tarbert which was unveiled in 1923 by Sir Samuel Scott, Baronet, the second generation of his family to own the North Harris Estate. The Scottish baronial tower measures about 10 feet square at the base and rises to a height of about 25 feet. The granite used came from the Isle of Berneray, while the panels carrying 117 names of First World War dead are of Aberdeen granite. The design was by John G Chisholm, architect and surveyor, Inverness. Lord Leverhulme contributed half of the cost of the structure.

A public meeting was held in Stornoway in January 1920 at which it was decided to perpetuate the memory of the 1,151 Lewismen known to have made the supreme sacrifice. The proprietor of the island at that time, Lord Leverhulme, was elected chairman of an appeals committee, with joint secretaries George Macleod and Colin J Maciver and honorary treasurers Kenneth Mackenzie and John Macritchie Morrison.

From January to July 1920 the pages of the *Stornoway Gazette* carried advertisements appealing for subscriptions towards the building costs of a suitable memorial that would cost at least £10,000 and, more probably, £20,000. As a spur to generous donations, it was announced that an anonymous resident was willing to double the amount subscribed up to £5,000. This resident was later discovered to be Lord Leverhulme himself.

The response was overwhelming and by May 1923 there had been a competition for the design of the memorial, won by Mr J H Gall of Inverness. The contract to begin work was awarded and, by June 1924, the masonry work was complete, creating a striking landmark at the already prominent Cnoc nan Uan, a 300-foot hill just outside the town. The memorial tower is in Scottish baronial style, rising a further 85 feet from the hilltop, the years 1914-19 engraved above the entrance door. Within, an entrance hall leads to four upper chambers, each dedicated to one of the four districts of Lewis – which can be seen from the memorial itself. 16 bronze plaques carried the names of Lewismen lost, including victims of the *Iolaire*. The bronze plaques are missing a number of names and there is also duplication, some men listed more than once under different parishes.

The internal work at the Lewis War Memorial was completed by August 1924 at a modest cost of £4,000 and, on 5th September 1924, over 2,000 people witnessed the unveiling of the memorial by Lord Leverhulme. In almost a century since there have been renovations and additions – firstly in response to the losses of the Second World War, and most recently a major renovation completed in 2017. The bronze plaques listing the names of the war dead are now mounted outside the tower, on granite stones, with a viewing path and seating for visitors.

Fundraising for the Isle of Berneray's memorial commenced in the spring of 1920, with Kenneth MacLean of the schoolhouse as secretary/treasurer. It took over a decade before the Berneray monument was unveiled at Church Road, listing 18 First World War dead, including the two young friends Donald Paterson and Norman Mackillop, both lost on the *Iolaire* at the age of just 18.

Memorials to the dead of two World Wars have been erected in villages around Lewis and Harris over the years – from the St Moluag's cross in 1918 to the most recent, at Barvas and Brue, in 2016. Those which list names of *Iolaire* men are listed below in date order, together with their date of unveiling and the number of First World War dead, and of *Iolaire* victims, whose names are there inscribed.

Lewis War Memorial was unveiled by Lord Leverhulme before a large crowd on 5th September 1924 and has dominated the Stornoway skyline since.

*Small memorials were unveiled around the islands, including this one in Breaclete,
Great Bernera, seen on the day of its dedication in 1925.*

Memorial	Year Unveiled	WW1 Names	Iolaire Names
Tolsta Chaolais	1921	18	1
Pairc (Kershader)	1922	49	8
Harris (Tarbert)	1923	117	5
Lewis (Stornoway)	1924	1,151	171
Isle of Great Bernera (Breaclet)	c1925	28	4
Isle of Berneray (Church Road)	c1930	18	2
The Nicolson Institute	1932	147	7
Carloway (Knock Carloway)	1989	58	5
Tolsta (North Tolsta)	1998	52	11

(Plaques originally sited at Tolsta School, rededicated in 1998)

Memorial	Year Unveiled	WW1 Names	Iolaire Names
Uig (Baile na Cille)	1999	49	9
North Lochs (Crossbost)	2000	82	21
North Lewis (Cross)	2001	152	23
North Lewis (Borve)	2001	61	6
Back (Back)	2001	79	9
Point (Garrabost)	2004	191	39
Kinloch (Laxay)	2004	41	3
Arnol/Bragar/Shawbost (Bragar)	2005	84	22
Loch Roag (Callanish)	2006	40	2
Barvas & Brue (Barvas)	2016	32	1

There are a number of other memorial plaques and tributes to men lost, both during the war itself and as a result of the *Iolaire* disaster. A plaque commemorating 148 boys who had attended The Nicolson Institute and were lost during the war was unveiled by former Rector of the school, William Gibson, in 1932. The plaque names seven members of the Royal Navy who died on the *Iolaire* – William Mackay, John Macaskill, John (Jack) A. Macaskill (RNVR), Alexander J. Macdonald, John Macdonald, Angus Macleod and Donald Macleod – and can still be seen in the school's former Francis Street Building, now the headquarters for eSgoil. There are other indoor plaques commemorating the fallen, such as those at the Uig Community Centre and within local churches.

Despite all of the memorials which have been raised, some names were not commemorated by 2018. Malcolm Macleod of 2 Crossbost and 42 Keith Street, Stornoway, Alexander D Maciver of 42 Church Street and William K. Wilson of Beach House, South Beach Street do not appear on any memorials in Lewis. Murdo Mackinnon of 18 Brenish does not appear on the Lewis War Memorial.

Remembering individuals

Every home of a man lost on the *Iolaire* had their own way of preserving memories. For many, the focus would have been around the so-called 'Dead Man's Penny' issued by the British Government. After the First World War, a bronze plaque measuring around five inches in diameter, showing Britannia with a lion and inscribed, "He died for freedom and honour", was given by the government to the next of kin of every serviceman killed in the Great War. In houses around the country, these "pennies" became a shrine to family members who had made the supreme sacrifice in the war. A service photograph of the loved one, objects recovered from his body or from the shore, his coat, his kitbag or a bible in which he had written his name would also have been among the objects carefully preserved, displayed or hidden away, as treasured memories of a lost man.

Every family received a bronze plaque, the so-called 'Dead Man's Penny', commemorating their lost relative. Often the focus of remembrance within a home, this example was given to the family of Angus Crichton of 12 Knock, Point. His body was never recovered.

Just a few individual servicemen had named memorials in more public places. One such was a memorial at St Peter's Episcopal Church in Stornoway, dedicated to the popular young signalman John Alexander (Jack) Macaskill, before the war well-known to many as a junior clerk at the Harbour Office, and a member of Stornoway Naval Corps, who had died on the *Iolaire* aged just 19. The memorial specifically states that Jack was 'drowned in the *Iolaire* disaster' and is dedicated: "In affectionate remembrance of John Alexander Macaskill, on whose dear soul kind shepherd have mercy."

Exactly one year after the disaster, the pages of local newspapers carried echoes of the deep-seated grief still felt by so many. Small notices placed by parents, siblings and widows in the *Stornoway Gazette* and the *Highland News* in the first week of January 1920 commemorated 14 lost men. They included a memorial for Londoner Albert Matthews from 'his chums' and this tribute to teacher Malcom Maciver of 28 Aignish, placed by his 'devoted sisters and brothers':

> *'In my home you are fondly remembered*
> *Such happy memories cling round your name*
> *True hearts that loved you with deepest affection*
> *Always shall have you in death just the same.'*[3]

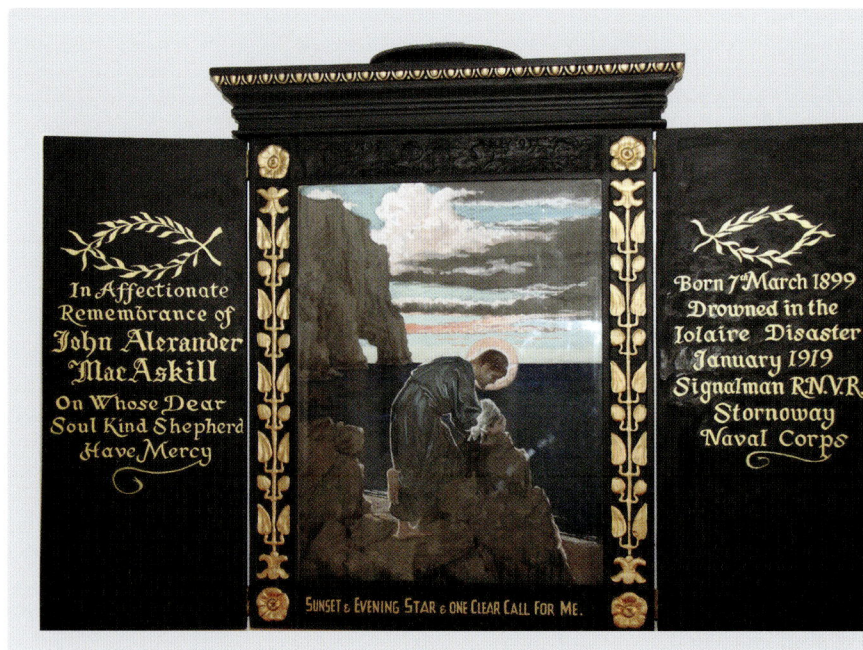

The ornate and colourful memorial plaque at St Peter's Episcopal Church in Stornoway, dedicated to 19-year-old Jack Macaskill.

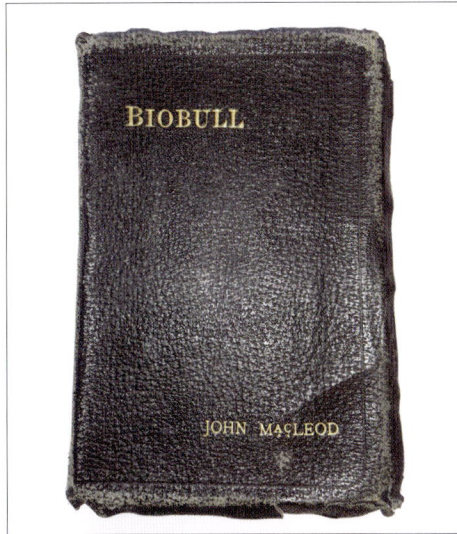

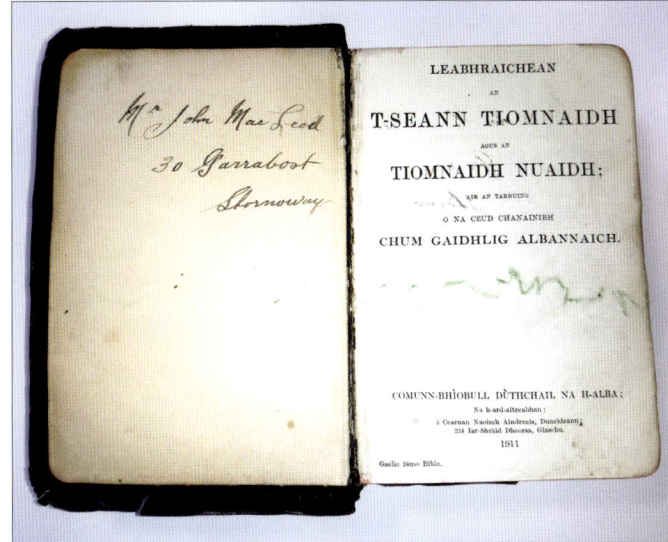

The bible belonging to John Macleod of 30 Lower Garrabost was kept by the family as a private memorial. It is believed to have later been taken to Vancouver by one of his sisters and returned to the Isle of Lewis only in 2015.

A report in the *Highland News* tells us of the dedication of the monument in November 1919:

"…..The memorial in St Peter's is on oak triptych in the centre panel of which is a painting representing rock scenery with the sun setting across the water. In the foreground the Shepherd is seen bending over a lamb of his flock that has evidently been drowned, the picture thus emphasising the Good Shepherd's care for his flock – underneath is a quote from Tennyson:

'Sunset and every star
And one clear call for me'

"The design was carried out with advice from the Royal Academy and executed by Estella Canziani whose paintings have more than once attracted considerable attention. The memorial had been on show at the Victoria and Albert Museum where several London Lewis people had the opportunity to see it."[4]

Memorials to the *Iolaire*

Despite the evident enthusiasm post-war for memorialising those lost between 1914 and 1919, the silence which shrouded memories of the loss of the *Iolaire* was so dense, so well-observed, that no comparable attempts were made at first to mark the site of the sinking on 1st January 1919, or to specifically commemorate in stone the men lost on that night.

Nevertheless, people did silently pay tribute at the spot from which the wreck could most clearly be seen, with a cairn of rough stones, placed upon the cliff-top where

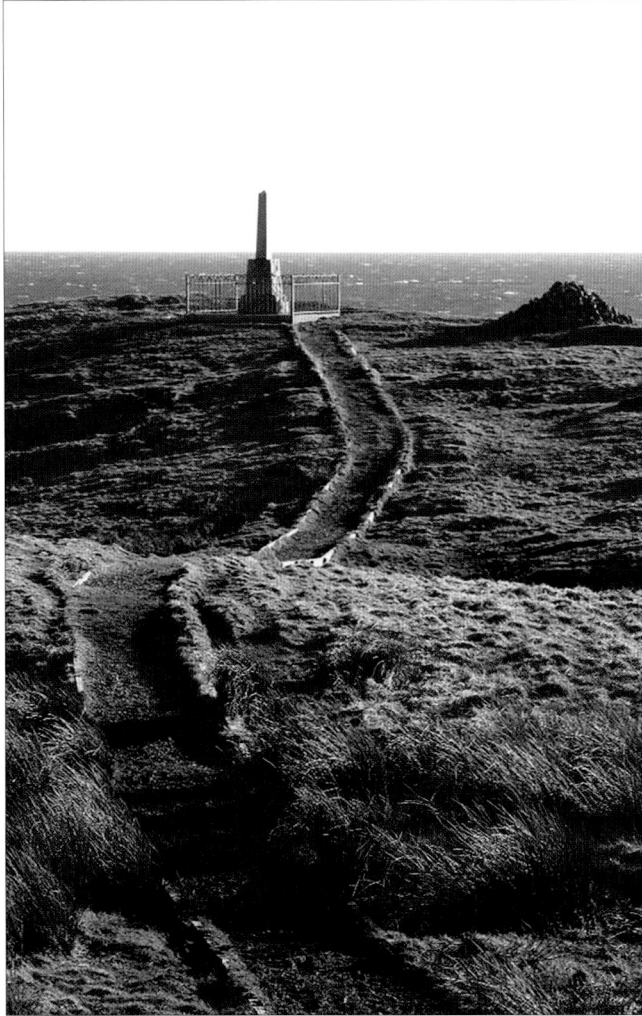

In this picture of the Iolaire memorial the original stone cairn can still be seen close beside.

relatives gathered to gaze upon the site of their great loss. It's not known whether the cairn was begun on 1st January 1919, but it was certainly a notable landmark by the late 1920s, as evidenced in a poem written by Alex John Nicholson, of nearby Holm Farm (born 1911) who is known to have written the poem as a teenager in 1928.

> *"On a cliff across the bay,*
> *Just two miles from Stornoway,*
> *Stands a cairn of stones above a jagged reef;*
> *It's a tragic souvenir,*
> *Of that cold and sad New Year,*
> *When a crowd of Lewis sailors came to grief."*[5]

The cairn, which is still clearly to be seen close to the site of newer monuments to the *Iolaire* disaster, is a roughly pyramid-shaped structure of loose stones, each of which would have been brought to the site and laid individually, over time, by grieving relatives and friends. The building of cairns was an ancient, well-established custom in the islands and across Scotland. Similar cairns are still to be found along the routes taken by funeral processions towards the cemeteries, and were constructed on hilltops as way-finders for travellers by land and sea. The significance of the cairn here is that such a marker was often formed to mark a grave, or to commemorate the passing of a loved one. With so many men's bodies never to be recovered from the sea, this simple monument would have been the first recognised place of remembrance for many.

On 6th January 1939 a letter appeared in the *Stornoway Gazette* suggesting a memorial be erected to the *Iolaire*. There was strong initial opposition to this proposal from those for whom the idea stirred painful memories. "*Their names are already on the Lewis War Memorial!"* was one plaintive cry. The tide of opposition eventually receded, after these initial strong emotions subsided, but it was not until nearly 20 years later, on 25th August 1958, that it was mooted at a meeting of Stornoway Town Council that a cairn for the *Iolaire* should be built overlooking the scene of the tragedy.

The idea at that time was promoted initially by County Councillor Allan Cameron, a former RNR sailor from North Tolsta who had served in the Great War. His idea was reported in the *Stornoway Gazette* of 6th June 1958 and taken up by Stornoway Town Council. On 16th December 1958, at a meeting of the Lewis District Council, it was decided to set up a committee to collect money for a suitable monument to be erected near the spot where the ship went down. The money was to be collected from the people of Lewis and Harris, and from natives living away from the island. The meeting stressed that that the names of those lost were already on the Lewis War Memorial, but it was felt that a monument should be placed at the scene of the disaster. Councillor Cameron said:

> "The idea is to erect something quite simple to mark the spot, but I would like to see a substantial sum collected, so there would be a balance in reserve to keep up the memorial after it is erected".[6]

When the fundraising closed at the end of October 1959, a total of £781 had been raised. A year later, on 26th October 1960, a 10-foot high granite obelisk, mounted on a two-step base and plinth, was unveiled on the headland at Holm Point. The new memorial was only yards from the original cairn, on land made available by Angus MacDonald of Holm Farm, Chairman of the Lewis District Council. Ex-Provost Alastair J. Mackenzie unveiled the memorial and both he and Provost Donald James Stewart of Stornoway Town Council laid a wreath. Both had served in the Royal Navy – Mackenzie in the First War and Stewart in the Second. The *Stornoway Gazette* reported:

> "It was with feelings of great sorrow that the several hundred people of Lewis gathered there that day thought of their kith and kin who had gallantly fought for king and country only to meet their end coming home on leave after winning the victory."[7]

Rev Murdo Murray of Carloway dedicated the monument, on the plinth of which is inscribed:

> "Erected by the people of Lewis and friends in grateful memory of the brave men of the Royal Navy who lost their lives in the *"Iolaire"* Disaster at the Beasts of Holm on the 1st January, 1919. Of the 205 persons lost, 175 were natives of the island and for them and their comrades Lewis still mourns. With gratitude for their service and in sorrow for their loss.

> "Do cheuman tha san doimhneachd mhòir
>   Do slighe tha sa chuan:
>   Ach luirg do chas chan aithnich sinn,
>   Tha siud am falach uainn.
> *Sailm LXXVII, 19."*

The Gaelic words are from Psalm 77, verse 19. One translation is:

> *"Thy way is in the sea and in the waters great thy path: Yet are thy footsteps hid, O Lord, None knowledge thereof hath."*

The monument does not list the four men from Harris, two from Berneray and one from Scalpay. All of these seven are listed on their home monuments (five in Tarbert and two in Berneray).

In 2001 a decorative plaque was placed at the beginning of the path accessing the monument by Scottish Water. It was unveiled on 4th January 2002 by Lord Lieutenant of the Western Isles, Alexander Matheson. Although the text contains a few inaccuracies, it gives a good account of the events of the night when the *Iolaire* sank, and the subsequent impact on the islands. The tubular railing surrounding the monument was replaced and the monument was restored by Sandwick Community Association at a cost of £2,500 in the summer and autumn of 2003.

Since 1960 the *Iolaire* memorial, and the vantage point where it stands, overlooking the Beasts of Holm, has become the location for anniversary events. The passage of years has made the anniversaries more poignant and a time has now been reached where no-one is alive who can remember the events of the tragic day. Mòr Macleod (née Smith), the last of the *Iolaire* children, attended the 90th anniversary service held at the memorial at Holm when some 300 people gathered in the cold dawn of New Year's Day 2009. Mòr died on 7th January 2012 aged 97. Sandy Macleod from Garrabost, the second last of the children to pass away, also attended that 90th anniversary New Year's Day.

The tragedy of the *Iolaire* is also commemorated in Stornoway itself, at Battery Point (also called Inaclete Point, behind the power station), where in 1995 a plaque was erected between two of the long guns used by men of the Royal Naval Reserve. The plaque pays tribute to the men who trained there, and to the use of the depot as a mortuary in 1919. It states:

> "This plaque is erected on the site at Inaclete Point to commemorate the establishment of the largest RNR Battery and Training Depot in Great Britain. During the 43 years of its existence many thousands of men from Lewis, Harris and Wester Ross received their training for service in the Royal Navy. The Battery was established in 1876 and decommissioned in 1919.

> "On 1st January 1919 it was from this depot that the Coastguard Lifesaving Apparatus was despatched to the scene of the wreck of the "*Iolaire*" on the "Beasts of Holm" 2000 metres south-east of this plaque. Two hundred and five lives were lost and many of the one hundred and thirty-eight bodies recovered were laid out here for identification by their relatives who had travelled from all parts of Lewis and Harris.

> "In subsequent years the site was used by HM Coastguard as a look out station …. And from 1943 to the present time by the Hydro Board, now Hydro Electric, by whom this commemorative plaque was erected in 1995."

The plaque was unveiled on the 50th anniversary of VE Day by Ivor M Murray and Lt Cdr WAJ (Peter) Cunningham RNR. Ivor's grandfather John Mackenzie (Iain 'An Anndra), Portvoller, was a survivor of the *Iolaire*.

The Iolaire memorial was unveiled at Holm on 26th October 1960 by ex-Provost Alastair J. MacKenzie. Both he and Provost Donald James Stewart of Stornoway Town Council laid a wreath.

Events and celebrations

The plaque at Battery Point records that Stornoway naval base – HMS *Iolaire* – was decommissioned in 1919. It had played a large part in the life of the town and of so many of the island's men, since it was opened in 1915. At the Sailors' Institute on Keith Street a farewell concert to the base was held on Wednesday 2nd April 1919. Vice Admiral RF Boyle MVO was present and among the artistes was Lt Cdr William DT Morrish singing "Up from Somerset".

Also in April, the first recognition came for one of the unassuming heroes of the *Iolaire* disaster, John Finlay Macleod. John Finlay (Iain Mhurdo) of Port of Ness was a carpenter to trade, and had been demobilised from the Stornoway base just days before, on 5th April, when on 9th April he was awarded the Royal Humane Society's parchment and silver medal for an act of gallant bravery. The day was a celebration for many in Stornoway, as the *Highland News* reported:

"Wednesday was a gala day in Stornoway. In the afternoon games were held in the park immediately below the Castle, and were attended by a large concourse of people from the town, as well as a considerable sprinkling of visitors from the surrounding district. The weather conditions were perfect, and the various events followed each other in rapid succession and with a smoothness that reflected the utmost credit on the Committee in charge of the arrangements.

"In the course of the afternoon the proceedings were suspended while an interesting function was performed, namely, the presentation of the Humane Society's parchment and silver medal to John Finlay MacLeod RNR, for a deed of gallant

John Finlay was presented with the Royal Humane Society medal (top and bottom right), the Lloyds silver medal (top and bottom left) and a vellum certificate by the trustees of the Carnegie Hero Fund.

A large crowd gathered on the Castle green in 5th April 1919 to see John Finlay Macleod presented with the Royal Humane Society parchment and silver medal by Provost Murdo Maclean. With them on the platform are Lord Leverhulme (looking behind him), his guests Mr Robert Tootill (MP for Bolton 1914-22), Sir Albert Parkinson (MP and Mayor of Blackpool 1918-22), Coastguard Divisional Officer Lt Frederick Boxall and Baillie Roderick Smith, who became Provost of Stornoway later in 1919.

bravery performed by him in connection with the melancholy disaster to HMS *Iolaire* (sic) on the morning of New-Year's Day last. MacLeod was one of those on board the ill-fated vessel when she struck on the rocks at Holm. With swift perception of the danger, but with superb coolness and judgement and daring intrepidity, he seized a line, plunged boldly into the water amidst the inky darkness and swam ashore, thereby enabling a hawser to be landed, by means of which a large number of lives were saved that would otherwise have gone to swell the already heavy roll of loss.

"Provost Maclean, who was arrayed in the full panoply of his official robes and chain of office, in a few well-chosen and appropriate sentences, made the presentation, pinning the medal on Macleod's breast amid enthusiastic manifestations of pleasure

369

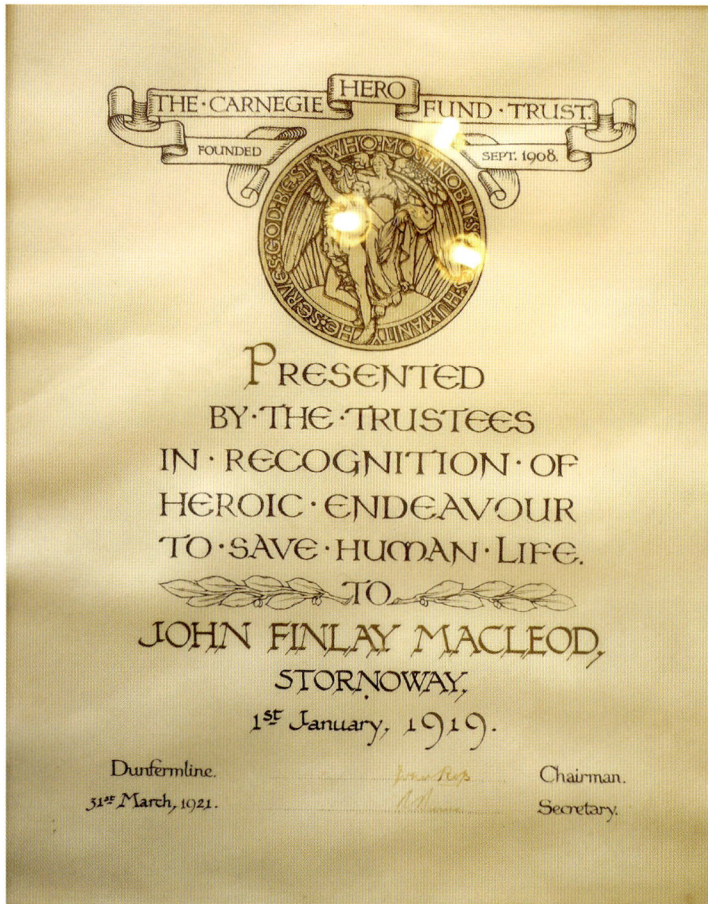

John Finlay's vellum certificate presented from the trustees of the Carnegie Hero Fund.

from the crowd gathered round the platform. On the platform, besides Provost Maclean and the hero of the hour, were Lord Leverhulme and a distinguished party, including, among others, Mr Toothill, MP, and Mayor of Blackpool; Lieut Boxall, Divisional Officer, Coastguard; the Misses Lever, Baillie Smith, etc."[8]

The Royal Humane Society award was not the only honour which marked John Finlay's heroism. He was also presented with Lloyd's Medal and the Carnegie Parchment. A mainland newspaper reported (incorrectly) that he was responsible for the rescue of 79 passengers from a stricken vessel, when he was rewarded by the Trustees of the Carnegie Hero Fund at Dunfermline on Thursday 31st March 1921. The newspaper went on to say:

> "Immediately after the crash, Macleod volunteered to swim ashore with a heaving line. With great difficulty he succeeded in reaching the land and, with assistance, hauled over the hawser, by means of which 79 passengers were landed. Macleod was awarded an honorary certificate and a sum of £50."

Captain George Watt, Newmarket, the Admiralty's port pilot at Stornoway during the war was made an MBE in April 1920. He had a strenuous war when berthing and piloting steamers – sometimes over 40 large vessels were being berthed at one time. He did it without a hitch or accident. He had gone to sea as a young lad at the end of the 1860s, being a Master on sailing ships and then transferring to steamships, before he retired in 1913. He was called back to serve during the war.

Another MBE in 1920 went to Miss Ada Maud Crow, Seamen's Mission, Esplanade Road for services in the Mission, probably to distressed seamen during the war. Royal

Navy Padré Rev S. Morris Crow (her father or her brother) was Chaplain to the Mission from 1915 until the war's end.

Decades would pass before any commemorative event brought people together in memory of the tragedy, the island shrouded in a dark silence. From the 1960s the clouds began to part and the unveiling of memorials began to create opportunities for remembrance and thanksgiving in memory of those lost.

The 70th, 80th and 90th anniversaries gathered pace, with publications and radio or television programmes re-awakening memories, especially as an urgency to gather living memories inspired reporters and local historians. A 90th anniversary memorial service was conducted at Hogmanay 2008/09 by Port Missionary Superintendent Finlay Macleod of the Royal National Mission to Deep Sea Fishermen, with 300 people gathered at the memorial at Holm. At the same time the Stornoway RNLI lifeboat *Tom Sanderson* held a memorial service at sea, with wreaths laid around the Beasts of Holm.

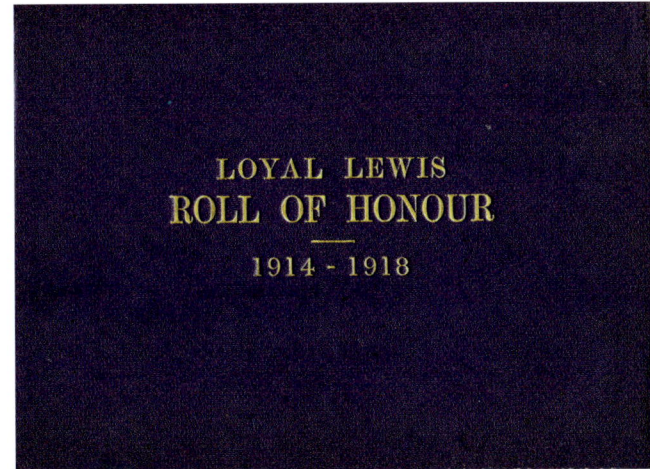

Loyal Lewis Roll of Honour 1914-1918 – front cover

Publications, press and media commemoration

After the first wave of reporting of the tragedy itself had died down, it would be some time before the silence of grief would be penetrated by any attempt to summarise the events of 1st January 1919, or to make sense of what had happened.

The first printed record of the story of the *Iolaire* was produced in the final edition of William Grant's *Loyal Lewis Roll of Honour* in 1920. In a separately titled section the story of the *Iolaire*, including pictures of men lost and an

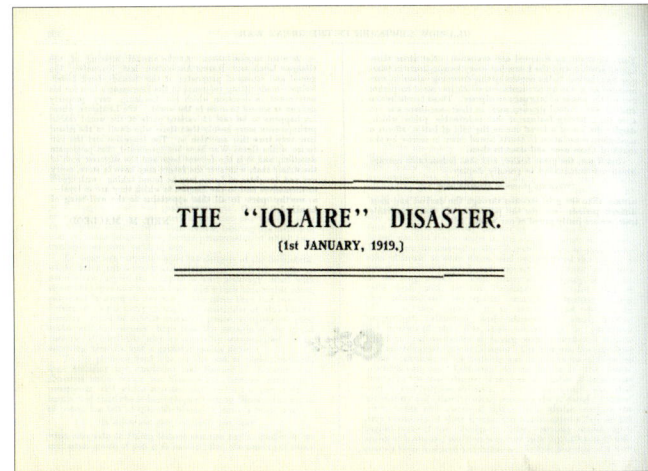

Loyal Lewis Roll of Honour 1914-1918 – Iolaire title page.

account of the Public Inquiry, were prefaced by remarks from Grant:

"THE overwhelming catastrophe of 1st January, 1919, which plunged Lewis into bitterest sorrow, sent a thrill of horror and a wave of sympathy throughout the English-speaking world. Apart from the great loss of life, the whole surrounding circumstances – the place, the time, the season, the mystery as to the cause of the disaster – were calculated to touch a responsive chord in every feeling heart .... For the four and a half years of war, Death's messenger had been no stranger in the homes of Lewis, for hundreds of our gallant Islesmen had fallen on battlefields in foreign lands or found their last resting place in the silent depths of war-swept seas. But the Armistice was signed and the perils of war were past when the crowning sorrow fell on Lewis. It was New Year's Eve, too, and the whole ship's company, in festive mood, were homeward bound for the glad re-union so long and so lovingly anticipated, and well they knew how eagerly their homecoming was awaited and what preparations were even then being made to welcome them. All this, only to be shipwrecked at the very entrance to Stornoway Harbour with appalling loss of life. What a tragedy!"[9]

As reporters sought to capture the events and emotions of the *Iolaire* disaster over the years, survivors and children would increasingly be asked to recall their own memories for public consumption,

especially as the significant anniversaries arrived – forty, fifty and sixty years after the events. The mortality of survivors, the last of whom was thought to have died in 1992, and the passing of the few remaining widows and orphans – the last of these in 2012 – also stimulated renewed interest in recording personal memories of the events for posterity. In some cases the individuals interviewed were encouraged to visit the memorial to have their picture taken or to be filmed at the site of the tragedy. Some of the words of those interviewed are included in Chapter 8.

Significant milestone publications were produced from 1960, when the *Stornoway Gazette* book *Sea Sorrow: The Story of the Iolaire Disaster* was published. This was based on a contemporary account of the disaster which appeared

Survivors John Finlay Macleod (left) and John Murray ('Ain Help) seated in front of the Iolaire memorial in the 1960s, soon after the unveiling of the monument. It was the first time they had returned to the site since the sinking.

in the newspaper itself in July 1959. The leaflet was just 24 pages long and included an account of the tragedy, some poetry and a list of the Lewismen lost in the disaster. It was reprinted in 1972.

In 1961 the journalist Fred Macaulay made a programme for BBC Radio Highland (now BBC Radio nan Gàidheal) in which he interviewed *Iolaire* survivors and descendants, producing a vivid account of the events and their subsequent impact on the islands. Extracts from these interviews appear in Chapter 8.

In January 1969, to commemorate the 50th anniversary of the tragedy, BBC Radio produced a programme titled *Case C93*, presented by Martin Macdonald. This was repeated in June 1970 and a TV documentary for the BBC2 *Yesterday's Witness* series, *The Iolaire Disaster* was produced in September 1973. In those days BBC2 was not available in the islands, so it was first seen when it was repeated on BBC1 in October 1973.

In 1978 the book *Call na h-Iolaire* by Tormod Calum Dòmhnallach was published by Acair, in Gaelic with an English summary, and with a significant evaluation of the navigational issues (which is reproduced in full in Appendix 2 of this book). Grampian TV's documentary *Home at Last* was first aired for the 70th anniversary of the disaster in 1989 and included interviews with descendants. BBC Alba also marked the 90th anniversary with a one-hour TV documentary, *An Iolaire* (later screened by BAFTA at the Glasgow Film Festival 2009) and a radio documentary, broadcast on Hogmanay on Throughout the years newspapers and media have commemorated the anniversary of the wreck with individual accounts from survivors, descendants and historical commentators, and many of their words have helped to shape the narrative of this latest book, which is published to mark the centenary of the *Iolaire* disaster.

Artefacts and memorabilia

The few precious items recovered from the wreck and from the shore, either with or without the remains of their owners, now form our tangible link with a scene of unimaginable horror. In some cases the small gifts carried in the kitbags and pockets of drowned men remained with their families, handed down and, sometimes, taken from the country as relatives and descendants emigrated for Canada, Australia and other destinations worldwide. Survivors, too, might cling to a relic of the wreck.

The lifebelt that Donald Maciver, am Bèicear, of New Tolsta wore as he escaped the sinking ship is in the keeping

The bell and engine plate recovered from the sea bed by divers.

373

The bell was presented to the people of Stornoway at a ceremony at the Town Hall in 1971.

Pictured left to right: Survivors John Maclennan and Neil Nicolson, Provost of Stornoway Sandy Matheson, survivor Donald Murray and customs officer and receiver of wrecks WAJ (Peter) Cunningham.

of Museum nan Eilean at Lews Castle. At Ness Historical Society's local history museum at the former Cross School, there is a ditty box[10] belonging to Donald Macdonald of 13 Swainbost, inscribed with his name and containing coins from Japan, India, Ceylon and Egypt, as well as a record of the ships and bases where he and his brother Murdo served – Murdo also drowned. The box is all that remains of Donald, whose body was never recovered. Neither was the body of Angus Mackinnon of Caversta in Lochs, who married Dover lass Ethel Ratcliff and left her expecting their only child when he drowned on the *Iolaire*. His greatcoat was found, in its pocket a sealed tin containing a lock of Ethel's hair, which is now on display at the local history museum at Ravenspoint, in South Lochs.

Some of the few remaining artefacts recovered from the seabed at Holm, after the Navy had concluded salvage operations, were presented to townsfolk, attended by memorial events. A presentation in Stornoway Town Hall marked the recovery of the bell and plate of the sunken yacht, recovered by Mr C A Robb, a diver from Easdale, near Oban and presented to the then Stornoway Town Council. These objects are now with Museum nan Eilean at Lews Castle.

A fragment of ensign from the *Iolaire*, made of red plain weave wool fabric and measuring approximately 4 x 1½ inches has been conserved and mounted in an ash wood frame and is now preserved by Stornoway Historical Society. It was retrieved by the crew of HM Motor Launch *J F Spence* immediately after the wreck. The crew were James Crockett, Alex Macleod (Cando), Donald G. Mackenzie and Donald A. Macleod, all local RNR sailors.

What remains on the seabed – the wreck site

Over the years several divers have visited the wreck site and recovered items. As well as the yacht's bell and name-plate recovered in the early 1970s, the flare gun was recovered from the seabed by former Royal Navy diver Chris Murray in April 2012. It is displayed at Museum nan Eilean at Lews Castle. Chris, who now lives in Stornoway, gives this account:

"I first dived on HMY *Iolaire* in the late eighties and not much has changed over the years. She lies more or less up against the shoreline rocks just to the west of the memorial in a depth of around 35 feet. Some people imagine a wreck lying on the sea bed and rotting away, but in fact the truth is a lot different, as what was once a recognisable shipwreck changed dramatically when the Admiralty sent a salvage team, some time in the late 1920s, to recover anything that was deemed valuable, such as the bronze propeller, deck guns and engine. During this operation it seems almost certain that explosives and underwater cutting equipment were used, as the twisted and tortured metal plates on the seabed suggest.

"The only recognisable part of what was once a proud ship is the prop-shaft and boiler, now collapsing into the sea bed. What we have is a debris field about 50 metres in diameter, strewn with metal plating, ammunition shells, shards of broken glass, ceramics, ship timber, lead piping, and anything else that may have been on board including the odd sole of a shoe. There is a small section of black and white tiles which was perhaps the deck of the galley. I have recovered various bits such as naval tunic buttons, coins, china plate, brass taps, a stone pastry board and other items.

"Down on the seabed there is an overwhelming feeling of sadness which lingers around the remains of the *Iolaire*."[11]

The *Iolaire* is only one of many wrecks around the Beasts of Holm, treacherous rocks which have brought numerous ships to grief over the centuries. Chris Murray recounts:

"A few years ago while diving in the area out near the marker pole at Holm I came across a brass nameplate with *NIMBLE* engraved. Further out, in 100ft of water, lies the wreck of the steam drifter *Enzie*, still in good condition after sinking following a collision with the trawler *Barracuta* in 1948. There are large anchors in and around the Beasts – over the years it seems that a few vessels came to grief around this area. Numerous broken bottles and window panes dating from around 1830 onwards may indicate what we call the Bottle Wreck."

The so-called Bottle Wreck was a favourite site for local scuba divers, but there remained a strong disinclination for any local diver to visit the sacrosanct remains of the *Iolaire*. Recreational diver Alasdair Macleod of Swordale explains:

"In the early 1990s I trained to be a scuba diver with the Lewis and Harris Sub-Aqua Club. During my diving career, I was lucky enough to visit many historic wrecks in the Hebrides, including the iconic SS *Politician* of Whisky Galore fame and the historic wreck HMS *Lively*, which transported the Napier Commission round the Highlands and Islands until it came to grief on the Chicken Rock, off Swordale, in 1883.

The site of the Iolaire wreck pictured by diver Chris Murray, showing a fragment of china from the galley, the flare gun as discovered on the sea-bed, the Iolaire's propeller shaft – sheared off by the salvage team for salvage of the propeller – and the propeller shaft, ribs and boiler as they now appear (2018).

"There was an unwritten rule within the club at that time that we would avoid the *Iolaire*, for obvious reasons. However, there was an interesting wreck on the inner side of the Beasts of Holm which we called the Bottle Wreck – no-one had established its real name. It was a wreck in outline only, due to the pounding it had received over the years in this exposed location. Every spring, after the winter gales, the Bottle Wreck was a favourite dive, as often there was a bounty of old bottles on the seabed near the wreck. The bottles were made of thick, green glass and had rounded bottoms which dated them at over 100 years old. Fairly close to the Bottle Wreck lay the remains of the *Iolaire* and we were always careful to avoid it. As I knew the history of this tragic vessel, I was careful to stay well away.

"However one day, by accident, my dive buddy and I landed on the wreck of the *Iolaire*. I immediately realised where we had landed and indicated to my buddy that we should move away. This is what I wrote in my dive log-book that day, 27th August 1994: 'Dropped down onto the *Iolaire* by mistake and immediately wanted to get away from it as quickly as possible. I knew that it was the *Iolaire* from the mass of crumpled metal on the seabed, totally unlike the Bottle Wreck. I felt a real sense of unease and indicated to my buddy to move away from it. He was from the mainland and probably not as aware as I was of the significance of the wreck. Luckily, he understood my desire to move away and we headed for our planned dive site. He probably didn't understand why I wanted to scram. As soon as I saw the *Iolaire*, I felt a deep sense of unease and just didn't want to be there.'

"During my years of diving, I never felt frightened or afraid underwater apart from that time on the *Iolaire*. It was not a pleasant experience that day, although I can say that I have seen the wreck of the *Iolaire* at first hand. Some years ago BBC Alba sent divers with underwater cameras down to the watery grave of the *Iolaire*. The visibility on that day wasn't good and the hazy images of the wreck captured the scene on the seabed perfectly."[12]

Artistic responses to an island tragedy

"The *Iolaire* disaster stretches our vocabulary to its limits and can only be articulated further through art."[13]

Many have turned to creative means to express strong emotions and to respond to their feelings on the tragedy and its impact on the islands. Most particularly, the island traditions of poetry and song were called upon to give voice to emotions which could not be spoken or otherwise articulated. A representative collection of poetry and song about the *Iolaire* tragedy is presented in Chapter 10.

From the powerful imagination of Murdo Macfarlane, the Melbost Bard, who as a young man had seen the bodies strewn along the shore a short distance from his own home, came the poem *Raoir Reubadh an Iolaire*. Macfarlane's song was part of a great wealth of music and poetry which was produced, and continues to be produced, in response to the sinking of the *Iolaire*. In 2014 the poem *Banntrach Cogaidh* (War widow), written by National Mòd bard John Macleod was set to music by Erik Spence and premiered at the Royal National Mòd in Inverness, as part of the Great War centenary commemorations. John Macleod was the son of Norman of 13 Arnol and it was his mother's grief after the death of his father, her repeated washing of his uniform and laying it to dry on the wall outside the house, which inspired the verses.

In 2014, as Britain commemorated the beginning of the Great War, a pipe tune written in tribute by Pipe Major Donald Macleod of Lewis won the memorial competition held each year in his name. PM Donald Macleod was born in Stornoway eighteen months before the tragedy, in 1917. The 2014 winner of the competition was Roddy Macleod, playing PM Macleod's piobaireachd *Lament for the Iolaire*.[14] The pipes and the ceòl mòr (great music) tradition of Highland piping formed a central feature of one piece of music commissioned for the centenary commemorations in 2018 by the Stornoway arts centre An Lanntair, as part of the 14-18 NOW programme of arts events commemorating the Great War. Composer Iain Morrison is the great-grandson of John Morrison of 10 Coll, who was lost on the *Iolaire* leaving eight children, of whom Iain's grandfather John Eona was one.

Iain was to perform his new work *Sàl (Saltwater)* with Scottish artists Dalziel + Scullion on 31st December 2018. Also being performed as part of a live programme of events was a new collaboration by Gaelic singer Julie Fowlis and fiddler Duncan Chisholm. *An Treas Suaile (The Third Wave)*, was inspired by the heroic story of John Finlay Macleod and the rope by which he saved so many lives.

There are numerous artistic representations of the *Iolaire* disaster in physical form – a panel of the Great Tapestry of Scotland, made by ladies from South Harris unveiled at the Scottish Parliament in Holyrood, Edinburgh in 2013, depicts 'The sinking of HMY *Iolaire* off Stornoway, 1919' and shows scenes including hands gripping the life-saving rope, women gathered on the shore in grief and a cart carrying a shrouded body across the moor to a crofthouse. As part of the centenary commemoration of the disaster in 2018, one hundred portraits of men lost on the *Iolaire* were created by Stornoway artist Dr Margaret Ferguson, and at the CalMac ferry terminal in Stornoway a scale working model of the *Iolaire*, built by John Campbell from Portvoller, is displayed, having undertaken her maiden voyage at Loch an t-Siumpain in Portvoller on 1st January 2013.

Portrait of Malcolm Macdonald, 57 South Bragar, completed in 2018 by artist Margaret Ferguson

Individuals had their own ways of commemorating the Iolaire. John Campbell of Portvoller created this scale model of the yacht and launched her at Loch an t-Siumpan, near his home, on 1st January 2013.

The *Iolaire* Centenary: 31st December 2018 – 1st January 2019

In March 2013 the Scottish Government announced the formation of the Scottish Commemorations Panel, to oversee the programme of events marking 100 years since the Great War, and to ensure that the contribution of Scotland would be appropriately recognised.

Among events to mark the passing of 100 years since the islands' tragic postscript to the story of the war, the unveiling of new sculptures, exhibitions, musical commissions and the publication of this book formed significant milestones. The centenary of the *Iolaire* disaster was to be the final formal event in the official, national four-year programme commemorating the centenary of the Great War. Recognised as a time for deep reflection, it would also create the opportunity for a significant memorial to give the tragedy the national profile and place in history it merits.

Among the acts of commemoration, a design was therefore sought for a new memorial. The Stornoway-based arts centre An Lanntair, with financial assistance from local authority Comhairle nan Eilean Siar, opened a call for

In 2018 the young people of the islands designed a memorial to the dead of the Iolaire, gathering a stone for every man lost from the town or village where he was born. These included stones from as far afield as London and the Isle of Wight. It was devised with help from the Nicolson Institute, Stornoway Historical Society and Stornoway Amenity Trust and placed, together with a memorial bench provided by Stornoway Port Authority, in Carn Gardens, overlooking South Beach and the harbour.

artist submissions, consulted on the shortlisted ideas and commissioned Royal Scottish Academicians Will Maclean, Marian Leven and Arthur Watson to produce a sculpture of bronze and stone bearing the names of those lost and the communities they came from. The statue features a coiled rope, symbolising the rope on which 40 sailors were rescued from the stricken yacht. Part of the preparations for the event included re-instatement of the path leading down to the 1960 *Iolaire* monument.

The Western Isles local authority, Comhairle nan Eilean Siar, planned a programme of events including a civic event and clifftop vigil in remembrance of the *Iolaire* disaster on 31st December 2018 into 1st January 2019. There were also to be opportunities for participation by schools – the Stornoway secondary school, The Nicolson Institute, worked with Stornoway Amenity Trust and Stornoway Historical Society to create a new memorial in the town centre, for which pupils collected 201 stones from all over Lewis and Harris and parts of Scotland and England, each representing one of the men lost. It was unveiled in 2018. An *Iolaire* Working Party was formed late in 2017 and the Comhairle also worked with the Royal Navy and Scottish Commemorations Panel. A Facebook page elicited public contributions throughout 2018.

Cllr Norman A Macdonald, convener of Comhairle nan Eilean Siar and chairman of the *Iolaire* Working Group, said:

> "This commemoration is of major significance for our Islands. The events of that terrible night in January 1919 impacted on communities throughout the Western Isles and remain a poignant reminder of the sacrifices made by our young men in the service of their country. It is the worst tragedy to befall our Islands and its effect reverberates to this day."[15]

The new pathway to the Iolaire memorials and original cairn of stones, completed in 2018 ahead of the centenary commemorations

Marian Leven's impression of the Iolaire Centenary Sculpture by Will Maclean RSA, Arthur Watson PRSA and Marian Leven RSA, commissioned by An Lanntair. Contained within the stone structure are a bronze wreath and a coiled rope representing the lost and saved, and a bronze installation with the names of all who perished.

To record the official events and significant physical memorials which set in stone the traumatic events of New Year's Day 1919 is not to overlook countless individual acts of remembrance which have taken place at cemeteries, in homes, and quietly at places of public remembrance over the past century. In many island homes the night of December 31st each year was a time for quiet reflection, to shed a tear and to speak in muted tones of those lost, perhaps sharing the painful memories with a fellow survivor or another bereaved parent or widow.

"Every New Year's Eve since that time had a special poignancy for my mother. No matter how late we came home, she'd be sitting up and she would say: 'Oh, well, you're alright', to which we would reply: 'Yes' and then, in her own quiet way, she would say: 'Well, I have other memories of this night.' And she would say: 'Go to your beds.'"[15]

The men who had direct, personal experience of the tragic night were still alive, with their personal memories, well into recent history. The last known survivor was Neil Nicolson, Lemreway, who died in 1992 at 95 years of age. A month earlier Donald Murray from Tolsta passed away, having reached the greatest age, 96 years, of all of the survivors. They were known and related to many of today's island fishermen and mariners, who seldom pass the Beasts of Holm without casting a lingering glance at the rocks and the marker, thoughts of the lost souls there given a moment of remembrance.

383

Chapter 9 Footnotes

1. Roddy Murray, *Stornoway Gazette*, 11th January 1994

2. As reported by the *Stornoway Gazette*, 25th January 1919

3. *Stornoway Gazette*, week ending 10th January 1920

4. *Highland News*, 22nd November 1919

5. *The Iolaire Disaster,* 31st December 1918 by A J Nicholson, Holm Farm

6. *Stornoway Gazette*, 6th June 1958

7. *Stornoway Gazette*, November 1960

8. Reported in the *Highland News*, April 12th 1919

9. William Grant in Loyal Lewis, final edition, *Stornoway Gazette*, 1920

10. Ditty box – a box for the personal possessions of sailors or soldiers, in this case a small tin

11. Personal account of diver Chris Murray to author, 2017. Two seabed films of the Iolaire wreck made by Chris were posted on YouTube in 2009 and images from his dives on the wreck appear in this book

12. Personal account of Alasdair Macleod to author, 2017

13. Roddy Murray, founding director and head of visual arts, An Lanntair, at www.lanntair.com

14. *Lament for the Iolaire*, Pipe Major Donald Macleod OBE

15. Press statement from Comhairle nan Eilean Siar, 2018

16. Peggy Gillies, daughter of John Murray, 36 Lionel

Chapter 10

Poetry, Verse and Song

A considerable number of poems have been written over the years following the *Iolaire's* loss, both in Gaelic and in English. Many were published within weeks of the tragedy, in newspapers around Scotland, illustrating the shock felt nationally at the terrible circumstances of the loss. The selection in this chapter is of the most well-known and significant works.

We have provided translations to help those readers who may not be literate in Gaelic, conveying the sense and feeling of the poems, rather than a literal or poetic translation.

Further titles and references, especially to recent compositions, are given in Appendix 3.

The HMY *Iolaire* Disaster

By R. A. Stephen, 9 Keith Street, Stornoway

This poem was thought to have little poetic merit when first published in February 1919 but, despite its critics, this is undoubtedly the widest-known poem about the loss of the *Iolaire*. It was in circulation in several different versions. A version compiled by James Shaw Grant in 1959 was published in the *Stornoway Gazette* and in the *Eilean an Fhraoich Annual*. This is the poet's original.

'Twas nineteen hundred and eighteen,
December's latest day,
When the HMY the Iolaire,
From Kyle did sail away.

The ship was bound for Stornoway,
A port in Lewis Isle,
On board 300 Navy men,
The best of rank and file.

They shipped on board the Iolaire
To cross the raging main,
And little dreamt they of their friends
They'd never see again.

Out on the briny sea once more,
There goes the jolly tar,
To cross the Minch to Stornoway –
The distance is not far.

Up on deck and down below,
Was full of mirth and glee,
When thinking of the friends they'd meet
When once they crossed the sea.

The South wind blew in vengeance wild,
The waves aloud did roar,
And soon the light of Rona dipped
As they neared the Western shore.

So, then gleamed out the Arnish Light,
As with a welcome smile,
And each successive flash would say;
"Stornoway in a while."

Then on she sped on her fateful course,
And passed the point of turning,
She left behind the Arnish Light;
A light well-trimmed, and burning.

The lights of Stornoway did loom -
"See! Yonder is the pier,
And we'll be greeted by our friends
And wished a glad New Year."

The old year slowly swept away,
With all its joy and sorrow,
And thus the New Year did appear,
With sadness on the morrow.

'Twas early in the morning,
On the first day of the year,
When such a sad disaster.
Was unexpected here.

At last she reached the spot of fate,
Near by was South Holm Head,
When o'er two hundred lives were lost,
And numbered with the dead.

Right early did the herald come,
The saddest news to tell,
Of the HMY the Iolaire,
And all that there befell.

They'll roam no more the mountain side,
The valleys and the dells;
Nor by the brooklet's heathery banks,
Whose chorus softly swells.

They'll travel not the rock-bound coast,
Where sea birds softly cry,
Nor yet along the sandy beach
Where they did live near by.

They fought for Britain's glory,
And sailed the oceans o'er,
At last they died like heroes
On the threshold of their door.

But now their warfare's ended,
They've laid their armour down,
They have won the British laurels,
And to-day a heavenly crown.

Their storms in life are over,
Their anchor's safely cast
In that celestial harbour
With God himself at last.

Highland News 1st February 1919

A Mother's Lament: for the empty chair that was found in every part of Lewis on January 1st, 1919

By Canon Henry Anderson Meaden, Stornoway

Canon Meaden was the curate at St Peters Episcopal Church of Scotland and formed the Boys' Naval Brigade in 1912. Two former members of the brigade were among those drowned. Canon Meaden officiated at the funeral of 18-year-old messenger boy Donald Macleod of Murray's Court, and at the memorial service from HMT *Kimberley* over the wreck site on 14th January 1919.

There's just one less in this busy world —
One less to bear with its strife;
For one has passed to the great Unknown
To learn of a restful life.

There's only one empty place to fill —
Then all goes on as before;
It's only a footfall long delayed,
And one less hand on the door.

Just one less heart to respond to heart,
And one less soul to be stirred;
Only one ripple of laughter less,
And one less voice to be heard.

Yes! Only one in a crowded world,
With many to solace me;
But still there is one each day I miss,
And one that I long to see.

So, often now in the evening time,
When the light is growing dim,
I look away to the Western sky,
And long to be Home with him.

Isle of Sorrow

By Neil Munro

Dr Neil Munro (1863-1930) of Inverary is best-known as author of the Para-Handy series of stories. The poem was written for a matinee held in the King's Theatre, Glasgow, in April 1919 for the Lewis Naval Disaster Fund. It was recited by stage and film actor John Martin-Harvey, son of a yacht designer and ship-builder, who had spent the war touring to recruit for the military and raise funds. The performance raised almost £250.

April has come to the isles again, blythe as a lover,
Shaking out birdsong and sunshine and soothing the tides;
April has come to the Hebrides, filled them with frolic,
Only in Lewis of sorrow, bleak winter abides.

Always they went to battles, the people of Lewis,
And always they fell, in the wars of a thousand years;
Peace never to Lewis brought springtime of joy or of season,
The wars might be won, but the women were destined to tears!

That is, to-day, why in Lewis the lark sings unheeded,
The sparkle of waves in the sea-creeks gladdens no eye;
No dance to the pipe in the croft, and no mirth in the shieling,
Cheerless and leaden the hours of the spring go by.

They had lit up their windows for beacons, the women of Lewis,
The peat fires were glowing a welcome, the table was spread;
The sea brought their sons back home from war and the long
*   years of tumult,*
And cast them ashore, on the cliffs of their boyhood – dead!

We are but players in motley, brief moths of a season,
Mimicking passion and laughter, and loving and grief;
But yet we are kin to all souls that are sad and enduring,
Acquainted with sorrow ourselves, we would bring them relief.

Far, far is the cry to the Lews and its storm-bitten beaches,
To the isle of lamenting, that lies on the sea like a gem,
If aught be of feeling profound in this place of our playing,
'Tis because we remember the widows, our thoughts are with them!

Stornoway Gazette 11th April 1919
Highland News 12th April 1919

Leòdhas an dèidh a' Chogaidh

Le Dòmhnall Macaoidh, 2 An t-Acha Mòr

Tha Leòdhas tùrsach bho thaobh gu taobh
Ri caoidh nan òg-fhear nach pill don tìr
A' cheart cho cràiteach 's a bha Ràicheil
Nuair a chualas an Ramah i gul 's a' caoidh.

Ri caoidh nam fiùran thug iad nan ìobairt
Air altair sìobhaltachd clann nan daoin'
Thug iomadh Sìofort a cheann na ìobairt
Nan grunnan prìseil an tìrean cèin.

Gach fine Gàidhealach bha ann mar b' àbhaist
Tha 'n ainm 's gach àite air rola sgrìobht'
Na gillean àlainn nach pill don àite
Thuit cuid gu tràth dhiubh is phàigh a' phrìs.

Ach 's e bhliadhna ùir ud a rinn an ciùrradh
Nuair chaidh an Iolair' air sgeirean Thuilm
Cha chuireadh cainnt air na b' urrainn innse
Gach cridhe briste 's gach sùil fo dheòir.

Lewis After the War

By Donald Mackay, 2 Achmore

*Lewis is in mourning
And grieving for the young men that will not return to shore
Just as tortured as Rachel was
When she was heard in Ramah weeping and grieving.*

*Grieving for the handsome youth who made their sacrifice
At the altar of civilization of mankind
Many of the Seaforths were sacrificed
As a precious group in foreign lands.*

*Each Highland clan was there as usual
Their names in many places are written in the roll of honour
The beautiful boys who will not return home
Some fell early and paid the price.*

*But it was that new year that caused the torture
When the Iolaire struck the rocks of Holm
Words cannot describe the situation
Every heart broken and tears in every eye.*

Highland News 3rd May 1919

The *Iolaire* Disaster, 31st December 1918

by A.J. Nicholson, Holm Farm, Isle of Lewis

Alex John Nicholson (1911-1971) was a child at Holm Farm on the night of the wreck and wrote the poem as a teenager in 1928. During the Second World War he was awarded the George Medal for bravery at Stornoway Airport when, on 8th August 1941, he received burns while pulling a fellow airman out of a blazing 220 Squadron Hudson plane. The pilot was killed and the crew were all injured.

On a cliff across the bay,
Just two miles from Stornoway,
Stands a cairn of stones above a jagged reef;
It's a tragic souvenir,
Of that cold and sad New Year,
When a crowd of Lewis sailors came to grief.

In the history of the Lews,
Never did such dreadful news,
Bring the brave God-fearing people to despair;
Boys who fought upon the seas,
That their country might have peace,
Lost their lives in that disastrous Iolaire.

In the "Queen of all the Isles"
Every one wore welcome smiles,
For the Armistice was signed across the foam;
Young and old wives full of cheer,
Celebrating this New Year,
For their boys who'd been at war were coming home.

'Twas a wild December night,
When the Iolaire went down,
Without warning to the gallant souls aboard;
Some were sleeping where they could,
Never dreaming that they would
Find a watery grave without a farewell word.

Happy parents lined the pier,
For they thought their sons were near,
Till the mailboat Sheila tied up at the docks;
Then the dreadful news went round,
That their brave sons had been drowned,
And the Iolaire was wrecked on Holm rocks.

Some were standing on the deck,
Of that sad ill-fated wreck,
When she struck the cruel rocks on Holm shore;
Screams and cries soon rent the air,
Here and there a dying prayer,
To the friends and families they would see no more.

Just one rending grinding crash,
It was over in a flash,
And the jagged rock soon tore her open wide;
Then the death cries, ghastly, grim,
As the waves went pouring in,
And the Iolaire slid over on her side.

Bolder men in that grim band,
Tried to swim a rope to land,
But their brave and desperate efforts only failed;
For the ocean with a roar,
Dashed them senseless on the shore,
While the wild wind o'er the moorland whined and wailed.

Of two hundred men or more,
Only sixty got ashore,
The flower of Lewis perished in the foam;
Those brave boys who came so far,
Through the dangers of the war,
By the irony of fate were drowned at home.

Broken hearted parents tried,
To distinguish those who died,
As the morning tide brought in its gruesome toll;
Toys and presents strewed the shore,
Meant for friends they'd see no more,
For their names were upon that great death roll.

Raoir Reubadh an *Iolaire*

Murchadh Macphàrlain, Bàrd Mhealaboist, Leòdhas

Last Night the *Iolaire* was Torn Asunder

By Murdo Macfarlane, Melbost, Lewis

Born in 1901, Murdo was the fifth son of a fisherman, Malcolm MacFarlane. As a young man he saw the bodies of *Iolaire* sailors washed up on the shores near his home, and it had a profound effect on him. The loss of so many villagers and islanders affected Murdo and the tragedy prompted him to write both this and his longest poem, *Mar a Chailleadh an Iolaire*. Celebrated in later life as 'the Melbost Bard', Murdo wrote much poetry and song, and was also noted as a champion of Gaelic and an activist. He spent some time in Canada and served in the Second World War. Murdo died in 1982.

’S binn sheinn i, a’ chailin,
A-raoir ann an Leòdhas,
I fuineadh an arain
Le cridhe làn sòlais
Air choinneamh a leannain
Tha tighinn air fòrladh,
Tighinn dhachaigh thuic’ tèaraint’,
Fear a gràidh.

Last night in Lewis the maiden sang tunefully, happily baking bread in anticipation of her sweetheart, who is coming on leave: coming home to her safely, her loved one.

Tha ’n cogadh nis thairis
’S a’ bhuaidh leis na fiùrain
Tha nochd ri tigh’nn dhachaigh,
Tha ’n *Iolaire* gan giùlan.
Chuir mòine mun tein’ i
’S an coire le bùrn air,
Ghràidh, chadal cha tèidear
Gus an lò.

The war is now over, the heroes victorious, coming home tonight; the Iolaire *carries them. She put peats on the fire and a kettle of water: my dear, we’ll not sleep till daybreak.*

Bidh iadsan ri 'g aithris
'S bidh sinne ri 'g èisteachd
Ri euchdanaibh bhalaich
Na mara 's an fhèilidh
'S na treun-fhir a chailleadh,
A thuit is nach èirich
Ò, liuth'd fear deas dìreach
Chaidh gu làr!

Cluinn osnaich na gaoithe!
O, cluinn oirre sèideadh!
'S ràn buairte na doimhne,
Ò, 's mairg tha, mo chreubhag,
Aig muir leis an oidhch' seo
Cath ri muir beucach.
Sgaoil, Iolair', do sgiathaibh
'S greas le m' ghràdh.

Ri 'g èirigh tha 'n latha
'S ri tuiteam tha dòchas,
Air an t-slabhraidh tha 'n coire
Ri pìobaireachd brònach,
Sguir i dhol chun an dorais
'S air an teine chuir mòine,
Cluinn cruaidh-fhead na gaoithe
A' caoidh, a' caoidh.

They will be talking and we will listen to the feats of the sea-faring Gaels; and the brave ones who were lost, who fell and won't rise – so many upright, handsome men felled to the ground.

Hear the wind sighing! Oh, hear it blowing! and the troubled cry of the sea – pity, my goodness, those at sea this night fighting a roaring ocean: Iolaire, *spread your wings and make haste with my loved one.*

Day is breaking and hope is fading; the kettle on the chain-hanger piping sadly; she stopped going to the door and putting peat on the fire; hear the wind whistling loudly mourning, mourning.

Goirt ghuil i, a' chailin,
Moch madainn a-màireach
Nuair fhuair i san fheamainn
A leannan 's e bàthte,
Gun bhrògan mu chasan
Mar chaidh air an t-snàmh e,
'N sin chrom agus phòg i
A bhilean fuar.

Raoir reubadh an Iolair',
Bàtht' fo sgiathaibh tha h-àlach,
O na Hearadh tha tuireadh
Gu ruig Nis nam fear bàna.
O nach tug thu dhuinn beò iad,
A chuain, thoir dhuinn bàtht' iad,
'N sin ri do bheul cìocrach
Cha bhi ar sùil.

The maiden wept bitterly the following morning when they found her loved one drowned in the seaweed, no shoes on his feet as he had taken to swimming; then she crouched and kissed his cold lips.

Last night the Iolaire *was torn asunder, her brood drowned beneath her wings; there is mourning from Harris to Ness. Since you did not deliver them alive, oh sea, give them to us drowned, then from your ravenous mouth we'll expect nothing.*

War Widow

By Rev. John Macleod, 13 Arnol, Isle of Lewis.

Before John Macleod was a year old his father, Norman Macleod of Arnol, was drowned in the *Iolaire* disaster, his body washed ashore at the Braighe near Stornoway. John's mother, Christina, never got over the loss of her husband and died at a young age, probably from a broken heart. She was buried beside her husband at Bragar Cemetery, Isle of Lewis. John Macleod joined the Royal Navy in the Second World War and, in 1945, was ordained by the Presbytery of Glasgow for service as a chaplain in the Royal Navy. He later served in the Presbyterian Church in Canada, at St Paul's Newington, Edinburgh and finally at Kilbride Oban Old Parish Church. He died in Oban in 1995. *Banntrach Cogaidh/War Widow* was set to music by Erik Spence as part of *Mac-talla Cogaidh/Echoes of War* at the Royal National Mòd in Inverness, in October 2014.

Banntrach Cogaidh

Sgaoil i aodach air gàrradh;	*She spread clothes on a garden wall*
Briogais bhàn is lèine gheal.	*Tropical trousers and a white shirt,*
Crios gorm leathann,	*Broad blue belt,*
Còrd geal caol.	*White lanyard.*
Bha mi air clach ri taobh,	*I sat on a stone beside her*
Bonaid cruinn air mo cheann,	*A round bonnet on my head,*
Bonaid m' athar.	*My father's bonnet.*
Deise ghorm na stiallan	*The blue suit in strips*
Mar reub iad bho chorp i	*As they tore it from his body*
Nuair fhuair iad e	*When they found him*
Fuar bàite air an tràigh,	*Cold, drowned on the shore,*
Air a pasgadh le làmhan gràidh	*Folded by hands of love*
Is cridhe brist	*And a broken heart*
Mar deise rìgh dol gu banais.	*Like a royal dress for a wedding.*

Carson tha thu dol uair sa mhìos	*Why do you go once a month*
Don post office nad aodach dubh	*To the post office in your black clothes,*
Le cridhe trom	*With a heavy heart*
Is leabhar a' pheinnsein nad làimh?	*And the pension book in your hand?*
Carson a thog thu mi nad uchd	*Why did you take me in your arms,*
'S do cheann crom,	*With your head bowed*
Is fhluich thu m' aodann le do dheòir	*And wet my face with your tears,*
Nuair thuirt mi,	*When I said,*
"Mhàthair, cà' il m' athair?"	*"Mother, where's my father?"*
Aon là san sgoil	*One day in school*
Sheas sinn sàmhach dà mhionaid	*We stood in silence for two minutes*
A' cuimhneachadh	*Remembering*
Air laoich a' Chogaidh Mhòir,	*The heroes of the Great War*
Is ruith mi dhachaigh na mo dheann	*And I ran home at speed*
A dh'innse dhi,	*To tell her*
"Cha bhi cogadh tuilleadh ann."	*"There will be no more war."*
Oidhche gheamhraidh rinn i snìomh.	*On a winter's night she was spinning*
Shuidh mi ri taobh;	*I sat beside her;*
Bha ceann dol liath	*Her head was turning grey*
'S i fhathast òg.	*though still young*
An lùib an t-snàth chaidh	*Among the strands was twisted*
fuiltean mìn,	*a tender hair,*
Mar shìoda measg an dubh.	*Like silk amidst the black.*
Thuirt is, "Glèidh cuimhne	*She said, "Remember me*
Nuair chì thu m' fhalt an lùib an t-snàth	*When you see my hair among the thread*
'S nach bi mi ann",	*And I'm not here",*
'S mar thuirt, bha.	*And as she said, it was.*

Rinn iad d' uaigh ri taobh nan tonn,
Cha chlisg thu chaoidh aig gaoth
no stoirm.
Sibh sin cho rèidh, thu fhèin 's an cuan.
Cha toir e tuilleadh uat
do ghràdh.

Nach math gun tug am bàs thu tràth,
'S nach fhac' thu cogadh ùr
nad latha,
'S nach fhac' thu mise falbh
don bhlàr,
Le deise ghorm is bonaid cruinn
Mar bh' air m' athair
Nuair fhuair iad marbh e,
Aig a' Bhràigh.

They dug your grave beside the waves,
You will never be afraid of wind
or storm,
Now reconciled, you and the ocean.
It will never take from you,
your beloved.

It's good that death took you so early,
And that you did not live to
see a new war
And that you did not see me leaving
for the battles,
In blue uniform and round cap
As my father was dressed
When they found him, dead,
At the Braigh.

Oran na h-*Iolaire*

A' bhàrdachd air a dèanamh is Eachainn Macfhionghain,
Bàrd Bheàrnaraigh.

Nach cianail Eilean Leòdhais
'S nach brònach e san uair,
Is e ri caoidh nan àrmann sin
Chaidh àrachadh ann suas;
Tha peathraichean is bràithrean ann
Is pàrantan fo ghruaim
'S gu sònraichte na màthraichean
Lem pàistean beaga truagh.

Bidh madainn na Bliadhn' Ùire ud
Cho ùr dhuinne gu bràth,
A' cuimhneachadh nam fiùran sin
Chaidh sgiùrsadh far nach tràigh;
B' i sgeul bha ro-thùrsach i
A dh'ùraicheadh san àit'
'S nach gabh e cur am briathran dhomh
Na leudachadh le bàrd.

Nach iomadh ceàrn a shiubhail iad,
Shiubhail 'ad deas is tuath
Is chaidh iad tro na h-àmhghairean
'S na gàbhaidhean bha cruaidh;
Bha 'n nàmhaid is e 'n tòir orra
A Dhòmhnaich is a Luain
Ged 's ann air cladach Leòdhais
Chaidh an òrdachadh don chuan.

The Song of the *Iolaire*

By Hector Mackinnon, Berneray

How terrible for the Isle of Lewis
And how sad it is for them now
As they mourn for the brave men
That were brought up there.
There are sisters and brothers there
And parents under a gloom,
And especially the mothers
With their poor young children.

That New Year's morning
Will be new to us forever
Remembering the handsome youths
That were banished to where there is no tide;
The story was too distressing
As told in each place,
And I cannot put it into words
Or elaborate with poetry.

How many corners they travelled to
They travelled south and north,
And they made it through adversity
And dangerous perils
The enemy was in pursuit of them
On Sunday and on Monday
Although it was on the shores on Lewis
They were ordered to the sea.

Tha 'n *Iolaire* na sìneadh ann
'S na croinn aice an-àird,
Air creagan corrach millteanach
Chuir crìoch oirre cho tràth,
Le fiùrain a bu chiataiche
'S a choisich riamh air sràid
B' i bhanaltram neo-thruasail i
Sa chluasag nach eil blàth.

Nach duilich mar a thachair
Do na gaisgich ud a bh' ann
A thàinig air an astar ud
'S an dachaighean cho teann;
Bha càirdean is luchd-eòlais ann
Gu sòlasach san àm
A' cuimhneachadh nan òganach
A phògadh iad air làimh.

Cha b' fhada chun an cuala sinn
An fhuaim a bha le bròn,
Is dhùisg e mar am bruadar sinn
An truaighe thàinig òirnn';
Bha greadhnachas air fhuadachadh
Nuair chualas mu na seòid,
'S bha cridheachan ro luaisgeanach
Is dh'fhuasgail e na deòir.

Bha peathraichean is bràithrean ann,
Is pàrantan ri caoidh,
'S luchd-eòlais a bu chàirdiche,
Is nàbaidhean na tìr',
'S na leanaba' caomh bu ghràdhaichte
Aig màthair air a cìch,
Gun dual dhaibh bhith air allaban
'S an athraichean gan dìth.

The Iolaire is lying there
Her masts raised up high,
On dangerous steep rocks
That ended her so soon,
For those handsome young
That ever walked along a street
She was an unsympathetic nurse
And a pillow that is not warm.

How awful what happened
To the heroes that were there
That came that distance
And their homes so close by;
Friends and companions were there
Comforting them and
Remembering the young
Who would kiss their hand.

It wasn't long until we heard
The noise that came with grief
That woke us like a dream
The misery that came to us;
The rejoicing was displaced
When we heard about the heroes
And our hearts were agitated
And it caused our tears.

There were sisters and brothers
And parents in mourning
And companions who were related
And neighbours from the community,
And the much loved young children
At their mother's breast
May yet become orphans,
With their fathers missing.

Tha Na Hearadh far an eòlach mi
Gu brònach mar tha càch,
Tha bhliadhna seo neo-shòlasach
Aig mòran feadh an àit',
Tha ionndrainn agus iargain ann
'S nach dìochuimhnich an càs,
Na càirdean a bhith dealachadh
A chailleadh air ar sgàth.

Cha bhàrd gu dèanamh òrain mi
'S cha chòir dhomh dol nan dàil
Gun eachdraidh tha seo innse dhuibh
Na sgrìobhadh le mo làmh,
Ach 's duilich mu na h-òganaich
'S nach còmhlaich sinn gu bràth;
Bha Tarmod agus Dòmhnall innt'
À eilean feòir mo ghràidh.

Ach guidheam anns an dealachadh
Mun aithris mi nas mò,
'S e Crìosda a bhith maille ribh
A neartaicheas am bròn,
'S E 'n caraid is fear bhios dhuibh
Na bràthair anns an fheòil,
Oir fanaidh E gu sìorraidh leibh
Is siabaidh e gach deòir.

Harris, the place I am familiar with,
Is sad like the rest,
This year is mournful
For many throughout the island,
There is longing and grief
That will never be forgotten,
The friends who are separated
Who were lost for our benefit.

I am not a bard who writes songs
And I should not delay
In telling you this history
Written in my own hand,
But how difficult for the young
That will be together no more;
Norman and Donald were on board
From my own beautiful grassy island.

But I pray that in the parting
Before I say any more,
That Christ will be with you
to give strength in the sorrow,
He is a friend who will be
A brother in the flesh,
For He will remain with you forever
And will wipe away each tear.

Cumha nan Leòdhasach an Dèidh Call na h-*Iolaire*

Niall Macilleathain, Caolas, Tiriodh

Lament of the People of Lewis Following the Loss of the *Iolaire*

Neil Maclean, Caolas, Tiree

Thàinig naidheachd bhon tuath, dhùisg gu mulad bhios buan
'S a dh'fhàg mòran dhen t-sluagh fo èislean,
Gun robh Gàidheil mo rùin 's iad nan sìneadh sa ghrunnd
'S iad gun chlaistneachd, gun lùth, gun lèirsinn.

News of everlasting sadness has come from the north, leaving many of us sorrowful: namely that our fellow Gaels lie at the bottom of the sea, without hearing, strength or sight.

'S ann an Leòdhas tha 'm bròn, 's iomadh cridhe tha leòint
'S iad a' sileadh an deòir gu deurach
Mu na gillean bha còir bhith nan sìneadh gun deò
'S gur e 'n cuan a thug oirnn an lèir-sgrios.

There's sadness in Lewis, many hearts are wounded. They weep for the able lads who now lie lifeless, the sea having taken them.

'S ann mu àm na Bliadhn' Ùir fhuair iad cead bhon a' Chrùn
Tilleadh dhachaigh bho dhùthchannan cèine,
'S fàth mo sgaraidh gu fìor mun do ràinig iad tìr
Gu robh cuid dhiubh aig crìch an rèise.

Around New Year they got leave from the Crown to return home from foreign lands. Sadly many of them lost their lives before they reached land.

Tha e nàdarra dhuinn gum biomaid gan caoidh,
Chaill sinn ceatharnaich ghrinn na fèille,
Bha daonnan gar dìon air muir is air tìr
'S thug ar nàimhdean fo chìs le 'n euchdan.

It is proper for us to mourn them. We lost generous, handsome warriors who always protected us on sea and on land and through their bravery defeated our enemies.

Bidh cuimhne 's gach dòigh air na dh'fhàgadh ri bròn,
Tha iad sean agus òg gun dèis-làimh,
'S an cùl-taic air thoirt bhuap' ann an gàirich nan stuagh,
Leam is cràiteach ri luaidh an sgeul ud.

All who mourn will be remembered and the old and young who are left without support. Those who protected them were lost in the roaring waves: it hurts me to tell the story.

Cuimhneachan, Acair, 2015

Cuimhneachan, Acair, 2015

Call na h-*Iolaire*

Aonghas Caimbeul, Am Bocsair, Nis, Leòdhas

'S mi 'g amharc air na Biastan
'S am fiacla corrach cruaidh
Le an-iochd an dùbhlain
Tha 'g ùrachadh am smuain
An oidhche dhubh Bliadhn' Ùire
Chuir driùchd air iomadh gruaidh,
An Iolair' cha do ràinig i
'S ràn-bàis aic' air do ghruaig.

Cò thuigeadh meud an gàirdeachais
'N Caol Àcainn dol air bòrd,
Thug ceithir bliadhn' an àmhghair
Fo sgàil a' bhàis d' an deòin,
An leas an Rìgh 's an dùthaich,
A' dìon a cliù 's a còir,
Is dhòirteadh fuil nam mìltean
San ìobairt a bha mòr.

Bha an t-athair caomh san àireamh
A sgaradh tràth bho chlann,
Le taingealachd don Àrd-Rìgh
Gun robh gach cìs aig ceann,
'S e dèanamh dealbh na smaointean
Air bean a ghaoil sa ghleann
'S mar phògadh e gu gràdhach i,
'S gach cridhe làn san àm.

The Loss of the *Iolaire*

Angus Campbell, Ness, Lewis

As I look at the Beasts with their hard, jagged teeth, so cruel and defiant, it brings back thoughts of that dark New Year's Eve which brought grief to many, the Iolaire not reaching harbour but coming to rest on your head with the screech of death.

Who could imagine their thankfulness as they went aboard in Kyleakin, having suffered four years of torment, under the shadow of death, for the sake of king and country and in defence of its reputation and rights? The blood of thousands was spilt in that great sacrifice.

There was the loving father, separated early from his children, thanking God that hostilities had ceased and conjuring up a picture in his mind of his beloved wife and how he would lovingly kiss her, their hearts full of joy.

Bha aon mhac na màthar ann
'S a dealbh air clàr a chrìdh',
'S e deiseil gu a fàilteachadh
O thobar làn a ghaoil,
'S e cuimhneach' sgiath a càirdeis
'S a gràdh nuair bha e maoth
'S a deòir bha goirt nuair dh'fhàg e i,
'S e leath' mar chlach a sùl.

'S e seo am fuidheall thill dhiubh
On chuibhreach a bha mòr,
Seòl'dairean is saighdearan
'S gum b' aoibhneach iad air bòrd.
Bha dìochuimhn' ac' an oidhche sin
Air iomadh teinn is leòn
Is cùrsa dìreach cinnteach ac'
Air bhàrr nan tonn gu Leòdh's.

A Leòdhais, bha thu mùirneach
Is d' ionndrainn tighinn gu ceann,
Bha iomadh bean an oidhch' ud
'S a cridhe seinn le taing,
A' sileadh deòir an aoibhneis
'S a' cuimhneachadh d' a clann
Gu faiceadh iad a-màireach iad
Tighinn sàbhailt' gu luchd-dàimh.

There was the mother's only son, her image engraved on his heart, getting ready to greet her from the full well of his love, remembering how she loved and shielded him when he was young and helpless and her tears when he, the apple of her eye, left for war.

This was all that was left of the large contingent that had gone - the sailors and soldiers - all of them now happily on board. They forgot that night about the suffering and injuries, being now on course for Lewis.

Lewis, you were joyful as your waiting was coming to its end. Many a woman's heart that night was singing with gratitude, shedding tears of joy and reminding their children that they would see their fathers tomorrow, back safely with their loved ones.

407

Bha peathraichean is màthraichean
Cur fàrdaichean air dòigh,
Ag ullachadh gu mànranach
Gach nì a b' fheàrr fo 'n còir.
Bha iomadh bodach liath–ghlas
Gu briathrach dèanamh spòrs,
Dol faoin le meud an gàirdeachais
Gu robh na h-àrmainn beò.

Sisters and mothers were getting their homes ready,
singing as they prepared the best welcome possible.
Grey-haired old men joked verbosely, overcome by
joy that the warriors were alive.

Mo chall! mo chall! An cuala sibh
An èighe chruaidh gach taobh?
An Iolair' air a cliathaich
Fo riaghladh mara 's gaoith,
Na sìneadh ris na Biastan,
Gun do shiabadh i o cùrs',
Toirt uaigh sàil do cheudan
Am fianais tìr an gaoil.

Alas! Alas! have you heard the loud cry on all sides?
The Iolaire has been blown off course and is lying on
its side on the Beasts at the mercy of wind and sea,
imposing a watery grave on hundreds within sight
of their beloved land.

Mo thruaighe, cha b' sgeul dhìomhain i,
Nach cianail bhith ga h-inns',
Bha tost an-iochdmhor dubhachais
Is bior an grunnd gach crìdh',
Bha gul an àit' a' ghàirdeachais
'S an dòchas àrd gun chlì,
A' cluinntinn guth na h-èiginn,
"Mo chreach! Tha 'n sgeula fior."

Alas, it was no rumour, sad to say. The cruel silence
of sorrow descended, every heart feeling a pang of grief.
Joy gave way to weeping and high hopes were dashed
on hearing the unwelcome words, "Alas! The news
is true."

Is iomadh òigear calma bh' innt'
Nach tug an stoirm air smaoin,
Na sruthan toinnt' 's an onfhadh
Is gorm-thuinn dol nan smùid.
'S ann bha 'n cridhe 's aiteas orr'
Tighinn faisg air Tìr an Fhraoich,
A' faicinn solais Steòrnabhaigh
Cur sòlas air gach gnùis.

'S ann bha 'n sealladh uabhasach
Nuair fhuair i buille bhàis,
Snasail air na cruaidh-sgeirean,
Muir fuaraidh tighinn na làid.
Gu beucach, dos-cheann, bruailleanach,
Neo-thruasail bha do nàmh,
Cur crìdh' a' ghaisgich luaisgeanach
Is gruaidhean a' dol bàn.

Cò 'n crìdh' tha blàth a' bualadh
Nach leagh le truas ri 'm beud?
Cò an t-sùil a chunnaic luaidh
Air nach sileadh bhuaip' an deur?
An uair bu chinnteach sàbhailteachd
'S iad làmh ri 'n dachaigh fèin,
'S e am bàs a rinn am fàilteachadh
'S a bhàth iad ris a' Bhèist.

Cuimhneachan, Acair, 2015

There were many hardy youths on board who thought nothing of the storm or of the rough swells and currents. Their hearts were happy, approaching Lewis and seeing the lights of Stornoway.

What a terrible sight when the death-blow struck, the ship resting firmly on the hard reef and the sea to windward coming at it in shoals. Your foe was roaring, foam-topped, tumultuous and merciless, unsettling the heart of heroes and turning their faces pale.

What beating heart is not affected by their loss? Who could hear a description of it and not weep? When safety seemed assured, so close to home, it was death that welcomed them and which drowned them at the Beasts.

Cuimhneachan, Acair, 2015

Fir Thrèin na h-*Iolaire*

Coinneach Mac a' Ghobhainn, Iarsiadair

Chaochail athair Coinneach, Coinneach Mac a' Ghobhainn, Coinneach Iain Mhoireach Mhurchaidh, air an *Iolaire* air oidhche na bliadhna ùire. Chaidh am bàrdachd seo fhoillseachadh trì fichead bliadhna as deidh call na h-*Iolaire*. Bha Iain Fionnlagh MacLeòid, Iain Mhurdo, a thug an loidhne gu tìr, dìreach air bàsachadh. Chaidh seo fhoillseachadh ann an *Gazette Steòrnabhagh* air an 6mh Foilleach 1979.

Ged tha àireamh gach bliadhna sìor dhol seachad,
Leth cheud air imeachd is còrr,
Cha leig sinn air dì-chuimhn' cliù nam fearaibh
A dh'eug 's gun cobhar air dòigh
Gun fhasgadh no dìon dh'aindeoin meud an cunnairt
'S gun rian air pilleadh bho bhròn,
'S an cala bu mhiann le rian gam feitheamh
'S tha shìos fo chomhair an sròin.

Is e fiùghalaich ghleusta, eudmhor, fallain
Bha gu lèir air turas san long;
'S na tìrean tha cèin cha do ghèill iad idir
'S ri streup is buillean nan nàimhd',
Gun chog iad gu treun 's gun ghlèidh iad uile
Fìor bheusan ceanalt' is grinn,
'S nach b' oglaidh an sgeul chaidh sheuladh dhuinne
Nach fheudaichte 'n aiseag gun chall.

The Heroic Men of the *Iolaire*

Kenneth Smith, Earshader

Kenneth was the son of Kenneth, one of the sailors lost on the *Iolaire*. It had been sixty years since the *Iolaire* struck the Beasts of Holm when this poem was published. John Finlay MacLeod, who pulled the line to shore, had just died, aged 90. The poem was published in the *Stornoway Gazette* on 6th January 1979.

Although the number of years grow,
Fifty and more gone,
We will not forget the reputation of the men
Who perished and had no help
With no shelter or protection despite the severity of the danger
And with no way to return from the sadness,
And the harbour waiting in order to greet them
That was so close to them.

Those were worthy, skilled and healthy men
Who had all been at sea;
And had survived foreign lands
And struggles with the enemy,
They fought so bravely and survived
Handsome and with kind virtue,
And how dismal the story told to us
That their ferry was lost.

Nuair a ghairmeadh air tùs fìor flùr nam fearaibh
Gun stiùir gun ceannard air ball,
Is ghabh iad mar chùrs bhith cliù is urram
Don chrùn bhith toirt ùmhlachd gun mhoill;
'S nuair a chaidh iad an ùin' don chrùn toirt spionnadh
Le sùrd 's am beatha nan làimh,
Aig deireadh na cùis mar bhrùchd no feamainn
Chaidh an sgaoileadh sa chladach 's na tuinn.

Bha laoich innt' air bòrd bha òrdail, duineil
'S bhiodh a' seòladh longan a' chuain;
'S bhiodh luchd-faire mar bu chòir rèir òrdugh longan
Toirt treòir mar a chitheadh iad shuas
Ach nuair thàinig na seòid air fòrladh thugainn
'S gach còmhstri nis air a ruaig,
Cha robh fear-faire ann air chòir faicinn leòn is cunnart
'S a' cur dò-bheart thairis fon cual.

Do na h-uile bh' air bòrd bha 'n còmhrag seachad
'S an còrr cha dèanadh iad ann,
'S cò cheileadh orra sògh 's iad seòladh thairis
Gu sòlas cuideachd an dàimh;
'S cha bhiodh cuimhn' air gach leòn agus bròn agus mulad
Bha aca fo òrdugh nan nàimhd'
Nuair laigheadh iad stòld fo dhòigh na dachaigh
'S am fear fòirneirt a bh' aca, 's e caillt'.

When these choice men were called
Without direction or leaders,
And they took their course with respect and dignity
In obedience to the crown;
And after giving the Crown their sacrifice
Eager and full of life,
At the end like a pile of seaweed
They were dispersed on the shore and in the waves.

There were heroes on board
Who sailed the seas on ships;
And they were watchful as they were seamen
Giving guidance as they would see fit
But when the heroes took their leave to come to us
And every conflict now over
There was no watchman
who could see the approaching danger.

For everyone on board the battle was over
And they could do no more,
And who would keep from them the pleasure
Of sailing to the comfort of their families;
There would be no memory of every injury and sadness and sorrow
That came from the enemy
When they lay down still in the happiness of the home
And the oppressor they had, now lost.

Bha cuid innt' 's bha gràs bhon àrd nan anam
Tre fhàbhar beannachd Mhic Dhè,
'S mar ghadaich thàinig am bàs mun coinneamh
'S gun dàil gan toirt Thuige Fhèin;
'S ged bu duilich an càs bhith fàgail gach caraid
'S gach gràdh bha aca fon ghrèin,
Bha lànachd A Ghràis gun dàil toirt barrachd
'S iad sàbhailte tron a' chrann-ceus.

Bha cuid innt' bha pòst' 's bha bòrd gam feitheamh
A rèir òrdugh mhnathan is chlann;
'S cha robh èis air gach nòs chuireadh dòigh air cagailt
Gu solas a bhith ga thoirt dhaibh;
Ged nach robh dachaighean mòr le sògh anns gach baile
Bha coibhneas bha òr-dhearc ann;
'S cha bhiodh gainne air a' chòrr ach fa-dheòidh iad tighinn
Is gach lòn a ghabhail air ball.

Bha òganaich innt' bha dàimheil, fearail
A dh'fhàg coibhneas dachaigh is pàirt,
'S a chaidh thogail os làimh tre ghanntair duine
'S na nàimhdean ag agairt ar slàint';
Chaidh cuid dhiubh a chall san ainneirt dhuilich
Sna tuinn a bha faramach àrd,
'S nach b' oillteil an t-seinn am broinn gach baile
Nach do thill na balaich gu slàn.

Cha b' e buille bhon nàmh a chràidh na fearaibh
Bha làidir, duineil 's gach dòigh;
Cha b' e peileirean pràis no stàrnach gunna
A dh'fhàg a' bhuille cho mòr;
Ach cion-faire san tràth 's iad sàr mì-shuimeil
Mu shàbhailteachd na bh' aca air bòrd,
A dh'adhbhraich a' chràidh a sgàin gach baile
'S a dh'fhàg sinn falamh gun treòir.

There were some on board who had grace in their souls
Those who would favour the blessing of God's Son,
And as if robbed, death was meeting them
Without delay taking them to Himself;
Although it was hard leaving each friend
And every love they had under the sun,
Grace was providing more
And they were safe through the cross.

There were some married and the table was waiting
Prepared by women and children;
And there was nothing left out while preparing the hearth
To give them light;
Although there were no large homes with luxury in each village
There was kindness to behold;
And there was nothing missing except for the men to return
And to eat all that was prepared.

There were youth on board who were friendly and manly
Who left the kindness of their homes,
Who were chosen despite the scarcity of men
And the enemy claiming their health;
Some of them were lost in the difficult violence
In the loud noisy waves,
And how terrifying the sound of sorrow from each village
When the boys didn't return whole.

It wasn't a blow from the enemy that pained the men
That were strong men is every sense;
It wasn't brass bullets or a gun
That left the blow so enormous;
But not being watchful
And caring for the safety of all they had on board,
That caused the torment that split each village
And left us empty and weak.

Ach mo thruaighe mhòr nuair bhuail i fearann
Cha b' e fàilt no furan bha ann;
Bha creagan ro chruaidh toirt fuaim m' a slige
'S cha robh fuasgladh idir dhi ann;
Bha Biastan gun truas nach gluaiseadh duine
Ri bualadh a-staigh fo a druim,
'S cha tàinig facal no fuaim a-nuas bhon drochaid
Gu riaghladh a ghabhail os làimh.

Ach gaisgeach mo rùin bha lùthmhor duineil
'S a stiùir tro ainneart nan tonn,
'S a shnàmh tro mhuir-cùil bha brùchdadh thairis
'S a shlaod gu fearann am ball;
Tre na ghleidheadh gach aon a chaomhain am beatha
Measg saothair is an-shocair throm
Tren d' fhuair cuid dhiubh gu tìr tre shrì agus calaist
Agus duibhre is doineann na h-oidhch'.

Cha do dheònaicheadh dhuibh tighinn fa-dheòidh gu dachaigh
Gu fàilt' agus furan bhith ann;
Gu fois agus gràdh agus blàths na cagailt
Agus fàbhar cuideachd luchd-dàimh;
Ach tha sibh san tràth gu sàbhailte sona
Ann an comann is gràdh Fear na Bainns';
'S nuair thig gairm oirnn bhon Àird 's a bhitheas an gàrradh abaich
Cha bhi àite falamh dhuinn ann.

Stornoway Gazette 6th January 1979

But how terrible when she struck the land
There was no welcome;
The rocks hard against the hull
And there was no solution to be had;
There were Beasts without pity that no one could move
That struck her under her back,
And not a word or a noise came from the bridge
To provide some direction.

But my hero was strong
And steered through the violence of the waves
And swam through rough seas that were rushing forward
And pulled people to land;
And each one who's life was saved
Amidst hard labour and discomfort
And some managed ashore from his efforts
In the gloom and storm of the night.

They were not granted the opportunity to be home safe at last
To welcome and hospitality
To the peace and love and warmth of the hearth
And the support of the family;
But in the morning there is peaceful safety
In the love and companionship of the Christ;
And when the cry comes from High the garden will be ripe
And there will be no empty places for us.

Stornoway Gazette 6th January 1979

An *Iolaire*

Tarmod Macleòid, Tarmod Bàn Aonghais 'Ic Tharmoid,
Cuidhdinis, Na Hearadh

The *Iolaire*

Norman Macleod, Quidinish, Harris

Nuair a dh'fhuasgail iad na ròpan
'S a sheòl i às a' Chaol,
'S e 'n *Iolair*' 'm bàt' bu luaithe
Dh'aindeoin luaisgean muir is gaoith.
Is iomadh òigear fuasgailt' bh' innt'
An uair sin nach do shaoil
Cho goirid 's a bha chuairt ac',
Beagan uairean anns an t-saogh'l.

*When the ropes were cast off and it sailed out of Kyle,
the Iolaire was the fastest, despite the stormy sea and
wind. There were many carefree youths on board who
never thought then that their sojourn in this world was
going to be as short as a few hours.*

Chaidh a h-uile nì cho fàbharach
Gun tàinig meadhan-oidhch'
Nuair bhuail i air na creagan grànd'
A bha neo-bhàidheil greann.
Fhuair an *Iolair*' buille bàis
'S na ràin a' tighinn o com,
'S ged bha fearann làmh rithe
Rathad teàrnaidh cha robh ann.

*Everything went favourably until midnight when it
struck rocks of the most dangerous kind. The Iolaire
received a death blow and its body screamed. Although
land was near them, there was no means of escape.*

Cha b' fhada sheas a' chliathaich aic'
Ri biastan biorach Thuilm
'S an *Iolair*' chaidh i sìos leotha
San oidhche fhiadhaich dhorch'.
B' e siud an sealladh cianail,
Bha na ceudan ghillean calm'
A' strì ri 'm beatha dhìon
Am measg siantannan is stoirm.

*Its hull did not long survive the sharp Beasts of Holm
and the Iolaire sank with them in the dark and stormy
night. It was a horrific sight to see hundreds of strong
lads struggling to survive in the storm and wild sea.*

An oidhch' ud thall an Steòrnabhagh
Gun chòmhlaich mòran sluaigh,
Dùil ac' ris na h-òigearan
Bh' air fòrladh bhar a' chuain.
Bha athraichean 's bha màthraichean
Is bha pàistean beag' gun ghruaim,
Bha peathraichean 's bha bràithrean ann
Gus fàilt' chur orr' san uair.

Mo chreach, mo chreach-sa thàinig,
Chaidh an gàirdeachas gu tùrs'!
Mun d' èirich grian a-màireach
'S iomadh gàirdean bha gun lùths.
Chaidh fios air feadh gach àite
Gun robh na h-àrmainn ri robh dùil
Air cladach tìr an àraich
Air am bàthadh anns a' ghrunnd.

Cha shaoilinn-sa cho brònach e
Nan òrdaicht' e le Dia
Gun tugaist suas an deò leoth'
Ri aghaidh còmhstri dhian.
Nuair shaoil leotha a bhith sàbhailte
Bho gach gàbhadh agus pian,
'S ann ghoid a-staigh am bàs orra,
'S neo-bhàidheil a bha Bhiast.

That night across in Stornoway a large crowd had gathered waiting for the youths who were on leave from the sea. There were fathers and mothers and happy young children, sisters and brothers, all eager to greet them.

Alas, to our great sorrow, the joy turned to grief. Before the sun rose next day many had lost their lives. Word went round the place that the heroes who were expected were lying on the shores of their native island, having drowned in the sea.

I wouldn't have thought it so sad had it been ordained by God that they would die in combat. Instead, when they thought they were free from danger, death caught them unawares on the fearsome Beasts.

'S iomadh caileag àlainn
Bha 's a leannan gràidh ga dìth,
Piuthar a chaill bràthair,
Chaill a màthair mac a cùim.
O, 's iomadh bean tha 'n-tràth seo
Le pàistean beag' a' caoidh
Na dh'fhalbh 's nach till gu bràth thuca,
'S an osann chràidh nach cluinn.

Many a beautiful young woman has lost her loving sweetheart, many a sister has lost her brother, many a mother her son. Women with young children mourn those who left and won't return and who won't hear their sighs of sorrow.

Tha Leòdhas is na Hearadh,
Tha 'd an-diugh fo sprochd 's fo ghruaim,
Caoidh nan gillean tapaidh,
'S ann dha 'n aindeoin chaidh toirt bhuap'.
'S e dithis a b' aithne dhòmhsa
Dhe na seòid ud chaidh dhan chuan,
Mac Nèill Choinnich às an t-Òb
'S mac Dhòmhnaill san Taobh Tuath.

Today Lewis and Harris are sad and low in spirit. Many are heartbroken and many weep. I knew two of the heroes who drowned in the sea – Niall Choinnich's son from Leverburgh and the son of Donald from Northton.

Nis crìochnaichidh mi 'n còmhradh seo
Bhon 's sgòideach cainnt mo bhèil,
Cha bhàrd gus dèanamh òran mi
Ged is còir dhomh dhol na ghleus.
Ach innsidh na tha beò an-diugh
Dhan òigridh thig nan dèidh
Mar dh'èirich dha na seòid ud
A bh' air bòrd an '*Iolaire*'.

Now I'll conclude what I have to say as my verse is unpolished, I am no poet although I've made the effort. Those alive today must tell the young who come after them what happened to those heroes who were on board the Iolaire.

Cuimhneachan, Acair, 2015

Cuimhneachan, Acair, 2015

Eachdraidh na h–*Iolaire*

Cairstìona A. Nicleòid, Pabail, An Rubha, Leòdhas

Bha còmhlan den a' chabhlaich
Air slighe dhachaigh anns a' Chaol,
'S bha 'n *Sheila* cus ro luchdaichte
Le cudrom bathair 's dhaoin',
Sin thàinig fios le òrdugh
Gheata mhòr a cur fo aont'
A ghiùlaineadh na seòl'dairean
Do Steòrnabhagh an gaoil.

Bha an oidhche gruamach iargalt' ac'
Le siantan agus gaoth
Ri tighinn teann bhon iardheas orr'
'S na chliathan an Cuan Sgìth.
Cò am fear am measg nan ceudan ud
A dh'iadh e air a smaoin
Gun robh a thuras crìochnaichte
No shìorraidheachd cho dlùth?

B' e coigreach anns an àit' bha leath'
Ach càit' an robh chàirt-iùil?
Bha seòl'dairean sa bhàt' aige
A bha an t-àit' ud air an sùil,
Ri togail Rinn na Càbaig
'S solas Àranais air cùrs',
Ach cha bhi fios gu bràth air
An e fàilneadh rinn an stiùir.

The Story of the *Iolaire*

Christina A. Macleod, Bayble, Point, Lewis

A group of navy men were in Kyle on their way home but the Sheila was overloaded with cargo and people: an order came to commandeer a large yacht to take the sailors to their beloved Stornoway.

The night was gloomy and blustery with a strong south-west wind and the Minch was rough. Who among those hundreds thought that his journey was at an end or that eternity was so close?

The captain was a stranger to the place but did he not have a chart? On board were sailors who knew the area. They plotted a course by Càbag Head and the Arnish light. It will never be known if the rudder failed.

417

Bha eachdraidh ann bha 'g ràitinn
Gun robh làmh aig' anns a' chùis
Ach bha sin an aghaidh nàdair
'S na h-àithne bh' aig' bho thùs.
Air madainn an là-mhàirich
Bha chnàmhan anns an tiùrr,
Na bannan air na gàirdeanan
'S a sheacaid-àirc' air dùint'.

Bha ceithir bliadhna luasganach
A' bhuairidh air an cùl
A chaidh seachad iarganach
Air cuantan agus raoin,
Ceartas air a riarachadh
Le buaidh ga thoirt air daors',
'S a' Ghearmailt fo riaghladh ac'
Le fallas dian an gnùis.

Is iomadh cridhe mànranach
Bha bualadh blàth le mùirn,
Ri sgioblachadh nam fàrdaichean
Airson sàir ris an robh dùil
Tilleadh dhachaigh sàbhailt'
Bhon a' bhlàr thuca le 'n saors',
'S a' choinneamh bhiodh cho aoibhneach ac'
Air oidhche na Bliadhn' Ùir.

There was a story that he was partly to blame but that was contrary to nature and his orders. The following morning his bones were found in the seaweed, the stripes on his sleeves and his lifejacket fastened.

Four unsettled years were behind them, spent dangerously on sea and land. Justice had been done with victory over evil: Germany had been conquered by the sweat of their brows.

Many happy hearts beat warmly with joy, as they prepared the homes for the heroes who were returning from battle safe and free. Their reunion would be a happy one on New Year's Eve.

Ro sgarachadh nan tràthan
Chaidh an gàirdeachas ma sgaoil,
Nuair bhriseadh sgeul a' ghàbhaidh ud
Le guth a' bhàis gach taobh.
Cha tug i mach an t-àite
Chaidh an-àirde oirr' anns a' Chaol,
A' chaladh anns an fhàire
'S i sàbht' air Biastan Thuilm.

Nach bu dhorch' an neul
A bha còmhdach grian gach sgìr',
Le dubhachadh is cianalas,
Le tiamhaidheachd is glaodh.
Dilleachdain is dàimhean
Is banntraichean gun mhaoin,
'S a' chosgais bh' air a' chunntas ud
No an t-sùim cha tèid am prìs.

Teaghlaichean le tuill annta
Ri caoidh na bha d' an dìth
A chunnaic crìoch na h-aimhreit
Agus bonntachadh na sìth.
Làraich lom na muinntir sin
Nach togadh ceann an tìm,
Is ged a b' fhaisg am fonn orra
Nach d' fhuair am bonn air tìr.

Before daybreak their joy vanished when the tragic news broke that death was all around. The Iolaire did not reach the place it set out for in Kyle: with the harbour in sight it was torn to pieces on the Beasts of Holm.

A dark cloud covered the sun everywhere. There was sadness and gloom and many plaintive cries. The lasting effect on orphans and poor widows cannot be described.

The deprived families mourn what they lost, having witnessed the end of hostilities and the foundation of peace. They view the empty spaces left by those who will never now return and who, though land was close by, couldn't step ashore.

Cha deachaidh 's cha teid àireamh
Gu bràth don àite 'n call,
Cha ghleachd gàirdean làidir
Ris a' bhàs a thig na àm.
An Niseach còir a dh'fhàg
Cuid de làmhan anns a' chrann
'S bha fear na mheadhan teàrnaidh innt'
A shnàmh aist' leis a' bhall.

Nach iomchaidh do na h-àil
Iomradh sàr-fhir ghlèidheadh beò
A dhìon sinn bhon an nàmhaid
'S a choisinn blàir na h-Eòrp'.
Na dorsan ged a ràinig iad
'S an tràigh bha gràdhaicht' leòth',
Nach daor, nach daor a phàigheadh
A' chàin le Eilean Leòdh'is!

Cuimhneachan, Acair, 2015

*Their loss to the island cannot be described.
Strong arms cannot fight death when the time comes.
We remember the Nessman who was stuck on the
mast and the one who saved others by swimming
ashore with a rope.*

*It is right that generations to come should keep alive
the story of the heroes who protected us from the enemy
and won the battle for Europe. Though they reached
their doorsteps and their beloved shore the Island of
Lewis has paid an expensive toll!*

Cuimhneachan, Acair, 2015

Chapter 11

Could the Tragedy Have Been Avoided?

"A child could have brought her into harbour that night."[1]

"The Lewismen were all sailors, who knew the sea.
I don't suppose there was one of them who couldn't
single-handedly have sailed her safely into Stornoway."[2]

Since the very first news of the sinking of the *Iolaire* reached Lewis, the single question asked – and never satisfactorily answered – has been "How did it happen?" From that flow all the other questions – were the crew competent and sober? What route did the vessel follow towards Stornoway, and how did she come to such a dangerous position? Was it safe to send HMY *Iolaire* to sea with so many passengers and with so little safety provision? What equipment was in working order, on the yacht and on the land? Was the shore response swift and effective enough? Who was to blame?

There is also the question: "What if?" which remained with the population then and now. If the trains had been on time, if the previous and faster *Iolaire* had been available, if the naval authorities had made better and safer provision and if there had not been a gale at the crucial time, how differently might history have remembered the end of the Great War in the islands.

One of the greatest ironies of the disaster is that the vast majority of the passengers aboard were not only skilled and hardy seafarers, but that many were also intimately familiar with the very waters in which they came to grief. There can be few maritime disasters anywhere in the world where those who perished were so well-qualified to save themselves from destruction. Yet circumstance and coincidence added to lack of foresight and planning, and to probable lack of competence, all reaching a peak at a time when weather, darkness, sea and shore conditions would render most of their skills inadequate to save their lives.

However flawed the Public Inquiry process, most of the jury's conclusions were clear and unequivocal. They found:

"That the *Iolaire* went ashore, and was wrecked on the rocks inside the Beasts of Holm, about 1.55 am on the morning of 1st January, resulting in the deaths of 205 men.

That the officer in charge did not exercise sufficient prudence in approaching the harbour.

That the boat did not slow down.

That a look-out was not on duty at the time of the accident.

That the number of lifebelts, boats and rafts was insufficient for the number of people carried.

That no orders were given by the officers with a view to saving life.

That there was a loss of valuable time between the signals of distress and the arrival of the life-saving apparatus in the vicinity of the wreck."[3]

The jury's first four points rest on the issue that has preoccupied mariners and historians ever since. How did the ship's captain and navigator come to be in that position? How did they make such a catastrophic mistake in navigation on a route so well-known to all on board, and within such a short distance of safe harbour? Why did they not observe the danger they were in, in time to correct the course and bring the vessel safely to port?

View of the entrance to Stornoway harbour from Holm, showing clearly how close the wreck of the site was to the safe passage guarded by Arnish lighthouse.

Navigation and the course steered

Two men were in charge of the bridge on the night of the disaster, Commander Richard Gordon William Mason and Lieutenant Edmund Cotter, the navigating officer. Cotter took over command at 1am and it was he who took the yacht towards the Beasts.

A suggestion was made at the Public Inquiry that the *Iolaire* had not entered Stornoway harbour at night before, leading to the possibility of confusion in navigating. However, the HMS *Iolaire* naval base log records the daily movements of HMY *Iolaire* and, during the period from 17th December to 31st December, she entered the harbour a total of four times, the last of which was at half past midnight, 0030 hours on 29th December. During research for this book, a letter from the Curatorial Officer of the Admiralty Library confirmed that 1st January 1919 was Lt Cdr Mason's third night entry into Stornoway.

All the subsequent commentators on the disaster, like the jury at the Inquiry, are hampered by the fact that the key players in the question of navigation did not survive the sinking. The Captain, Lt Cotter and Acting Quartermaster Leggett all drowned, leaving 39-year-old assistant quartermaster James MacLean as the only survivor who had witnessed the course steered and some of the decisions made. MacLean was experienced at sea, and had served on the *Iolaire* since 1916 (when she was still the *Amalthaea*). There has never been any suggestion that his testimony is other than reliable, so the information that he gave at the time is critical to our understanding of what happened. However, the Inquiry did not follow up either his or other witness testimony with questioning that could have provided greater clarity on the exact circumstances which led to the grounding. Opportunities missed on that day could never be regained, and significant information was provided, much later, by survivors among the passengers and by witnesses from other vessels.

From the time when she left Kyle, the *Iolaire*'s course was well-known and clearly marked. As they left Kyle, the officers had two coastlines with two prominent lighthouses on the starboard side – Rubh Re north of Gairloch and Stoer Head on the west coast of the mainland. With a clear night, despite rain showers becoming more regular during the voyage, the lights would give a fix and the yacht's position could easily be established. Between there and Stornoway the following lights were visible on the port side: Rona on the Isle of South Rona, Eilean Glas on the Isle of Scalpay, Gob na Milaid (Minor Light) south of Kebbock Head, Pairc and Tiumpan Head on the Isle of Lewis and Arnish at the entrance to Stornoway harbour.

In the 1978 book *Call na h-Iolaire (The Loss of the Iolaire)* by Tormod Calum Dòmhnallach[4], Alex Reid proposed three possible courses steered by the *Iolaire* prior to her striking the Beasts of Holm. He plotted these as:

Course A – the official 'Admiralty' theory as given at the Inquiry. *Iolaire* is half a mile off course

Course B – the 'Eastward' theory. Captain John Smith, Master of the *Loch Seaforth* 1948-1972, gives his interpretation of an eastward error of five miles or so.

Course C – the '*Spider*' theory. The *Iolaire* is off course due to overtaking the fishing-boat *Spider*.

Alex Reid's full navigational explanation is given in **Appendix 2** and is used by kind permission.

James MacLean stated at the Inquiry that, when he took over at midnight, "She was steering north – easterly – just a touch easterly." He went on to say that "at 12.30 a.m. the course was altered to north." Reid states that a course change is only made if there is some reason to believe it necessary, usually after establishing that the vessel is off course. At night, in 1919, this would be by observing the bearings of light-houses, if land was not visible. MacLean saw and reported the lights of Stornoway to Lieut. Cotter, who said 'All right,'" So between 1am and 1.25am hours the *Iolaire* was about on course, the town lights seem to have been where they were expected to be, which favours the suggested courses Reid identifies as A and C.

Captain Smith's suggested course (course B) would only make sense if Tiumpan Head light had been confused for Arnish, and if Arnish had been similarly confused for Milaid (Kebbock Head). Each lighthouse has a distinctive flash 'signature' well-known to navigators – Tiumpan gives two flashes every 30 seconds, Arnish one flash at 10 seconds and Milaid one flash at 15 seconds. Several passengers referred to seeing the light at Cabag/ Kebbock, seeming to indicate that visibility was not poor as the vessel approached Lewis.

The testimony of passengers – who as we have seen were well informed both on seamanship and on the local sea and coast conditions, as well as extremely familiar with passage in and out of Stornoway – adds extra detail to the position of the *Iolaire* before she struck the Beasts of Holm. Passenger Norman Maciver stated that about an hour before striking (12.50am) he saw land to starboard at about 600 yards – "We were going along the land at the time" – the strongest evidence for course B, as it is the only explanation for land being seen at that distance so long before Holm, although Maciver's stated times are not precisely right for this explanation.

Angus Macdonald saw Arnish Light on the port bow at 1.40am, confirming the time by the ship's clock, as well as seeing the town lights just to the right of Arnish. At the same time, according to John Macinnes, there was land ahead – Holm would have been just within visibility, at 2½ miles. John Montgomery said that about five minutes before striking – 1.50am – he saw Arnish Light "broad on the port bow," and at just that time *Iolaire* altered course to port, bringing Arnish right ahead. He had come on deck 10 minutes before striking and the first land he saw was the east side of Holm Bay. Donald Maciver said that about three minutes before striking land was visible 200 yards to starboard, but the harbour lights were not visible. Just before striking the *Iolaire* "slewed" to port, he said.

The sudden change of course just before the vessel struck is widely verified. In addition to the testimony of seamen aboard the *Iolaire* given at the Inquiry, there are later accounts from survivors, who in some cases told their tale many years later. Even allowing for the passage of years, their familiarity with the island coast adds to the credibility of their accounts. Donald Morrison of Knockaird (Am Patch) said:

> "The *Iolaire* was sailing straight and steady until she changed course to port. If she had changed four or five minutes earlier, she would have gone right into Stornoway, but she changed too late because the rocks of Holm were right in front of her."[5]

Donald Murray of North Tolsta recalled:

"I could see the Stornoway Lighthouse flashing. You'd think there was no possibility of anything going wrong ... when we felt her altering course out to the west – instead of going in --- I didn't understand."[6]

And John Maclennan of Kneep ('Ain Geal) gave his opinion:

"The mistake was made when we changed course. All it required was less than half a point, it just needed to be slightly to the West. The lighthouse was visible, but the man at the wheel (sic)[7] didn't alter course when he should have."[8]

So the change of course is agreed, but not the reason why it became necessary. We then come to the proximity of the fishing vessel *Spider*, which was in the immediate vicinity and from which at least one person saw the *Iolaire* heading towards the rocks. The main Inquiry witness for the interaction between the two vessels was that man, the mysterious James Macdonald, engineer on board the fishing-boat. He is reported as saying:

"When sailing past the mouth of Loch Grimshader on our way back to port (from the Shiant banks), a steamer passed us on the starboard side – we followed immediately in her wake and when approaching Arnish Point I noticed that the vessel did not alter her course but kept straight on in the direction of the Beasts ... it went too far off its course to make the harbour in safety."[9]

Seaman John Macinnes, an *Iolaire* survivor, said that the fishing vessel crossed the *Iolaire*'s bow from starboard to port. Although no other passenger testimony supported that account, Donald Macdonald from Upper Bayble was on deck and said:

"Between Cabback and Arnish I noticed a fishing vessel, but I did not know whether it was a motor boat or a drifter. She was on our starboard side. I saw her afterwards on our port side."[10]

These accounts indicate that *Iolaire* was first over-taking *Spider* to port and altered course to starboard to cross her stern. This supports the idea of Reid's course C, and he also suggests it possible that Lt. Cotter's preoccupation with completing this manoeuvre, at 1.30am, could have meant that he would not reduce speed, would not call the Captain and would probably be navigating by eye, without time to refer fully to compass and chart.

Alex Reid concludes that course C, the *Spider* theory, is the likeliest, making sense of the conflicting evidence. Course B would require incompetence or incapacity on the part of all officers and crew in the wheelhouse for the last hour and a half of the voyage, which is difficult to accept. He believes course A, the Admiralty theory, is possible, especially given the conditions and Lt Cotter's lack of experience, but even those circumstances do not seem to explain that degree of incompetence in a naval officer.

But Alex Reid concludes:

"The addition of *Spider* as a third element in the equation, however, transforms a straightforward navigational exercise into a complex problem, involving the mental calculation of relative courses, speeds and position, highly taxing in that night's conditions. That Lieut. Cotter failed to judge the manoeuvre successfully would not then be so surprising, and the basic criticism against him is his lack of judgment or caution in deciding to overtake without referring to his Captain (then, however, only 20-25 minutes off watch). If *Iolaire* had reduced speed to 5 knots when half a mile behind *Spider* and followed her in, she may perhaps have been delayed by fifteen minutes."[11]

There is an anecdotal footnote to the question of navigation errors on the night. One account suggests that Lewis fisherman Roderick Mackenzie went up to the bridge and offered to take the yacht into harbour, but was ordered off the bridge by Lt Cotter. Roddy was from Swordale, from which village Holm Point is in view, and he knew the approaches to Stornoway harbour well. He also had the credentials to offer his services, as a mature man with Second Hand rank, equivalent to a Mate or Petty Officer. Lower-ranked deck ratings would have been nervous of making such an offer, for fear of naval discipline. Yet one of the descendants of a man lost on the night would say nearly 90 years later:

"The local sailors on that ship knew they were on the wrong course and they told the captain so, but he just wouldn't listen to them. If he had, it would have saved a lot of heartbreak and we wouldn't be talking about it today."[12]

This illustrates a widely-held belief, confirmed by some survivors, that some of the Lewis sailors on board had told the crew that they were on the wrong course. There was no attempt made by the Royal Navy to verify these accounts and they were not mentioned to the jury at the *Iolaire* inquiry. In those days, a naval officer would not have taken advice from a rating, far less one on leave. He may even have charged the rating with insolence or for querying an order issued by an officer. As Donald Morrison (Am Patch) said many years later: "Who was going to tell a Royal Naval Commander and Navigator – nobody aboard!"

The belief that the skipper had navigated the ship astray and that many passengers could have brought her safely into harbour, would persist down the years.

"They would talk about it... they put the blame on the commander, the skipper on the boat, as there were many on the *Iolaire* who would have taken the boat into Stornoway. The majority of them were fishermen, who were used enough to the place and they could tell, when they were coming in, those who survived, they could tell that they were on the wrong course."[13]

Looking for a scapegoat – the lights

Very soon after the disaster, it was evident that the Admiralty were seeking people and factors to blame for how the tragic events came about. In a memo on 20th January 1919 the Admiralty's head of naval law, Thomas Walter Hobart Inskip, 1st Viscount Caldecote, stated that the Lord Advocate had:

"suggested as a possibility that the shore lights might not have been in order. The proposed enquiry will be able to investigate the facts as to this."[14]

Although there's no evidence that his suggestion was taken as a hint, it is possible that it had an influence on the way the Inquiry was conducted. Considerable emphasis was placed on the lights, their visibility and their positioning.

In this context 'lights' most probably means the lighthouses and other navigating beacons. Other lights ashore would have been individual gas lamps on the harbour and streets, unlikely to aid in navigation. In addition to the lights at Tiumpan Head and Kebbock on Lewis, which help to position vessels on their approach to the great sweep of Stornoway harbour, there are two lights much further into the harbour at Arnish – the Arnish Point lighthouse – which showed a white light in the directions of safe approach and red where there was danger – and a beacon at the end of rocks leading out from Arnish Point.

In an early report on the disaster, Captain John Webster, Director of Navigation at the Royal Navy Hydrographic Department, suggested that 'the brightness (of the lights) was probably affected by the drizzling rain'. The implication was that a navigator might have found it hard to judge his distance from the lights. At the subsequent Public Inquiry crewman James Maclean, who had been on the bridge just before the *Iolaire* struck, was asked whether his view of the lights was obscured. He replied:

"No, there was nothing to obscure the view, and that night I could see all the lights clearly".

He reported telling the navigator, Lt Cotter, when he saw the light at Arnish. Passenger Donald Macdonald from Upper Bayble also testified:

"When we were approaching Lewis I saw all the lights, Cabback (Kebbock Head), Tiumpan and Arnish – quite clearly."

Later in the Inquiry the master of the MacBrayne mailboat *Sheila*, which followed *Iolaire* towards Stornoway harbour on the same night, was questioned about the difficulty of entering Stornoway harbour:

"**Q** Is Stornoway a difficult harbour to enter at night?

A Well, it is for the man that does not know it, a man who has not actually taken a vessel in .....

Q Do you think it is a difficulty to a stranger in these waters not to have a light on the Holm side of the harbour?

A I don't miss it myself; I keep closer to the lighthouse side."[15]

Under such questioning, the Inquiry could not find any significant issues with the lights – they were well-known to mariners and they had been clear on the night of the disaster, even so, they recommended when the Inquiry closed:

"That the Lighthouse Commissioners take into consideration the question of putting up a light on the Holm side of the harbour."[16]

Where was the lookout?

The question of a lookout is an issue which continues to arise in Marine Accident Investigations. Even small vessels must keep adequate watch for danger of collision, whether with rocks or with other vessels. On a ship carrying hundreds of passengers, approaching a harbour in darkness and gale, a lookout is indispensable.

At the Public Inquiry in February 1919, Captain Cameron of the *Sheila* stated that it was normal procedure when approaching the harbour to have two lookouts. On the *Iolaire* only one, survivor James MacLean, was on duty and he had gone below to rouse the anchoring crew. MacLean stated clearly: "I was the only one keeping a look-out." He was questioned by both the Admiralty's representative, Edinburgh advocate James Pitman, and by the lawyer for the *Iolaire* widows and children, Lewisman John Norrie Anderson. Mr Pitman asked:

"**Q** Who put you on look-out?

A Nobody

Q You were just looking out on your own?

A No, not on my own: it was a rule to have a look-out

Q How did you come to go on look-out?

A It was the hands' duty, but the vessel was shorthanded on that voyage."[17]

Without a lookout, the immediate danger from the looming land could not be warned of and the *Iolaire* also had a physical deficiency when it came to keeping watch, as Alex Reid has pointed out:

"*Iolaire*'s bridge and wheelhouse seem to have been more than half her length, or 100ft, from her bowsprit, due to her yacht lines – a time-lag of six seconds at 10 knots."[18]

The bridge and wheelhouse were not well-positioned for good visibility ahead, and there was no facility for a watch to be kept at the bow or masthead. MacLean confirmed: "There was no one stationed at the boat's head – not during this voyage at all." He also confirmed that Lt Cotter was inside the wheelhouse at the time of the collision, below the bridge and therefore not only 100 feet from the bow, but physically lower down, in a poorer position for visibility.

The authors of this book believe that it is significant that Lt Cotter was inside the wheelhouse with Ernest Leggett the helmsman. The helmsman's principal duty was to steer the course, looking at the compass in front of him, until ordered by voice tube to change course – he would not have been tasked with looking forward or keeping watch. With Cotter not on the bridge and MacLean below, the crew were unaware that the yacht was approaching the Beasts. Even the few seamen on deck as passengers would have had a clearer idea of impending danger.

Just as baffling is the question of where all the other crew members were as the yacht neared harbour, when Commander Mason departed from the bridge leaving Cotter in charge, Leggett at the helm and MacLean as lookout. Any of the deck crew – Dewsbury, Mariner, Moore, Ramsay, Stanley or Willder – could have been posted on lookout and should have been on duty well before the yacht came in towards land. After taking on the role of lookout, MacLean's departure compromised the safety of the yacht when he went below to rouse the other anchoring crew. Why did he not go earlier and, when he did go, why did he take so long and why did he have to go below twice? Why did those crew members not report on deck themselves? In such conditions, coming close to the harbour, it was imperative that one man should not be on the bridge alone. At least one other of the deck crew should have been on lookout with MacLean and Cotter.

Over the years islanders have queried such aspects of the disaster and the Inquiry that followed. Charles Kingsbury, an *Iolaire* crew member, who was on leave the night that the *Iolaire* sank, wrote in 1977:

> "Surely the need for vigilant lookout was all the more necessary entering a strange harbour at night with the risk of increased volume of shipping in the vicinity.... The ship would be slow to answer the helm and was steaming full speed on a flowing tide into a harbour estuary, going to leeward, and without a pilot or a lookout, and there was a drowsy crew in their bunks, after two days rail travel to Kyle... I count myself fortunate to be able to write the foregoing, and to be alive."[19]

The sea and weather conditions

Even the navigational errors which might be attributed either to Commander Mason or to Lt Cotter, the short-handedness of the vessel and the lack of a lookout would not have been as catastrophic, were it not for the uniquely unfavourable combination of natural circumstances on the night of the tragedy. There was to be a new moon on 2nd January 1919, and it was midwinter, meaning that this was literally one of the darkest nights of the year, and cold. There was rain at sea which fell as sleet after midnight. Survivors all attested that it was extremely dark and bereaved relatives ashore would later recollect the darkness and the wild weather. There was no natural light available and heavy cloud cover obscured even the faintest glimmer of starlight.

The *Highland News* for that week published Stornoway's tide table, showing high tide on the evening of 31st December at 6pm, and on the morning of 1st January 1919 at 6.08am. Low water would therefore have been around midnight, exposing the Beasts of Holm which would then have been gradually submerged again between midnight and 6am. The *Iolaire* grounded at 1.55am on a rising tide.

The HMS *Iolaire* naval base log records prevailing weather conditions, showing a pattern all too familiar to island residents – relative calm, followed by a few hours of gale and storm, rapidly dropping away to renewed calm. At 8pm on the night of 31st December, just after the *Iolaire* had departed from Kyle, the wind was blowing mildly from the south at just force 2. On the Beaufort scale this is a light breeze of between four and seven miles per hour, with wave heights between one and two feet. Between then and midnight the wind rose to force 8, gale force, with winds up to 46mph and wave heights up to 25ft. By 4am the conditions had grown still worse – winds to force 10, (storm force, 55-63mph) and waves of 29-41ft. The scale describes dense foam blown across the water, while the rolling of the sea becomes heavy and visibility is affected. In these conditions the *Iolaire* went aground, and in these seas men fought to survive. The wind was from the south, driving hard onto the shore and possibly compounding the navigation errors which headed the vessel north. Between 1.55am, when the

Iolaire struck the Beasts of Holm, and the time she sank at 3.25am, men were flung towards a shore of chaotic, sharp conglomerate rock on high waves driven by storm force winds. Then the base log also shows a sudden improvement in conditions. Before daylight came, at around 8.30am, the storm was already abating, winds reducing until by noon it was simply breezy, at force 4.

A failure of leadership

When the *Iolaire* struck, some salvation could have come from a calm, orderly response from the yacht's officers, with orders for abandoning ship given and signals for help made to the shore. But the Inquiry concluded:

> "That no orders were given by the officers with a view to saving life."[20]

Instead many passengers and crew acted independently to save themselves and others, or to complete their duties to the best of their ability. Among these were telegraphist Leonard Welch, who tried to get the wireless set working again even as water swirled around his feet, and engineers Charles Rankin and John Hern, both drowned, who struggled to maintain and restore power for the lights and other equipment. Among the passengers, Angus Nicolson of Stornoway shouted to the bridge to blow the steam whistle and urged the crew to drive the yacht astern; John MacInnes of North Tolsta blew the whistle on the bridge; Alexander Maciver from Shulishader was seen trying to fire rockets and John Mackay searched the bridge for rockets. Individual crew members helped launch the

boats – there were no boat parties at their stations and no orders given for organised launching of the boats.

Responsibility was taken by many individual islanders – chief among them Ness man John Finlay Macleod, who swam ashore with a heaving line and made fast a six-inch hawser which saved 40 lives. John Maclennan of Kneep fixed the rope more firmly to the *Iolaire*, and John Murray (Iain Help) and Robert Mackinnon of Tarbert were among four men who helped to secure the hawser at the landward end. Men queued in an orderly fashion to use the rope, and others helped comrades back aboard from the sinking lifeboats, or onto the rocks as they fought through the waves. None of these were acting under any orders. Few even saw the officers after the vessel struck, although Alex Dan Maciver of Church Street, Stornoway, told the *Inverness Courier* soon afterwards that he had seen both the master and the navigator on the bridge just before he dropped overboard.

But witness testimony both at the Inquiry and in later interviews and broadcasts told a sad tale of responsibility abdicated by the officers. Fireman Ernie Adams made it abundantly clear under questioning:

A   I went to the boat deck and I saw the leading hand – Dewsbury – and I asked him if he could try to get the big boat out – the whaler, port side.

Q   What did Dewsbury say?

A   He said, "This is terrible", I said, "Yes", and he went away.

Q   When you were on board at any time did you hear any orders given by anybody?

A   None at all…

Q   When you spoke to (acting bo'sun) Dewsbury on the deck, was he in the act of doing anything?

A   No.

.......**Q**   You could hear any orders from the bridge quite distinctly from that position?

A   Yes, if there had been any given; but I did not hear any…"[21]

Lifesaving equipment

Questionable decisions on the bridge, an unresponsive crew, officers who did not provide leadership and a conspiracy of natural circumstances therefore brought the *Iolaire* to grief. But had she been well-provided with the equipment needed for the saving of lives, perhaps the scale of the tragedy could have been much reduced. The jury at the Public Inquiry were quite specific in their conclusion:

> "That the number of lifebelts, boats and rafts was insufficient for the number of people carried."[22]

After the *Titanic* disaster, which had occurred only seven years earlier, a public inquiry recommended that the number of lifeboats on a ship, and their carrying capacity, should exceed the maximum number of passengers and crew. The recommendations of the *Titanic* inquiry were incorporated into the first version of the international Maritime Convention on the Safety of Lives at Sea (SOLAS), a treaty signed in 1914, but which did not at that time pass into law due to the outbreak of the war.

Commander Mason of the *Iolaire* had been asked at Kyle if he could take 300 men across to Stornoway. He reportedly replied that his lifeboats could take that number easily enough, though the *Iolaire* had lifeboat capacity – in perfect conditions – for just 100 men, and only 80 lifebelts. The yacht had two open wooden rowing boats, whalers, one on the starboard side and one on the port side, each about 27 feet long and six feet across. They could each carry 22 men in comfort in good conditions, 30 crammed together or 15 in foul weather. There were two smaller lifeboats (dinghies) aft on either side of the vessel.

Crew member Charles Kingsbury was on leave the night that the *Iolaire* sank. He later wrote:

> "I would suggest that …. Commander Mason was not accurate in his statement that the boats could accommodate 100 men, and that there were about 80 lifebelts available, when it was acknowledged that the *Iolaire* only carried sufficient equipment for the ship's normal complement of forty odd men. Certainly, when I was aboard, I never saw a superfluity of lifesaving equipment, and during the weeks on the *Iolaire* as a member of the crew I was not assigned to any one of the boats, took no part in any boat drill (we did not have any) and I was not given a lifebelt in person, for use in emergency."[23]

During the Inquiry, deckhand James MacLean, who had been a crew member on the *Iolaire* for nearly three years said:

"She carried four boats. These boats could accommodate 60 men. We had at least a dozen lifebuoys. I could not say whether there would be as many as 80 lifebelts and lifebuoys."[24]

The *Iolaire*'s lifeboat carrying capacity was anyway substantially reduced, when the tragedy occurred, by the list of the yacht and the heavy seas, which made launching from the port side impossible. As it transpired, the gale also rendered the starboard boats useless. Crewmen MacLean and Adams, both survivors of the wreck, gave evidence at the Inquiry that they had helped to get boats out. Their evidence paints a picture of inadequacy of orders, passengers setting their hands to getting boats into the water themselves and boats instantly overwhelmed by the sea, men drowning as they were washed away. Survivor Alex Dan Maciver estimated that 20 men went into each of the two boats launched, but they were soon swamped and most men in them lost. Donald Macdonald, of Cromore in South Lochs described seeing the boats and their destruction:

"I .... descended to the bulwarks to jump into one of the boats. Thank goodness I missed it by seconds. It was loaded. I watched it churning and swirling and in an instant down it went. ... Something determined me from jumping into the second boat. I gazed at it as it shoved off, then a mighty back wash wave seemed to fill the boat. It seemed to glide up to their shoulders, their heads – and then no more. I could not see any survivors from any of the boats."[25]

If the boats were useless, the chance for any man to be saved by a lifejacket or lifebelt was negligible. James MacLean gave evidence about lifejackets, saying that the crew kept them under their bunks and there were a few spares in the lifeboats. This very likely means that many were simply washed away. They certainly were not issued to passengers. Some passengers did go looking for lifebelts, as Donald Macdonald of Upper Bayble would later recount:

"After she struck I .... went and looked for a lifebelt for myself. I didn't find one. Others were looking for lifebelts too and they could not find them, I went a second time and I saw two of the crew in the galley and I asked if there were any spare lifebelts. They said, 'No'."[26]

Only a few men can be specifically identified who did have these life-saving devices. The lifebelt that survivor Donald Maciver, am Bèicear, of New Tolsta wore was kept by North Tolsta Historical Society and is now in safekeeping at Museum nan Eilean at Lews Castle. Donald Macaskill of Shulishader found a lifejacket but gave it to his older brother Duncan – Donald was swept away and his body never recovered. Telegraphist Leonard Welch, a crew member who survived, recalled many years later that his money was still soaking wet from the pocket of his lifejacket when he went to buy a razor a few days later.

Whether lifejackets would actually save lives was also questionable – Welch also testified that he had given a lifejacket to Londoner Albert Matthews, who was returning from leave to his posting as a storekeeper at HMS *Iolaire* naval base. Matthews did not survive. Accounts from some islanders say that the vessel's Captain, Commander Mason, was seen dead on the shore, wearing two lifejackets, and survivor John Maclean of Borrowston recalled seeing men wearing more than one lifejacket being swept to their deaths from the rope – perhaps the jackets even hampered their survival.

Of potential help in saving lives were other devices on board. John Macinnes of North Tolsta blew the whistle on the bridge and then asked Lt Cotter if he had a searchlight, the strong light from which would have helped those in the water to scale the storm-lashed rocks. He was told that the searchlight would not work, as the dynamo was broken. Crew member Charles Dewsbury was asked by Lt Cotter to try and mend the light, according to Maclean's testimony. The *Iolaire*'s guns were not fired to attract attention to her desperate plight – there were two three-inch guns mounted fore and aft, plus a recently fitted three-pounder anti-aircraft mounting amidships. In the dark and with the yacht listing heavily, loading ammunition and firing would have been a difficult task. Later when the yacht stabilised it could have been attempted, especially with the high-elevation gun amidships. It would have needed the crew to do this as the passengers would not know where the locked magazine was.

The 15 or so flares or rockets launched were seen from the land, but widely misunderstood as being celebratory lights for the New Year. Yet perhaps the flares provided the best chance for those aboard to find assistance. At Battery Point, Stephen Saunders, Yeoman of Signals, saw a blue light between 1.50 and 2am and reported it as a vessel requiring a pilot. He saw another blue light, then a third one, around 2.20am, which was red. He reported that there was a vessel in distress. The yacht fired white flares thereafter. As soon as she struck, men aboard the *Iolaire* were signalling their distress, and now came the chance to rush to their aid.

The land response – was it too slow?

While the men aboard the *Iolaire* were struggling with the shock and turmoil of the wreck, people ashore were, for the most part, completely unaware of what was happening within yards of their homes. During the inquiries, focus was placed on the deficiencies of the civilian landward response, although no blame was apportioned to Admiralty men. Yet there's evidence to show that a slow response at the naval base was, at least in part, to blame for the late arrival at the scene of those who might have been able to help.

By sea, there might have been some chance of giving assistance had the conditions not been so atrocious. The naval drifter *Budding Rose* was standing by to pilot the *Iolaire* into the harbour, and indeed did set out at 1.55am when the blue 'pilot required' rocket was seen. It took the *Budding Rose* a full 25 minutes, until 2.20am, to reach the scene, where she saw the situation and stopped 300 yards away. Her commander, Lieutenant W B Wenlock, reported later that he:

> "Was unable to render any assistance owing to the heavy seas running. I approached to the edge of the breakers but found it was impossible to communicate with the ship in any way."[27]

He went back into the harbour, took orders from Admiral Boyle at the Imperial Hotel, and then went out again and stood by at a distance from the wreck. Apart from taking on board 'the man on the mast' after his rescue the next morning, he did not provide any assistance, light the scene or take anyone aboard.

Budding Rose and *Rorqual*, steam-driven vessels which were stoked up and ready to depart, could not approach the *Iolaire*, according to the Admiral's later report 'owing to the heavy sea'. Yet in the same message to the Admiralty he finds it only 'doubtful' whether the lifeboat could have rendered any service. The lifeboat was powered by oars and by civilian volunteers, and would have taken a couple of hours to even reach the harbour mouth in the prevailing conditions. If *Budding Rose* was 'unable to render assistance' the lifeboat would certainly not have won through. Yet this line of enquiry was given precious time in the Public Inquiry and it was the locals that were blamed for not being able to muster a crew.

Still, Sub Lt Charles W Murray received orders at 2.45am to raise the lifeboat crew and get assistance to Holm. He made heroic efforts to do so, running about the town centre in a storm for over two hours and banging on doors to try and rouse the crew. The Inquiry did not establish whether there was a normal system for calling out the lifeboat – a rocket, siren, bell, or some other means other than knocking on doors.

At the time of the disaster the RNLI volunteer lifeboat *Janet* was on station, but until 1920 there was no regular crew to man her and the vessel was only tasked to 'come to the rescue of ships and boats in distress which could be sighted from Stornoway and its immediate neighbourhood.' The RNLI had no wireless or telephone communications, the vessel had no engine and the crew of working fishermen was often depleted. With young, fit and able men away in the war, the issue was much worse than normal at the war's end. Acting coxswain John "Shonnachan" Maclean was responsible for mustering a crew but, on this night, was unable to do

so. He tried to round up a crew from ships lying in the harbour, "but no crew could be got." Three soldiers and the coxswain himself were the only men who could be raised, but the lifeboat needed eight men and a cox. The last lifeboat practice had in fact been with a naval crew and with John Maclean as Cox. Murray went back to the Imperial Hotel to report his lack of success at 4.30am.

With the sea boiling and churning in the strong winds, rescue from land was really the only possible hope for the poor souls aboard the *Iolaire*. The shore-based life-saving apparatus (LSA) was based at Battery Point and operated by the Coastguard service, itself overseen by the Admiralty. But the naval commander was slow, horses could not be found and the LSA could not reach the shore at Holm by road. A distress flare fired from the *Iolaire* was recorded at 2.20am, but the message was then delayed 40 minutes in reaching Coastguard Warrant Officer William Barnes, who lived just 300 yards from the Battery. He was woken with a message from the Rear Admiral that there was a ship in distress at Holm, but not until 3am. Under his direction 19 men harnessed themselves to the one-ton apparatus and set out towards the wreck location, at 3.50am. This was already much too late, for the vessel had sunk at 3.25am, 90 minutes after going aground, and 70 minutes after her signals of distress were understood by the Battery Point signalman.

The jury at the Inquiry stated there had been a loss of valuable time between the signals of distress and the arrival of the life-saving equipment in the vicinity of the wreck, and recommended that drastic improvements should be made immediately for conveying the life-saving apparatus in future to give assistance in cases of ships in distress. The delays now seem inexplicable, but then, Rear Admiral Boyle was never called to explain them. Why had he not immediately despatched a party of men with lights and ropes when the signals reached him? The Imperial Hotel was connected by wireless to the barracks, from where men could have gone along the Sandwick shore and been at the scene within 40 minutes. At that time, lives could have been saved or men recovered from the shore in time to revive them.

Even the primitive means by which the LSA was hauled towards the scene of the wreck seem incredible now. Horse-drawn emergency vehicles were not unusual in 1919 – ponies and gigs, horses and carts were still the main means of transporting heavy things. In 1915 Lewis Hospital had acquired a horse-drawn ambulance and the Burgh Fire Brigade still had a horse-drawn appliance until 1929. But the first motor car had arrived at Stornoway on Langland's *Princess Ena* on 21st August 1899, so the lack of the Admiralty's own motor provision nearly 20 years later is inexplicable. 19 men were harnessed to draw a cart weighing a ton, when the Rear Admiral would have had a staff car, the base an ambulance or a lorry. No plan was in place for conveying men or equipment in an emergency – and this immediately after a war. The horses and carts meeting the *Sheila* and *Iolaire* at the pier on the night were allowed to disperse before the Admiral and his office woke to reality. Even the lorries, procured from Messrs Ross and Mackenzie on James Street to carry the bodies back into town the next day, would have been of so much more use if a stern naval commander had requisitioned their support in the early hours of the morning. It is fair to say that, even with the moorland terrain, the gale and darkness, had motor transport been available, the Life Saving Apparatus would probably have arrived at just about the time the *Iolaire* sank. The road only reached

the farms in 1919 and did not go on further towards the shore. It is doubtful whether it could have brought men ashore even had a team been standing by and ready to go.

The naval response on land was chaotic, yet the Admiralty were not criticised or blamed at the Inquiry. Quite why the Admiralty were allowed to get away with it is hard to comprehend.

So there the *Iolaire* was – on rocks unseen by lookouts, steered there by uncertain navigators, her passengers without protection from lifesaving equipment and her half-strength crew uncoordinated under inadequate commanders. There the returning servicemen of the islands were, battered by some of the worst weather their islands could endure and without hope of rescue from sea or land. It remains only to ask – how did this situation come to arise in the first place?

Moving servicemen – the lessons not learnt

The jury at the Inquiry showed they were not afraid to pass responsibility for the tragedy up the chain of command when they recommended:

> "That the Government should in future provide adequate and safe travelling facilities for naval ratings and soldiers."[28]

For this issue – how to get large numbers of men between their homes and their postings in the armed services – was very far from new or unusual. In April

1906, about 750 reservists in the 3rd Battalion Seaforth Highlanders were summoned from Lewis to Fort George, to go on to Montrose for training. On the first night about 400 men tried to board the *Sheila*, but only 250 tickets were issued as that was her carrying capacity. The men became agitated and Supt Hector Smith was summoned to restore order by the purser of the *Sheila*. Smith sent a telegram to Fort George asking for money to look after the soldiers left behind and to keep them off the street. In reply, he was told to spend what he thought fit (and be duly recompensed). The *Highland News* referred to the case as 'military mismanagement'. Provost John Norrie Anderson was involved in that incident, at which time, while rebutting the claim that men had been left to fend for themselves on the street, he did agree there had been total mismanagement by the organising authorities. It seems strange that Mr Anderson did not seem to recollect these early concerns about conveying service personnel when he was present as a solicitor at the Public Inquiry into the loss of the *Iolaire*.

As the war approached, Lewis trainees from the RNR returned from Chatham docks in the last week of January 1912 – exactly 250 men, showing that the authorities knew how many could be safely transported on the vessel available. The *Sheila* could only accommodate 250 servicemen. Although a sturdy little ship and a good sea boat, the *Sheila* was far too cramped for the duties expected of her in wartime, when servicemen coming and going travelled alongside civilian passengers. In March 1918, when Lord Leverhulme purchased the Isle of Lewis, he promised that within six months that he would have a bigger, better and faster mailboat.[29] Sadly this promise failed to materialise –

if it had, it would probably have prevented the need for the *Iolaire* to sail the following Hogmanay.

A few days before the *Iolaire* disaster, two herring drifters had to be chartered to assist the cargo steamer *Plover* to transport all the naval reservists that had arrived at Kyle. This was on Friday 27th December 1918. On Saturday 28th December both *Plover* and HMY *Iolaire* were used together to transport sailors, soldiers and civilians home from Kyle of Lochalsh. They both arrived in Stornoway in the early hours of Sunday. According to HMS *Iolaire* (base) records, the *Iolaire* arrived at half past midnight with 200 navy men aboard and the *Plover* berthed three quarters of an hour later at 1.15am. It's worth noting that, on 31st December, *Iolaire* carried half as many men again. MacBrayne's *Plover* was, on the night, making for Stornoway, where she berthed on 1st January 1919. She could have called at Kyle to collect extra passengers, but why she did not was never raised at the Public Inquiry.

Not only was HMY *Iolaire* overloaded, then, but the strain on the military transport system was predictable. The men pouring onto the station platforms from naval bases the length of Britain were desperate to get home but it would, with the benefit of hindsight, have been prudent to have held a number of men back at Inverness – where accommodation and food could have been much more easily provided. It would appear that a 'get them home at all costs' rationale was operating and the men were not going to argue, especially as they all wanted to get home to warmth and peace with their families.

The wrong ship?

The yacht *Iolaire* which came to Kyle from Stornoway on 31st December 1918 to carry men home was newly detailed to serve the Stornoway naval base, HMS *Iolaire*. She had arrived in Stornoway on 9th October 1918 as HMY *Amalthaea*, and swapped names with her predecessor *Iolaire* when the former departed the base for Greenock, eventually to be decommissioned from her naval service and returned to her owner, Lady Currie, widow of the Glasgow shipowner who had her built. The changeover happened only on 5th November 1918, as the war was drawing to a close.

There were substantial differences between the two yachts and the *Iolaire* which arrived to transport the men home on New Year's Eve was not ideally suited to her task. She was older than the previous ship by over 20 years, less than two thirds of the size and much slower – her engine consisted of three furnaces which produced a working pressure of 80lbs and her top speed was 10 knots. She suffered, as did many vessels converted for war service, from the imposition of guns on a structure not originally designed to carry them. Her iron hull made her solid, but the three guns mounted on her decks made her top-heavy and liable to pitch and wallow in heavy seas. She was also a single screw vessel, under-powered for foul weather conditions, as had been evidenced on an uncomfortable mission to St Kilda in November 1918. The first *Iolaire* was much faster, with a twin-screw speed of 17.5 knots, and she was better equipped for the conditions.

We must consider what the impact was of this change of vessels on the outcome of the tragedy. The first *Iolaire* might have carried a larger number of men, with more spacious accommodation. She would have travelled faster, arriving in Stornoway before the worst of the weather struck, and she would have coped better with deteriorating sea conditions, raising the possibility that she could have been steered out of danger. Although this is supposition, and although it does not remove the issues around navigation errors, the authors of this book consider this to have been one of several significant factors in the disaster.

The New Year factor

Amidst the pathos and heart-rending chain of events of the *Iolaire* tragedy, three factors combine to make the circumstances almost unbearable. War had ended – these men had survived. They were coming home and it was upon their own shore that they died. And it was New Year, a time of especial significance to Gaels and Scots alike – a time for family, for greetings, gifts and warm good wishes, for hopes and good intentions.

But New Year also contributed tragically to the way that things turned out. In small details and by larger influences, it simply would not have been such a disaster if it had not been Hogmanay and Oidhche na Bliadhna Ùr (The night of New year). Service personnel would not have been heading home in such large numbers, for one thing, and the *Iolaire* might not then have been needed to carry them. Even if she were, her crew might have been at full complement, since almost half were on leave at the time. Those crew who were aboard the vessel seemed strangely absent as she drew towards Stornoway harbour, and this brings us to the inevitable question of drink.

The jury at the Inquiry stated that they were satisfied no one aboard was under the influence of intoxicating liquor, but Admiral Boyle was sufficiently concerned about this possibility to telegraph the harbour authorities at Kyle asking their view on whether officers were inebriated. The Inquiry in fact concentrated their questions on the sobriety of the officers, not querying the condition of other crew members. Had there been failure by some crew to fulfil their duties and ensure the vessel docked safely due to the New Year? As they did not appear to launch the lifeboats, it raises doubts that will never be answered. The Inquiry did not ask, and the men themselves did not survive.

After the Inquiry had concluded, it was claimed that the First Officer of the mailboat *Sheila* was summoned to stand by to go with the *Iolaire*, as Lt Cotter was late reporting for duty. He had left the yacht after crossing from Stornoway and gone ashore at Kyle. He did report for duty in time to sail, and navigated the yacht for the latter part of the voyage. That was not brought to light in court and there is no other report that substantiates the claim.

Alexander Macleod of South Bragar (known as Murdo) emigrated to Australia after surviving the tragedy, but he wrote to his cousin Alex Macaulay, who contributed to an article about the *Iolaire* in the late 1990s:

> "My cousin, Alexander MacLeod, who later emigrated to Australia, spoke of seeing liquor bottles being thrown from the bridge into the sea, and how, if the Captain survived, he would be in dire trouble."[30]

His was not the only anecdotal account of drinking on the bridge. People talked among themselves, and there were strong opinions on the causes of the tragedy. Murdo Macdonald, who was in the crew of the whaler *Rorqual* on the night, later said:

> "The skipper was said to have been under the influence of drink. …. A very bad skipper he was! He was wearing two lifebelts when they found his body. The skipper himself was."

Widespread celebratory drunkenness ashore could also have stolen precious minutes from the race to save lives. When Anderson Young of Stoneyfield Farm reached Naval HQ at the Imperial Hotel, the sentries would not, at first, let him enter to raise the alarm. Once they admitted him, he had difficulty convincing the inebriated naval officers that a disaster had occurred. Sub Lt Charles W Murray went about the town for two hours, hammering on doors and throwing stones at windows, trying to raise a crew for the lifeboat and to get a car in which a first aid party could reach Holm. He was faced with an impossible task for one man, shut doors and householders impossible to rouse – many probably sleeping off a celebration that had taken them through midnight. On the morning of 1st January early risers were faced with the sight of shoeless, staggering men coming into the town, or knocking on their doors. They suspected these men of being drunk, given their incoherent speech and bedraggled appearance. Drink and its effects were clearly assumed to be inevitable on this night of all nights.

The Public Inquiry did not call as a witness Imperial Hotel manager Frank Pierre Carnegie who, with his bar staff, could have provided insight regarding the New Year celebrations within the hotel. The Imperial Hotel was the location for naval base command, and those who were there were celebrating the first peaceful New Year since 1914. It is hard to be critical of these celebrations – for all they knew,

Steam Yacht Iolaire
pre-war as a private yacht.
A twin screw yacht, she had a
greater length and beam than
the Amalthaea. Her forward
superstructure, shelter deck and
broader funnel distinguish her
from the vessel which sank.

HMY Iolaire, in her war colours
and carrying deck guns fore and
aft. Her bridge, funnel and shelter
deck are still prominent. This
faster and more modern yacht left
Stornoway after serving at the
base for three years. She exchanged
names with the Amalthaea on
6th November 1918 and left to be
decommissioned.

Steam Yacht Amalthaea pre-war as a luxury yacht. The image is post 1907 as she has two masts. A single screw vessel, she had a deck saloon forward with her bridge amidships forward of the funnel and she had a counter stern.

HMY Iolaire (ex-Amalthaea) in battleship grey and fitted out with deck guns. A new bridge structure has been added with her bridge ventilators raised during her conversion as an armed yacht. Note the crosspiece on the main mast that Donald Morrison sat upon during the gale after the yacht sank.

this was a night of the greatest rejoicing, not an immediate and significant emergency. But if the question of drink aboard the *Iolaire* was of significance, so too, surely, was the question of drink among those in command at the naval base.

The subtlest impact of New Year on the disaster, though, did not arise from drink, or even from the suspicion of it. This was an island where tragedy at sea was familiar, and where many knew how to set their hands to the saving of lives if such a thing were to happen near their shore. The blowing ship's whistle, the 15 or more flares which were set off, on any other night might have brought people to the scene to do what they could, but in every tale where these incidents are recounted the inevitable deduction was that it was Hogmanay, and that people were celebrating.

"If people had come half an hour before this they would have saved many people. But the night it was, it was New Year's Eve and no one was taking any notice of what was going on."[31]

The final analysis of the great disaster that befell Lewis and Harris

When we come to examine the disaster of 1st January 1919, we see many contributing factors to the final tragic outcome. The ultimate blame for the *Iolaire* disaster and for the deaths that resulted must, though, be laid at the door of the Admiralty. They granted the island seamen New Year leave without ensuring that they had adequate transport to arrive home safely. It was their procedures which meant that nobody checked the number of ratings arriving at Inverness, heading onwards to Kyle of Lochalsh for Stornoway and other destinations.

The despatch of the *Iolaire* to carry those who could not get on board the *Sheila* was an emergency attempt to solve a problem created by the Royal Navy. It was a problem the naval authorities should have foreseen, as the *Plover* and drifters had to transport over 300 servicemen from Kyle to Stornoway the two nights before the *Iolaire* disaster. No additional trawlers and drifters were sent across on 31st December and no attempt was made to alert David MacBrayne to supply additional vessels – although *Plover* was in the area at the time. In the years prior to and during the war there had been problems with transporting large numbers of service personnel, yet no lessons were learned and the *Sheila*, with her sparse accommodation and carrying capacity, continued to plough across the Minch unsupported.

Crossing the Minch, the Commander of the *Iolaire*, a Royal Navy officer, was ultimately responsible for the safe passage of the vessel and the security of the men on board. In this capacity he singularly failed to carry out his duty. Additional lifejackets were not procured, lifeboats were inadequate, no lookout was posted and the Commander did not supervise entry to Stornoway harbour in a gale. When the vessel struck, orders to save lives were not given. It was, literally, every man for himself – only island bonds brought men to each other's aid in their final hour.

The Admiralty's callous disregard of local sensitivity, landing the bodies like dead fish and selling the yacht's wreck before all the human remains were recovered, alienated them from the locals. At the Public Inquiry they tried to blame the volunteer Stornoway lifeboat, Coastguard Life Saving Apparatus team and civilian car owners, losing still more respect from the community. Meanwhile they failed to shoulder responsibility for the poor response by the naval authorities ashore, the loss of time, their inability to supply motor transport and many other failings.

The Admiralty also failed abysmally to recognise unique aspects of the loss of this vessel in both the location of the wreck and the vast majority of the casualties they were dealing with. Normally ship's companies came from dispersed areas of the United Kingdom and Empire, and wartime sinkings would have been far from the homes of almost all those lost. Similarly, all the previous island losses over four years of war took place far from home, island relatives unable to witness what actually happened.

But this was an island community. When the *Iolaire* was lost drowned men were pulled from the seas of their own home. Strong emotions were brutally exposed within a small, tightly interwoven community, where the feelings of families and village neighbours amplified each other. All understood each other's grief. Anger, distress and the urgent call for answers were correspondingly magnified.

The haste with which the Inquiries were held, the secrecy with which the process was shrouded and other obvious lacks in transparency left the islanders feeling that they had been cheated, not only of their men, but of answers as to why they had lost them. Why were only a select number of survivors chosen for the Public Inquiry and why were dispositions relating to each survivor not made available to all sides and to the public afterwards?

The lack of documented statements from all survivors is regrettable, as it seems to evidence the cover-up that the island public of the day expected. People wondered whether the Admiralty feared collusion between survivors, who might blame those in command. Perhaps they wanted to process the evidence before men were demobilised and free to speak openly.

It is easy with the hindsight of a century later, but it would appear that those conducting the Inquiry were ill-prepared for such an undertaking. The questions asked of the witnesses look almost crass at times, but then they had so little time to familiarise themselves with the circumstances. Representatives for the Crown and the families were not given enough time to assimilate the bewildering facts, in order to conduct themselves appropriately in court and establish what had happened. The Inquiry significantly left out crucial areas of information – they did not comment on the officers and crew's failure to distribute lifesaving gear and to man their lifeboat positions, or on the searchlight and wireless failures. Significant witnesses were omitted, such as the skipper of the *Spider*, the fishing vessel which crossed the *Iolaire* just before she grounded.

In 1919 the Admiralty proposed that the papers relating to Case 693, the *Iolaire* Disaster, be closed for fifty years. Even once the papers were released for public view, 50 years later, it was found that, apart from the verbal evidence given by witnesses at the Public Inquiry, only the dispositions from the Crown agent were kept. The dispositions made by the other survivors were not retained for the National Archive and so their evidence as to how the yacht was lost can never be re-examined. Burying the *Iolaire* papers in a dusty vault meant there would be no accusations or publicity denigrating the Royal Navy for the loss of the boat, the lives, or a huge part of the future of a whole island community.

Since the date when the case was closed, the *Iolaire* disaster has been virtually absent from reports and books on British maritime disasters. Over the decades, it has puzzled many people why the *Iolaire* disaster has virtually been cleansed from accounts of disasters at sea. As an example, when the MV *Herald of Free Enterprise*, a roll-on roll-off ferry, sank just outside Zeebrugge in 1987, leaving 193 passengers and crew dead, news reports referred to the tragedy as the worst peacetime British sea disaster since the *Titanic*. But more lives were lost on the *Iolaire*, in peacetime, in home waters. *Titanic* is remembered, Zeebrugge is remembered, but the sinking of the *Iolaire* has too often been forgotten.

The name HMY *Iolaire* will never be forgotten in the islands that lie in the Atlantic, off the north-west coast of Scotland. The men aboard were practically all fishermen who, as naval reservists, wished to serve their King and country at sea. After four years of war they drowned on the threshold of their own homes. Such cruel fate will, we pray, never knock at island doors again. The enormity of the loss and the impact it had on the islands is still strongly felt. Islanders still talk in hushed tones and look downwards when discussing it, many have tears in their eyes when the name *Iolaire* is remembered, as it will be remembered for many years to come.

For still alive in island memories are the many, many individual tragedies that lay within the greater disaster – the child sitting bewildered as her grandfather's tears fall upon her face, the brothers laid to rest side by side, the young woman buried beside her drowned father and the bride waiting vainly on the pier for her returning husband. Again and again, in homes around the island, we remember the wife or mother who, like Peggy Macdonald of Leurbost, combed the sand from the hair of a drowned boy, his face speckled black by the shore against which he was dashed, his fingernails torn away as he tried to grasp the rock of home.

> *"Gone, now they're gone; though they've gone from
>   here,
> Bright shining we see them in visions clear;
> The faithful who watched for that lightened shore,
> Rest in the peace that will last evermore."*[32]

From **In Memoriam: Iolaire**, by A Mackenzie, Branahuie, Lewis
Published in the *Highland News*, 15th February 1919

Chapter 11 Footnotes

1. John Maclennan interviewed by Maga Mackay, translated by Maggie Smith for *Hebridean Connections*, 2005

2. Mòr Macleod (née Smith) interviewed in *Seanchas*, No 53, Winter 2006

3. PRO Admiralty file 116/1869

4. Navigational Appendix *Call na h-Iolaire* Acair, 1978

5. Donald Morrison, *Stornoway Gazette*, 4th January 1992

6. Donald Murray, *Stornoway Gazette*, 4th January 1992

7. Ernest Leggett, the quartermaster, who was at the wheel, did not make the mistake. The commander was responsible for setting the course

8. John Maclennan interviewed by Maga Mackay, translated by Maggie Smith for *Hebridean Connections*, 2005

9. PRO Admiralty file 116/1869

10. PRO Admiralty file 116/1869

11. Navigational Appendix *Call na h-Iolaire* Acair, 1978

12. 103-year-old Catherine Macaskill, interviewed in *Back in the Day*, May/June 2007

13. John Smith, Captain of the *Loch Seaforth*, speaking to BBC Radio nan Gàidheal

14. Memo in PRO Admiralty file 116/1869

15. Testimony of Captain Cameron in PRO Admiralty file 116/1869

16. Recommendations of Public Inquiry in PRO Admiralty file 116/1869

17. James Maclean Inquiry evidence, PRO Admiralty file 116/1869

18. Navigational Appendix *Call na h-Iolaire*, Acair, 1978

19. Charles Kingsbury *Eilean an Fhraoich Annual*, *Stornoway Gazette*, 1977

20. Recommendations of Public Inquiry in PRO Admiralty file 116/1869

21. Testimony of Fireman Ernest Adams in PRO Admiralty file 116/1869

22. Recommendations of Public Inquiry in PRO Admiralty file 116/1869

23. Charles Kingsbury, *Eilean an Fhraoich Annual*, *Stornoway Gazette*, 1977

24. James Maclean Inquiry testimony. PRO Admiralty file 116/1869

25. *Stornoway Gazette*, 10th August 1956

26. Donald Macdonald Inquiry testimony. PRO Admiralty file 116/1869

27. Lt Wenlock report to Rear Admiral Boyle. PRO Admiralty file 116/1869

28. Recommendations of Public Inquiry in PRO Admiralty file 116/1869

29. *Highland News*, 12th April 1918

30. James Shaw Grant in *Stornoway Gazette*, 17th April 1997

31. Donald Maciver (Am Beiceir) interviewed on *Càil san Amharc*, BBC Radio nan Gàidheal. Presenter Kenneth Maciver (Coinneach Maciomhair), 1986

32. From *In Memoriam: Iolaire,* by A Mackenzie, Branahuie, Lewis. Published in *Highland News,* 15th February 1919

Appendix 1 –

People and Profiles

Iolaire family members – brothers aboard the *Iolaire*, brothers killed in action during 1914-18 war, children living at the time of father's death in tragedy.

This appendix provides additional detail about significant personnel involved in the *Iolaire* disaster, on board and ashore, and bereaved descendants. Further biographical details about survivors and those who were lost in the wreck appear in the sections 'Roll Call of the Lost' and 'Roll Call of Survivors'.

Naval base personnel

Naval base commanders, HMS *Iolaire*

Two commanders were in operational control of the Stornoway naval base, HMS *Iolaire*, during the period of the First World War:

Rear Admiral Sir Reginald Godfrey Otway Tupper was born on 16th October 1859 and joined the Royal Navy in 1873. He remained in the Senior Service for a total of 48 years. During the First World War he served as Rear Admiral West Coast (Scotland and Hebrides), then Vice Admiral Atlantic Blockade, then Admiral Northern Patrol. He was stationed at Stornoway from late 1914 until February 28th 1916. He was promoted to Rear Admiral when based at Stornoway in January 1916 and left for a new command at the end of the following month. He died on 5th March 1945.

Rear Admiral Robert Francis Boyle MVO was in command of the Stornoway base at the time of the *Iolaire* disaster, He was born in December 1863, the third son of the 5th Earl of Shannon, Henry Bentink Boyle and Lady Blanche Emily Lascelles, daughter of the 3rd Earl of Harewood. His mother died two weeks after his birth and his father was to remarry, with further children following. Robert joined the Royal Navy at the age of just 13, at 17 he was a midshipman aboard the Royal Navy ship *Monarch* and was promoted to Captain in December 1903. In 1904 he was awarded membership of the Royal Victorian Order (MVO) while in command of HMS *Colossus*, guardship at Cowes.

He had married Cerise Champion DeCrespigny in 1889 and they had two sons and two daughters.

He had a widely varied naval career, including being dangerously wounded in action, mentioned in despatches and specifically named for gallantry, but he was court-martialled in 1910, as Captain of the *Duke of Edinburgh*, and found guilty of a charge of negligence after stranding his vessel. In 1911 he was still Captain of HMS *Duke of Edinburgh* and suffered further disciplinary action following 'omissions of a very serious nature' in gunnery tests. Promotion came with the outbreak of war and he had progressed to the rank of Rear Admiral by April 1914. He succeeded Tupper as naval base Commander at Stornoway in April 1916. Rear Admiral Boyle was not asked to appear at the Public Inquiry despite his direct involvement with the events of 31st December to 1st January. On the day of the Inquiry, 10th February 1919, he was promoted to Vice Admiral and he was placed on the retired list the next day, leaving his command as the base closed in April 1919.

After leaving Stornoway, he retired to the village of Catisfield near Fareham in Hampshire and twice received messages from the Admiralty expressing 'appreciation of his services during the war in command of north bases at Larne and Stornoway.' He was appointed Nautical Assessor to the House of Lords in June 1920. He died on 11th September 1922, at the age of 58, at the family seat, Harewood House in North Yorkshire, of emphysema and heart disease. His son Vivian Boyle, RN, was with him when he died

Both Boyle and Tupper presented trophies to the Stornoway Golf Club – Boyle's trophy was won outright and is now in Canada, while the Tupper Cup is still competed for.

Other naval personnel on duty at Stornoway naval base (HMS *Iolaire*) on 1st January 1919

Lt Robert Robinson Ansdell RN was officer of the watch until 9am, when relieved by **Lt A Stableford**.

Sub Lt Frederick E Townend was placed in charge of the temporary mortuary. He was born in Hull in 1892 and his job in wartime was to make compass adjustments for the armed trawlers and other small naval vessels in Stornoway. He spent nearly all of the war in Stornoway, posted in March 1915. He was initiated into Lodge Fortrose on 19th May 1916 and lived at Croistean House. He was married to Christina Anne MacLean and became Principal of the Grimsby Nautical School on leaving the Royal Navy. Also on watch were Lt Frank Divine Reynolds and CPO Macdonald (stand-in).

Signalman Stephen Saunders saw the flares from the *Iolaire* and reported a call for a pilot, then a distress call. He had been a Naval Instructor pre-war. Also on duty were signalmen Wileman, Seaton, Mullarkey and Gibson.

Sentries on the night were M MacLeod, I MacLeod, J MacLeod, A MacDonald, K MacDonald, M MacDonald, MacKenzie, Murray, A Kerr.

Diver **Victor Gusterson** dived to the wreck on 1st January and made his report, subsequently refusing to dive at the site for a second time. His wife's uncle, Kenneth Smith, who left a widow and two children, was one of eleven men from the village of Leurbost who was drowned on the *Iolaire*. Gusterson, who had served in the Royal Navy

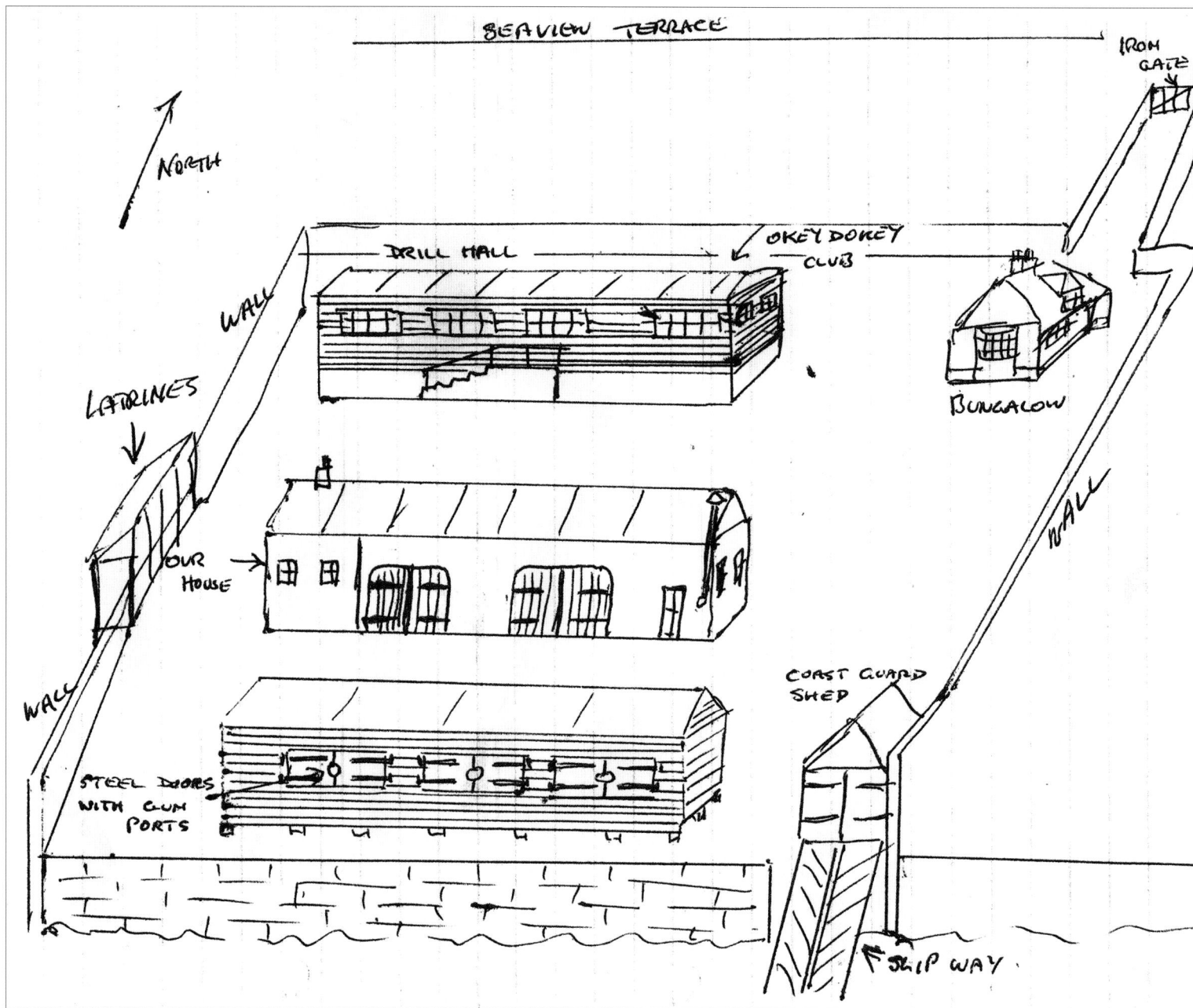

SEAVIEW TERRACE

NORTH

IRON GATE

WALL

DRILL HALL

OKEY DOKEY CLUB

BUNGALOW

LATRINES

WALL

OUR HOUSE

WALL

COAST GUARD SHED

STEEL DOORS WITH GUN PORTS

SLIP WAY

Plans of the buildings at the Battery, now Battery Point, as it was in the 1920s-30s.
The drawings were made from memory by Benny Walton, who was among those who lived there temporarily during his childhood.

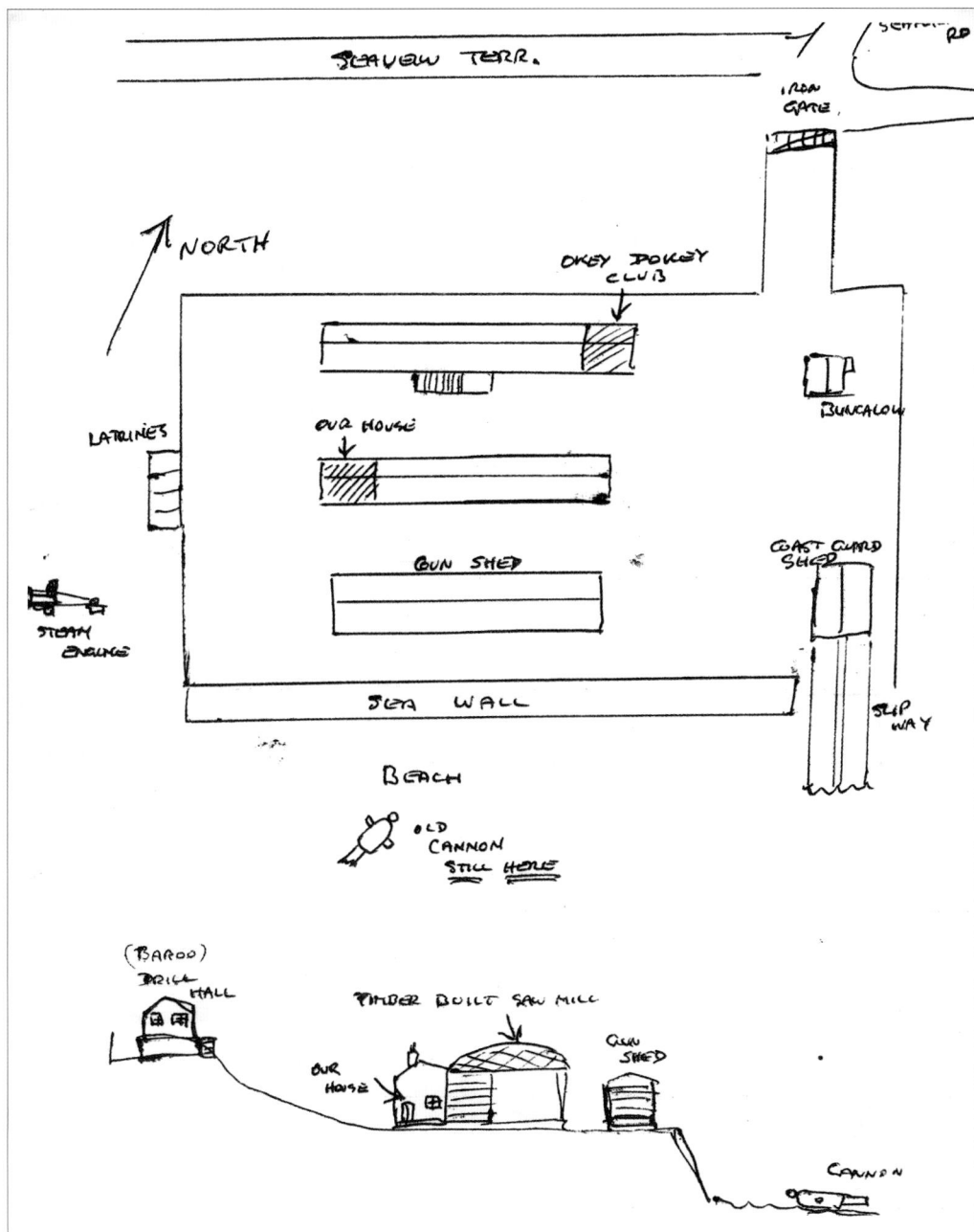

SEAVIEW TERR.

SCHOOL RD

IRON GATE

NORTH

OKEY DOKEY CLUB

BUNGALOW

LATRINES

OUR HOUSE

COAST GUARD SHED

GUN SHED

STEAM ENGINE

SEA WALL

SLIP WAY

BEACH

OLD CANNON STILL HERE

(BAROO) DRILL HALL

TIMBER BUILT SAW MILL

GUN SHED

OUR HOUSE

CANNON

from 1915 until 1922, married Jessie MacLeod and they had 12 children. They lived at Essex Cottage, Sandwick. He died on 11th September 1955 aged 62. Also on duty was diver Edward William Spencer.

Sub Lt Charles W Murray RNVR received orders at 2.45am to get assistance to Holm. He spent several hours attempting to rouse Lifeboat crew and transport to reach survivors

Warrant Officer William Barnes, Chief Officer of the Coastguard was called from his house at Seaview Terrace at 3.15am and took charge of getting the Life Saving Apparatus from Battery Point to Holm.

Divisional Chief Officer of Coastguard Frederick Boxall arrived at Battery Point about 3.40am and went around the coast to Stoneyfield Farm.

Surgeon Lt Thomas Owen RN was a temporary Surgeon Lieutenant who had been posted to Stornoway in August 1917. He was a member of the Royal College of Surgeons and a Licensee of the Royal College of Physicians. He was called to accompany Sub Lt Murray at 4.30am and went with him to Stoneyfield Farm. First to provide medical attention to casualties at farm.

Lt Walter Benjamin Wenlock RN, aged 56, from Lexden, Essex was Coaling Officer and undertaking naval harbourmaster duties at Stornoway. He was posted to HMS *Iolaire* in August 1916 and was in command of HMD *Budding Rose*, on standby to meet the *Iolaire* and act as a pilot boat and tender. He and his crew took the

vessel out to the location of the vessel but were unable to approach the sinking yacht due to sea conditions. He was mentioned in despatches in May 1919 for his duties at Stornoway: "He has carried out the duties of Coaling Officer and Naval Harbour Master with marked ability and judgement. On any occasion of emergency he has always rendered assistance when required at all times of the day or night. Any duty which he undertakes, he carries out in a most conscientious manner. He has materially assisted in the efficiency and work of the base."

The crew of the *Iolaire*

The *Iolaire*'s full crew complement was 40 officers and men, but 16 members of the crew were on New Year's leave and the crew available had just come off Christmas leave. A few men were seconded from other vessels. The *Iolaire* sailed with 24 crew on December 31st 1918.

Navigating Officers:

Lt Cdr Richard Gordon William Mason – From Newry in Ireland, Mason was a vastly experienced seaman. He was apprenticed to Carmichaels, a Greenock company, under sail and was with the British India Steam Navigation Company for four years before joining the Union Steamship Company. He served with the RNR, firstly as a Midshipman from October 1889 and later as Sub Lieutenant from November 1897. He sailed with the White Star Line from July 1901 as 1st and 2nd Officer on routes to New York and Australia. His ships included *Teutonic, Cevic, Gothic, Suevic, Dovic, Oceanic, Cretic,*

Cedric and Megantic and his home address from then until the outbreak of war was in Liverpool. During this time and leading up to the war, he had trained in manoeuvres, torpedo and gunnery and did a year-long course as officer of the watch. He remained in the Mercantile Marine on the outbreak of war, refreshing his gunnery with the RNR in 1914. He sailed in the Mediterranean with the Mercantile Marine on the Italy to New York routes but in March 1917 was called to serve and appointed Lt Commander with HMY Amalthaea. During his time with her, she was attached to the shore bases of HMS Zaria at Longhope, Orkney on three occasions, HMS Brilliant in Shetland, HMS Kingfisher at Yarmouth and finally HMS Iolaire at Stornoway.

Lt Leonard Edmund Dillistone Cotter – Cotter was a yachtsman and an RNVR officer. He had been in the Mercantile Marine at the turn of the century and before the war was in charge of the steam yacht Christabel in America. After HMS Victory at Portsmouth, he was made a Temporary Sub Lieutenant in March 1916 and Temporary Lieutenant with HMY Goissa, navigation his recognised ability, though he was cautioned by a Naval Court of Inquiry for an error of judgement after a collision with Granton West Pier. HMY Goissa had also accidentally collided with the battlecruiser HMS Invincible earlier in 1916, killing crewman Donald MacLeod, RNR, of 1a Upper Bayble in Lewis, three other crewmen and one of the Invincible crew. There is a break in Cotter's service record from the date of his caution until he was posted to HMY Amalthaea (later Iolaire) on 28th June 1918. He had been on leave at home for Christmas and had returned to the Iolaire four

days before she sank. On 31st December he reported late for duty after leaving the vessel at Kyle, causing the First Officer from the mailboat Sheila to be placed on standby to replace him, but he reported in time to sail.

The rest of the crew were:

Engineering Officers: Lt Rankin RNR, 2nd Eng Hern
Telegraphist: Welch
Signal Boy: Macdonald RNR.
Galley/Lamps: Henley, Brown (Loaned RNR Trimmer/Cook from HMT William Jones).
Stewards: Humphry, Taylor
Carpenter: McCarthy.
Deck Crew: Acting Boatswain L/DH Dewsbury, Leggett, Acting QM DH Maclean, Mariner, Moore, D. Ramsay, Stanley, Willder.
Engines/Stokehold: Harris (Greaser), Adams (Fireman but was Acting as Greaser), George (Fireman), G. Ramsey (Fireman), Topham (Loaned RNR man from HMS Armageddon - Trimmer)
All Mercantile Marine Reserve unless stated.

The Inquiries

Personnel conducting the Naval Inquiry made into the disaster on 8th January 1919

William Bradley, Commander RNR. Aged 52, he had been awarded the DSO for duties for the Northern Patrol in 1917. He was appointed to the Stornoway base on 28th March 1918.

Ivan Gordon Humphreys, Commander RNR. He was posted to HMS *Iolaire* in January 1917. From Wandsworth in London, he died early in 1920.

Lt William Armstrong Westgarth, Lt RNR. The only one of the three with a local connection, he was married in Stornoway to Isabella, daughter of the banker Ebenezer Ross. He served at the Stornoway naval base for the last three years of the Great War, commanding the minesweeper HMS *Pavlova*, he had been awarded the DSC and became a Master in the Merchant Navy later in life. He died at Belfast in 1942 aged 56.

Personnel involved in the Public Inquiry on 10th and 11th February 1919

The Public Inquiry was heard before a Sheriff Principal and Sheriff Depute, with a jury of seven. **John MacIntosh**, MA BA KC of Ross, Cromarty and Sutherland (served 1912-1940) – was Sheriff Principal. He was born in Forres in May 1857 and lived in Inverness. He had donated £10 to the *Iolaire* Disaster Fund in January 1919. **William Dunbar**, resident in Stornoway (1917-21) was Sheriff Depute.

Seven Stornoway men were on the Jury. Women over 30 had just received the vote in 1918 and were not permitted to sit on a Scottish Jury until 1920.

Malcolm Maclean was known as 'Calum Sgiathanach'. He lived at Uignish House, 1 Goathill Road. His father Ronald had come to Stornoway from Skye. A baker and grocer, his shop was at 41-43 Point Street and the bakery

was on Bank Street, part of the original Stag Bakeries, which still flourishes today. Malcolm died in November 1938, aged 74.

Alexander Roderick Murray, draper, was known as 'the saddler' and lived at 66 Bayhead Street. His shop, stable and garage were at 55-57 Cromwell Street. He was a town councillor before and after the Great War. His father Kenneth was a fishcurer from Port of Ness and Alexander died at Callicvol Cottage, Port of Ness, aged 76, on April 15th 1948.

George Morrison lived at 61 Cromwell Street next door to his shop at No 59. His son Donald Duncan Morrison, known as 'Hilton', took over the shop after the Second World War and, as DD Morrison's, it was a pionéer supplier of radios and televisions. George died in December 1948 aged 85.

John Ross lived at 63 Bayhead Street and was the Estate Clerk of Works for Lord Leverhulme.

Malcolm Ross was a grocer from Skye with a shop at 17 Francis Street, near the corner of Keith Street. He and his family lived at 20 South Beach Street.

Kenneth Mackenzie lived at 81 Keith Street and was a house painter. He was tenant to Mrs Jessie Macfarlane of Edinburgh.

Angus Macleod lived at 47 Keith Street and was a mason/contractor. He was a town councillor from 1933 until 1937. He died at 15 Scotland Street in December 1937 aged 81.

The Inquiry was conducted with witnesses presenting evidence and being questioned by three parties. Representing the Admiralty was **James Campbell Pitman** (Counsel), an Edinburgh Advocate with vast experience. Born in Edinburgh in 1864, he was married to Jemima Helen Pitman (née Chancellor) and they had a daughter. He was later made a Senator of the College of Justice and died in East Lothian in 1941 aged 77.

Working with him was **William Alexander Ross**, a practicing solicitor since 1892, who had offices at 50 Kenneth Street, Stornoway. He had built Wandene on Goathill Crescent and was a Stornoway town councillor from November 1904 until November 1916. On December 28th 1917, his 13-year-old son Conrad had been lost tragically in a boat fire in Stornoway Harbour, while several little boys were aboard the motor fishing boat *Children's Trust*, SY438, watching the crew. Conrad's brother Douglas was also badly burnt. William Ross left Lewis in 1921 to move to Edinburgh and died at Bucksford Manor, Kent, in December 1958 aged 94.

Pitman and Ross were under instructions from Thomas Carmichael, Edinburgh (Solicitor in Scotland to the Admiralty) and had received, by the First Sea Lord's approval, a full set of Court of Inquiry papers.

Presenting the case for the Crown was **John Charles Fenton**, born in Edinburgh in 1880 and educated at George Watson's College, Edinburgh University. He was admitted a member of the faculty of Advocates in 1904, served in the war and was appointed a King's Counsel in 1923. He became Solicitor General for Scotland in the first ever Labour government in 1924. He was later Sheriff of Fife and Kinross from 1926-1937, of Stirling, Dumbarton, and Clackmannan from 1937-1942 and of the Lothians and Peebles and Sheriff of Chancery in Scotland from 1942. He was knighted in 1945. He was married to Catherine Fenton (née Coutts) and died in Edinburgh in 1951, aged 70.

Alongside him was the first generation of a dynasty of Procurator Fiscals in Stornoway, **Colin George Mackenzie**. He was born in Stornoway in 1860 and served as Procurator Fiscal from 1899-1936. Both his son Colin Scott Snr (1936-1971) and grandson Colin Scott Jnr (1971-1989) followed on in the position, between them fulfilling those duties for over 90 years. The family lived at Park House on Matheson Road and still do. Colin George died in May 1936 aged 77.

The widows and children of the *Iolaire's* victims were represented by **John Norrie Anderson**, who had worked for Donald Munro, the notorious factor for former island landowner Sir James Matheson. Born in 1844, he was first elected to Stornoway Town Council in November 1881. He later became Notary Public and was a founding partner in the law firm Anderson, Macarthur and Co, which is still in existence. John Norrie was Provost of Stornoway from 1897-1909 and said to be the ablest Lewisman of his time. He lived at Plymville on Lewis Street and was married to Mary Walters Peake. Like Ross, he left Lewis soon after the Inquiry, in 1920 and died at Portobello in 1925 aged 80.

Other Court Officials

Taking the official record of proceedings at the Inquiry was **William Grant**, editor of the *Stornoway Gazette*. An Inverness man, he came to Stornoway in 1899 as reporter to the *Highland News*. He supplemented his income by combining the duties of reporter with part-time work at The Nicolson Institute, as well as with the roles of official short-hand writer to the Sheriff Court, local observer for the Meteorological Office, and for a period Burgh treasurer. He established the *Stornoway Gazette* in 1917 and provided in his paper some of the most detailed and well-informed reports on the loss of HMY *Iolaire*. He also reported for other newspapers on the tragedy and compiled the admirable *Loyal Lewis Roll of Honour*. He married Johanna Morison in 1906 and died in 1932 aged 59. His younger son James Shaw Grant (1910-1999) took over the *Gazette* and carved a niche for himself as a formidable writer and historian.

The Sheriff's clerk depute was **William John Clarke**, born in 1861 and fulfilling this role from 1911 until his death in 1926.

Also at the Inquiry was Archibald Munro, Town Clerk of Stornoway from 1897-1931, who was born in 1848 and resided at 18 Bayhead Street. He was a familiar figure in the town, with his round glasses and old-fashioned attire. He died in March 1931, aged 82.

Naval witnesses – Stornoway Naval Base

Lt Robert Robinson Ansdell RN (aged 35) from Sculcoates, Officer of the Watch at the Stornoway naval base on 31st December 1918 until 9am on 1st January. The Court of Inquiry notes have him incorrectly named as Ainsdale.

Lt Cdr William Douglas Travers Morrish RN (aged 36) from Kensington, paymaster in Stornoway and to become Secretary to the Rear Admiral in Stornoway from February.

Sub Lt Charles W Murray RNVR had been posted to HMS *Iolaire* on April 27th 1918. It was he who was sent to call out the lifeboat and to arrange transport to Holm.

Surg Lt Thomas Owen RN, temp Surgeon Lieutenant, had been posted to Stornoway on 13 August 1917. He was a member of the Royal College of Surgeons and a Licensee of the Royal College of Physicians.

Lt Frederick Edward Townend RNR (aged 27). He was in charge of the temporary mortuary at the RNR Battery

CPO Stephen Saunders RN (aged 47) was Yeoman of Signals at the naval base at Stornoway.

Lt Walter Benjamin Wenlock RN, (aged 56) undertaking naval harbourmaster duties at Stornoway and in command of HMD *Budding Rose* on the night.

Witnesses at Kyle

Lt Cdr Arthur Hepburn Walsh RN, (aged 51) from Canterbury. Based at HMS *Lavatera* he was the officer meeting the men off the train sections.

CPO William John Wyman RN (aged 52) from Westbury-on-Severn was Master at Arms in Kyle. He met the train as an assistant to the commander.

Lt Charles Wayles Hicks RNR (aged 50) appointed temporary Lieutenant in June 1917. At Kyle, he had ascertained the passenger availability on both *Sheila* and *Iolaire*.

Kyle of Lochalsh railway porters **Donald Campbell** (52) from Drumbuie and **John Beaton** (43) from Erbussaig.

Stornoway Coastguard Witnesses

Divisional Commanding Officer Frederick Boxall (aged 50) from Midhurst, Surrey. He had been based at Stornoway for one month.

Chief Officer William Barnes (aged 46), depute to Boxall, first to be called from his home on Seaview Terrace.

John Macsween, Volunteer Coastguard (aged 51), waiter. Lived at 22 Battery Park with his wife Catherine and family. He tried to get horses to pull the Life Saving Apparatus and also guided Barnes to the shore holding an oil lamp.

Hugh Macleod, Volunteer Coastguard, (aged 47), joiner. Lived at 37 Newton Street with wife Bella and their family.

Hugh Munro, Volunteer Coastguard (aged 47), baker. Lived at 30 Newton Street with his two sisters.

Thirteen survivors were called as witnesses: Angus Nicolson, Kenneth MacLeod, John Montgomery, John MacKay, Alexander MacIver, John MacInnes, Alexander Smith, John MacKenzie (Iain Anndra), James MacLean (crew) - witnesses called by Crown. Archibald Ross - witness called for bereaved. Norman MacIver, Donald MacDonald, John MacPhail – witnesses for Crown.

Contributions to the Inquiry were provided in letter and telegram form by:

Thomas Walter Herbert Inskip, head of the Naval Law branch 1918-19. He was later Viscount Caldecote CBE PC KC, Lord Chancellor (1939-40), then Lord Chief Justice for England (1940-46).

Dr Thomas James Macnamara, Parliamentary and Financial Secretary to the Admiralty.

Sir Rosslyn Erskine Wemyss GCB, CMG, MVO, First Sea Lord of the Admiralty.

John William Stewart Anderson, Assistant Secretary at the department of the Secretary to the Admiralty.

H Eastwood, Secretary to the Fourth Sea Lord at the Admiralty.

Capt. John Alexander Webster CBE MVO, Director of Navigation at the Royal Navy Hydrographic Department 1916-1919

R Walton, secretary

Civilian personnel involved on the night of the disaster

Dr Donald Murray was the first MP to represent the Western Isles at Westminster, confirmed in the new position just three days before the *Iolaire* disaster. The General Election was held on 14th December 1918, but the count was delayed until 28th December to allow votes from servicemen overseas to be included in the totals. Dr Murray assisted at the temporary mortuary at the Drill Hall at Church Street on 1st January and insisted on accompanying the policeman who brought the official sad news to many of the homes affected. His daughter Aleen recalled, many years later, the grey pallor of her father's face as he travelled between the Drill Hall and their home.

Dr Murray lived at The Cottage on Church Street, where he was married to Janet and had two sons and three daughters. Donald met Janet while he was working at his first job as an assistant in the shop of Alex Macpherson, 'the Druggist', on the site where Boots the Chemist is today. He graduated from Glasgow University in 1890 and went to work as an assistant doctor in Brora for five years. While in Brora, he was invited to stand for parliament as the Liberal candidate for Sutherland, but was persuaded to stand down shortly afterward with the promise that he would be short-listed for another constituency. He had always been keen on politics; his hero was Gladstone and he was known to be a passionate debater at university where he had been president of the Liberal Club. He returned to Lewis in the mid 1890's and set up in partnership with Dr Murdoch Mackenzie. He married Janet in 1898.

Having taken time out to gain a D.Phil. from Aberdeen University in 1910, he decided about the same time to give up private practice. In that same year Dr Murray was appointed Lewis Medical Officer of Health and Medical Officer for Stornoway Burgh. He was also medical officer for the Infectious Diseases Hospital at Mossend and had been joint medical officer for Coulregrein House with Dr Mackenzie from 1906-11.

His brother, Hugh Brown Murray died in the First World War, serving with the Royal Navy. During the post-war general election campaign of 1918, Donald Murray stood as an Asquithian Liberal under the slogan of 'An Islesman for the Isles'. He campaigned on the issues of crofting and unemployment and on the hustings was not afraid to criticise the development plans of the new proprietor of Lewis, Lord Leverhulme. His chief rival was Sir William Dingwall Mitchell Cotts, a Glasgow shipowner who was standing as a coalition Liberal candidate with Leverhulme's personal support. In the end, Dr Murray won by 3765 votes to 3375, a majority of 390. He soon established for himself a fine reputation as a speaker and debater in the House of Commons, and did not shy away from raising the issue of the *Iolaire* and keeping it in political consciousness, especially where it related to returned servicemen and the conditions of their lives. In his maiden speech on 10th March 1919 he pleaded for the right of returned servicemen to have smallholdings (crofts) from which they could make a living.

Despite his undoubted abilities and personal popularity, he was surprisingly defeated by Cotts in the 1922 General Election. He died in London in July 1923 and was buried in Old Sandwick Cemetery. His funeral was one of the largest seen in Lewis, a fitting testament to the admiration and respect in which his fellow islanders held him.

William Anderson Young Jnr (known as Anderson Young) and his wife Margaret – were the farmers at Stoneyfield Farm, where survivors first appeared on foot directly from the wreck around 3am. With family members and servants including Annie Nicolson, they provided food, drink and dry clothing to the survivors. Anderson Young then cycled to Stornoway to raise the alarm. At the official inquiry into the loss of the vessel, the jury put on record their appreciation of the hospitality shown to the survivors by Mr and Mrs Young.

Anderson Young was born at Sandwick Cottage in 1881 and was a piper in the original Stornoway Pipe Band (formed 1904), later Pipe Major. He married Margaret Young (née Hunter), youngest daughter of John Hunter from Coll Farm on 11th March 1913 at Dingwall. The Youngs, with son John Hunter Young (known as Ian), emigrated from Greenock aboard SS *Laurentic* on 27th April 1929, to Montreal and on to Vancouver. Margaret Young died aged 79 in March 1961 at Richmond, Vancouver. Anderson died at Richmond in September 1972, aged 91.

Iolaire family members

Aboard the *Iolaire* there were many cousins, brothers-in-law and other relatives travelling together as they returned home, but there were also 25 men who travelled in company with their own brothers. They were:

George and Murdo Macarthur, of 10 Cromore. Both survived.

Donald and Allan Macaskill, 9 Gravir. Donald drowned and Allan survived.

Donald and Duncan Macaskill, 14 Shulishader. Donald drowned and Duncan survived.

Donald and Murdo Macdonald, 13 Swainbost. Both drowned.

Donald and Murdo Macdonald, 1 North Tolsta. Donald drowned and Murdo survived.

John Snr and John Jnr Macdonald, 20 Sheshader. Both drowned.

Alexander and John Mackenzie, 16 Leurbost. Both drowned.

Alexander and John Mackenzie, 1 Aird and 8 Portvoller. Alexander drowned and John survived.

John and Murdo Maclean, 17 and 6 South Bragar. Both drowned.

Donald and Malcolm Macleod, 58 North Tolsta. Both drowned.

Angus, John and Norman Macphail, 13 Doune and 32 Knock Carloway. Both Angus and John survived but Norman drowned.

Angus and Donald Morrison, 7 Knockaird. Angus drowned and Donald survived.

Also, **John Mackenzie and Allan Macleod** were cousins brought up as brothers by John's parents at 11 Leurbost. Both drowned.

Donald and Malcolm Macleod of 2 Crossbost were uncle and nephew, but Malcolm was brought up from boyhood by his uncle and aunt at Crossbost – his Aunt Mary given as next of kin on Malcolm's naval record. Both drowned.

Many of the families of men drowned in the *Iolaire* had already lost one or more sons during the war. These brothers of *Iolaire* victims were:

James Beaton, 40 Coll – 43rd Btn Canadians, 17 April 1917, aged 27. Son of James and Isabella Beaton (née Maciver) and brother of Alexander.

Malcolm Campbell, 2nd Btn, KOSB, 7 June 1915, aged 30, and **Norman Campbell,** Royal Engineers, 23 March 1916, aged 27. 41 Habost, Ness – Sons of John and Isabella Campbell (née Mackay) and brothers of Alexander John.

Donald Campbell, HMS *Otway*, 22 July 1917, aged 32 and **Angus Campbell**, SS *Antui*, 29 May 1918, aged 31. 54 North Tolsta. Sons of John and Isabella Campbell (née Graham) and brothers of Kenneth.

Reece Head, Church Hill, Monks Eleigh – 12th Btn W.Yorks. Regt., 16 August 1916, aged 21. Son of George William and Catherine Sophia Head (née Lewis) and brother of Herbert.

Alexander Macaskill, Lighthill, 1st Btn Gordon Highlanders, 7 May 1915, aged 19. Son of Murdo and Anne Macaskill (née Macdonald) and brother of John.

John Macaulay, 4 Hacklet, 2nd Btn Seaforth Highlanders, 24 April 1915, aged 23. Son of John and Christina Macaulay (née Macdonald) and brother of Donald.

Murdo Macaulay, 1 Shulishader, 43rd Btn Canadians, 13 November 1917, aged 29. Son of John and Annie Macaulay (née Murray) and brother of Donald.

Peter Macaulay, 13 Sheshader, 4th Btn Seaforth Highlanders, 23 April 1917, aged 24. Son of John and Christina Macaulay (née Mackenzie) and brother of Donald.

Donald Macdonald, 10 Holm, HMS *Ascot*, 10 November 1918, aged 25. Son of Alexander and Margaret Macdonald (née Maciver) and brother of John.

Donald Macdonald, 44 Lower Bayble, SS *Euphorbia*, 1 December 1917, aged 24. Son of Donald and Catherine Macdonald (née Macleod) and brother of William.

Neil Maciver, 40 Breasclete – 2nd Btn Seaforth Highlanders, 5 May 1915, aged 22. Son of Neil and Chirsty Maciver (née Macaulay) and brother of Malcolm.

Colin Mackay, 22 Sheshader – 1st Btn Seaforth Highlanders, 14 December 1917, aged 27. Son of John and Magdalene Mackay (née Macleod) and brother of Donald.

Murdo Mackay, 14b Crowlista – 2nd Btn Seaforth Highlanders, 28 March 1918, aged 30. Son of Donald and Margaret Mackay (née Maclean) and brother of Malcolm.

Angus Macleod, 43 Ranish – 2nd Btn Seaforth Highlanders, 25 April 1915, aged 25. Son of Leod and Joan Macleod (née Macleod) and brother of Allan, 11 Leurbost.

John Macleod, 28 Swainbost – 2nd Btn Seaforth Highlanders, 28 March 1918, aged 23. Son of Murdo and Margaret Macleod (née Macleod) and brother of Malcolm.

John Macleod, 13 Arnol – 200th Machine Gun Corps, 7 October 1918, aged 40. Son of Norman and Margaret Macleod (née Macleod) and brother of Norman.

Alexander Macleod, 1st Btn Gordon Highl'ders, 14 December 1914, aged 20, Angus MacLeod, HMS *Victory*, 24 June 1916, aged 27 and William Macleod, HMT *Sanda*, 25 September 1915, aged 28, all of 10 Portnaguran. Sons of Donald and Christina Macleod (née Macleod) and brothers of Norman.

Angus Murray, 30 South Bragar – HMS *Vivid I*, 7 May 1916, aged 26. Son of Donald and Henrietta Murray (née Smith) and brother of John.

Kenneth John Murray, 2nd Btn Seaforth High., 20 February 1915, aged 40 and Kenneth Roderick Murray, 9th Btn Gordon High., 30 April 1918, aged 28, of 43 South Shawbost. Sons of John and Mary Murray (née Maclennan) and brothers of Donald.

Donald Nicolson, 20 Ranish – SS *Portloe*, 20 April 1917, aged 30. Son of John and Marion Nicolson (née Mackinnon) and brother of Malcolm.

Donald Nicolson, 1 Crowlista – 8th Btn Seaforth Highlanders, 7 August 1917, aged 26. Son of Donald and Catherine Nicolson (née Macaulay) and brother of Murdo.

The fatherless children of *Iolaire* victims

The disaster left many children fatherless, and in some cases orphaned as their mothers had already died. The children of *Iolaire* victims living at the time of the disaster, listed under the name of the father they lost, were:

Alexander Campbell, 8 Vatisker (wife Jessie) – Maggie b 30 October 1908, Norman b 12 July 1911, Alexander and Jessie, twins b 13 March 1919 (Jessie died 19 March 1919)

Angus Campbell, 31 Lionel (wife Susan) – Dolina b 9 September 1909, Alick b 20 March 1911, Roderick b 1 March 1912.

Donald Campbell, 3 Vatisker (wife Catherine) – **William Macdonald** stepchild/nephew b 31 July 1902, Jane Macdonald stepchild/niece b 27 January 1904, Jane b 2 January 1907.

Kenneth Campbell, 30 North Tolsta (wife Mary) – John b 29 December 1913, Kenina b 6 November 1918.

Leonard Edmund Cotter, Cranmore House, Park Road, Cowes (wife Margaret) – Mabel Violet b 14 August 1901, Ena May and Leonard Edgar, twins b 27 July 1906. The mother died three months after the disaster leaving the children as orphans.

Angus Crichton, 12 Knock (wife Jane died 1907 and second wife Mary) – Hugh Snr b 1 February 1903, Murdo b 1 February 1905, Donald Angus b 20 October 1913, Hugh Jnr b 22 October 1914.

Murdo Ferguson, 3 Lemreway (wife Betsy) – John Angus b 29 September 1905, Murdo b 4 March 1907, Kenneth b 3 December 1908, Christina b 6 December 1910, Mary b 2 December 1912.

Joseph W. George, 120 Headlam Street, Byker, Newcastle (wife Jane) – Stepchildren Esther Annie, 22, Ivy 20, Florence 18, Sydney 15.

Herbert W. Head, Monks Eleigh, Suffolk (fiancée Catherine Wares) – Elizabeth (Betty) Head Wares b 13 June 1919. Catherine returned to Pulteneytown, Wick after her fiancé was drowned and her daughter was born there six months later.

Alfred Henley, Burnham, St Helens, Isle of Wight (wife Elizabeth) – Roy Alfred b 9 October 1907, Madge b 14 August 1909, Elsa Grace b 1 October 1910, Ernest Richard John b 17 September 1911, Basil b 23 September 1913.

Ernest Leggett, 27 Queen St, Emsworth, Hampshire (wife Maud died 1918) – Violet Rose (18), Sydney (18), George (17) Maud (15), Ernest b 4 April 1908, Dorothy b 15 January 1911, Fred b 13 April 1913, William b 13 March 1915 all orphaned.

Donald Macaulay, 1 Shulishader (wife Rachel) – Annie b 7 November 1911, Kate Ann b 26 January 1914, Donaldina b 29 June 1917.

John Macaulay, 11 Grimshader (wife Alexina) – Angus b 10 July 1895, Chirsty b 13 June 1900, Alexander b 29 January 1903, Bella Mary b 9 April 1906, Neil b 12 January 1912.

Alexander Macdonald, 28 Lower Bayble (wife Margaret) – John b 19 January 1909, Dolina b 11 September 1911, Mary b 4 July 1913, Johanna b 27 July 1918.

Angus Macdonald, 42 Leurbost (wife Mary) – Murdina b 8 December 1902, Roderick b 5 December 1905, Allan b 19 November 1910, Angus b 12 September 1914, John b 3 September 1916.

Donald Macdonald, 13 Tobson, Bernera (wife Catherine died 1914) – Maggie Ann b 21 April 1911, Angus b 6 August 1912.

John Macdonald, 16 Crowlista (wife Rachel) – Johanna b 10 February 1919.

John Macdonald, 1a North Tolsta (wife Catherine died 1915) – Donald b 16 August 1905, Marion b 2 August 1910, Mary b 16 September 1912, died 2 February 1919, Catherine b 5 February 1915, all orphaned.

Malcolm Macdonald, 57 South Bragar (wife Mary died 1911, second wife Isabella) – Angus b 14 February 1906, John b 16 December 1907, Mary Ann b 13 August 1913. The two boys went to separate homes after their father's death.

Alexander Maciver, 19 Shulishader (wife Mary) – Mary b 16 September 1911, Henrietta/Effie b 25 March 1913, Alexandra b 30 June 1918.

Angus Maciver, 45 Arnol (wife Catherine) – Maggie Ann b 4 February 1902, Chirsty Mary b 9 September 1904, Norman b 23 July 1909, Maggie b 2 November 1912, Agnes b 28 December 1918.

John Maciver, 69 North Tolsta (wife Margaret died 1904, second wife Catherine) – Isabella b 6 August 1898, Murdo b 29 November 1900.

John Maciver, 19 Lower Bayble (wife Margaret) – Johanna b 16 September 1903, John Murdo b 1 January 1906, Donald b 4 December 1911, Maggie b 2 April 1914, Alexander b 26 April 1916.

Murdo Maciver, 36 Lower Bayble (wife Ann) – Ann b 26 September 1896, Colin b 16 January 1898, Murdo b 16 June 1900, Effie b 25 August 1902, Alexander b 6 February 1905, John b 9 October 1906, Peggie b 8 May 1909.

Angus Mackay, 11 Shulishader (wife Annie) – William b 23 January 1905, Murdo 3 July 1908, Norman b 9 February 1911, Donald b 16 April 1913.

Malcolm Mackay, 36 South Bragar (wife Kate) – Donald Malcolm b 20 November 1910, Donald b 1 June 1912, Murdo b 16 December 1914, Malcolm and Mary, twins b 18 November 1918).

Alexander Mackenzie, 1 Aird (wife Marion) – William b 7 September 1906, Donald b 6 December 1908, John Alick b 12 November 1910, Catherine b 25 December 1912, Alexina b 19 December 1914.

Alexander Mackenzie, 5 Aird (wife Margaret) – Catherine Ann b 28 August 1903, Evander b 2 November 1906, Malcolm b 7 June 1909, Donald b 12 October 1911.

Donald Mackenzie, 22 Upper Bayble (wife Peggie) – Jessie b 28 December 1899 (died 14 February 1919, aged 19), Johanna b 22 August 1902, Catherine b 1 January 1906, Murdo b 1 July 1909, Roderick b 28 August 1913.

John Mackenzie, 8 Breaclet, Bernera (wife Mary) – Catherine b 25 December 1913.

Murdo Mackenzie, 15 Garenin, Carloway (wife Chirsty) – Son Murdo b 8th May 1919).

Murdo Mackenzie, 15 Sheshader (wife Dolina) – Nancy b 1 February 1913, Mary b 12 September 1914, Murdo b 4 August 1916, Jessie Ann b 24 November 1918.

Roderick Mackenzie, 5 Swordale (wife Mary) – Murdo b 18 October 1913, Malcolm b 2 April 1918, Christina Macaulay adopted 1 February 1907.

Angus Mackinnon, 4 Caversta (wife Ethel). Ethel was living at 158 Mayfield Avenue, Dover when her daughter Nellie Iolaire May was born on 16 April 1919, three months after her father drowned.

Donald Maclean, 35 Leurbost (wife Annie) – Catherine b 30 June 1899, died 6 January 1919, five days after the disaster, George b 25 March 1902, Christina b 25 October 1903, John b 2 October 1905, Murdo b 9 August 1907, Isabella b 12 July 1909, Isabella Ann b 5 October 1912.

John Maclean, 17 South Bragar (wife Murdina) – Donald b 14 July 1906, Chirsty Ann b 16 June 1908, Angus b 1 May 1911, Margaret/Peggy b 14 August 1914, John b 1 December 1917.

Murdo Maclean, 6 South Bragar (wife Effie) – Angus b 28 December 1906, Norman b 13 December 1908, Malina b 27 December 1910, John b 4 September 1913, Murdo b 1 July 1917.

Angus Macleay, 33 Lower Shader (wife Katy Ann) – Mary and Marion twins b 25 October 1912, John b 20 February 1917, Angus b 17 June 1918.

Alexander Macleod, 21 Ranish (wife Marion) – Murdo b 29 February 1904, Annie b 21 October 1905, Isabella b 28 April 1909.

Angus Macleod, 1 Portnaguran (wife Maggie) – Dolina b 22 July 1905, Malcolm b 17 November 1906, Matthew b 10 September 1908, Alick b 26 August 1910, Donald b 25 August 1912, Henrietta b 16 September 1914, Alex Donald b 31 May 1919.

John Macleod, 31 Ranish (wife Maggie) – Donald Snr b 19 February 1908, Catherine b 14 August 1910, Donald Jnr b 19 January 1913, John Murdo b 13 September 1915.

John Macleod, 43 Upper Bayble (wife Catherine) – Mary b 10 December 1908, Murdo b 6 February 1911, John b 5 December 1912, Donald John b 4 July 1916, Barbara b 6 July 1918.

John Macleod, 30 Lower Garrabost (wife Maggie) – Alexander b 9 April 1915, Alex Angus b 28 January 1917.

Murdo Macleod, 30 Coll (wife Annie died 1915) – Angusina b 4 June 1914, orphaned.

Murdo Macleod, 10 Aird (wife Annie) – Mary b 9 February 1902, Murdina b 4 September 1904, Alick b 21 February 1907, Peggy b 19 August 1912.

Norman Macleod, 13 Arnol (wife Christina) – Norman b 15 January 1915, John b 14 January 1918.

Malcolm Macmillan, 51 Upper Bayble (wife Catherine) – Malcolm b 3 July 1900, Dolina b 15 June 1902, Annie b 20 September 1904, Chirsty b 29 March 1907, Mary b 22 December 1909, Jessie Ann b 9 July 1912.

Donald Macphail, 11 Borriston, Carloway (wife Mary) – Chirsty b 9 September 1902, Johan b 2 July 1904, Katie b 3 July 1906, Dolina b 5 December 1908, Murdina b 5 July 1914.

Norman Macphail, 32 Knock Carloway (wife Maggie) – Katie Ann b 14 July 1913, Maggie b 3 November 1914, Jane Ann b 1 June 1916, Norman b 5 December 1918.

Donald Macritchie, 46 Keith Street, Stornoway (wife Jeanie) – Davidina b 2 October 1916.

Norman Martin, 8 Lower Shader (wife Annie) – Marion b 19 February 1910, John b 18 June 1912, Donald b 13 February 1914.

Angus Montgomery, 2 Garyvard (wife Mary) – Annie b 6 September 1903, Kenneth b 29 June 1905, Angus John b 29 June 1907, Alexander b 4 April 1909, Isabella b 8 June 1911, Donald b 1 June 1913, Maggie b 16 May 1915, Katie Ann b 29 December 1917.

Norman Montgomery, 6 Sheshader (wife Bella) – Willina b 12 February 1909, Margaret b 16 December 1910, Norman b 5 December 1912, Nora b 27 September 1914, Norman Malcolm b 9 July 1918.

Harold Moore, 8 Myrtle Road, Southend (wife May) – Harold A. b 19 March 1917.

Farquhar Morrison, Scott, Stockinish (wife Rachel died 1909) – Rachel b 27 February 1908, orphaned.

John Morrison, 10 Coll (wife Kate) – Maggie b 21 June 1901, Jessie b 20 June 1903, Murdo b 15 July 1905, Johanna b 2 September 1908, Donald b 30 September 1910, Annie b 20 December 1913, Katie Bell b 23 November 1915, John b 15 November 1917.

Roderick Morrison, 2 Back Street, Habost (wife Gormelia) – Margaret b 19 October 1901, Angus b 29 December 1903, Malcolm b 5 February 1907, Murdo and Mary twins b 28 September 1909, Kenneth b 15 January 1912, Roderick and Donald twins b 11 October 1914.

Donald John Murray, 43a South Shawbost (wife Murdina) – Katie b 14 July 1906, Dolina Snr b 27 July 1908, Jane b 2 August 1910, Dolina Jnr b 1 February 1919.

Evander Murray, 45b North Tolsta (wife Margaret died 1914, second wife Margaret) – Catherine b 22 October 1899.

John Murray, 36 Lionel (wife Annie) – Norman Snr b 7 September 1908, Norman Jnr b 1 August 1912, Peggy b 17 July 1914, John b 25 January 1917.

Donald Nicolson, 10 North Shawbost (wife Catherine) – Kenneth b 29 December 1900, Murdo b 22 August 1902, Chirsty b 30 July 1904, Mary b 22 September 1906, Kate Ann b 6 October 1908, Donald b 13 July 1911, Kenneth Malcolm b 8 January 1915.

David Bisset Ramsay, 4 Townhead, Auchterarder (wife Martha) – Bessie Robertson b 7 December 1907, Charlotte Douglas b 2 September 1909, Margaret Angus b 28 October 1913, David Bisset b 7 September 1916.

Charles Ritchie Nairn Rankin, 4 Moveabe Lee, Penzance (wife Gladys) – Sheila Niven b 11 June 1919

John Smith, 11 South Shawbost (wife Kate) – Catherine b 28 October 1909, John b 6 October 1911, Maggie b 5 February 1913, Mary Ann b 12 July 1916.

John Smith, 17 Upper Bayble (wife Catherine died 1914, second wife Annie) – John b 14 November 1915, Malcolm b 20 January 1919, died 20 April 1919.

Kenneth Smith, 1 Earshader (wife Christina) – Marion b 23 December 1914, Kenneth John b 23 May 1918.

Kenneth Smith, 28 Leurbost (wife Annie) – Marion b 17 October 1905, Murdina b 7 October 1907, Kenneth adopted 26 October 1918, at less than 14 weeks old.

William Kirk Wilson, Beach Ho., 36 South Beach, Stornoway (wife Mary) – Mary Crawford b 7 March 1917, Helen Millar b 4 April 1918.

Appendix 2 –

Technical Information

- Three ships named *Iolaire* – technical details and history Building costs of HMY *Iolaire* (1881)

- Other ships at Stornoway naval base

- An Analysis of Courses steered by the *Iolaire* by Alex Reid

- *Iolaire* Disaster Fund monies received and disbursed

Three ships named *Iolaire*

The naval shore base at Stornoway during the First World War was named HMS *Iolaire*, after the first yacht which served the station (rather than the usual tradition of naming the vessel after the shore base).

The first HMY *Iolaire*, ship no. 115838 built in 1902, was a yacht of 999 gross register tonnage (GRT), built by Beardmore and Company in Glasgow, for the Scottish shipowner Sir Donald Currie. She was hired from the widow of Sir Donald by the Admiralty for wartime service. A twin-screw vessel with a speed of 17.5 knots, she was better equipped than her successor, armed with two three-inch guns, mounted fore and aft. A third gun was added later in the war and was an anti-aircraft gun believed to be mounted amidships. She was also equipped with depth charges, mine ramps and wireless and arrived in Stornoway in May 1915. She was renamed *Amalthaea*, swapping names with the second *Iolaire*, on 6th November 1918. This first vessel left Stornoway on 5th November 1919 and briefly served at Dundee in the Granton Area. She was decommissioned at Greenock and, following refurbishment to her pre-war glory, was returned to her owner later in January 1919, when she took back her name *Iolaire*. The *People's Journal* of 21st June 1919 reported: "Lady Currie's fine steam yacht *Iolaire* has arrived in Oban bay. Captain Maclean is in charge. He is one of the best navigators in western waters". This *Iolaire* served in the Second World War as an accommodation vessel and was at Dunkirk, where she lost the top half of her mainmast. Renamed HMS *Persephone*, she carried on as an accommodation ship at Greenock until 6th February 1946. She was sold and broken up in 1948.

The second HMY *Iolaire*, the subject of this book, was ship no. 85043, built in 1881, a yacht of 634 GRT. Launched on 30th April 1881 by Ramage and Ferguson, Leith, she was number 28 in a yard which had only commenced building vessels three years earlier. Her engine consisted of three furnaces which produced a working pressure of 80lbs. She had an iron hull and was a single screw vessel, which meant she was only able to achieve 10 knots. She was sometimes described as a poor sea-boat, liable to roll and pitch in heavy seas, partly due to the guns which were later added fore and aft and on the promenade deck. The *Iolaire*, like all requisitioned vessels, was not designed for this added weight and it made her top heavy.

Thomas James Waller owned her when she was launched and registered in London as the *Iolanthe*. Waller sold her in 1889 to Sir Adam Mortimer Singer KBC, of New York, son of the Singers of sewing machine fame, and three years later Sir Donald Currie acquired her. In November 1897 she was renamed *Mione*, but reverted to her original name in October 1899 when purchased by the Duke of Montrose. She was bought by James Horlick (later Baronet Horlick), inventor of the malted milk drink, in 1902 and then by Mrs F Calvert in 1906. The yacht was registered as having three masts then but, after another change of hands in 1907, she was re-named *Amalthaea* and became a two-masted yacht. Her new owner was the racehorse enthusiast and owner of three Grand National winners, Sir Charles Garden Assheton-Smith, Bart. (né Duff) of Vaynol in Anglesey, North Wales. Assheton-Smith based his yacht at Port Dinorwic near his estate and carried out other design changes, to the stern and promenade deck and the

addition of a new smoking room, the work done by Cox and Kings, Naval Architects of London.

Sir Charles died at Claridge's hotel in London in September 1914 and his son and heir, Lt Sir Robin Duff, died a matter of days later on active service with the 2nd Life Guards in Flanders. Their yacht was requisitioned by the Admiralty in March 1915 and sailed from Port Dinorwic on 5th April, arriving at Portsmouth on the 8th to be given pennant number O-65 and armed with two three-inch guns, situated fore and aft. She also had added to her original armament a three-pounder anti-aircraft gun amidships. As *Amalthaea* she operated in the Portsmouth Area until August 1916 when she was sent north to Area II, Shetland Islands. Lt Cdr Richard GW Mason RD RNR was appointed to command her in March 1917 and engaged a U-boat off Shetland on 30th July 1917, when escorting a Lerwick to Holmengraa convoy. The yacht moved to Area X, Yarmouth, on 19th December 1917 and from October 1918 was at Area 1, Stornoway. She swapped names with the first *Iolaire* on 6th November 1918 and this was the vessel which stranded and sank on 1st January 1919.

A third *Iolaire* came into being immediately after the sinking of the *Iolaire*, as naval practice required that each Naval base should have a vessel of the same name. The hired screw tug *Lady Windsor*, built in 1891, 81 gross register tons, had been in service from July 1914 and served until July 1919. She would serve again as HM Tug *Iolaire* in the Second World War.

Building costs of the *Iolaire* at Ramage and Ferguson, Leith in 1881

Built as steam yacht *Iolanthe* for Thomas James Waller, London. The profit on the *Iolanthe* was only beaten by one of the preceding vessels. No building plan for the vessel could be located.

WAGES

Storekeepers	10-8-2
Ironbuilders at hull, spars and tanks	994-7-1
Blacksmiths	135-9-0
Carpenters	378-10-11
Labourers	90-2-6
Sawing and C.	13-10-11
Joiners and Cabineteers	870-0-4
Painters and Cementers	185-7-7
Riggers	55-2-10
TOTAL:	2732-11-1

MATERIALS

Iron in hull (221 tons)	1625-10-11
S. 9.17	29-11-0
Castings and Ballast	111-10-6
Screws, Bolts and Nuts	31-13-9 ½
Smith's Iron	64-11-7 ½
Carpenter's Wood	537-3-0
Joiner's wood	791-10-7
Paints and Cement	143-7-9
E.P. Goods	46-4-7
Store Goods	160-7-1 ½
TOTAL:	3510-13-10 ½

FURNISHINGS

Steam Pipes	23-15-0
Windlass	130-0-0
Steering Gear	135-5-7
Blocks	41-8-1
Boats	113-7-9
Brass Sd Lights and Plumberwork	407-5-2 ½
Carving and Glazing	91-18-3
TOTAL:	942-19-10 ½

OUTFIT

Rigging Chains (6 cwt)	7-13-8 ½
Hemp Rope (34 cwt)	108-11-0
Wire (20 ½ cwt)	24-1-7
Sailmaker work	225-13-6
P.Bells	27-17-0
Chains and Anchors	163-0-0
Upholstery	219-9-8
Optician Stores	21-6-0
Chandlery	232-15-8
Cabin Outfit (bedding)	93-6-0
Bunker Coals and Stores	70-7-8
Cash Payments	143-1-0
Engineers' Sundries and Condenser	252-0-8
TOTAL:	1589-3-5 ½

Working Expenses 6% of £8775-8-3 ½	526-7-6
Cost of Boiler (RandF)	743-6-2
Machinery (JMP and Co)	2800-0-0
TOTAL	£12,845-1-11 ½
PRICE RECEIVED	£13,900-0-0
PROFIT	£1,054-18-0 ½

Other ships at Stornoway Naval Base

Stornoway was the shore-base of Area 1 of the Auxiliary Patrol. The number of vessels based there rose from 30 in 1915 to a high of 99 in 1918. The Auxiliary Patrol flotilla at Stornoway at the beginning of 1919 consisted of two yachts, 13 trawlers, 31 drifters, five motor launches and six boom defence vessels. The destroyers *Spear* and *Laeartes* had been stationed in the harbour for specific operational duties at sea and were still at Stornoway on 1st January 1919.

The following ships served from Stornoway in 1918 (with skipper where known): HMY *Adventuress* (Lt Richard S. Durham DSC RNR), HMY *Maid of Honour* (Lt Leopold G.P. Verecker RNR), HMT *City of Carlisle* (E.C. Know RNR), HMT *Pointz Castle* (William T. Smith RNR), HMT *Sasebo* (W. Key RNR), HMT *Stanley Weyman* (G. Oag RNR), HMD *Mary Stephen* (John Buchan (b) RNR), HMT *Scotsman II* (W. Smith RNR), HMD *Kicheel*, HMD *Commodore* (John Thomson RNR), HMD *Oriole II* (James S. Harris RNR), HMT *Armageddon* (F. Walster RNR), HMT *Newhaven* (A. Brown RNR), HMT *Pavlova* (James Farquhar RNR), HMD *Budding Rose* (Lt W. B. Wenlock RNR), HMT *Snowdrop* (Joseph Mair RNR), HMD *John Watt*, HMS *Kildonan*, HMS *Spear*, HMD *Kimberley* (Alexander Reekie RNR), HMT *William Jones*, HMD *Daisy IV* (Joseph Mair RNR), HMD *Elgar* (Alexander King RNR), HMT *Goosander* (T.D. Reid DSO, RNR), HMD *Honeysuckle II* (John Buchan (d) RNR), HM Whaler *Rorqual*, HMD *Vale o'Moray* (James Flett RNR), HMD *Renown*, HMD *Watchful*, HMD *Welland II* (John Mitchell RNR), HMD *Alert II* (F.K. Mair RNR), HMD *Hawthorn Bud*, HMS *Laeartes* and MLs 177, 179, 205, 266 and 301.

The *Iolaire* was not the only loss among naval ships based at Stornoway. HMT *Rhodesia*, a requisitioned Hull steam trawler (H443) was wrecked on 19th April 1915 off the north coast of Skye. HMY *Hersilia* was wrecked in Loch Torridon, on 6th January 1916 with no lives lost. Lt Frederick Edward Townend RNR, who was later to run the mortuary after the *Iolaire* sinking, was skipper of HMT *Edison*, an Admiralty trawler hired as a minesweeper and armed patrol trawler which ran aground near Arnol in Lewis in July 1916.

In order to get comparisons with the vessels plying the Minch from Kyle to Stornoway before, during and after 1919, dimensions of some of the vessels are listed here:

The first *Iolaire* (1902) 236.8 feet long by 30.1 feet beam, 999 GRT.

Amalthaea (1881) – the second *Iolaire* – 189.3 feet long by 27.0 feet beam, 634 GRT.

Sheila (1904) 150.2 feet long by 23.1 feet beam, 280 GRT.

Plover (1904) 136.8 feet long by 21.1 feet beam, 208 GRT.

Clansman II (1870) 211.3 feet long by 27.3 feet beam, 600 GRT.

Claymore I (1881) 227.0 feet long by 29.6 feet beam, 726 GRT.

Lovedale (1867) 220.4 feet long by 25.2 feet beam, 466 GRT.

Clydesdale (1862) 180.2 feet long by 24.1 feet beam, 403 GRT.

Lochness (1929) 208.8 feet long, by 34.1 feet beam, 777 GRT.

Loch Seaforth (1947) 229.4 feet long, by 36.1 feet beam, 1,126 GRT.

An Analysis of Courses steered by the *Iolaire* prior to her striking the Beasts of Holm by Alex Reid.

Course Steered from Rona (40 Miles to Holm) ref. Chart 1

In the following analysis Course A is the official Admiralty view at the Inquiry, *Iolaire* being half a mile off course; Course B is Captain Smith's interpretation of an Eastward error of five miles or so, shared also at the Inquiry and by others; Course C is a theory of *Iolaire* being off course through overtaking the fishing-boat *Spider*.

The chart course from a mile or so East of South Rona Light to Arnish Light is 340° True (North 20° West). Magnetic variation at 1918/19, according to the Geomagnetism unit of the Institute of Geological Studies (Edinburgh) is estimated to have been 18°51'W, at Gareloch. Commander Bradley stated that magnetic variation was 19°40'W. in 1917, decreasing 9' annually, leading to 19°22'W. in 1919.

It can be assumed then that variation was in the order of 19°W. (341° True), and Captain Cameron's evidence of its being 11°22' is not understandable, unless it is a typing error for 19°22'. Captain Smith's statement that the "correct line" to Arnish is North, 7°W., is based on a magnetic variation of 12-13°, which was the case in 1959 (according to charts current). Captain Cameron is therefore quite in order to say that he "steered North (by the compass) all the way across for Stornoway."

Helmsman James MacLean stated, in cross examination, that when he took over at midnight, about two hours from Rona or 20 miles, half-way across, "She was steering North — Easterly — just a touch Easterly."

In subsequent analysis this seems to have led to the view that the course (Course B) may have been North-East (as in fact suggested at the Inquiry), which is not in any way a logical heading. In my view the typing dash (—) indicates a pause, rather than a link, in the evidence transcription, so that he meant the course was basically North, with a qualifying "Easterly" being further modified by "just a touch." This is confirmed by his subsequent statement that *Iolaire* was making "to the East of North about 2 degrees," which is the course officially held as steered by the Admiralty Minute (Course A).

The compass in any steel or iron ship is affected by the influence of her own magnetism which is called 'deviation,' and as Commander Bradley says, consequently "The compass course of all vessels differ." It could well be that *Iolaire* required 2° Easterly deviation applied to steer a course of North magnetic, which would account for this slight difference from the correct heading, which I believe she followed. (Note: an angular departure of 2° from a line leads to a difference of roughly 1 mile in 30, or 1.4 miles in 40 miles, e.g. Rona—Arnish.)

Position at 0030 hours (13 Miles to Holm) ref. Chart 2.

Helmsman MacLean stated that "at 12.30 a.m. the course was altered to North," the only alteration while he was on watch and on deck from midnight to 0125 hours, that is, at 10 knots (speed estimate from other evidence), about 20 miles to 5 miles from striking at Holm. He further stated that Arnish Point Light "would be about half-a-point on the port bow, as far as I can recollect," at about 12.30. (Note: a compass 'point' is 1/32 of the compass rose or 11¼°, a usage from sailing-ship days when half-a-point (5½°) was about the most accurate course-keeping possible. In angular bearing estimates by eye, a 'point' is about a palm's width at arm's length, eight to the quarter-circle 90°).

A course change is only made if there is some reason to believe it is necessary, which in navigation is usually after establishing a position estimate or 'fix' which shows that the vessel is off-course. At night, in 1919, this could only be by observing the bearings of light-houses, if land was not visible.

If *Iolaire* was fairly close to her calculated course at 0030 hours she would be about 13 miles short of Arnish Light and 5 miles ESE of Milaid Light (near Kebbock Head); Tiumpan Head Light may also have been visible at about 17 miles distance on the starboard bow (depending on the range of the light in 1919). This would be an ideal position to obtain a good 'fix', with lights well-located at wide bearings from each other; but on the other hand MacLean gave evidence that no bearings were taken.

However, at this point it would certainly be an obvious alteration to correct the vessel's heading directly towards Arnish, when the Light was well visible for correct identification and when Milaid showed she was clear of the Lewis eastern shore (courses A/C), and I can see no other reason for the alteration by the skipper. The fact that she required this slight correction (2° to port) is not unusual when tide, wind and sea could well have pushed her a mile or so to starboard in the 25 miles from Rona.

Captain Smith (Course B) maintains that she was then 8½ miles from Kebbock (Milaid), bearing S.70°W. (approximately W.S.W.), which places her 5 miles East of the correct course, heading for Point, but the 2° course alteration makes no sense if Arnish was correctly identified, as the Light

would then be about 35° to port. However, Course B can be argued for, if Tiumpan Head Light (two flashes every 30 seconds) had been confused for Arnish (one flash at 10 seconds), as Tiumpan could then have been near the vessel's heading, about 12 miles distant, and if Arnish had been similarly confused for Milaid (one flash at 15 seconds), which itself would have been near the limit of its visible range at that estimated position and could have escaped notice.

Course made from 0030 hours to 0125 hours (5 Miles to Holm) ref. Chart 2.

Helmsman MacLean stated that Arnish Light remained about "half-a-point" on the port bow at 1 a.m. and again, just before calling the hands for anchoring, at 1.25. Half a point, though theoretically 5½° to port, is in visual terms the minimum definition for the equivalent of "just to the left" in my view. He further states that "when on the bridge after leaving the wheel I reported the lights of Stornoway to Lieut. Cotter, who said 'All right,'" that is between 0100 and 0125 hours when *Iolaire* was between 9 and 5 miles from Holm, which would seem to indicate that the town lights were where expected on the vessel's heading (Course A/C).

Seaman John Montgomery (passenger), at the Public Inquiry, stated: "As we were coming towards Stornoway, I could see Tiumpan Head Light well on the starboard bow and Arnish Light a little on the port bow — perhaps three points on the port bow. I also saw Kebbock Head Light when we passed it on our port beam." If *Iolaire* was following Course A/C she would lose Tiumpan Light about 9 miles short of Holm (0100 hours) when it would be bearing about 37° to starboard (3½ points).

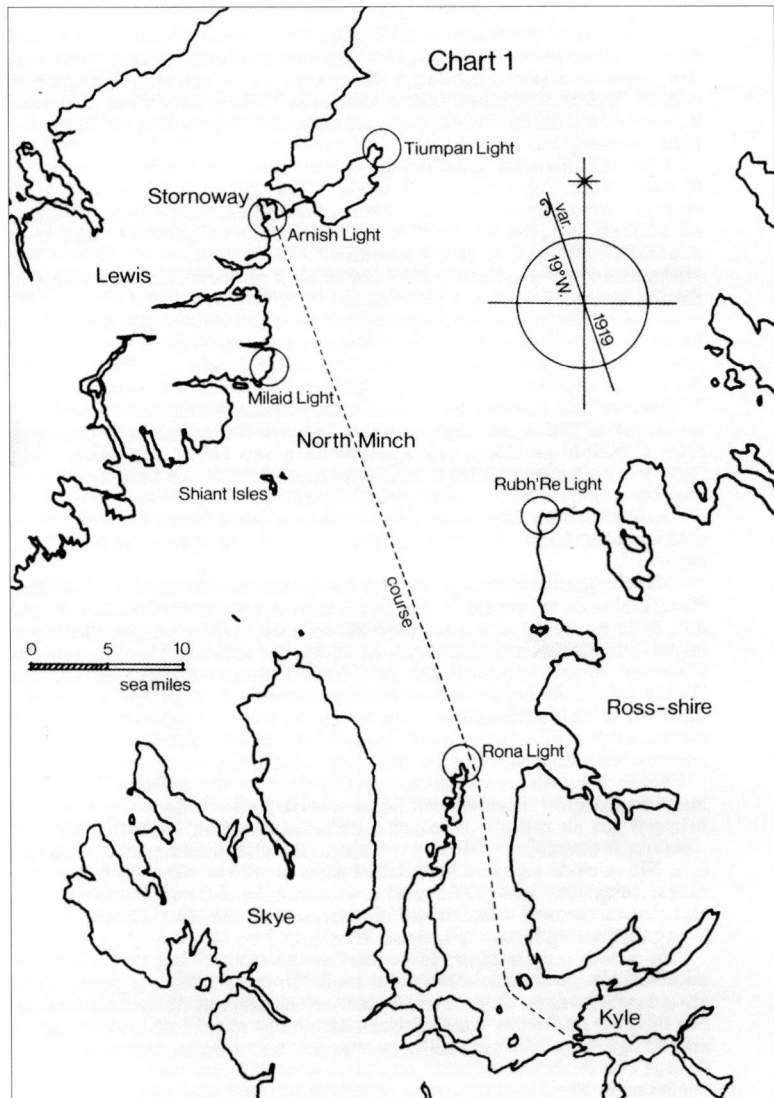

Chart 1

Tiumpan Light

Stornoway

Arnish Light

Lewis

Milaid Light

North Minch

Shiant Isles

Rubh'Re Light

Ross-shire

Rona Light

Skye

Kyle

Var.

19°W.

1919

0   5   10
sea miles

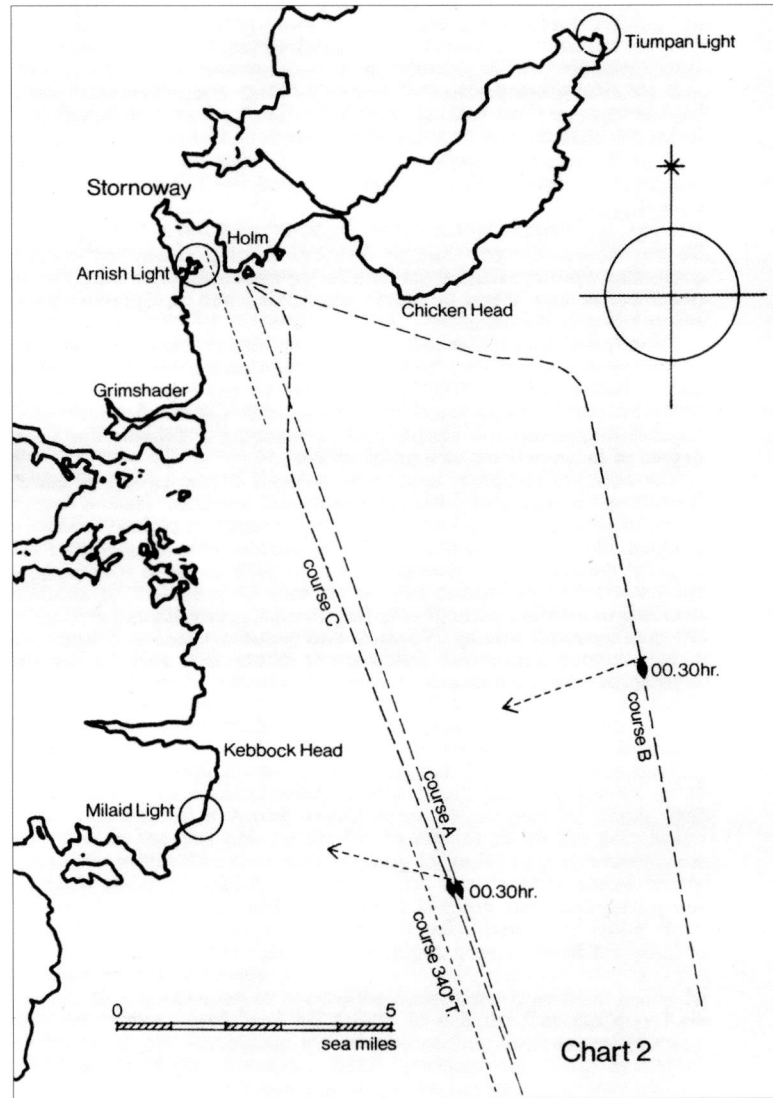

Chart 2

Tiumpan Light

Stornoway

Holm

Arnish Light

Chicken Head

Grimshader

course C

00.30hr.

course B

Kebbock Head

course A

Milaid Light

00.30hr.

course 340° T.

0   5
sea miles

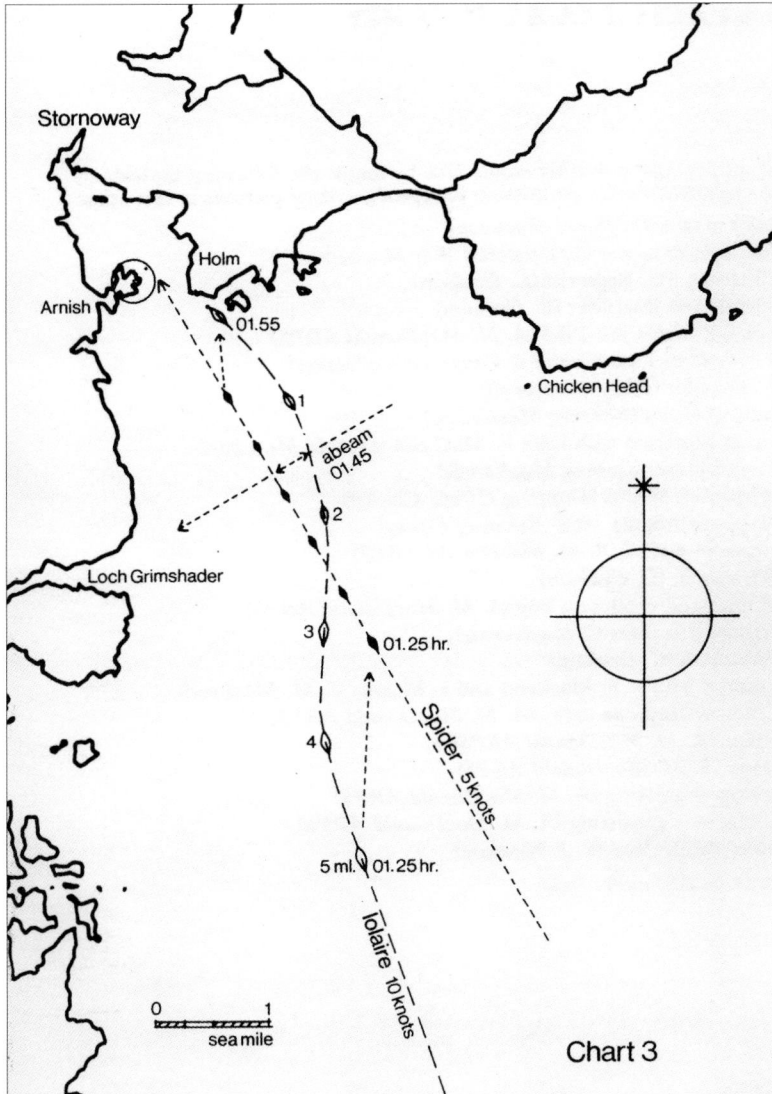

Chart 3

Stornoway
Holm
Arnish
01.55
Chicken Head
1
abeam
01.45
2
Loch Grimshader
3
01.25 hr.
4
Spider 5 knots
5 ml. 01.25 hr.
Iolaire 10 knots
0 1
sea mile

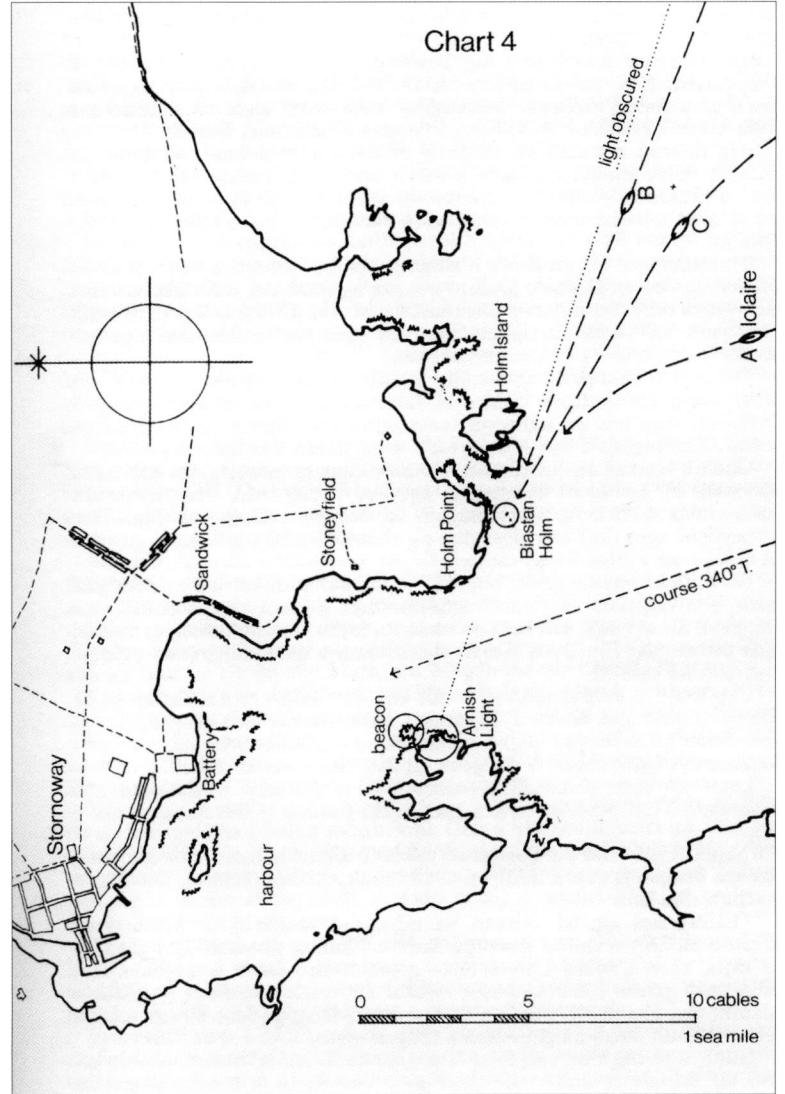

Chart 4

light obscured
B
C
A Iolaire
Holm Island
Holm Point
Biastan
Holm
Sandwick
Stoneyfield
course 340° T.
Stornoway
Battery
beacon
Arnish Light
harbour
0 5 10 cables
1 sea mile

If following Course B (Captain Smith), she would lose Arnish Light (obscured by Holm) 35° to port at about the same time (0100 hours), and would then make a large turn to port to open it up again, the skipper having realised his mistake, and Tiumpan would then be directly abeam to starboard and would be obscured shortly after, 5 miles from Holm at 0125 hours. However, following Course B on a heading of approximately 290° (True) to keep Arnish open ahead, the lights of Stornoway would be obscured by Holm at all times, as the headland rises to 75 ft. and most of the town in 1919 would be below that, the height of an observer on *Iolaire* bridge being approximately 30 ft. above water-line at the most.

Passenger Norman Maciver stated that he saw a white light two points on the starboard bow about an hour before striking Holm (0050 hours); at that time Tiumpan would have been about 35° (3 points) to starboard on Course A/C or about 6° starboard (½ point) on Course B; or conceivably this could have been the fishing-boat *Spider*'s stern light ahead.

Maciver also stated he saw land to starboard at about 600 yards — "We were going along the land at the time" (again about an hour before she struck) — for a quarter of an hour to twenty minutes. This to me is the main evidence for Course B, the approach by Chicken Head, as it is the only explanation for land at that distance so long before Holm. However, on Course B, she would be passing Chicken Head 3½ miles from Holm only at 0130 hours with Bayble maybe visible at 5 miles, 0125 hours.

On Course C, Chicken Head would have been 2 miles to starboard at 0135 hours, and it may be that the land or village lights were visible before then, but I feel Maciver's times are not reliable.

Overtaking Spider ref. Chart 3.

James Macdonald, engineer of fishing-boat *Spider*, is reported as saying: "When sailing past the mouth of Loch Grimshader on our way back to port (from the Shiant banks), a steamer passed us on the starboard side – we followed immediately in her wake and when approaching Arnish Point I noticed that the vessel did not alter her course but kept straight on in the direction of the Beasts ... it went too far off its course to make the harbour in safety."

Seaman John Macinnes (*Iolaire* passenger) stated: "I can only say a word about a light I saw going on the same headway as ourselves. I first saw the light on the starboard bow, just before we came abreast of Grimshader Loch. Shortly after that it was coming broader on the starboard bow, until after we passed Grimshader Loch, it came to the port bow. He crossed our bow from starboard to port. Ten or twelve minutes before the ship struck I saw this craft's green light on our port beam ... as far to the port side of us as Arnish Point when we struck."

If seaman Macinnes' otherwise unsupported evidence is accepted, this very well made statement can only indicate that *Iolaire* was first over-taking *Spider* to port and altered course to starboard to cross her stern (*Spider* appearing to cross *Iolaire*'s bows) and overtake on the starboard side of *Spider* (Course C). "Coming broader" to starboard means that the bearing was increasing, that is, *Spider* was apparently dropping back on *Iolaire*'s starboard bow, and ironically if that was a steady increase *Iolaire* could well have safely overtaken to port.

However, the International Regulations for Prevention of Collision at Sea are quite explicit in these circumstances: "Any vessel overtaking any other shall keep out of the way of the vessel being overtaken," and "when two vessels are crossing so as to involve risk of collision, the vessel which has the other on her own starboard side shall keep out of the way and shall, if the circumstances of the case admit, avoid crossing ahead of the other vessel." *Spider*'s course returning from the main (East) Shiant Bank would place her to the North of *Iolaire*'s course, thus converging from starboard, at possibly half *Iolaire*'s speed, being overtaken say at 5 knots (1 mile in 12 minutes).

We know that they were abreast of each other and abeam of Loch Grimshader at the same time, at about ten minutes before the *Iolaire* struck (i.e. 0145 hours, 2 miles from Holm). If *Iolaire* was previously on course for harbour and the two vessels were converging at about 15° and 5 knots, Lieut. Cotter would only have to alter course about 20° to starboard (approximately 2 points), when a mile or so behind *Spider*, to pass behind her stern (MacInnes states he saw *Spider* first 2 points to starboard). If this alteration was made just after 0125 hours as likely, when helmsman MacLean was sent below, the change of course could have been gentle enough not to have been noticed as such by him or the passengers on deck.

To go from 1½ miles behind to ½ mile ahead of *Spider*, at an overtaking speed of 5 knots, would require 24 minutes and 4 miles, *Iolaire*'s distance from Holm at 0130 hours.

Course made from 0125 hours to stranding 0155 hours ref. Chart 3, 4.

Seaman Angus Macdonald (passenger) stated that at about twenty to two (0140 hours) he saw Arnish Light 4 points (45°) on the port bow, and confirmed the time by the ship's clock, as well as seeing the town lights just to the right of Arnish.

Seaman John Montgomery (passenger) stated that about five minutes before striking (0150 hours) he saw Arnish Light "broad on the port bow, about 4 to 5 points," just at the time *Iolaire* altered course to port, bringing Arnish right ahead. He came on deck 10 minutes before striking (0145 hours) and from starboard side the first land he saw was the East side of Holm Bay, at 0150 hours. At the Public Inquiry he stated: "After she altered course the Beacon light at Arnish was right ahead and Arnish Light would be one point to port."

Seaman John Maciver (passenger) stated that about 3 minutes before striking land was visible 200 yards to starboard, the harbour lights were not visible, and (3 or 4 minutes) before striking she "slewed" to port towards the beacon light, "about ¾ of a point." Seaman John Macinnes (passenger) stated he saw "land ahead" about a quarter of an hour before striking (i.e. 0140 hours, Holm 2½ miles distant — indicates visibility?)

There is thus a fair agreement of evidence that Arnish was approximately 45° on port bow (Macdonald/Montgomery/others), five or ten minutes before striking, followed immediately by the pronounced course alteration to port to bring the Light ahead, at least five minutes before stranding; followed by a steady course, during which the Holm Bay headlands and island were seen close to starboard, and possibly a last-minute alteration again to port too late to avoid the Beasts.

If Course B was directed towards Arnish from close South of Chicken Head, she would have Arnish ahead for at least twenty minutes (from 0135 hours), the town lights would not be visible, and there would have been no further alteration to port in that period.

The Admiralty's theory (Course A) is that she was simply off course 6 cables to starboard (0.6 sea miles) and that Lieut.

Cotter, coming on watch at 0100 hours, was working off a bearing on Arnish Light close on the port bow. On this reasoning, with Arnish approximately 25° to port, heading North by compass still, he thought he was ½ mile from the Light on the correct line, whereas he was 1½ miles off heading for Holm when he realised his mistake, caused perhaps by rain diffusion. However, Arnish would only come 4 points to port (45) on this course, if she was about 2½ cables (500 yards) from Holm Island (1½ iminutes before stranding) and not yet turning. There is no explanation for his failing to reduce speed and call the Captain, standard procedure when within ½ mile of harbour, although he did burn the blue light for a pilot.

Course C (off course and overtaking *Spider*) would require *Iolaire* to alter 20° to starboard, about 25 minutes and 4 miles before stranding (0130 hours), onto approximately a true North heading for 10 to 15 minutes, during which Arnish would come 45° to port (at about 0145 hours) just as she was passing *Spider*, ½ mile or so on the port beam. Lieut. Cotter would then alter the necessary 45° to 50° to port, when he was reasonably ahead of *Spider*, to bring Arnish Beacon close ahead on the port bow, but taking too wide a sweep in keeping clear and setting too close to Holm. Ironically, if the turn had been even later Holm Head would have obscured the light and he might have realised his position and continued turning clear.

Due to his commitment to overtaking *Spider*, made at 0130 hours, he would not reduce speed, and his failure to call the Captain may have been due to his pre-occupation with the immediate navigational problem (as well as MacLean, his spare hand, perhaps not being available). During this manoeuvre he would probably be navigating by eye, without time to refer fully to compass and chart. The relative angles of the Arnish Light and Beacon, approximately 1 cable (200 yards) apart, provide little assistance to assessing the angle of approach, although the town lights' relationship beyond give more guidance to those familiar with the harbour. I presume that the red sector of Arnish Light over the Beasts was not then in existence as it is not mentioned.

It should be noted also that *Iolaire*'s bridge and wheelhouse seem to have been more than half her length, or 100 ft., from her bowsprit, due to her yacht lines – a time-lag of 6 seconds at 10 knots.

Conclusion

To me, Course C (the '*Spider*' Theory), putting *Iolaire* off course by overtaking *Spider*, satisfies the conflicting evidence better than the other two theories and seems a more satisfactory and acceptable chain of events towards the disaster.

Course B (Eastward) would require an incompetence or incapacity on the part of all officers and crew in the wheelhouse for the last hour and a half which is difficult to accept. In the prevailing conditions and with lack of experience by Lieut. Cotter, Course A (Admiralty) is possible but seems over-simple and an inadequate explanation for that degree of incompetence in a naval officer.

The addition of *Spider* as a third element in the equation, however, transforms a straightforward navigational exercise into a complex problem, involving the mental calculation of relative courses, speeds and position, highly taxing in that night's conditions. That

Lieut. Cotter failed to judge the manoeuvre successfully would not then be so surprising, and the basic criticism against him is his lack of judgment or caution in deciding to overtake without referring to his Captain (then, however, only 20-25 minutes off watch). If *Iolaire* had reduced speed to 5 knots when ½ mile behind *Spider* and followed her in, she may perhaps have been delayed by fifteen minutes.

Iolaire **Disaster Fund monies received and disbursed**

The *Iolaire* Disaster Fund Committee registered under the War Charities Act was formed on 7th January 1919 by Provost Murdo Maclean (merchant), the chairman; ex-Provost John Mackenzie (fishcurer), vice-chairman; Baillie Peter Macleod (baker), vice-chairman; councillor Angus Macleod (harbour collector), secretary; and Mr Angus Cameron (National Bank of Scotland, Stornoway), treasurer. Ex-Provost John Norrie Anderson (solicitor) was joint chairman. The rest of the committee was: Dr Donald Murray MP, Baillie Roderick Smith (chemist), ex-councillor John Macritchie Morrison (fish salesman), councillor Norman Stewart (merchant), councillor Alexander R Murray (draper), Rev George Macleod (UF Church, Garrabost), Rev Roderick Macleod (Free Church, Knock), and Mr John Mackenzie (school board clerk, Tarbert).

National donations (and those of note below £50) received by Angus Cameron, Stornoway, Treasurer of the *Iolaire* Disaster Fund as at 31st January 1919 were:

	£
Navy League Overseas Relief Fund, London	2,000
Lord Leverhulme, Lews Castle, Stornoway	1,000
Mrs Wiseley, Orpington	500
William D Mitchell-Cotts, London	500
Association of Highland Societies, Edinburgh	500
Collected by John Duff, Glasgow	292+
Gilbert W Fox, Edinburgh	250
Trustees of Pater Coates, Paisley	200
Messrs David MacBrayne Ltd, Glasgow	200
Trawler Fund of the Orkney Trawlers (RNR)	110
Glasgow and West of Scotland Branch, Navy League	100
Officers and Men of Granton naval base	100
Ship's Fund, HMS *Venerable*, Portland	100
HS Lowdell, Guildford	100
TJ Hurst, Huddersfield	100
Alexander William Macrae, Yateley, Hants	100
John Wallace Taylor, Sunderland	100
J and W Campbell and Co, Glasgow	100
Roderick Morrison, Westcliff-on-Sea	100
"A Friend", Aberfeldy	100
Kenneth Mackenzie, "Fernlea", Stornoway	50
Mrs Jessie Platt, Eishken Lodge, Isle of Lewis	50
"A Friend", Kilmarnock	50
Lewis and Harris Association	50
"DH.", Argyllshire	50
Mrs MC Thomson, Glasgow	50
Messrs John Mitchell and Son, Ltd, Peterhead	50
D Coats, Alvesford, Hants	50
Oswald L Carnegie, Beckenham, Hants	50

Clan Morrison Society	50
James Mackenzie, Glasgow	50
Mann, Byers and Co, Glasgow	50
Officials and Foremen, Fairfield S and E Company, Govan	50
Provost Murdo Maclean, Stornoway	20
Bain, Morrison and Co, Stornoway	20
James Mackenzie and Sons, Stornoway	10+
Servants of Eishken Lodge, Isle of Lewis	10+
Mr and Mrs Duncan Mackenzie, Royal Hotel, Stornoway	10
John Matheson, Caledonian Hotel	10
Bailie Roderick Smith, Stornoway	10
Captain George Watt, Stornoway	10
Dr Donald Murray MP, Stornoway	10
William C Mackenzie, London	10
Sheriff Mackintosh, Edinburgh	10
Admiral Tupper, Fareham	5
Captain Corbett RN, Imperial Hotel, Stornoway	5
Ship's Company, HMS *Zaria*	5

Iolaire Disaster Fund Account – Abstract of Account from 1st January 1919 to 31st December 1919

	Charge £	Discharge £
Confirm monies received	29,116 -7- 0	
Allowance paid to Dependants		2,198-11-4
Interest	196-1-10	
Advertising, printing, stationery, post		887-1-9
Amount drawn from Bank	65,064-13-1	
Miscellaneous payments		4-0-0
Victory Bonds purchase		19,975-0-0
Amount lodged in Bank		71,312-8-10
	94,377-1-11	94,377-1-11

As an example of how the worldwide diaspora of islanders contributed to the fund, below is a list of *Iolaire* Disaster Fund donors in January 1920 from Vermont, USA. Each is listed according to the 'home' address given in the covering letter, but all were resident in the USA: Mr and Mrs Alexander A Stewart, 47 Coll; Mr and Mrs Donald Macaskill, 6 Doune, Carloway; Malcolm Macaskill, 6 Doune, Carloway; Mrs Alexander Mackenzie, 15 Swainbost; William Macritchie, 46 Lower Barvas; Mr John Macaulay, Port of Ness; Mrs Murdo Macinnes, 22 Leurbost; John Maclean, 19 Tong; John Murray, 17 South Dell; Mr and Mrs Norman Graham, 18 South Dell; Mr and Mrs Donald I Murray, 22 South Dell; Malcolm Macleod, 9 Upper Garrabost; Mrs Chrissie Mackenzie, 18 South Dell; Mrs Mary Macinnes, 14 Lower Barvas; Mrs John Mackenzie, 17 South Dell; Mr Robert Hamilton, Aberdeen, Scotland; Mr DG Macdonald, Portage la Prairie and Mr P Stewart, Claremount, Perth.

The following figures relate to the disbursement of funds:

Year	Discharged	Treasurer	Auditor
1924 - £2703.00	Angus Cameron	Hugh Macleod
1925 - £2623.00	Donald Mackay	Hugh Macleod
1926 - £2552.00	Donald Mackay	Colin G Mackenzie
1927 - £2462.00	Donald Mackay	William McNab
1928 - £2407.00	Donald Mackay	William McNab
1929 - £2345.00	Donald Mackay	William McNab
1930 - £2259.00	Donald Mackay	William McNab
1931 - £2157.00	Donald Mackay	William McNab
1932 - £2049.00	Donald Mackay	William McNab
1933 - £1965.00	Donald Mackay	William McNab
1934 - £1852.00	Donald Mackay	William McNab
1935 - £1793.00	Donald Mackay	Donald J. McIver
1936 - £1687.00	Donald Mackay	Donald J. McIver

The final meeting of the trustees of the *Iolaire* Disaster Fund was held towards the end of 1938.

Payments to descendants amounted to £43,854 14s 5d. Funeral expenses amounted to £345 and administrative expenses to £2159 17s 5d. Court expenses of 314 18s 10d left a balance of £33 4s 7d remaining when the last payments were made in January 1938. That last balance was handed over to the Lewis Hospital.

The Steam Yacht Amalthaea anchored at Menai Strait, North Wales prior to the First World War.

Nicolson Institute pupils at the site of the tragedy in 2018.

Appendix 3 –

Poetry and songs of the *Iolaire*

Some of the poems written in Gaelic on the subject of the Iolaire appeared in Acair's 2015 publication *Cuimhneachan – Remembrance*. As well those in the Chapter 10, these include:

Òran na h-Iolaire/Song of the Iolaire
By John Macleod, Shawbost, Lewis

Marbhrann (Òran don Iolaire)/Elegy (Song to the Iolaire)
By John Campbell, Habost, Ness, Lewis

Other poetry:

Call na h-Iolaire / The Loss of the Iolaire –
John Smith, 1919

The Wreck of the Iolaire - J. Graham Macaskill, 1919

Iolaire – A. Mackenzie, 1919

The Lewis Disaster – 'Conyan', 1919

Mar a Chailleadh an Iolaire - Murdo Macfarlane (Bàrd Mhealaboist), date unknown

The Wreck of the Iolaire ('Twas Early in the Morning) – recited by Belle Macintosh 1957

Màiri Iain Mhurch' Chaluim - Anne Frater, 1990

The Iolaire Disaster – William Smith McKechnie, first published 1995

The Iolaire - Iain Crichton Smith

Songs and tunes in commemoration of the *Iolaire*

The Iolaire - Iain Macdonald. On the vinyl album **Beneath Still Waters** Greentrax 1986

Iolaire (*The Eagle*) – Willie John Macaulay. Released on the vinyl album **From Lewis to Lochindaal**, 1987. (Lismor Recordings LCOM5056. Available as a digital download).

Oran An Iolaire – Catherine-Ann Macphee. *Canan nan Gaidheal*, Greentrax recordings 1993.

The Loss of the Iolaire – Allan Henderson/Ingrid Henderson. *The Perpetual Horseshoe*, 2000

Lament for the Iolaire – Pipe Major Donald Macleod MBE. Donald was born in Stornoway in 1917, and this piobaireachd (pipe tune) is included in his *Classic Collection of Piobaireachd Tutorials (Vol 2)*. A shortened version was included by the piper James Duncan Mackenzie of Back in Lewis on his 2013 solo album.

Raoir Reubadh an Iolaire, by the Melbost Bard Murdo Macfarlane (see above), was included in a tribute recording produced in collaboration between An Lanntair arts centre and the Hebridean Celtic Festival in 2007. On the album **Dhachaigh/Home: The Murdo Macfarlane Songbook**, the song is performed by Ness singer Mary Smith. (Birnam CD LANNCD003).

Lewis Love – Written by Isle of Skye musician Blair Douglas, a founder member of the Gaelic rock group Runrig, the song is performed by vocalists Rory Macdonald and Vivien Scotson on Douglas's 2008 album **Stay Strong/Bithibh Laidir/Rester Fort**. (Ridge Records RR052).

The Iolaire (Sons & Fathers) - Gillian Murray, single (digital release), 2014

An Iolaire – by Lewis singer/songwriter Calum Martin, from Back. Sung by his daughter Isobel Ann Martin and included on the 2016 album *An Dealachadh (The Parting)*. (Ridge Records RR062).

The Iolaire – Angus Macphail and Robert Robertson. Recorded by the Scottish traditional band Skipinnish with lead vocals by Norrie Tago Maciver (Carloway, Isle of Lewis) and additional vocals by Ceitlin L. R. Smith (Ness, Isle of Lewis). The song appears on the 2017 album **The Seventh Wave** (Skipinnish Records, SKIPCD26).

The Iolaire – Folky MacFolk Face. From the 2017 album **When Night Falls**. Songwriter Dougie Torrance is a descendant of John Finlay Macleod, who brought the rope to shore and saved some 40 souls on the night of the tragedy.

In 2018 a number of commemorative songs and pieces of music were released as part of the centenary events. These included:

Sàl/Saltwater – Iain Morrison and Dalziel + Scullion. Commissioned as part of 14-18 NOW, the Scottish national commemoration programme, this piece of music is rooted in Ceol Mor, the traditional 'great music' of the pipes. Composer and piper Iain Morrison is the great-grandson of John Morrison of 10 Coll, who was drowned on the Iolaire, leaving eight children fatherless including Iain's grandfather, one-year-old John Eona Morrison. The music includes collaboration with Iain's father, pipe major Iain Murdo Morrison.

An Treas Suaile/The Third Wave – Julie Fowlis and Duncan Chisholm. An audio-visual suite of music performed by musicians and poets, including voices from Lewis and Harris, and based on the central concept of 'the third wave' caught by John Finlay Macleod as he brought the rope ashore.

My Time Wasn't at Hand – Willie Campbell. One of several songs composed by the Lewis singer songwriter as part of Comhairle nan Eilean Siar's *Dileab* project, focusing on four themes of central importance to the Isle of Lewis, of which the loss of the *Iolaire* is one. Willie comes from Tolsta in Lewis.

Songs and poetry in English and Gaelic can be heard on the website www.tobarandualchais.co.uk. Most of the songs, including those originally recorded on vinyl, are available via digital platforms. The book *Cuimhneachan – Bàrdachd a' Chiad Chogaidh/Remembrance – Gaelic Poetry of World War One* is available from Acair (ISBN: 9780861525447) www.acairbooks.com

Appendix 4 –

Bibliography, sources and acknowledgements

KEY PUBLICATIONS:

Loyal Lewis Roll of Honour – 1914 and After.
William Grant 1915

Loyal Lewis Roll of Honour. William Grant.
Stornoway Gazette Ltd 1920

Sea Sorrow: the story of the Iolaire disaster
Stornoway Gazette Ltd 1960/1972

Call na h-Iolaire Tormod Calum Domhnallach.
Acair 1978

Children of the Black House. Calum Ferguson.
Birlinn Ltd 2003

When I Heard the Bell: the loss of the Iolaire.
John Macleod. Birlinn Ltd 2009

Around the Peat-Fire Calum Smith. Birlinn Ltd 2010

FURTHER READING:

Bardachd a' Bhocsair.
Aonghas Caimbeul. C Macdhomhnaill 1978

The Hub of my Universe. James Shaw Grant.
Thin/Grant 1982

Surprise Island: true stories from the Western Isles.
James Shaw Grant. James Thin 1983

A Hebridean Heritage. Myra M Hoar and William S Hoar,
Tangled Roots Press 1991

Fallen War Heroes of Stornoway and District.
Malcolm Macdonald, Stornoway Historical Society 2014

Island Heroes: The Military History of the Hebrides.
Presentations from a conference including from Donald John
MacLeod and Malcolm Macdonald. Islands Book Trust 2010

North Lochs Roll of Honour (WWI). North Lochs
Historical Society Publications 2000

Dusgadh - Special Edition (WWI). Comann Eachdraidh
Ceann A Tuath Nan Lochs

The Dark Ship. Anne MacLeod. Neil Wilson Publishing 2012

IOLAIRE and the Beasts of Holm. Colin E Demet.
Wordcatcher 2009

Iolaire. Karen Clavelle. Turnstone Press 2017

Lewis And Other Verses. H. Anderson Meaden.
(Private Publication, pre-1953)

Place Names of Lewis and Harris. D MacIver FEIS.
John Bartholomew and Son Ltd 1934

Ships of the Royal Navy. J J Colledge.
Revised by Ben Warlow. Greenhill Books 1970/2010

Shore Establishments of the Royal Navy. Ben Warlow.
Maritime Books 2000

The Merchant Navy: World War I at Sea, vols 1-3.
Archibald Hurd. Murray/IWM 1921, 1924 and 1929.

Old Stornoway Revisited. W H Macdonald.
Stornoway Historical Society 2001

History of the Royal Naval Reserve. Frank C Bowen.
Lloyds 1926

Stornoway Lifeboat RNLI Centenary, 1887-1987.
Frances and Angus M Macleod 1987

British Vessels Lost at Sea 1914-18. Thorsons Publishing
Group - HMSO 1919

Devil in The Wind. Charles MacLeod. G Wright 1979

Scotland's War Losses. Duncan Duff. Scottish Secretariat
1947

The Ship That Hunted Itself. Colin Simpson.
Stein and Day 1977

*Sailing the Strait: Aspects of Port Dinorwic and the Menai
Strait.* Reg Chambers Jones. Bridge Books 2004

The Going Down of the Sun/Dol Fodha na Grèine.
Comann Eachdraidh Nis. Acair 2014

Archive and other sources

The National Archive/Public Records Office (PRO)

Evidence in Public Inquiry re Wreck of HM Yacht *Iolaire* ADM 116/1869

HMS *Iolaire* (attached vessel logs) ADM 1494

Stornoway naval base ADM 53/44910 to 44925 *IOLAIRE* 9th June 1915 - 5th March 1919

Royal Marines' service records ADM 159

Royal Naval Division service records ADM 339

Royal Navy ratings' service records ADM 188

Royal Naval Volunteer Reserve service records ADM 337

Royal Naval Reserve officers' service records ADM 240

Royal Naval Reserve service records BT 164 and BT 377

Lt Commander Richard Mason service record ADM 340/94/43

Lt Edmund Cotter service record ADM 240/44/39

Rear-Admiral Boyle service records ADM 196/20/484 and ADM 196/88/28

Registry of Shipping and Seamen Central Register of Seamen: Seamen's Records (Pouches) BT 372

Registry of Shipping and Seamen Index of First World War Mercantile Marine Medals and the British War Medal (1914-1925) BT 351

Registry of Shipping and Seamen Central Register of Seamen: Special Index, Alphabetical Series (CR 10) BT 350

Registry of Shipping and Seamen register of seamen, Central Index, Alphabetical Series (CR1): 1921-1941 BT349

Merchant Seamen's campaign medal records 1914-1918 BT 351/1/1 and 351/1/2

The National Records and Archives of Scotland:

Napier Commission - The Royal Commission of Inquiry into the Condition of Crofters and Cottars in the Highlands and Islands 1884

Ramage and Ferguson and Co Ltd GD339

Stornoway *Iolaire* Disaster Fund IRS21/1338

Other Record Sources

The National Maritime Museum, Greenwich

Museum nan Eilean: *Iolaire* Disaster Fund application forms

Stornoway Pier and Harbour Commission (Now Stornoway Port Authority): arrivals and departures logbooks

John MacQueen Collection (Stornoway Historical Society)

Frank Thompson Collection (Stornoway Historical Society)

Iolaire Disaster – Captain Donald John Smith's dissertation

Local and historical society publications (Lewis and Harris)

Seanchas – Comann Eachdraidh Tholastaidh bho Tuath/ North Tolsta Historical Society

Dùsgadh – Comann Eachdraidh Cheann a Tuath nan Loch/ North Lochs Historical Society

Tional – Comunn Eachdraidh na Pàirc/Pairc Historical Society

Fuaran – Comann Eachdraidh an Taobh Siar/West Side Historical Society

Sop às Gach Seid – Comann Eachdraidh Chàrlabhaigh/ Carloway Historical Society

Cuimhnich - East Loch Roag Local History Society

Dioghlum - Comunn Eachdraidh Ceann a' Loch/ Kinloch Historical Society

Fios a' Bhaile - Comann Eachdraidh Bharabhais agus Bhrù/Barvas and Brue Historical Society

Loch a Tuath News – Back community magazine

The Rudhach – Point community magazine

Water Under the Bridge – Great Bernera community newsletter

Lochs News – Magazine

De Tha Dol – The Harris Community Newsletter

SY Gone By – Stornoway Historical Society magazine

Criomagan – Comunn Eachdraidh Nis/Ness Historical Society magazine

Fios – Ness community newspaper

Websites

All local historical society/Commun Eachdraidh sites – some links are available via hebrideanconnections.com

stornowayhistoricalsociety.org.uk

Iolaire Centre Working Group/CnES – www.facebook.com/AnIolaire

Commonwealth War Graves Commission – www.cwcg.org

Scottish National War Memorial – www.snwm.org

The National Archives – nationalarchives.gov.uk

Scotland's People – scotlandspeople.gov.uk

Find my past – www.findmypast.co.uk

cracroftspeerage.co.uk

Ships Nostalgia – shipsnostalgia.com

naval-history.net

uboat.net

The Dreadnought Project, naval history wiki 1880-1920 – dreadnoughtproject.org

ww100scotland.com – commemorating 100 years since the Great War

Photograph acknowledgements:

Landscapes and buildings

Blackhouse interior – Dawn Nicolson, Vancouver Island, Canada

Croft house exterior, North Beach quay, King Edward wharf, naval flotilla in Stornoway harbour, YMCA canteen in wartime, Imperial Hotel, RNR Battery, Arnish lighthouse – Malcolm Macdonald

Kneep township – Comunn Eachdraidh Uig

Muirneag fishing vessel and fishing boat launch, wreck site January 1919 – Roddy Murray, An Lanntair

Fishing boat beaching – North Tolsta Historical Society

Views of Stornoway town centre, Sandwick Bay, Stornoway Post Office, horse-drawn carts in Ness, Sandwick cemetery crosses, memory map of Stornoway naval base – Stornoway Historical Society

Pictures of HMY *Iolaire* (ex-Amalthaea) and HMY *Iolaire* – Stornoway Historical Society (John Macqueen Collection), Reg Chambers-Jones

Troop train at Kyle and Kyle railhead – reproduced by permission of Duncan Macpherson collection, Skye and Lochalsh Archive Centre (High Life Highland).

Sea views of Beasts of Holm and Holm shore – Chris Murray, John J Maclennan, Iain A Maciver, Stornoway Historical Society

Arnish lighthouse and Tiumpanhead lighthouse, dive pictures of Iolaire wreck site – Chris Murray

Stoneyfield Farm – John Maclean

Sandwick cemetry gravestones – Ian Maclennan

Lewis War Memorial – Rodney Long

Bernera War Memorial – Bernera Historical Society

Iolaire memorial wreath-laying – Stornoway Gazette

Carn Gardens memorial – Fiona Rennie

Pathway to Iolaire monument (2018) – Comhairle nan Eilean Siar

Artist's impression of 2018 memorial – Marion Leven

Young people at Holm – Stornoway Amenity Trust

Artefacts:

1911 Admiralty navigation chart – approaches to Stornoway harbour. Reproduced by permission of the National Library of Scotland

Iolaire sweetheart badge – Malcolm Macdonald

Press cuttings – Malcolm Macdonald and Donald John MacLeod

HMY *Amalthaea* propeller – Reg Chambers-Jones

Iolaire flare gun, bell and plate – Alick Matheson, CnES Multimedia Unit, by permission of Museum nan Eilean

Iolaire lifebelt – Mark Elliott

Cigarette tin and photo frame – Marion Mary Mackenzie

Lock of hair and tobacco pouch – Pairc Historical Society

Watch – Roddy Nicolson

Letters from Roderick Murray's pocket – Rhoda Macleod

Funeral directors' record book – Archibald Macrae Funeral Directors

Iolaire Disaster Fund documents – Museum nan Eilean

Fundraising flags – Stornoway Historical Society

Dead man's penny given to family of Angus Crichton – Jane Mould

Monument to Jack Macaskill – Ian Maclennan

John Macleod's bible – Margaret Mackay

John Finlay Macleod's awards – Iain Macleod

Iolaire portrait – Dr Margaret Ferguson

People:

Two women carrying peat, 1913 – Bernera Historical Society

Rear Admiral Boyle – copyright National Portrait Gallery, London. Robert Francis Boyle by Walter Stoneman

RNR on parade – Stornoway Historical Society (John Macqueen collection)

Donald Murray in trenches – Catherine Maclennan

Leonard Welch on HMY *Amalthaea* and Leonard Welch portrait – Paul Hern

Armistice day in Stornoway – Stornoway Historical Society and Stornoway Amenity Trust

HMY *Amalthaea* football team – Fiona Maccallum

Anderson Young, John Maclean, Dr Donald Murray, Lt Westgarth, John Norrie Anderson, Donald Murray and politicians at Liberal Club, John Finlay Macleod award presentation – Stornoway Historical Society

Captain Cameron – reproduced by permission of Duncan Macpherson collection, Skye and Lochalsh Archive Centre (High Life Highland).

Victor Gusterson – Margaret Nicolson

Henley children – Di Burford

Smith family – North Lochs Historical Society

Wilson family – William Macleod

Alexander Macleod – Point Historical Society

Mackinnon family – Colin N P Mackenzie

Catherine Wares and Betty Head – Elizabeth Wood

Donald Maciver – Tolsta Historical Society

John Maclennan – Comunn Eachdraidh Uig

John Finlay Macleod – Dan Morrison

Donald Morrison, John Finlay Macleod and John Murray – Comunn Eachdraidh Nis

Robert Mackinnon – Robert Wemyss

Katie Watt – Alison White

Marion Macleod – Leila Angus

Bell presentation – Sandy Matheson

John Campbell with *Iolaire* model – John J Maclennan

Portraits of men appearing in the Roll Call of the Lost and Roll Call of Survivors were also provided by:

Malcolm Macneil, Alexander Campbell, Alexina Graham, Malcolm Macdonald, Margaret Macleod, Catherine Bjarnsson, Malcolm Smith, Angus Macdonald, Effie Macdonald, Janice Campbell, Donald Ferguson, Maggie Mackenzie, Jean Maciver, Angus Macleod, Catherine Mackay, Helen Friars, David Mackenzie, Donald John Macleod, Christine Murray, Norman Mackenzie MacFarlane, Fiona MacCallum, Mrs M. Macleod, Margaret Macaulay, Calum Macleod, Karina Macleod, Donald John Macleod, Anna Frater, Calum Morrison, Kenneth M. Macleod, Kathreen Hunter, Donald J. Macaulay, Moira Maclean, Iain Henri Morrison, Margaret Nicolson, Sandy & Cathie Bruce, Alexander Morrison, Peter Morrison, Donald Mackay, Roderick J. Nicolson, John Macdonald, Dena Macleod, Donna Macleod, Agnes Macleay, Duncan Macaskill, Jean Mackenzie, Morag Macdonald, Rod Macdonald, Fiona Maccallum.

Pictures of individuals were also sourced from the *Loyal Lewis Roll of Honour* (*Stornoway Gazette*) and the *People's Journal*

Grateful thanks to all who provided help gathering information from:

Barvas and Brue Historical Society

Bernera Historical Society

Berneray Historical Society

Carloway Historical Society

Harris Historical Society

Kinloch Historical Society

Comunn Eachdraidh Nis

North Lochs Historical Society

Commun Eachdraidh Pairc

Point Historical Society

Stornoway Historical Society

Tolsta Historical Society

Uig Historical Society

Hebridean Connections

Grateful thanks and acknowledgements to:

Nick Smith, Mark Elliott and Museum nan Eilean staff, Mary Ferguson and Stornoway Library staff, Effie Macdonald and Registration Service staff, Matthew Sheldon and Royal Navy Museum Portsmouth, Margaret Nicolson, William Foulger, Ken Galloway, Peter Bell, Iain Campbell, Karen Clavelle, Willie Cross, Monty Dart, Calum Ferguson, Dr Margaret Ferguson, Les Jobbins, Bill and Chris Lawson, Fiona Maccallum, Cathie Macdonald, Rod J. Macdonald, Chrissie Elise Macfarlane, Colin N P Mackenzie, Mairi Mackenzie, Marion Mackenzie, Chrissie Bell Maclean, Hugh Maclean, Catherine Margaret Maclennan, Alasdair Macleod, Angus "Eubaidh" Macleod, Donna Macleod, John Macleod, John K. Macleod, Marion Mary Macleod, John Macqueen, Alex Dan and Chrissie Macrae, Annie Macsween, Alex Morrison, John Murdo Morrison, Jane Mould, Chris Murray, Roderick J. Nicolson, Tommy Ralston, Angus Smith, Norman Smith, Roddie John Smith, David Seeney, Michael Skelly, Ernest Adams, Marcus Bedingfield, Bernard de Neumann, Mary Evans, Angus Graham, Mòr Macleod, Alasdair Macrae, Rev Donald J. Morrison, Captain Roderick Murray, Sandra Roberts, Maggie Smith, Catherine M. Watt, Elizabeth Wood, Roddy Nicolson, Colin Scott Mackenzie, Calum Graham, Ernest George Adams, Ian Maclennan, Donald Martin, Katie Macinnes, Johann Macleod, Ealasaid Chaimbeul.

Anna Mackinnon, Anna Mairi Martin, Maggie Smith, Andrew Mackinnon, Annie Macsween, Annella Macleod.

Special thanks to Eileen Macleod, Christopher Macleod and Matthew Maciver.

Some of those who provided help have passed away during the research leading up to the publication of this book.

The authors would like to thank the people of Lewis and Harris, and the wider community connected with the islands, for their support in the creation of this tribute.

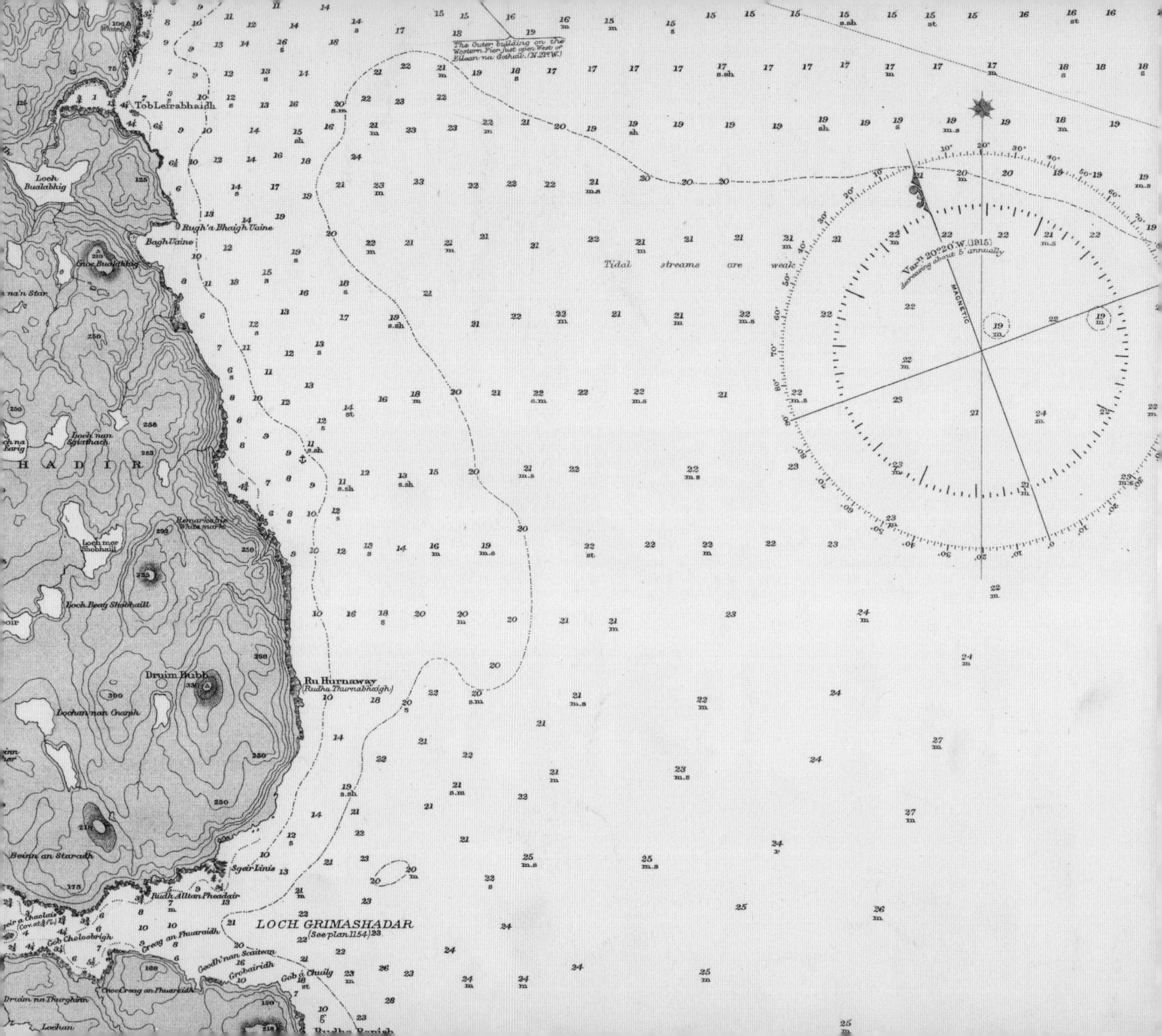

The Outer building on the Western Pier just open West of Eilean na Gothail. (N.27 W.)

Tidal streams are weak

Var. 20°20′ W. (1915)
decreasing about 5′ annually

MAGNETIC

Loch Bualabhig

Tob Leirabhaidh

Rugh'a Bhaigh Uaine

Bagh Uaine

Cnoc Bualabhig

na'n Star

Loch nan Sgiathach

HADIR

Loch mor Shobhaill

Loch Beag Shobhaill

Remarkable White mark

Druim Bubh

Lochan nan Cnamh

Beinn an Staradh

Sgar Linis

Rudh Alltan Pheadair

Gob Cholosbrigh

Creag an Fhuaraidh

Druim na Thorghinn

Geodh'nan Scaitean

Grobairidh

Gob a Chuilg

Chnoc Creag an Fhuaraidh

Loch na Barig

LOCH GRIMASHADAR
(See plan 1154)

Ru Hurnaway
(Rudha Thornabhaigh)